Granville L Howe

The Golden Key to Prosperity and Happiness

A complete educator embracing thorough instruction in every branch of knowledge. An encyclopedia of useful information, comprising every essential to success in all departments of business and social life

Granville L Howe

The Golden Key to Prosperity and Happiness
A complete educator embracing thorough instruction in every branch of knowledge. An encyclopedia of useful information, comprising every essential to success in all departments of business and social life

ISBN/EAN: 9783337219963

Printed in Europe, USA, Canada, Australia, Japan

Cover: Foto ©Thomas Meinert / pixelio.de

More available books at **www.hansebooks.com**

THE GOLDEN KEY TO PROSPERITY AND HAPPINESS.

A COMPLETE EDUCATOR

EMBRACING

THOROUGH INSTRUCTION IN EVERY BRANCH OF KNOWLEDGE.

AN ENCYCLOPEDIA OF USEFUL INFORMATION, COMPRISING EVERY ESSENTIAL TO SUCCESS IN ALL DEPARTMENTS OF BUSINESS AND SOCIAL LIFE.

ILLUSTRATED.

EDITED BY G. L. HOWE,

AUTHOR OF "THE SECRETS OF SUCCESS," "THE COMPLETE ACCOUNTANT," "ELEMENTS OF BOOKKEEPING," AND "THE SCIENCE OF ACCOUNTS."

CHICAGO:
METROPOLITAN PUBLISHING COMPANY,
79 MADISON STREET,
1885.

As this book is sold only by subscription, and cannot be found at the bookstores, parties desiring a copy should address the publishers, when an agent will call upon them.

CONTENTS.

INDEX OF SUBJECTS.

LIST OF TABLES OF REFERENCE.

INDEX TO POETRY.

INDEX OF AUTHORS QUOTED.

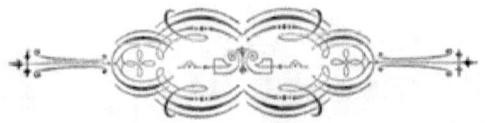

LIST OF ILLUSTRATIONS.

INDEX.

PREFACE

THE publishers, in offering this work to the public, do not feel that any apology is necessary for its appearance. It was conceived and entered upon to meet a general and well-defined want, and in carrying out this object the publishers have not only brought to bear, in every branch of knowledge treated within these covers, painstaking labor and industrious research on the part of the best attainable talent, but have studiously endeavored to improve upon personal experience in kindred publications, and upon the experience of others who have labored in the same field.

It is in very recent years only that the importance and advantage have been realized of placing within the reach of all a comprehensive compendium of every branch of knowledge, useful in the practical duties of life, elevating in its moral aspect, and softening and refining in the exercise of those qualities which go to embellish and adorn social intercourse.

The unreserved and more than anticipated favor which our "Secrets of Success" won for itself at the hands of a public whose wants it went very far to meet, did not prove its perfection. On the contrary, the experience of that, and of the few other publications of a similar character, convinced us that there was still something wanting to cover and completely occupy the field, and to offer what may be strictly and without exaggeration characterized as a book, a thorough acquaintance with which will constitute, in its best and broadest sense, "a liberal education."

This work is designed to cover a broader field than any of its predecessors, and to furnish not only all the information of a utilitarian nature essential to the successful prosecution of the practical affairs of life and the knowledge necessary to enable the student of its pages to comport himself with propriety in every calling and condition of life, but also those rules for the government of mind, morals and manners which both form the bases of success in practical affairs and are essential to the perfection of Character, the attainment of those characteristics which elevate and beautify it, command admiration, affection and esteem. and which unite to form the only avenue by which personal, domestic and social happiness is to be reached, and true and real prosperity made to crown the labors of Life.

The object here briefly set forth, has, we believe, been successfully attained in these pages, and they are offered to the Public as a volume of real, tangible and appreciable value to every person who possesses it, as a source of self-improvement and elevation of mind of incalculable importance to those who make a study of its contents, and as, indeed, in its most practical and realistic sense, as its name implies, The Golden Key, which will surely unlock for every student of Life who masters the knowledge here set forth for his most convenient and easy acquirement, those Treasures of Prosperity and Happiness which comprise the highest ambitions and the best rewards of human existence and labors.

G. L. H.

CHICAGO, FEBRUARY 1, 1885.

WHAT CONSTITUTES SUCCESS.

THE person who asks himself this question will jump to the conclusion, at the first glance, that it is one of so complex a character, and to be viewed from so many diversified aspects, as to be incapable of a general answer of universal application. It naturally appears to the casual inquirer that the various avenues to success and the prizes at the end of them, differ so widely in their conditions and characteristics that the word "success" cannot be invested with any general interpretation. Those who labor for distinction in the field of science, who strive for prominence in the domain of politics, who seek eminence in the social world, or who make it the goal of their ambition to distinguish themselves beyond their fellows in commercial enterprise and the accumulation of wealth, would seem at the first blush to be so far separated in their various paths that there can be no universal estimate of success which will apply equally to all. Yet a proper reflection will soon lead to the conclusion that they have a common goal, "success in life," and that, though they travel by widely divergent roads to reach it, the conditions which are throughout essential to its achievement are identical. No matter to what pursuit either natural inclination or the force of circumstances may impel the young man who is setting out in life, the success to which he looks forward in the spring-time of his career, and which he will most surely reach if he observe the conditions which the experience of others has marked out for him, and his common sense approved, may be briefly summed up as an honorable place in the esteem of his fellow-citizens, the accumulation of sufficient means to place himself and his family beyond the reach of want, physical capacity to enjoy with appreciation and satisfaction the rewards of life, and that moral self-respect which an honest and upright life affords, and which alone can render of any real value either the possession of wealth or the enjoyment of reputation.

The earlier the young man makes up his mind to enter upon his equipment for the struggles of life, the more effective he will find his efforts during the whole course of his career, and it is a duty which he owes to himself, at the very outset of that career, first, to thoroughly realize how absolutely and imperatively necessary to success is Character; next to comprehend fully what are those qualities and attributes which combine to form and complete character; and finally to set himself to work with steadfast resolution to so shape his habits of morals, of mind, of person and of manners, that he may attain in his individuality the harmonious whole of true Character. He will in this light, and with this end in view, cultivate and practice the qualities of Honesty, Industry, Sobriety, Fidelity, Economy, Frugality, Perseverance, Patience, Determination, Cleanliness and Self-cultivation. With Character founded upon and embracing these qualities, the young man is fully equipped with those weapons by means of which all difficulties are to be overcome, and by which, and which alone, in the history of modern civilization, every successful man, in whatever walk of life, has scaled the heights of greatness and prosperity.

CHARACTER.

THE corner-stone of the edifice of success is Character—the possession of those moral and mental habits and characteristics which guide the footsteps of the student of life in the boundaries of honor and probity, and without which neither wealth, nor ability, nor friends, nor opportunity, nor any adventitious circumstance whatever in his favor can avail. Without Character, well formed and secured against peril of loss by a full realization of all that it means, as the weapon with which success in life is to be achieved from even the humblest condition, and of all of the wreck of hope and ruin of high aspiration which its absence or its loss involves, there is no such thing as success, permanent, real and lasting, to be attained. And this is something in which every man holds his destiny in his own hands, from the period at which he arrives at years of sufficient discretion to recognize his moral responsibilities. No advantages of moral surroundings, of pious training, of education, or of affluence will insure the young man Character who himself neglects to fulfill those conditions which are necessary to create and retain it; and no difficulties of birth, poverty, neglect nor misfortune, will be sufficient to restrain from advancement, and all the benefits which Character bestows on its possessor, the young man who realizes what constitutes Character and its importance to his future advancement, and who armors himself with an inflexible determination to cultivate and practice those habits—of body, and mind and morals—which form the elements of Character.

HONESTY.

THE keystone in the arch of Character is Honesty, and he who would win and wear the crown of success cannot too earnestly appreciate the fact when he places his foot upon the lowest rung of the ladder of life. And it is well not to mistake what Honesty is. It is not that superficial kind of Honesty which is the mere creation of a habit of education, a sentiment which vaguely recognizes that dishonesty is disgraceful, and which too often, in after life, degenerates into belief that the disgrace consists only in being found out. It is not that self-satisfied feeling which attends prosperity reached without passing through the crucible of adversity. Honesty, in the sense in which Character is founded, is based upon the bed-rock of moral principle, and should be the supreme and governing impulse of action, even where necessity was most strongly appealed to by temptation. It is a quality which, though quiet and unobtrusive, and modest from its inherent nature, never fails in the course of life to make itself recognized, and to bring its reward to its possessor, in trust, confidence, promotion, and opportunities for advancement, which the unstable or doubtful character will not find open to it. He who strives to form his character so that he may grasp confidently for success, will be honest because it is right; because it is a moral obligation with rewards and penalties in a higher code of laws than those of business; and because it pays to be honest. There never was a truer axiom than that which says, "Honesty is the best policy." It is not only the best policy, but it is the only policy upon which to found Character on a basis which will uphold a superstructure of success.

INDUSTRY.

PERHAPS the attribute of Character next in importance to Honesty is Industry. And in no respect does a young man's future rest so entirely with himself as in this. No matter how honest or faithful the young man may be; no matter how bright his intellect, nor how promising his opportunities; if he have allowed the fatal habit of indolence and sloth to grow upon him, his efforts will be in vain. Industry is the working partner in the firm of attributes which constitute Character. It is the aggressive weapon in the battle of life, and it is trenchant, effective, and victorious in its progress just in proportion to its quality. If it be vigorous, persistent and in constant exercise, no difficulties will stay its course. If it be feeble, spasmodic and irregular in its application, a meagre measure of success, or more likely total disappointment, is the certain result. It is the quality above all others which attracts attention, which most readily enlists sympathy, insures confidence, and brings material assistance to him who constantly displays that faculty in every work to which he applies his hand or his head, whether for himself or others. There is nothing of greater importance to the youth who sets out in the journey of life with an ambition for success, than that he should early so cultivate habits of industry that they become a second nature to him. Such a habit makes the whole work of a life easier, renders obstacles less difficult to overcome, and success more easy of attainment. It commands confidence, inspires respect, and is the best assurance a man can give to himself of his ability to grasp the prizes of life.

SOBRIETY.

NO one who is ever likely to take a prominent position in competition for honor and place in the race of life, needs to have it impressed upon him that Sobriety must go hand in hand with Honesty and Industry in the constitution of that Character by means of which success alone can be attained. No person of years of discretion and matured judgment needs to have pointed out to him, in the face of the experience with which he is daily confronted, the fatal results which invariably attend the absence of a strict and uncompromising observance of an undeviating habit of Sobriety. Anything less than that is dangerous to all, and fatal to most men. To the young man who desires to succeed in life, Sobriety is absolutely essential; and, aside from the fact that without that quality he can seek in vain for the confidence which leads to trust and promotion, or which will give to his abilities the scope of favorable opportunity, he who deliberately ignores this condition, in the face of the warning beacons with which his course is surrounded, and deliberately risks the breakers of failure and disappointment and the rocky shores of ruin, is not deserving of sympathy, much less of success. It is, at the beginning of a career, the easiest of all the elements which make up Character to have under control; because the resort to insobriety is, at the first, a violence to nature, at which every faculty and sense rises in revolt and repugnance. It is a false and unnatural habit, which is only to be attained by vicious cultivation, which blights the promise of life in the bud. Aside from these and higher moral considerations, the dictates of selfishness and common-sense say to the young man, that sobriety is desirable because it is essential to his success. Insobriety is to be avoided because it is a profligate of time; because it is injurious to the health; because it involves a senseless expenditure of money; because it destroys the possibility of attaining confidence, and puts barriers in the way of advancement; and because it creates contact with associations injurious to personal reputation and prospects. In the individual case it is in the period of early manhood in which his conduct, in this respect, is subjected to the closest criticism and scrutiny. His movements, his personal tendencies, his companionship, and his associations, are more narrowly observed than he dreams by his elders, already engaged in the serious affairs of life, and to whom presently he will have to owe his opportunities for advancement and success. And this is the case in every walk of life, commercial or professional, but more strictly so, perhaps, among business men. It is not necessary that the young man should be a recluse or an anchorite; convivial and social qualities are esteemed with favor in the business world, if they lead a man to clean and rational amusements, to honorable and elevating companionship, and to the avoidance of contact with all that is low, vicious and degrading, or even questionable. But it is a rule that, long before the youth knocks at the door of the business world for admission and seeks to be assigned a place there, older heads have scrutinized this feature of his character, and will meet him with welcome and favor, or with doubt and distrust, according to whether or not he has approved himself, at the threshold of life, a sober young man. Let it be solemnly and earnestly borne in mind that Character cannot be complete unless it be marked by the habit of Sobriety, and that, while a young man must be content to use and improve the intellect with which nature has endowed him, and may only overcome the difficulties of poverty and want of influence, by a struggle of time, it is in his own power, by the simple exercise of his will, and proper regard for his self-respect and self-interest, to engrave at once and for his lifetime the attribute of Sobriety upon his Character.

FIDELITY.

FIDELITY is one of the most beautiful traits in the human Character, and is not the least regarded, nor the least important among its composite elements. The man who holds faithful to the principles of honor, who aspires to stamp upon his career the royal insignia of true nobility, who aims to be esteemed as one of "nature's gentlemen," will be found faithful to every trust. He will by his conduct in life establish in his daily progress his fidelity to every duty, to his employer, to his family, and to himself. He who has earned, in whatsoever sphere of life he may elect to move, a reputation for fidelity, has already placed his foot firmly upon the ground of success. It is a quality which commands universal respect, and which most speedily begets confidence and regard, even from the least susceptible, and where it is exhibited so as to be unmistakable in its genuineness, it is an infallible passport to advancement and preferment. No young man who proves himself steadfastly and unswervingly faithful to every trust, however small or humble, will ever fail to find friends in his course, who will take pleasure in helping him forward in the battle of life. Fidelity in a man is a touchstone which invariably develops its like when brought into contact with other natures, and while, in a higher sense, it is its own reward, the young man who enters the conflict of existence with nothing but talent and Character as his capital, will find in after life that Fidelity, in whatever measure of success he has achieved, has been one of his most effective instruments.

ECONOMY AND FRUGALITY.

ECONOMY is a feature of character which solely affects the individual and reflects upon his prospects and opportunities. How frequently are we led to wonder that Mr. A. or Mr. B., whose silvering locks betoken that age is growing upon him, and whom we have known ever to be honest, industrious, sober and faithful, is still a clerk at the desk, or a professional man in a rented house, with always a hard struggle to make both ends meet. It is not in these cases always, or even often, a lack of ambition. It is that there has been on the part of such a person a something wanting in the foundation of his career—a flaw in an otherwise excellent character, which makes him capable of doing his duty in life to everyone's advantage but his own. Economy and frugality are qualities which must be acquired, if ever, in early life, and which are only to be affixed to the character, so as to be borne without being a burden, by painstaking self-denial in youth till they become settled habits of nature. It is natural to man to be luxurious, to take all the comforts and enjoyments out of life which his pecuniary resources will permit, and where this feeling is not restrained by the cultivation of Economy, it becomes a fixture in the Character, and the man who gives way to it will go on through life, without seeming extravagance, yet self-indulgently limiting his outlay only by his income. The young man should take strict care to be master of his own appetites and wants, and while penury and parsimony are among the passive vices, he should, at all times in life but particularly in youth, always maintain a balance to the credit of each month's income, and year by year increase the store which will, when the time and the opportunity arrive, form a capital for the commencement of business. He who has shown his capacity to thus lay up for a rainy day, will find always credit and business friends, while at all events common prudence advises every one to make a provision for the future, for any calamity or untoward fortune that may befall; and if this be done in youth, the habit of Economy is insensibly acquired, a lasting benefit through life.

PERSEVERANCE.

AMONG the leading features of Character, which chiefly fit it to beget success, is Perseverance. It is by no means one of the virtues the most easy to practice, but it is one that is perhaps the most surely of all, certain to find a rich reward in results. Youth is the season of hot blood, of vivid imagination, and of impatient ambition. Nature is at that period more volatile—liable to unreasonable inflation of expectation upon slight foundation, and still more to unreasonable periods of depression and despondency on the occasion of every reverse or unfavorable circumstance. But the man who starts out in life with the necessity for Perseverance against all difficulties, so thoroughly impressed upon his mind by his habit of thought as to be a fixed part of his Character, is equipped for every emergency, and has as certain a prospect of success before him as it is possible to compass in the scope of human effort. It is a quality that should be early cultivated and ingrained into the character so as to be ineradicable. Over the sea of human life it is not all nor always smooth sailing. Upon the fairest sky the clouds will arise, and the serenity of its beauty be, without warning, distorted by the anger of the tempest. So it is in life, and when all seems smooth for the path of progress, difficulties spring up, and perhaps disasters befall, in spite of every precaution and of every desert, and it is at such times as these that he who lacks Perseverance is tossed like a ship without ballast, oftimes to utter destruction, while the vessel with Perseverance at the helm will weather the gale in safety, and, if shaken in the struggle, will still keep on the course and finally reach the haven of Prosperity and Success.

PATIENCE.

IMPATIENCE is a habit which often and seriously interferes with the progress of the most deserving young man, and jeopardizes the whole future of his career. Like Perseverance, it is one of the virtues of self-denial, and requires self-control and determination and early practice, before it can be reckoned a part of Character, or be proof against the assaults of temptation. It is a part of good temper, which is essential not only to a man's own comfort through life, but to that of those with whom he is brought into contact. It is slow to anger, and quick to forgiveness. It cements friendship, strengthens old ties, and creates new ones. It is the quality which at the beginning of a young man's career is the most likely to be tried, and to be tried most frequently. It guards against seeing affront where none was intended, and curbs the rising temper, and prevents hostility, where others give way to anger. The man who has patience is far superior to him who loses his temper, and his superiority is soon recognized in the world in which he moves. It avoids at the outset of his career difficulties which otherwise deprive men of useful and influential friends, in employers, and those in authority over him, and is an attribute of Character which, while it requires constant watchfulness through life, is one of its greatest beautifiers.

DETERMINATION.

EVERY young man should set out in life with the distinct understanding that he who is not master of himself will be the slave of many weaknesses and follies which will beset his course through life with difficulties and dangers. The young man should early cultivate the exercise of his will-power, so as to acquire, as a habit, an inflexible Determination in the pursuit of all that is upright, honorable, elevating and profitable, and in the shunning of all that is ignoble, degrading, frivolous or vicious. "He cannot say, 'No!'" Upon the tombstones of how many brightly-dawning lives, high ambitions and brilliant prospects, is this confession of weakness the pitiable epitaph! No young man can do justice to himself, to his opportunities, or to his prospects in life, unless he early acquires and practices this thorough command and mastery over the weaknesses and frailties of nature. He who is his own master—that is, the master of his own impulses, passions, appetites and prejudices—has a safeguard against temptation through life of invaluable importance, and which will not only prove a profit and advantage to himself, but will command the respect of men of weaker will. It is a guard against the infirmities of temper, against the demands of extravagance, against the risks in which indulgent good nature would involve a business man, against the insidious approach of vicious or undesirable habits and evil and unprofitable associations. Determination is in itself a virile virtue, and it develops and strengthens every other mental and moral faculty.

CLEANLINESS.

CLEANLINESS, in the proverb, is placed next to Godliness. It is not the least desirable and important of those personal attributes which constitute Character, and is a most essential feature of the conditions which go to make up *mens sana in corpore sano*. It is not only essential to physical health and comfort, but it is an indicator of the habits of mind as well. The young man who is careless about his personal appearance and attire, can hardly be expected to have the exact and tidy habits which become a well-ordered counting-room, while he is open to suspicion, perhaps, and generally no doubt, of being a moral as well as a personal "slouch." He who does not see that his apparel and personal habits are clean, if not dandified, and tidy, if not expensive, will find that he will labor from the first at a disadvantage in making his way through the world, and will have himself to blame if he be suspected by others—more particularly by those in the social and business world with whom he most desires to (with whom it is most important to him he shall) stand in good estimation—of lack of proper pride and self-respect, and indifference to the suggestions of good taste and a desire to please. And the young man cannot be too mindful of the fact that this cleanliness must not only mark his habits of dress and person, but also of mind, manners, language and morals.

SELF-CULTIVATION.

THIS is a subject whose importance no young man who sets out in life with an ambition to make his mark in the world, can afford to overlook. How frequently in after life a man finds cause to regret bitterly those leisure hours of youth wasted beyond recall in idleness or in social frivolity, in which he might have improved his mind, expanded his intellect, perfected his education, widened his sphere of knowledge and information, and lessened ten-fold the difficulties which he has had to surmount in the road to prosperity and success in life. Youth is the period at which the mind is in the plastic condition; when it receives impressions most readily and retains them most faithfully and permanently; when knowledge is acquired with the least labor and exertion. It is the period, too, when the student is less oppressed with the cares of life, with the responsibilities of business, and with those anxieties and perplexities which come later in life to fill up the whole current of existence. Some of the best men of our day, who began life in the most humble circumstances, with but the barest rudiments of an education, and amid all the discouragements which beset poverty and friendlessness, have become learned and widely read men of the world, capable of taking a creditable position in the circles of men of letters, when their advancement in life threw them into such society, by devoting a few hours in the evening of each day to persistent, determined and industrious effort at self-improvement. The advantages enjoyed by the present generation for this object are incalculable. The golden treasury of knowledge is open wide to all who choose to avail themselves of its priceless stores. The printing press, the great educator of the day, by its marvelous labor, places within the reach and within the means of every young man the facilities by which his mind can be stored with every description of knowledge, whether calculated to aid him in the practical struggle with the world, or to equip himself with those graces and accomplishments of intellect which embellish and adorn his intercourse with others, and are a source of indescribable pleasure and satisfaction to him who—in the full enjoyment of the wider fields of interest, amusement, speculation, contemplation, thought and action, thus opened to him—can look back and thank God for the wisdom which led him to the task of improving the idle hours of youth to self-cultivation, and for the determination which enabled him to persist in the pursuit of knowledge until it became no longer a task, but a pleasure and delight.

RISE AND LABOR.

I had drank with lips unsated
  Where the founts of pleasure burst,
I had hewn out broken cisterns,
  But they mocked my spirit's thirst;

And I said, life is a desert,
  Hot, and measureless and dry,
And God will not give me water,
  Though I thirst, and pant, and die!

Spoke there a friend and brother:
  "Rise and roll the stone away:
There are wells of life upspringing
  To thy pathway every day."

But I said: "My lips are sinful,
  Very sinful in my speech,
And the wells of God's salvation
  Are too deep for me to reach."

Then he answered: "Rise and labor;
  Doubt and idleness are death;
Shape thee out a goodly vessel
  With the strong hand of thy faith.'

Then I rose and shaped a vessel
  And knelt lowly, humbly, there,
And I drew up living water
  By the golden chain of prayer.

THE WORLD'S LETTER-BAGS.

THE statistics of the Universal Postal Union for last year, collected and published by the International Bureau at Berne, Switzerland, shows that in number of postoffices the United States ranks first, with 45,512 offices, and Great Britain next, with 14,918 offices. Japan is far in advance of Russia, British India, Austria, Italy and Spain, in the number of her postoffices, having 5,094. Switzerland ranks first in the relative portion between the number of her postoffices and the population, having an average of 985 inhabitants to each postoffice; the United States has 1,126; Norway has 2,054; and Great Britain has 2,362 inhabitants for each office. In the number of letters conveyed by mail Great Britain ranks first, with 1,229,354,800; the United States next, with 1,046,107,348; then Germany with 563-, 225,700; and France with 535,541,373. The Argentine Republic stands at the bottom of the list. The United States conveys more postal cards than any other country; Germany comes next, followed by Great Britain and Austria.

In completeness and perfection of arrangements, the mail service of the United States, notwithstanding the magnificent distances to be overcome, is with its railway mail system, admittedly the best in the world.

In respect to the number of letters and postal cards to each inhabitant, the countries rank as follows: Great Britain, 38.7; the United States, 27.3; Switzerland, 19.9; Germany, 15.8.

The United States has 91,571 miles of railroad; Germany has 20,573; France 16,822, and Russia 14,439 miles.

In number of newspapers conveyed in domestic mails, the United States ranks first, with 852,180,792; Germany second, with 439,089,900; France third, with 320,188,636, and Great Britain fourth, with 140,789,100.

In respect to the amount of gross postal revenue, Germany takes the lead with $41,064,843; the United States next, with $38,-926,088; Great Britain third, with $35,138,000; and France fourth, with $30,593,713.

Great Britain, Germany and France had a net revenue in 1881 ranging from $13,705,020 to $3,980,088; but the United States, Russia and Japan had a deficiency in revenue, the same year, ranging from $2,883,615 to $264,168.

THE FOUR SEASONS.

THE SEASONS.

These, as they change, Almighty Father, these
Are but the varied God. The rolling year
Is full of Thee. Forth in the pleasing SPRING
Thy BEAUTY walks, thy TENDERNESS and LOVE.
Wide flush the fields; the softening air is balm.
Echo the mountains round; the forest smiles,
And every sense, and every heart, is joy.

Then comes thy GLORY in the SUMMER months
With light and heat effulgent. Then thy SUN
Shootest full perfection through the swelling year;
And oft thy VOICE in dreadful thunder speaks,
And oft at dawn, deep noon, or falling eve,
By brooks and groves, in hollow-whispering gales.

Thy BOUNTY shines in AUTUMN unconfined,
And spreads a common feast for all that lives.

In WINTER, awful Thou! with clouds and storms
Around thee thrown, tempest o'er tempest rolled.
Majestic darkness! On the whirlwind's wing,
Riding sublime, Thou bidst the world adore,
And humblest Nature with thy northern blast.

THE mysterious round of the Seasons, which Thompson, in his Hymn, apostrophizes as the manifestation of the Creator in the things of Nature, is one of the most beautiful forms in which the inscrutable Power which controls and directs the grand harmonies of the universe, is presented to the finite minds of men. Nor has all the wisdom of man, in the most profound and indefatigable labors of science, pursued with ardor and determination for centuries, been able to bring us even to the threshhold of knowledge and comprehension of these mysteries, which lie beyond the curtain through which all must pass at the close of their earthly career, but from which none has ever returned to enlighten the unceasing and unavailing curiosity of mankind. Even with all the knowledge which science has placed within our reach, we can but scan as "through a glass darkly" the shadowy portents of the Infinite, and the only lesson we are enabled to learn with certainty from the endless circles of the Seasons, is that which teaches us, in an unerring and awe-inspiring voice, the immortality of all animate nature—that that which we call Death is but the gateway to Resurrection, reproduction and development into a new life of higher perfection. The beauty and fragrance of the flower fades away and perishes from our sight and sense; the blooming meadows, on whose verdant bosom the modest daisies are kissed by the grateful dews and caressed by the Æolian zephyrs, become black and bare and desolate before the chill breath of inexorable Winter. The grateful trees which hang their blossoming garlands upon the beauteous brow of virgin Spring, and interpose their umbrageous shade to the hot and amorous breath of sighing Summer, yield their golden favors and ripened beauties to the Autumn, and relapse into the bareness and blackness of apparent dissolution. But we know, as surely as we know that the Seasons return in their appointed courses, that this Death is a delusion; that the fetters of Winter's dissolution will be broken in the resurrection of the coming again of Spring, and that once more the laughter-laden vernal breezes will waft the fragrance of the blushing blossoms abroad upon the flowering meads, and that again from out the bonds of the sleep of nature will burst in triumph the foliage, the flower and the fruit. The four seasons, Spring, Summer, Autumn and Winter, proceeding in their unfailing round, typify, in a manner and with a significance which is more than an accident, as well the course of existence of humanity, as of the plant, the tree and the flower; and their recurrence, after undergoing the process of apparent decay and death, conveys in language not to be misunderstood the great and awful lesson of Immortality. In the life of man there are distinctly marked the four Seasons—the Spring, the Summer, the Autumn and the Winter—the bud, the blossom, the fruit, and the sere and yellow leaf which ushers in life's winter, Death, from which the immortal part of that which expires passes to the resurrection of a new Spring, the knowledge of which is shut out from our present existence by the impenetrable veil which the hand of inscrutable wisdom holds before our eager and inquiring gaze. These four seasons of life have each their peculiar and separate conditions and course of existence, and we pass in order from the one stage to the other—from the helplessness of infancy to the promise of youth, the materializing fruition of maturity, and thence again to the decay of old age, and the grave—through whose grim and dreadful portals each must pass in his appointed time, and by whose shadowy vale of tears lies the only avenue to the promise of the new Spring-time in the life beyond. As the varying seasons have their peculiar vicissitudes and accidents, their sunshine and storm, their periods of calm repose and tempestuous turbulence, so the Seasons of Life are made up of smiles and tears, of joys and sorrows, and delights and disasters. And as we know, even in the limited scope of the visual horizon of human knowledge, that there is nothing in this universe left to Chance—that the vicissitudes which the varying currents of the seasons present, are the results of well-defined laws under which distinct conditions will evolve definite effects—so we know, too, that in the seasons of our lives, whatever of light or shadow, of sunshine or of tempest, may fall across our pathway, these accidences are governed by undeviating laws, under which the conditions to which we expose ourselves or are exposed, produce inevitable and certain results. And it is in this respect that man is the superior of all created things,—that by the gift of reason which makes him kin to divinity, he can so order his own life in all its courses that he may sow the seed in his Spring time with the full knowledge of what the harvest of his Autumn will bring to his reaping.

In the perfectly ordered life, there is, as in the eternal round of the Seasons in the march of nature, a perfect rhythm and harmony. The Spring melts imperceptibly away into the bosom of Summer, which in its turn gilds the borders of autumnal glory with its expiring rays, while the Autumn lends a halo to mellow the gray advance of winter. So in life. Childhood advances with a stealthy and imperceptible step toward Youth, and we have scarce had time to note and become accustomed to the change, when the youth assumes the duties and dignities of Manhood. The whole of life is a harmony in which there are no sharp or rudden divisions, and it is only when we survey the whole ground, that we can properly separate the distinct periods which constitute existence.

These four Seasons, then, constitute the field of every man's life, and it is a duty which prudence suggests to young and old alike, that they should study well its every feature, both for example to emulate, monuments to guide, and beacons to warn away from danger—the old that they may add their own experience to that of others, and apply it to the guidance of the youth, and the young that they may learn how best to lay hold upon the securities and safeguards of their future happiness. Experience is the great teacher of life. It is the principle of progress. By it alone each succeeding generation mounts to a higher plane of moral and material, mental and physical development. In the labors of life it is to the pilgrim upon that journey through its four revolving Seasons, what his chart and compass is to the mariner who sets out toward a boundless horizon in the sure faith and confidence that these guides will lead him unerringly to the haven he seeks.

SPRING.

"Our wean's the most wonderful wean I e'er saw;
  It wad tak' me a lang simmer day to tell a'
His pranks, frae the mornin' till night shuts his ee,
  When he sleeps like a peerie, 'tween father and me;
For in his quite turns siccan questions he'll spier!
  How the moon can stick up in the sky that's sae clear?
What gars the wind blaw? and whar frae comes the rain?
  He's a perfec' divert—he's a wonderfu' wean!

"But, 'mid a' his daffin sic kindness he shows,
  That he's dear to my heart as the dew to the rose;
And the unclouded hinnybeam aye in his ee
  Makes him every day dearer and dearer to me.
Though Fortune be saucy and dorty, and dour,
  And gloom through her fingers like hills through a shooer,
When bodies hae got a bit bairn o' their ain,
  How he cheers up their hearts!—he's a wonderfu' wean!"

CHILDHOOD is the spring-time of life. It is the period when the physical, mental and moral capabilities are in the tender bud, and gently unfolding their beauties and graces to the genial influences and beneficent atmosphere of their domestic surroundings, or developing the infancy of defects and blemishes cultivated by an unhealthy air devoid of the warmth which should glow at the fireside of every true home. The child has been rightly called by Wordsworth, "the Father of the Man," and those who have assumed the grave and solemn responsibilities of parentage should remember that it is they who are to be held to account for the manhood or womanhood which is to be developed from the tender infant, the guidance of whose growth and formation of whose character is committed to their charge. From the first dawn of the new life the work of parents in the education of the child begins, and it may be divided into three departments: first, the physical development; second, the formation of healthy moral and mental habits; third, the study of the happiness of the child. And these departments of duty, care and labor, offer to those upon whom they devolve a pleasure in the performance and a satisfaction in the result, than which there are no higher to be attained in any other of the supreme rewards of a well spent life. In early infancy the sole care of the child falls upon the mother, and in these duties the instincts of the mother-love may be relied upon to secure their full performance. That mother fails to realize the true nobility of womanhood, who would commit the nourishment of her offspring to the breast of a stranger, and who

BOYHOOD.

Ah! then how sweetly closed those parting days,
The minutes parting one by one like rays
  That fade upon a summer's eve.
    But, oh! what charm or magic numbers
    Can give me back the gentle slumbers
  Those weary happy days did leave?
When by my bed I saw my mother kneel,
    And with her blessing took her nightly kiss,
    Whatever Time destroys, he cannot this—
E'en now that nameless kiss I feel.

WASHINGTON ALLSTON.

in the first two years of the infancy of her child leaves the tender blossom to the cold attention, or even the rude caresses, of careless dependents, in which the very earliest infancy of the child detects the absence of that maternal sympathy and care, which is as essential to its healthy growth as air and sunshine to the tenderest plant that grows.

As the dawn of intelligence begins to assert itself, and reason takes possession of its kingdom in the mind of the child, the duties of parentage begin to be divided between the mother and father, and each should vie with the other in cultivating for themselves the serene and happy fireside joys, which spring from the proper performance of them. It is at this period of life that an unvarying love and tenderness, careful consultation of the happiness of the child in its childish sphere, accompanied by judicious firmness, will secure the habit of obedience founded on love, and save the parents many a painful experience which they will certainly encounter, if this simple rule, which ought itself to be a mutual delight between parent and child, be overlooked, and the lessons of authority have to be enforced by fear as the child advances toward youth. Let every parent remember that the period of childhood is the only one in life in which perfect and unalloyed happiness, untainted by a single anxiety and unalloyed with any responsibility, are possible to any human being between the cradle and the grave. To make the lives of children joyous and happy is a duty which every parent should observe, and lays the best foundation that can be placed under a stable character, a buoyant temperament, and an amiable disposition, which are sure to follow such a course.

It is in this period of life that the early work of forming character begins, and the simple lessons which may be indelibly impressed upon the white pages of the childish mind will cling to it through life, strengthening and confirming the more serious teachings which the expanding intelligence, discretion and reason call for. The first lessons to be taught, and which are the more easily conveyed because nature has made the virgin soil congenial for the reception of healthy sentiments, are the habits of truthfulness, of kindness and tenderness, of sympathy, and of abhorrence of anger and passion. These things should be watchfully kept ever before the child till they fix themselves upon its mind as a habit, and make the lessons of morality more easily learned, more readily understood and more gratefully received, when they come to be presented at the years of early discretion, on other and higher grounds to its reason and intelligence.

The period of school life is, or ought to be one of the most anxious to the parents. While the public school is best for the child, tending to instill into it early the lessons of self-reliance, and to give the impulse of emulation to its ambition, it is also attended with many dangers for the child first fluttering from the parental nest. Endeavor should be made to divert the current of the childish frendships and associations into wholesome and healthful channels. Encourage it to take pride in the company of children whose parents are known to be governed by piety and uprightness, and teach it to despise and avoid the company of idle and vicious playmates. In this you may be certain, from your knowledge of the parents, whether the child be a desirable companion.

Too great care cannot be exercised, not only in those things which concern the present health of the young child, but in the formation of habits which will make even its daily round of pleasures, and the outcome of its instincts of activity and love of pleasure, auxiliaries ever at work in the development of its physical health and strength. Habits of cleanliness are among the first. The child should be not only taught to submit to be "washed" with docility, but should be educated to find its bath one of its most congenial pleasures. Rough or careless handling of children of tender years by servants, and even by careless and too vigorous mothers, often creates a sentiment of repugnance to the bath that makes the duties of cleanliness irksome through life, and leads to their abandonment in time of youth, when they can be avoided, just at the period when the careful observance of the habits of cleanliness of the person are of the greatest importance to the development of robust and vigorous manhood and womanhood. It is the nature of the child to find its earliest pleasures in activity. It is an instinct implanted there by nature to secure the harmonious growth of physical health, strength and perfection. Encourage the child at play. Teach it to find its favorite diversions in active exercise. Bring to its favor pastimes which take it much into the open air and sunlight. Avoid any mistaken kindnesses which are calculated to foster the false habit of effeminacy, which, if permitted to usurp the supremacy of the healthy instincts of nature, will surely to a greater or less degree dwarf and stunt the whole physical being and rob it of the complete development to which it is entitled. By observing these rules, the parent may safely count upon witnessing the progress of the Child to the period of Youth, and its transition from the Spring to the Summer of life, attended by all the conditions most favorable to the higher stage of development upon which it now enters.

MAIDENHOOD.

Maiden with the meek, brown eyes,
In whose orbs a shadow lies
Like the dusk in evening skies!
*   *   *   *   *   *
Standing with reluctant feet,
Where the brook and river meet,
Womanhood and childhood fleet!

Gazing with a timid glance,
On the brooklet's swift advance,
On the river's broad expanse!
*   *   *   *   *   *

Bear a lily in thy hand.
Gates of brass cannot withstand
One touch of that magic wand.
*   *   *   *   *   *
Bear through sorrow, wrong and ruth
In thy heart the dew of youth,
On thy lips the smile of truth.
*   *   *   *   *   *
And that smile like sunshine dart
Into many a sunless heart,
For a smile of God thou art.

LONGFELLOW.

SUMMER.

"A breeze 'mid blossoms straying,
Where Hope clung feeding like a bee—
Both were mine! Life went a-Maying
With Nature, Hope and Poesy
When I was young!

* * * * * * *

"O'er aery cliffs and glittering sands,
How lightly then it flashed along:
Like those trim skiffs, unknown of yore,
On winding lakes and rivers wide;
That ask no aid of sail or oar,
That fear no spite of wind or tide
Naught cared this body for wind or weather
When Youth and I lived in't together.

"Flowers are lovely; Love is flower-like;
Friendship is a sheltering tree,
Oh, the joys that came down shower-like
Of Friendship, Love and Liberty,
Ere I was old!

—*Coleridge.*

YOUTH is the Summer season of life. It is the season when the joys of independence, the sweets of friendships, the pride of intellect, the elastic pleasures of conscious health and strength, the realization by the mind of the fair expanse of the empire of reason over which it wields the sceptre, come in the first flush of the pleasure of enjoyment to the fullest capacity for grateful appreciation. It is the period when life is a garden of roses, and the happy youth will follow the advice of the poet:

"Gather the rosebuds while ye may."

The old time theories of ascetic philosophy and ascetic religion have in these days of progress and advancement given place to a higher and better creed, that youth, health, beauty, flowers and sunshine, in the things of life and nature, are given us to be enjoyed to the fullest degree consistent with innocence and integrity. The teacher who advises:

"Remember now thy Creator in the days of thy youth,"

is the same who also says to us:

"Rejoice, oh young man in thy youth."

The school of the duties of life, in which our youth should be spent, is no longer to be regarded as a cave of gloom, which the youth or maiden has to endure, with an impatient longing for the emancipation that the advent to maturity brings. On the contrary, where it has true guidance, the summer of youth will find the parental authority a garland of roses; will discover in every duty a delight; will distinguish true pleasures from the false and vicious, and tread in safety the fields of innocent enjoyment with an elastic and buoyant measure. The youth should find in the father the "guide, philopher and friend," and the maiden, in the mother, the companion and confidante. Sympathy and confidence should mark every relation between the Summer and the Autumn seasons of life. The parent will reap the grateful rewards of filial obedience, respect and confidence, from the love and consideration bestowed upon youth, and the light with which he is able enhance its sunshine; and youth will find it a pleasure to render the tribute of obedience to the paternal rule and observance of its advice and admonition, in grateful recognition of the affection and tender regard of the parental effort to beautify and brighten its buoyant existence.

Youth should always remember that this is the season of preparation for the more serious duties and responsibilities of life, and it has, in its early period, arrived at years of sufficient discretion to comprehend fully how entirely the vigor, strength, pride and success of maturity is dependent upon the formation of character, the acquisition of knowledge and the cultivation of physical, mental and moral health, in that time of life which is left wholly free to pursue this course of healthful preparation. Do not imagine that the most devoted attention to these prerequisites of your future success in life will interfere with the fullest enjoyment of the pleasures of life's Summer. On the contrary, rightly appreciated and conducted, these important duties are among the best of pleasures, and go to make up the variety which is the spice of life in all stages of its enjoyment. The youth devoted wholly to aimless amusements, to the neglect of solid accomplishments, will soon find that his sweetness clogs upon him, and his sense of enjoyment palls, while he has perchance lost the faculty of application and the capacity of appreciation for the things of higher importance. Remember that the choicest fruit, the healthiest plant, the flower of rarest beauty and fragrance, is not that which draws its growth and inspiration of life from artificial light and heat, but that which is the true offspring of nature, nurtured by the free air of heaven, and fostered by the genial rays which come direct from the centre of light and life in the universe. "Work while you work, and play while you play," is a homely but a good and wholesome adage, and contains a whole volume of wisdom if rightly interpreted. When you devote yourself to physical exercises, either for recreation or for improvement, put your whole mind and strength into it. Remember that "health

THE MOTHER'S LOVE.

Is there, when the winds are singing
  In the happy summer time,
When the raptured air is ringing
With earth's music heavenward springing,
  Forest chirp, and village chime;
Is there of the sounds that float
Minglingly, a single note
Half so sweet, and clear, and wild,
As the laughter of a child?

Yes; a mother's large affection,
  Hears with a mysterious sense,
Breathings that evade detection,
Whispers faint, and fine inflection,
  Thrill in her with power intense.
Childhood's honey'd tones untaught,
Heareth she in living thought!
Tones that never thence depart,
For she listens—with her heart.

LAMAN BLANCHARD.

is the vital principle of bliss," and is essential to the highest and most perfect enjoyment of every pleasure of life. In the time allotted to study and mental improvement devote yourself to the task with undivided attention and industry, and an appreciation of not only its future importance but of the present pleasures which are to be found by the earnest student among the treasures of knowledge. In the pastimes and social pleasures of youth, give your powers of enjoyment full scope and play, and you will find your capacity for the enjoyment of innocent and healthful pleasures redoubled by the wholesome appetite which will have been created by diligent attention to the duties owed to mental, moral and physical development. Bear in mind always the words of the wise man:

"Wisdom is the principal thing: therefore get wisdom: and with all thy getting, get understanding."

"Her ways are ways of pleasantness, and all her paths are peace."

AUTUMN.

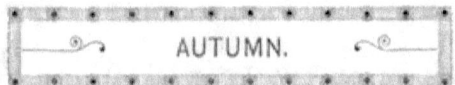

"Season of mists and mellow fruitfulness!
Close bosom-friend of the maturing sun!
Conspiring with him how to load and bless
With fruit the vines that round the thatch-eaves run
To bend with apples the moss'd cottage trees,
And fill all fruit with ripeness to the core—
To swell the gourd and plump the hazel shells
With a sweet kernel—to set budding more,
And still more, later flowers for the trees,
Until they think warm days will never cease,
For Summer has o'er-brimm'd their clammy cells."

—*John Keats.*

MANHOOD and womanhood are the Autumn of life, the season of perfection and fruition. The boundaries of youth have been passed, the stately vessel, fully equipped for the sea of life, laden with its precious cargo of hopes, duties, aspirations, ambitions and responsibilities, cuts adrift from the moorings in the placid river which flows alongside the parental home, and steers its course bravely out upon the broad expanse of ocean, to seek that unknown shore which Fortune may appoint. The ties of childhood and home are severed and the youth of yesterday goes out into the world to-day in the strong and conscious vigor of manhood to set up new altars and found new destinies of which he himself shall be the head. The maiden will have attained to that womanhood to whose boundaries she has been led by the hand of modest and reluctant maidenhood, and will have joined her fortunes with the man toward whom her heart and her inclinations have directed her, and thenceforth through the Autumn period of life, these two streams will flow in one channel onward to the sunset, which ushers in the repose of the evening and winter of life. In this golden age are gathered the fruits of the labors of life, and to those who have attended to the duties of youth—who have founded character upon enduring principles, who have brought to their aid industry and perseverance, and the higher guidance of sound morality—the harvest of that season is one continued return, which honors every draft made upon it in the course of life—a fragrant flowering plant which is in perennial bloom. But whatever may have been the successes of life in material things—and these are generally in proportion to the industry, fidelity and enterprise brought to bear upon them—whatever fortune may have attended the efforts for personal distinction, for commercial success, or for public ambition, the highest prizes of life will always be found to be those which cluster around the domestic altar. It is at the shrine of home that the most fragrant incense of our lives is sought and found, and it is here that we live our higher and better life. In his own house every man is a sovereign, and in a well ordered Christian home, where the domestic virtues are cultivated, where the fireside graces hover round, where culture and refinement pervade every relation, and where love and courtesy abound, the household monarch and his consort have a court in which there is more honor, truth and loyalty than in the glittering circle which surrounds the crown and sceptre of the proudest throne. Here in mutual respect and honor, cemented by the experiences of life, the man and wife pass the golden Autumn days, in the serenity of personal comfort and bountiful surroundings which flow in from labors and duties faithfully performed in the outer world; here they live again in their children the loves and joys of their own childhood and youth; here they watch with thankful pride the stately growth of sons and daughters, whose infancy was tended with anxious prayers, and whose childhood nurtured with tender care and loving hope.

In this happy harvest time of life, in which the gilded hours are divided between public, business, social and domestic duties, the too common error of the age is towards excess of kindness in dealing with the following generation. The father who has made his way to affluence and prosperity against early discouragements and adversities, who can remember vividly the cruelties of poverty, and who still feels the frosts which sometimes chilled the growth of springtime, is too frequently prone, in his anxiety for the welfare and comfort of his children, to over-indulgence. No greater mistake can be made in life, nor is there any greater refinement of cruelty, than the infliction of incapacity upon a young man through the mistaken kindness of parents. While it is fit and eminently proper that the parent should accustom the young man to every reasonable indulgence suited to his fortunes, every young man should be as thoroughly equipped for the stern realities of life, as if he had the world to win for himself. There should be no difference in the physical and mental education of the son of the mechanic and that of the millionaire, except in the degree of luxury of living. Every man should become the master of some calling, art or profession, without regard to fortune. The present generation presents a most memorable and melancholy example, in the family of the most illustrious military figure of his age, the second savior of this great republic, of what sad and gloomy skies may come to cloud the ripe Autumn days of life, by that undue kindness to children which unfits them for the practical duties of existence.

If there be a fault to be found with the progressive, vigorous, energetic mode of life which is distinctively American, the characteristic of the healthy vitality of our people and of their institutions, it is the tendency, too often developed, to allow the mind to become wholly engrossed in the cares of business, to the neglect of that large fund of resources for the higher enjoyments of domestic and social life, which every man with a sound mind in a healthy body inherently possesses. And this, when it does occur, invariably encroaches upon that period of life in which the capacity for rational enjoyment and wholesome pleasures is in its most vigorous stage. It is the too common mistake of the man of business to put off for the future day, when he shall have reached the affluence at which he aims, the exercise of that faculty of enjoyment, which he robs of its present gratification with a promise to pay in the indefinite future, in order that he may double his attention to material pursuits. This is doubly a mistake, in that the future may never be reached, and if it be, then may be found that the time has gone by; that the capacity has perished in its neglect; that it is impossible to rekindle the fires of youth in the ashes of old age, and when once resolved to devote the remnant of life to pursuit of pleasure fairly won by arduous toil, there remains only the desire without the realization, able to "clip Elysium, but to lack its joy." He, who keeps life well balanced, neither evading its duties nor refusing its passing rewards, will find in the end that he has made as satisfactory progress in worldly prosperity, and has lived a better and a brighter life.

WINTER.

"Only waiting till the shadows
Are a little longer grown,
Only waiting till the glimmer
Of the day's last beam is flown;
Till the night of earth is faded
From the heart once full of day,
Till the stars of heaven are breaking
Through the twilight soft and gray.

* * * * * *

"Only waiting till the shadows
Are a little longer grown,
Only waiting till the glimmer
Of the day's last beam is flown;
Then from out the gathered darkness
Holy, deathless stars shall rise,
By whose light my soul shall gladly
Tread its pathway to the skies."

THE Winter season of life is essentially that of the home and the fireside. It is not given to many men like Gladstone, Montefiore or Peter Cooper, of green and happy memory, to carry the cross of duty to the very door of the tomb; nor is it for the happiness and comfort which is the just due and the chief enjoyment of a "green old age," that it should be so. Winter is the season of tranquility and repose. The turgid, ambitious and sordid cares of the world will have ceased to trouble the placid existence of old age. It heeds not the storms and the hardships which drive upon the outer world, for among them it has no duties to perform. In its cozy corner by the fireside of life's household, its time is passed in the mellow light of domestic affection, in the serenity of contemplation, and in the soothing attentions of those upon whom the cares of its existence have been bestowed. The prattling innocence of the little children recall again the days of early manhood and the infancy of the matron who fondly hovers round the armchair set apart for the grandfather, and the tasks taken up again for the second generation, enable the old to live again the best days of their youth and strength. For a life well spent, which has had experience in weighing the empty vanities of the world, and of estimating the comparative worthlessness of the pleasures of ambition and worldly success, there comes a realization of the great rewards which are garnered up by the fireside in plenteous store, and to which the old man turns with grateful relief when his worldly tasks are done. His silver locks are indeed a crown of glory, and life's last days a serene and mellow sunset, diffusing a softened

YOUTH AND AGE.

O Youth, for years so many and sweet
  'Tis known that thou and I were one,
I'd think it but a fond conceit—
  It cannot be that thou art gone!
Thy vesper-bell has not yet toll'd;—
And thou wer't e'er a masker bold;
What strange disguise hast now put on
To make believe that thou art gone?

*   *   *   *   *   *

I see these locks in silvery slips,
  I see this drooping gait, this alter'd size—
But springtide blossoms on thy lips,
  And tears take sunshine from thine eyes!
Life is but Thought; so think, I will,
That Youth and I are housemates still.

COLERIDGE.

radiance upon the circle which surrounds him. His latter life is a book of wisdom, full of counsel, admonition, encouragement and hope for the sons and daughters who, with children in their train, are fast following the footsteps of the fading life. Happy that old age which, in the full possession of all the enjoyments which belong to material comforts and a ripened intellect, can add the consolations of hope and of religion to the proud consciousness of immortality—he who can reckon up his life with the thankful self-consciousness that to the best of his power he has fairly met every duty, and trace his footsteps upon the sands of his nearly completed course without a regret. For such the passing hours are laden with the full cup of serene contentment. In sweet and grateful repose and placid enjoyment he realizes

"How noiseless falls the foot of Time
That only treads on flowers,"

and with calm resignation and untroubled conscience, awaits the "privileged chamber" where "the good man meets his fate." To such an one, who possesses

"A peace above all earthly dignities,
A still and quiet conscience,"

the period of life's decline is a season to be envied of all. His

"Old age is a lusty winter,
Frosty, yet kindly."

His days are a perfect harmony, without care for the present, regret for the past, nor fear for the future, and amid the olive branches of his family tree he is the oracle, venerated, respected, beloved, diffusing in his leisure hours from out of the treasury of ripe experience,

"Sydnean showers
Of sweet discourse, whose powers
Can crown old Winter's head with flowers."

THE AUTOGRAPH ALBUM.

THE little souvenirs of affection or friendship written on the pages of an album do not possess their greatest value when first written. But when absence has separated the friends who wrote from the owner of the album, or when, perhaps, the hands that penned the words are folded in the embrace of death, tender memories of those loved and lost are recalled by its pages. The past is brought back, and scenes long forgotten reappear before the mental vision with the distinctness of the present. It is then that the album is most highly prized, and its pages scanned with moistened eyes; while some serve to cheer sadness, and others as guide-posts on the road to eternity.

DEDICATORY VERSES.

(Suitable for inscription on the first pages of Albums.)

My album's open, come and see!
What! won't you write a line for me?
Write but a thought, a word or two,
That memory may revert to you.

To My Friends:
My album is a garden spot
Where all my friends may sow,
Where thorns and thistles flourish not,
But flowers alone may grow.
With smiles for sunshine, tears for showers,
I'll water, watch and guard these flowers.

Go, album! range thy gay parterre
From gem to gem, from flower to flower.
Select with taste, and cull with care,
And bring your offering, fresh and rare,
To this sweet maiden's bower.

When years elapse
It may, perhaps,
Delight us to review these scraps,
And live again 'mid scenes so gay,
That Time's rough hand has swept away;
For when the eye, bedimmed with age,
Shall rest upon each treasured page,

These pleasant hours,
That once were ours,
Shall come again, like Autumn flowers,
To bloom and smile upon us here
When all things else seem sad and drear;
'T will tune our hearts and make them sing,
And turn our Autumn into Spring.

Go, little book, thy destined course pursue,
Collect memorials of the just and true,
And beg of every friend so near
Some token of remembrance dear.

As life flows on from day to day,
And this, your book, soon fills,
How many may be far away
From treasured vales and hills.

But there is joy in future time
To turn the pages o'er,
And see within a name or rhyme
From one you'll see no more.

SENTIMENT AND AFFECTION.

The gem cannot be polished without friction, nor man perfected without adversity.

Time advances like the slowest tide, but retreats like the swiftest current.

Daily we write our autographs on the minds and hearts of those around us.

I have tried for a week, and vainly I seek
Words of wisdom to write for you here.
So, wishing you life free from sorrow and strife,
Nor wanting in friends and good cheer,
With health—perhaps wealth—
Love better than self,
And truth, for the best, to the end;
Since content it maintains
While existence remains,
I subscribe myself, truly, your friend.

He is the true nobleman who can work right on, quietly waiting for recognition, if it comes; if not, yet right on.

As you travel through life, scatter kind words and gentle deeds; in so doing, you will enrich your soul. Withhold them, and it tends to poverty.

May your life be like the day—more beautiful in the evening; like the summer—aglow with promise; and like the autumn—rich with the golden sheeves, where good work and deeds have ripened on the field.

Be blessings scattered o'er thy way,
My gladsome, joyous, laughing sprite;
Be thy whole life one summer's day
Without the night.

Desire not to live long, but well;
How long we live, not years, but actions, tell.

Meanness shun, and all its train;
Goodness seek, and life is gain.

LIFE ENDS NOT IN DEATH.

Through days of doubt and darkness,
In fear and trembling breath,
Through mists of grief and sorrow,
In tears of woe and death;

Through days of light and gladness,
Through days of love and life,
Through smiles of joy and sunshine,
Through days with beauty rife,

The Lord of life and glory,
The King of earth and sea,
The Lord who guided Israel,
Keep watch, sweet friend, o'er thee.

Among the many friends who claim
A kind remembrance in thy breast,
I, too, would add my simple name
Among the rest.

When the name that I write here is dim on the page,
And the leaves of your Album are yellow with age,
Still think of me kindly, and do not forget
That, wherever I am, I remember you yet.

If the recollections of friends brighten moments of sadness,
What a fund of delight is here treasured for thee!
If advice and kind wishes bring goodness and gladness,
How perfect and happy thy future must be.

The tissues of the life to be,
We weave with colors all our own;
But in the field of Destiny,
We reap what we have sown.

HUMOROUS.

In the storms of life,
When you need an umbrella,
May you have to uphold it
Some handsome young fellow.

If you wish to laugh,
Glance at my autograph.

Sliding down the stream of life,
In your little bark canoe,
May you have a pleasant trip,
With just room enough for two.

As sure as comes your wedding day,
A broom to you I'll send;
In *sunshine*, use the bushy part;
In *storms*, the other end.

CHRISTMAS AND NEW YEAR.

Health and prosperity
Your life to cheer,
With every blessing
For the bright New Year.

On this New Year's morning
My wishes take their flight,
And wing to thee a greeting
That would make all things bright.

O, bright be the day,
Sweet echoes resounding,
Love lighting the way,
And warm hearts surrounding.
May the breath of His peace
In thy spirit remain,
Till Christmas revisits
The round world again.

Now Christmas comes with hearty cheer,
May kindly thoughts go round,
And bring to you a glad New Year,
With peace and plenty crowned.

BIRTHDAYS.

Love in every bosom live,
And the truest pleasure give,
And happy smiles each lip adorn
On this happy birthday morn.

This is thy birthday, may it be
A source of happiness to thee.
And may each birthday yet in store,
Be brighter than the one before.

As beauteous flowers in garlands twine,
May peace and love to cheer thy heart combine,
To give you a happy birthday.

If words could all my wishes say,
Oh! how my tongue could talk away.
I wish this day, and many more,
Might on dear ——— blessings pour.
May health and wealth, love and peace,
With each succeeding year increase;
And, oh! the last, come when it may,
Be unto thee a happy day.

MASTERPIECES OF ELOQUENCE.

THE following masterpieces of elegiac eloquence are unsurpassed in the repertory of the English classics, for lofty and noble sentiment, exquisite pathos, vivid imagery, tenderness of feeling, glowing power of description, brilliant command of language, and that immortal and seldom attained faculty of painting in the soul of the listener or reader a realistic picture whose sublimity of conception impresses the understanding with awe and admiration, and impels the mind to rise involuntarily for the time to an elevation out of and above the inconsequent contemplation of the common and sordid things of life.

AT HIS BROTHER'S GRAVE.

The following grand oration was delivered by Hon. Robert G. Ingersoll on the occasion of the funeral of his brother, Hon. Eben C. Ingersoll, in Washington, June 2:

My friends, I am going to do that which the dead oft promised he would do for me. The loved and loving brother, husband, father, friend, died where manhood's morning almost touches noon, and while the shadows were still falling towards the west. He had not passed on life's highway the stone that marks the highest point, but being weary for a moment he lay down by the wayside, and using his burden for a pillow fell into that dreamless sleep that kisses down the eyelids. Still, while yet in love with life and raptured with the world, he passed to silence and pathetic dust. Yet, after all, it may be best, just in the happiest, sunniest hour of all the voyage, while eager winds are kissing every sail, to dash against the unseen rock and in an instant to hear the billows roar, "A sunken ship;" for whether in mid sea or among the breakers of the farther shore, a wreck must mark at last the end of each and all, and every life, no matter if its every hour is rich with love, and every moment jeweled with a joy, will at its close become a tragedy as sad and deep and dark as can be woven of the warp and woof of mystery and death. This brave and tender man in every storm of life was oak and rock, but in the sunshine he was vine and flower. He was the friend of all heroic souls. He climbed the heights and left all superstitions far below, while on his forehead fell the golden dawning of a grander day. He loved the beautiful, and was with color, form and music touched to tears. He sided with the weak, and with a willing hand gave alms. With loyal heart, and with the purest hand he faithfully discharged all public trusts. He was a worshiper of liberty and a friend of the oppressed. A thousand times I have heard him quote the words, "For Justice all place temple, and all seasons summer." He believed that happiness was the only good, reason the only torch, justice the only worshiper, humanity the only religion, and love the priest. He added to the sum of human joy, and were every one for whom he did some loving service to bring a blossom to his grave, he would sleep to-night beneath a wilderness of flowers. Life is a narrow vale between the cold and barren peaks of two eternities. We strive in vain to look beyond the heights. We cry aloud, and the only answer is the echo of our wailing cry. From the voiceless lips of the unreplying dead there comes no word, but the light of death. Hope sees a star, and listening love can hear the rustle of a wing. He who sleeps here when dying, mistaking the approach of death for the return of health, whispered with his latest breath, "I am better now." Let us believe, in spite of doubts and dogmas, and tears and fears, that these dear words are true of all the countless dead. And now, to you who have been chosen from among the many men he loved to do the last sad office for the dead, we give his sacred dust. Speech cannot contain our love. There was, there is, no gentler, stronger, manlier man.

AT THE GRAVE OF A CHILD.

Colonel Ingersoll upon one occasion was one of a little party of sympathizing friends who had gathered in a drizzling rain to assist the sorrowing friends of a young boy—a bright and stainless flower, cut off in the bloom of its beauty and virgin purity by the ruthless north winds from the Plutonian shades—in the last sad office of committing the poor clay to the bosom of its mother earth. Inspired by that true sympathy of the great heart of a great man, Colonel Ingersoll stepped to the side of the grave and spoke as follows:

My friends, I know how vain it is to gild grief with words, and yet I wish to take from every grave its fear. Here in this world, where life and death are equal kings, all should be brave enough to meet what all the dead have met. The future has been filled with fear, stained and polluted by the heartless past. From the wondrous tree of life the buds and blossoms fall with ripened fruit, and in the common bed of earth the patriarchs and babes sleep side by side. Why should we fear that which will come to all that is? We cannot tell; we do not know which is the greater blessing—life or death. We cannot say that death is not a good; we do not know whether the grave is the end of this life or the door of another, or whether the night here is not somewhere else a dawn. Neither can we tell which is the more fortunate, the child dying in its mother's arms, before its lips have learned to form a word, or he who journeys all the length of life's uneven road, taking the last slow steps painfully with staff and crutch. Every cradle asks us "whence," and every coffin "whither?" The poor barbarian, weeping above his dead, can answer these questions as intelligently and satisfactorily as the robed priest of the most authentic creed. The tearful ignorance of the one is just as good as the learned and unmeaning words of the other. No man, standing where the horizon of life has touched a grave, has any right to prophesy a future filled with pain and tears. It may be that death gives all there is of worth to live. If those we press and strain against our hearts could never die, perhaps that love would wither from the earth. May be this common fate treads from out the paths between our hearts the weeds of selfishness and hate, and I had rather live and love where death is king, than have eternal life where love is not. Another life is naught, unless we know and love again the ones who love us here. They who stand with breaking hearts around this little grave need have no fear. The larger and the nobler faith in all that is and is to be, tells us that death, even at its worst, is only perfect rest. We know that through the common wants of life, the needs and duties of each hour, their grief will lessen day by day, until at last these graves will be to them a place of rest and peace, almost of joy. There is for them this consolation, the dead do not suffer. If they live again, their lives will surely be as good as ours. We have no fear; we are all the children of the same mother, and the same fate awaits us all. We, too, have our religion, and it is this: "Help for the living; hope for the dead."

BEAUTIFUL HOME LIFE.

THE word "Home" comprises and implies all that is best and highest in the sum of earthly existence. Taking it in its widest interpretation, it embraces the attainment of all the best ambitions of life. It means a perfect existence, and he who has attained to its possession enjoys as much of Heaven as is permitted to visit earth. Cowper writes:

> "Domestic Happiness, thou only bliss
> Of Paradise that has survived the fall!"

It is the duty of every young man to seek to realize what true Home is, of what it consists, how sought and how to be acquired; the more so because the happiness which is to be found at the domestic fireside comes not accidentally, unsought nor undeserved, to any man, and also because, both in its creation and its enjoyment, its perfection depends so largely if not so entirely upon the seeker and the possessor. Nathaniel Cotton, in his "Fireside," strikes the true chord when he exclaims:

> "If solid happiness we prize,
> Within our breast this jewel lies;
> And fools they are who roam:
> The world has nothing to bestow;
> From our own selves our joys must flow
> And that dear hut, our Home."

The home which the poet had in view was not, it will be observed, within the stately walls of a palace. The gilded abodes of wealth and luxury are not always, nor indeed often, the dwelling places of Home and Happiness.

> "Well may your hearts believe the truths I tell;
> 'Tis virtue makes the bliss, where'er we dwell."—*Collins.*

THE TRUE HOME.

THE true home, whether lofty or humble, is the abode which the industry of a man provides for the shelter and comfort of the domestic circle of which he is the head. It is the shrine of which he is the patron saint, bringing for the adoration of those who put their faith and trust in him, the virtues of honor, probity, purity, honesty and integrity, faithfulness in every duty of life, and the example of obedience to every moral law, and receiving in return,

> "That incense of the heart
> Whose fragrance smells to Heaven,"

in the love and devotion of the wife, the confidence, respect and filial affection of children, and in that pure and unalloyed happiness which attends the approval of a conscience which appreciates and meets the responsibility of the head of the household, as the sun of the little world which revolves around him, and which upon him depends for the diffusion of the light, heat, and enjoyment of human existence. The industry of the husband and head of the home will fix the place in the scale of material comforts, but does not in any way affect or limit those moral attributes which govern its higher characteristics. His daily walk and conversation form the pattern upon which the young children found themselves, for whose present welfare and preparation for the future before them the father labors, and should be marked by purity of mind, manners and morals. In all things he should have a care to remember that by the example which he offers, other young lives are shaping themselves for the future, and guide himself by the responsibility which the fact involves. To the sharer of his hearth and home he should present always the uniform life-picture of manly devotion, chivalrous courtesy and connubial fidelity. His children should love him with an affectionate zeal into which no temper of fear enters, and should have the most thorough, explicit and unreserved confidence in his uprightness and integrity. The wife will be the care of his life, and it will be his desire to see that the winds of heaven do not visit her too roughly. At all times he will treat her with tender and respectful consideration, calculated to smooth away all difficulties from her path, and to render the burden of her duties less trying and more easy to bear. True husband and true wife have everything in common, and should, from the very outset of the joint journey through life, recognize this fact, and in all things act up to that understanding. Remembering by his own experience the perils that snare the feet of youth and the temptations which beset them, he will strive to so equip his own children, both mentally and morally, as will best enable them to successfully engage in the struggle which he himself has gone through in his own career. He will reap a rich reward in the love, respect and gratitude of those who surround his hearthstone, and in all those other benefits which go to sum up the total of life's happiness. Pursuing the course of duty, he will find his home a true one in every sense of the word. He will find there, always, the warmth and glow of real happiness. He will enter his household knowing by experience and intuition that all of love and comfort it boasts are for him alone, and returning to the field of his daily labors, he will go forth in renewed strength, courage and vigor. The husband and head of the family should watch carefully over the education of the little ones whom God has given him, should maintain his authority unquestioned in the household, keep his dignity always in view, and exact from others that respect which is due to his position and authority.

The true Home has Rest and Peace to guard its portals. Happiness and Contentment sit by its fireside. The angels of domestic bliss, Conjugal Love and Filial Affection, take up their abode beneath its roof; while Christian piety, like a fragrant incense, pervades all its relations. The sordid cares of life, the fever of unrest, which attend the steps of worldly ambition, the gnawing cares and perplexities of those who live no higher life than the strife of "the world and all its motley rout," these have no place in the Home whose head is an honest and upright man, and whose heart a tender, loving and Christian woman, wife and mother. The man who is blessed with such a home—whose helpmeet, besides being tender and affectionate, is faithful and prudent—and who, as the father of children, having given "hostages to fortune," has that additional stimulation to his industry and his ambition, need not despair of any future to which he directs his efforts, and his life will prove in its results that, as old John Fletcher, just three hundred years ago, wrote:

"Man is his own star, and the soul that can
Render an honest and a perfect man
Commands all light, all influence, all fate.
Nothing to him falls early, or too late.
Our acts our angels are, or good or ill,
Our fatal shadows that walk by us still."

SELF-CONTROL.

IN the government of the household, the head of the family will occasionally find, in his way, little rifts of unpleasantness in the domestic atmosphere, occasioned by the rebellion of children, the conduct of servants, or possibly the extravagance of the wife. On occasions such as these he will have need to remember that if, while asserting his authority, he would also maintain his dignity and not endanger his personal respect and affection, he must keep his mind, judgment and all his faculties under control. The little difficulties of domestic discipline are oftimes very trying to the temper, especially where the mind is worried by the contact with the world during the day's business. On such occasions it is that the practice of habitual self-control comes to the assistance of the head of the family, makes his duty easy, and preserves him from mistakes calculated to weaken his authority, and injure his respect in the household as well as his own self-esteem.

The parent who never corrects a child except when his self-control gives way, or who yields to fits of unreasonable anger, and so chastises the child in wrath, and not in justice, commits a terrible breach of parental duty. The parent who fully appreciates the solemn gravity of the duties which devolve upon him in that capacity, will watchfully avoid letting his temper interfere with any domestic duty. The child is generally keenly susceptible to the truth in a case like this, and is quick in perceiving that it has been wrongfully or unreasonably punished, and has been made the victim of anger, not of justice. The result is that he is hardened in his disposition, and confirmed in the vicious habit which has brought punishment upon him. The habit of self-control should be cultivated by the future head of a family while forming his Character in the period of youth, so that it will be so firmly implanted in his habit of thought and action, that he will never be tempted to rash courses when he comes to the responsibility of the head of a family,—so weakening the paternal authority and exposing flaws in the symmetry of the paternal character which the child has been taught to reverence. Self-control is desirable, moreover, in every walk of life, and in every relation of business. It enables a man to receive and retain bad news without alarming others by its premature disclosure, or giving others in business competition the advantage of a tell-tale nervousness, or a too frank countenance. It will enable a man suffering under the knowledge of some serious business calamity to carry to the bedside of an invalid wife, child or parent, to whom the shock of distressing news might be fatal, a cheerful and smiling countenance, and to administer comfort and consolation where he who possessed not this quality would be a source of danger rather than of comfort. It will, too, enable the man to be the master of his own emotions, and nerve him to a sense of duty where the enforcement of household discipline becomes a greater pain to him who administers it than to those who receive it. It will also enable the head of the house to preserve that equanimity and imperturbability of temper which are essential to his dignity, and to the respect of his household. Self-control will be practiced in its completest extent by every one who wishes to maintain the dignity and integrity of the household relations, and to complete that symmetry of character which makes home happy.

The parent who has studied the laws which govern the formation of character will not fail to have been early impressed with this duty which in every condition and sphere of life he owes to himself. When, however, he reaches that stage of existence where the government of his conduct is invested not only with his personal responsibility, but with that of the formation of the character and lives of those whom he has brought into being—when he must in bounden duty appear in his daily walk and conversation a living model and example of the truth of those principles and rules of conduct which he seeks to instill into the hearts and minds of his children—the duty of self-control will assume a higher, graver and more solemn aspect, and he will endeavor by undeviating and uniform mastery and control of his own temper, passions, appetites and weaknesses to give to those precepts which he offers to the child as the only key to the treasury of success, prosperity and happiness, the strengthening influence of a bright and consistent example.

CONFIDENCE OF CHILDREN IN PARENTS.

THE confidence of the child in the parent, where it exists as nature implanted it in the infantile breast, a God-given virtue typifying the trust which man himself should feel toward his Creator is one of the greatest joys of that higher and purer existence, which a man leads in the confines of his home—in spirit, if not in fact, "far from the busy haunts of men." It is the delicate germ that, through after years, if its growth be not in youth stunted by the chilling winds of unkindness, develops to the maturity of a robust and vigorous sentiment, and whose blossom is that of filial affection. That parent must have a soul dead to the finer instincts, if he be not touched by the faith and confidence extended to him or her by the simplicity and trust of prattling innocence, and surely it ought to be a pleasing duty to keep this innocent faith of the child in the parent unshaken till it can be justified to the expanding intelligence of the youth by its own knowledge of the parent. But while this faith springs naturally from the uncorrupted fountain of infantile affection, it is accompanied by that indefinable wisdom or instinct of simplicity, which is oftimes the magic mirror in which insincerity and unworthiness, however craftily concealed, are faithfully revealed. It should be the effort of the parent not only to appear to be worthy of the faith of the child, but also to deserve it, so that there will be no illusion to be destroyed as the child grows older, and the fruit of the tree of knowledge reveals the parental idol as it really is. The child should be met in all things by a reciprocal faith. It should never be deceived, even in the most trivial matters. A promise made to a little one should be more sacredly kept even than an engagement with one of more mature years, for in its little world its disappointment at being deceived is in proportion to its trust, and where shall we find in the world of maturity faith in our word so complete, so entire, so wholly without doubt or reservation? It is too much the habit among thoughtless young and old married people to make little account of the promises made to children. Let them reflect upon the shock to the little innocent and trusting mind on discovering that "papa" or "mamma" has told them a deliberate falsehood, and upon the effect of the further discovery that this disregard of the truth is a habit and not an oversight!

"Confidence is a plant of slow growth in an aged bosom," said the elder Pitt, but in the tender heart of childhood, unspoiled by contact with the world, it springs spontaneously into being, and if watchfully guarded against abuse in its infancy, will take strong root and flourish apace with increasing years, and so shelter the virgin soil in which the graces and virtues of life are to be planted, that the poisonous weeds of doubt, distrust, envy, malice, and uncharitableness can find no root there. The parent who—recognizing the importance of thorough confidence on the part of the child, in his honor, his truth and his judgment, to his parental influence in the coming years—sedulously takes care in the smallest things of the crude and elementary life which it is his duty, as it should be his pride and anxious care, to shape to a perfect character, will have lightened and made easy the responsibilities which increase upon him as the child advances toward maturity. From the seeds thus sown in the little things of early life, he will reap a rich reward in filial obedience and confident reliance in the paternal counsel, when the dangers and temptations of life assail the approach of youth to manhood—that critical period in the career of the young when, without experience of the world, so many, in the impetuous temerity of youth, who have not been thoroughly imbued with filial respect and confidence, are swept away in their too confident rashness into the vortex of dissipation and ruin.

EDUCATION OF CHILDREN.

TO the parents who are rightly imbued with the proper spirit of their obligations to their children the task of waiting upon the budding intelligence, and shaping its growth into perfect symmetry, is not only a duty but a pleasure—a pleasure not only in its performance, but in the sure and certain rewards which it treasures up for the enjoyment of later years. "The child is the father of the man," is a truism which should be ever present in the mind of the parent, associated with the proverb, "As the twig is bent the tree is inclined." The education of the child is but the seed sown in a fertile soil, from which life is to reap a rich and bounteous harvest—of honor, happiness and moral and material prosperity, or of vice, disappointment, disgrace and ruin, according as the seeds implanted under the eye of the parent are those of honor, truth, probity, industry and integrity, or of carelessness, willfulness, selfishness, sloth, disregard of truth and indifference to honor. The happiness and wellfare, as well as the interest, of the parent is, too, bound up inseparably in this future. A man may be never so successful in the material objects of his career; he may have reached every goal of ambition for public or social distinction; he may enjoy the inestimable boon of the unfaltering love and devotion of wife; he may have the rich reward which comes to him who wears the "white flower of a blameless life;" and yet to all these may come "the worm, the canker and the grief," if compelled to realize

"How sharper than a serpent's tooth it is
To have a thankless child,"

and to find all the high hopes which parental fondness and anticipation had formed of a reproduction and higher development of his own successful career in the person of a son, dashed to the ground by irreclaimable waywardness, moral baseness, vicious habits and companionships, shameful weaknesses or a degraded life. And how bitter to such an one, who finds this gall of misery in his cup of well-earned happiness, must be the self-reproaching reflection that such a shattering of his fond aspirations of living again in his children the life of honor, truth and probity, is to be traced by the unerring and inexorable finger of a self-condemning conscience, to the errors and faults of the parent in the early education of the child—to his irremediable carelessness in laying the foundations of character. The parent, then, who would not reap in tears this melancholy harvest of bitterness, disappointment and self-reproach, must see his duty clearly from the early beginning of his responsibility, and perform it vigilantly and faithfully. Into the warp and woof of the young life intrusted to his guidance he must weave the strong and enduring fibers of every virtue. Above all things he must see to it that false love is not permitted to impose that damning blight upon the development of character which the too common expression "a spoiled child" implies. There is no greater cruelty possible to be stamped upon the character and inflicted upon the developing career of the child than that misdirected tenderness which restrains the hand of deserved punishment, weakens in its vital point the dignity and control of parental authority and paves the way for its final overthrow and destruction, and gives a lodging-place in the young mind and an influence in the forming character, to those willfulnesses and waywardnesses which may be, even at first, "pretty," "interesting" and "charming," but which all too soon will unfold themselves to the misguided parent in the shape of vices which defy his love and anxiety, and distort and disfigure beyond redemption the character, which hardens and becomes permanent as manhood is approached. It is in this regard that the man should assert himself as the head of the household, responsible and controlling, for it is generally from woman's tenderness and weakness that these dangers proceed. The husband and father should be as firm and inflexible in the performance of his duty and the assertion of his authority as he is gentle and tender in all his relations with the child. Even in the punishment, which is sometimes necessary, it is love for the child which should be the controlling spirit. The wisdom of Solomon, which says "he that spareth his rod hateth his son," does not mean that harshness should be the rule of paternal authority. On the contrary, undue harshness leads to the same deplorable results as undue weakness. It means that while the paternal government should be founded on love, it must not hesitate to correct the faults of childish conduct or disposition by fear, when necessary, in order that he may be so thoroughly grounded in true habits of character, that they will safely develop into natural governing impulses as he passes to years of discretion, and through youth to maturity. It is by the exercise of this watchful firmness that,—like the gardener who by gentle force corrects the deformity of the growing tree till it matures into straight and perfect symmetry,—the parent by the firm performance of his duty corrects the natural infirmities of the child's temper and disposition, and has the satisfaction of seeing those correct habits into which the child is led by love or guided by authority crystallized into the perfect and stable character. One other point in the education of the children should engage the parents' attention. Never attempt to prevent the young from forming friendships. Man, even in the elementary existence of childhood, is a gregarious animal. The child seeks friendships and companionships of its own age and sympathies as naturally as the rosebud unfolds its blushing beauties to the sunlight. The child which is allowed to make in the early years of discretion one congenial friend, may be safely trusted not to seek miscellaneous and therefore undesirable company. The parent who watches carefully over the developing character of the child will be content, without apparent pressure, to direct the child's friendship to another which he is assured has the advantage of careful moral training, and the influence of pious parents. Such a friendship he will find to be not only an aid to him in forming the character of the child, but a safeguard to the latter against many evil companionships and dangerous associations. And endeavor in the inculcation of every virtue, to imbue the mind of the child and the youth with a sensitive and realizing spirit, in every relation of life for which he is being fitted, of what Burke describes as "that chastity of honor which feels a stain like a wound."

FILIAL AFFECTION.

ONE of the most beautiful, because the most unselfish and most honorable, of the many virtues which gather round the domestic hearth, is filial affection, and he who does not possess it, can scarcely be credited with the possession of the finer qualities of the human heart, soul and understanding. In every system of philosophy, mythology, morality and religion that has ever prevailed in the world throughout the various phases of progressing and developing civilization and enlightenment, filial affection has always been accorded the highest place. It is the natural instinct of man, where not perverted by false education or vicious tendencies on the part of the child, or cast off by the forfeiture of his claim to respect and confidence on the part of the parents. It is the peremptory command of the Mosaic law, and is numbered among the strictest injunctions of the Gospel dispensation. It is the reward which the parent has earned by years of anxious care and devotion from the hour of the mother's travail, by shelter and protection afforded through the helplessness of childhood, by the best years and the highest affections of life freely bestowed, and by the cares and tears and labors which have been ungrudgingly given, that the child may be put forward in the race of life always with greater advantages than the parent was ever conscious of having enjoyed. It is the acknowledgment which justice and common gratitude, as well as nature, demand from the child to be rendered to the parent. In all ages the ingratitude of children to parents, the setting at naught of the dictates of filial affection, has ever been pictured as the blackest and most disgraceful kind of turpitude. It is a duty which religion and honor alike impose, and it is one to which all the higher and holier instincts and feelings will naturally lead. No man can go through life and expect to rank in his own conscience and self-approval, or in the respect of the world, among the happy number of those "whose yesterdays look backward with a smile," who has any reproach resting—visible, perhaps, only to the eye of his own conscience, or to the sorrowful soul of a neglected and ill-requited parent—upon his mind and conscience. As the young man advances in years and strength, and the parent who has been his shield and protection and guardian angel through the period of his weakness and helplessness, goes down the decline of life and casts his lengthening shadow toward the grave, this duty becomes more and more imperative, and he who looks forward in his own turn to the common lot, and who would have his conscience and his record clear when his accounts come to be cast up by an arbiter who knows no errors and acknowledges no excuses, will take care that the same kind and considerate love which sheltered him in his infancy, shall smooth and brighten and make grateful the sunset of the parent's life. Young says:

"The chamber where a good man meets his fate
Is privileged beyond the common walk
Of virtue's life, quite to the verge of Heaven."

Every man and woman who possesses Christian hope, and who believes in a higher, nobler and purer existence hereafter, may well pray for such a deathbed as this, from which to pass the narrow portals of time into the mysterious vista of eternity. Let all such remember that of all the sins of omission or commission which may rest upon the conscience of man, weak and erring at the best, there is none more inexcusable, none for which remorse will more vehemently rend his heartstrings when the day of reparation and atonement has gone by, than the reflection that he has in life withheld from parents those tributes of filial affection which were their due. No man, however, who cultivates the other virtues of a Christian and upright life will overlook the solemn claims of the parent upon his love, respect and gratitude. That feeling will have been inculcated in him in youth, and it will have been indorsed by the judgment and sense of justice of maturer years. To the man or woman of proper feeling and true integrity this filial affection, in affording some slight return to parents for all their long years of watchful care and attention, will be a gladness and a pleasure. As parents, perhaps, themselves, they will recognize in their duty to *their* parents in the decline of life, what they themselves must look forward for in a few fleeting years, as the only reward, beyond that which a duty performed bestows, which they will receive for the affection they in turn are lavishing upon their offspring. Happily filial attention is honored in the world even by those who do not regard or comprehend its higher motives. It is the parental heart alone which perceives whether that attention is a cold and formal duty, merely, or whether it is that living, ripe and warm affection which blesses both the giver and the receiver. To bring its real reward, in a conscience at peace with itself, the parental affection should be earnest, grateful and real, springing from the heart and overflowing with respectful love and gratitude.

SIGNERS OF THE DECLARATION.

Following is a List of Members of the Continental Congress Who Signed the Declaration of Independence.

Names of the Signers.	Delegate from	Born at	Died.
Adams, John	Mass.	Braintree, Mass., Oct. 19, 1735	July 4...1826
Adams, Samuel	Mass.	Boston, Mass., Sept. 27, 1722	Oct. 2...1803
Bartlett, Josiah	N. H.	Amesbury, Mass, Nov. 1729	May 19..1795
Braxton, Carter	Va.	Newington, Va., Sept. 10, 1736	Oct. 10..1797
Carroll, Charles, of Carrollton	Md.	Annapolis, Md., Sept. 20, 1737	Nov. 14..1832
Chase, Samuel	Md.	Somerset County, Md., April 17, 1741	June 19..1811
Clark, Abraham	N. J	Elizabethtown, N. J., Feb. 15, 1726	Sept.....1794
Clymer, George	Penn.	Philadelphia, Pa., 1739	Jan. 23..1813
Ellery, William	R.I. & Prov.	Newport, R. I., Dec. 22, 1727	Feb. 15..1820
Floyd, William	N. Y.	Suffolk Co., N. Y., Dec. 17, 1734	Aug. 4...1821
Franklin, Benjamin	Penn.	Boston, Mass., Jan. 17, 1706	April 17 1790
Gerry, Elbridge	Mass.	Marblehead, Mass., July 1, 1744	Nov. 23..1814
Gwinnet, Button	Ga.	England, 1732	May 27..1777
Hall, Lyman	Ga	Connecticut, 1731	Feb 1790
Hancock, John	Mass.	Braintree, Mass, 1737	Oct. 8....1793
Harrison, Benjamin	Va.	Berkley, Va	April....1791
Hart, John	N. J	Hopewell, N. J., 1715	—— ...1780
Heyward, Thomas, Jr.	S. C	St. Lukes, S. C., 1746	March...1809
Hewes, Joseph	N. C	Kingston, N. J., 1730	Oct. 10..1779
Hooper, William	N. C.	Boston, Mass., June 17, 1742	Oct......1790
Hopkins, Stephen	R.I. & Prov.	Scituate, Mass., March 7, 1707	July 13..1785
Huntington, Samuel	Conn.	Windham, Conn, July 3, 1732	Jan. 5...1796
Hopkinson, Francis	N. J.	Philadelphia, Pa., 1737	May 9...1790
Jefferson, Thomas	Va.	Shadwell, Va., April 13, 1743	July 4...1826
Lee, Richard Henry	Va.	Stratford, Va., Jan. 20, 1732	June 19..1794
Lee, Francis Lightfoot	Va.	Stratford, Va., Oct. 14, 1734	April....1797
Lewis, Francis F	N. Y.	Landaff, Wales, March, 1713	Dec. 30..1803
Livingston, Philip	N. Y.	Albany, N. Y., Jan. 15, 1716	June 12..1778
Lynch, Thomas, Jr.	S. C.	St. George's, S. C., Aug. 5, 1749	Lost sea.1779
McKean, Thomas	Del.	Chester Co., Pa., March 19, 1734	June 24..1817
Middleton, Arthur	S. C	Middleton Place, S. C., 1743	Jan. 1. 1787
Morris, Lewis	N. Y	Morrisania, N. Y., 1726	Jan. 22..1798
Morris, Robert	Penn.	Lancashire, England, Jan. 1733	May 8...1806
Morton, John	Penn.	Ridley, Pa., 1724	April....1777
Nelson, Thomas, Jr	Va.	York, Va., Dec. 26, 1738	Jan. 4...1789
Paca, William	Md.	Wye Hill, Md., Oct. 31, 1740	—— ...1799
Paine, Robert Treat	Mass.	Boston, Mass., 1731	May 11..1804
Penn, John	N. C.	Caroline Co., Va., May 17, 1741	Oct. 26..1809
Read, George	Del	Cecil Co., Md., 1734	—— ...1798
Rodney, Cæsar	Del.	Dover, Del., 1730	—— ...1783
Ross, George	Penn.	New Castle, Del., 1730	July.....1779
Rush, Benjamin, M. D	Penn.	Byberry, Pa., Dec. 24, 1745	April 19.1813
Rutledge, Edward	S. C.	Charleston, S. C., Nov. 1749	Jan. 23..1800
Sherman, Roger	Conn.	Newton, Mass., April 19, 1721	July 23..1793
Smith, James	Penn.	Ireland	July 11..1806
Stockton, Richard	N. J.	Princeton, N. J., Oct. 1, 1730	Feb. 28..1781
Stone, Thomas	Md	Charles Co., Md., 1742	Oct. 5....1787
Taylor, George	Penn.	Ireland, 1716	Feb. 23..1781
Thornton, Matthew	N. H.	Ireland, 1714	June 24..1803
Walton, George	Ga	Frederick Co., Va., 1740	Feb. 2...1804
Whipple, William	N. H.	Kittery, Me., 1730	Nov. 28..1785
Williams, William	Conn.	Lebanon, Conn., April 8, 1731	Aug. 2...1811
Wilson, James	Penn.	Scotland, about 1742	Aug. 28..1798
Witherspoon, John	N. J	Yester, Scotland, Feb. 5, 1722	Nov. 15..1794
Wolcott, Oliver	Conn.	Windsor, Conn., Nov. 20, 1726	Dec. 1...1797
Wythe, George	Va.	Elizabeth City Co., Va., 1726	June 8...1806

MOUNT VERNON.

MOUNT VERNON, once the home, is now the last resting-place, of George Washington. The house is in a charming situation, overlooking the river, with beautiful and extensive views. The building itself is a plain structure of wood, in imitation of stone. On the second story, at the south side, is the bedroom of Washington, the bed in this apartment being the same on which the great warrior, statesman and patriot breathed his last, on December 17, 1799. Near it is the room occupied by Lafayette while Washington's guest. In the dining-room are several portraits of Washington, besides the famous picture by Rembrandt Peale, "Washington before Yorktown." There are several interesting relics in the house, among them being the key of the French Bastile, presented to Washington by Lafayette. Near the house, on the road from the steamboat-landing, stands the TOMB OF WASHINGTON and MARTHA, his wife. Their remains repose, side by side, in marble sarcophagi, which are surrounded by a plain, brick inclosure, entered through a barred, iron gate.

Subsequent to the death of Judge Washington, in 1826, the Mount Vernon estate descended to John Augustine Washington, his nephew, who died in 1832, when his widow, Jane Washington, became the next heir. John A. Washington, her son, was the last of the family to hold possession of the estate, in 1855. Not having the means to keep it in proper order, he disposed of it in 1860 through the State of Virginia to the Mount Vernon Association for $200,000. The association was incorporated for the special purpose of acquiring Mount Vernon, and its charter provides that the estate must never pass from its possession. Supervision over the estate is retained by the state of Virginia, that appoints a board of visitors whose duty is that of making an examination each year and reporting if the conditions of the charter have been complied with.

A southern woman named Pamelia Cunningham became the originator of the project to purchase Mount Vernon and save the home of Washington from decay. She obtained the refusal of it for a time, when its last owner made manifest his intention to sell the estate. Having made an appeal to Congress for money to be used for its purchase, and without success, she appealed to the women of America, under the title of "The Southern Matron," for aid in the commendable work. The Virginia legislature granted a charter, at

MOUNT VERNON.

her request, when she organized an association, and became the regent of it. Vice-regents for the different states were appointed by her, and these began to raise funds for the object. Large and small contributions were made throughout the United States, the largest single contribution, $68,000, being made by Edward Everett. The effort met with success, and Mount Vernon, sacred to every American, became the property of the people.

TIME TABLE Showing the Time in Months or Days from Any Day in one Month to the Corresponding Day in Any Other Month.

FROM	TO												
		Jan.	Feb.	Mar.	Apr.	May	J'ne	July	Aug	Sept	Oct.	Nov	Dec.
JAN.	Mos.	12	1	2	3	4	5	6	7	8	9	10	11
	Days	365	31	59	90	120	151	181	212	243	273	304	334
		Jan.	Feb.	Mar.	Apr.	May	J'ne	July	Aug	Sept	Oct.	Nov	Dec.
FEB.	Mos.	11	12	1	2	3	4	5	6	7	8	9	10
	Days	334	365	28	59	89	120	150	181	212	242	273	303
		Jan.	Feb.	Mar.	Apr.	May	J'ne	July	Aug	Sept	Oct.	Nov	Dec.
MARCH	Mos.	10	11	12	1	2	3	4	5	6	7	8	9
	Days	306	337	365	31	61	92	122	153	184	214	245	275
		Jan.	Feb.	Mar.	Apr.	May	J'ne	July	Aug	Sept	Oct.	Nov	Dec.
APRIL	Mos.	9	10	11	12	1	2	3	4	5	6	7	8
	Days	275	306	334	365	30	61	91	122	153	183	214	244
		Jan.	Feb.	Mar.	Apr.	May	J'ne	July	Aug	Sept	Oct.	Nov	Dec.
MAY	Mos.	8	9	10	11	12	1	2	3	4	5	6	7
	Days	245	276	304	335	365	31	61	92	123	153	184	214
		Jan.	Feb.	Mar.	Apr.	May	J'ne	July	Aug	Sept	Oct.	Nov	Dec.
JUNE	Mos.	7	8	9	10	11	12	1	2	3	4	5	6
	Days	214	245	273	304	334	365	30	61	92	122	153	183
		Jan.	Feb.	Mar.	Apr.	May	J'ne	July	Aug	Sept	Oct.	Nov	Dec.
JULY	Mos.	6	7	8	9	10	11	12	1	2	3	4	5
	Days	184	215	243	274	304	335	365	31	62	92	123	153
		Jan.	Feb.	Mar.	Apr.	May	J'ne	July	Aug	Sept	Oct.	Nov	Dec.
AUG	Mos.	5	6	7	8	9	10	11	12	1	2	3	4
	Days	153	184	212	243	273	304	334	365	31	61	92	122
		Jan.	Feb.	Mar.	Apr.	May	J'ne	July	Aug	Sept	Oct.	Nov	Dec.
SEPT	Mos.	4	5	6	7	8	9	10	11	12	1	2	3
	Days	122	153	181	212	242	273	303	334	365	30	61	91
		Jan.	Feb.	Mar.	Apr.	May	J'ne	July	Aug	Sept	Oct.	Nov	Dec.
OCT	Mos.	3	4	5	6	7	8	9	10	11	12	1	2
	Days	92	123	151	182	212	243	273	304	335	365	31	61
		Jan.	Feb.	Mar.	Apr.	May	J'ne	July	Aug	Sept	Oct.	Nov	Dec.
NOV	Mos.	2	3	4	5	6	7	8	9	10	11	12	1
	Days	61	92	120	151	181	212	242	273	304	334	365	30
		Jan.	Feb.	Mar.	Apr.	May	Ju'e	July	Aug	Sept	Oct.	Nov	Dec.
DEC.	Mos.	1	2	3	4	5	6	7	8	9	10	11	12
	Days	31	62	90	121	151	182	212	243	274	304	335	365

EXPLANATIONS.—Suppose the time be required from July 10 to September 10. Find July in the left hand column, and follow out the line to the right until you come to September; the number of months is 2; of days, 62. If the date *to* which we reckon be either greater or less than the one *from* which we reckon, the difference should be added or subtracted, as the case may be. For example: How many days from February 1 to August 31? By following out the February line to the August column, we find the time from February 1 to August 1 to be 181 days, to which if we add 30, the difference between 1 and 31, the time required will be 211 days. If the time be required between February 28 and August 1, we find the time from February 28 to August 28 to be 181 days, from which, if we subtract 27, the difference between 1 and 28, we get for the number of days, 154. The table is one of quite common use, but is none the less important. It may be used to great advantage in the processes of averaging.

Length, Breadth and Superficial Areas of the Principal Lakes.

NAME.	Length.	Breadth	Superficial Area.	NAME.	Length.	Breadth	Superficial Area.
Athabasca	200 miles	20 miles	4,000 sq. m.	Great Slave	300 miles	45 miles	13,500 sq. m.
Baikal	360 miles	35 miles	12,600 sq. m.	Huron	250 miles	90 miles	22,500 sq. m.
Cayuga	36 miles	4 miles	144 sq. m.	Ladoga	125 miles	75 miles	9,375 sq. m.
Champlain	123 miles	12 miles	1,476 sq. m.	L. of the Woods	70 miles	25 miles	1,750 sq. m.
Constance	45 miles	10 miles	450 sq. m.	Maracaybo	150 miles	60 miles	9,000 sq. m.
Erie	270 miles	50 miles	13,500 sq. m.	Michigan	330 miles	60 miles	19,800 sq. m.
Geneva	50 miles	10 miles	108 sq. m.	Ontario	180 miles	40 miles	7,200 sq. m.
George	36 miles	3 miles	108 sq. m.	Superior	380 miles	120 miles	45,600 sq. m.
Great Bear	150 miles	40 miles	6,000 sq. m.	Winnipeg	240 miles	40 miles	9,600 sq. m.

Dimensions and Surface Measurement of Oceans, Lakes and Seas.

SUPERFICIAL AREAS OF OCEANS.	SUPERFICIAL AREAS OF OCEANS—CONT'D.
The Arctic Ocean contains... 5,000,000 sq. m.	The Pacific Ocean contains... 80,000,000 sq. m.
The Atlantic Ocean contains.. 40,000,000 sq. m.	The Southern Ocean contains 10,000,000 sq. m.
The Indian Ocean contains... 20,000,000 sq. m.	

METEOROLOGICAL.

TABLE Showing Annual Mean Temperature at Various Points in the United States.

STATION.	State.	Average Temperature.	STATION.	State.	Average Temperature.
St. Paul	Minnesota	42	Fort Boise	Idaho Territory	52
Montpelier	Vermont	43	Portland	Oregon	53
Helena	Montana Territory	43	Columbus	Ohio	53
Madison	Wisconsin	45	Trenton	New Jersey	53
Augusta	Maine	45	Wilmington	Delaware	53
Concord	New Hampshire	46	Harrisburg	Pennsylvania	54
Sitka	Alaska	46	Baltimore	Maryland	54
Fort Randall	Dakota Territory	47	St. Louis	Missouri	55
Detroit	Michigan	47	Washington	District of Columbia	55
Providence	Rhode Island	48	San Francisco	California	55
Albany	New York	48	Louisville	Kentucky	56
Boston	Massachusetts	48	Richmond	Virginia	57
Denver	Colorado	48	Nashville	Tennessee	58
Omaha	Nebraska	49	Atlanta	Georgia	58
Des Moines	Iowa	49	Raleigh	North Carolina	59
Camp Scott	Nevada	50	Fort Gibson	Idaho Territory	60
Springfield	Illinois	50	Columbia	South Carolina	62
Hartford	Connecticut	50	Little Rock	Arkansas	63
Sterlacoon	Washington Ter	51	Jackson	Mississippi	64
Santa Fé	New Mexico Ter	51	Mobile	Alabama	66
Leavenworth	Kansas	51	Austin	Texas	67
Indianapolis	Indiana	51	New Orleans	Lousiana	69
Romney	West Virginia	52	Jacksonville	Florida	69
Salt Lake City	Utah Territory	52	Tucson	Arizona Territory	69

THE SOCIAL CODE.

THE importance of a thorough, or at least a competent acquaintance with the usages of good society, has been recognized in all ages, and has even commanded, with graver subjects, the study of philosophers, who have given a place to the graces of courteous bearing and conversation and polite deportment, as among the essentials of thorough education. Confined originally to ceremonious regulations governing the intercourse of people of rank, the laws of etiquette assumed a wider scope and a more authoritative shape, with the progress of refinement, the elevation of the female sex and the general diffusion of knowledge. In these modern days, a knowledge of the requirements of etiquette is not only an important element of success, but a potent factor in determining the degree of esteem in which a man is held among his fellows. The young man who sets out early in life to grapple with its serious problems, is too often prone to esteem too lightly, and even to look with contempt upon, the graces of personal conduct, conversation and deportment as the exclusive heritage of the "gilded youth," and among the frivolities to be despised, rather than the accomplishments to be courted. After life, when they have risen to high public or social responsibilities, causes them, to regret in their awkward and brusque habits, abrupt conversation and *mauvaise honte* where ease and affability are imperative duties, their neglect of the social graces, which are so easily acquired by the simple mastery and observance of the laws of custom in good society, which constitute Etiquette. Of vastly greater importance is it to woman, the principal aim of whose existence it is to shed light and grace upon the sterner realities of life, to adorn the home, and embellish her particular circle of society, that she should be not only conversant with the usages of society, but carry them into constant practice, and be thus thoroughly equipped for the performance of domestic and social duties and obligations, into whatever sphere of life her lot may be cast, or in whatever circle or surroundings circumstances may place her. The cultivation of courtesy is, too, a moral duty, as well, and runs side by side with the practice of the Christian virtues. In its general aspect, it is essential to the harmony of society at large and of our mutual relations in the world; and for the individual, it affects his own comfort, his enjoyment of life, his esteem in the world, and the extent and character of his friendships and associations. Recognizing these facts, let those who are ambitious to find life a pleasure as well as a profit, in cultivating the resources of their minds and the quality of their morals, not overlook the care of their manners, which are regarded as the outward evidence of mental and moral refinement.

CONCERNING DRESS.

THE first essential of a good appearance in polite society is that of suitable dress. This by no means involves that in order to be properly equipped for the best society, the apparel of a lady or gentleman requires either profuse or the most rigid adherence to the extreme of fashion. To a certain extent, of course, dress must conform to fashionable requirements, but even these requirements, imperious as are the dictates of Madame Fashion, are subject to the rules of good taste and harmony, which have come to be recognized as permanent laws, no matter what may be the caprices of evanescent fashions. Formerly, the commands of fashion were supreme, and her dictates, no matter how absurd her fancies, had, perforce, to be obeyed to the letter. But the growing refinement of later years, the general cultivation of artistic tastes, the more elevated idea that the grace and symmetry of the human figure are the highest perfection, and that dress is a mere accessory, to relieve and adorn it, and to contribute to its comfort, have banished the theory that dress must be consulted for itself alone, and rendered it impossible that we shall ever recur to any of the hideous and fantastic styles of garnishing the person in which fashion formerly delighted to disport her fine fabrics and rare laces. Permanence in the general scope and design of all fashions have made startling and radical innovations an impossibility, and this fact, coupled with the wonderful cheapening in the cost of everything that goes to make up fashionable attire, has rendered a degree of economy attainable, which places pleasing and fashionable costumes and garments within the reach of all, and hence the more imperative the duty imposed upon a man, and still more upon a woman, to consult the fashion in his or her apparel, as far as good taste will permit.

FOLLOWING THE FASHION.

In this regard the lady who studies effect and refined and ladylike appearance, will be careful to study discretion, in regarding new innovations, in the style of leading articles of attire. In many cases a new fashion may be wholly unsuitable to the "style" or figure of the lady, and in this case good taste will impel her to refrain as long as possible from adopting it, and then to so modify it as to consult her own peculiarities of size, figure, or complexion. In any event, the lady of refined breeding is never the first to "set" a fashion. Many new fashions promulgated prove to be utter failures, and after a brief struggle with adverse judgment, are abandoned, to the great expense and mortification of those who in seeking to lead the fashion have only succeeded in making themselves conspicuous. Wait sufficiently long to make certain that the new fashion is accepted by polite society for the season. Then consult your own personal requirements, and adapt the new fashion to what is indispensable to your personal appearance. In this way, while never forcing the fashion, or presenting a *bizarre* or *outre* appearance, you will always be sufficiently in the fashion and always present the most effective and elegant appearance.

EFFECTS IN COLORS.

As it comes natural to the female sex to desire to please the eye, most women are gifted with that good taste which distinguishes her natural harmonies in color, and in the combinations of colors, which are presented in dress, and these again when borne in relation to the shade of the hair and the tendency of the complexion and eyes. Others not gifted with this faculty, which is of such momentous importance to the success with which a woman dressed for society undergoes the ordeal of criticism, have to depend on the suggestions of friends or their *modistes*, not always better capable of judging than themselves. A few simple rules, however, will prevent anyone who observes them, from straying far from the boundaries of good taste; and this is most important in an economical sense, for the simple incongruity of a single ribbon or bow, or the color of a feather, is sufficient to destroy the *tout ensemble* of a costume otherwise the most exquisitely faultless.

For Blondes.—The blonde can stand the test of most all colors except bright shades of red and crimson, but will prefer generally the lighter shades of color, as well as neutral tints, such as drab and gray, in all the delicate shades. The full complexioned blonde, with golden or bronze hair, will add to her charms by giving prominence to the darker shades of blue, violet, lilac, or green, while the pale blonde with transparent complexion will appear to better advantage in lighter green and paler shades of other colors.

For Brunettes.—Dark green and red, scarlet, orange and yellow are the colors which must be consulted by the brunette. The lighter colors should be used by persons of sallow complexion, and the darker by the fuller complexioned. Scarlet or deep red flowers for the hair, if dead black.

Suitable to All.—Either blonde or brunette can wear pure white or plain black, but in ribbons, flowers or ornaments must conform to the colors above given, as, for a brunette, a red rose in the hair and scarlet ribbon, or for a blonde, violet flowers and light ribbon or bow.

ARTISTS' HARMONIES OF COLORS.—The following are artists' harmonies in colors, and may be accepted in making contrasts and combinations:

White.—With black, blue or red.

Black.—With white, orange, scarlet, lilac, pink, maize, buff and slate, or in combinations of crimson, yellow and white, or blue, yellow or orange, and white.

Green.—With gold, yellow, ecru, orange and crimson, or combined with scarlet and yellow or crimson and yellow.

Blue.—With gold, orange, drab, salmon, white, gray, black, mauve, ecru, straw, corn, chestnut and brown.

Crimson.—With gold, orange, maize, drab, purple and black.

Lilac.—With gold, maize, cherry, scarlet and crimson.

Purple.—With maize, orange and gold.

Yellow.—With violet, brown, red, black and crimson.

Red.—With gold, white or gray, or combined with green and orange, or yellow, black and white.

ARRANGEMENT OF THE COIFFURE.

This is a matter in which good taste is supreme over fashion. While it is the rule to follow certain fashions provided by so doing the classic contour of the head and the general effect is not deteriorated, custom permits every lady to dress her hair in such manner as will best relieve defects or improve advantages of appearance. A tall person can with safety adopt the modes founded on the Grecian models, which would be absurd on a *petite* figure, and vice versa, the latter will dress her hair so as to add to the effect of her stature. The effect of the arrangement of the hair upon the face is also to be considered. Round faces require the hair dressed back close to the head, while oval or long faces are relieved by abundance in the same way. It is a matter, however, in which every woman can be safely left to her own judgment.

JEWELRY.

It is in the wearing of jewelry, that the generally best test of refinement is to be had. The vain desire of obtrusive display, in season and out of season, which is too frequently indulged in the excessive use of jewelry, is the most tangible and offensive badge of vulgarity which can be presented to the polite world. For a gentleman, the wearing of a profusion of jewelry is in the worst possible form; good taste forbids the use of more than one ring, and regards with favor small and plain studs and sleeve-buttons, and a chain of modest dimensions, which it is strictly essential shall be of genuine gold. Young ladies should not affect jewelry, beyond a simple brooch and earrings. Ladies generally should avoid the display of jewelry in the day time. Strict etiquette confines the use of precious stones to the evenings or to occasions of important public ceremonial, to which ladies are invited, and where *costume de rigueur* is imperative.

BALL DRESSES

May be made of any rich material, and are limited in style and expensiveness by the purse of the wearer. They do not, however, involve extravagant outlay. A simple dress of white tarletan, with natural flowers in the hair and ribbons to suit the complexion is often as effective and as greatly admired as the most expensive creation of the modiste's art. In Europe custom prescribes rigidly the *decoleté* dress for balls and all full dress occasions. American custom very sensibly leaves this a question of choice. A lady who has elegant arms and shoulders is an ornament in a ball-room, but too free an exhibition of the charms of the bust is not in good taste, and is not favored in the most refined American circles, though the rules of European courts prescribe a display which is indelicate if not indecent.

The gentleman's ball dress is the stereotyped black suit, with swallow-tail coat and white vest, cut low to display the shirt bosom. The vest may be of satin, and if desired of delicate mauve or slate color. Coral and pearl buttons are sometimes used, and are in strict good taste. Patent leather or plain low-cut light shoes are worn.

GLOVES AND BOOTS.

No matter what may be the quality of a lady's raiment, there is one point in which refinement and good breeding are most scrupulously exacting, and that is in regard to her gloves and boots. Perfect gloves and perfect boots are indispensable. These require to be of fashionable make, of good quality, and to fit snugly, without the appearance of straining. It is worth a lady's while to reflect that a pair of gloves or boots half a size too small for her, while they destroy her physical and mental comfort, instead of producing the effect desired, in reality give the feet and hands a larger appearance than the properly fitting article.

ESSENTIALS FOR GENTLEMEN.

A man is said to be "well dressed," that is to present the unmistakable distinguishing marks of a gentleman, when his linen, hat and boots are in irreproachable style and condition. With these essentials, he can be indifferent, to a degree, in every respect but that of tidiness, in regard to the rest of his attire. There is no excuse for a man whose linen is not irreproachable, and on this test most people judging a stranger, will estimate at once his mind, his manner, and his morals.

PERFUMES.

Fastidiousness in the use of perfumes is a fine test of delicacy and refinement. Excessive use of perfumery is not only vulgar in the extreme, but excessively offensive and annoying to well-bred people of sensitive olfactory nerves, while the indiscriminate use of vile preparations, calculated to cover some worse defect of the breath, is disgusting. The person whose habits or condition of health afflicts his breath, should cure his habits or his infirmities before invading the drawing-room. Perfumes, when used, as they may always advantageously be, should be of the finest fragrance, according to choice, and should be but faintly perceptible about the person.

HINTS TO GENTLEMEN.

Avoid over-dressing. Do not affect the fashions too closely. Be particular about the cut and style of your garments, rather than about the quality of the material. Avoid too much jewelry, and beware of all flashy imitations. A heavy chain or guard so large as to attract attention by its apparent expensiveness, is the mark of the retainer of the turf or the faro table. Be scrupulously careful to cultivate habits of personal cleanliness. The sponge and flesh-brush every day, and the tub once a week, is a good rule. Clean the teeth after each meal, and if you would avoid an offensive breath, after smoking. No gentleman of fastidious habits will chew tobacco. Keep the hair and beard neatly trimmed, and shave as frequently as necessary to avoid an untidy appearance. Make frequent resort to the lavatory when the hands are liable to become soiled in business, and see that the nails are kept clean and neatly pared. In all things avoid the appearance of foppishness, which is the certain sign of ignorant vulgarity or weak-minded vanity.

CONDUCT IN PUBLIC PLACES.

THE first thing to be considered in the appearance on the street, or in public places, is the deportment. The lady of refinement, on her way through the street, may be noted by a free, light, graceful "gliding" motion, as it has been described, not so rapid as to indicate haste, nor so slow as to suggest languor. She will never look around, and will, in company with others, of either sex, avoid exclamations, and laughter or conversation that will be audible to others, or be liable to attract attention. She will have a pleasant nod and smile for acquaintances and pass on her way, quietly and unobtrusively.

MEETING ON THE STREETS.

Ladies meeting lady friends on the street do not stop to engage in conversation. A pleasant recognition is sufficient unless there be special reason, and then merely sufficient for explanation and future appointment, as in the case, for instance, of friends unexpectedly encountered. Do not bow first to a lady whom you may have only casually met, if she be your elder or superior in social position. Leave the recognition to her. Acquaintances and even intimacies at summer resorts are not expected to continue unless by special request or mutual agreement. If the lady who has precedence desires to continue the acquaintance, or otherwise, she will indicate her wish by her manner on meeting. When meeting any person whom you know by employing them as seamstress, dressmaker or milliner, good breeding requires that you recognize them pleasantly, though not familiarly. Bow to a lady first whom you wish to recognize and over whom you have precedence of age or social position. Bow first to a gentleman acquaintance. If you have had formal introduction to a gentleman whom you do not wish to number among your acquaintances, bow coldly on the first time of meeting, so that your intention may be apparent, and after not at all. It is allowable, but not desirable, to shake hands with a gentleman on the streets. Never permit a gentleman to stop you for conversation on the street.

GENTLEMEN'S RULE OF CONDUCT.

On the streets, and in public places, as indeed always and at all times and places, the laws of politeness and good-breeding exact from gentlemen toward ladies the most punctilious courtesy. On meeting a lady acquaintance, respond to her recognition by raising the hat—not merely touching it, but raising it quite off the head—and pass on. If it appears to be her pleasure to converse with you, or if you are on sufficiently intimate terms and desire to do so, do not stop on the street, but turn and accompany her for a short distance, and on leaving salute her by raising the hat. A cigar should be removed from the mouth if you expect recognition from a lady approaching, and if you enter her company should be thrown away. Always give the lady the inside of the pavement. Do not offer the arm in the daytime, except in case of a dangerous walk, or up the steps of a public edifice, or to a lady for whom age or physical infirmity demands the courtesy as an assistance. At night the arm should always be tendered. Precede the lady into the church, theatre or concert room, because you can so best avoid crowding and assist in procuring her seat. In attending a lady from the street to the shop, open the door wide and let her precede you. In coming out, hold the door quite wide open till she has passed through. Should you see a lady acquaintance unattended, about to alight from a carriage or conveyance, if the driver does not indicate his intention of assisting her, go at once to attend her by opening the door, offering the hand, and protecting the dress from the wheel. When the service is rendered, salute her by raising the hat and proceed quietly on your way. This service may be rendered to a stranger, if she appears to be in a difficulty, but must be offered with an apology and performed without the slightest approach to familiarity. In walking with a lady, take charge of her book, or parcel, or any such small burden.

FOR GENERAL GUIDANCE.

Never talk across the street nor hold conversation with another party in a vehicle, except both parties be on the same seat. Always accommodate your step to that of the lady whom you are accompanying. To stare at a lady is the height of offensive vulgarity. In giving information to a lady who has addressed a question to you on the street, and with whom you are unacquainted, do so with some phrase of politeness and respect, and do not afterward presume upon the incident unless the lady recognizes you. If you wish to address a lady with whom you are acquainted, on the street, preceding you, do not startle her by calling out in an abrupt manner, and when she recognizes you on being overtaken, ask permission to accompany her in a polite manner, indicating the distance of the walk which will be sufficient for your conversation, and take formal leave of her at the point indicated unless she should otherwise express a desire. Never join a party of two—gentleman and lady—except by joint invitation, given in such a manner that you need have no fear of being *de trop*. Make no mistake in being sure of the recognition of a lady before saluting or addressing her. To make a mistake of this kind is the most offensive kind of intrusion, and a gentleman will carefully avoid it.

GENTLEMEN'S STREET INTERCOURSE.

Gentlemen should be careful in their intercourse with others who are engrossed in business, not to intrude upon their attention or time during business hours. A friendly "good-morning," or other form of salutation, is sufficient. If you have anything of a serious or business nature to impart, draw aside from the crowd and state it as briefly as possible. To engage the valuable time of a business man by detaining him on the street for frivolous or inconsequent conversation is a most ill-bred act, and will speedily earn for a man the undesirable reputation of a bore. Do not stay to remove the glove in shaking hands if the action occupies time. Always speak a kind or pleasant word on passing a servant or inferior who is not entitled to ceremonious salutation.

THE THEATRE AND CONCERT ROOM.

Always endeavor to be early at a concert, theatrical or other public performance. Entering after the performance begins is annoying to the audience and attracts attention to the person, which every gentleman, and certainly every lady, should shun. If you have not engaged seats, the reasons for going early are increased. Boisterous applause should be avoided by gentlemen, and a lady should be careful in expressing approbation or giving way to merriment, not to do so in a manner to render herself conspicuous. It is a vulgar sign of ill breeding to make audible remarks unfavorable to the entertainment, or to indulge in derisive laughter in pathetic or tragic parts, even where accident or incompetence is evident. Conduct or conversation, that will interfere with the appreciation of the performance, by those surrounding you, is most reprehensible.

PLACES OF WORSHIP.

Of all the situations in which a gentleman or lady may be placed, there is none where the obligations of true politeness are more imperative, or where genuine regard for decorum will be more studiously evinced than in attendance at divine worship. The mind which is truly refined cannot by any possibility permit its possessor to be guilty of irreverence or unseemly levity in a sacred edifice, where people are gathered for the purposes of devotion. Even if the persons have no share in the pious and devout feelings which the very attendance even should express, he must be callous to every true principle of common courtesy, who would allow frivolity to mark his conduct in such a place on such an occasion. The most common breach of decorum in places of public worship is carelessness, which should be scrupulously guarded against. The gentleman or lady who is guided by refined instincts and polite habits will observe the following rules: Always enter church before the services begins. If unavoidably late, wait and make your entry between the exercises. Enter the church and take your seat as noiselessly and quietly as possible. The gentleman will remove his hat on crossing the threshold. Let the demeanor be marked by reverence and attention. Avoid salutations with acquaintances whom you may happen to notice. Even if a church is not of your own denomination, conform to the best of your ability with the ceremonial. Talking, whispering and laughing in church indicate gross vulgarity. In entering a strange church, avoid error and confusion by waiting in the vestibule till an usher or church member shows you to a seat. In case you are afforded the freedom of a pew not your own, under no circumstances introduce a friend without previous permission, and never take a child with you. Never leave the church before the benediction is pronounced except in cases of illness or absolute necessity.

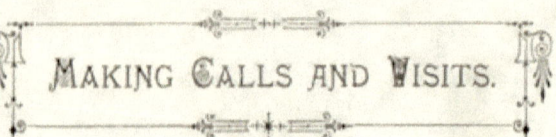

MAKING CALLS AND VISITS.

THIS branch of the usages of polite society is one of which every young gentleman and lady should make a careful study, and in whose rules, regulations and *convenances* they should be thoroughly informed, even if at that period of life there does not appear to be any special reason for thorough acquaintance with it.

CALLING.

MORNING CALLS.—Morning calls are made at any time in daylight in which you are quite certain the lady called upon is prepared to receive. It is a rule of good breeding, however, not to call earlier than 2 o'clock, p.m., nor later than 4 p.m., in winter and 5 p.m., in summer—the object being to afford time for luncheon or dinner, as the case may be, to be removed, and to allow the lady time to make her dinner or evening toilet. Calls before noon should only be made on express invitation, or where warranted by unusual intimacy. Should the lady be absent, leave your card. If the call is designed for a visitor, or particular member of the lady's family, leave a second card with the name of the person written on the top left hand corner.

It is a general custom for a lady to set apart a certain day or days of the week for receiving callers, indicated on her cards. In such case a formal call should not be made on any other day. It is proper where a social invitation has been received and unavoidably declined, to call within one week for acknowledgment and regret. Formal calls should be as brief as courtesy will admit, and on special calling days the visitor should retire upon another being announced.

Gentlemen's Etiquette in Making Morning Calls.—After properly announcing yourself, on entering leave your cane or umbrella in the hall. On being ushered into the reception room, advance with the hat in the left hand, and retain it during the stay, indicating the formality of the call. If the lady offers her hand, advance and return the salutation briefly and respectfully. If the hostess merely bows, respond in like manner to the salutation, and take the seat which she may indicate. If other ladies or members of the family are present, speak to each in succession, according to age and precedence, and if there be a stranger present, bow slightly in acknowledgment of their presence. If an introduction ensues after you are seated, rise and bow to them—if gentlemen are introduced they advance mutually and shake hands. If conversation does not at once become general, or you observe that you are interrupting a special circle, pass a few words of ordinary courtesy with the hostess and take your leave. In taking leave a formal bow to a stranger to whom you have been introduced, is sufficient.

In Attending Ladies.—Gentlemen who attend ladies in making morning calls, will assist them up the steps, ring the bell, write cards where necessary, relieve them of shawls, etc., where it will conduce to their convenience. If stairs are to be ascended, offer the lady the arm on the wall side. On entering, follow them into the drawing room and wait to pay your own respects, or for introduction, till the lady has finished her salutations. If you have to introduce the lady to the hostess, advance with her into the drawing room a little in advance. Do not seat yourself or remain seated while they are standing. If they are required for any purpose to change position, place a seat for them, and study with courtesy to relieve them from anything likely to involve discomfort or effort. The duration of the visit is always determined by the pleasure of the lady.

Evening Calls.—Evening calls should not be made later than 9 p.m., and unless you are familiar with the hours observed by the family, under no circumstances protract a call longer than to 10 p.m. Where not on terms of familiarity, the hat and gloves should be retained in one hand unless requested to lay them aside. Where familiar, and if accompanied by a lady friend, the wraps may be laid aside in the hall.

Ladies Receiving.—The lady receiving does not advance to greet her caller, except where special attention is designed. If the caller be a lady, she will arise and advance a step, either extending the hand or bowing, according to the degree of respect intended, and remain standing till the caller shall have taken the seat to which she shall direct. Receive a gentleman seated. If engaged at the piano or with a book, the occupation should be laid aside during the visitor's stay. Fancy work which does not distract the attention from the duties of conversation may with propriety be continued. The hostess will direct her conversation during the visit with a view to put the visitor at ease, and will show her good breeding by implying a welcome in her conduct. If several visitors are entertained together she will display her tact by making the conversation general, and placing all upon a pleasant and easy footing. It is not necessary to accompany the guest to the door where there is a servant to attend.

VISITS OF CONDOLENCE.—A visit of condolence should be paid within a week after the event which occasions it, or in case of slight acquaintance immediately after the family appear at public worship. Unless intimacy or relationship is sufficient to give you a personal interest, it is a more delicate way to express sympathy to merely leave a card. If the visit be deemed necessary, go in a quiet dress—any dark colors are usually chosen. In case of relationship the slightest mourning is considered necessary.

CARDS.

The rules of observance for the style and forms of visiting cards, and for their proper use, demand the strictest adherence. Any deviation from the most exact compliance with these forms and customs, betrays at once a want of familiarity with the usages of good society, which on the threshold of acquaintance creates an unfavorable impression. There are three sizes of cards, with which every stationer and engraver is familiar—the larger being used for married ladies or couples, the medium for unmarried women, and the smaller for gentlemen. The printing or engraving in all cases should be neat and plain, as are also the cards, and entirely devoid of flourishes or ornamentation.

THE LADY'S CARD.—On a married lady's card her own name may appear alone, or as is more strictly *en regle*, with that of her husband in this shape:

> *Mr. and Mrs. Edwin H. Lawrence.*
>
> 271 CEDAR STREET.

Married ladies who use cards which do not include the husband's name, in making visits of ceremony, should in all cases leave the card of her husband with her own. Where there are unmarried daughters included in the call, the card should include their names with those of their mother, as:

> *Mrs. Edwin H. Lawrence.*
>
> *Miss Lawrence.*

or where there is more than one daughter, "The Misses Lawrence," or "Miss Lawrence, Miss Julia Lawrence, Miss Sarah Lawrence."

YOUNG LADIES' CARDS.—In the case of young ladies, the mother's name should precede their own, according to the strict rules of etiquette, though it is common in America to a large extent to honor it in the breach rather than the observance. Where there is no mother, the father's name should precede, as:

> *Mr. Edwin H. Lawrence.*
> *Miss Lawrence.*

A card bearing the name of an unmarried lady without the prefix "Miss," is not acknowledged in good society.

GENTLEMEN'S CARDS.—The gentleman's card may give simply the name, which must invariably have the prefix "Mr." or it may give his residence or club address, as:

> *Mr. Edwin H. Lawrence.*
>
> 271 CEDAR STREET.

or,

> *Mr. Edwin H. Lawrence.*
>
> UNION CLUB.

It is allowable for a physician to use his professional title either as "Dr. L. M. Jones," or "L. M. Jones, M.D." Officers of the army or navy have their cards engraved thus:

Capt. Spangler, U. S. A.

THE USE OF CARDS.—When a lady calls upon another and finds her absent, she leaves a card to denote that she has called. Or, if she desires a visiting acquaintance with a lady with whom she is not so intimate, she leaves cards without inquiring whether the lady visited is at home or not. Under either circumstance the number of cards left is the same. If the lady have a husband, but no daughters in society, the caller will leave one of her own cards and two of her husband's, one of the latter for the gentleman of the family called on, or two cards if they include the husband's name with the wife's. This rule, though in strict etiquette, is not generally observed, and a lady may make calls with perfect propriety by leaving her own card alone. If there are other lady members of the household, another of the lady's cards should be left also. If the lady lives alone, the card of husband and wife, or the joint card, should be left. In case the caller finds the lady called on at home, she does not leave her card, but will leave two of her husband's cards, one for the husband of the lady called on. If the latter be at home when the call is made, leave one of the husband's cards only. In leaving a card where the answer is "not at home," turn down the card at the end to indicate that it has been left in person. When contemplating an extended absence, it has become the custom to notify one's friends by having the letters "P. P. C." printed on the lower left hand corner of cards sent out, though a card turned down at the lower right hand corner will answer the purpose.

AFTER SOCIAL ENTERTAINMENTS.—After a dinner party, cards should always be left—if not on terms of intimacy, the following day after a dinner party, without inquiry; otherwise within ten days. After a ball, reception, etc., whether the invitation has been accepted or not, cards should be left within a week. It is not allowable, under any circumstances, to send cards by mail.

SPECIAL CARDS.—In calling on a lady who is ill, and who for that reason cannot be seen, the lady will leave a card with the words "to inquire," and also a card of her husband, if the occasion be other than the birth of a child. On recovery, the lady called on acknowledges by issuing cards as follows: "Mrs. Lawrence returns thanks for [blank to be filled in with name of caller] kind inquiries."

SOCIAL VISITING.

Thorough knowledge of the etiquette of Visiting as distinguished from Calling is essential to all who desire to conform to polite usages, and also consult their own comfort and their social popularity, the following notes should be carefully observed in this branch of social intercourse:

INVITATION.—No well-bred person will think of paying a visit to a friend without either a distinct invitation or giving due and timely notice of an intended visit. The visitor who consults his own comfort and pleasure, as well as his social duty, will never presume upon a "general invitation," which does not present the certainty that the visit is desired. Many such invitations are merely intended as formal courtesies, though good breeding will prevent them from being offered. "Chinese hospitality" is not polite. If your acquaintance or relationship with the family visited is sufficient to insure a welcome without invitation, send notice to the hostess giving the date of your intended visit and its duration. This will enable her to prepare for your proper entertainment and avoid disturbing her domestic or social arrangements, in which she might by an unheralded arrival be embarrassed and annoyed. The "surprise visit," like the "surprise party," is neither popular nor in good taste.

RULES OF CONDUCT DURING VISIT.—On the first evening of arrival, ascertain the hours of meals and general household regulations so far as they concern you as for the time being a member of the family, and conform to them with exactitude and punctuality. Be careful to have your toilet completed in time for the first meal. If you have time on your hands before it is called occupy yourself in your own room, in the garden, or in the library, but do not enter a room used for ordinary, domestic or social purposes. To keep the family waiting at any meal time is an unpardonable breach of propriety. Do not accept too literally any invitation to "make yourself at home." Remember that it is your duty to devote your whole time to your hostess, and to make your visit agreeable, and at the same time you must exercise discretion and consideration, so as not to interfere with her domestic or social duties. Under no circumstances either invite, or suggest the invitation of a friend. Your friend is at liberty to call on you at your hostess' residence. Do not accept social invitations in which your hostess is not included during your stay. In case of illness occurring in the house, unless you can be of real service, you should take your departure at once. Be considerate in your relations with the children and servants. Do not allow your hostess to pay for any incidental expense that may be incurred on your account, such as removal of baggage, etc. Before leaving it is proper to make a present as a souvenir to the lady visited. Children may also be remembered in this way, and any servant who has been specially attentive. On returning home always write to the hostess expressing your acknowledgment of the pleasure afforded by your visit.

LADY GUESTS.—The lady guest should be prepared to put out and pay for her own washing, if that is the rule of the family. Have two clothes bags; one to be sent to the laundry, the other to receive soiled linen in its absence. Be careful to have your own work-box, so as to avoid troubling members of the family by borrowing scissors, etc. Take with you also a small writing box, with sufficient stationery and stamps for your visit. Where possible, assist your hostess in any of the lighter duties of the household. Before leaving, express cordially the pleasure and gratification which the visit has afforded, and where practicable extend a reciprocal invitation.

HINTS TO GENTLEMEN.—In visiting country friends, send a telegram announcing the day and hour of your arrival at the nearest station, so that, if they have conveyance, they may be able to meet you. In visiting a friend in the city, where notice has not been given, go first to a hotel. Then call and leave your card, and the formal invitation will follow as a matter of course, if the visit be desired. Be careful to give reverent attention to any religious observances of the house visited.

THE HOSTESS.—When a visitor is expected, learn the exact time of arrival and have some male representative of the family at the station to attend them. Provide such means of conveyance as are within your power. On arrival, have the guest's baggage sent to her room at once, and when a lady guest goes to her room, send a servant to furnish assistance in unpacking, and render any service that may be required. The room should be prepared in advance, with every possible reference to the guest's comfort, and also to their habits and peculiarities, if known to the hostess. The guest's room should receive the first attention in the morning, and when it is done the hostess should visit it to see that it has been properly attended to, but at no other time. While taking care that no appearance of unusual effort is made, provide in every way possible for the pleasure and entertainment of the guest. Never make apologies for the absence of anything which you would like to but are unable to provide. When the guest departs, send a servant to assist in packing and preparations for the journey. If in the morning, provide an early breakfast, and see that some member of the family is present at the table. Have the family or other conveyance at the door in time, and let some male representative of the family accompany the guest to the starting place, and see them off; if a lady, procuring tickets, attending to baggage and checks, and seeing her to a comfortable seat in the car, boat or coach.

INTRODUCTIONS AND SALUTATIONS.

THE forms of salutation proper for polite society in this country are: bowing, shaking hands and address. Kissing cannot, with propriety, be indulged in in public, except under peculiar circumstances, and is not to be regarded as a form of salutation. A parent, on the point of a lengthy separation from a child, may exchange a kiss in public. The common mode of recognition is by a bow, to which every acquaintance is entitled. To omit to return a salutation offered in this way is an unpardonable rudeness, even where the person has bowed under misapprehension or by mistake of identity, or belongs to the humblest rank.

RULES FOR GUIDANCE.—It is the prerogative of the lady to bow first, and the cordiality of her salutation is governed by the degree of intimacy she is disposed to accord to the gentleman honored by recognition. The gentleman returning the bow will raise his hat.

In the country, where people are not so thickly hived together, it is a pleasant custom to nod to every person met, and this should be borne in mind by city visitors to the country who do not wish to be set down as snobbish and haughty.

On horseback, the gentleman who is recognized will either remove the whip to the bridle hand and acknowledge the salute by raising the hat, or he may salute with the whip in military fashion, bringing the whip to the position of the sword of a military officer at the "present." The latter is considered best form.

If the gentleman recognized by a lady be accompanied by a friend, the friend should also raise the hat, but without regarding the lady.

If a gentleman meet a friend in company of ladies, he will acknowledge the presence of the ladies by raising his hat, but without regarding them, and the gentleman acting as the ladies' escort will also raise his hat in recognition of the courtesy.

Good breeding will restrain a lady from recognizing a gentleman on the street from a window.

In hand-shaking every person has a characteristic of his or her own. The general rule is to give the whole hand, and to give a gentle but firm grasp for the space of a second, in mere salutation.

Hand-shaking is, however, susceptible of many expressions—respect, sympathy, love, and gratitude.

Never give a hand like a fish, nor one or two fingers. Such a salutation is snobbish and impertinent.

Never offer the left hand. It is not necessary to remove the glove, unless quite convenient, but if the other's hand be bare, pray to be excused for the glove.

In addressing a man give him his full title, as "Judge," "Senator," "Doctor," "Major." In addition to the title given with the name use the ordinary form of salutation, "Good-morning," "Good-day," "Good-evening," or such conventional salutation as may occur. Never exercise familiarity with a friend in addressing him on the street. Address children and servants by their full Christian names, and never use a nickname in salutation. The wife will address her husband, and *vice versa*, in society just the same as she would any other gentleman, and in speaking of him, mention his name in the same way.

THE ART OF CONVERSATION.

THIS is the crucial test not only of fitness of a man for the social circle by thorough knowledge and observance of the laws of etiquette, but of the rank which is to be awarded, according to his capacity to embellish and adorn social intercourse. One may possess all the attributes of refinement and true gentility, he may be *au fait* in every art and accomplishment of etiquette, may be irreproachable in his manner, and in punctilious observance of the *minutiæ* of all the regulations provided for social harmony; but if he lack either the wit to hold his tongue with eloquence, and so conceal his deficiencies of education, tact and talent, or the good taste, discretion and discernment which mark the finished and accomplished conversationalist, he will find himself far behind the front rank in social popularity. To possess the graces of a cultivated mind, and the art and ability, without ostentation, to share its treasures with others, is a far more potent weapon, for the achievement of social success, than charms of person or elegance of manner and deportment. But it is one thing to possess the wit, knowledge and learning, and the mental powers necessary to the successful conversationalist, and another to be master of the art of using these advantages in accordance with the dictates of refinement, delicacy, decorum and propriety.

REQUISITES OF A SUCCESSFUL CONVERSATIONALIST.—The successful conversationalist must be a man of good education, should be fairly acquainted with the laws of elocution, must have an extended knowledge of the world and of books, as well as being thoroughly conversant with the current literature of the day. He must be a constant student of the magazines and newspapers, and possess the faculty of imparting the knowledge so gathered, in the course of conversation upon any subject that may arise. He must be modest in asserting opinions, avoid dogmatism and any approach to pedantry, be genial and sympathetic in his manner, and cultivate an easy temper. He must talk with his tongue and not with his teeth nor his throat, and must practice a distinct and deliberate, but not drawling utterance. He must modulate his tones according to the circle addressed and the circumstances of the room. A too loud talker is offensive; an indistinct enunciation is an annoyance. He must not dwell too long on one subject, and adapt his style of dealing with it as nearly as he can judge to the capacity or information of his audience. He must take up promptly any subject introduced by another, listen with respectful and interested attention, and advance his opinions with modesty and deference. A popular conversationalist must be also a patient and discerning listener.

POLITE HABITS OF CONVERSATION.—In conversation, confine your talk and adapt your voice to a limited circle in your immediate vicinity. No matter how many may be interested in the conversation, do not appear to presume that every one is desirous of listening to you. Be careful not to disturb any conversation in progress in another part of the room. Do not address a person across the room; if you have something special to say to him, wait till you can conveniently join him. Remember that all guests appear upon an equal footing. In whatever company you may be, for the moment strive to make your conversation agreeable and exercise tact in adapting it to the scope of your companion's interest. If there be a guest of special prominence, be careful not to engross an undue share of his conversation, no matter how agreeable it may be to you personally. Never absolutely contradict, and where your statement or opinion is contradicted, after mildly expressing confidence in your own opinion, lead the conversation away from the disputed point. Always endeavor to seek a common ground of discussion, from which none in the circle by prejudice or want of information may be excluded. Above all things avoid any utterance which will painfully impress upon another a sense of inferiority.

HABITS TO BE AVOIDED.—Endeavor to be as careful as possible in your choice of language. Be as far as your knowledge will permit strictly grammatical. Carefully avoid the use of slang or cant phrases—they are the distinguishing marks of vulgarity of mind and habit. Never make complimentary speeches which can be construed into flattery. Flattery is offensive and even painful to people of refined minds, and is embarrassing to the sensitive. Be careful equally to avoid speeches which might be construed into a desire to receive a compliment in return. Avoid long arguments, and endeavor to change the current of conversation frequently in order to give variety to its interest. Avoid religious topics, and where they are indiscreetly introduced, and the expression of opinion cannot be avoided, do so in such a manner as not to give offense to any one who may be present. In referring to any doctrine or creed, speak as if there were some one present whose sensibilities would be wounded by harsh criticism, or absolute condemnation of the religious theory they might entertain.

EXCEPTIONALLY REPREHENSIBLE PRACTICES.—There are some rules of conduct, the violation of which is specially ill-bred and offensive, and with many would exclude offenders from a second admission to the circle in which the breach of decorum occurs. Among such offenses are: Loss of temper in argument. Absolutely disputing a statement of fact by another, even if you be assured that he is in error. Introducing scandal of any description, or taking part in its discussion when another has the bad taste or ignorance to do so. Propounding puns which reflect personally or by their professional allusion upon any other guest. Interrupting another guest while he is speaking in a general conversation.

UNPLEASANT TOPICS.—Both skillful tact and watchful care should be exercised to see that no unpleasant topics are introduced or continued by you. When you observe that such an element has been introduced in discussion, it is a part of good breeding to endeavor to lead the course of conversation into another channel. Among subjects which are carefully to be avoided are religion and politics. In the case of the former, it is one upon which people feel deeply, and upon which their sensibilities are more acute than upon ordinary matters. No matter how small the circle to which conversation is limited, there will most certainly be some one to be hurt or offended by an adverse reflection upon his or her religion, and true politeness will avoid the subject altogether. Discussion of politics is to be avoided, because it is prone to lead to collisions of opinion which are liable to disturb the harmony of the intercourse for which the company has been brought together.

DINNER CONVERSATION.—In taking a lady in to dinner, even though a perfect stranger beyond the introduction, remember that you are the deputy of your hostess for her entertainment. While it is allowable to exchange occasional remarks with your *vis-a-vis*, or with your left-hand neighbor, your conversation belongs to your partner. When the cloth is withdrawn, and the ladies have retired to the drawing-room, conversation becomes general, and is allowed more latitude and freedom than in the drawing-room. A good anecdote related is generally listened to by the whole table if the company be not too large, and recollections of foreign travel, remarkable experiences, enlivened by sallies of wit, are favorable to general enjoyment.

PRIVILEGED CONVERSATION.—Etiquette strictly forbids repetition by any guest of what has transpired in conversation under the roof of another. Harmless jokes, or expressions entirely without significance, by being repeated soon assume an entirely different form and give rise to grave offense and serious social trouble. The guest, therefore, who betrays the laws of hospitality by relating conversations which occurred in another's house, is justly adjudged worthy of expulsion from the pale of good society. Offenses are not infrequent in this respect through carelessness or thoughtlessness, but it should be borne in mind that the consequences are so grave that carelessness is no palliation.

SARCASM AND WIT.—No man is more welcome in the social gathering than he who has the reputation of *un homme d'esprit*—who possesses a fund of humor, the faculty of sharing it with others, and the discretion to so use it as to judiciously flavor conversation without spoiling it by extravagance or overdoing. Wit should be so tempered as to avoid offense, as well as excessive frivolity. The man who is forever on the point of exploding a joke becomes a nuisance and a bore. So with regard to puns. While not desirable, an occasional pun, if it have originality and humor without offense, is not objectionable; but the habitual punster is shunned. Sarcasm and raillery, however, are two spoilsports in social conversation, which should be rigidly excluded from polite society. He who has a biting tongue ought to keep it completely under control. It is the affliction of a diseased temper and an unnatural acerbity of disposition, which has no proper place in society, whose laws are framed wholly for the comfort, ease and enjoyment of mutual intercourse among its members. To attempt to be sarcastic at the expense of another guest, or of his opinions, is the depth of ill-breeding. Repartee, if conducted with genuine good nature, and not pressed to an undue limit, will interest and amuse, but prolonged unreasonably, or descending to personal retort or reflection, it is very bad taste indeed.

SMALL TALK.—The airy nothings which constitute the vapid intercourse which brainless frivolity chooses to dignify as conversation, is not without its uses even in society of a more elevated standard. No one can be without a sufficient fund of it, to adjust his conversation to all with whom he comes in contact with ease. Entering into conversation with a stranger, it bridges over the gulf of want of mutual acquaintance and leads you easily and naturally to the proper ground of your neighbor's tastes and intellectual capacity, while not infrequently you may be compelled in good breeding to devote yourself conscientously to the entertainment and amusement of a fair neighbor whose mental ambition and understanding does not soar beyond the limited region of small talk.

COURTSHIP AND MARRIAGE.

THE contemplation of courtship and marriage, and all that the subject involves, embraces, it may almost be said, the whole scope of a young girl's life. Therein is included for her all that life holds in store, of happiness, prosperity, rank and station. It is a sweet and solemn mystery, this mystic urn of Fate, from which, with her own hand, of her own choice, but not, happily, with blindfold eyes, she must draw forth the prize of destiny, domestic happiness, connubial felicities, social ambitions, and every aspiration in the direction of all that makes life worth living; and, it is little to be wondered that, when she reaches that period of life when

> "Standing with reluctant feet,
> Where the brook and river meet,"

she feels that she is rapidly drawing near to the crisis which is to change the whole current of existence. She should approach this grave and solemn question with timidity and hesitation. Yet every true woman, when she does arrive at that age, cannot avoid the duty of taking into serious consideration how best to comport herself to meet the inevitable, and how, in doing so, to consult her intelligence, discretion and discernment, as well as her heart, so as to secure for herself the best prospect of future and permanent happiness.

COURTSHIP.

THE INITIAL STEP.—When a young girl first "comes out" into society, or is "introduced," as the expression is, she will find herself the subject, in her social intercourse, of a great number and variety of flattering attentions. She will, however, take all these without trepidation or serious thought. They are her due, and natural tact and woman's wit will soon lead her to distinguish between those attentions which are purely complimentary, and those which indicate a desire to lead to warmer regard. Indeed, it is not infrequent that the young *debutante* receives an offer of marriage before she has been allowed a breathing time in the social world. She should, however, keep her affections strictly within her own control till she has had ample time to judge by observation and reflection what is best for herself. There will be some one among those the tendency of whose advances she receives, but may not recognize, whom she will in time come to regard as worthier than others, of more congenial temperament and disposition, and to whom those subtler instincts of nature which are governed by no rule, will draw her. She should never, under any circumstances, give the slightest encouragement to one whose advances are distasteful to her, and whom she is certain she could never wed, and she should, if such advances are pressed, make this so coldly manifest as to leave the unfavored suitor no excuse for the mortification and pain of a direct refusal. Her manner towards the one whom she is ready to acknowledge as a lover, when he shall express his suit, should be in consonance with maidenly dignity and reserve, but not repellant. The dignity which is too chilling on the part of the lady, and the doubt which leaves the lover without courage to declare his passion, too often lead two loving hearts into separate roads of misery.

UNEXPECTED AVOWALS.—It often happens, through the sensitiveness and secretiveness of a man, and a very delicate modesty, he finds himself very earnestly in love with a lady, who has not had the slightest reason to suspect the nature of his feelings. In such a case, when the avowal is made, it will require all the tact and good feeling of the lady to acquit herself in justice and honor. If she be "heart whole and fancy free," she should consider well if it is possible that she could honestly lead mere esteem into the warmer latitudes of affection. If she doubt, she may fairly ask time to consider; but, if she have no doubt, it is her duty to at once give a final answer.

PROPOSAL BY LETTER.—This is a form of proposal frequently resorted to by those who fear to face the ordeal of possible rejection, and, in most cases, the proposal, if not the form of it, will not have been unlooked for. The lady should answer as soon as possible after due consideration, if she be not sure of her own heart. If the proposal be agreeable, to keep the lover in suspense is needless cruelty. If it is otherwise, she will be governed in her reply by the esteem in which the wooer is held. In some cases a simple and unmistakable refusal is sufficient. If she highly esteem the person refused, she should couch her language so as to assure him of regard and friendship, explaining the impossibility of entertaining any more tender regard for him. In any case, the letter of proposal should be returned, and the lady's lips sealed on the subject thereafter.

REFUSALS.—To a true woman, a lady of delicate and refined instincts, the duty of refusing the proffer of a sincere and honorable affection is one of the most painful that could be imposed upon her. She will remember that the suitor upon whom she is compelled to visit pain, mortification and bitter disappointment, has paid her the highest honor and compliment in the power of a man to bestow upon a woman, and while the best kindness is to be so firm in the refusal as not to give rise to bootless hopes, she will, by the delicacy of her language, show that she appreciates the honor done her, and extend sympathy with the pain which she has to inflict. It will be due to him that, except to parents, she shall keep his secret, and will make it a point to meet him thereafter with the frankness and cordiality of friendship, entirely ignoring what has passed between them.

THE ENGAGEMENT.—When the suitor has proposed and been accepted, his courtship being always presumed to have had the sanction and approval of parents or guardians, it is first announced to the family through the head of the household, and the fact becomes generally known in society. On acceptance, the suitor will, according to custom, place upon the third finger of the right or left hand the engagement or betrothal ring, which is not removed till marriage. If on the left hand, it is removed when the wedding ring is placed on the finger, and thereafter becomes its guard. If on the right, it is transferred to the corresponding finger of the left hand upon the wedding ring being put on. Engagement rings may be either of chased gold, often bearing the Hebrew word, "Mizpah" ("Fidelity"), or "A. E. I." ("Ever"). Rings set with precious stones are also favored. The opal should not be used, being the symbol of misfortune.

AFTER BETROTHAL.—After the engagement the position of the betrothed will be respected by others in society who are imbued with true good-breeding. If the familiarities of gentlemen friends, however, are continued, the lady must mark her conduct by unmistakable displeasure and resentment. No true woman will flirt after being engaged, nor should the gentleman, while being courteous and gallant, as becomes a gentleman to be, to other ladies, allow his attentions to give rise to jealousy in the mind of his betrothed. He will make her the object of his special devotion and attention, will visit her frequently, and extend his courtesies to all members of her family. Expensive presents from the engaged gentleman to his betrothed are not in good taste, but flowers, books, music, etc., constitute suitable and unobjectionable attentions.

MARRIAGE.

FEW topics are more interesting to all classes of society than weddings. From the young girl just budding into womanhood, to the grey-haired matron surrounded by prattling grandchildren, the subject of marriage is one which awakens in the female breast an interest which nothing else but maternity can arouse. In cottage or castle, the feminine sisterhood preserve the same instinct, never blunted by lapse of years.

No fixed and inflexible rules can be laid down governing the subject of weddings, yet among the better class of society a certain similarity of usage prevails. After the day for the marriage has been set and announced, the next subject that engrosses the attention of the engaged couple is the number of persons to be invited to attend the ceremony, where it shall be performed, and what shall be the form of invitations.

In answering these questions, each family must have regard to appropriateness in reference to their circumstances and surroundings. Nothing excites more just criticism than to see persons of small means attempt a cheap imitation of the display made by their wealthier (yet not necessarily happier) neighbors. Parade is not always a prelude to peace, and many a bride, the magnificence of whose wedding has excited the envy of all of her female acquaintances, has been ready, within a few short months, to exchange all her grandeur for the quiet happiness that fills the humble home of one of the poorest of her sisters. Another circumstance to be considered is the surroundings of the families of both bride and groom with reference to domestic affairs. A recent bereavement, or some similar cloud overhanging the home, will, of course, render improper any elaborate preparations for the wedding, even were the heart disposed toward festivity. Under such circumstances a quiet marriage, in presence of relatives, or, at most, a few intimate friends, is every way "in better form," as well as, probably, more congenial to the feelings of the principal participants.

WEDDING PREPARATIONS.—Where, however, the wedding is to be a joyous one, and no tinge of sadness colors the feelings of those who are to be united, or of those who are to "set forth the marriage feast," the affair may be made as ceremonious as good taste and the wishes and circumstances of the parties may dictate. If it be determined to invite any outside of the circle of very near friends, it is better to make the list long enough to include all those who may not unreasonably feel slighted by the omission of their names. At such an epoch in life, the heart should feel sufficiently enlarged by its newly found happiness to find room for every generous impulse, and yet too small for bitterness or resentment to find a hiding place. It may be, however, that the circle of acquaintance of the families of the bride and groom is so large, and embraces social elements so diverse, as to render even a representative assemblage of those whom one might wish to invite too large to be conveniently entertained or too mixed in its composition to be agreeable. In such a case, a happy way is afforded between the horns of the dilemma by having the ceremony solemnized at the church, where all may meet on one common level, while only those need be invited to the reception whose names affection, or regard, or inclination may suggest.

Having determined upon the number and names of the guests, the next topic that engages the attention is the invitation. The most usual method of conveying invitations is by cards. The style of these little heralds of Cupid's conquests varies greatly in different years and even with individual tastes. In case of small, or comparatively private weddings, cards are unnecessary and are seldom used, although it is not uncommon, in such cases, to issue cards of announcement after the marriage, containing the names of the bride and groom, their conventional wedded title, and sometimes a card announcing when they will be "at home." The following forms will illustrate what is meant:

Miss Edith Jordan.

Mr. Frank W. Fay.

Mr. and Mrs. Frank W. Fay.

or, if preferred, in place of the latter card may be substituted the following, which should be larger than those accompanying it.

Mr. and Mrs. Frank W. Fay.

At Home,

Wednesdays in March

from

8 to 10 p. m.

Written wedding cards are preferable, printer's ink being not so commonly used as formerly. Written cards are more expensive, but the outlay is one which will not need to be repeated, in most domestic histories. The note of invitation should be on a whole sheet of heavy paper of creamy, satin finish, and when folded once should just fill the envelope in which it is inclosed. The accompanying reception cards should be exactly half the size of one page of the note. The letter may or may not be headed by a monogram or initial, the more fashionable element of society at the present time giving the preference to placing the design on the envelope only or omitting it altogether. If it be used on the paper, however, it should always be on the envelope.

The following are among the most modern and approved forms:

FOR INVITATIONS.

Mr. and Mrs. Alfred Terry

desire your presence at

the marriage of their daughter

Louise B.

to

Charles B. Lawton,

On Thursday Evening,

February 20, 1885, at seven o'clock,

Saint John's Church,

Chicago.

H-N.

Mr. and Mrs. John W. Norris
request your presence at
the marriage of their daughter
Ella
to
William S. Hudson,
Monday, April 9th, 1885,
at nine o'clock a. m.
Dixon, Ill.

FOR THE CARDS.

At Home
Tuesday and Thursday,
March 20 and 22.

401 Elbert Street,

Chicago, Ill.

If a wedding reception is to be held immediately after the marriage, the hour named should be half an hour after that fixed for the ceremony.

> *At Home,*
> *Monday Evening, April 9th,*
> *from*
> *9:30 to 11 o'clock,*
> *896 South Edwards Street.*

The following form of invitation will be used when the wedding ceremony is to take place at a church.

> *Mr. and Mrs John W. Norris*
> *request your presence at*
> *the marriage of their daughter*
> *Ella*
> *to*
> *William S. Hudson.*
> *Ceremony:*
> *First Presbyterian Church,*
> *Chicago.*
> *Monday, 9 to 11 a. m.*
> *April 9, 1885.*
>
> At Home after June 23d. 127 Grace Street.

The announcement of the future residence of the couple and of their "at home," may be made in the way indicated at the bottom of the above form of invitation, or by separate cards according to preference.

Invitations to weddings should be issued two weeks before the day set for the ceremony, and those intended for persons in the same city or town should be conveyed by a private messenger rather than sent through the mail. Shortly before sending out the invitations, the prospective bride should make ceremonious calls on her acquaintance. Invitations to weddings need not be answered, unless a wedding breakfast is to be given, in which case, replies should always be returned, as in the case of dinner parties. Ordinarily, however, if no letter of regret be sent, the invitation is considered as accepted. Where the ceremony is performed in church, it is customary to send cards of admission to the building, which are usually about three inches in length and two in breadth. Two or three of these cards are commonly inclosed for distribution among the friends of the invited guests, or for the use of servants who may accompany them. These cards are usually in the following form:

St. Mark's Church,

Forty-Second Street,

Wednesday, April, 20, 1884,

at 8 o'clock p. m.

WEDDING PRESENTS.—The custom of making presents to the prospective bride and bridegroom, is almost generally observed, and is one which is, if properly carried out, of no little benefit to the couple just starting in life, fitting the table, the sideboard and the drawing-room with many useful articles, and articles of virtu, which aid the bride in giving her new home a home-like aspect. It is customary to send presents from a fortnight previous down to the evening preceding the wedding. If practicable, learn indirectly what articles have been received to avoid duplicating as much as possible. Select gifts either with a view to ornament or utility, and use discretion in their character.

THE CEREMONY.

THE date for the solemnization of the ceremony should always be fixed by the bride. All details of the ceremony should be left to her choosing. She stands at the threshold of a new life; its paths are to her untrodden and unknown; trustfully, she is about to enter, knowing that however long or thorny may be the way before her, she must walk in it to the end. It is due to her that the archway through which she passes into this new existence should be erected at her own command.

All forms of marriage ceremonies may be grouped under two classes—civil and religious—while in France and other nations of continental Europe a double ceremony is commonly performed, one before a civil magistrate, the other before a minister of religion.

The statutes of every state in the American Union contain provisions that marriage may be solemnized by any minister of religion, as well as by certain civil officers connected with the executive department of the government. In every state, the governor, any judge of a court of record, or any justice of the peace, is empowered so to act. In most states the law requires that notice of the parties' intention to marry be given by applying to a designated officer for a marriage license. The omission to do this, however, although it subjects the parties themselves, as well as the person solemnizing the marriage, to a penalty (usually a fine), does not affect the validity of the marriage itself. The "publication of bans of matrimony"—in other words, the public announcement in church on three successive Sundays of the intention of the parties to marry—is, in some states, made a legal substitute for the obtaining of the marriage license.

In the Roman Catholic Church marriage is considered a sacrament, and no member of that communion considers himself properly married unless the nuptial blessing of his clergyman has been pronounced upon his union.

Marriage by a civil magistrate is comparatively infrequent, and extremely rare in polite society.

The "wedding-ring" is an institution which has come down to us with all the respectability that attaches to antiquity. It is difficult to trace its origin. Probably its symbolical significance is to be sought in its form; being a circle, it is *endless*, being thereby typical of the union of which it is the outward sign. In all churches using a liturgical form of worship, the form prescribes a ring, and in the Roman Catholic Church it is indispensable. Where a ring is used, the groom should always endeavor so far to keep his faculties at command as to be able to find and produce it at the moment when it is called for; a delay or "hitch" at this stage of the ceremony is always extremely embarrassing, and has even been said to be a "bad omen."

The groomsmen are, of course, chosen by the groom, the bridesmaids by the bride. The latter are usually selected from the sisters or other near relatives of both parties Their bouquets are presented them by the groom, while the bride frequently gives to each a memento, in the form of a ring, or bracelet, or locket, etc., which, however, need not be expensive.

At weddings in church, the attendance of ushers is a necessity. They are selected by the bridegroom from among his personal friends. Their gloves, bouquets and favors are gifts from the bride. It is common for the groom to present each with a scarf-pin, charm, or some other trifling souvenir of the occasion. Their duties are to see that no improper persons are admitted (and where admission is by card, to exclude all those not holding the coveted pasteboard); to seat the invited guests; to keep the middle aisle free for the entrance of the bridal party. A white ribbon is

LEAVING THE CHURCH.

sometimes stretched across this aisle at a little distance back, the pews in front of the silken barrier being reserved for the families and immediate relatives of the parties. The ushers should also precede the bridal procession as it moves to its position in front of the altar or pulpit. It is not infrequent, in order to avoid the awkwardness and embarrassment natural to finding one's self in an unaccustomed position, to have one or more rehearsals of the entrance into and exit from the building, a custom which tends to facilitate ease by practice.

The passage of the bridal party to the altar should be in the following order: First, the ushers, two and two; following them, the bridesmaids with their attendant groomsmen, the "best man" and "first bridesmaid" coming last; next, the groom with the mother of the bride; and lastly, the bride, leaning on the arm of her father, or other natural or legal male protector. On reaching the chancel the procession divides, one-half of the ushers, with the bridesmaids, going to the left, the remaining ushers, with the groomsmen, going to the right. The ushers stand back, allowing the remainder of the party to pass and stand before them. The bride and groom (she standing on his left) take their places immediately before the officiating clergyman, who meets them at the chancel rail. [A custom has found favor in England by which the groom and his "best man" advance with the clergyman from his sacristy (or dressing room) as the procession enters the other end of the church.]

In leaving the church after the ceremony, the order of march is reversed, the bride walking first, taking her husband's right arm, the rest of the party following, as has been said, in the reverse order of their entry.

All incidental expenses attendant upon the ceremony itself, such as clergymen's fees, etc., etc., should be defrayed by the groom, who commonly intrusts their liquidation to his first attendant. The amount paid depends, in many particulars, upon the option of the donor, who should show a liberality consistent at once with the occasion and his purse.

If it be desirable to insert a notice of the marriage in the newspapers, the groom should see that this is done. Such notices should be sent to the newspapers accompanied by the usual charge for insertion, and should be confined to a simple announcement of the performance of the ceremony, giving the names of the parties, the date and place of the marriage, and the name of the officiating clergyman.

The following forms will be found convenient for reference:

MARRIED.

BROWN—HOLDER.—At the Church of the Epiphany, on Wednesday evening, by the rector, REV. ROBERT BRUCE, FREDERIC J. BROWN, of Boston, Mass., to ADA, youngest daughter of GEORGE HOLDER, Esq.

GREEN—TALBOT.—On Monday morning at 10 o'clock, at the residence of the bride's parents, HARRY S. GREEN to MISS ALICE TALBOT, both of this city.

HITCHINGS—MORSE.—On Thursday evening, December 18th, at St. Paul's (M.E.) Church, by the REV. EDWARD GRAY, assisted by the REV. HENRY DEWITT, MR. GEORGE HITCHINGS to MISS GERTRUDE MORSE, daughter of MR. JOHN F. MORSE, all of this city.

When the marriage has been a private one, and formal invitations have not been sent out, the notice of marriage should contain, at the close, the words "No Cards."

If either party has friends at a distance, and desires the marriage to be noticed by local papers of the town or city where they reside, it is usual to add the words "Boston (or other locality, naming it) papers please copy."

THE WEDDING BREAKFAST.—This very important event follows directly after the ceremony and before the happy couple start out upon their bridal tour. The breakfast may be simple or elaborate, according to taste, economy, or convenience. It may be partaken of standing or sitting, and it is a matter of choice whether the bride appear or not. The custom is, however, to have a sitting-down breakfast with the bride present. The bride is placed at her husband's right hand, with her father and his mother next, and the bride's mother to the left of the groom with his father next. The breakfast may be simple or may take the nature of lunch, according to the suitability of the hour, and wine is generally provided. When the meal is approaching conclusion, the bride takes a knife and makes an incision into the cake before her, which is then cut and passed around. The bride's father proposes the health of the newly united couple, which is responded to by the bridegroom, who in his turn proposes the health of the bridesmaids, which is responded to by the "best man," and other toasts may follow. The bride then retires to assume her traveling dress, and as the couple proceed to the carriage they are escorted by the party. In accordance with custom, signifying "good luck and good wishes," the guests usually sprinkle the bride with rice and send after the carriage showers of rice and satin slippers.

WEDDING ANNIVERSARIES.

A writer upon the usages of society says that formal celebrations of each return of the wedding day is not common among the best families. In the privacy of home such days are usually observed by kindly family greetings, by an interchange of gifts between husband and wife, and by the giving of presents from children to parents.

But after a certain number of years have passed, many households celebrate the marriage anniversary by social hospitality. Custom has selected certain of these anniversaries as epochs in matrimonial life, designating them by fanciful names.

Of course, as the wedded pair descend the hill of life, such entertainments are marked by more dignified formality than is expected of young husbands and wives.

Probably the return of the wedding anniversary would be more frequently observed by social gatherings were it not for the fact that so many persons consider an invitation to such a celebration very much as a request to "stand and deliver." A cynical writer has stigmatized such invitations as being "upon the contribution plan;" and while it may be a pleasure to offer a souvenir of our good wishes to a bride, it is not always agreeable to be asked for a contribution toward her sustenance after marriage. As a consequence of this sentiment, many who would be glad to make the wedding anniversary a gala entertainment often relinquish the idea of so doing, from a delicacy of feeling, or else announce on their cards of invitation that no gifts will be received. It is to be hoped that we shall soon reach a point in our social observances where such entertainments as these will no longer be viewed as "donation parties," and where giving will signify something more than mere compliance with an unwritten law.

Where the invitation contains an intimation that no gifts are desired it is a gross breach of etiquette to send anything save flowers or a mere trifling souvenir (such as a book). Intimate relatives and very old friends may, of course, take the liberty of disregarding the injunction; but on the part of others, such disregard will only be impertinence, and is liable to be resented accordingly.

The following style of invitation, clearly engraved in script, is at once simple and thoroughly proper:

Mr. and Mrs. J. B. Jones
request the pleasure of your company
Thursday Evening,
February 21,
on the
Third Anniversary of their
WEDDING.

R. S. V. P. 241 Locust Street.

Sometimes the year of marriage and the year of the anniversary are added to the card, as:

> *Mr. and Mrs. J. B. Jones*
> *request the pleasure of your company*
> *Thursday Evening, February 21,*
> *on the*
> *Third Anniversary of their*
> WEDDING,
> *February 21, 1882. February 21, 1885.*
>
> R. S. V. P. 241 LOCUST STREET.

If, as is occasionally done, there is to be a re-celebration of the marriage ceremony, it is usual to add, at the bottom of the invitation, the words, "Ceremony at nine o'clock."

Invitations of this character should be answered. An acceptance or declinature (with regrets) should always be sent, accompanied by such congratulations and expressions of kind wishes as the acquaintance of the parties may render suitable.

If a formal supper be served it is proper that the host and hostess lead the way to the dining-room, followed by the guests as at ordinary parties. If, however, the refreshments are served in buffet style, the host and hostess remain in their first position during the entire evening, unless to lead the first set (if there be dancing); the first set, under such circumstances, usually being a quadrille.

Guests should depart before midnight, after an expression of their wishes for a longevity of health and joy to their hosts.

The following table shows the designations given to the various marriage anniversaries:

One year—Cotton.	Twenty years—China.
Two years—Paper.	Twenty-five years—Silver.
Three years—Leather.	Thirty years—Pearl.
Five years—Wooden.	Forty years—Ruby.
Ten years—Tin.	Fifty years—Gold.
Fifteen years—Crystal.	Seventy-five years—Diamond.

BAPTISMAL CEREMONIES.

BAPTISM, CHILDHOOD AND BIRTHDAYS.

THE birth of a child in the household is always an event of the first importance in any family. It is the first great epoch, after marriage, of the domestic history, and, involving as it does the holding of two lives trembling in the balance, is a period of the most supreme anxiety and the most profound interest, not only in the household and the family, but throughout the whole circle of acquaintance in which the family move. The event, therefore, if it have unfortunately an untoward result, is an occasion for the usual methods of condolence from friends and acquaintances, whose members in close connection with the family should not have omitted, during the period of illness, to show their concern by leaving cards "to inquire." But as is happily generally the case, the event is one of congratulation and rejoicing, and cards of felicitation are in order. In response, the lady, as soon as she feels prepared to receive visitors, returns cards expressive of her thanks for the intimations of solicitude on the part of her friends. Calls are in order immediately thereafter, when the baby is presented, and congratulations personally extended to the mother.

BAPTISM.—There is no fixed rule of date at which baptism or christening shall take place, but it is customary to have the ceremony as soon after birth as the health of mother and child will permit. In most religious societies, the customs of the church favor the public ceremonial in the church. In the Roman Catholic and Episcopal churches, the rubrics make this rule imperative, except for special and urgent reasons.

SPONSORS.—In the Roman Catholic, Episcopal, and Lutheran churches, sponsors are necessary to the completeness of the ceremonial. In the two former, the male child will have two godfathers and one godmother, and the female child two godmothers and one godfather. These are supposed to assume responsibility for its moral welfare, until the child arrives at years of sufficient discretion to renew personally the vows of fidelity to the laws of the church. In foreign countries the relation of godfather or godmother is generally held to be almost as close as a tie of blood, and generally, if possible, some person of near kin, having a personal interest in the welfare of the child, is chosen. The sponsors generally are the most important contributors to the christening presents, according to their means.

NAMING THE BABY.—This momentous question is generally the subject of anxious domestic consideration, and it is indeed of the greatest importance to the unconscious and unnamed member of the family which, though it affects its whole future, has no voice in the matter. In case of a male child the name of the father is generally conferred, and vice versa with the female infant. It is customary, too, to confer the name of a god-parent or relative, especially where the latter has signified the intention of making a legatee under will of the little stranger. In choosing names the parents will consult the future comfort and gratitude of the child if care be taken not to give names of fantastic or grandiloquent character, to avoid strange names of uncouth sound, and especially names which are liable to give rise to "nicknames," likely to be a source of annoyance and offense to the child through life. In choosing second names it is customary to give the family name of the mother and other branches of the family of special pride or interest, and to remember intimate friends, or persons to whom special honor or gratitude is intended to be shown.

THE CEREMONY.—Whether the ceremony be performed in church or at the nome, the infant which is being received in the church, and taking the elementary

place in society, is attired for the occasion in a christening robe of white, generally elaborately embroidered and trimmed with lace, according to the means, and the religious ceremony being completed according to the ritual of the denomination to which the officiating clergyman belongs. The infant is then retired in custody of the nurse to the nursery.

LUNCHEON AND PRESENTS.—On the occasion of christening it is customary for relations and friends of the family to give presents commemorative of the occasion, which are stored away to be given over to the child when it arrives at an age when the presents can be appreciated. It is also proper at the conclusion of the ceremony to celebrate the event by a luncheon or even more elaborate dinner party, to which the near friends of the house, including first the officiating clergyman and donors of gifts are invited. The health of the child is proposed and its future welfare toasted, to which the god-father, if there, will usually respond.

FEES.—The father is generally expected, on the occasion of a christening, to give a fee over and above the customary amount to go to the church, according to his means. A nurse whose services are appreciated will also receive a *douceur* on the occasion.

CHILDHOOD AND YOUTH.—The maternal tenderness and pride in her children of a young mother is too frequently the occasion of many gross violations of the social code. The lady who values her social popularity and desires to consult the comfort of her guests, will never allow children to be admitted to the table or to the company at a dinner party, and even when visiting guests are temporary members of the household, the child should never be brought to the table till it is able to feed itself. Even then they should be made to understand that if they do not keep quiet and refrain from talking, they will be sent into the nursery. The chatter of children will destroy the harmony of the best regulated dinner party. Children should be early taught not to repeat the conversation of their elders, and parents will encourage and confirm them in the habit by refusing to listen to tales brought home from school, or accounts of what occurred if they have been visiting neighbors.

CONFIRMATION.—In those religious denominations of whose observances the rite of confirmation forms a part, this ceremony is the first public appearance of the young girl beyond the shelter of the motherly wing, even temporarily. Whatever be the sex of the youth going up for confirmation, they should be duly impressed by the parents with the solemnity of the occasion, even if they do not appreciate it. An indication of levity on the part of the young person during the ceremony not only jars upon the sense of propriety of those gathered in the church, but is a direct reflection upon both the morals and good breeding of the parents.

CONFIRMATION TOILET.—The mother of the young girl going up for confirmation should take care that the most rigid simplicity is displayed in the dress provided for the occasion, both because the spirit of the ceremony is one of humility, from which all display of worldly pride should be banished, and because candidates for confirmation are gathered from all ranks and conditions of life, who meet on a common footing at the altar, and it would be contrary both to Christian courtesy and social propriety to put to shame the modest garments of the poor by a display of luxury in dress. The dress should be of pure white without frills, slashings, puffings, or any fashionable garniture whatever, a neat and quiet tucking being the limit of ornamentation. Either veils or caps may be worn, according to preference, it being necessary that the head of the female shall be covered in the church. The material should be muslin, barege, cashmere, or flannel, or some similar material not expensive, according to the season.

BIRTHDAY ANNIVERSARIES.

THE observance of birthdays is yearly growing in favor. American life is essentially so practical, so utilitarian, so prosaic, that we naturally seek some pretext for the multiplication of our holidays; and what fitter time for rest and recreation can we find than that which marks a fully rounded period in our lives? Each birthday closes one completed cycle in our lives; these anniversaries are the milestones on life's journey, and it is only natural that we should celebrate their annual recurrence as days of joy.

So common is this sentiment, so almost universal has become the observance of birthdays, that the social world is already coming to recognize certain formalities as peculiarly appropriate to entertainments given on such occasions. In other words, birthday parties have an etiquette of their own; while governed by no inflexible rules, there are recognized "proprieties" peculiar to such occasions.

HOW CELEBRATED.—Children's birthday parties are becoming more and more general. These way-marks in the lives of the little ones are made full of pleasant memories to them. The most natural mode of giving pleasure to children is "a party," which in childhood is almost a synonym for joy. The child's playmates are invited to a feast; but, for obvious reasons, the number invited should, in most instances, be confined to the number that can be *seated* at the tables.

Daintiness and (above all) abundance should characterize the banquet, rich food being unsuitable. A birthday cake should always be a prominent feature, and it is a pretty practice to adorn this with lighted wax candles, the number of which should correspond with the number of years in the life of the childish host. When candles are used, it is usual to place them in little tin tubes, sunken near the cake's outer edge, or (if the number be sufficient) to arrange them in a rim about it. They should be lighted just before the children enter.

The cutting of the birthday cake closes the supper, and is performed by the child whose birthday is celebrated, if age and strength will permit. After the supper follow plays and dances. Celebrations of this character may continue until the child is too old to find pleasure in them. The fact that the family is in mourning need not prevent them, although the gaiety of the occasion may be less marked.

As the members of a household grow older, the return of a birthday is celebrated more privately, only immediate relatives usually being present. In the case of gentlemen, however, the twenty-first anniversary is very frequently made the occasion of a breakfast, a dinner, a ball or some other social festivity. The repugnance of young ladies (however natural or however absurd) to allow her age to be known, renders this practice unusual in the case of the female members of the household.

As a rule, persons who retain (or believe they retain) the vigor of youth dislike to call attention to their progress toward old age. But as the lengthening shadows fall athwart the pathway of life's decline, and the twilight calm wraps its soft mantle around the form of age, each added year seems but a new thread in the silver wreath woven by Time with which to crown a well-spent life. After a lady or gentleman has grown old enough to feel proud of their age, their birthdays are marked by the most beautiful attentions by their young friends as well as by those who were the friends of their childhood.

Flowers, congratulatory letters, cards of respect and inquiry, and gifts valuable more from the interest which attaches to them than from their intrinsic worth, are appropriate mementoes. At this period of life, breakfast and dinner parties, as well as receptions, are usual.

A few words may be added as to the reception of presents. If you accept a gift, it is your duty to let the donor see that you make use of it in the manner intended. An article of dress or personal adornment should be worn in the giver's presence on the first convenient and suitable opportunity. If the gift be a book, it should be read with the least possible delay, and on the first occasion possible, you should speak of it to the giver in as favorable terms as you conscientiously can. If the present be of a perishable nature—such as fruit or flowers—refer to it the next time that you meet the party sending it.

One universal rule, applicable to all gifts not delivered by the donor in person, is to send a message of thanks (verbal, at least, if not written) at once.

There are persons who believe that a gift is always prompted by mercenary motives, and who make it a rule to return a present of equal (or greater) value at once. Such a practice is open to objection. To make an *immediate* return of an article of equivalent value always implies suspicion of the donor's motives, and if he or she be sincere such a course cannot fail to wound their tenderest sensibilities.

FUNERALS AND MOURNING.

DEATH is the common lot of man, and sooner or later in every household, sorrow will take up its abode for a season. Yet, even in that season of woe, the grief of the stricken household is not allowed to overlook the usages by which the circle in which the bereaved family move is apprized of the affliction which has befallen them, and enabled with due and customary decorum to testify their respect for the departed, or sympathy with the stricken and sorrowing.

NOTICE OF DEATH.—As soon as the dreaded event is known, the person in the house next in authority to those immediately prostrated by the visitation will see that the blinds of the afflicted residence are drawn, and that notice that there is "death in the house" is further given by hanging crape on the door knob or bell—black, if announcing the death of an adult person; white, if of a child. Similar notice is given at the place of business, if any, of the head of the family, which will remain closed for the day, and also on the day of the funeral generally. Obituary notices should also be forwarded (if by post, prepaid, according to the tariff of the newspaper) to one or all of the newspapers of the community. The following is the usual and best form:

DIED.—On Thursday, 2d inst., at the residence of his father, 227 Grosvenor street (cause of death may here be inserted, as: "of consumption," or "after a lingering illness,") EDMOND, second son of MR. CHARLES A. BENTLEY, aged 17 years. Funeral announcement by cards (or "to-morrow," if the date be not fixed, or if it is to be publicly announced).

Funeral announcement may be either public or by cards.

For a funeral announcement the following is the best form:

DIED.—On Thursday, 2d inst., at the residence of his father, 227 Grosvenor street, EDMOND, second son of MR. CHARLES A. BENTLEY, aged 17 years.

The funeral will take place from the late residence of the deceased, as above, on Saturday next, at 2 p.m., to the Presbyterian Church, Bay street, and thence to Oakgrove Cemetery. Friends and acquaintances are respectively invited to attend without further intimation.

The same form will answer the purpose of announcement by card.

PREPARATIONS.—Preparations for the funeral are mainly left to the undertaker, whose instructions will be carried out by the person in charge of the household. The better taste which has prevailed of late years has gradually and almost entirely abolished the senseless, and in cases of families of limited circumstances, almost ruinous ostentation which was formerly considered strictly essential to respectability. Funeral ceremonies should be without unnecessary parade or public show, and adapted to the means of the afflicted.

FLORAL OFFERINGS.—In cases of persons of prominence and wealth, or where the deceased has been especially popular in the social or business world, or in the circle of relationship, floral offerings are common. These should be of natural flowers, of pure white, and are generally made up in various designs symbolic of the solemn event, or of Christian hope. In case of youth, a broken column is a favorite and expressive design. Crosses hung with immortelles, or plain, anchors, etc., are among the most suitable designs. Floral offerings should be sent to the residence of the deceased with a card bearing the name of the donor, on the morning of the day set apart for the funeral.

THE FUNERAL.—The relatives and friends invited, pall-bearers, and chief mourners, will arrive at the house from one to two hours before the hour of the funeral, and assemble in the most convenient room, where they will be invested by the undertaker with hatband, scarf and gloves. Ladies assemble in their own rooms, and proceed immediately to their conveyances, when they attend the procession (which is the custom in many communities), except where services are held at the house, when they will gather in the mourning room. The funeral procession should be arranged to depart promptly at the time announced, and should be in the following order:

THE HEARSE.
PALL BEARERS.
THE FAMILY PHYSICIAN.
CHIEF MOURNERS.
FRIENDS OF DECEASED.

The chief mourners should follow in the order of their nearness of relation to the deceased. If the funeral services take place at the church, the pall-bearers remove the coffin from the hearse and are met at the door by the officiating clergyman, who, on the conclusion of the ceremony, follows the pall-bearers to the door of the church. The formal attendants are then at liberty to depart, without any fixed order, those who are related or most intimate with the family gathering around the grave, according to their nearness of relation, awaiting with uncovered heads the last words of the clergyman. The sound of the earth upon the coffin is the signal for dispersion.

MOURNING.—The garments or badges of mourning are worn both in duration of time and in depth of expression, according to the age or propinquity of relation to the deceased. For minors, the family should wear mourning from three to six months, according to age. For a parent, adult child, brother, or sister, mourning is usually worn for one year, the rule being imperative for husband or wife. The wife who mourns the loss of her husband will wear black, unrelieved, except by the minutest show of white at the neck, for one year, at the end of which half mourning, black, relieved with lilac, or some neutral shade, is worn for three months, when, and not before, it is permissible for the subject of remarriage to be considered. The husband, during the period of a year, will wear plain black, with black studs, sleeve-buttons and chain or guard.

CORRESPONDENCE.

THE use of the pen is something which requires on the part of every person who has occasion to resort to it, the greatest care and caution, and this is particularly the case with regard to young ladies. As a general rule, and except when writing to a friend whom you may trust as confidently as your own conscience, govern your letters by the same rules as you would your conversation in the drawing room. As the letter is regarded as an exposition of the mind, be careful about its grammatical construction. See that you begin the sentence with a capital letter and conclude with a period; that the period is always followed by a capital letter, and that names of places and persons are capitalized. If you are in doubt about the spelling of a word or the construction of a sentence, have your dictionary or grammar handy for consultation, rather than risk being suspected of inexcusable ignorance. After the usual prefatory remarks, come directly to the principal topic for which the letter is written. Devote a new paragraph to each change of subject. Do not cross your writing—it looks as if you were endeavoring to economize paper and postage; use another sheet if necessary. Be careful to date your letters. Refrain from expressing harsh opinions of others, as your judgment is liable to be wrong, or influenced by erroneous impressions or information, and you never know when, if too freely expressed in correspondence, it may rise up against you.

WITH SCHOOL FRIENDS.—Many young ladies, after leaving school, undertake to keep alive a voluminous correspondence with class-mates. This is not objectionable where the topics are wholesome and live, and the friendship real and healthy, but where there is a tendency to morbid sentimentalism or romantic and imaginative nonsense, avoid it. If your school friend's letters turn altogether upon lovers and beaux, love and hate, drop it as speedily as you conveniently can.

WITH GENTLEMEN.—It is a safe rule which does not permit young ladies to correspond with any gentleman unless he be either her betrothed lover or a near relative. It is a dangerous thing for a young lady to place her written signature in the hands of one of the opposite sex. Such correspondence implies an intimacy which modesty forbids should be extended to any man outside the family circle, except him who is looked upon as your future husband. For all necessary correspondence respecting social intercourse, society furnishes the forms, which are merely forms, and should never, by any circumstances, be exceeded. Where correspondence on business matters is necessary with a gentleman, confine the letter strictly to the subject in hand, and under no circumstances which may arise, which necessitate your writing to a gentleman, write a sentence which you would not willingly permit your mother or father to read.

PRIVACY INVIOLABLE.—It is one of the cardinal points in the code of honor that the statement of one gentleman to another (and how much more in the case of a lady), when communicated by letter, is the secret of the sender, which is not to be repeated or divulged without gross breach of every instinct of honor. Under ordinary circumstances, the wife will show her letters to her husband, and vice-versa in case of the latter, if the letters are of a social character; but that rule is not always either proper or permissible. The lady's letter may contain her friend's secret, to which her husband has no right, and concerning which he should have no curiosity. If a husband receive a letter from a lady, or the wife from a gentleman, it should be shown to the other under all circumstances. For young people, it is well that correspondence should be under the supervision of the parents, but grown-up young people should be left to their own discretion, if carefully trained in the laws of propriety.

INVITATION NOTES.—Be careful in writing notes of invitation always to put the day of the week as well as the day of the month. This is a duty in which the young lady generally assists her mother, and she should be particular that her calligraphy is neat and distinct. Always answer a note the same day, and if anything should occur after accepting an invitation to prevent, write a second note explanatory.

LETTERS OF INTRODUCTION.—Letters of introduction should never be sealed. In addition to the address, they should contain on the lower left hand corner the words, "Introducing Mr. ——." This enables the person whose civilities are requested for the bearer to address him by name and request to be excused while the letter is read. It is proper always to deliver letters of introduction in person, but if sent they should be accompanied by a card giving your name and place of residence.

LETTERS BY HAND.—Letters are frequently sent by hand, in which the bearer has no concern. The letter, sealed of course, should contain, besides the address, in the lower left hand corner, the words "Politeness of Mr. ——," or "By favor of Mr. ——." The person addressed will thus have an opportunity of thanking the bearer by name. The letter should not be read till the visitor has departed unless he has some interest in it.

In writing to strangers for personal information always inclose a stamp, as also in writing to a poor person.

ADDRESSES.—In addressing a letter, give the full title of the person addressed, if he have any public station or professional title. As "A. W. Smith, Esq., M. D." or "Dr. A. W. Smith," "Right Reverend Bishop McQuade," "Rev. J. W. Brown, D.D." or "Rev. Dr. J. W. Brown," "Captain Amos Jones, U. S. A." In addressing naval officers on active service, address "Captain H. W. Morton, Commanding U. S. S. *Clyde*," or "Lieutenant James A. Garland, on board U. S. S. *Clyde*." People without title or office are addressed "Mr. John Jones," or "John Jones, Esq." according to fancy.

PRESENTS.

There is an art in giving presents which comes intuitively to people of refined instincts, but for which no rule can be laid down. The person offering the gift should study in doing so to give the greatest amount of pleasure and satisfaction. In a gift to a poor person, while it is preferable to give some article of utility, care should be taken that the gift is not a reminder of poverty. Some article both useful and ornamental for the table is the most suitable. The most expensive present is not always the most welcome. If possible, ascertain without suspicion something for which the person in question has expressed a special desire, but has been unable to secure. The gift in this case will be a surprise and a real gratification.

In wedding presents care should be taken about the suitability of the articles selected for presentation. Articles of perspicuous unsuitability or absurd incongruity, will only excite amusement and derision, which cannot very well be avoided, in place of the gratitude designed to be evoked. Donors should never be present when their presents are being received.

In acknowledging presents endeavor to convey *appreciation* of the friendship which the gift indicates rather than mere *gratitude* for the gift itself. Express your thanks simply without profusion of words or effusion of sentiment.

INVITATION BOOK.

No lady with a large circle of acquaintances will attempt to trust to memory for the issuance of her invitations, as unintended omissions, construed as intentional slights, are the frequent and inevitable result. The lady who desires to avoid this, and to consult her own comfort and convenience, and the success of her social *menage*, will have a regular invitation book, in which will be inscribed the names of all whom she wishes to retain in the circle of her acquaintance, and classified according to the scale of intimacy which is accorded to them. For instance, a lady may extend invitations to an evening reception, which would be confined to a much smaller circle for a dinner party. Lists of eligible parties should be kept for each form of entertainment, and as the accommodation available to a lady of an ordinarily large circle of friends, will not permit of a dinner party to which all can be invited, it is proper to decide at the beginning of the season upon a certain number of dinners during the season, and care should be taken to extend at least one invitation during that period to every person whose name appears on the visiting list.

DINNER PARTIES

THERE is no social responsibility which rests with greater anxiety upon the mind of the mistress of an establishment, than that of giving dinner parties, and there is hardly any branch of her social duties where success is attended with greater satisfaction. It is, therefore, of supreme importance to her that before marriage she should not only acquire skill in the ordinary duties of the household, but have a thorough knowledge of the etiquette which governs polite society in the art of dinner giving, and the rules by the observance of which a successful dinner party can be assured. The matter of numbers invited may vary according to the extent of the hostess' convenience and the circle of acquaintance, but, according to the old rule, there should never be "more than the Graces, nor less than the Muses;" that is to say, not more than nine nor less than three. If, however, the hostess have space at her table she will find that six guests for each side of the table will make up a very pleasant circle, giving sufficient numbers to insure variety in the conversation. To have *thirteen* at the table is, by tradition, forbidden. It is a rule of faith with a great many among the French, that where there are thirteen at the table, death will surely claim a victim from their number before the year is out.

SELECTING THE COMPANY.—The dinner party is the highest social distinction which can be conferred in polite society upon one's neighbor. Unlike other social entertainments, the dinner party is given in the joint name of the host and hostess, and the first essential to success is the proper selection of the company.

WHO TO INVITE.—Having decided upon the number to be invited, the hostess will bear in mind that the party must consist of an equal number of ladies and gentlemen. From her acquaintances she will then proceed to select those who will be most likely to be pleased to meet each other, bearing in mind at the same time that a successful conversationalist, a good relator of anecdotes, or a gentleman with a polite and refined sense of humor is a great acquisition to a dinner party. Care should be taken not to invite people to meet each other who are not on agreeable terms, or people in public or political position who hold violently opposing views. So far as can be attained harmony of ideas, of friendships and of interest should be secured. If there be young ladies in the house, young people should be invited to meet them, but otherwise it is not customary to invite young ladies to meet married people at a dinner party. Where this is done, however, care should be taken to provide a suitable and congenial escort for them.

ISSUING INVITATIONS.—The next thing in order is the issuing of the cards. If the party be small, the hostess will simply dispatch a written note in the following form:

"*Dear Mrs. Doe*,—Will yourself and Mr. Doe give us the pleasure of your company at dinner, on Monday, the 19th inst., at a quarter before eight?"

For the formal dinner, however, regular cards of invitation are used, and the invitations are sent out in the following shape:

> Mr. and Mrs. James Everett
> request the pleasure of the
> company of
> Mr. Edward Hawley
> At Dinner,
> On Tuesday, March 27th 1885,
> At seven o'clock.
>
> 357 Vine Street.

It is customary in the very highest circles to have these invitation cards printed or engraved, leaving only the names and dates to be filled in. In replying to the first form of invitation, the answer will be in a friendly note of acceptance or declination. In replying to the formal card, the answer is sent in the following shape:

"Mr. and Mrs. Leroy Jones have (not will have) much pleasure in accepting Mr. and Mrs. Lawrence's kind invitation to dinner on Monday, the 19th inst., at 8 o'clock."

Cards should always be sent out two weeks before the time set for the dinner, and the replies should be made promptly, so as to enable the hostess to issue further invitations, in case of a declination, or to complete her arrangements in event of acceptance. A refusal to accept an invitation cannot be made a mere conventional matter, as in case of a party. There must be some real or substantial previous unavoidable engagement where an invitation can be declined with propriety. Otherwise the refusal is insulting to the party who issues the invitation.

DRESS FOR DINNER PARTIES.—The gentlemen have no choice in this respect, having only one style of permissible full dress, and no such thing as a *demi toilette*. For ladies, however, although the dinner party is a full-dress occasion, it is not strictly *de rigueur*. The dinner dress is now usually made quite low, the square, or heart-shaped corsage being adopted. The sleeves should reach the elbow, and be trimmed with lace or frillings. The gloves are retained on the hands till the lady has taken her seat at the table. Where lace mittens are worn, they need not be removed. It is quite permissible to wear dresses made high to the throat, but they should be of rich material, of full-dress style, and be generously trimmed with lace. Strict attention to the requirement of the toilet is exacted from both hostess and guests.

PRECEDENCE TO THE DINING-ROOM.—The hostess will have arranged the precedence of her guests, and also taken care to assign escorts to the lady guests, with a view to their comfort and wishes, so that when dinner is announced they are promptly assigned to their places, without confusion or delay. The host offers his right arm to the lady of highest rank or consideration in the company, and hands her to the seat on the right hand of the head of the table. Gentlemen will invariably offer the *right* arm. The gentleman of second rank takes the seat to the left of the host, and so on. In case of married couples the hostess will take care that ladies are placed in charge of gentlemen other than their husbands. Where a young couple, whose engagement is publicly known, are present, they should not be placed together, but, where practicable, *vis-a-vis*. The hostess is the last to enter the room, and is accompanied by the gentleman of the highest rank. Rank, of course, will be understood to be governed by social prominence, or public, professional, or official position.

THE GUESTS.—Guests will bear in mind that they are required to observe the strictest punctuality. The last guest should be fully five minutes before the time set for announcing dinner, as conveyed on the invitation card. To be late at a dinner party is a gross breach of etiquette. At the table while devoting yourself assiduously to your partner, be careful to be interested when the conversation is general, and take a part in it. No more wraps should be taken in going to a dinner than can conveniently be left in the hall, so that the guest passes almost directly into the drawing room. Go directly to the hostess and receive her greeting before acknowledging the presence of any other person. Join in the conversation and do your best to make the waiting time pass cheerfully, and find a bright and pleasant word for your partner on the way to the dining room.

AT THE TABLE.—Considerations of health, comfort and seemliness, suggest that the dinner eating be done leisurely. To eat with haste or avidity is a sure token of ill-breeding, and leaves the guest in the uncomfortable position of having nothing to do while others are finishing the courses. The gentleman should time his movements by those of the lady in his charge. He should see that she has such attendance as he can afford, such as handing the salt and giving instructions to the waiter. Avoid questions involving lengthy answers or explanations. In the intervals of the dinner fill up the time with light and agreeable conversation, endeavoring to adapt yourself to the comfort of your charge. Do not refuse soup; you may partake of as little as you please. If you take sherry with your soup, refuse hock when offered with the *entrees*. Never drink a whole glass of wine. It is courteous to take wine, even if it be merely tasted, except it be understood that you have conscientious objections to doing so. If asked at table what part of the fowl you prefer, answer promptly, as nothing is more embarrassing to the host, if he be the carver, than two or more guests who have "no preference." Good breeding will instinctively lead you to thank the servant. True refinement is always courteous to inferiors.

REMOVING THE CLOTH.—On the "removal of the cloth," which has come to be a mere figurative expression, implying the bringing on of the dessert, and the hostess thinks a suitable time has elapsed, she rises, bows to the lady of highest consideration, and leads the way from the dining-room, the gentlemen rising as they leave the table. A gentleman may excuse himself to the male company and ask leave to join the ladies, but it is not good form to do so. Coffee is handed to the ladies in the drawing-room ten to fifteen minutes after retiring, and to the gentlemen after a somewhat longer interval. The host should not allow more than thirty minutes to elapse before giving the signal for joining the ladies in the drawing room, after which tea is handed. A hostess, if musical, may entertain her guests at the piano or harp, or may ask any of her guests to do so, if she knows they have the accomplishment and are not averse.

TABLE DEPORTMENT.—While it is unnecessary here to repeat as injunctions in etiquette, the simple habits of decency which are learned in the nursery, such as "Do not leave the table with food in your mouth," "Do not put your fingers in your mouth," or "Do not come to the table in your shirt sleeves," which may be found in some books which profess to give the rules of polite society, there are some general observations which it will be well to bear in mind, as, for instance: In crude society it is not considered *au fait* to take the last piece of bread or cake from the plate, but in the polite world it will be taken as a matter of course, because hesitation would imply the absurd suspicion that there was no more in the house. While if asked during the carving your preference as to a part of the fowl you do not hesitate to state it, it should not be expressed without request. Stones and seeds of fruits and skins of grapes should be removed from the mouth with the spoon and deposited on the plate. Be careful, while judiciously praising any dish that affords you special enjoyment, not to occasion suspicion of your sincerity by overdoing it. Avoid fulsome or indiscriminate praise of everything presented. Do not rise from the table, even where summoned by telegram, message, or other necessity, without asking to be excused, addressing the request to the company through the hostess.

THE MENU CARDS.—While for a very small party the carving by the host and placing of the dishes upon the table may be adopted with propriety, the dinner *a la Russe* may now be considered to be the universal rule, as, indeed, the superior convenience which the system affords entitles it to be. For this dinner *en ceremonie menu* cards are indispensable. As these are, on exceptional occasions, generally taken away by the guest as a souvenir, it is fashionable to have them of as elegant design as possible. One card is provided for every couple. The card should show two soups, one or two kinds of fish, the choicest in season, two *entrees*, two kinds of meat and fowl, in boiled and roast, cold meats, some preparation of cheese, and a variety of dessert, fruit, and confections.

ORDER OF WINES.—With the soup and fish the waiter will pass round sherry, taking care to inquire of each guest, and if wine be not declined, to fill each glass about four-fifths full. If hock is not provided for the *entrees*, the sherry should be passed round again. With the dinner proper champagne is supplied, in the bottle, as a matter of course, the waiter simply seeing to it that there is wine within convenient reach and removing empty bottles. In sultry weather ice in a glass dish with ice tongs should be passed around. In pouring the wine the waiter will take the neck of the bottle with a clean napkin. At dessert sherry, port, claret or Madeira may be provided, one or all, but generally two varieties. As the standard after-dinner beverage claret has generally supplanted port, which was formerly *en regle*. The host, after filling the glass of the lady on his right, if she wishes, passes the bottle, which makes the detour of the table to the host, where it remains till the ladies leave the table, when the bottle is circulated according to pleasure. Champagne, ales or stout should be kept in the sideboard, or on the ice, according to season. Wines in decanters are placed on the table.

SETTING THE TABLE.—In arranging the table for a dinner-party, at each place there should be placed a knife and fork for dinner and dessert, soup spoon and dessert spoon, napkin, finger bowl and salt.

For ordinary domestic dinners, knife, fork, soup spoon, napkin and salt should be at each place. The cruet is usually the centre piece, and the table arranged according to the taste of the lady of the house. The plates are placed on the table after soup, with the joint, by the servant to the right of the host at the head of the table. Plates for all hot meals should be always heated. The head of the family will carve the joint, and the servant will wait upon those at the table in the same manner and order as prescribed for larger dinner parties.

SHAPE OF THE TABLE.—A table should not be so wide that a guest is unable to carry on conversation with his *vis-a-vis*. For that reason, except for the very smallest number, a round table is inadmissible. The most convenient shape is an oval table, where the whole circle can see and be seen.

TABLE DECORATIONS.—The decoration of the table is something which tests the good taste and artistic skill of the hostess. The dinner *a la Russe* gives scope for a pleasing effect at the table not attainable where the board is crowded with viands. Care should be taken not to be too profuse nor elaborate. The center piece may be a floral design, or an epergne, tastefully arranged with fruit and crowned with flowers. Where the table is lengthy, the center piece should be supported by two side pieces containing pyramids of fruit tastefully arranged. Vases of flowers should be arranged to fill the table with taste, and with regard to the general effect. Nothing is more elegant than bowls of fresh blown roses. Where the table is large enough to warrant, and the choice of a conservatory is available, a floral favor, in glass or silver holder, placed before each guest, or between alternate covers, has a pleasing effect. These should be of the most simple design, such as a rosebud with spray of maiden hair, or pink and white or yellow and red buds delicately relieved with foliage.

THE SIDEBOARD.—The arrangement of the sideboard will occupy the attention of the hostess scarcely less than the table. The silver necessary to the service, salvers, etc., knives, forks and spoons, cheese plates, dessert plates, etc., should be neatly arranged, both for effect and for the facilitation of the work of the waiter. The champagne (and beer ale or stout, where provided), except when the weather requires it to be kept on the ice, is generally placed upon the sideboard.

THE WAITING.—The lady who is anxious for the success of her dinner, and what lady is not alive to the supreme importance of the event in a social sense, will be exceedingly careful about the waiting, as the best dinner in the world will be spoiled by clumsy, uninstructed or ill-trained waiters or waitresses. In large establishments where the services of a butler are retained, that duty is taken off the lady's hands, but in the generality of cases the responsibility is left upon the lady of the house. As a rule women are preferred to men for this work. The waiter requires to be prompt, vigilant, noiseless and quick of perception. For a party of more than twelve and less than twenty, two waiters are indispensable, and the services of a temporary butler should be provided to guard against blunders. He will superintend the work of the waiters and take charge of the sideboard. The waiters of course, must receive the hot dishes at the door from some invisible agency connected with the culinary department, which also removes the dishes as fast as they may be dispensed with.

DUTIES OF WAITERS.—When there is a small party and only one waiter (the term is applied to either male or female), he takes his place behind the chair of the host on the left hand side. At a signal from the host he removes the cover of the soup tureen, and then proceeds to hand soup to each person, commencing with the lady on the right hand of the host. During the course he will hand round the sherry. He will then, as the guests finish the course, pass a clean plate to each, removing the soup plate with the spoon in it. When all have finished, the tureen is removed and placed with the soiled plates in the receptacle provided for the purpose. The fish received at the door from the cook is then placed on the table. Each dish should be ready for the waiter at the door as required for the table. The cover is removed as before, and the fish served, the waiter taking in his left hand the sauce tureen. If a cruet be used, it should also be passed round, but the rule is that salt, pepper and sauces are provided on the table. He then goes round with the sherry again during this course, which will be removed as before. The same routine is to be observed, with the *entrees*, joints, etc. Cheese is usually placed on the table, where it is cut by the person helping in small pieces on a plate, which the waiter, who has previously placed cheese plates, with biscuits, butter, and celery, will pass around. The waiter will then remove everything from the table except the dessert and flowers, carefully removing the sidecloths, where used, crumbs, etc. The dessert plate and glasses are then placed before each guest, and the wine before the host or gentleman presiding. The waiter should hand round two or three dishes of dessert, after which his duties terminate with the removal of the box or bucket containing the plates, knives, etc. Where there are two waiters one should be assigned to each side of the table. In passing the *entrees*, each should have a separate dish which will be exchanged at the foot of the table, the second being proffered to such guests on each side as have refused the first.

FRUIT.—In arranging the fruit for the occasion, the housewife will find it a great convenience to her guests to make an incision round the circumference of the orange. By introducing a spoon, the half of the peel can be neatly removed so far that when handed to the person partaking, it is conveniently got rid of, and the orange thus eaten with comfort, and without the danger of spoiled clothes, which makes so many ladies reject this choicest of fruit at dinner. Sugar, in the granulated form, should be placed on the table for those who prefer it with oranges.

THE MENU.

THE following examples in various forms of menu cards may be advantageously followed both in form, and for programme, for correct, elegant and fashionable menus:

MENU FOR LADIES' RECEPTION.

Cream of Terrapin, Puff Paste.
Cutlets of Minced Quail, with French Peas in Cream.
Chicken Salad. Fresh Lobster Salad.
Bread and Butter Sandwiches.
French Sponge Rolls.
Coffee, with Whipped Cream.
Nesselrode Pudding, Kirsch Glacé and Coffee Ice Cream,
Macaroon Tart Cake. Jellies, in Paper Cases.
White Chocolate. Tea.

ANOTHER.

Cream of Oysters.
Escaloped Partridge in Shells. Fricadelle of Game, with Truffles.
Sweetbread Salad. Assorted Glacés.
Walnut and Orange Tart Cakes.
French Sponge Rolls.
Bread and Butter Sandwiches.
Coffee, with Whipped Cream. White Chocolate. Oolong Tea.
Lemonade Frappé, or Punch.

ANOTHER.

Bisque of Lobster.
Cutlets of Minced Chicken, with French Peas.
Fricadelle of Game, Truffle Sauce. Sweetbread Salad.
Glacés, in Paper Cases. Walnut and Orange Tart Cakes.
French Sponge Rolls.
Bread and Butter Sandwiches.
Coffee, with Whipped Cream. White Chocolate. Oolong Tea.

MENU FOR DINNER PARTY.

Blue Points.
Bisque of Lobster.
Baked Blue-fish, Port Wine Sauce. Fried Parisienne Potatoes.
Patties of Sweetbreads.
Fillet of Turkey, with Truffles and Chestnuts.
Asparagus.
Croquettes of Potatoes.
Victoria Punch.
Broiled Quail, Currant Jelly.
Lettuce Salad.
Glacés. Cakes.
Café.

MENU FOR CHILDREN'S EVENING PARTY.

Escaloped Chicken. Sweetbread Salad.
Rolls, Sandwiches. Coffee, with Whipped Cream.
Assorted French Creams and Ices.
Assorted Cakes.
Center Piece, Mottoes and Flowers.
Lemonade Frappé.

MENU FOR WEDDING BREAKFAST.

Cutlets of Minced Lobster, a la Hollandaise.
Fricadelle of Turkey, with Truffles.
Sweetbread Patties.
Chicken Salad. Fresh Lobster Salad.
Ices. Creams. Glacés. Tart Cakes.
Jellies.
Bride's Cake. Groom's Cake. Wedding Cake Boxes Filled.
Center Piece Natural Flowers.
French Sponge Rolls. Bread and Butter Sandwiches.
Coffee. Tea. Sauterne Punch Frappé.

ANOTHER.

Chicken Croquettes.
Crab Salad.
French Sponge Rolls. Bread and Butter Sandwiches.
Coffee, with Whipped Cream. Oolong Tea.
Bride's Cake. Groom's Cake.
Wedding Cake Boxes Filled. Assorted Cakes.
Assorted French Creams and Ices. Jellies.
Lemonade Frappé.

CHOICE RECIPES.

The following recipes, furnished by Kinsley, of Chicago, will no doubt be fully appreciated by the ladies at the head of many households:

Chicken Croquettes for Eight Persons.

Ingredients.—Select one good hen; ¼ lb. butter; ½ pint sweet cream; 3 tablespoonfuls sherry; a very little ground nutmeg; 3 tablespoonfuls flour; ½ pint chicken stock; salt and white pepper to taste; the juice of half a lemon, and ½ can mushrooms.

Boil the chicken, and let it cool; remove the meat from the bone, cut it in small pieces, and chop the mushrooms. Then melt the butter in a saucepan, stir in the flour, cream and stock, and continue stirring for about two minutes: then take it off the fire, add the wine and seasoning, chicken and mushrooms. Spread thin on a platter, and let it cool. When quite cold, shape in the form of pears, dip them in egg and cracker crumbs, and fry in boiling-hot lard, two or three at a time.

Green or French peas, or mushroom sauce, can be served with croquettes.

To Broil a Steak, Chop, Chicken, Game, Fish, or Anything.

Season the meat with pepper and salt; place it in a double wire broiler, and put the broiler in a baking-pan containing about ½ inch cold water; put the pan on the top shelf of the oven, which should be very hot. For sirloin steak, eight to ten minutes; other articles, according to size and heat of the oven.

Coffee.

Ingredients.—1½ quarts boiling water; ¼ lb. best ground coffee; 1 egg.

Break the egg into the dry coffee; stir together until the coffee has entirely absorbed the egg, then put into the boiling water and let it boil five minutes. Strain through a flannel into a china or porcelain coffee-pot, and it is ready to serve.

Tea.

One teaspoonful best tea to one cup water. Pour boiling water into a china or earthen tea-pot; let stand till heated through, then pour off the water; put in the tea, pour boiling-hot water over it, and serve in three minutes.

Cafe Brule for Six.

Ingredients.—Take 1 pint strong coffee; 1 oz. whole spices (consisting of allspice, cloves, cinnamon, mace and lemon-peel) in a linen sack; 3 oz. old-fashion loaf sugar, in one piece.

Pour the coffee into a small bowl; place the sack of spices in the coffee, and the sugar on top of the spices. Pour cognac over the sugar and coffee, and set on fire. Stir to keep it in a blaze for some minutes.

Salad Dressing, or French Mayonnaise.

Ingredients.—Take the yolks of 2 eggs; the juice of half a lemon; a small pinch of cayenne pepper; ½ teaspoonful fine salt; 3 tablespoonfuls of vinegar; ½ pint best olive oil; 1 teaspoonful dry mustard (Colman's).

Put the eggs in a china bowl, salt and mustard them, stir with a fork, and drop in the oil slowly until it thickens; then add the vinegar and lemon-juice, stirring all the time till well mixed.

Whitefish a la Point Shirley.

After cleaning the fish, lay it open and remove the backbone, placing it in a buttered baking-pan, skin next to the pan. Season freely with pepper and salt, a little lemon-juice, and butter. Put two cups water in the pan, around the sides of the fish. Bake in a hot oven. A four-pound fish should cook fifteen minutes. Large white-fish are superior to small ones.

Muffins.

Ingredients.—1 pint sifted flour, 1 pinch salt, 3 eggs, ½ pint milk, 1 teaspoonful powdered sugar, 2 teaspoonfuls baking powder.

Beat the eggs and milk together, put in the salt and sugar; sift the flour and baking powder together into the first mixture, and stir well together. Butter the irons and fill about half full. Have a medium hot oven.

French Puff Paste.

Ingredients.—1 lb. flour, 1 lb. best butter.

Mix the flour with one quarter of the butter by rubbing it together, and add enough cold water to make it the consistency of ordinary bread-dough. Roll this out to the thickness of half an inch; put the balance of the butter on this in one lump, and fold the four corners of the dough over the butter, entirely covering it, then roll it out to the thickness of a quarter of an inch, as nearly square or oblong as possible; then fold the ends over to the center until the sheet is about four inches wide, then roll it out again. Let it rest one half hour each time, and roll out four times.

Peach or Apricot Omelette for Four Persons.

Ingredients.—4 eggs, 2 oz. sugar, ½ can fruit, ½ tea-cup sweet cream, pinch salt.

Beat the whites of eggs separate, then beat the yolks and cream together, add the salt and mix all well together. Melt two ounces choice butter in an 8-inch frying-pan, pour in the mixture; when well set on the bottom place in the oven two minutes; then place the fruit on and fold over like a turn-over. Serve plain or put on a platter. Sprinkle fine sugar over it, pour rum around it, and set on fire.

Corned Beef Hash.

Ingredients.—½ lb. cooked corned beef, chopped fine, double quantity in bulk of cold boiled potatoes chopped fine, 6 drops Tobasco pepper, ½ teacup water, 2 oz. butter, salt and black pepper to taste.

Melt the butter in the water, then add the other ingredients and cook till thoroughly heated through, then put into a baking-pan and place in the oven till brown on top. Serve with or without poached eggs. Onions may be added if desired.

Hamburg Steak.

Ingredients.—2 lbs. round of beef, raw, 1 medium size onion, ¼ lb. beef suet, pepper and salt to taste.

Chop the beef and suet very fine; chop the onion very fine; mix well together size of a fish-ball and fry slow in butter till thoroughly cooked through, about five minutes. Mushroom, tomato or truffle sauce may be served with the above.

Sauce Hollandaise.

Ingredients.—2 oz. butter, ½ pint sweet cream, pepper and salt, 3 tablespoonfuls flour, juice of 1 lemon, yolk of 3 eggs.

Melt the butter, stir in the flour, boil the cream and stir it in, and then add the lemon, pepper and salt; whip the eggs and add to the above. If too thick, thin it with fish broth.

White Sauce.

Same as above, leaving out the lemon and eggs.

Tomato Soup.

Ingredients.—1 can best tomatoes, pinch red pepper, ½ teaspoonful sugar, 2 teaspoonfuls flour, equal quantity water, salt to taste, 1 oz. butter, ½ wine glass sherry.

Melt the butter and stir in the flour, then add the tomatoes, water and seasoning; stir well to mix, and bring to a boil. When ready to serve put in the sherry. Fried bread crumbs may be added if desired.

THE ART OF CARVING.

EVERY gentleman should early make himself master of the art of carving. It is a necessary accomplishment, not only for the young man who contemplates himself as the future head of a household, but for everyone. Every young man who has social habits, is liable at any moment to be asked by his hostess to undertake the carving of a dinner, and and he will make a poor figure, especially in the eyes of those who look upon him with a view to his "eligibility," if he have to plead ignorance. Unscientific carving, like ignorant waiting, will ruin the best efforts of the hostess and cook. Young men should take lessons from properly qualified instructors in carving, where available, or from their elders, when possible. For those who have to depend upon their own aptitude and ingenuity, with practice, for their acquaintance with the art of carving, a few rules borne in mind will enable them to carve with the best advantage, and to cut meats so as to give the greatest satisfaction to the guests and to do the greatest measure of justice to the *cuisine*.

RULES FOR CARVING.

Serve small fish whole. Mackerel should be quartered. Salmon should be cut in slices, down the middle of the upper side and across on the lower side; codfish is cut in the same manner. The larger fishes, such as the turbot, should be halved down the centre from head to tail, and then served in slices across. The fin of a turbot is esteemed by many a rare delicacy.

A sirloin of beef is carved downward to the bone, the inside or tenderloin part being sliced thin lengthwise. Ask each guest the preference, for outside or inside, and serve a small piece of fat with each piece. Otherwise a small piece of the inside should be helped with each piece, being esteemed the choicest portion.

A round of beef should be cut in thin, smooth, and even slices.

Cut a leg of mutton in the middle, being the most juicy part, making the slices thin and deep, and helping each plate to a little of the fat and a portion of the outside brown. Be careful not to press too hard with the knife, as the succulent juices, which form the chief merit of a well-cooked leg of mutton, will be squeezed out.

If a fillet of veal is stuffed, cut clean through the stuffing, and serve a portion with each piece. If not stuffed, cut in the same way as a round of beef. Ask each person whether the brown or outside is preferred.

The most economical way to carve a ham is to cut from the large end. The common way is to cut down the center, to the bone, carving out thin, circular slices, with the fat and lean as evenly distributed as possible.

Carve a shoulder of mutton in slices lengthwise from knuckle to joint.

Separate the shoulder of a forequarter of lamb from the breast and ribs by passing the knife through and under it. Help from the ribs, or the other part, according to choice.

Carve a saddle of mutton in thin slices, beginning close to the backbone, and cutting from tail to end. Help, with each plate, to some of the fat from the sides.

Roast pig is sent to the table halved from end to end. Begin by severing the shoulder, and then divide the joints and ribs. The neck end and ribs are considered the choicest parts.

Cut a haunch of venison close across to the elbow, after which slice lengthwise.

Tongue should be cut across, beginning an inch and a half from the small end, diminishing the slices toward the larger part.

Small game is sent to the plate whole, or halved, according to size.

In carving a goose or turkey, cut off the apron, or part under the neck and outside the "merry thought," or "wishbone." With the neck end towards you, then cut off the breast in slices from each side down to the bone. In cutting off a wing or a leg (the former first) with the knife, holding the small end of the bone or pinion, press close to the body, and separate the joint with the knife. The wing, sidebones and thighs are next separated, holding the fowl with the fork on the breastbone and pressing the bone out with the knife till the joint separates, when it is easily removed. Cut the back in two crosswise. The breast and thighs are choice pieces, but a piece of the breast goes with each plate.

Chicken or fowl are carved by separating the leg and wings whole. Divide the breast from the body by cutting through the tender ribs. Cut the breast in two lengthwise and the back crosswise.

Never pour gravy over white meat, on a plate, as it destroys its delicate appearance.

BALLS AND PARTIES.

THE BALL.

BALLS and parties are the occasions where people of both sexes, more especially the young and pleasure-loving, meet for mutual enjoyment and the innocent and exhilarating pleasures of social intercourse, of which, as a rule, dancing forms the chief feature. And here let it be remarked that many young men of sober thought and serious aspirations are accustomed to look upon dancing as a frivolous amusement, to be indulged in only by the empty-headed. It should be remembered, however, that a few lessons in dancing necessitates but a small expenditure of time and money, and they do not involve the promiscuous attendance and waste of the precious hours of youth, at balls and dancing parties, in which too much indulgence is often permitted. The young man should be sufficiently master of the standard dances to be able, later in life, when business success shall have imposed social duties upon him, to make a creditable appearance upon the the ball-room floor.

Balls are of three classes, private, public, and fancy dress, the latter of which may be either public or private. Public balls are generally to subserve some practical object, and are in charge of committees of lady patronesses, who supervise the issuing of invitations, where they are not offered for public sale, and consider applications for tickets, and of stewards who assist them, and act as masters of ceremonies. Public balls usually extend from 10 p.m. to 4 a.m. For a private ball the principal requisites are a room suitable for dancing, and a hostess with sufficient tact not to allow her hospitality to overcrowd the room at her disposal. In the dancing room, where there is not an apartment specially devoted to that purpose, the carpet should be removed. A newly waxed floor is not pleasant for dancers; still floors have to be waxed the first time. In case of an uneven floor, a cover made of strong brown holland stretched tightly over the floor, makes an excellent dancing surface.

THE MUSIC.—For a small party a piano, or piano and violin, is sufficient, but a large party in a room of corresponding dimensions requires at least a piano, cornet, violin and violoncello.

CLOAK-ROOMS.—Rooms will be set apart for ladies' and gentlemen's dressing rooms, where the attendants should have duplicate tickets to be given with each article of attire received, so as to avoid confusion at the close. The maids in the ladies' dressing room should have a supply of needles, pins, cotton, hairpains, etc., and there should be mirrors and other toilet accessories.

DECORATION AND REFRESHMENTS.—In the cities the decorations can be best left in the hands of a professional, who will supply everything and be responsible. The chief requisite is a profusion of flowers artistically arranged, plenty of mirrors and abundant light. For refreshments there should be a lunch-room on the same floor as the dancing room, where light refections are served out by attendants from a table, with ices and champagne cup, or claret punch.

PROGRAMMES.—Each invited guest should be supplied with a card, with programme of dances to be followed, and blanks for filling in the names of partners, to which a small pencil is attached by a silk cord and tassel.

SUPPER.—Supper should be provided in a separate room, and is generally the subject of care on the part of the hostess. It will comprise cold turkey, fowl, game, ham, tongue, salads, *patés*, soufflés, trifles, etc., and Moselle, claret, sauterne and lighter wines are the beverages. Everything as far as possible is iced.

INVITATIONS AND RECEPTION.—Invitation cards for Balls, At Homes, etc., are all in very much the same form, which may be generally procured from stationers and the blanks filled in. One example will suffice for all :

MRS. JAMES EVERETT

requests the pleasure of your company

At..

On Monday, November 23d inst.

Dancing at 9:30 o'clock.

The blank may be filled in with the words, "A Ball," or "At Home," or otherwise as the occasion varies. The lady of the house should remain in the vicinity of the door till all the guests have arrived, to welcome them by bow or handshake. She should be assisted by sons or daughters, or friends, in the task of performing introductions, finding partners for late arrivals, and generally endeavoring to make the event one of as much pleasure as possible to the guests.

AT HOMES.

OF VARIOUS KINDS.—The term "At Home," is nowadays applied to nearly every kind of evening entertainment. The invitation may be worded as follows:

> MRS. JAMES EVERETT
>
> requests the pleasure of your company
>
> on
>
> Monday Evening, November 23d,
>
> from 8 to 11 o'clock.
>
> Dancing.

As the leading feature of the event, the words, Music, Charades, Theatricals, may take the place of Dancing. The invitations are usually sent out two weeks in advance of the date, and require the same punctilious attention and form of reply as in other social events alluded to.

THE INVITED GUEST.—If the "At Home" be held in the afternoon, if there be dancing or not, ladies will retain their bonnets during the stay, but will avoid large hats which would incommode themselves or others in dancing. The guest on being announced will endeavor to make his way to the lady of the house to pay his respects, but may salute acquaintances on his way. It is good form to arrive a short time after the hour fixed on the invitation card, and to retire some time before the close. Receptions are, of course, attended in full evening dress.

INTRODUCTIONS.—The "At Home" being of a more promiscuous nature than other social events, general introductions are neither necessary nor desirable. The hostess in this matter will exercise tact and discretion. If a guest have a desire for an introduction to a stranger of either sex he may, in the absence of a mutual acquaintance, apply to his hostess for it. The hostess should be watchful, however, to see that no person is left entirely to his or her own resources for amusement.

REFRESHMENTS.—These are provided in the dining-room, whether at ceremonious "Teas" or "At Homes." No plates are necessary, except where ices are served. The edibles provided comprise sandwiches, bread and butter, biscuits and cake, with tea and coffee and wine "cups," if desired. Fresh fruit may also have a place on the refreshment list. Strawberries and cream in season are always appreciated.

AFTERNOON TEAS.

THE same regulations will apply to afternoon teas as to "At Homes," and the provision for refreshments will be made in the same manner. For a small five o'clock tea party, the hostess herself dispenses tea or coffee, and the ladies are waited on by the gentlemen present, or, in the absence of gentlemen, by young lady members or friends of the hostess. The gloves are not removed, as a rule, but in some circles the sensible custom of ungloving the right hand is adopted.

AFTERNOON PARTIES.—For more formal afternoon parties, which are popular in the months of June, July, and August, cards are issued in the following manner:

> CREST
> or
> MONOGRAM.
>
> *Mrs. S. B. Gill*
>
> At Home
>
> *Tuesday, June 5th inst.,*
>
> *3 to 6 o'clock p. m.*

The name of the invited guest is written across the top of the card, and the date is generally written on a blank line left for the purpose. In the refreshment room, tea, coffee, and ices will be presided over by the lady's maid, and the salads, biscuits, sandwiches, rolls, cakes, fruit, and champagne or claret cup is dispensed by waiters.

Where music of a professional character is included, chairs should be arranged in concert-room order, and guests furnished with programmes; also in the case of theatricals; in either case "Music," or "Theatricals" being denoted on the card. The guests should leave cards with the hostess the day succeeding the party.

PICNICS.

AMONG social amusements limited to the summer months, there is none more deservedly popular than the Picnic. The healthful, exhilarating influence of such an event, when a good deal of the stiffness of conventional etiquette is relaxed, usually gives the picnic an air of hilarious festivity, which, indeed, indicates its true character, and for this reason care should be taken to have the company invited selected with care and discrimination.

SELECTING THE SPOT.—The site selected for a picnic should be not so remote as to be inconvenient of access, nor so near the "busy haunts of men" as to invite intrusion or impertinent curiosity. It should combine the attributes of utility and the picturesque; should afford shade from the meridian heat, and open lawn for afternoon amusements, and, above all, if possible, should be near a stream of living water. Prudence will also take into account the proximity of some convenient shelter in which refuge can be had in the event of unpropitious weather.

PICNIC TOILETS.—An expensive toilet at a picnic betokens neither good taste nor good breeding. Boots and gloves should, as at all times, be unexceptionable, and the style in which the dress material is made up may be of the most approved fashion The material itself should be of some cheap and strong washing material, white being given the preference. If the weather be cool, flannel, serge, or mohair is suitable; if hot, cotton, linen, or holland. The dress should be short enough for convenience and comfort in walking. Gentlemen may wear shooting-coats and wide-awake hats if desired.

INVITATIONS, CONVEYANCES AND LUNCH.—The most agreeable way of selecting a picnic party is for two or three friends to join the hostess in making the necessary provisions. The invitations are to be written, as there are so many points to be explained that no stereotyped form can be adopted. The guests may be requested to meet at the spot selected at a given hour, or they may be rendezvoused at an appointed time for conveyance by rail or carriage. In this case the party issuing the invitations is expected to furnish the conveyances and to make all needful arrangements. The guests will, as a rule, pay for their own tickets and traps. The luncheon should consist of an abundance of cold fowl, ham and tongue, salads, canned fish, meats and sardines, sandwiches, patés, cold salmon, bread, butter and cheese, tarts, fruits and cake, and a generous supply of cider, claret and champagne—in the "cup" preparation. The party, on reaching the destination, will disperse, leaving the hostess and her chosen attendants to prepare the lunch, a time for which is set, generally about one hour from time of arrival. The gentlemen will wait upon the ladies, and the lunch is altogether *sans ceremonie*.

THE FANCY DRESS BALL.

CARDS for the *bal masque*, a form of entertainment which the hostess, if she have ample accommodation, may give once, but not oftener, in a season, should be of exceptionally elegant and expensive design, marking the more than ordinary character of the event. Invitations are in the following form:

> Mask.
>
> Mr. and Mrs. Ralph Winters
>
> request the pleasure of your company in
>
> Fancy Dress
>
> On Monday Evening, December 22d.
>
> at 9 o'clock.
>
> R. S. V. P. Gorham Place.

No introductions are possible, and guests are presumed to maintain conversational intercourse in accordance with the character assumed. A gentleman in mask may beg the favor of attending the masked lady without an introduction. Masks are removed on the announcement of supper. The fancy dress ball most in vogue in America dispenses with masks, which is the French custom. The ordinary regulations for a ball prevail.

ENTERTAINING.

THE lady at the head of a household has not only the social reputation of the house on her shoulders in her general management of the domestic economy, and her success in providing the substantial elements of comfort, but much also depends upon her personal knowledge of the proprieties, her tact in being in the right place at the right time and saying the right thing to the right person. She should have a distinct understanding of the programme necessary to be followed upon the various social events, and in carrying this out she will not fail to meet the expectations of society.

MORNING RECEPTIONS.—For receiving morning visitors the hostess will rise to receive ladies, but will, as a rule, receive a gentleman seated, shaking hands with each visitor. When the guests depart she will shake hands with each, without rising if a gentleman, and ringing the bell for the door as she does so. If, however, her visitor is a lady unattended, the hostess will accompany her to the door of the drawing-room, and close it after her. If two parties are present in the room at the same time, the hostess may introduce them to each other, or not, at her discretion.

RECEPTION OF DINNER GUESTS.—In preparing for the reception of guests for a dinner party, the hostess should be in the drawing room for some little time previous to the hour appointed for the arrival of guests, to see that every arrangement has been properly executed, and, also, lest a difference in time pieces might announce some guest, who would not find her prepared for the occasion. She will rise on the arrival of each guest, but generally takes a position seated near the door, where she greets the guest, exchanging a few words of conversation, in which the gentleman should be informed whom he will escort to the table, and passes the guest on to some other visitor or coterie where he will be entertained. When the host offers his arm to the *premier* lady, the hostess, in the order of consideration, mentions the name of each gentleman, instructing him which lady guest to attend to the table. She will give the signal for the conclusion of the dinner by rising and bowing to the partner of the host, and will follow the ladies to the drawing-room. She will there devote herself to the entertainment of the ladies by introducing general conversation till the gentlemen reappear. In the drawing-room the hostess will endeavor to divide her attentions and conversation impartially among her guests.

EVENING RECEPTIONS AND BALLS.—At afternoon and evening receptions the first guests are received by the hostess seated in the drawing-room, rising to greet each. As the arrivals become more frequent, and the rooms begin to fill, she takes her stand at the drawing-room door, or on the landing, greeting the guests as they reach the top of the stair-case or the vestibule leading to the drawing-room, passing a word with each, and intimating on occasion that a particular friend of the guest will be found within. She will not leave the drawing-room for the refreshment room till the majority of the guests have done so.

If the entertainment be a concert, the hostess must accord a pleasant reception to the performers, see that they are comfortably disposed at the piano, and have everything that they require, such as wine and water.

At a ball the chief duty of the hostess, after seeing that everything else is in order, is the reception of her guests, as for an afternoon party. It is not necessary to introduce people to each other generally, but where a young lady is observed who is not

COUNTRY VISITING.

dancing the hostess will ask permission from her chaperon to introduce a partner, or from herself, if the young lady is alone, and she will generally endeavor to find partners for those whose want of acquaintance or diffidence keeps them in the background. When supper is announced, and the host leads the way with the *premier* lady, the hostess will make introductions so that the company is duly paired off.

HOUSE VISITORS IN THE COUNTRY.—The duties of the hostess in town are comparatively slight. It is when entertaining a party of friends at her country residence that she feels the full anxieties and responsibilities of her place. The first anxiety is the assembling of a suitable party of people, that is persons who will be likely to be pleased to meet each other, to join in the same recreations, and who sometimes by diversity of special talents, such as music, singing, conversation or humor will contribute to each other's mutual entertainment and to the fund of common pleasure.

Invitations should be worded so as to leave no suspicion of mere formality in the mind of the recipient, and should state the day on which the guest is expected, and the duration of the visit. When the acceptance is received, write naming the station, and whether a friend or carriage will be in waiting Guests generally arrive late in the afternoon, and the hostess should, if not engaged in driving with other guests, be ready to welcome them, and have tea ready for their refreshment. When sufficient time has thus elapsed to allow the guests' baggage to be deposited in the room prepared for them, to which the hostess will previously personally have attended, she will accompany the guests, to their rooms, and having informed them of the hour for dinner, and indicated the bell to summon the maid, will leave them to rest.

When the guests assemble in the drawing room, before dinner, the hostess will introduce them to each other, if on the first assembling, or introduce any new addition to the circle. The hostess in pairing off for dinner will give the latest comer due precedence, and will endeavor to alternate the company as much as possible, so that there shall be, if possible, a different order on each evening. After dinner, she will divide the company for various amusements, arrange tables for whist, and other round games, matching those at chess who prefer it, and utilizing those who are musical in playing and singing for the entertainment of the company. When the tray with wine and water makes its appearance, at the hour fixed by the custom of the house, the lady suggests the propriety of retiring, and accompanies to their rooms such guests as are new on that day, leaving with polite hopes for their comfort, and intimations to ring or ask for anything desired.

In the morning, the hostess is the first down, and will preside at the breakfast table. Tea is generally made and handed round by the butler or servant, instead of being made at table by the hostess, as was formerly the custom.

Formerly it was the duty of the hostess not to lose sight of her guests for a moment, but more rational customs now prevail. At and after breakfast the hostess, will impart to her guests such society news as may have reached her by mail, and after giving such information as may aid the guests to enjoy themselves, will leave them free to follow their own inclinations. She will indicate what points of interest are in the neighborhood, and what horses and conveyances are available, what friends of members of the party are within visiting distance, etc., while the host, if in the shooting season, will take charge of those who desire to engage in shooting. The hostess is thus left free to hold counsel with her cook as to the *menu*, give orders respecting rooms, to give instructions to the gardener as to flowers required for house use, to attend to her correspondence, write *menus*, rearrange the order of her guests for dinner, and plan the programme of the evening's entertainment. She reappears before luncheon, at which she presides, afterward drives or walks with guests, and is on hand to welcome any fresh guests, before retiring to dress for dinner. When guests are departing the hostess will be on hand early to bid them good-bye, and will inquire the address to which to forward their mail matter, if any should come after their departure.

When taking her guests to a neighbor's house for a ball or other party, the hostess should arrive in the first carriage so as to be ready to introduce members of her party to the lady of the house visited.

When accompanied by guests to church, the hostess will stop at the door of her family seat, and wait till they have entered, before taking her seat.

The really good hostess is she who attends to those trifles which go so far to make up the pleasure of existence. Nearly every person has some peculiarity or preference in their habits of life, eating or drinking, or daily custom, the means of gratifying which, in a strange house, is always particularly grateful. The good hostess will study these trifles, and endeavor to meet the comfort of her guests by providing for them.

INTRODUCTIONS.

THE ceremony of introduction is one which should never be looked upon as trivial or formal. Though it is in itself the simplest and the most frequent of social ceremonies, it is at the same time one of the most important. There are, of course, occasions when introductions are a mere formality, rendered necessary by the exigency of the occasion, where the introduction is not designed to, and does not warrant, the foundation of acquaintance, but the true meaning in etiquette of an introduction is that the person who introduces the stranger to his (or her) friend takes upon himself the warranty for the worthiness of the person introduced of that friend's esteem. The hostess at a social event should never introduce to a young lady, or cause to be introduced, a gentleman whom she does not consider worthy of her own regard. The conveniences of society ofttimes make it necessary to invite the company at a social gathering of a gentleman whom the hostess would not select for the acquaintance of her own daughters, and she has a moral duty not to be the means of introducing such an one to the respect of a young lady friend by the indorsement of an introduction.

FORMS OF INTRODUCTION.

In making an introduction; the person of the higher social consideration is always the person to whom the introduction is made. If the parties are lady and gentleman, it is the gentleman who is introduced to the lady. If two ladies, the one having the higher social standing, or of the greater age, is given the place of honor. At a party where a lady or gentleman is the guest of the evening, all the other guests are introduced to her or him, as the case may be.

The mutual friend or hostess will, in making an introduction, say: "Mrs. Jones, permit me to make you acquainted with (or, to introduce to you) Miss Robinson; Miss Robinson, Mrs. Jones." If there are others in the group, the introducer will add: "Mrs. Martin, Miss Robinson; Miss Featherstone, Miss Robinson; Mr. Hardy, Miss Robinson," waiting in a short pause between each introduction, the formal salutation, by bow, or otherwise, between the parties introduced.

In introductions, always give the full title of either party, military, naval, judicial or professional. As, for instance, "Mr. Grace, allow me to introduce to you, Captain Patton, of the United States ship *Warrant;* Captain Patton, the Rev. Mr. Grace, rector of St. Alban's Church;" or, "Dr. Blade, permit me to make you acquainted with Senator Harvey, of the state of Iowa; Senator Harvey, Dr. Blade, Professor of Anatomy, in the University of Bonesville."

Introductions are frequently made with a business object, which should be fully stated by the introducing party, as, for instance: "Mr. Marley, allow me to introduce to you Mr. Yarrow, of the Ebbw Vale Steel and Iron Company, of Bristol, England, who is seeking to extend the business of the company in the West; Mr. Yarrow, Mr. Marley, President of the Missouri Valley Railway Company, who is well qualified to give you any information you may desire." Or, in other words: "Mr. Bernard, let me make you acquainted with Prof. Driscoll, Professor of Mathematics, of the Toronto University, Canada, who is taking advantage of his holidays to study the systems in the leading colleges of the United States; Prof. Driscoll, Mr. Bernard, President of the Faculty of the Mount Allison University."

Gentlemen will take care to bear in mind that an introduction necessitated by accidental circumstances is not made the ground of obtruding acquaintance. In the same way ladies, who at home move in different social spheres, often meet on a common ground at watering-places and other places of public resort; but it should always be left to the person of higher social standing to indicate whether the acquaintance so formed shall be continued.

TITLES—HOW TO USE THEM.

IN foreign countries the necessities of etiquette impose quite a task upon the memory in keeping it stored with the numerous titles conferred by governments or by educational institutions. In our own land the constitution prohibits the conferring of titles of nobility, yet even our democratic customs and tendencies do not cause an entire disuse of titles. Many of them, however, are mere abbreviations, while others indicate a profession or avocation. Nevertheless, there remains among superficial people a tendency to make the most of their limited opportunities of wearing titles, and if they have earned none they are tempted to assume them. More than this, a title once borne is made to cling ever after to the name which it has adorned in the past. One must use his own judgment in conceding to a man a title to which he has not a right, and the tendency ought to be toward limiting, rather than enlarging, the use of titles. It is rudeness, however, amounting to insult, to withhold a title which a man has acquired with unquestioned right, and which the public freely gives him. In matters of ceremony, especially, this rule must be rigidly observed. In addressing, or even in writing of, the possessor of an honorary title, offense may be given or inferred as being intended, if the usual title is not attached to the name.

Following are some examples of titles as used in the United States:

MILITARY.—Gen. U. S. Grant; Major-General Winfield Scott; Lieut-General Philip Sheridan; Captain J. J. Lambert, Post Commanding; Adjutant-General Stimpson; Major O. J. Smith; Francis S. Dodge, Lieutenant Commanding; Colonel M. H. Fitch.

NAVAL.—Admiral David G. Farragut; Rear-Admiral Andrew H. Foote; Commodore Isaac Hull; Commander John Paul Jones; Captain George H. Preble; Post-Captain Jacob Jones.

CIVIL.—Hon. John A. Logan; Hon. William R. Grace; Governor Richard J. Oglesby; Attorney-General James Brewster; His Excellency, Chester A. Arthur; Chief-Justice Marshall; Judge H. D. Scott; Consul-General Edwin A. Merritt; Alderman Henry Jamison.

SCHOLASTIC.—Prof. Joseph Luce; Louis J. R. Agassiz, A.M.; Edward Hitchcock, B.A.; William McDonald, M.D.; Dr. J. C. Lay; J. S. Greene, C.E.; John G. Smith, M.E.; Rev. James Edmondson; Rev. J. C. Reid, D.D.

SOCIAL.—Mr. Joseph Medill; Mrs. E. B. Russell; Miss Sallie Smith; Master John Brown; Messrs. J. V. Farwell & Co.; John Boggs, Esq.; Dear Sir; Gentlemen (used in the plural); Madam, etc.

The above titles are too frequently used to need explanation. In their use, but one should be applied to the same name. To say "Mr. William Hyde, Esquire," would be useless and absurd. To say "Dr. M. A. Wilcox, M.D.," would be an equally absurd repetition. An exception is where one title does not imply or include another; as, "Rev. Matthew Simpson, LL.D."

The title "Mr." is one which every respectable man may claim as his due. It is the part of politeness to make use of it in all cases where no higher title is known. Any man who places a value upon courtesy will have "Mr." at his tongue's end when addressing all kinds of men, rich or poor. It is in much better taste, placed before a name, than the anglicism "Esquire" placed after it.

"Honorable" is a title applied to persons who have been elected to seats in the United States congress or a state legislature; also to members or ex-members of the president's cabinet, or of a governor's staff, and mayors of cities.

Plural titles are written as follows: Messrs. (for Messieurs, meaning "Gentlemen"); Misses (plural of Miss); Mesdames (plural of Madame).

The term "His" or "Your Excellency," is applied to the president of the United States, the governor of any state, and the minister plenipotentiary to any foreign country.

The address to a man and his wife, in case the man has a title, should be as follows: His Excellency and Mrs. A. Lincoln; Governor and Mrs. F. Pitkin; Hon. and Mrs. George Steel; Rev. and Mrs. F. M. Pavey; Dr. and Mrs. F. H. Sutherland; Rev. Dr. and Mrs. W. H. Thomas. If the person have no title, other than the social, let it be given; as, "Mr. and Mrs. M. J. Bigelow."

OUT-DOOR EXERCISES.

AMONG the active exercises in which the polite world is accustomed to indulge, and in which pleasure and profit are combined, the physical health being as much consulted as social intercourse, are riding, driving and boating. Of these exercises, the most elegant, suitable and beneficial, for the lady especially, is that of horseback riding, and its popularity is gradually and perceptibly spreading in American society.

HABIT FOR THE SADDLE.—The lady's riding habit may be either long or of moderate length, according to taste. The long habit is certainly preferable in point of appearance. It should be of dark colored stuff of some woolen material, black, dark green or brown, made plain, and fitting closely to the figure. Strong buff gloves should be worn. The left hand, or the "rear" side is the whip hand, and the right or "off" side the bridle hand. A lady who is accustomed to riding exercise will do well to familiarize herself with the accoutrements of the horse, so as to be able in event of necessity to remedy an accident.

THE LADY'S HORSE.—The head of the household will, usually either personally or through some person of proper experience, use care and judgment in the selection of a lady's horse. The horse should be selected of good stock, of fair symmetry, and handsome appearance, of good temper, and free from vicious or nervous habits, such as biting, kicking, bolting, shying, or stumbling. He should be free in action, spirited in temper, though gentle under control. He should walk well, trot swiftly and steadily, and canter lightly, and be obedient but not too sensitive to the bit. A horse which has the stumbling habit should never be mounted by a lady. For a lady of petite form, a tall horse should not be provided, nor should a lady of full stature be mounted on a diminutive animal.

MOUNTING.—The art of assisting a lady to mount her horse is one of which every gentlemen should be master. It is a grateful courtesy to a lady if gracefully performed, but one in which awkwardness or clumsiness, which is liable to expose a lady to ridicule, is not easily overlooked. The lady prepared to mount is stationed on the near side of the horse with her right hand grasping the reins, and holding the head of the saddle. The cavalier, facing her, stoops and offers his clasped hands as a stirrup into which she places her foot, then placing her left hand on his shoulder by a simultaneous movement, she is placed lightly and easily in the saddle. If necessary, the gentleman should adjust the stirrup, which should hang just below the ankle bone.

ON HORSE BACK.—In the saddle the lady should sit erect, facing squarely to the front, and not depending entirely for her seat either upon the stirrup or crutch. She should accustom herself to the movement of her horse, and at all times keep him under thorough but gentle control of the bit. If a horse stumble or slip, the rider should instantly detach her foot from the stirrup, to avoid disaster in case of being thrown.

On the road always keep to the near side in passing.

The gentleman will usually take the off side in escorting a lady on horseback.

In dismounting the lady will free her knee, placing one hand on the saddle head and the other on the gentleman's shoulder, and spring lightly to the ground.

The gentleman in escorting a lady on horseback will attend her on the right hand side. He will offer such assistance in mounting and dismounting as has been described, and will study her comfort by every means at his command, attending to errands and commissions, and opening gates. After the lady has been mounted for a time he should see that the saddle girth does not require tightening as is frequently the case.

In absence of other escort, the lady should always be attended by a groom, who will ride a respectful distance to the rear.

CARRIAGE EXERCISE.

Let it be borne in mind that you never go for a ride except on horseback. When you take carriage exercise you always go for a drive. The etiquette of the road, which is in the hands of the driver, consists in not driving at an unseemly pace, and keeping to your own side of the road, both in meeting and passing vehicles.

If gentlemen accompany ladies in a two-seated carriage, the ladies will be given the seat facing the horses. The deportment in the carriage should be unaffected and unostentatious. Avoid loud talking and undue hilarity. Enter a carriage gracefully. If there is one step, place the left foot upon it, the right reaching the floor, and the seat being thus easily and naturally reached. If there are two steps, place the right foot first, and the seat is reached in the same manner.

BOATING.

Many ladies are excellent oarswomen, and, though many in the medical profession set their faces against the practice as too violent for female health, used in moderation it is an invigorating and health-developing exercise. The lady who is attired for rowing should have substantial boots and loose corsets. The costume is a matter of taste, but is generally of blue serge, trimmed with white braid, and a sailor hat. There are many other picturesque and elegant costumes worn. The gentleman's rowing costume is of white flannel, and he should take a pea jacket in the boat to put on when heated with rowing and resting from the oars. Gentlemen should hand the ladies to their seats, and see that they are comfortably bestowed and placed so as to have their garments clear of accidental splashing from the oars. Where ladies are timid, the gentlemen should reassure them. The accidental rocking of a boat by the swell of a passing steamer is alarming to the novice, and if the absence of danger be not explained by the escort, she is liable to a panic from which serious results may occur.

GENERAL OUT-DOOR EXERCISES.

For archery, an out-door amusement which of late years has become quite popular, special costumes are generally provided by the ladies. For other out-door exercises, such as croquet, lawn tennis, etc., ladies should be attired in a suitable, cheerful costume, without train or unnecessary encumbrance, and having regard to the degree of exertion involved in the amusement to be engaged in. Conversation should be light and cheerful, and should be general among parties engaged in a game.

MISTRESSES AND SERVANTS.

THE rules which govern the relations between mistresses and servants, belong to the domain of domestic economy rather than that of etiquette, but there are one or two more or less important points with which etiquette has to deal, and upon which no lady should fail to perform the duty which she owes to society.

In the first place in her relations with the servant the lady represents society, and has no right to relax the respect due to herself in that capacity by permitting undue familiarity or freedom of intercourse with the servant, and so turn the servant loose upon society to annoy others with offensive breaches of place and impertinent familiarity. The lady of good breeding treats her servant with the same gentle and considerate courtesy which she extends to all, but the servant must understand that a request is a command, that his or her duty is prompt, explicit, and respectful obedience.

In engaging a servant, she should not accept a recommendation from a lady who is unknown to her. Where practicable, the servant who brings a letter of recommendation, should be asked to arrange with the former employer an hour for an interview with the lady with whom service is sought; the lady will then ascertain how far the "character" is deserved, and how much of it was due to good nature, and also the characteristics of the intended employee. If "characters" are given from persons whom she only knows from reputation, a note should be addressed to the party for direct confirmation of the character given. Servants should be received into the household with the greatest caution.

When you discharge a servant for cause, never give a character. You have no right to furnish the false pretenses by which such servant shall gain undeserved confidence in another household. Let your recommendation, if you are warranted in giving a character, be strictly in accordance with the deserts of the employee. If he or she be especially worthy of trust and confidence, word the "character" furnished so as to be of the greatest benefit to the servant. It is as proper to help a deserving servant as it is wrong and improper to cover up the slothful, impertinent or dishonest proclivities of another, with the guarantee of your name and station.

SHOPPING.

THE lady who desires to carry respect with her wherever she goes, and who would be considered a gentlewoman, even among strangers, and in the pursuance of every avocation of life, will pay strict attention to her conduct while shopping, and in all her dealings with tradesmen.

The first thing to be impressed upon the mind is the importance of thoroughly making up your conclusions, before setting out, as to exactly what you want, and about to what expense you are prepared to go in the purchase.

When you enter a store speak frankly and courteously to the clerk. Tell him plainly what class of goods you require, what grade of color, and about what range of cost, and ask to be shown something in the line indicated.

In examining the goods, unless you are ambitious of distinction for vulgarity, do not say to the clerk that the goods could be got cheaper at another store, or that you could get better value elsewhere for the same money. If the goods do not suit for any reason, state it frankly, and leave the store.

Never ask to be shown goods if you do not intend to purchase on the occasion, without previously stating to the shopman that you merely wish to examine goods with a view to future purchase, if suited.

Remember, in handling goods, more especially in those of delicate construction, that if you treat them roughly you are liable to destroy their salableness.

Remember that the time of the clerk is of value to his employer, and that it is only yours while you are engaged in doing business. Consequently, while you are engaging his time do not keep him waiting while you indulge in social chatter.

Never attempt to engage the attention of a clerk while he is waiting upon another person. That is both unreasonable and ill-bred.

If you have no account at the store where you are purchasing, and are not confident that you are so well known that your credit is unquestioned, always pay cash for goods, or instruct the clerk to send the bill with them.

If either before or after leaving the store you find that an error in change has been made in your favor, always return and rectify it. This is not only rendered necessary to your self-esteem by your sense of honesty, but it is an imperative duty from the fact that the clerk or cashier may be unjustly suspected of dishonesty as a reason for the shortage in cash which the mistake involves.

Invariably be polite and courteous to clerks. It is the natural instinct of good breeding, and will be observed if you would avoid a reputation for snobbishness.

PUBLIC TRAVEL.

NOT only is the conduct and deportment of a person traveling in public of the strictest account, but an acquaintance with the rules which govern them will affect the comfort of the inexperienced traveler. To the traveler who is governed by a few simple rules, a journey on the cars is undertaken with as much confidence and certainty of enjoyment, as would attend his passage from his place of business to his dinner table. On the contrary, to the person, particularly if a lady, who is both a stranger to the experience and to the rules which should be observed, a journey from home is a subject of apprehension and anxiety, which only go to increase the difficulties to be encountered.

TICKETS.—The first essential to the traveler is the possession of a reliable Railway Guide. As soon as a journey is contemplated consult the Guide, and make up your mind by what route you will travel and also by what train you will leave. If you have sufficient leisure, never leave the purchase of the ticket until the arrival of the train. Send out and get your ticket during the day. If the journey be a prolonged one, take the sleeping car, and secure your berth before starting. In selecting the berth, if the lady be alone, she will do better to take the whole section (two berths), as she will thus avoid even a chance disturbance of her privacy. Remember that the best berths are those in the center of the car, where the jar of the wheels is less perceptible, and that lower berths are always preferable to the upper.

BAGGAGE.—Unless it be a lady, when a friend or traveling companion takes the responsibility, always personally supervise the checking of baggage. Have your ticket in your hand when you approach the baggageman, and indicate the baggage to be checked, mentioning also its destination. It is a safe rule to compare the coupon check with that attached to the baggage to see that they correspond; but the baggageman may be generally trusted to avoid error in that respect. Once you have your check in your satchel, no further concern need be given to the baggage till the destination is reached.

In your personal baggage include nothing that is not absolutely necessary to your comfort and requirements on the journey. A lady who enters a railway carriage with a hand-satchel, a band-box, a bird cage, and a miscellaneous collection of parcels is at once set down as ill-bred, no matter how charming in appearance, or how much her accoutrements and apparel may indicate the possession of wealth.

TRAVELING COSTUME.—This should invariably be of some quiet material, of texture that will not attract nor retain dust, of a color that will not weary the eye by its perspicuity, and of substance that will shake out into its natural shape after a day's wear, without acquiring permanent folds. It should be suited to the season, but always bearing in mind that even summer nights are chilly, and require a dress of woolen fabric, even if of the very lightest material.

Upon every loose article of dress, and of baggage, always have the name and address of the owner, either by card attached or in some other way.

THE LADY ON BOARD BOAT OR CAR.—Upon entering a car glance round for a vacant seat, and take possession of the most convenient one that offers, choosing in summer if available the shady side and the seat next the window. If a lady is alone and the car is but sparsely filled endeavor to secure a seat as near as possible to any other lady on the car, and if there are none, seat yourself so that you may not be suspected of desiring the proximity of gentlemen.

If an overcoat, satchel or parcel is observed upon an apparently vacant seat accept it as an indication that the seat is occupied, and the owner temporarily absent.

A lady traveling alone should invariably resent any attempt on the part of a stranger to engage her in conversation, as an impertinence of which no person, with the title of gentleman, would be guilty. If the lady is in want of any information let her seek it from the conductor, and never accost a strange gentleman except under unavoidable circumstances.

If, however, a gentleman who is on a long journey observes a lady whose continued presence indicates that she also is on a protracted journey, and apparently unattended, he may with respectful courtesy offer any assistance which is likely to conduce to her comfort. Conversation is in such a case permissible; but the gentleman should never take a seat along side the lady so addressed, but the seat in front of her. If an approach to familiarity is made on part of the gentleman, the lady will promptly check it, by freezing out the conversation, and withdrawing from the acquaintance with quiet dignity.

HINTS FOR THE CARS.—Never loll in the seats. Do not monopolize a double seat when you see others standing—you pay only for a single seat. Never open a window without first inquiring from those about you if the draught would be too much for them. If the car is overheated do not open the door without first appealing to the general sense of the passengers.

HOTEL DEPORTMENT.

The conduct of a lady traveling alone should be a subject of constant care and anxious watchfulness to her. In European countries no lady may travel alone without either escort or servant, but in America much greater freedom of movement is given, and any well-bred lady can travel alone in this country without being misapprehended or experiencing the least want of courteous attention.

On arriving at a hotel from the cars, the lady traveling alone will enter by the "ladies' entrance," and proceed to the ladies' parlor, where she will ring the bell and send the servant for the hotel clerk or proprietor, to whom she will give her card, explaining the reason for her traveling alone, giving the length of her stay, and ask them to see to the registering and locating of her room.

On going down to dinner, notice should be sent to the clerk, who will escort her to the head-waiter, who will assign her a permanent seat.

At breakfast it is permissible to read a paper, while waiting to be served, but not at any other meal.

She will not permit any conversation at the hotel table to be addressed to her, except from friends, nor will she ask any one to pass anything from the table. The waiter is at hand for that purpose.

No lady should ever use the public parlor piano, nor sing in the apartment unless entertaining a company of friends or callers.

It is not good taste to sit at the hotel window, and in passing on the stairs or corridors do so quietly and intently, paying no attention to anything or person on the way.

Dress quietly and unassumingly, even for dinner, for which a plain black silk, relieved with fine white lace is the most suitable.

THE WONDERS OF AMERICA.

The following is a list of the chief Natural and Artificial Wonders of the United States, with their location.

Niagara Falls.—In the Niagara River, between Lakes Erie and Ontario; breadth, three-quarters of a mile, height, 175 feet.

Natural Bridge.—A natural arch of rock, spanning Cedar Creek, Virginia.

Split Rock.—A rock of great height, in Virginia, having a fissure formed by nature extending from top to bottom.

Mammoth Cave.—In Kentucky. Supposed to be the largest cave in the world.

Yosemite Valley.—Sixty miles from Coulterville, California. The length of the valley is about nine miles, and its average width about a mile. It abounds in natural wonders, containing waterfalls from 700 to 1,000 feet in height, a perpendicular precipice 3,000 feet high; slopes of great steepness and a height of 3,500 feet; and a nearly perpendicular rock of 3,270 feet in altitude.

Lake Superior.—Between Canada and Michigan; the largest lake in the world.

Croton Aqueduct.—An aqueduct over thirty miles long, bringing water to New York city.

East River Bridge.—A suspension bridge, hung on cables of steel wire, connecting the cities of New York and Brooklyn.

The National Capitol.—At Washington, D. C.

The New York Capitol.—At Albany, N. Y.

Washington Monument.—At Washington, D. C.

City Park.—At Philadelphia, Pennsylvania.

Central Park.—In New York city.

THE GAUGER'S GUIDE.

The following are rules for ascertaining the number of bushels of shelled corn in a crib, or of apples, potatoes, etc., in a bin, or the number of tons of hay in a mow:

Multiply together the length, breadth and height of the crib, bin or mow, to ascertain the number of cubic feet in whichever one is to be measured. Then proceed as follows:

To find the number of bushels of shelled corn that the crib holds, divide its cubic contents by two.

To learn the number of bushels that the bin contains, divide its cubic contents by eight, and point off the right hand figure as a decimal fraction.

To ascertain the number of tons that will fill the mow, divide its cubic contents by five hundred and twelve.

TABLE Showing the Altitude and Location of the most Celebrated Mountains in the World, arranged according to their height.

Mountain.	Location.	Altitude (in Feet.)	Mountain.	Location.	Altitude (in Feet.)
Mt. Everest (Himalaya Range)	Thibet	29,000	Mt. St. Helena	Washington Ter., U. S.	13,475
Dhawalaghiri (Himalaya Range)	India	25,500	Mt. Ararat	Armenia	12,700
Sorata	Bolivia	25,400	Temeriffe Peak	Canary Islands	12,000
Chimborazo	Ecuador	21,000	Mt. Millazin	Morocco	11,498
Hindoo Koosh	Afghanistan	20,544	Purdu Mountain	France	11,300
Cotopaxi (the highest volcano in the world)	Ecuador	18,900	Mt. Hood	Oregon, U. S	11,220
Mt. St. Elias	Alaska	17,900	Mt. Ætna	Sicily	10,000
Popocatapetl	Mexico	17,700	Mt. Lebanon	Syria	10,000
Mt. Boa	Sandwich Islands	17,500	Mt. Sinai	Arabia	8,200
Brown Mountain (Rocky Mt. Range)	U. S.	16,000	Shehattan	Norway	8,100
Mt. Blanc	Switzerland.	15,900	St. Bernard	Switzerland	8,000
Mt. Geesh	Africa	15,100	Mt. Olympus	Greece	6,600
Mt. Whitney	California, U. S.	14,865	Black Mountain	N. Carolina.	6,500
Mt. Fairweather	Alaska	14,475	Mt. Washington	New Hampshire, U. S.	6,293
Mt. Ramier	Washington Ter., U. S.	14,445	Mt. Parnassus	Greece	6,000
Mt. Shasta	California, U. S.	14,440	Mt. Hecla.	Iceland	5,500
Antiusua	Ecuador	14,300	Mt. Marcy	New York, U. S.	5,400
Pike's Peak	Colorado	14,215	Ben Nevis	Scotland	4,400
Mt. Ophir, Sumatra	India	13,800	Mt. Mansfield	Vermont, U. S.	4,275
Jungfrau	Switzerland.	13,700	Peaks of Otto	Virginia	4,250
Fremont's Peak	Wyoming Ter., U. S.	13,575	Vesuvius	Italy	3,900
			Round Top	New York, U.S.	3,800
			Stromboli	A volcano in the Mediterranean Sea.	3,000

TABLE Showing the Various Sizes of Tacks and Nails, the length of each Size, and the Number per Pound.

TACKS.

Commercial Name.	Length.	Number per pound.	Commercial Name.	Length.	Number per pound.
1 oz.	One-half inch	16,000	10 oz.	Eleven-sixteenths inch	1,600
1½ "	Three-sixteenths inch	10,666	12 "	Three-quarters inch	1,333
2 "	One-quarter inch	8,000	14 "	Thirteen-sixteenths inch	1,143
2½ "	Five-sixteenths inch	6,400	16 "	Seven-eighths inch	1,000
3 "	Three-quarters inch	5,333	18 "	Fifteen-sixteenths inch	888
4 "	Seven-sixteenths inch	4,000	20 "	One inch	800
6 "	Nine-sixteenths inch	2,666	22 "	One and one-sixteenth inches	727
8 "	Five-eighths inch	2,000	24 "	One and one-quarter inches	666

NAILS.

Commercial Name.	Length in Inches.	Number per pound.	Commercial Name.	Length in Inches.	Number per pound.
2 penny, fine.	One and one-eighth	760	16 penny, fine.	Three and one-quarter	32
3 "	One and one-quarter	480	20 "	Three and one half	24
4 "	One and one-half	300	30 "	Four	18
5 "	One and three-quarters	200	40 "	Four and one-half	14
6 "	Two	160	50 "	Five	12
7 "	Two and one-quarter	128	6 " fence	Two	80
8 "	Two and one-half	92	8 "	Two and one-half	50
9 "	Two and three-quarters	72	10 "	Three	34
10 "	Three	60	12 "	Three and one-half	29
12 "	Three and one-quarter	44			

DOMESTIC ECONOMY

WHATEVER may be the opinion of the "butterflies of fashion," housekeeping is, of all the arts, the one which has the most important bearing on the real life of women. It is more than an art: it rises to the dignity of a science. All that goes to make up a well-ordered home is comprehended in it. Considered as an accomplishment, it is of more solid, practical value than any of those showy attainments that serve to adorn rather than to build up. It is acquired only by study and experiment; like liberty, "eternal vigilance" is the price of it; and it is only through great tribulation that the young and inexperienced housekeeper enters into success. Nothing tends more to insure comfort, peace and attractiveness in home than good housekeeping. The mother who desires her daughter's real happiness will not fail to instruct her in household duties, and no maiden who looks forward to being one day the mistress of her own home will grudge the time spent in mastering their smallest details.

It is a common error of young girls to believe that because they are able (or expect to be able) to keep servants, it is, therefore, unnecessary for them to become familiar with household cares. "Hired help" are quick to discern the ignorance and incapacity of a mistress, and, as a rule, are equally ready to take advantage of it. A capable housekeeper, however, soon makes her capacity appreciated and respected by her servants.

No department of domestic economy is less understood or more neglected than ventilation. Sunlight and pure air are the worst foes to disease. Grates and open fire places are of great value as ventilating flues. The heavy, impure air naturally sinks toward the floor, and openings of this kind create a draft which tends to carry it off. If no grates or fire-places are used, throw open the windows and let in the outer air; do not rely on the air in the halls. Plenty of sunlight—floods of it—should enter the living-rooms of the family. It is better (and cheaper) to replace a faded carpet than to pay a doctor's bill.

To sweep and dust properly is "not so easy as it looks," and in this, as in nearly every other department of the housekeeper's care, system will secure the best results. Statuettes, books and articles of bric-a-brac which are difficult to dust should, before sweeping, be covered with "dusters" made of old calico or other convenient material. Admit as much light as possible into the room before sweeping. Scan the ceilings for cobwebs and remove them by means of a broom, around which a towel has been pinned. The housekeeper will be repaid for care in sweeping and dusting by the longer wear of her carpets and by the brightness and freshness of their colors.

The "siege" of housecleaning is one of the epochs in household life, and is a most trying period in the housekeeper's existence. The first bright sunshine of spring reveals unsuspected dust and cobwebs, and to her imagination, even the brooms and scrubbing-brushes seem anxious to begin the campaign. In northern latitudes, however, it is not wise to begin too early. Spring breaks her promises of pleasant weather and gives us many days when it will be anything but comfortable to sit, shivering, in a fireless room, when children become unmanageable and husbands growl. So, for the sake of health, peace and comfort, don't remove the stoves before the middle of May.

To combat the ravages of the everlasting moth is one of the most tiresome of the housekeeper's duties. The moth works in the dark. During the winter the worms are torpid. Early in the spring they change into chrysalids, and in three weeks afterward they are transformed into winged moths, which fly about the house in the evenings of May and June. They lay their eggs (which are too small to be distinguished by the naked eye) in dark corners, and immediately thereafter die. The eggs hatch in about a fortnight, and the young worms at once devote their energies to business. The owner of a cedar closet (or even a cedar chest) is secure against their ravages; those who do not own either will find camphor, cedar chips, cut tobacco and cayenne pepper, laid in the folds of the garment, valuable preventives. It is a good plan to wrap articles in heavy brown paper and seal the packages closely. Moths will not touch brown paper. Furs should be combed, beaten and aired, sprinkled with camphor gum, sewed up in linen and then put in a paper bag. It is a prudent course to examine the furs once or twice during the summer.

To many housekeepers, servants constitute the "greatest plague of life." The incompetent servant is perpetually repeating her (or him) self. The nurse who tyrannizes over the children, or upsets the baby carriage in the park; the waitress who drinks the cherry brandy and fills the bottle with weak tea; the cook who stimulates her fiery temper with whisky; all these are more or less familiar examples of the "trained servants," whom the intelligence offices daily send forth to vex the souls of their employers.

And yet, after all, for how many bad servants are those employers honestly responsible? Servants have a creed of their own, the first article of which is "I *do not* believe in my mistress;" and is not this distrust often the result of an experience of injustice? In your intercourse with your servants remember that they are *human.* Bridget, or Gretchen, or Dinah is as susceptible of fatigue and as capable of enjoyment as her employers. Their pleasures are (and should be) separate from yours, but recreation in some form is as necessary for them as for you. At the same time bear in mind the old adage, "familiarity breeds contempt," and do not place yourself and them on the same level by making them your confidantes and associates. Make no rules which you have not carefully considered, and a compliance with which you intend to enforce. Don't tell "Mary" to follow a certain line of conduct, unless you have fully made up your mind that she *shall* follow it, and if you have, insist upon obedience. In one word, the same principles should control you in the management of your servants as in the government of your children—firmness, joined to consideration and gentleness. Remember, always, that they have the same desires and are subject to the same temptations as yourself; and you will find them, as a rule, ready to meet you fully half-way in your efforts to secure a well-ordered household.

HEALTH-GIVING FOOD.

IN every living human being there is an incessant waste and repair. The body is every moment yielding up its particles to destruction, like the coal which is burned in the furnace. Hunger is the instinct which teaches us that the furnace needs to be replenished. Properly speaking, every ingredient of the body constantly requires to be replaced, and every ingredient which goes to make up the body must, therefore, form a part of food. All food substances are accordingly divided into groups, each of which has some distinguishing characteristic.

The first group comprises what are called *inorganic* substances, namely, water and what are known as mineral salts. Of these, water is the most abundant, as it is the most indispensable. It forms from two-thirds to three-quarters of the entire body, and is being constantly discharged by perspiration, etc. Of the mineral salts, the most important are the chloride of sodium (or common salt) and phosphate of lime. Salt is found in lean meat in small proportions; phosphate of lime is also found in lean meat, fish, oysters, and eggs, the cereal grains, vegetables, and even in fruit. Alkaline salts (carbonate of soda, etc.,) are also necessary for the nourishment of the body, in order to repair the waste of the secretions of the blood. These salts are found in many of the summer vegetables and fruits.

The second group of food-substances comprises starch and sugar. Starch is found in the form of minute round grains in a vast number of vegetable products. It is very abundant in wheat-flour, rice, Indian corn, rye, barley, potatoes, peas and beans, and enters, in smaller proportion, into nearly every article of vegetable food. Sugar is not so plentiful in nature as starch, but it forms an ingredient of the sweet juice of nearly all the fruits and most of the vegetables. Wheat flour has five per cent of sugar; milk nearly as much; beets, nine per cent., etc., etc. Vegetable foods containing starch and sugar, are always useful in maintaining health.

The third group comprises the fats, which are of both animal and vegetable origin. Twenty-five per cent of the yolk of eggs, and all of the butter obtained from cow's milk, belong to this class of food, as well as the natural fat of animals.

The fourth group of food substances is known as the albuminoid class. One of the most familiar of this class is the white of an egg, which is pure albumen. Albumen is also found in lean meats as well as in a few vegetables.

The articles of food containing most of the substances needed in the body are as follows: For fat and heat making—butter, lard, sugar, and molasses; for flesh, blood or muscle-forming—lean meat, cheese, peas, beans, and lean fish; for brain and nerves—shell fish, lean meat, peas, beans, and very active birds and fish which live on food in which phosphorus abounds. Green vegetables, fruits and berries furnish additional supplies of the acids, the salts and the water needed. Water, coffee, tea, cocoa, and other drinks, are simply liquid foods, each supplying nutriment in greater or less amounts and repairing waste. Alcohol, in all its forms, is generally excluded from the list of foods; but taken in limited quantities and under certain conditions, it is thought by some authors to promote digestion and stimulate the conversion of food into tissue and blood. It is, however, as a rule, a wiser plan to allow the process of digestion to proceed under the guidance of nature, unassisted by artificial stimulation of this kind. Whatever may be the usefulness of alcohol under proper restrictions, the danger of its abuse is too great to render its use prudent or wise.

STRANGE POST OFFICE NAMES.

SOME genius with an eye to the double meaning of words has compiled the following list of queer names of post offices in the United States:

One hundred and thirty-five Cedar, 124 Pine, 216 Oak, 25 Chestnut, 100 Maple, 36 Locust, 61 Elm, 28 Apple, 10 Spruce, 38 Hickory, and 27 Poplar. Four have only two letters in their names: Po, Ok, Oz, and Ai. Two are Poor and 106 are Rich; 81 High and 72 Low; 113 Big and 106 Little; 11 Short and 100 Long; 42 Upper and 24 Lower; 16 Great and 3 Small. The lightest town is Pound, in Wise county, Va. The town that holds the least is Gill, in Franklin county, Mass. There are 240 names of post offices beginning with Rock, 42 with Stone, 106 with Sand, 68 with Clay, and 15 with Mud. There are 200 beginning with Spring, 28 with Summer, 39 with Fall and 17 with Winter. Eight are Hot and 38 Cold; 13 Wet and 41 Dry; 47 Clear and 15 Muddy. One is Violet, 65 are Blue, 230 Green, 27 Yellow, 42 Orange, 123 Red, 300 White, 105 Black, and 36 Gray.

HOUSEHOLD VADE MECUM.

THE following recipes and hints upon various matters of household economy are carefully collated from the most reliable and valuable sources, and will be found of advantage in regulating the domestic economy. The housewife who refers here in a difficulty will find herself extricated from the horns of many little dilemmas, which invariably arise to perplex her.

USEFUL RECIPES AND PRACTICAL HINTS.

For Sprains.—The white of an egg and salt mixed to a thick paste is one of the best remedies for sprains, bruises or lameness, for man or beast. Rub well the parts affected.

Salve for Cuts and Burns.—To one-half pound of sweet lard add one-fourth pound of beeswax and the same of resin. Beat all together till well mixed, and pour into small tin box. Apply a little to the wound on a soft cotton cloth.

To Cure Chilblains.—Soak the feet fifteen minutes in warm water, put on a pair of rubbers, without stockings, and go to bed.

To Procure an Appetite.—Take a slice of fresh cut bread, not too new, rub it all over with garlic, and pour a little fine olive oil over it. This eaten just previously to a meal induces an astonishing appetite. For such as dislike the raw oil, the bread may be lightly fried in butter or oil.

Cure for Hiccough.—Hold your nose, and in the meantime drink of any liquid you please. This will cause hiccoughs to cease instantly.

White Teeth.—A mixture of honey with the purest charcoal will make the teeth as white as snow. At rare intervals pumice stone, powdered, on the tooth-brush, may be used, but cautiously, so as not to destroy the enamel.

To Stop Bleeding.—Apply to a fresh cut wet tea leaves, or wetted scrapings of new sole leather. Both of these substances contain *tannin*, which is an astringent. A strong decoction of white oak bark is still better.

Eruptions of the Face.—Smear the face over with oil of walnuts at night on going to bed, and wash it off in the morning by means of a little oat meal or Indian meal in the water, instead of soap.

A Smoky Lamp.—A smoky lamp not only emits a disagreeable smell, but also spoils the furniture and blackens the ceiling. The simple preventative for this is to soak the wick in vinegar and dry it before using. See that the air has free passage up through the bottom of the chimney.

To Destroy Ants.—Take a large sponge, wash it well, press it very dry. By so doing it will leave the small cells open. Lay it on a shelf where the ants are most troublesome, and sprinkle sugar lightly over the sponge. At intervals plunge the sponge into boiling water to kill the ants, which will gather by thousands in the cells of the sponge.

Uses of Ammonia.—To wash paint, put a tablespoonful of ammonia into a quart of moderately hot water; dip in a flannel cloth, and with this merely wipe over the woodwork; no scrubbing will be necessary. For taking grease spots from any fabric, use the ammonia nearly pure, and then lay white blotting paper over the spot and iron it lightly. For washing laces, put twelve drops in a little warm suds. For cleaning silver, mix two teaspoonfuls of ammonia in a quart of hot soap-suds, put in your silver and wash it, using an old nail-brush or tooth-brush. For cleaning hair-brushes, etc., simply shake the brushes up and down in a mixture of one teaspoonful of ammonia to one pint of hot water, and when they are cleaned rinse them in cold water and stand them in the wind or in a hot place to dry. For washing finger marks from looking-glasses or windows, put a few drops of ammonia on a moist rag and make quick work of it. If you wish your house plants to flourish, put a few drops of the spirits in every pint of water used in watering. A teaspoonful in a basin of cold water will add much to the refreshing effects of a bath, and for those who have a sour or sweet smell it will be an absolute remedy for some time. Nothing is better than ammonia water for cleansing the hair. In every case rinse off the ammonia with pure water.

Varnish for Hard Wood.—Two parts linseed oil, one part spirits of turpentine, one and a half parts copal varnish. Mix well together, apply with a piece of linen rag, and polish with a soft cloth.

To Silence Snorers.—If a person snore in your vicinity to such a degree that you cannot go to sleep, steal gently out of bed, seize the water-jug, approach his bed side, catch hold of his hand and plunge it into the water. It is strange, but true, notwithstanding, that after this he will never snore again. The reason of this is that although asleep we still possess a certain amount of moral consciousness, which exercises its influence over the actions; and thus the snorer instinctively associates the shock with the act of snoring, and this dread is sufficient to control him so as to escape the penalty.

Burns and Scalds.—In case of scalding by hot water, dash on cold water instantly, and lift off from the skin any clothing that may cover the scald, as quickly as possible. Cold milk is still better. If the scald or burn is not serious, keep upon it a cloth wetted with equal parts of lime-water and linseed oil, with a little spirits of turpentine. If it is a severe burn, cover it with simple dry flour. Keep the flour heaped and packed down tightly, so as to wholly exclude the air, and send for a physician. The danger from a burn depends upon the extent of the surface injured. If flame is inhaled into the lungs the patient is not likely to recover, although but little outward mark of the fire may be found.

Illusion of Taste.—If the nose be held tightly while the most nauseous medicine is being administered, no taste will be perceptible; and if the eyes be shut while a person is smoking, he will not be able to tell whether his cigar or pipe is lighted or not.

To Look at the Sun Without Injury.—Provide a wine-glass filled with plain water, which will keep off the heat so effectually that the brightest sun may be viewed some time through it without any inconvenience.

Reviving Withered Flowers.—Flowers that have been twenty-four hours out of water and are withered, may be revived by plunging their stems into hot water, and as the water gradually cools they will become quite fresh again.

Boots and Shoes.—As soon as you buy a pair of boots, and before wearing, rub into the leather with the hand a mixture of equal parts of neats-foot oil and castor-oil, well shaken. Before applying the oil wet the leather slightly with a moist rag, to keep the oil from soaking through into the stockings. The following is an excellent water-proof for coarse boots: Beef tallow, 12 ounces; resin, 1 ounce; beeswax, 6 ounces; neatsfoot oil, 1 gill; castor oil, 1 gill. Mix well, and apply as hot as the leather will stand without burning. Remember that a very moderate degree of heat will scorch leather and ruin it. The following is another valuable leather preservative, good for boots and shoes and for leather belting: Melt 21 parts tallow with 3 parts resin, and mix well. In another vessel put 70 parts rain-water and 7 parts good washing-soap, dissolved in the water by boiling. Add the first mixture and again bring to a gentle boil. When cool it is ready for use. Apply only what will enter the leather in a reasonable time.

A Cheap Aquarium.—Cut a narrow groove in a board the size you wish. Set four panes of glass on edge in the grooves. Put a piece of zinc in the bottom. Make a light frame of wood or zinc, with grooves to correspond, for the top. Pass rods through the frame down the inside of the corners, through the bottom, and screw up tight. Put into the joints and corners the following:

Water-Proof Cement.—One part, by measurement, of litharge; one of plaster-Paris; one of fine sand; one-third of finely powdered resin. Keep dry, ready for use, in a well-corked bottle. To use, make into a putty with boiled linseed oil. A little *patent drier* may be used.

Another.—White lead and red lead, equal parts, mixed with boiled linseed oil.

For Dandruff.—One ounce flour of sulphur to one quart of water. Shake at intervals of a few hours. Next day pour off the clear water, and use it to saturate the hair every morning. Shampoo, gently, once a week, with mild soap, not rubbing the scalp very hard. Do not use preparations of carbonate of potass. for dandruff, as it will cause the hair to fall out.

To Remove Grease.—If simple benzine, followed with soap suds, is not sufficient, make the following preparation: Alcohol, one-half pint; sulphuric ether, 2 ounces; pure carbonate of potash-salts of tartar, 10 grains; soft water, 2 ounces; oil of bergamot, one-fourth ounce. Dissolve the carbonate in the water, and put the oil of bergamot in the alcohol. Mix all together and cork for use. (The bergamot is only for flavor.) In using, apply with a clean sponge, rubbing patiently. If the paint or grease has been long on the goods it will be more difficult to remove than when fresh.

To clean Brussels carpets when down, thoroughly sweep, and then scrub with a stiff brush.

To clean zinc, or indeed any metal, use kerosene. Remember that kerosene is not harmful to any metal, and is a foe to all rust, grease and paint.

To clean saws or tools from rust, when petroleum will not do, scrub with pumice stone and diluted muriatic acid, afterward washing with water, drying and slightly heating. You must keep your fingers out of the acid.

Stimulating Flowers.—To hasten the blooming of flowers, the following liquid has been used with advantage: Sulphate or nitrate of ammonia, 4 oz.; nitrate of potash, 2 oz.; sugar, 1 oz.; hot water, 1 pint. Dissolve and keep it in a well-corked bottle. For use, put eight or ten drops of this liquid into the water of a hyacinth glass or jar, for bulbous-rooted plants, changing the water every ten or twelve days. For flowering plants in pots a few drops must be added to the water used to moisten them. Rain-water should be used. If you have only well-water, remove the lime by boiling.

Flowers in Winter.—Flowers may be produced in winter by taking up the plants, trees or shrubs, in the spring, at the time when they are about to bud, with some of their own soil carefully preserved among the roots, placing them upright in a dark cellar till October. Then, with the addition of fresh earth, they are to be put into proper tubs or vessels and placed in a hot-house or warm window, where they must be moistened every morning.

Natural Flowers in Winter.—Choose some of the most perfect buds of the flowers you would preserve, such as are latest in blooming and ready to open. Cut them off with a pair of scissors or a knife, leaving to each, if possible, a piece of the stem about three inches long. Cover the end of the stem immediately with Spanish wax. When the buds are a little shrunk and withered, inclose and seal each of them separately in a piece of paper, perfectly clean and dry, and preserve them untouched in a box or drawer. Well-sized paper, or paper coated with wax, must be used. In winter, or at any other time when you would have the flowers bloom, take buds over night and cut off the ends of the stems sealed with Spanish wax, and place them in water wherein a little nitre or salt has been dissolved, and the buds will open the next day, the same as on their native bushes.

Snake-Bites.—In 900 cases of snake-bites in India, reported by an English surgeon, aqua ammonia was administered internally, and over 700 of them recovered, although the average time that had elapsed after the bite, before the ammonia was given, was 3½ hours; and in those who died, 4½. The dose in administering ammonia is 5 to 30 drops, well diluted with water.

Nose-Bleed.—Wet a small, soft linen cloth in water, roll it in a convenient size, dip and rub it in tannic acid in the dry powdered form, and pass it into the nostril as high up as will allow the tannic acid to reach the point where the blood is issuing. If the acid will not adhere to the cloth, make an ointment of it with a very little lard, and apply as before. Monsel's persulphate of iron is also highly recommended as a *styptic*, or astringent for causing contraction of the blood vessels. In case of severe nose-bleed it is well to soak the feet in hot water, to draw the blood away from the head. Compress the little artery in the side of the face leading to the nostril, just where it passes over the jaw bone.

To Relieve Asthma.—Wet blotting paper in a strong solution of saltpetre, dry it, and burn a piece three inches square on a plate in the sleeping room, and it will afford quick relief.

To Remove Warts.—Touch the warts with caustic potassa, or liquor potassa, or acetic acid. The operation is not painful, does not discolor the skin, and removes the warts in a short time, leaving the skin perfectly smooth.

PUZZLES OF HOUSEKEEPERS.

Clean brass ornaments by washing with roche alum boiled to a strong lye, afterward scouring with tripoli.

Extract grease from papered walls by washing lightly with spirits of wine.

Remove medicine stains from silver spoons with sulphuric acid, diluted somewhat.

Remove stains from the hands by washing in water containing a very little sulphuric acid.

To clean knives and forks rub with

sweet oil, let them lie forty-eight hours, then scour with powdered unslaked lime.

Sharpen light, thin-edged tools by putting them half an hour in water with one twentieth part of muriatic acid.

Remove strong vegetable odors from kitchen utensils by rinsing with powdered charcoal.

A spoonful of oxgall to a gallon of water will set the colors of almost any goods soaked in it previous to washing. A tea cup of lye in a pail of water will improve the color of black goods. Nankin should lie in lye before being washed, as it sets the color. A strong tea of common hay will preserve the color of French linen. Vinegar in the rinsing water for pink or green calicoes will brighten them, and soda answers the same end for both purple and blue. To bleach cotton cloth take one large spoonful of sal-soda and one pound of chloride of lime for thirty yards; dissolve in clear soft water; rinse the cloth thoroughly in cold soft water, so that it may not rot. That amount of cloth may be bleached in fourteen or fifteen minutes.

SUNDRY BRIEF ITEMS OF INTEREST.

In 1492 America was discovered.

In 1848 gold was found in California.

Invention of telescopes, 1590.

Elias Howe, Jr., invented sewing machines in 1846.

In 1839 envelopes came into use.

Steel pens first made in 1830.

The first watch was constructed in 1476.

First manufacture of sulphur matches in 1829.

Glass windows introduced into England in the eighth century.

First coaches introduced into England in 1569.

In 1545 needles of the modern style first came into use.

In 1527 Albert Durer first engraved on wood.

1559 saw knives introduced into England.

In the same year wheeled carriages were first used in France.

In 1588 the first newspaper appeared in England.

In 1629 the first printing press was brought to America.

The first newspaper advertisement appeared in 1652.

England sent the first steam engine to this continent in 1703.

The first steamboat in the United States ascended the Hudson in 1807.

Locomotive first used in the United States in 1830.

First horse railroad constructed in 1827.

In 1830 the first iron steamship was built.

Coal oil first used for illuminating purposes in 1836.

Looms introduced as a substitute for spinning wheels in 1776.

The velocity of a severe storm is 36 miles an hour; that of a hurricane, 80 miles an hour.

National ensign of the United States formally adopted by Congress in 1777.

A square acre is a trifle less than 209 feet each way.

Six hundred and forty acres make a square mile.

A "hand" (employed in measuring horses' height) is four inches.

A span is 10¾ inches.

Six hundred pounds make a barrel of rice.

One hundred and ninety-six pounds make a barrel of flour.

Two hundred pounds make a barrel of pork.

Fifty-six pounds make a firkin of butter.

The number of languages is 2,750.

The average duration of human life is 31 years.

PHYSICIANS' DIGESTION TABLE.

SHOWING THE TIME REQUIRED FOR THE DIGESTION OF THE ORDINARY ARTICLES OF FOOD.

SOUPS.

Chicken, 3 hours; Mutton, 3½ hours; Oyster, 3½ hours: vegetable, 4 hours.

FISH.

Bass, broiled, 3 hours; Codfish, boiled, 2 hours; Oysters, raw, 3 hours; Oysters, roasted, 3¼ hours; Oysters, stewed. 3½ hours; Salmon (fresh), boiled, 1¾ hours; Trout, fried, 1½ hours.

MEATS.

Beef, roasted, 3 hours; Beefsteak, broiled, 3 hours; Beef (corned, boiled, 4¼ hours; Lamb, roast, 2½ hours; Lamb, boiled, 3 hours; Meat, hashed, 2½ hours; Mutton, broiled, 3 hours; Mutton, roast, 3¼ hours; Pigs' feet, soused, 1 hour; Pork, roast, 5¼ hours; Pork, boiled, 4½ hours; Pork, fried, 4¼ hours; Pork, broiled, 3¼ hours; Sausage, fried, 4 hours; Veal, broiled, 4 hours; Veal, roast, 4½ hours.

POULTRY AND GAME.

Chicken, fricasseed, 3¾ hours; Duck (tame), roasted, 4 hours; Duck (wild), roasted, 4½ hours; Fowls (domestic), roasted or boiled, 4 hours; Goose (wild) roasted, 2½ hours; Goose (tame), roasted, 2½ hours; Turkey, boiled or roasted, 2½ hours; Venison, broiled or roasted, 1½ hours.

VEGETABLES.

Asparagus, boiled, 2½ hours; Beans (Lima), boiled, 2½ hours; Beans (string), boiled, 3 hours; Beans, baked (with pork), 4½ hours; Beets (young) boiled, 3¾ hours; Beets (old) boiled, 4 hours; Cabbage, raw, 2 hours; Cabbage, boiled, 4½ hours; Cauliflower, boiled, 2½ hours; Corn (green), boiled, 4 hours; Onions, boiled, 3 hours; Parsnips, boiled, 3 hours; Potatoes, boiled or baked, 3½ hours; Rice, boiled, 1 hour; Spinach, boiled, 2½ hours; Tomatoes, raw or stewed, 2½ hours; Turnips, boiled, 3½ hours.

BREAD, EGGS, MILK, ETC.

Bread, corn, 3¼ hours; Bread, wheat, 3½ hours; Eggs, raw, 2 hours; Cheese, 3½ hours; Custard, 2¾ hours; Eggs, soft-boiled, 3 hours; Eggs, hard-boiled or fried, 3½ hours; Gelatine, 2½ hours; Tapioca, 2 hours.

SUSTAINING POWER OF ICE.

The sustaining power of ice at various degrees of thickness is given in the following paragraphs:

At a thickness of two inches, will support a man.

At a thickness of four inches, will support man on horseback.

At a thickness of six inches, will support teams with moderate loads.

At a thickness of eight inches, will support heavy loads.

At a thickness of ten inches, it will support 1,000 pounds to the square foot.

Principal Nations of the World, With Their Population, Area, Form of Government, Religion, and Present Ruler.

Countries.	Capitals.	Population.	Area square miles.	Inhabitants to square mile.	Prevailing Religion.	Government.	Ruler or Head.	Title.	Public debt. (dollars).
Argentine Republic	Buenos Ayres	2,400,000	827,177	2.90	Catholic	Republic	Julio A. Roca	President	$ 57,068,949
Austria-Hungary	Vienna	37,741,413	240,415	156.98	Catholic	Monarchy	Franz Joseph I	Emperor	1,582,322,008
Australia	Seven Capitals	2,850,000	2,983,396	.97	Protestant	Colonies		Governors	462,760,515
Belgium	Brussels	5,476,668	11,373	481.71	Catholic	Monarchy	Leopold II	King	351,967,293
Bolivia	La Paz	2,080,000	500,740	4.51	Catholic	Republic	Nicolas Campero	President	30,000,000
Brazil	Rio de Janeiro	10,108,291	3,218,166	3.14	Catholic	Monarchy	Pedro II. Alcántara	Emperor	407,716,027
Canada (Dominion)	Ottawa	4,352,080	3,204,381	1.35	Protestant	Self-gov'd col'ny	Marquis of Lansdowne	Governor-General	199,125,323
Ceylon	Colombo	2,758,166	24,702	111.65	Buddhist	Colony		Governor	6,650,000
Chili	Santiago	2,400,396	124,084	19.34	Catholic	Republic	Domingo Santa Maria	President	77,654,298
Chinese Empire	Pekin	400,000,000	4,500,107	95.31	Buddhist	Empire	Kwong Shu	Emperor	64,500,000
Colombia, U. S. of	Bogota	2,951,323	320,678	9.20	Catholic	Republic	R. Nuñez	President	19,971,219
Denmark	Copenhagen	1,969,454	14,784	133.21	Protestant	Monarchy	Christian IX	King	46,798,190
Ecuador	Quito	1,146,000	248,312	4.61	Catholic	Republic	José de Vintimilla	President	18,350,400
Egypt (Turkish depen'cy)	Cairo	17,419,980	1,152,048	15.19	Mohammedan	Province	Tewfik Pasha	Khedive	411,820,700
France	Paris	36,905,788	204,030	180.88	Catholic	Republic	François P. Jules Grévy	President	3,700,800,700
Germany	Berlin	45,194,172	208,624	216.62	Protestant	Empire	Wilhelm I	Emperor	1,100,000,000
Great Britain and Ireland	London	35,246,633	121,571	289.92	Protestant	Monarchy	Victoria I	Queen, Emp. India	3,843,518,400
Greece	Athens	1,679,775	20,018	83.91	Greek Church	Monarchy	Georgios I	King	58,572,730
India (British)	Calcuttta	252,541,210	810,542	311.57	Hindoo	Monarchy	George F. S. Robinson	Viceroy	754,979,810
Italy	Rome	28,209,620	114,380	246.63	Catholic	Monarchy	Humbert I	King	2,042,000,000
Japan	Yeddo	34,338,404	146,568	234.28	Buddhist	Monarchy	Mutsu Hito	Mikado	388,721,778
Mexico	Mexico	9,389,461	741,598	12.66	Catholic	Republic	Porfirio Diaz	President	144,953,785
Morocco	Morocco	6,370,000	313,560	20.31	Mohammedan	Sultanate	Muley-Hassan	Sultan	
Netherlands	The Hague	3,981,887	12,727	312.86	Protestant	Monarchy	Wilhelm III	King	376,908,500
Norway	Christiana	1,806,900	122,823	14.71	Protestant	Monarchy	Oscar II	King	24,705,000
Paraguay	Asuncion	293,844	91,980	3.19	Catholic	Republic	Gen. B. Caballero	President	12,098,417
Persia	Teheran	7,000,000	636,265	11.00	Mohammedan	Monarchy	Nasr-ed-deen	Shah	No debt.
Peru	Lima	3,050,000	72,413	42.11	Catholic	Republic	Montero (acting)	President	254,000,000
Portugal	Lisbon	4,348,551	34,596	125.69	Catholic	Monarchy	Luis I	King	387,659,525
Russian Empire	St. Petersburg	82,330,864	8,138,541	10.11	Greek Church	Empire	Alexander III	Emperor	2,081,417,802
Roumania	Bucharest	5,376,000	50,159	107.17	Greek Church	Monarchy	Karl I	King	114,210,075
Servia	Belgrade	1,589,650	18,781	84.64	Greek Church	Monarchy	Milan IV., Obrenovic	Prince	29,248,000
Siam	Bangkok	9,750,000	280,564	20.49	Buddhist	Monarchy		King	
Spain	Madrid	16,333,293	193,171	84.55	Catholic	Monarchy	Alfonso XII	King	2,504,571,684
Sweden	Stockholm	4,531,863	170,927	26.51	Protestant	Monarchy	Oscar II	King	62,196,184
Switzerland	Berne	2,831,787	15,981	177.10	Protestant	Republic	Numa Droz	President	6,120,780
Turkey	Constantinople	25,036,480	860,222	29.10	Mohammedan	Monarchy	Abdul-Hamed Khan	Sultan	1,289,565,600
Uruguay	Montevideo	447,000	72,151	6.19	Catholic	Republic	F. A. Vidal	President	47,861,042
United States	Washington	50,155,783	3,602,990	13.92	Protestant	Republic	Grover Cleveland	President	1,800,000,000
Venezuela	Caracas	1,784,197	439,119	4.06	Catholic	Republic	Guzman Blanco	President	67,309,990

OUR COUNTRY'S CAPITAL.

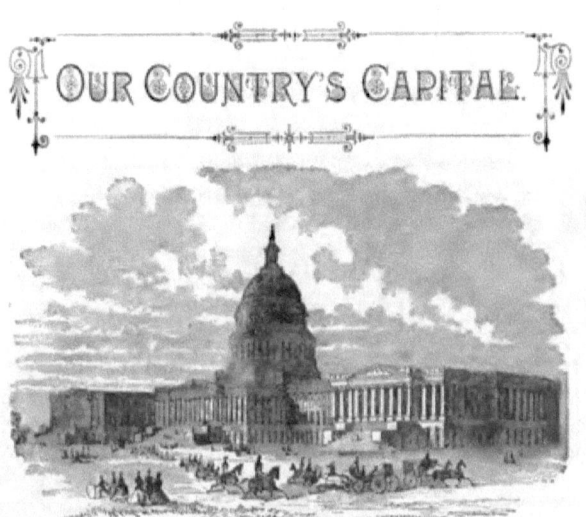

THE CAPITOL AT WASHINGTON.

WASHINGTON City, the capital of the United States, occupies a central position in the District of Columbia, on the left bank of the Potomac, 105 miles from its mouth. The site was selected by Washington himself, whose choice was ratified by Act of Congress in 1790.

The city is laid out upon a somewhat unique plan. Its streets run parallel with the meridian, or at right angles with it, while a number of avenues intersect these in diagonal directions. The main street is known as Pennsylvania Avenue, and extends from the Capitol to the White House, which are about a mile apart, and which are themselves the centers around which several of the broad diagonal avenues radiate. The streets are from 70 to 110 feet in width, and the avenues from 130 to 160 feet. The city, although it has become one of the largest in the country, with a population, in 1880, of 147,300, is laid out on so grand à scale that it will be many years before all the streets are lined with buildings. It has acquired the name of the "City of Magnificent Distances." It is said that Washington in his early days, and being before he dreamed of the august destiny and glorious career which awaited him, predicted that somewhere in that vicinity would one day stand a great city, and time is rapidly developing the fulfillment of that youthful dream of the saviour of his country.

PUBLIC BUILDINGS.

THE building of the greatest importance in Washington, if not in America, is the NATIONAL CAPITOL. It is situated on an elevation known as Capitol Hill, a mile east of the Potomac. The building faces to the east, and before it extends a wide plaza, used for reviews and for some of the inauguration ceremonies.

The first building on this site was commenced in 1793, General Washington laying the corner stone, but was destroyed by fire during the British occupancy of the city in 1814. The present edifice was commenced in 1821, its corner stone being laid by Daniel Webster, then Secretary of State. It consisted at first of what is now called the central building, but two wings were added in 1851. The cost of this splendid structure has been about $15,000,000 up to the present time. Its entire length is 750 feet. The central building is of freestone, whitened; it is approached by a flight of steps, on which stand statues of the discovery and first settlement of America. A portico, supported on lofty Corinthian columns, extends across the front of this portion of the building, in front of which stands a colossal statue of Washington. The building is surmounted by a lofty iron dome, on whose summit stands a bronze statue of Liberty, also of colossal size, being twenty feet in height. The height to the top of this figure is 307½ feet, being 36 feet less than that of St. Peter's at Rome.

Underneath the dome, in the interior of the building, is the Rotunda, an enormous hall, 96 feet in diameter and 168 feet in height. Over its doors are marble bas-reliefs, representing scenes in American history; and on its walls hang pictures of historical interest. Adjoining the Rotunda is the famous Library of Congress, which occupies three large halls with fire-proof walls and shelving. It contains more than 525,000 books and pamphlets, and about 15,000 are annually added to its numbers.

To the north of the Rotunda extends the Senate wing of the building. The Senate Chamber itself is rectangular in form, being 114 feet long, 82 feet wide, and 36 feet high. The ceiling is of cast-iron, paneled with richly ornamented stained glass skylights. Galleries capable of seating more than 1,000 persons surround the hall, to which the visitor ascends by spacious staircases of white and colored marble. Adjoining this chamber are reception rooms, retiring rooms for senators, etc., etc., all furnished with great magnificence, with walls and columns of white and red marble, and the ceilings frescoed and gilded.

Hall of Representatives.—This is in the opposite wing of the building. It is of fine proportions, and is richly decorated. It is 139 feet long and 93 feet wide. Spacious galleries surround is for the diplomatic corps, the public and the reporters for the press, capable of seating 1,200 persons. The roof is similar to that of the Senate Chamber, and on its glass panels are painted the arms of the States.

The Executive Mansion.—This building, known as the White House, is constructed of whitened sandstone, in the style of architecture called Ionic. It is 170 feet long. Its main entrance is through a portico supported by columns, on the north side of the building; on the south side a semi-circular portico overlooks the Potomac. On the ground floor are the public rooms, consisting of the East Room, the Blue Room, the Green Room and the State Dining Room. The first named is adorned with portraits of former presidents and is sumptuously furnished, its floor being covered by a Turkish carpet presented to the Government by the Sultan. On the upper floor are the executive offices and the private apartments. Presidential levees, to which the public are admitted, are held frequently during the congressional sessions.

Smithsonian Institute.—This is one of the most important and interesting of the public buildings. It is of red sandstone, and ornamented by seven towers at its extremities. It was erected with money bequeathed to the United States by James Smithson, a natural son of the Duke of Northumberland, at a cost of $450,000. It contains very valuable and extensive collections of minerals, animals, skeletons, shells, costumes, weapons, medals, fossils and photographs. The building is surrounded by spacious and well-kept grounds.

Department Buildings.—These are huge piles of marble, granite, or sandstone. Those of special interest are the Treasury, the State, War and Navy Department and the Patent Office. Of these, the Treasury is the largest, being 589 feet long, and 300 feet wide. The north and south porticos and eastern portion are supported by immense columns, 31 feet in height, and 4 feet in diameter. The north part opens upon a tesselated plateau containing a fine fountain, and the south portico commands a view over beautiful gardens of the Potomac. The stair-cases and offices are lined with marbles and richly decorated. To most visitors, however, the most interesting portions of the building are the marble Cash Room and the Gold Vaults with their thousands of millions of dollars, so readily seen, yet so difficult to reach!

State, War and Navy Departments.—The building occupied by these departments is one of the most beautiful specimens of architecture in the United States. It is built of granite, and is believed to be absolutely fire-proof. Its length is 567 feet, its width 342 feet, and its cost was $5,000,000. The Hall of the Secretary of State, the Ambassadors' Hall and the Library, are sumptuous apartments.

Patent Office.—This is also a beautiful piece of architectural work—perhaps it is, architecturally considered, the most perfect in the city. It is built of white marble and sandstone. Here are deposited models of every patent issued. The Model Rooms are filled with objects of the greatest interest, inclosed in cases, the contents of each case being described on a label attached. The original Declaration of Independence may be seen here, and various interesting historical relics, originally belonging to Washington, Lincoln, and other patriots.

WASHINGTON MONUMENT.

THIS stupendous work was commenced in 1848 and completed in 1884, although work upon it has been suspended from time to time. The suspension has been due, sometimes, to lack of funds, and again because the foundations were found to be insecure. Its design is a circular temple, from which springs a lofty shaft in the shape of an obelisk, the whole structure reaching a height of 557 feet. The shaft is of Maine granite, faced with white. The interior contains various stones presented by foreign powers, as well as by the different States and by distinguished American societies. Some of the blocks bear inscriptions and are richly ornamented with carving. This monument, which has been called "earth's greatest cenotaph," is the loftiest structure in the world, towering far above the Capitol, and even exceeding in altitude, by 69 feet, the great Pyramid of Cheops in Egypt. It is intended that an elevator, as well as a spiral staircase, shall be used for ascent, and that the interior of the shaft shall be brilliantly illuminated, as the only natural light admitted will be through star-shaped windows at the top. The prospect from the top is sublime beyond conception. On the west, the range of vision extends to the Alleghanies; on the south, across the blue waters of Chesapeake Bay to the Atlantic; and on the north and east, far over the fertile valleys of Maryland and Pennsylvania.

PARKS AND STREETS.

NO description of Washington could pretend to be complete which failed to include some mention of its parks and statues. The squares are numerous and beautiful, the largest covering an area of nineteen acres. They not only beautify the city and please the eye, but also serve as delightful resting spots for tired pedestrians and charming play grounds for whole troops of laughing children. Almost all of these parks are adorned with statues of persons famous in American history, among whom might be named Lafayette, Greene, Scott, Lincoln, and many of the heroes of the Civil War. Besides the parks, another feature which tends greatly to beautify the city should be noticed. On the majority of the streets, the houses stand from forty to fifty feet back from the curbstone, each house having nearly twenty feet of garden in front of it. The result is, that in the vernal season Washington is dotted by innumerable gardens filled with the choicest of Southern flowers.

POPULATION—SOCIETY.

PROBABLY no city on the American continent has a population of so cosmopolitan a character as Washington. Hither flock people from all climes and countries, whose interests and tastes are as diverse as their habits and civilization. The rosy-faced, blonde-haired European from the steppes of Northern Russia is jostled by the tawny-skinned, black-browed South American; the delicate features of the Caucasian present a daily contrast to the thick lips and high cheek-bones of the native African; while the polished Parisian learns new lessons in life from the "cow-boy" of our Western plains. In addition to its cosmopolitan character, the population of Washington may be fairly characterized as *migratory*. The number of "old settlers" is comparatively small, and even the "oldest inhabitant" will hardly strain his conscience by telling you stories of his personal recollections of General Jackson. A very large majority of Washingtonians are office-*holders*, and a considerable percentage of the remainder are office-*seekers*, known in Washington as "tide-waiters." The advent of a new political party, or even of a new administration, or the assembling of a new congress, renders necessary very material alterations in the directory.

Washington society is of every grade, and no variety of social entertainment can be imagined which cannot be found there, from the "state dinner" with its distinguished guests, its elaborate *menu*, and its gorgeous appointments, to the far humbler, but perhaps equally happy, "tea" given in the quiet home of the department lady-clerk, who thinks herself rich on an income of $75 per month. In a word, whatever may be your intellectual tastes, or financial circumstances, or religious creed, or social standing, you may find in some one of the many *strata* of Washington society a congenial circle. No capital of the New World can vie with it in gayety during what is known as "the season," as none can surpass it in beauty.

Art and nature vie with each other in affording a situation and surroundings worthy of the highest ambition of the capital for the future, and on so generous and noble a plan have the improvements of the naturally picturesque site been conducted, that it is difficult to decide which of the two has most contributed to the imposing *coup d'oeil* which the Washington of to-day presents.

More than half a century ago a distinguished writer penned these lines, which are even more true to-day than when first written: "The Nation has founded a city which bears and will transmit to posterity the name of Washington and his renown. It is a living, intelligent monument of his glory, and will reflect, as it grows in wealth and splendor, the inestimable consequences resulting to the country from his martial qualities and patriotic virtues."

LIST of State and Territorial Capitals, with the Salaries and Length of Terms of the Governors.

I.—STATES.

State.	Capital.	Salary of Governor.	Governor's Term of Office.	State.	Capital.	Salary of Governor.	Governor's Term of Office.
Alabama	Montgomery	$3,000	2 years	Missouri	Jefferson City	$5,000	4 years
Arkansas	Little Rock	3,000	2 "	Nebraska	Lincoln	2,500	2 "
California	Sacramento	6,000	4 "	Nevada	Carson City	5,000	4 "
Colorado	Denver	5,000	2 "	New Hampshire	Concord	1,000	2 "
Connecticut	Hartford	2,000	2 "	New Jersey	Trenton	5,000	3 "
Delaware	Dover	2,000	4 "	New York	Albany	10,000	3 "
Florida	Tallahassee	3,500	4 "	North Carolina	Raleigh	3,0 0	4 "
Georgia	Atlanta	3,000	2 "	Ohio	Columbus	4,000	2 "
Illinois	Springfield	6,000	4 "	Oregon	Salem	1,500	4 "
Indiana	Indianapolis	5,000	4 "	Pennsylvania	Harrisburgh	10,0 0	4 "
Iowa	Des Moines	3,000	2 "	Rhode Island	Providence and Newport	1,000	1 "
Kansas	Topeka	3,000	2 "	South Carolina	Columbia	3 500	2 "
Kentucky	Frankfort	5,000	4 "	Tennessee	Nashville	4,000	2 "
Louisiana	Baton Rouge	4,000	4 "	Texas	Austin	4,000	2 "
Maine	Augusta	2,000	2 "	Vermont	Montpelier	1,000	2 "
Maryland	Annapolis	4,500	4 "	Virginia	Richmond	5,000	4 "
Massachusetts	Boston	4,000	1 "	West Virginia	Wheeling	2,700	4 "
Michigan	Lansing	1,000	2 "	Wisconsin	Madison	5,000	2 "
Minnesota	St. Paul	3,300	2 "				
Mississippi	Jackson	4,000	4 "				

II.—TERRITORIES.

Territories.	Capitals.	Salary of Governor.	Governor's Term of Office.	Territories.	Capitals.	Salary of Governor.	Governor's Term of Office.
Arizona	Prescott	$2,000	4 years	New Mexico	Santa Fé	$2,000	4 years
Dakota	Bismarck	2,000	4 "	Utah	Salt Lake City	2,000	4 "
Idaho	Boisé City	2,000	4 "	Washington	Olympia	2,000	4 "
Indian	Tehlequah	2,000	4 "	Wyoming	Cheyenne	2,000	4 "
Montana	Helena	2,000	4 "				

TABLE showing the length of the Longest and Shortest Day and Night in various Capitals of the World.

Time.	Amsterdam.	Berlin.	Boston.	Cairo.	Calcutta.	Cape Town.	Constantinople.	Copenhagen.	Dublin.	Edinburgh.
	H. M.	H. M.	H. M.	H. M.	H. M.	H. M.	H. M.	H. M.	H. M.	H. M.
Longest day	16 44	16 38	15 16	14 0	13 26	14 22	15 4	17 20	16 56	17 32
Longest night	16 27	16 20	15 2	13 41	13 18	14 22	14 48	17 6	16 42	17 10
Shortest day	7 33	7 40	8 58	10 19	10 42	9 38	9 12	6 54	7 18	6 50
Shortest night	7 16	7 22	8 44	10 0	10 34	9 38	8 56	6 40	7 4	6 28

Time.	London.	Madrid.	Naples.	Paris.	Panama.	Pekin.	Stockholm.	St. Petersburgh.	Vienna.	Washington.
	H. M.	H. M.	H. M.	H. M.	H. M.	H. M.	H. M.	H. M.	H. M.	H. M.
Longest day	16 23	15 0	15 3	16 6	12 36	14 58	18 30	18 44	15 58	14 52
Longest night	18 16	14 48	14 48	15 50	12 26	14 44	18 6	18 18	15 43	14 38
Shortest day	7 44	9 14	9 14	8 10	11 34	9 16	5 54	5 42	8 17	9 22
Shortest night	7 37	9 0	8 57	7 54	11 24	9 2	5 30	5 16	8 2	9 8

GEOGRAPHICAL TABLE

A Table Showing the Height of the Most Celebrated Buildings and Monuments of the World, Arranged According to their Altitude.

Name of Edifice.	Ht. Ft.	Location.	Name of Edifice.	Ht. Ft.	Location.
Washington Monument	555	Washing., D.C	Milan Cathedral	355	Milan, It.
Pyramid of Cheops	486	Egypt.	Notre Dame Cathedral	348	Munich, Bav.
Cathedral of Antwerp	476	Antwerp, Bel.	St. Mark's Church	328	Venice, It.
Strasbourg Cathedral	474	Strasb'rg, Gr.	Trinity Church	284	New York Cy.
Pyramid of Cephrenes	456	Egypt.	Asinelli Tower	272	Bologna, It.
St. Peter's Church	448	Rome, It.	Delhi Column	262	Delhi, India.
St. Martin's Church	411	Landshut, Gr.	Porcelain Tower	260	Nankin, China
Saulsbury Cathedral	400	Saulsb'y, Eng.	Notre Dame Cathedral	224	Paris, France.
Cremona Cathedral	396	Cremona, It.	Bunker Hill Monument	221	Boston, Mass.
Florence Cathedral	387	Florence, It.	Leaning Tower of Pisa	179	Pisa, It.
Church at Fribourg	386	Fribourg, Gr.	Washington Monument	175	Baltimore, Md
St. Paul's Church	365	London, Eng.	Vendome Column	152	Paris, France.
Seville Cathedral	360	Seville, Spain.	Trajan's Pillar	151	Rome, It.
Pyramid of Sakurah	356	Egypt.	Obelisk of Luxor	110	Paris, France.
Utrecht Cathedral	356	Utrecht, Hol.			

LENGTH OF SEAS.

Baltic Sea	Length 600 miles	Mediterranean Sea	Length 2,000 miles
Black Sea	" 932 "	Okhotsk Sea	" 600 "
Carribean Sea	" 1,800 "	Red Sea	" 1,400 "
Caspian Sea	" 640 "	Sea of Aral	" 250 "
China Sea	" 1,700 "	White Sea	" 450 "
Japan Sea	" 1,000 "		

Table Showing the Solid Contents of Boxes of Various Sizes, in Cubic Feet or Inches, with the Equivalent in Dry and Liquid Measure.

Dimensions of Box.	Solid Contents. Cubic In.	Equivalent.	Dimensions of Box.	Solid Contents. Cubic In.	Equivalent.
4 in. x 4 in. x 4⅕ in.	67⅕	1 quart.	16 in. x 16 in. x 8⅖ in.	2,150⅖	1 bushel.
8 in. x 4 in. x 4⅕ in.	134⅖	2 quarts ½ (gal)	16 in. x 16 in. x 12⅚ in.	3,285⅗	½ barrel (1½ bu)
8 in. x 8 in. x 4⅕ in.	268⅘	1 gallon.	24 in. x 16 in. x 16⅘ in.	6,451⅕	1 barrel (3 bu).
8 in. x 8⅖ in. x 8 in.	537⅗	1 peck.	4 ft. x 3$\frac{5}{12}$ ft. x 2⅓ ft.	36⅓ cu. ft.	1 ton of coal.
8 in. x 8⅖ in. x 16 in.	1,075⅕	2 pecks (½ bu).			

SYNONYMS.

SYNONYMS are words that have not the *same*, but *similar*, meaning. One word can seldom be explained otherwise than roughly by any other word in the same language. Even if two words are identical in meaning there is a constant tendency to differentiate their meaning, a process aptly termed by Coleridge as desynonymizing. No other language is more open to the charge of superfluity of words than the English, and yet rarely do synonyms, which in their literal sense signifiy words of precisely the same meaning, occur.

By synonyms, then, we mean that there are words which, with great and essential resemblances of meaning, have at the same time small, subordinate, and partial differences, these being such as either originally, on the ground of their etymology, inhered in them, or differences acquired by universal usage, or such as, though nearly latent, they were capable of receiving at the hands of wise masters of the tongue. Synonyms are neither on the one hand absolutely identical, nor on the other remotely related to one another. They are words more or less liable to confusion, but which ought not to be confounded.

The main source of synonyms in our language arises from modern English, being the result of a compromise between Norman-French and Anglo-Saxon, while to this may be added the words imported into our early literature by writers familiar with foreign tongues. And even in one race, such as the Anglo-Saxon, there was a coalescence of various tribes speaking different dialects. As an illustration of how English has enriched itself from various quarters we may instance these words, trick, device, finesse, artifice and stratagem, which are respectively from Anglo-Saxon, Italian, French, Latin and Greek.

As society advances from a simple to a complex state, and language as an instrument for the conveyance of thought becomes more and more an object of attention, it is felt to be a waste of resources to have more than one sign for one and the same object, and men feel that with a boundless world lying both without and within them, with an infinity of shades of thought and meaning, such extravagance as two signs for one object must be counterbalanced by a scantiness and straitness in another direction, and hence arises the desynonymizing process.

It will serve as a guide to the choice of synonym in numberless instances to know that of two words, the Anglo-Saxon is generally used in its plain, literal, primary meaning, and relates to the external world of sensation, while the Latin or Greek equivalent, is used in a secondary or figurative sense. The pure English word is concrete, the foreign term is abstract; the former is the language of primitive nature; the latter of the scientific world. Thus *shepherd*, the Anglo-Saxon word, is generally confined to its primary meaning as a keeper of sheep, while *pastor* is exclusively confined to its figurative sense of one who keeps the flock of God, and so in numberless other cases.

While the habit of nice discrimination in the use of words is valuable even for its intellectual training, it brings what is of more value, an increase of mental wealth in the ability to discern between things which really differ, but which we have hitherto confused in our minds, and we have made these distinctions permanently our own in the only way they can be made secure, that is, by assigning to each its own appropriate word and peculiar sign. What a help to the writing of a good English style is the ability instantly to choose from a list of words presented to the mind that one which expresses the exact shade of meaning we wish to give. When a writer says either more or less than he means, or has said something beside what his intention was, it shows a lack of dexterity in the employment of the instrument of language. Nor is this power of expressing exactly what we mean a mere elegant mental accomplishment; it is something far higher—it is nearly allied to morality, since it is closely connected with truthfulness. How much that is false has become current by the use of words carelessly or dishonestly employed. While one may sometimes feel tempted, like Shakspeare's clown, to say that "Words are grown so false, I am loath to prove reason with them," we cannot forego their employment, and this falseness arises rather from their abuse and not from their proper use. Learn to distinguish between words, for, as Hooker observes, "The mixture of those things by speech, which by nature are divided, is the mother of all error."

The natural way to distinguish the meaning of a word is by the method of induction. Thus we hear the word *oppression* repeated in a context so as to convey to our mind the idea of *violence;* then we hear it in another context and perceive that it does not exactly mean *violence*, but it seems now rather to suggest *injustice;* but again some further mention of the word makes it evident that while *oppression* is always *unjust*, yet it is not identical with *injustice*. If we are accustomed to live in society where words are correctly used, or if we read words by the best masters of English, in course of time we learn to reject incorrect notions of the word and arrive at its exact meaning. The process of rejection may technically be termed *elimination*. The whole process by which, by *introducing* the different instances in which a word occurs, we arrive at the meaning it has in every instance is called *induction*. Thus, if we say, "The tenant *oppressed* his landlord by defrauding him of his rent," we feel this is incorrect, as oppression can only be exercised by the superior on the inferior, by the strong on the weak. Then, again, if we say that, "The robber oppressed the traveler by robbing him of his purse," we see that this is incorrect because oppression denotes conduct more public and self-reliant than the violence of a robber who may at any time be punished by the law. Then, "The tyrant oppressed his steward by giving him a blow," is also incorrect as oppression implies systematic injustice, not a single isolated instance. Hence we can eliminate from the broad ideas of *injustice* as inherent in all *oppression*, all injustice that is (1) not practised by the strong against the weak; (2) public and self-reliant; (3) systematic. The residuum i. e., "injustice more or less open and systematic, practiced by the strong upon the weak," is a fair definition of *oppression*.

To illustrate how the list following should be used, should for instance the word *pride* be under consideration, it is well to make a list of the synonymous group, which is, vanity, conceit, arrogance, assurance, presumption, haughtiness and insolence, and ascertain first what is the common quality pervading all these synonyms, and second what are the special qualities in which *pride* differs from each of the others. This common quality is an exaggerated sense of one's own worth as compared with others; but *pride* differs from *vanity* in being more indifferent to the opinion of others; the *proud* man has a more solid foundation of merit than the *conceited* man; he is not so selfishly exacting as the *arrogant*; not so brutally unfeeling as the *insolent*; and far too dignified to be accused of *assurance.* He is too certain of his own merits to *presume* upon them, knowing that time will bring their acknowledgment without pushing, and the same feeling of merit will lead him to beware of the open contempt of others which the *haughty* affect. Hence from this analysis will flow a correct definition as follows: (1) *Pride* is a high opinion of one's own merits, or of something connected with one's self; (2) it is not pushing like *presumption*, nor brutal like *insolence*, nor openly contemptuous like *haughtiness*, nor influenced by a desire of admiration like *vanity*, etc.

We append below a full list of synonyms.

LIST OF SYNONYMS.

A

Abandon—relinquish, give up, desert, forsake, forego, yield, cede, surrender, resign, abdicate, leave, retire, withdraw from.
Abandoned—reprobate, profligate, forsaken.
Abase—degrade, humble, disgrace, lower, depress.
Abate—reduce, subside, diminish, lessen, decrease.
Abbreviate—curtail, compress, abridge, condense, epitomize, shorten, lessen, reduce.
Abettor—accomplice, aid, accessory.
Abhor—abominate, hate, detest, loathe.
Ability—capacity, power, talent, skill, means.
Able—capable, competent.
Abode—dwelling, habitation, residence.
Abominate—detest, hate, loathe, abhor.
Abridge—contract, curtail, diminish, lessen, shorten.
Abrogate—abolish, cancel, annul, repeal, revoke.
Abrupt—hasty, harsh, steep, rough, sudden, rugged, unceremonious.
Absent—Abstracted, heedless, inattentive.
Absorb—engulf, engross, imbibe, swallow.
Abstain—forbear, refrain, withhold.
Abstruse—difficult, hidden, obscure.
Absurd—foolish, preposterous, silly, ridiculous, unreasonable.
Abundant—ample, copious, plentiful.
Abusive—disgraceful, insolent, offensive, scurrilous.
Abyss—chasm, gulf.
Accede—agree, acquiesce, assent, comply, consent, yield.
Accept—admit, receive, take.
Acceptable—agreeable, grateful, welcome.
Accession—addition, augmentation, increase.
Accommodate—adapt, suit, adjust, serve, fit.
Accompany—attend, escort, wait on, go with.
Accomplice—abettor, ally, accessory, associate, assistant.
Accomplish—execute, effect, finish, achieve, fulfill, realize, complete.
Accordingly—agreeably, consequently, therefore, suitably.
Account—description, explanation, recital, narration.
Accumulate—amass, collect, gather, heap.
Accurate—correct, exact, nice, precise.
Accuse—arraign, asperse, detract, defame, impeach, calumniate, villify, censure.
Achieve—accomplish, realize, effect, complete, execute, fulfill.
Acknowledge—avow, confess, own, grant.
Acknowledgment—admission, avowal, confession, concession, recognition.
Acquaint—communicate, disclose, inform, make known.
Acquiesce—accede, assent, agree, comply, consent, yield.
Acquire—attain, obtain, gain, procure, win.
Acquirement—attainment, gain.
Acquit—clear, discharge, free, forgive, pardon.
Active—agile, busy, vigorous, brisk, quick, industrious, nimble, prompt.
Actual—real, positive, certain, genuine.
Actuate—move, impel, incite, rouse, instigate, animate, induce.
Acute—penetrating, pointed, keen, piercing, subtle, shrewd, sharp.
Adage—apothegm, aphorism, maxim, saying, proverb, axiom.
Adapt—accommodate, adjust, fit, suit.
Add—join, annex, increase.
Addition—accession, augmentation increase.
Address—ability, courtship, direction, utterance, skill, speech.
Address—accost, salute, harangue, speech, oration, direction, superscription, dexterity.
Adept—skillful, apt, quick, expert.
Adhere—attach, cleave, hold, stick.
Adherent—disciple, partisan, follower, upholder.
Adhesion—attachment, sticking, adherence, union.
Adjacent—adjoining, contiguous, near, close.
Adjourn—postpone, defer, delay, put off.
Adjust—accommodate, adapt, fit, settle, suit.
Administer—give, manage, dispense, supply, serve, execute.
Admiration—amazement, esteem, regard, wonder, surprise.
Admission—entrance, admittance, access, concession, initiation.
Admit—allow, concede, grant, permit, tolerate.
Admonition—advice, caution, counsel, reproof, warning.
Adore—revere, reverence, venerate, worship.
Adorn—deck, embellish, beautify, decorate, ornament.
Adroit—agile, clever, dexterous, skillful.
Adulterate—corrupt, defile, debase, pollute.
Advancement—improvement, furtherance, progression.

Advantage—benefit, good, profit, use.
Adventure—occurrence, incident, casualty, chance, contingency.
Adversary—opponent, enemy, antagonist.
Adverse—hostile, contrary, repugnant, unfortunate, opposed.
Advert—allude, notice, regard, turn.
Advertise—publish, proclaim, announce.
Advice—instruction, admonition, counsel.
Advise—admonish, consult, deliberate, consider.
Advocate—argue, defend, plead, support.
Affability—civility, courteousness, urbanity.
Affable—courteous, civil, pleasing, urbane.
Affair—business, concern, matter, transaction.
Affect—aim, assume, arrogate, move, pretend.
Affecting—feeling, pathetic, touching.
Affection—tenderness, love, kindness, fondness, attachment.
Affiliate—adopt, associate, initiate, receive.
Affinity—conformity, alliance, relationship, kindred, attraction.
Affirm—assert, aver, assure, protest, declare.
Affliction—sadness, sorrow, bereavement, calamity, distress, pain, grief, trouble, tribulation.
Affluence—opulence, wealth, riches, abundance, concourse, influx, plenty.
Afford—impart, grant, give, produce, spare, yield.
Affray—disturbance, broil, feud, fray, quarrel.
Affright—alarm, appall, frighten, terrify, shock, dismay, intimidate, dishearten.
Affront—insult, offend, provoke, outrage.
Afraid—fearful, timid, timorous, terrified.
Aged—old, elderly, senile, advanced in years.
Agent—deputy, factor, representative.
Aggravate—tantalize, provoke, exasperate, irritate.
Aggregate—accumulate, mass, collect, pile.
Agile—nimble, brisk, alert, lively, quick, active, sprightly.
Agitate—disturb, shake, move, discuss.
Agitation—trepidation, tremor, disturbance.
Agony—distress, pain, anguish, torture, suffering.
Agree—consent, assent, accede, concur, comply, acquiesce.
Agreeable—suitable, acceptable, pleasing, grateful.
Agreement—bargain, covenant, accordance, contract, concurrence, harmony.
Aid—assist, help, succor, relieve.
Aim—aspire, endeavor, level, strive, point.
Air—mien, look, manner, appearance, aspect.
Alarm—apprehension, terror, surprise, summons fright, fear, dread, consternation.
Alienate—withdraw, estrange, transfer.
Allay—soothe, mitigate, appease, assuage.
Allege—assert, advance, adduce, affirm.
Alleviate—mitigate, relieve, soothe, ease, lessen, diminish, abate, lighten.
Alliance—union, league, confederacy, coalition, combination.
Allot—assign, apportion, appoint, distribute.
Allowance—wages, salary, pay, stipend, grant, concession.
All to—very much, entirely, completely, altogether.
Allude—refer, intimate, hint, suggest.
Allure—decoy, attract, seduce, tempt, entice.
Alter—change, vary, modify, rearrange.
Altercation—difference, dispute, quarrel.
Always—continually, incessantly, consantly, ever, perpetually.
Amass—heap, pile, accumulate, collect, gather.
Amazement—surprise, astonishment, admiration, wonder.
Ambiguous—equivocal, doubtful, uncertain, obscure.
Amenable—answerable, responsible, accountable.
Amend—rectify, reform, mend, better, correct, improve.
Amends—restitution, restoration, recompense, reparation.
Amiable—kind, agreeable, obliging, charming, delightful, lovely.
Ample—abundant, large, copious, spacious, extended, plenteous.
Amusement—pastime, recreation, diversion, sport, entertainment.
Ancestors—progenitors, forefathers.
Anecdote—tale, story.
Angry—passionate, resentful, hot, hasty, irascible, wrathful, furious.
Anguish—distress, pain, agony, suffering.
Animate—urge, enliven, exhilarate, encourage, impel, cheer, incite, inspire.
Animation—life, spirits, gayety, buoyancy, vivacity, liveliness.
Animosity—enmity, hatred, hostility, malignity.
Annals—memoirs, anecdotes, chronicles, narrations.
Annex—attach, add, affix, subjoin.
Announce—proclaim, publish, advertise, declare.
Annul—cancel, destroy, revoke, repeal, abolish, annihilate.
Answer—reply, rejoinder, response.
Answerable—accountable, responsible, amenable.
Antagonist—foe, adversary, opponent, enemy.
Antecedent—foregoing, former, previous, anterior, prior, preceding.
Anterior—antecedent, previous, prior, former, foregoing.
Antipathy—aversion, dislike, detestation, abhorrence, hatred.
Antique—ancient, old, antiquated.
Anxiety—uneasiness, caution, care, perplexity, solicitude, disquietude.
Apathy—insensibility, indifference, unconcern, unfeelingness.
Aperture—cavity, hollow.
Aphorism—adage, maxim, apothegm, axiom, proverb, saying.
Apology—plea, excuse, defense.
Appall—daunt, dismay, reduce, depress, discourage.
Apparent—evident, visible, plain, clear, distinct.
Appeal—refer, invoke, call upon.
Appearance—aspect, air, manner, look, mien, semblance.
Appease—assuage, allay, soothe, pacify, calm, tranquilize.
Applaud—extol, praise, commend, approve.
Applause—acclamation, approval, shouting.
Appoint—provide, allot, constitute, fix, ordain, prescribe, depute, order.
Appraise—estimate, value.
Appreciate—value, esteem, prize, estimate.
Apprehension—suspicion, alarm, seizure, terror, fear, fright, dread.
Apprise—make known, acquaint, disclose, inform.
Approach—admittance, access, passage, avenue.
Approbation—approval, concurrence, confirmation consent, sanction.
Appropriate—set apart, assume, usurp.
Appropriate—adapted, exclusive, peculiar, suitable.
Approve—allow, applaud, commend, like, esteem.
Apt—fit, meet, quick, ready, prompt, liable.
Arbitrator—arbiter, referee, judge, umpire.
Archives—annals, records, registers, chronicles.

Ardent—eager, fervent, fiery, hot, passionate, vehement.
Arduous—difficult, trying, laborious, hard.
Argument—debate, dispute, proof, reason.
Arise—ascend, mount, rise, stand up.
Arraign—accuse, charge, impeach.
Arrange—class, adjust, dispose, place.
Arrogance—assumption, haughtiness, pride, presumption, self-conceit.
Artful—artificial, cunning, crafty, dexterous, deceitful.
Articulate—speak, utter, pronounce.
Artifice—stratagem, deceit, cheat, finesse, imposition, deception.
Assembly—assemblage, collection, group.
Associate—companion, friend, mate.
Atrocious—heinous, flagrant, flagitious.
Attitude—position, posture, gesture.
Attract—allure, charm, captivate, entice, win, draw.
Audacity—hardihood, impudence, effrontery, boldness.
Auspicious—favorable, fortunate, lucky, propitious, prosperous.
Austere—rigid, rigorous, stern, severe.
Authentic—genuine, authorized, true.
Authority—dominion, force, power, sway, influence, ascendancy.
Avarice—greed, covetousness, cupidity.
Averse—loath, reluctant, repugnant, unwilling, unfavorable, unfortunate.
Aversion—abhorrence, antipathy, detestation, dislike, repugnance.
Avidity—eagerness, greediness.
Avocation—occupation, profession, trade, employment, calling, office, business.
Avoid—shun, elude, eschew.
Avow—acknowledge, own, confess, recognize.
Awake—arouse, excite, provoke.
Awe—dread, fear, reverence.

B

Babbling—chattering, idle talk, prattling, loquacity.
Backward—unwilling, averse, loath, reluctant.
Baffle—disconcert, elude, confound, defeat, confuse.
Balance—equalize, adjust, settle, regulate, poise.
Banter—deride, jest, ridicule, taunt, rally.
Bare—naked, unadorned, stripped, destitute.
Bargain—buy, purchase, contract.
Base—low, vile, mean, evil.
Bashful—modest, diffident, shy, timid.
Basis—pedestal, base, foundation.
Bastard—illegitimate, spurious.
Battle—engagement, combat, fight.
Bear—suffer, undergo, carry, sustain, bring forth, support, endure, yield.
Beat—strike, overthrow, defeat, hit.
Beau—gallant, dandy, sweetheart, fop.
Beautiful—fine, handsome, pretty.
Beautify—decorate, ornament, embellish, adorn, deck.
Becoming—comely, decent, fit, graceful, suitable.
Beg—beseech, request, ask, crave, supplicate.
Begin—enter upon, originate, commence.
Beguile—mislead, amuse, impose upon, deceive.
Behavior—carriage, deportment, address, conduct.
Behold—observe, see, view.
Beholder—observer, spectator, looker on.
Belief—assent, conviction, confidence, certainty, faith, trust.
Below—beneath, under.
Bend—bow, distort, incline, lean, subdue.
Beneath—below, under.
Beneficent—helpful, benevolent, generous, bountiful, liberal, munificent.
Bent—crooked, awry, prepossession, curved, inclination.
Bequeath—devise, give by will.
Beseech—urge, beg, implore, solicit, supplicate, request, crave, entreat.
Bestow—grant, confer, present, give.
Better—improve, ameliorate, reform, mend.
Bias—warp, prepossession, bent, prejudice.
Blame—inculpate, reprove, upbraid, condemn, censure, reproach, reprehend.
Blameless—guiltless, innocent, spotless, faultless, unblemished, irreproachable.
Blast—split, wither up, desolate, destroy.
Blemish—flaw, defect, stain, fault, spot, speck.
Blend—mix, mingle, confound.
Bliss—happiness, felicity, beatitude, blessedness.
Blunt—dull, uncouth, brusque, insentient, abrupt.
Blunder—error, mistake.
Boaster—vaunter, blusterer, braggard, braggart.
Boasting—parade, ostentation, vaunting.
Boisterous—violent, vehement, furious, impetuous.
Bold—courageous, daring, insolent, impudent, intrepid, fearless, audacious.
Bondage—servitude, confinement, slavery, imprisonment.
Booty—plunder, spoil, prey.
Border—edge, side, verge, brink, brim, margin, rim.
Bore—penetrate, perforate, pierce.
Bound—define, circumscribe, confine, restrict, limit, terminate.
Bounty—liberality, beneficence, generosity, benevolence, munificence.
Brace—support, pair, couple.
Brave—bold, intrepid, fearless, undaunted, heroic, daring, courageous.
Breach—chasm, break, gap, opening.
Break—destroy, shatter, batter, demolish, tame, dissolve, crush, rend.
Breaker—covered rock, surge, wave, sandbank, billow.
Brief—short, epitomized, concise, summary, succinct, compendious.
Bright—lucid, glistening, resplendent, brilliant, glittering, clear, shining, sparkling, vivid.
Brilliancy—brightness, luster, radiance, splendor.
Brittle—crisp, frail, fragile.
Broad—far-reaching, wide, ample, extensive, large.
Broil—fight, affray, altercation, feud, quarrel.
Bruise—break, crush, squeeze, pound, compress.
Build—erect, establish, found, construct.
Bulk—magnitude, dimensions, greatness, extent, size, largeness.
Burden—load, cargo, weight, freight.
Burning—ardent, hot, scorching, fiery.
Burst—split, crack, rend, break.
Business—avocation, occupation, employment, trade, work, calling, profession.
Bustle—confusion, hurry, tumult, disorder.
But—notwithstanding, nevertheless, except, however, still, yet, save.
Butchery—havoc, carnage, massacre, slaughter.
Buy—procure, purchase, bargain, obtain.

C

Cabal—coalition, intrigue, plot, combination, league, conspiracy.
Cajole—fawn, wheedle, coax.
Calamity—mishap, misfortune, disaster, mischance.
Calculate—count, reckon, estimate, compute, number.
Call—subpœna, summon, name, cry, bid, invite, exclaim.
Calling—trade, employment, avocation, occupation, profession, business.
Calm—soothe, assuage, allay, appease, compose, tranquilize, quiet, peace, pacify.

Cancel—erase, revoke, destroy, annul, abolish, repeal.
Candid—frank, honest, ingenuous, open, artless.
Capable—able, skillful, fitted, qualified, competent.
Capacity—capability, talent, faculty, genius, ability.
Caprice—fancy, humor, whim, freak, notion.
Capricious—notional, whimsical, variable, fantastical, fickle, changeable.
Captivate—charm, fascinate, take prisoner, enslave, enchant, attract, enrapture.
Captivity—servitude, imprisonment, bondage, confinement.
Capture—prize, seizure.
Care—disquietude, management, worry, anxiety, concern, attention, regard, solicitude.
Careful—provident, circumspect, guarded prudent, cautious, solicitous, attentive.
Careless—inattentive, unconcerned, negligent, thoughtless, remiss, heedless.
Caress—fondle, soothe, endear, stroke, embrace.
Carnage—massacre, slaughter, butchery.
Carriage—deportment, walk, bearing, demeanor, manner, behavior, mien.
Carry—bear, convey, transport.
Case—predicament, condition, state, plight, situation.
Cast—throw, fling, direct, turn, hurl.
Casual—accidental, contingent, incidental.
Catch—capture, grip, snatch, lay hold of, seize, grasp.
Cause—origin, inducement, reason, motive, source.
Caution—solicitude, notice, advice, circumspection, care, admonition, warning.
Cautious—careful, wary, prudent, watchful, circumspect.
Cease—leave off, stop, desist, discontinue.
Celebrated—illustrious, renowned, famous, honored.
Celebrate—praise; commend, extol, perpetuate
Celerity—velocity, swiftness, fleetness, quickness, rapidity.
Censure—rebuke, reproach, stricture, blame, reprimand upbraid, condemnation.
Ceremony—rite, form, observance.
Certain—actual, real, manifest, sure, constant.
Chagrin—vexation; mortification, fretfulness.
Challenge—object, demand, except, claim, defy, accuse, call, dare.
Chance—Casual, accident, fortune, fate, fortuitous, hazard.
Change—alteration, vicissitude, variety, conversion, mutation.
Changeable—uncertain, unsteady, inconstant, mutable, fickle, variable.
Character—manner, quality, mark, description, reputation, cast, letter.
Charity—kindness, beneficence, benevolence, generosity, good-will, liberality.
Charm—fascinate, captivate, bewitch, enrapture, attract, delight,
Chasten—chastise, afflict, correct, punish.
Chasteness—purity, simplicity, continence, chastity.
Chastise—afflict, correct, punish.
Chattels—effects, movable goods.
Cheat—fraud, imposition, deception, deceit, stratagem.
Cheer—encourage, incite, exhilarate, gladden, comfort.
Cheerfulness—sprightliness, liveliness, jollity, comfort, gayety, mirth, gladness.
Cherish—help, nurture, foster, shelter, indulge, warm.
Chide—scold, reprimand, rebuke reprove.
Chiefly—mainly, especially, principally, particularly.
Childish—simple, puerile, young, trifling.
Childhood—infancy, minority.
Children—issue, offspring, progeny.
Choke—suffocate, smother, stifle.
Choice—selection, option, election.
Choose—pick, select, elect, prefer.
Circulate—spread, pass, bruit, diffuse, propagate.
Circumscribe—limit, inclose, confine, bound.
Circumstance—situation, event, condition, state, incident.
Circumspect—vigilant, watchful, prudent, wary, particular, cautious.
Circumstantial—minute, accidental, particular, incidental.
Civil—obliging, well-bred, polite, polished, urbane, affable, courteous, complaisant.
Civilization—refinement, culture.
Claim—demand, ask, right, pretension.
Clamor—outcry, cry, uproar, noise.
Clandestine—hidden, secret, private.
Class—division, rank, order, degree.
Cleansing—purging, purifying, cleaning.
Clear—obvious, apparent, free, pure, vivid.
Clearly—visibly, manifestly, lucidly, distinctly, obviously, plainly.
Clemency—mercy, kindness, lenity, mildness.
Clever—adroit, expert, skillful, ready.
Climb—mount, ascend, rise, scale.
Cling—hang, clasp, cleave, stick, hold.
Close—confined, shut, near, firm, concise, compact.
Clothes—apparel, habiliments, raiment, covering, attire, garment.
Clouded—overcast, sullen, obscured, variegated, gloomy, dark.
Clumsy—uncouth, unhandy, bungling, awkward.
Coadjutor—colleague, ally, assistant.
Coalition—conspiracy, union, combination.
Coarse—gross, vulgar, rude, rough, inelegant, unrefined.
Coax—fawn, wheedle, tease, flatter, cajole.
Coerce—force, compel, restrain.
Cognomen—name, appellation, denomination.
Coherent—consistent, tenacious, adhesive.
Coincide—agree, harmonize, concur.
Cold—unaffecting, shy, frigid, chill, reserved.
Colleague—ally, partner, associate, coadjutor.
Collected—composed, calm, unruffled, placid, cool, gathered.
Collection—gathering, group, assemblage, contribution.
Colloquy—conference, talk, dialogue.
Color—hue, tint, stain.
Combination—confederacy, conspiracy, coalition, union, league, alliance.
Comely—handsome, becoming, graceful, agreeable.
Comfort—solace, enliven, encourage, console.
Comfortless—wretched, desolate, forlorn.
Comic—funny, laughable, ridiculous, ludicrous.
Command—direction, order, precept, behest, injunction.
Commanding—dictatorial, imperious, authoritative, imperative.
Commence—begin, undertake, originate.
Commend—approve, laud, praise, applaud, extol, recommend.
Commensurate—sufficient, adequate, equal, proportionate.
Comment—utterance, elucidation, remark, observation, annotation, note, explanation, exposition.
Commiseration—compassion, feeling for, condolence, pity, sympathy.
Commission—authorize, empower, enable.
Commodious—fit, large, suitable, convenient
Commodity—goods, wares, merchandise.
Common—general, low, mean, frequent, usual, vulgar, ordinary.
Commotion—perturbation, confusion, tumult, disturbance.

Communicate—tell, impart, reveal, disclose, report, make known.
Communication—commerce, intercourse, conference.
Communion—union, fellowship, converse, intercourse.
Commute—barter, exchange.
Compact—close, solid, firm.
Companion—partner, ally, confederate, accomplice, friend, comrade, associate, chum.
Company—assembly, congregation, crew, band, corporation, association.
Compass—consummate, attain, encircle, enclose, environ, invest.
Compassion—commiseratiom, sympathy, pity, tenderness.
Compensation—amends, requital, remuneration, reward, pay, satisfaction.
Competent—skillful, suitable, effective, fitted, efficient, qualified, capable, able.
Competition—emulation, rivalry.
Complaining—bemoaning, bewailing, lamenting, repining, regretting.
Complaisant—affable, civil, courteous, agreeable, obliging.
Complete—accomplish, consumate, conclude, execute, effect, finish, fulfill.
Complex—complicate, intricate.
Compliment—flatter, extol, praise.
Comply—accede, agree, assent, consent, yield, acquiesce.
Composed—calm, quiet, put together.
Comprehend—appreciate, embrace, comprise, understand.
Compress—bind, condense, squeeze.
Compulsion—coercion, restraint, force.
Compunction—contrition, repentance, penitence, regret.
Compute—calculate, reckon, count, estimate.
Concede—admit, allow, yield, grant, deliver.
Conceal—cover, disguise, hide, secrete.
Conceit—fancy, vanity, pride, notion, imagination, freak.
Conception—idea, notion, perception, fancy.
Concern—affair, matter, business, care.
Concert—adjust, consult, contrive.
Conciliate—reconcile, propitiate.
Conclude—finish, close, terminate.
Conclusive—convincing, decisive.
Concord—agreement, amity, peace, union, harmony.
Concur—agree, coincide, approve, acquiesce.
Condemn—reproach, doom, sentence, blame.
Condense—shorten, contract, abbreviate.
Condescension—submission, humility, deference.
Condition—stipulation, situation, state, rank.
Condolence—sympathy, commiseration, compassion.
Conduct—behavior, deportment, management.
Confederate—associate, ally, accomplice.
Confer—grant, bestow, give.
Confess—admit, disclose, acknowledge, own.
Confide—trust, depend, rely, repose.
Confident—assured, bold, positive.
Confined—imprisoned, circumscribed, limited, contracted.
Confirm—strengthen, corroborate, establish.
Conform—comply, yield, submit.
Congruity—consistency, agreement.
Connected—joined, united, related.
Conquer—overcome, subdue, vanquish.
Consent—agree, assent, comply, yield, accede.
Consider—ponder, deliberate, reflect.
Consistent—agreeing, accordant.
Conspicuous—noted, prominent, illustrious, distinguished.
Contract—build, erect, frame, form, make.
Consume—absorb, waste, destroy.
Contagious—infectious, epidemic.
Contaminate—corrupt, defile, taint, poison, pollute.
Contemplate—muse, meditate, consider.
Contend—contest, vie, strive, argue, debate.
Contentment—happiness, satisfaction, gratification.
Continuation—duration, continuance.
Contract—shorten, curtail, reduce, abbreviate, condense, abridge.
Contrary—opposite, adverse, inimical.
Contrivance—invention, plan, scheme, device, means.
Controversy—debate, disputation, argument, debate.
Convenient—suitable, adapted, handy.
Convey—transport, bear, carry.
Convivial—sociable, agreeable, festal, social.
Copy—duplicate, specimen, model.
Correct—mend, rectify, better, reform.
Costly—valuable, precious, expensive.
Countenance—uphold, sanction, support, favor, encourage.
Couple—connect, join, unite.
Courage—heroism, firmness, valor, bravery, fearlessness.
Covering—hiding, concealing, sheltering, screening.
Coward—poltroon, dastard, sneak.
Crave—beg, supplicate, solicit, request, beseech, implore, entreat.
Crime—sin, evil, vice, wickedness, guilt.
Cross—splenetic, ill-tempered, petulant, fretful, peevish.
Cure—remedy, restore, heal.
Curse—imprecation, anathema, malediction.
Curtail—abridge, shorten, abbreviate, contract.
Custom—manner, usage, habit, practice.

D

Dainty—choice, delicate.
Dampness—humidity, wet, moisture.
Dark—dismal, dim, gloomy, obscure.
Dead—lifeless, inanimate, deceased, still.
Dealing—commerce, trade, traffic.
Debase—degrade, lower, humble, abase.
Decay—consumption, decline.
Decent—comely, seemly, fit, becoming.
Decisive—conclusive, convincing, ending.
Decline—reject, refuse, decay.
Decoy—seduce, tempt, allure, entice, inveigle.
Dedicate—consecrate, set apart, devote.
Deed—feat, action, exploit, achievement.
Defect—blemish, want, imperfection, flaw.
Defender—protector, advocate, vindicator, pleader.
Deference—veneration, regard, respect.
Deficient—imperfect, lacking, wanting.
Defraud—cheat, swindle, deceive, rob, track.
Degree—class, rank, station, position.
Delay—postpone, protract, prolong, defer, hinder.
Delighted—grateful, pleased, charmed, joyful, glad.
Delinquent—offender, criminal, culprit.
Delude—beguile, mislead, cheat, deceive.
Demand—claim, ask, require.
Demonstrate—manifest, prove, show, evince.
Denote—mark, imply, signify.
Dependence—trust, reliance, confidence.
Deportment—behavior, demeanor, conduct, carriage.
Deprive—depose, strip, divest, hinder, prevent.
Deputy—delegate, agent, representative.
Deride—laugh at, mock, banter, ridicule.
Description—relation, detail, explanation, account, recital, illustration, narration.
Design—project, intend, sketch, plan, scheme, purpose.
Desist—discontinue, stop, leave off, cease.

Despicable—mean, outrageous, contemptible, pitiful, vile, worthless.
Despotic—arbitrary, self-willed, absolute.
Destitute—bare, forlorn, forsaken, poor, scanty, needy.
Desultory—loose, hasty, slight, roving.
Detail—account, recital, tale, description, narration.
Detect—discover, find, convict.
Determined—concluded, ended, firm, resolute, immovable, decided, fixed.
Detestable—hateful, loathsome, abominable, execrable.
Detriment—hurt, damage, injury, prejudice, loss, inconvenience, disadvantage.
Deviate—digress, err, wander, stray, swerve.
Devote—give, dedicate, set apart, apply, consecrate.
Devout—holy, religious, pious, prayerful.
Dialect—language, tongue, speech.
Die—expire, wither, perish, depart, languish.
Different—various, unlike, diverse.
Diffident—modest, retiring, hesitating, bashful, distrustful, fearful.
Diligent—persevering, laborious, attentive, industrious, active, assiduous.
Direct—show, sway, regulate, manage, guide, conduct.
Direction—command, order, address, superscription.
Disagree—quarrel, dissent, differ, dispute, vary.
Disappoint—fail, defeat.
Disavow—disown, deny, disclaim, repudiate.
Discard—cast off, discharge, dismiss.
Disclose—discover, reveal, divulge, promulgate.
Discord—dissension, contention, inharmony.
Discretion—judgment, prudence.
Disdain—scorn, pride, contempt, haughtiness, arrogance.
Disgrace—debase, degrade, abase, dishonor.
Disgust—loathing, nausea, dislike, aversion.
Dishonor—shame, disgrace.
Dismiss—divest, discharge, discard.
Disperse—scatter, deal out, spread, dissipate, distribute.
Display—parade, show, exhibit, ostentation.
Displease—offend, anger, vex.
Dispose—regulate, adapt, order, arrange.
Disseminate—scatter, spread, propagate, circulate.
Dissertation—discourse, essay, treatise, disquisition.
Distaste—aversion, disgust, contempt, dislike, loathing, dissatisfaction.
Distinguish—perceive, see, know, discern, discriminate.
Distress—affliction, misery, agony, pain, sorrow, anguish, sadness, suffering, grief.
District—county, circuit, locality, province, section, tract, region, territory.
Divide—part, share, separate, distribute.
Divulge—impart, disclose, publish, reveal, communicate.
Doctrine—wisdom, dogma, belief, principle, precept.
Doleful—awful, dismal, piteous, sorrowful, woeful, rueful.
Drag—pull, draw, bring, haul.
Dread—fear, apprehension.
Dress—array, attire, vestments, garments, apparel.
Dumb—silent, mute, still, inarticulate.
Dutiful—submissive, respectful, obedient.
Dye—stain, color, tinge.

E

Earn—gain, win, make, obtain, acquire.
Ease—rest, repose, quiet.
Eccentric—strange, singular, odd.
Ecstacy—happiness, joy, delight, rapture, transport, enthusiasm, elevation.
Edifice—fabric, building, structure.
Efface—expunge, erase, obliterate, destroy, eradicate.
Efficient—competent, effective, able, capable, effectual.
Effort—endeavor, trial, attempt, exertion, essay.
Elevate—raise, lift, hoist, exalt.
Eligible—worthy, fit, capable, suitable.
Emanate—issue, flow, arise, spring, proceed.
Embarrass—trouble, perplex, distress, entangle, puzzle.
Emblem—symbol, figure, type.
Emergency—exigency, casualty, necessity.
Emotion—feeling, tremor, agitation, excitement.
Empower—enable, commission, delegate, authorize.
Enchant—beguile, enrapture, charm, captivate, bewitch, fascinate.
Encomium—eulogy, praise.
Encroach—trespass, intrude, infringe.
Endeavor—effort, aim, exertion, attempt.
Endurance—fortitude, submission, patience, resignation.
Enemy—foe, opponent, antagonist, adversary.
Enervate—unnerve, enfeeble, deteriorate, weaken, debilitate.
Enjoyment—happiness, joy, pleasure, gratification.
Enlarge—extend, increase, lengthen, widen.
Enough—ample, plenty, sufficient, abundance.
Enrapture—charm, fascinate, attract, captivate, enchant.
Enterprise—business, adventure, attempt, undertaking.
Entice—tempt, allure, seduce, decoy.
Entirely—perfectly, wholly, completely.
Envy—jealousy, suspicion, grudging.
Epidemical—contageous, pestilential, catching.
Equal—uniform, adequate, commensurate.
Eradicate—root out, extirpate, exterminate.
Erase—expunge, cancel, efface, obliterate.
Error—fault, blunder, mistake.
Escape—elope, pass, avoid, fly, evade, elude.
Esteem—prize, love, respect, value, regard, appreciate.
Eulogy—encomium, panegyric.
Evade—escape, elude, shun, avoid, prevaricate.
Even—smooth, equal, plain, uniform, level.
Evidence—proof, witness, deposition, testimony.
Evil—wicked, bad, sinful.
Exact—enjoin, extort, demand, extract.
Exalted—high, sublime, dignified, magnificent, raised, refined, elevated.
Example—precedent, copy, pattern.
Exceed—transcend, surpass, improve, outdo, excel.
Except—but, object, besides, unless.
Excite—provoke, irritate, arouse, incite, awaken, stimulate.
Excursion—jaunt, trip, tour, ramble.
Execrable—hateful, detestable, contemptible, abominable.
Exercise—exert, practice, carry on.
Exhilarate—inspire, cheer, animate, enliven.
Exigency—necessity, emergency.
Expectation—belief, anticipation, confidence, hope, trust.
Expedite—hurry, quicken, hasten, accelerate.
Expel—banish, exile, cast out.
Experience—knowledge, test, proof, experiment, trial.
Explain—show, elucidate, unfold.
Explicit—clear, plain, express, definite.
Explore—hunt, search, examine.
Extensive—comprehensive, wide, commodious, large.
Exterior—outside, outward, external.
External—outward, exterior.
Extravagant—profuse, lavish, wasteful, prodigal.

F

Fabricate—invent, feign, falsify, frame, forge.
Fact—incident, circumstance.
Faculty—ability, power, talent, gift.
Failing—weakness, fault, foible, frailty, miscarriage, imperfection, misfortune.
Faith—fidelity, credit, trust, belief.
Falsehood—falsity, lie, untruth, fiction, fabrication, falsification.
Familiar—intimate, free, unceremonious.
Fanciful—ideal, hypochondriacal, whimsical, capricious, fantastical, imaginative.
Far—remote, distant.
Fashion—form, style, sort, practice, mode, custom, way, manner.
Fastidious—disdainful, particular, squeamish.
Favor—civility, benefit, grace, support.
Favorable—propitious, suitable, auspicious.
Faultless—guiltless, innocent, spotless, blameless.
Fearful—dreadful, timorous, horrible, afraid, awful, terrible.
Feasible—plausible, reasonable, practicable.
Feeble—infirm, weak, frail.
Feign—frame, forge, fabricate, invent.
Fertile—fruitful, productive, prolific, abundant.
Fervor—vehemence, warmth, zeal, heat, ardor.
Fetter—shackle, bind, chain.
Fiction—invention, untruth, lie, fabrication.
Fiery—hot, vehement, fervent, passionate, ardent, impulsive.
Finesse—stratagem, trick, artifice.
Firm—ready, partnership, strong, sturdy, solid, steady, immovable.
Fitted—suited, competent, qualified, adapted.
Flag—droop, faint, pine, decline, languish.
Flavor—odor, taste, fragrance, savor.
Fleeting—transient, swift, temporary, transitory.
Flexible—pliable, plaint, supple.
Fluctuate—hesitate, vary, waver, change, vacillate.
Fondness—affection, tenderness, love, attachment.
Forsake—relinquish, leave, desert, abandon, quit, abdicate.
Forbear—refrain, spare, abstain, pause.
Force—oblige, restrain, compel.
Forebode—augur, foretell, betoken, presage, prognosticate.
Forego—give up, quit, resign.
Foreigner—stranger, alien.
Forfeiture—penalty, fine.
Forgive—absolve, excuse, remit, acquit, pardon.
Form—rite, ceremony, shape, observance.
Fortunate—lucky, prosperous, successful.
Forward—immodest, progressive, ready, presumptuous, confident, bold, ardent, eager.
Fragile—brittle, tender, weak, frail.
Frailty—weakness, foible, failing, unsteadiness, instability.
Fraternity—brotherhood, society.
Fraught—loaded, filled.
Freak—whim, fancy, caprice, humor.
Free—deliver, liberate, rescue, clear, enfranchise, affranchise.
Freely—liberally, frankly, unreservedly, cheerfully, spontaneously, unhesitatingly.
Fresh—new, modern, cool, recent, novel.
Fretful—captious, angry, peevish, petulant.
Fright—terror, panic, alarm, consternation.
Frighten—terrify, alarm, daunt, scare, intimidate, affright.
Frivolous—futile, petty, trivial, trifling.
Frugal—careful, prudent, saving, economical.
Frustrate—defeat, disappoint, foil, hinder, nullify.
Furious—impetuous, boisterous, violent, vehement.

G

Gain—obtain, profit, get, acquire, attain, win.
Gale—breeze, hurricane, storm, tempest.
Gallantry—valor, bravery, courage.
Gay—dashing, cheerful, showy, fine, merry, sprightly.
Generally—commonly, frequently, usually.
Genteel—polite, cultured, mannerly, refined, polished.
Gentle—tame, peaceable, mild, quiet, meek.
Germinate—sprout, vegetate, grow, bud, shoot.
Gesture—action, attitude, motion, posture.
Giddiness—flightiness, levity, lightness, volatility.
Give—impart, yield, consign, grant, confer, bestow.
Glance—look, glimpse, sight.
Glitter—glisten, radiate, shine, glare, sparkle.
Gloom—dark, melancholy, morose, sullen, sad, cloudy, dull, dim.
Graceful—comely, neat, becoming, genteel, elegant.
Grant—sell, yield, give, bestow, confer, cede, concede.
Grateful—thankful, pleasing, agreeable, delicious.
Grave—sedate, thoughtful, important, solemn, slow, serious.
Greediness—ravenousness, covetousness, eagerness, rapacity, voracity.
Grieve—bemoan, mourn, sorrow, lament, hurt, afflict.
Group—collection, assemblage, cluster.
Guarantee—vouch for, secure, warrant.
Guard—protect, watch, defend, shield.
Guest—visitant, stranger, visitor.
Guilty—depraved, debauched, sinful, criminal, wicked.

H

Habit—custom, habitude, guise.
Hale—strong, hearty, robust, sound.
Happiness—contentment, bliss, luck, felicity.
Harbinger—precursor, forerunner, messenger.
Hardened—unfeeling, callous, obdurate, insensible.
Hardly—scarcely, with difficulty, barely.
Harm—evil, mishap, injury, ill, hurt, misfortune, damage.
Harmony—unison, accordance, melody, concord, agreement.
Hasten—hurry, quicken, expedite, accelerate.
Hasty—rash, passionate, quick, angry, cursory.
Hate—dislike, abominate, loathe, abhor, detest, abjure.
Haughtiness—vanity, arrogance, self-conceit, pride, disdain.
Hazard—trial, peril, danger, venture, chance, risk.
Heal—cure, remedy, restore.
Hear—harken, overhear, watch, attend, listen.
Heaviness—sorrow, gravity, dejection, weight, gloom.
Heighten—raise, aggravate, improve, advance.
Heinous—wicked, atrocious, simple, flagrant.
Help—provide, support, success, serve, aid, relieve, assist.
Heroic—bold, courageous, intrepid, brave, noble, valiant, fearless.
Hesitate—demur, pause, stammer, doubt, falter, wait, scruple, delay.
Hideous—awful, grisly, grim, ghastly, frightful, horrible.
High—tall, lofty.
Hinder—stop, thwart, oppose, prevent, retard, interfere, obstruct, impede, embarrass.
Hollow—empty, vacant.

Honor—exalt, venerate, reverence, dignify, esteem, respect, adorn, revere.
Hopeless—dejected, despairing, desponding.
Hostile—contrary, opposite, warlike, repugnant, unfriendly.
House—domicile, quorum, dwelling, race, home, family, habitation.
However—notwithstanding, still, yet, but, nevertheless.
Huge—vast, enormous, immense.
Humanity—benevolence, benignity.
Hurry—expedite, hasten, precipitate.
Hypocrisy—pretense, deceit, dissimulation.

I

Idea—notion, perception, thought, conception, imagination.
Ignorant—untaught, illiterate, unlearned, unlettered, uninformed, unskilled.
Illusion—deception, mockery, falsity.
Imbecility—weakness, impotence, debility, infirmity, languor, feebleness.
Imitate—copy, ape, follow, mimic.
Immediately—directly, instantly.
Immense—vast, huge, enormous, prodigious, unlimited.
Impair—lessen, injure, decrease, weaken.
Impatient—eager, restless, hasty, uneasy.
Impede—delay, hinder, obstruct, retard.
Impediment—obstacle, hinderance, obstruction.
Impending—imminent, threatening.
Imperious—tyrannical, overbearing, lordly, haughty, domineering.
Impetuous—hasty, forcible, rough, vehement, violent, boisterous.
Imply—involve, mean, infer, denote, signify.
Importunity—solicitation.
Imprecation—anathema, curse, malediction, execration.
Impute—ascribe, attribute, charge.
Inactive—sluggish, lazy, idle, inert, slothful, drowsy.
Inattentive—remiss, negligent, dilatory, careless, heedless, thoughtless, inadvertent.
Incident—circumstance, event, contingency, occurrence, adventure.
Inclination—disposition, bent, prepossession.
Incompetent—unsuitable, inapt, inadequate, incapable, insufficient.
Increase—accession, addition, augmentation.
Indicate—show, reveal, point out, mark.
Indigence—penury, poverty, want, need.
Indiscretion—folly, injudiciousness, imprudence.
Indistinct—dark, confused, doubtful, ambiguous.
Inevitable—certain, unavoidable.
Inexpedient—unfit, inconvenient, unsuitable.
Infamous—outrageous, scandalous.
Inference—conclusion, deduction.
Infested—annoyed, disturbed, plagued, troubled.
Influence—persuasion, authority, sway, power, credit.
Infringe—invade, intrench, encroach, intrude.
Ingenuity—talent, capacity, skill, genius, invention.
Inherent—inbred, inborn, innate.
Iniquitous—nefarious, unjust, wicked, evil.
Injure—harm, deteriorate, hurt, impair, damage.
Innate—natural, inborn, inherent, imbued.
Inordinate—immoderate, irregular, excessive, intemperate.
Inquisitive—curious, prying, anxious, inquiring.
Insensibility—dullness, torpor, imperceptibility, apathy, indifference, stupidity.
Insignificant—worthless, unimportant, trivial, meaningless, inconsiderable.
Insinuate—suggest, hint, intimate.
Inspire—animate, suggest, exhilarate, enliven, invigorate, cheer.
Instill—infuse, sow, impiant.
Insufficient—inadequate, unable, incapable, unfit, incompetent, unsuitable.
Integrity—purity, honesty, truthfulness, probity, uprightness.
Intellect—understanding, talent, capacity, ability, genius.
Intemperate—immoderate, inordinate, excessive.
Intercede—interpose, mediate, interfere.
Intermission—vacation, interruption, cessation, rest, stop.
Interpose—mediate, intermeddle, intercede, interfere.
Interrogate—question, inquire, examine.
Intervening—coming between, intermediate, interposing.
Intoxication—infatuation, inebriety, drunkenness.
Intrepid—fearless, brave, daring, bold, valiant, undaunted, courageous.
Introductory—preliminary, previous, prefatory.
Intrust—confide, commit.
Invade—intrench, infringe, attack, enter, encroach.
Invalidate—weaken, overthrow, destroy, injure, nullify.
Invent—discover, devise, feign, fabricate, conceive, frame.
Investigation—research, search, scrutiny, examination, inquiry.
Invigorate—restore, fortify, strengthen.
Invite—call, summon, bid.
Irascible—irritable, angry, hot, hasty, fiery.
Irksome—troublesome, vexatious.
Irrational—silly, foolish, absurd, unreasonable.
Irregular—intemperate, disorderly, inordinate.
Irruption—invasion, opening, inroad.

J

Jade—harass, weary, tire, dispirit, wench.
Jealousy—envy, suspicion, emulation.
Jest—fun, joke, sport.
Jocund—joyful, lighthearted, mirthful, merry, vivacious, gay, sprightly, sportive.
Joke—rally, sport.
Journey—trip, voyage, tour.
Judgment—discernment, sagacity, intelligence, doom, decision, sentence, opinion, discrimination.
Justify—clear, maintain, defend, absolve, excuse.
Justness—correctness, propriety, equity, accuracy, exactness.

K

Keen—shrewd, sharp, acute, cutting, piercing, penetrating.
Keep—guard, sustain, hold, reserve, support, maintain, detain, retain.
Kind—bland, benignant, lenient, courteous, gentle, indulgent, compassionate, tender, affable.
Kind—sort, way, genus, species, manner, race, class.
Knavish—deceitful, dishonest.
Knowledge—perception, acquaintance, erudition, understanding, skill, learning.

L

Labor—toil, exert, drudge, strive.
Lack—want, need.
Language—tongue, speech, dialect, idiom.
Languid—weary, faint, dull, drooping, exhausted.

Lassitude—prostration, enervation, fatigue, languor, weariness.
Last—latest, end, ultimate, final, hindermost.
Latent—unseen, secret, hidden.
Laughable—droll, comical, ridiculous, mirthful.
Lazy—indolent, inactive, idle, inert, slothful.
League—alliance, confederacy.
Lean—waver, totter, incline, bend.
Leave—resign, relinquish, bequeath, abandon.
Lengthen—continue, protract, extend, draw out.
Lenity—clemency, mercy.
Let—allow, permit, hire, leave, suffer.
Level—plain, flat, even, smooth.
Liable—exposed, responsible, subject.
Liberate—free, deliver, release.
Lie—untruth, falsehood, fiction, fabrication, deception.
Life—briskness, vitality, being, energy, vivacity.
Lift—exalt, erect, raise, hoist, elevate.
Like—similar, resembling, uniform, probable.
Liking—inclination, fondness, affection, attachment.
Linger—tarry, lag, delay, wait, saunter, hesitate, loiter.
Listen—overhear, attend, hearken, hear.
Live—dwell, reside, subsist, abide, exist.
Load—weight, encumber, clog, burden.
Lodge—shelter, harbor, entertain, accommodate.
Loiter—lag, saunter, tarry, linger.
Long—desire, hanker.
Look—see, view, inspect, behold, appearance.
Loquacious—talkative, garrulous.
Lot—doom, fortune, share, fate, destiny, portion.
Loud—noisy, vehement, clamorous, turbulent, vociferous.
Lovely—attractive, beautiful, amiable, elegant, fine, handsome, charming, delightful.
Lover—wooer, suitor, beau.
Low—despicable, debased, humble, dejected, base, abject.
Lucky—successful, fortunate, prosperous.
Lunacy—derangement, mania, insanity, madness.
Luxuriant—exuberant, voluptuous, excessive, abundant.
Luxury—abundance, excess, elegance, profusion.

M

Magisterial—august, prosperous, stately, majestic, dignified.
Magnitude—bulk, size, greatness.
Majestic—august, stately, dignified.
Malice—grudge, spite, rancor, pique.
Mandate—order, charge, injunction, command.
Manifest—apparent, plain, open, clear, obvious, evident.
Margin—border, rim, brink, verge, edge, brim.
Mark—imprint, observe, show, brand, impress, stamp.
Martial—soldier-like, military, warlike.
Massive—ponderous, heavy, large, bulky.
Mature—complete, ripe, perfect.
Mean—sordid, niggardly, penurious, low, miserly, abject, despicable.
Meanwhile—meantime, intervening, interim.
Meddle—touch, interfere, interpose, interrupt.
Meditate—contemplate, muse.
Meek—soft, humble, gentle, mild.
Meeting—congregation, company, auditory, assembly.
Melody—harmony, concord, happiness, unison.
Memory—reminiscence, recollection, remembrance.
Merchant—tradesman, trader.
Merciless—hard-hearted, pitiless, cruel, unmerciful.
Merry—lively, gay, sprightly, sportive, cheerful, happy, vivacious, mirthful.
Metaphor—trope, symbol, emblem, allegory, similitude.
Mighty—great, potent, strong, powerful.
Mindful—heedful, attentive, regardful, observant.
Miracle—prodigy, marvel, wonder.
Mischief—harm, hurt, damage, misfortune, injury.
Misfortune—calamity, ill luck, harm, mishap, disaster.
Misuse—pervert, ill-treat, abuse, misapply.
Mix—mingle, blend, confound.
Model—pattern, mould, sample, copy, specimen.
Modern—recent, new, novel, fresh, late.
Modify—re-arrange, alter, moderate, change, extenuate.
Mollify—ease, soften, assuage, appease, moderate, mitigate.
Morose—gloomy, sour, forbidding, sullen, peevish.
Motive—incentive, cause, reason, principle.
Mourn—sorrow, grieve, bewail, lament, bemoan.
Multitude—crowd, throng, swarm.
Murmur—complain, repine.
Mutable—irresolute, wavering, changeable, fickle, unstable, inconstant, variable, unsteady.
Mutinous—turbulent, seditious, insubordinate.

N

Naked—simple, unclothed, uncovered, nude, exposed.
Narrative—account, tale, story.
Nasty—filthy, foul.
Nautical—marine, naval, maritime.
Near—adjoining, adjacent, close, contiguous.
Need—indigence, poverty, penury, want.
Nefarious—wicked, evil, unjust, wrong, iniquitous.
Nevertheless—however, yet, notwithstanding.
Nice—exact, particular, delicate.
Noble—grand, exalted, distinguished, great, elevated, illustrious.
Noted—notorious, eminent, renowned, celebrated, distinguished, conspicuous, illustrious.
Notion—sentiment, perception, thought, whim, conception, opinion, idea.
Notwithstanding—in spite of, yet, nevertheless, however.

O

Obdurate—inflexible, obstinate, impenitent, hardened, unfeeling, callous, insensible.
Object—subject, end, aim, purpose, oppose.
Oblige—engage, bind, force, gratify, coerce, favor, compel, please.
Obscure—abstruse, concealed, hidden, indistinct, dark, dim, uncertain, difficult.
Observant—regardful, attentive, watchful, mindful.
Obsolete—disused, worn out, antiquated, ancient, old, old-fashioned.
Obstinate—headstrong, resolute, stubborn.
Obtain—gain, get, win, procure, secure, acquire, earn.
Obviate—prevent, preclude, avoid.
Occasional—frequently casual.
Occupy—use, hold, keep, possess.
Odd—singular, eccentric, strange, uneven.
Offense—injury, crime, transgression, outrage, trespass, misdeed, wrong, insult.
Officious—busy, active, forward, intrusive, obtrusive.
Omen—presage, prognostic, sign.

Open—disclose, reveal, unlock, unravel.
Operation—agency, performance, action.
Opinion—belief, sentiment, notion, idea.
Opponent—antagonist, adversary, opposer, foe, enemy.
Opprobrious—reproachful, insulting, scurrilous, offensive, insolent, scandalous, abusive.
Option—choice, selection.
Opulence—affluence, wealth, riches.
Ordain—prescribe, invest, appoint, order.
Order—mandate, command, injunction, precept.
Ordinary—usual, common, general.
Original—primary, first, pristine, primitive.
Ostentation—show, boast, display, parade.
Outlive—survive.
Outward—extraneous, apparent, extrinsic.
Overbearing—repressive, haughty, lordly, impertinent.
Overflow—fill, inundate, abound, deluge.
Overwhelm—up-turn, subdue, crush, overthrow, overpower.

P

Pacify—soothe, still, calm, quiet, conciliate.
Pain—hurt, afflict, distress, torture, suffer, torment.
Pair—couple, brace, two.
Palpable—apparent, plain, perceptible, gross, discernible.
Pang—sorrow, torment, anguish, torture, agony, distress.
Parade—show, ostentation.
Pare—strip, peel.
Part—concern, portion, piece, share, action, division.
Particularly—chiefly, mainly, principally, distinctly, especially, specifically.
Partner—associate, coadjutor, accomplice, colleague.
Passionate—excitable, hot, angry, hasty, irascible.
Pathetic—affecting, moving, touching.
Patience—endurance, fortitude, resignation.
Pay—salary, wages, stipend.
Penalty—punishment, chastisement, fine, pain, forfeiture.
Penitence—repentance, remorse, compunction, contrition.
Penury—poverty, need, want, distress, indigence.
Perceive—observe, discern, distinguish.
Perfect—done, complete, finished.
Perforate—bore, penetrate, pierce.
Perfume—smell, odor, scent, fragrance, exhalation.
Perish—die, decay.
Permit—tolerate, yield, allow, consent, suffer, admit.
Perpetrate.—commit.
Perplex—bewilder, confuse, involve, annoy, puzzle, harass, molest, entangle, embarrass.
Persist—pursue, prosecute.
Persuade—prevail upon, influence, induce, exhort, urge, entice.
Pestilential—epidemical, contagious, infectious, mischevious, destructive.
Petulant—peevish, cross, captious, fretful.
Pious—religious, devout, godly, spiritual, holy.
Pique—spite, grudge, malice, rancor, dislike, offense.
Place—post, site, ground, position, spot.
Plague—perplex, embarrass, annoy, tantalize, vex, importune, torment.
Plan—scheme, contrivance, device, design, project, stratagem, arrangement.
Play—game, sport.
Please—delight, satisfy, humor, gratify.
Pledge—hostage, deposit, security, pawn, earnest.
Pliant—limber, bending, lithe, yielding, pliable, supple.
Plight—state, condition, situation, case, conjecture.
Polite—well-bred, civil, courteous, polished, affable, genteel, refined.
Politic—careful, prudent, wise, artful, cunning.
Pompous—stately, showy, ostentatious, lofty, dignified.
Portion—part, share, piece, division, quantity, fortune.
Possess—hold, have, keep, occupy, enjoy.
Posture—gesture, action, figure, position, attitude.
Poverty—need, suffering, want, penury, indigence.
Practice—habit, custom, manner, use, form, style.
Prayer—suit request, entreaty, application, supplication.
Precedence—superiority, priority, preference.
Precept—rule, injunction, maxim, principle, law mandate, command.
Precious—costly, expensive, valuable, choice, rare.
Precise—exact, accurate, nice, careful, particular.
Predicament—position, plight, condition, situation.
Predominant—controlling, supreme, prevailing, prevalent.
Preference—priority, advancement, choice.
Prejudice—injury, disadvantage, bias, hurt.
Prepare—qualify, make ready, equip, arrange, fit.
Prerogative—immunity, privilege.
Preserve—maintain, save, uphold, protect, spare.
Presume—suppose, believe, guess, think, surmise.
Pretext—pretension, excuse, pretense.
Pretty—agreeable, lovely, fine, beautiful.
Prevent—hinder, obstruct, impede, preclude, obviate.
Price—expense, worth, cost, value, charge.
Pride—vanity, conceit, arrogance, assurance, presumption, haughtiness, insolence.
Primary—original, pristine, first, elemental.
Print—mark, impress, stamp.
Priority—precedence, pre-eminence, preference.
Privacy—solitude, loneliness, seclusion, secrecy.
Prize—esteem, value, reward.
Probity—uprightness, integrity, reliability, veracity.
Proclaim—publish, tell, declare, announce, advertise.
Procure—acquire, gain, obtain, get.
Prodigious—astonishing, large, great, vast, enormous.
Profession—employment, calling, vocation, work, business.
Profit—advantage, benefit, gain, lucre.
Profuse—wasteful, extravagant, lavish, prodigal.
Prohibit—proscribe, interdict, forbid.
Prolific—fertile, fruitful, productive.
Prolong—delay, extend, protract, postpone, retard.
Promise—engagement, agreement, pledge, word, obligation.
Prompt—ready, quick, assiduous, active.
Proof—argument, evidence, testimony.
Propensity—inclination, tendency, proneness, liking.
Propitious—auspicious, favorable.
Proportionate—adequate, commensurate, equal.
Proprietor—owner, master, possessor.
Prospect—landscape, view, survey.
Prosperous—lucky, successful, fortunate, flourishing.
Protract—retard, prolong, delay, postpone, withhold.
Prove—evince, manifest, demonstrate.
Provide—furnish, prepare, procure, supply.

Proviso—condition, stipulation, requirement.
Prudence—carefulness, discretion, judgment, wisdom.
Prying—inquisitive, curious.
Puerile—boyish, childish, infantile, juvenile.
Punctual—particular, prompt, exact, nice.
Purchase—procure, buy.
Puzzle—bewilder, confound, entangle, perplex.

Q

Quack—empiric, impostor, charlatan, pretender.
Qualified—fit, adapted, capable, competent.
Quality—attribute, property.
Query—interrogatory, inquiry, question.
Questionable—doubtful, suspicious.
Quiet—repose, rest, calm, tranquility, ease, still.
Quit—relinquish, depart, resign, forsake, leave.
Quota—share, rate, proportion.

R

Race—family, generation, lineage, breed, course.
Rage—fury, indignation, anger.
Ramble—stroll, rove, roam, wander, range.
Rank—degree, position, class, place, order.
Rapacious—ravenous, greedy, voracious.
Rapture—delight, ecstacy, joy, transport.
Rash—hasty, thoughtless, impulsive, violent, adventurous.
Ravenous—rapacious, greed, voracious.
Reach—extent, stretch.
Real—true, actual, certain, positive, genuine.
Reason—proof, argument, purpose, motive, origin, cause.
Rebellion—sedition, revolt, insurrection.
Recall—recant, retract, revoke, abjure.
Recede—retrograde, fall back, retire, retreat.
Reciprocal—mutual.
Recite—rehearse, repeat, narrate.
Reclaim—recover, correct, reform.
Recollection—memory, remembrance.
Reconcile—conciliate, propitiate.
Recruit—retrieve, recover, repair, replace.
Redeem—rescue, ransom, recover, restore.
Refer—suggest, intimate, hint, propose, allude.
Reform—amend, better, correct, improve.
Refrain—forbear, spare, abstain, forego.
Regale—entertain, gratify, feast, relish.
Region—quarter, country, section, district.
Regulate—rule, dispose, adjust, control, govern.
Reject—deny, repel, refuse, decline.
Relieve—succor, assist, mitigate, aid, help, support.
Relish—flavor, taste, enjoy.
Remain—stay, tarry, continue, abide, sojourn.
Remark—comment, observation, note.
Remiss—negligent, heedless, thoughtless, careless.
Remnant—residue, remainder, rest.
Renew—revive, renovate, refresh.
Renown—fame, reputation, celebrity.
Reparation—restitution, amends, restoration.
Repeat—rehearse, recite, detail.
Replenish—supply, fill, refill.
Repose—quiet, sleep, ease, rest.
Repugnance—dislike, aversion, hatred.
Request—demand, beseech, entreat, ask.
Research—inquiry, study, examination.
Residence—abode, home, house, dwelling.
Resign—forego, yield, renounce, abdicate.
Resist—endure, oppose, withstand.
Resort—haunt, frequent, visit.
Respectful—civil, dutiful, obedient.
Response—reply, rejoinder, answer.
Rest—ease, quiet, repose.
Restrain—repress, restrict, suppress, confine.
Result—event, effect, issue.
Retard—defer, delay, hinder, prevent.
Retract—take back, revoke, recall, annul.
Reveal—disclose, divulge, expose, impart.
Revere—adore, venerate, worship, reverence.
Revive—refresh, renew, renovate, enliven.
Reward—satisfaction, recompense.
Ridicule—laugh at, satire, irony.
Right—proper, honest, correct, direct.
Rigorous—rigid, rough, severe, harsh.
Rite—observance, form, ceremony, custom.
Roam—rove, wander, range, ramble.
Rough—harsh, uncivil, rude, uncouth.
Route—way, path, road, course.
Rugged—abrupt, rough.

S

Sacred—devoted, divine, holy.
Sagacity—discernment, penetration, perception, acuteness.
Salute—accost, address.
Sapient—wise, discreet, sage.
Satire—irony, sarcasm, burlesque.
Saucy—rude, insolent impudent.
Saying—by-word, maxim, adage, proverb.
Scarce—unusual, singular, rare.
Scent—perfume, odor, fragrance, smell.
Scoff—sneer, gibe, jeer, ridicule.
Scornful—contemptuous, disdainful.
Scrutinize—investigate, search, examine.
Search—inquiry, scrutiny, pursuit.
Seclusion—privacy, quietude.
Secret—quiet, hidden, still, latent.
Secure—certain, safe, sure.
Sedate—quiet, composed, still, calm.
See—examine, view, look, observe.
Select—choose, pick.
Sensitive—keen, appreciative.
Sentiment—feeling, opinion, notion, expression.
Serene—placid, calm.
Settled—conclusive, decided, confirmed.
Several—diverse, different, sundry, various.
Shake—totter, shiver, agitate.
Shame—ignominy, dishonor, disgrace.
Shape—mould, fashion, form.
Sharpness—cunning, acuteness, keenness.
Shine—glare, glisten, glitter, gleam.
Shocking—terrible, dreadful, horrible.
Shorten—curtail, lessen, reduce, abridge.
Showy—gay, gaudy, fine, grand.
Shudder—tumble, quake, shake.
Sickly—sick, ill, unwell, diseased.
Signify—express, imply, utter, declare.
Silent—mute, speechless, dumb, still.
Similarity—likeness, similitude, resemblance.
Simply—merely, solely, only.
Sincere—honest, frank, true, plain.
Situation—plight, locality, place, position.
Slander—vilify, defame, detract, asperse.
Slender—slim, thin, fragile, slight.
Slow—dilatory, tedious, tardy, dull.
Smooth—mild, easy, bland, even.
Snarling—snappish, waspish, surly.
Sneer—jibe, jeer, scoff.
Social—familiar, sociable, convivial.
Soft—yielding, pliant, mild, flexible.
Solemn—serious, grave.
Solid—firm, hard, enduring, fixed.
Soothe—compose, quiet, calm, assuage.
Sort—species, kind, order.
Sour—acid, sharp, acrimonious, tart.
Spacious—capacious, ample, large.
Species—kind, sort, order, class.
Specimen—pattern, sample, model, copy.
Speech—address, sermon, oration, lecture.
Sphere—globe, circle, orb.
Spite—malice, hatred, grudge.
Sport—recreation, pastime, game, play.
Spread—sow, disperse, scatter, diffuse.
Sprinkle—bedew, scatter, water.
Stability—firmness, fixedness, continuity.
Stammer—stutter, falter, hesitate.

Stare—gaze, gape.
Station—situation, place, post, position.
Sterility—unfruitfulness, barrenness.
Still—pacify, lull, quiet, appease.
Stop—check, hinder, delay, rest.
Straight—immediate, direct.
Stratagem—artifice, cheat, finesse, fine work.
Strife—contest, discussion, discord.
Stroll—ramble, rove, range.
Sturdy—firm, robust, strong.
Subdue—surmount, subject, conquer, overcome.
Subjoin—annex, attach, affix, connect.
Submissive—obedient, humble, compliant.
Substance—support, livelihood, sustenance.
Substitute—agent, change, exchange.
Subtract—deduct, withdraw, take from.
Successful—prosperous, fortunate, lucky.
Succor—defend, relieve, assist, help.
Suffer—endure, allow, permit, bear.
Sufficient—adequate, plenty, enough.
Suggest—propose, hint, allude.
Suitor—beau, lover, wooer.
Summon—cite, bid, convoke, call.
Superficial—slight, flimsy, shallow.
Supplicate—implore, entreat, ask, beg.
Sure—reliable, certain, confident.
Surmount—subdue, conquer, overcome.
Surprise—amazement, wonder, admiration.
Surround—incircle, inclose, encompass.
Suspense—doubt, hesitation.
Sustain—maintain, carry, support, bear.
Swarm—crowd, throng, multitude.
Symbol—emblem, type, figure.
Sympathy—compassion, agreement, condolence.
System—order, method.

T

Tale—anecdote, story.
Talk—conference, lecture, sermon.
Taste—relish, savor, flavor.
Tedious—tardy, tiresome, slow.
Temper—disposition, mood, humor.
Temporal—secular, mundane, worldly.
Tempt—allure, decoy, induce, entice.
Tenderness—fondness, affection, love.
Terms—language, expressions, words, condition.
Terrible—horrible, awful, terrific, fearful.
Test—standard, proof, trial, experience.
Testimony—proof, evidence.
Think—surmise, consider, imagine, ponder.
Thought—conceit, idea, fancy, reflection.
Thoughtless—unthinking, hasty, foolish, careless.
Throw—fling, hurl, heave, cast.
Time—epoch, era, season, date.
Timid—afraid, bashful, fearful.
Title—claim, name, appellation.
Tolerate—allow, suffer, permit.
Total—sum, gross, entire, whole.
Tour—trip, round, journey, jaunt.
Trade—occupation, traffic, dealing.
Tranquility—calm, quiet, peace, stillness.
Transcend—surpass, exceed, outdo, excell.
Transient—short, brief, transitory.
Tremendous—dreadful, terrific, fearful, terrible.
Trespass—transgression, violation, misdemeanor, offense.
Trip—voyage, journey, excursion, jaunt, ramble, tour.
True—upright, honest, plain, candid, reliable, sincere.
Try—attempt, endeavor.
Type—mark, illustration, emblem, figure, symbol.

U

Umpire—arbiter, arbitrator, judge.
Unbounded—infinite, unlimited, boundless.
Uncertain—precarious, dubious, doubtful.
Unconquerable—insuperable, insurmountable, invincible.
Undaunted—intrepid, courageous, bold, fearless.
Under—subordinate, subject, lower, beneath.
Unfaithful—perfidious, untruthful, treacherous, faithless.
Unhandy—awkward, ungainly, clumsy, uncouth.
Uniform—same, even, equal, alike.
Unite—combine, connect.
Unlike—different, dissimilar, distinct.
Unmerciful—cruel, hard-hearted, merciless.
Unravel—reveal, unfold, extricate, disentangle.
Unruly—ungovernable, unmanageable, refractory.
Unspeakable—unutterable, ineffable, inexpressible.
Untruth—falsehood, lie, falsity.
Upbraid—reproach, reprove, blame, censure.
Urbanity—civility, courtesy, suavity, affability.
Urgent—pressing, earnest, importunate.
Use—utility, advantage, custom, service, usage, habit.
Utterly—fully, completely, perfectly, wholly.

V

Vacant—unused, void, utterly, devoid, empty.
Vain—conceited, ineffectual, fruitless, useless.
Vanity—conceit, pride; arrogance, haughtiness.
Variation—vicissitude, deviation, variety, change.
Various—diverse, different, sundry, several.
Venal—hireling, mercenary
Venture—risk, hazard.
Verbal—vocal, oral.
Vestige—track, evidence, trace, mark.
Vicinity—section, locality, nearness, neighborhood.
Vile—mean, base.
Vindicate—depend, protect.
Virtue—efficacy, chastity, goodness, purity.
Vivid—bright, lucid, clear.
Vouch—attest, assure, protest, warrant, aver.
Vulgar—mean, low, ordinary, common.

W

Wages—allowance, salary, pay, hire, stipulation.
Wan—pallid, pale.
Want—lack, indigence, poverty, need.
Warlike—martial, military.
Warning—caution, notice, monition, advice.
Wasteful—prodigal, profuse, lavish, extravagant.
Way—route, means, road, fashion, plan, course, method.
Wealth—riches, affluence, opulence.
Wedding—nuptials, marriage.
Welcome—acceptable, desirable, grateful, agreeable.
Whimsical—fantastical, fanciful, capricious.
Wily—crafty, cunning, subtle, artful, sly.
Win—gain, obtain, earn, acquire.
Wisdom—understanding, foresight, knowledge.
Woeful—doleful, rueful, piteous.
Worthy—meritorious, deserving, estimable.
Writer—scribe, author.
Wrong—injury, injustice.

Y

Yearly—annually.
Yet—notwithstanding, but, still, nevertheless, however.
Youthful—juvenile, adolescent.

Z

Zeal—enthusiasm, warmth, fervor, ardor.
Zealous—warm, enthusiastic, earnest, anxious, fervent, ardent.

THE SIGNAL SERVICE.

SINCE the wonderful advance of the telegraphic system into all parts of the country, allowing the quick transmisssion of news to points widely distant, there has arisen the comparatively new feature of the War Department known as the Signal Service. This branch has been in existence many years, but was formerly confined principally, in its work, to the art of sending military messages from one point to another by means of flags of different colors. Gradually the transmission of other kinds of news was begun, or rather the sending of news which should be of importance not alone to the navy and the army, but to the merchant marine and those engaged in agriculture.

As now conducted, the signal office consists of a large corps of men and officers who devote themselves to the study of the weather. The headquarters of the chief signal officer are in Washington, and his office is furnished with every kind of apparatus, of the best known manufacture, and constructed on principles arrived at after years of careful experiment, for ascertaining the changes in the temperature, the amount of rain-fall and snow-fall, the moisture in the atmosphere, the direction and force of the wind, the rise and fall of the tides and of the principal rivers, etc. The more important facilities of the central office, however, are those of the telegraph, by which reports are received from and advice sent out in all directions.

At a great many points over the country, all the way from Maine to California and from the lakes to the gulf, are stationed signal officers and observers, who are more or less completely supplied with meteorological apparatus, and who from time to time send to the chief signal officer at Washington the reports of their observations. The "observers" are volunteers, who receive no salaries from the government, but in consideration of their services are supplied with a registering thermometer, dry and wet bulb barometers, wind-gauge and rain-gauge. Their reports are usually sent once a month, but meanwhile they send in special reports concerning heavy storms or other extraordinary phenomena. The reports of the "observers" are of no use in making predictions as to the future, but are of much value as contributions to the experience and general knowledge of the weather which is necessary to the officers at Washington. It is by experience of the past that the future can be judged.

The signal "officers," on the other hand, are regularly paid employes of the government, under the control of the signal service, into which they are detailed after being enrolled as recruits for the army. Each of these men is required to have a partial education at least, including some knowledge of science. He is supplied with an office fitted with all the apparatus necessary for his duties. He must take regular observations of the weather at stated times during each day. The rules for his guidance are very minute, even extending to the wearing and care of his uniform. His observations are very carefully made out, a copy is filed for record, and the result is promptly telegraphed to the chief at Washington every day.

Thus the corps at Washington have a bird's-eye view of the whole country, as it were, being instantly informed of every change in the weather at any point, the progress and character of every storm and every current of wind, the look of the clouds, the extent of every rainfall, etc. Having reduced to a science all the manifold features of atmospheric phenomena, they are enabled to deduct cause from effect, and from the information at hand they can predict the weather for many hours in advance, with an accuracy which has grown to be wonderfully reliable.

Besides the officers and observers there are persons stationed at different cities throughout the country, whose duty it is to supply all neighboring points with the reports of the service, which were formerly designated as "probabilities," but are now spoken of officially as "indications." These persons receive the midnight report by telegraph, make duplicates by means of type and a printing press, and send copies by mail to all surrounding postoffices, where these copies are displayed for the benefit of the public. The report is also furnished to the Associated Press, and thus telegraphed to all daily newspapers, both morning and evening.

Some years ago the proprietor of the New York *Herald* established a meteorological bureau, one feature of which was the exchange of weather news between New York and London. Out of this has grown an important adjunct of the marine service, by which warning is sent across the Atlantic, by cable, of the approach of any storm, the rate at which it is traveling, its direction, violence, etc., thus being the means of saving many lives and much valuable shipping.

OBEDIENCE AND POLITENESS.

AS STEPPING STONES TO GREATNESS.

THE love of personal freedom of action comes into existence simultaneously with the dawn of reason, and grows stronger as the years go by. The child, incapable of perceiving that the motive for parental restraint is the desire for his future happiness, is disposed to look upon his father's commands as the manifestations of caprice, or at least as arbitrary dictation; the schoolboy is prone to regard his master as a tyrant, and, therefore, his natural enemy; the boarding-school maiden resists and refuses obedience to the rules framed for her better protection against unseen dangers; and even among persons of maturer years, there is a constant chafing against control.

But "order is Heaven's first law." From the moment of his birth to the hour of his death, every man has, in a greater or less degree, to submit his will to the will of others. The foundations of government are laid in the lessons of obedience learned in childhood, and upon this basis is reared the superstructure of society. Without a "head" to exact and enforce obedience, the home would be the scene of turbulence and confusion, and the school-room would resound with shouts of riotous disorder; while without *law* to direct and govern, the ship of state would drift, rudderless, upon a tempestuous sea.

And yet, while none of the lessons of life are harder to learn, none are more salutary in their effects. What security would there be for life or property, if the strong arm of the law were not always uplifted, ready to punish disobedience? What would be the issue of a battle in which each private soldier undertook to wage a desultory warfare of his own, disregarding the command of his general? What would be the fate of the noble ship, with her costly cargo of merchandise, and her still more precious freight of human souls, if, in the moment of peril, every sailor did not promptly spring to obey the commander's orders? Or what business enterprise could hope for success if some one mind did not control the many hands employed,—if each subordinate were free to shape his course according to his own inclinations?

It is especially to the young that these remarks are addressed. It cannot be too strongly impressed upon their minds that obedience to rightful authority is their first and most imperative duty. The employé (be he ever so young) who yields a cheerful and unhesitating obedience to his employer's commands, is the one who gains that employer's confidence, and advances to positions of trust, of honor and of profit.

It is related of the late A. T. Stewart, the merchant prince of New York, that he once ordered a captain of a vessel, who was in his employ, to proceed to a certain port, there dispose of his cargo, and with the proceeds of the sale to buy a cargo of indigo, with which he was to return home. The captain, on reaching the port named, found that to dispose of his goods there would be to sacrifice them, by selling on a falling market. Accordingly, he proceeded to another port, where he sold the merchandise to great advantage, and, having procured his return cargo of indigo, set sail for New York. On reaching his destination, he hastened to report to Mr. Stewart the results of his enterprise, expecting to be praised for his sagacity and good judgment. But the merchant's reply was to demand his immediate resignation. 'But why?" asked the astonished captain. "You have disobeyed orders," said Mr. Stewart. "But you have gained ten thousand dollars by my exercise of judgment," said his employé. "I have gained this time, it is true," was the reply; "but I have learned that I cannot trust you. Another time, a similar act of disobedience on your part might cause me to lose ten times as much."

"Obey orders, if it breaks owners," is a common proverb among seafaring men, and it contains a whole volume of worldly wisdom. To follow this rule, is to lay the responsibility where it rightfully belongs—on the shoulders of the one who issues the orders.

> "Theirs not to make reply;
> Theirs not to reason why;"

says Tennyson, in describing the famous charge of the six hundred at Balaklava, and these words form a motto suitable for the adoption of every young man or woman, from whom obedience can be rightfully exacted. It may not be pleasant; many things must be met, disagreeable in themselves, and trying to your habits and patience. But no genuine or lasting success can be obtained without a readiness to subordinate your own will, your own judgment, to that of those who have a just claim to demand such a subordination.

Source and Value of Politeness.

ANOTHER most important—even essential—element of success, in the care of the young, is politeness. By the word *politeness*, as here used, is not meant an intimate acquaintance with every minute rule of conversational etiquette, but a more comprehensive signification is attached to it. Genuine good breeding proceeds from unselfish kindness of heart, and the hand that performs a genuine act of kindness, is equally beautiful, though not covered with the "regulation glove of fashion." And yet, kindness need not be linked with uncouthness. Gentleness of demeanor is attainable by all, and a polite man carries in his manners what is better than a letter of recommendation, for his manners are seen by all. Everyone loves to gaze on a beautiful picture or statue, and each look reveals beauties not before seen. The refined and beautiful in art awaken emotions of delight; and it is equally true that of two men, with equal talents and attainments, he who is refined and polite is regarded and remembered with vastly more pleasure than his equal, who is awkward, uncouth and boorish in his manners. The French lady who declared that she could never read her prayers except out of a prayer book beautifully bound and decorated, based her remark, not upon fancy, but upon true philosophy. That physician's image will be recalled with most pleasure by the feverish, suffering patient, whose kindly grace pronounced him a gentleman.

COMMON ERRORS RESPECTING POLITENESS.

Do not fear that politeness is inconsistent with independence. It is the man who only half respects himself, who reposes only half confidence in himself, who seeks to obtain from others by impudence what he feels they will not yield without. You may regard the convenience of others, and do all that politeness requires to secure it, and your own independence, so far from being endangered, will be actually strengthened by it.

Some persons regard it as a mark of genius, or of a great mind, to be slovenly in appearance or rude in their manners. If this be true, certainly the world has a superfluity of talent and genius. True, a man may rise to great eminence in spite of very bad manners; but so can an elephant accomplish wonders with his trunk. No lady can thread a needle with more ease than he can, but even the most ardent champion of boorishness would hardly think the lady improved by the substitution of the elephant's trunk for her hand.

No station, no rank, no talents, can excuse a man for neglecting the civilities due from man to man. When Pope Clement XIV. ascended the papal chair, the ambassadors of the several states represented at his court, waited on his Holiness to congratulate him. As they were presented, and severally bowed, he also bowed in acknowledgment of the compliment. The master of ceremonies told his Holiness that this act of courtesy, on his part, was unnecessary. "O, I beg your pardon," replied Clement, "I have not yet been Pope long enough to forget good manners."

ESSENTIAL ELEMENTS OF POLITENESS.

One essential element of politeness is to treat others with the respect due to their age, sex, and relative position toward yourself. Nothing sooner gains friends for a young man, among those who observe his conduct, than a reverence for age, and a chivalrous (not foppish) demeanor toward women. The little every day acts of courtesy cost but little, and no investment will lead a larger (or sometimes quicker) return.

Another element of politeness is cheerfulness. A gloomy, melancholy man is constantly thinking of himself, whom he cannot forget long enough to attend to others. When you cultivate cheerfulness, you cultivate the habit of politeness. There is, about some men, a keenness—a sort of razor-like irony—which assumes the air of cheerfulness, but which is, in reality, only another mode of snarling. Much that is impolite and really bitter, is said in this way.

Another element of true politeness is the faculty of being easily pleased. To appreciate the *motive* from which, rather than the *manner* in which, an act of kindness is rendered you, will prompt you at once to make a fitting acknowledgment and a suitable return.

It must always be remembered, also, that all politeness, to be genuine, must have a foundation of principle. The ancient Romans used the same term—"*boni mores*"—to express good manners and good morals. "Do unto others as ye would that they should do unto you," is the fundamental rule at once of morality and courtesy. Avoid showing rudeness to another, as you would wish him to avoid rudeness toward you. It is well nigh impossible to carry this rule into everyday life without becoming considerate, careful and gentle.

As a practical aid to success, politeness is invaluable. Combined with obedience, it forms the best of all recommendations. Its absence has been the cause of more than one ignominious failure.

CARE OF THE PERSON.

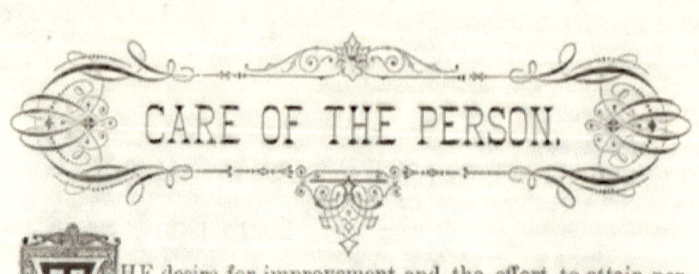

THE desire for improvement and the effort to attain perfection are nowhere to be more commended than when manifested in the care of the person. Refinement, as shown in other directions, is thrown away if the person be left in slovenly and unattractive condition. Young men are mistaken when they imagine that a reasonable time spent upon the toilet shows effeminacy, and young ladies who neglect the toilet cannot hope to be as attractive to others as they might be. The operations of the toilet should be as carefully performed for the home circle as for the public. The desire to make a good personal appearance is a natural one, and is commendable. * Not only that, but care of the person is an adjunct of good health, as certainly as that perfect health, more than anything else, is the brighest jewel in the crown of beauty.

Care of the Hands.—The worst looking hands are those which are not clean; next to that, chapped, bruised, or red hands are unsightly. The consideration of gloves becomes an important item in the cares of the toilet, when it is desired to keep the hands looking well. The best lotions for chapped hands are glycerine and linseed oil, applied at night on going to bed. After washing the hands with soap, always rinse them well in clear water. The nails should be neatly pared, not so short as to seem painful, nor so long as to look like talons. White spots which disfigure finger nails are caused by bruises. Stains may be removed with the juice of lemons or potatoes. The nail brush should not be forgotton.

Care of the Teeth.—It surpasses belief, to observe now many people suffer pain and inconvenience during the latter half of their lives, because during the first half they paid no attention to their teeth. It is also an absurdity to see, as we often do, a young man making an otherwise careful toilet, yet allowing his teeth to remain stained and unsightly, or perhaps blackened with tobacco, and his breath in consequence very repulsive. The use of the tooth brush should be as habitual as that of the comb. The simplest tooth powder is pulverized charcoal. Brush the backs as well as the fronts of the teeth. A dentist should examine them and put them in good condition at least every two years. Never crack nuts or hard candy with the teeth, or otherwise abuse them, for you will be repaid in pain. Do not suppose that after your natural teeth are gone the dentist can give you just as good a set, for he cannot do it. Artificial teeth are poor ones, at the best.

Bathing.—There is no such thing as a toilet, and no such thing as good health, without water, used frequently and regularly. The soap should be of good quality. Warm water removes dirt and sweat, and cold water, followed by brisk rubbing, revives the circulation. The sponge bath is almost as good as any other, and the whole person may be simply washed and rubbed with the hands, the same as the face.

The Hair.—The best care of the hair is cleanliness, which is attained by washing, better than by combing. Care should be taken in using the brush and comb, not to irritate the scalp too much. Pomades and hair oil should not be used too liberally. A good hair wash for ladies is made as follows: Beat up the yolks of two eggs with a spoonful of lemon juice and a spoonful of soft water, and with this rub the head and hair thoroughly. Then wash it with plenty of soft tepid water, and wipe it with towels. The hair may afterward be dried by spreading it loose a few seconds in the smoke of a little powdered benzoin, thrown upon a pan of lighted charcoal. The body reclines upon a sofa, while the hair is allowed to fall over the end of the couch in the smoke of the benzoin. This leaves in the hair a very agreeable perfume.

The Complexion.—The things which best promote the complexion are sleep, exercise and bathing. The use of cosmetics is a mistake, without question. They clog the pores of the skin, and are unnatural. The best cosmetics are sleep, exercise and health. Even the sunshine is better than too much darkness, which makes the face pale. Cosmetics as used by actresses consist of cold cream spread thin upon a perfectly clean face, and then gently rubbed with a soft cloth, so that it becomes almost dry without being rubbed away. Pure and fine powder is then puffed over the face, which is afterward softly patted with a cambric handkerchief, to remove any loose powder. It should be noted that the continued use of cosmetics will ruin the best complexion.

The Feet.—If the shoe fits perfectly, there will be little trouble with the feet; and those who choose shoes too small for them, through vanity, deserve to have trouble. Corns may be cured by paring, on going to bed, and binding upon them one of the many new salves containing petroleum as an ingredient. This must be continued night after night for a week or more. The same treatment will do for chilblains, if they have become broken, and if not they may simply be rubbed with spirits of turpentine. The feet should be washed, then well rubbed, every morning.

Perfumes.—One of the most attractive and harmless luxuries is that of sweet odors. It is but natural to wish for the continual breath of flowers. It has been said that "Even sound itself has less faculty of association with our ideas than the sense of smell. A waft of perfume in the air carries us back mentally to some scene of childhood or early youth. The favorite perfume of a mother, a sister, a friend, is forever associated with the thought of them, even if they themselves are but a memory." Care should be used not only in their selection, but also in their proper use.

On Dyeing the Hair.—Nature always tints the hair, beard and mustache in exact harmony with the complexion. To change the color of the hair, when the shade of the complexion cannot be altered to match it, produces inharmony, as unpleasant to the eye as a discord in music to the ear. Dyes are unnatural, unnecessary to the best possible personal appearance, dangerous in their effects, nearly all of them being poisonous, whether mineral or vegetable, and are not a requisite of the toilet. Still less to be commended are acids for bleaching the hair, which have in a number of instances caused insanity.

HOW TO PROLONG THE SIGHT.

IT is wonderful, how much hard work and steady use the human eyes will submit to when properly taken care of; and it is no less surprising, how small a thing will throw them so far wrong as to cause a great misfortune. The eye is most delicately constructed, yet, like the rest of our complicated organism, is perfectly adapted to its purpose, and will itself soon give notice if anything is not right with it.

The natural light of the sun is that best adapted for the organ of vision; yet even it may be too strong. The sunshine in the dry and cloudless countries bordering the Mediterranean, and in New Mexico, Arizona, and other parts of the west, is extremely trying to the eyes, and smoked or green glasses will be found a great relief. A long journey through snow should be similarly guarded against.

Working, reading or writing in insufficient or imperfect artificial light is the principal cause of most eye troubles. The artificial light should not be too strong, and should be perfectly steady. The electric arc light produces very severe effects upon the vison, but the incandescent light is not so unfavorable. The German student lamp, all things considered, gives the most satisfactory light, and gas light with an Argand burner is about the same. Both, however, may be made too strong, and it is well to use a blue glass chimney. The blue color has no special virtue, but it tones down the brilliancy of the light.

A very important matter is to regulate the focus at which the eye does its work. Many persons become so interested or earnest in their work as to bend down over it closely, thus bringing the eyes nearer than is natural. The natural focus is destroyed, and the eyes become tired very soon. It is always well to pause occasionally, during protracted work held near the face, and gaze for a moment at some distant object, so as to change the focus and relieve the eyes. Reading on the cars is very injurious, as they are too unsteady. The eyes should be little used during convalescence from sickness, as they are then very weak. A grateful relief to tired eyes is to dash pure cold water into them. On going to bed the eyes may be washed, even using soap slightly for a moment, to remove all sweat and dust, and then rinsing with pure water. The room should be dark during sleep. Never rub the eye with the hands or fingers. When there is any itching sensation, instead of rubbing them, hold them closed till the irritation ceases. Never use "eye cups," as they cause congestion. Tobacco smoke, and indeed any smoke, is injurious to the eyes. Do not read much immediately after eating a hearty meal, and never at dusk or in insufficient light. Do not sit at too high a desk, where your reading or writing is brought too near the face, and do not read by a jerking, unsteady light.

One of the most common and painful diseases of the eye is granulation of the lids. The most effectual treatment for it is dieting. The patient must eat very lightly of the most easily digested food, with no pepper or spices, no salt, no salty meats, not much meat of any kind, drink no tea nor coffee, no stimulants, use no tobacco, and must keep upon the eyelids a cloth constantly wetted with cold rainwater, or, better, distilled water, changing it frequently day and night, thus keeping the eyelids constantly cooler than the rest of the body. Such treatment will cure any case of granulated eyelids sooner than any medicine will do it.

List of Statutory Holidays.

The following is a list of the legal and bank holidays in the States and Territories of the Union:

INDEPENDENCE DAY—Fourth of July, in all States and Territories.

THANKSGIVING DAY, and all Fast Days appointed by Presidential Proclamation, in all States and Territories.

CHRISTMAS DAY—In all States and Territories.

NEW YEAR'S DAY—In all States and Territories except Arkansas, Delaware, Georgia, Kentucky, Maine, Massachusetts, New Hampshire, North Carolina, South Carolina and Rhode Island.

GOOD FRIDAY—In Florida, Louisiana, Minnesota and Pennsylvania.

SHROVE TUESDAY, in Louisiana, and the cities of Selma, Mobile and Montgomery, Alabama.

GENERAL ELECTION DAY—(Tuesday after the first Monday in November) in California, Maine, Missouri, New York, Oregon, South Carolina and Wisconsin.

WASHINGTON'S BIRTHDAY—(Feb. 22), in all States and Territories except Alabama, Florida, Illinois, Iowa, Indiana, Kansas, Maine, Missouri, North Carolina, Ohio, Texas, Oregon and Tennessee.

DECORATION DAY—(May 30), in Colorado, Connecticut, District of Columbia, Maine, Michigan, New Hampshire, New Jersey, New York, Pennsylvania and Rhode Island.

IN LOUISIANA ONLY—Anniversary of the battle of New Orleans (Jan. 8); Fireman's Anniversary (March 4); Lincoln's Birthday (Feb. 12).

IN TEXAS ONLY—Texan Independence Day (March 2); Battle of San Jacinto (April 21).

IN GEORGIA ONLY—Memorial Day (April 26).

NOTE.—Good Friday is the Friday next preceding Easter Sunday, and being the hypothetical anniversary of the Crucifixion, is set apart as the most solemn day of fast and prayer in the Lenten period. Shrove Tuesday, or Pancake Tuesday, as it is called in England, from the custom of eating pancakes on that day, is the Tuesday before Good Friday.

THE BICYCLE.

THIS has grown to be one of the recognized means of locomotion, and of late years bicycling has become very popular. Of the value of the bicycle for getting over ground no proof is now needed, when it is no uncommon thing for youths to ride sixty or seventy miles in a day, with no undue strain on the muscular powers. The bicycle interest is now assuming vast dimensions, and to a greater extent in the Old World than in America, thus far. In England there are 130 makers of bicycles, a million pounds sterling is invested in the business, and 60,000 bicycles are in existence in London and the British provinces. These are astonishing facts when we remember that only a few years ago the very name did not exist. One of the chief charms of the bicycle, as compared with other modern locomotive improvements, is that there is a privacy and an individuality about it in which the railway and steamboat are lacking. The bicyclist is as independent as the horseman, and is in some respects his superior, for his steed needs no watching, and though he miss his feed of oats can travel as long as the master's own strength holds out. The bicycle demands a more smooth and level road than the horse, and cannot explore woodlands or jump fences and ditches, but as the country is gradually improved, the streets and roads are more and more fitted for travel on the wheel.

In America the bicycle is manufactured in many different styles, the best of which are so perfect that no further improvement can be imagined. The old velocipede, the first machine of this kind which was propelled by treadles, had both its wheels of the same size, or nearly so; but the bicycle has a very small rear wheel, while the front wheel is made so large that its diameter stands as high as the rider's shoulder. This vastly increases the speed, for every revolution measures the increased circumference upon the ground.

The "wheel," as it is usually called, "for short," is not only found very useful by messengers and others who in their business have short, quick trips to make, but the sport takes rank with other kinds of competition in racing. The speed record of the bicycle has been constantly lowered, until now a mile is made in but little over three minutes. Sporting authorities preserve careful records of the speed made in one mile, three miles, six miles, ten miles, and other distances accomplished in the contests, which often attract large crowds of people.

In the large cities bicycle clubs are formed, which have the usual forms of society organizations, adopt a uniform and style of trumpet, hold meetings and races, and at times ride in procession. The authorities of many cities forbid the use of the bicycle on public streets. Its rapid, noiseless movement frightens many horses which are afraid of nothing else.

How Poor Boys Become Successful Men.

YOU want some good advice. Rise early. Be abstemious. Be frugal. Attend to your own business and never trust it to another. Be not afraid to work, and diligently, too, with your own hands. Treat every one with civility and respect. Good manners insure success. Accomplish what you undertake. Decide, then persevere. Diligence and industry overcome all difficulties. Never be mean—rather give than take the odd shilling. Never postpone till to-morrow what can be done to-day. Never anticipate wealth from any source but labor. Honesty is not only the best policy, but the only policy. Commence at the first round and keep climbing. Make your word as good as your bond. Seek knowledge to plan, enterprise to execute, honesty to govern all. Never overtrade. Never give too large credit. Time is money. Reckon the hours of the day as so many dollars, the minutes as so many cents. Make few promises. Keep your secrets. Live within your income. Sobriety above all things. Luck is a word that does not apply to a successful man. Not too much caution—slow but sure is the thing. The highest monuments are built piece by piece. Step by step we mount the pyramids. Be bold—be resolute when the clouds gather; difficulties are surmounted by opposition. Self-confidence, self-reliance, is your capital. Your conscience the best monitor. Never be over-sanguine, but do not underrate your own abilities. Don't be discouraged. Ninety-nine may say no, the hundredth, yes; take off your coat: roll up your sleeves, don't be afraid of manual labor! America is large enough for all—strike out for the west. The best letter of introduction is your own energy. Lean on yourself when you walk. Keep good company. Keep out of politics unless you are sure to win—you are never sure to win, so look out.

A CALENDAR for ascertaining Any Day of the Week for any given time within Two Hundred Years from introduction of New Style 1752* to 1952 inclusive.

Years 1753 to 1952.											Jan	Feb	Mar	Apr	May	Jun	July	Aug	Sep	Oct	Nov	Dec
1761 *1801*	1767 *1807*	1778 *1818*	1789 *1829*	1795 *1835*	*1846*	*1857* 1903	*1863* 1914	*1874* 1925	*1885* 1931	*1891* 1942	4	7	7	3	5	1	3	6	2	4	7	2
1762 *1802*	1773 *1813*	1779 *1819*	1790 *1830*	*1841*	*1847*	*1858* 1909	*1869* 1915	*1875* 1926	*1886* 1937	*1897* 1943	5	1	1	4	6	2	4	7	3	5	1	3
1757 *1803*	1763 *1814*	1774 *1825*	1785 *1831*	1791 *1842*	*1853*	*1859* 1910	*1870* 1921	*1881* 1927	*1887* 1938	*1898* 1949	6	2	2	5	7	3	5	1	4	6	2	
1754 *1805*	1765 *1811*	1771 *1822*	1782 *1833*	1793 *1839*	1799 *1850* 1901	*1861* 1907	*1867* 1918	*1878* 1929	*1889* 1935	*1895* 1946	2	5	5	1	3	6	1	4	7	2	5	7
1755 *1806*	1766 *1817*	1777 *1823*	1783 *1834*	1794 *1845*	1800 *1851* 1902	*1862* 1913	*1873* 1919	*1879* 1930	*1890* 1941	1947	3	6	6	2	4	7	2	5	1	3	6	1
1758 *1809*	1769 *1815*	1775 *1826*	1786 *1837*	1797 *1843*	*1854* 1905	*1865* 1911	*1871* 1922	*1882* 1933	*1893* 1939	*1899* 1950	7	3	3	6	1	4	6	2	5	7	3	5
1753 *1810*	1759 *1821*	1770 *1827*	1781 *1838*	1787 *1849*	1798 *1855*	*1866* 1906	*1877* 1917	† *1883* 1923	*1894* 1934	*1900* 1945 1951	1	4	4	7	2	5	7	3	6	1	4	6

Leap Years.								Jan	Feb	Mar	Apr	May	Jun	July	Aug	Sep	Oct	Nov	Dec
								..	29	..	..	..	..	..	..	..	..	..	..
1764	1792	*1804*	*1832*	*1860*	*1888*	1928	....	7	3	4	7	2	5	7	3	6	1	4	6
1768	1796	*1808*	*1836*	*1864*	*1892*	1904	1932	5	1	2	5	7	3	5	1	4	6	2	4
1772	....	*1812*	*1840*	*1868*	*1896*	1908	1936	3	6	7	3	5	1	3	6	2	4	7	2
1776	....	*1816*	*1844*	*1872*	....	1912	1940	1	4	5	1	3	6	1	4	7	2	5	7
1780	....	*1820*	*1848*	*1876*	....	1916	1944	6	2	3	6	1	4	6	2	5	7	3	5
1756	1784	*1824*	*1852*	*1880*	....	1920	1948	4	7	1	4	6	2	4	7	3	5	1	3
1760	1788	*1828*	*1856*	*1884*	....	1924	1952	2	5	6	2	4	7	2	5	1	3	6	1

1.		2.		3.		4.		5.		6.		7.	
Monday	1	Tuesday	1	Wednesd.	1	Thursday	1	Friday	1	Saturday	1	*Sunday*	1
Tuesday	2	Wednesd.	2	Thursday	2	Friday	2	Saturday	2	*Sunday*	2	Monday	2
Wednesd.	3	Thursday	3	Friday	3	Saturday	3	*Sunday*	3	Monday	3	Tuesday	3
Thursday	4	Friday	*4	Saturday	4	*Sunday*	4	Monday	4	Tuesday	4	Wednesd.	4
Friday	5	Saturday	5	*Sunday*	5	Monday	5	Tuesday	5	Wednesd.	5	Thursday	5
Saturday	6	*Sunday*	6	Monday	6	Tuesday	6	Wednesd.	6	Thursday	6	Friday	6
Sunday	7	Monday	7	Tuesday	7	Wednesd.	7	Thursday	7	Friday	7	Saturday	7
Monday	8	Tuesday	8	Wednesd.	8	Thursday	8	Friday	8	Saturday	8	*Sunday*	8
Tuesday	9	Wednesd.	9	Thursday	9	Friday	9	Saturday	9	*Sunday*	9	Monday	9
Wednesd.	10	Thursday	10	Friday	10	Saturday	10	*Sunday*	10	Monday	10	Tuesday	10
Thursday	11	Friday	11	Saturday	11	*Sunday*	11	Monday	11	Tuesday	11	Wednesd.	11
Friday	12	Saturday	12	*Sunday*	12	Monday	12	Tuesday	12	Wednesd.	12	Thursday	12
Saturday	13	*Sunday*	13	Monday	13	Tuesday	13	Wednesd.	13	Thursday	13	Friday	13
Sunday	14	Monday	14	Tuesday	14	Wednesd.	14	Thursday	14	Friday	14	Saturday	14
Monday	15	Tuesday	15	Wednesd.	15	Thursday	15	Friday	15	Saturday	15	*Sunday*	15
Tuesday	16	Wednesd.	16	Thursday	16	Friday	16	Saturday	16	*Sunday*	16	Monday	16
Wednesd.	17	Thursday	17	Friday	17	Saturday	17	*Sunday*	17	Monday	17	Tuesday	17
Thursday	18	Friday	18	Saturday	18	*Sunday*	18	Monday	18	Tuesday	18	Wednesd.	18
Friday	19	Saturday	19	*Sunday*	19	Monday	19	Tuesday	19	Wednesd.	19	Thursday	19
Saturday	20	*Sunday*	20	Monday	20	Tuesday	20	Wednesd.	20	Thursday	20	Friday	20
Sunday	21	Monday	21	Tuesday	21	Wednesd.	21	Thursday	21	Friday	21	Saturday	21
Monday	22	Tuesday	22	Wednesd.	22	Thursday	22	Friday	22	Saturday	22	*Sunday*	22
Tuesday	23	Wednesd.	23	Thursday	23	Friday	23	Saturday	23	*Sunday*	23	Monday	23
Wednesd.	24	Thursday	24	Friday	24	Saturday	24	*Sunday*	24	Monday	24	Tuesday	24
Thursday	25	Friday	25	Saturday	25	*Sunday*	25	Monday	25	Tuesday	25	Wednesd.	25
Friday	26	Saturday	26	*Sunday*	26	Monday	26	Tuesday	26	Wednesd.	26	Thursday	26
Saturday	27	*Sunday*	27	Monday	27	Tuesday	27	Wednesd.	27	Thursday	27	Friday	27
Sunday	28	Monday	28	Tuesday	28	Wednesd.	28	Thursday	28	Friday	28	Saturday	28
Monday	29	Tuesday	29	Wednesd.	29	Thursday	29	Friday	29	Saturday	29	*Sunday*	29
Tuesday	30	Wednesd.	30	Thursday	30	Friday	30	Saturday	30	*Sunday*	30	Monday	30
Wednesd.	31	Thursday	31	Friday	31	Saturday	31	*Sunday*	31	Monday	31	Tuesday	31

* 1752 same as 1772, from Jan. 1, to Sept. 2. From Sept. 14 to Dec. 31, same as 1780 (September 3-13 were omitted).

† To ascertain any day of the week, first look in the table for the year required, and under the months are figures which refer to the corresponding figures at the head of the columns of days below. *For Example*:—To know on what day of the week May 4 will be in the year 1883, in the table of years look for 1883, and in a parallel line, under May, is figure 2, which directs to column 2, in which it will be seen that May 4 falls on Friday.

POPULATION AND RANK OF THE SEVERAL STATES.

Rank	State.	Male.	Female.	Native.	Foreign.	White.	Colored.	Total.
1	New York	2,505,283	2,577,527	3,872,372	1,211,438	5,017,116	65,694	5,083,810
2	Pennsylvania	2,136,635	2,146,151	3,695,253	587,533	4,197,106	85,680	4,282,786
3	Ohio	1,614,165	1,584,074	2,803,499	394,743	3,118,344	79,895	3,198,239
4	Illinois	1,587,433	1,491,336	2,495,177	583,592	3,032,174	46,595	3,078,769
5	Missouri	1,127,424	1,041,380	1,957,564	211,240	2,023,568	145,236	2,168,804
6	Indiana	1,010,676	967,886	1,834,597	143,765	1,939,094	39,258	1,978,362
7	Massachusetts	858,475	924,537	1,339,919	443,093	1,764,004	19,008	1,783,012
8	Kentucky	832,676	816,032	1,589,237	59,471	1,377,187	271,521	1,648,708
9	Michigan	862,276	774,055	1,247,985	388,346	1,614,078	22,253	1,636,331
10	Iowa	848,234	776,386	1,363,132	261,488	1,614,666	9,954	1,624,620
11	Texas	838,719	753,855	1,478,058	114,516	1,197,496	395,078	1,592,574
12	Tennessee	769,374	773,089	1,525,881	16,582	1,139,120	403,343	1,542,463
13	Georgia	761,184	777,864	1,528,733	10,315	814,251	724,797	1,539,048
14	Virginia	745,839	766,967	1,498,139	14,667	880,981	631,825	1,512,806
15	North Carolina	688,203	711,844	1,396,398	3,679	867,478	532,569	1,400,047
16	Wisconsin	680,106	635,374	910,063	405,417	1,309,622	5,858	1,315,480
17	Alabama	622,890	639,904	1,253,121	9,673	662,328	600,466	1,262,794
18	Mississippi	567,137	564,455	1,122,429	9,168	479,371	652,221	1,131,592
19	New Jersey	559,828	571,160	909,398	221,585	1,091,947	39,039	1,130,983
20	Kansas	536,725	459,241	886,261	109,705	952,056	43,910	995,966
21	South Carolina	490,469	505,153	987,981	7,641	391,224	604,398	995,622
22	Louisiana	468,826	471,270	885,964	54,132	455,105	485,006	940,103
23	Maryland	462,104	472,628	851,984	82,648	724,718	209,914	934,632
24	California	518,271	346,415	572,006	292,680	767,266	97,420	864,686
25	Arkansas	416,380	386,181	792,269	10,295	591,611	210,953	802,564
26	Minnesota	419,262	361,544	513,107	267,699	776,940	3,866	780,806
27	Maine	324,084	324,861	590,076	58,869	646,903	2,042	648,945
28	Connecticut	305,886	316,797	492,879	129,804	610,884	11,799	622,683
29	West Virginia	314,479	303,964	600,214	18,129	592,606	25,887	618,443
30	Nebraska	249,275	203,158	355,043	97,390	449,806	2,627	452,433
31	New Hampshire	170,575	176,409	300,961	46,023	346,264	720	346,984
32	Vermont	166,888	165,398	291,340	40,946	331,243	1,043	332,286
33	Rhode Island	133,033	143,495	202,598	73,930	269,931	6,597	276,528
34	Florida	135,386	131,965	257,631	9,720	141,832	125,519	267,351
35	Colorado	129,471	65,178	154,909	39,780	191,452	3,197	194,649
36	Dist. Columbia	83,594	94,044	160,523	17,115	118,236	59,402	177,638
37	Oregon	103,388	71,379	143,327	30,440	163,087	11,680	174,767
38	Delaware	74,153	72,501	137,182	9,472	120,198	26,456	146,654
39	Utah	74,470	69,496	99,974	43,992	142,380	1,526	143,906
40	Dakota	82,302	52,848	83,387	51,763	133,177	2,003	135,180
41	New Mexico	63,751	54,679	108,498	9,932	108,127	10,303	118,430
42	Washington	45,977	29,143	59,259	15,861	67,349	7,771	75,120
43	Nevada	42,013	20,252	36,623	25,642	53,574	8,691	62,265
44	Arizona	28,202	12,239	24,419	15,022	35,178	5,263	40,441
45	Montana	28,180	10,977	27,640	11,515	35,446	3,711	39,157
46	Idaho	21,818	10,793	22,629	9,982	29,011	3,600	32,611
47	Wyoming	14,151	6,637	14,943	5,845	19,436	1,352	20,788
	Total	25,520,582	24,632,284	43,475,506	6,677,360	43,404,876	6,747,990	50,152,866

Slave Population in the United States in 1860.

States.	1850.	1860.	States.	1850.	1860.
Alabama	342,844	435,132	South Carolina	384,984	402,541
Arkansas	47,100	111,104	Tennessee	239,459	275,784
Delaware	2,290	1,798	Texas	58,161	180,388
Florida	39,310	61,753	Virginia	472,528	490,887
Georgia	381,682	462,230	Nebraska (Ter.)	....	10
Kentucky	210,981	225,490	Utah (Ter.)	....	29
Louisiana	244,809	332,520	New Mexico (Ter.)	26	24
Maryland	90,368	87,188	District Columbia	3,687	3,181
Mississippi	309,878	436,696			
Missouri	87,422	114,965	Total	$ 3,204,077	3,952,801
North Carolina	288,548	331,081			

Color Census of Four Decades.

	White.	Colored.		White.	Colored.
1880	43,404,876	6,577,151	1860	26,922,537	4,441,830
1870	33,589,377	4,880,000	1850	19,553,068	3,638,808

WORDS OF WIT AND WISDOM.

THE following selection of epigrams, proverbs, "wise saws," and original conceptions include some of the brilliant passages of standard authors—gleams of sunlight which here and there flash through the foliage of thought—as well as many gems of anonymous origin. They will be found not only full of entertainment and instruction, but useful where a pertinent quotation is required to illustrate ideas either in speech or writing.

WORDS OF WIT AND WISDOM.

'Tis strange the miser should his care employ,
To gain those riches he can ne'er enjoy.
—*Pope.*

If you would not have affliction visit you twice, listen at once to what it teaches.

Some sort of charity will swallow the egg and give away the shell.

A word of kindness is seldom spoken in vain. It is a seed which, even when dropped by chance, springs up a flower.

Mean souls, like mean pictures, are often found in good-looking frames.

A child is eager to have any toy he sees, but throws it away at the sight of another, and is equally eager to have that. We are most of us children through life, and only change one toy for another from the cradle to the grave.

Learning is wealth to the poor, an honor to the rich, an aid to the young, and a support and comfort to the aged.

Love is the strongest hold-fast in the world; it is stronger than death.

Hope and fear, peace and strife,
Make up the troubled web of life.

False friendship, like the ivy, decays and ruins the wall it embraces; but true friendship gives new life and animation to the object it supports.—*Burton.*

A man who hoards riches and enjoys them not is like the ass which carries gold yet eats thistles.

People should remember that it is only great souls that know how much glory there is in doing good.

Happiness is a perfume that one cannot shed over another without a few drops falling upon himself.

With love the heart becomes a fair and fertile garden, glowing with sunshine and warm hues, and exhaling sweet odors; but without it, it is a bleak desert covered with ashes.

Prosperity is no just scale; adversity is the only true balance to weigh friends.

To discover what is true, and to practice what is good, are the two most important objects of life.

Life has its hours of bitterness,
Its joys, its hopes and fears;
Our way is sometimes wreathed with smiles,
And then baptized with tears.

Prosperity is not without its trouble, nor adversity without its comfort.

As riches and favor forsake a man we discover him to be a fool, but nobody could find it out in his prosperity.—*Bruyère.*

Troubles are like babies—they only grow bigger by nursing.

You cannot injure any one by elevating poor fallen humanity. It is the noblest work man can engage in, not only to elevate himself but to elevate others.

Happiness is a butterfly, which, when pursued, is always just beyond your grasp; but which, if you will sit down quietly, may come and alight on you.

Purchase not friends with gifts; when thou ceasest to give, such will cease to love.—*Fuller.*

By humility, and the fear of the Lord, are riches, and honor and life.—*Proverbs.*

Life appears to be too short to be spent in nursing animosities or registering wrongs.

If thou wouldst be borne with, bear with others.—*Fuller.*

Ladies who have a disposition to punish their husbands should recollect that a little warm sunshine will melt an icicle much sooner than a regular northeaster.

A wise man knows his own ignorance; a fool thinks he knows everything.

Cyrus, the conqueror of Babylon, of whom we read in the Bible, was once asked what was the first thing he learned. "To tell the truth," was the reply.

Every man can and should do something for the public, if it be only to kick a piece of orange peel into the road from the pavement.

A rich man who is not liberal resembles a tree without fruit.

How brightly do little joys beam upon a soul which stands on a ground darkened by clouds of sorrow! So do stars come forth from the empty sky, when we look up to them from a deep well.

It is not going into the furnace, but the coming out, which demonstrates the metal.

Indulging in dangerous pleasures, saith a Burmese proverb, is like licking honey from a knife and cutting the tongue with the edge.

There are more poor willing to give charity from their necessity than rich from their superfluities.

Wealth does not always improve us. A man, as he gets to be worth more, may become worth-less.

The greatest friend of truth is time, her greatest enemy prejudice, and her constant companion is humility.—*Colton.*

Beauty unaccompanied by virtue is a flower without perfume.

Virtue, like a dowerless beauty, has more admirers than followers.

Never trouble trouble till trouble troubles you.

Whoso hath this world's goods, and seeth his brother have need, and shutteth up his bowels of compassion from him, how dwelleth the love of God in him.—*1 John.*

Every good deed is a benefit to the doer as sure as to the receiver.

We should value affliction as we do physic—not by its taste, but by its effects.

He that giveth unto the poor shall not lack, but he that hideth his eyes shall have many a curse.—*Proverbs.*

Most of the shadows that cross our pathway through life are caused by our standing in our own way.

Avarice is like a graveyard; it takes all that it can get and gives nothing back.

It is not wealth, but wisdom, that makes a man rich.

Virtue, like a rich stone, looks best when plainest set.

The duties and burdens of life should be met with courage and determination. No one has a right to be a wart on the fair face of nature, doing nothing useful, producing nothing of utility or value. It is a gross and fatal error to suppose that life is to be enjoyed in idleness. It can never be.

If a man be gracious to strangers, it shows he is a citizen of the world, and that his heart is no island cut off from the other lands, but a continent that joins them.—*Bacon.*

True friendship is like sound health, the value of it is seldom known until it is lost.

All our affections are but so many doors to let in Christ.

Much wanted more, and lost all.

Troubles are like hornets, the less ado you make about them the better, for your outcry will only bring the whole swarm upon you.

God lays us upon our backs that we may look heavenward.

The more liberal we are to others from a principle of faith and love, the more liberal God will be to us.

The flowers that breathe the sweetest perfume into our hearts bloom upon the rod with which Providence chastises us.

Be not stingy of kind words and pleasing acts, for such are fragrant gifts, whose perfume will gladden the heart and sweeten the life of all who hear or receive them.

Rare as is true love, true friendship is still rarer.—*Rochefoucauld.*

Learning by study must be won;
'Twas ne'er entailed from sire to son.
—*Gay.*

The violet grows low, and covers itself with its own tears, and of all flowers yields the sweetest fragrance. Such is humility.

We should not forget that life is a flower, which is no sooner fully blown than it begins to wither.

He who has other graces, without humility, is one who carries a box of precious powder without a cover on a windy day.

Heaven's gates are not so highly arched as princes' palaces. They that enter there must go upon their knees.—*Webster.*

God strikes not as an enemy to destroy, but as a father to correct.

This may be said of love, that if you strike it out of the soul, life would be insipid and our being but half animated.

It is better to be poor, with a good heart, than rich, with a bad conscience.

From the walks of humble life have risen those who are the lights and landmarks of mankind.

The universal lot,
To weep, to wander, die, and be forgot.
—*Sprague.*

The path of sorrow, and that path alone,
Leads to the land where sorrow is unknown;
No traveler ever reached that blest abode,
Who found not thorns and briars in his road.
—*Cowper.*

He that does good for good's sake seeks neither praise nor reward, though sure of both at last.

Living in the fear of God takes away the fear of death; for the sting of death is sin.

Nothing is more dangerous than a friend without discretion; even a prudent enemy is preferable.—*La Fontaine.*

The grand essentials to happiness in this life are, something to do, something to love, and something to hope for.

He that has never known adversity is but half acquainted with others, or with himself. Constant success shows us but one side of the world; for, as it surrounds us with friends, who will tell us only our merits, so it silences those enemies from whom only we can learn our defects.—*Colton.*

Base all your actions upon a principle of right; preserve your integrity of character, and, doing this, never reckon the cost.

Adversity is the trial of principle. Without it a man hardly knows whether he is honest or not.—*Fielding.*

Never be cast down by trifles. If a spider break his web twenty times, twenty times will he mend it. Make up your mind to do a thing and you will do it.

A covetous man lives without comfort, and dies without hope.

Whoso stoppeth his ear at the cry of the poor, he also shall cry himself, but shall not be heard.—*Proverbs.*

Value the friendship of him who stands by you in storms. Swarms of insects will surround you in sunshine.

Pleasures have honey in the mouth, but a sting in the tail, and often perish in the budding.

Religion teaches the rich humility, and the poor contentment.

It is far more easy to acquire a fortune like a knave, than to expend it like a gentleman.—*Colton.*

Excesses in our youth are drafts upon our old age, payable, with interest, about thirty years after date.

Riches and true excellence are seldom found together.

The use of money is all the advantage there is in having it.

Truth is a mighty weapon when wielded by the weakest arm.—*Fletcher.*

The greatest pleasure of life is love; the greatest treasure, contentment; the greatest possession, health; the greatest ease, sleep, and the best medicine, a true friend.

Wealth is not his who gets it, but his who enjoys it.

That man cannot be upright before God who is unjust in his dealings with men.

Little troubles wear the heart out, and it is easier to throw a bomb shell a mile than a feather, even with artillery. Fifty little debts of one dollar each will cause more trouble and dunning than one big one of a thousand.

Professing, without practicing, will bring neither glory to God nor comfort to ourselves.

He that follows pleasure instead of business will in a little time have no business to follow.

Fashionable christianity is not spiritual piety.

Fear God and keep his commandments; for this is the whole duty of man.—*Solomon.*

Pleasure as pleasure is not to be condemned, but only sinful pleasure; such as injures another is unjust, such as hurts ourselves is imprudent.

Natural blindness is bad, but spiritual blindnes is much worse.

The only avarice which is justifiable is that of love; the only ambition that is commendable is zeal in the cause of virtue and good actions.

Without entire confidence friendship and love are but mockeries, and social intercourse a war in disguise.

Contentment is a pearl of great price, and whoever procures it at the expense of ten thousand desires makes a wise purchase.

What is joy? A sunbeam between two clouds.

Who is wise? He that learns from every one. Who is powerful? He that governs his passions. Who is rich? He that is content.

Prosperity without God's presence is full of trouble; but trouble with the presence of God is full of comfort.

PAST, PRESENT AND FUTURE.

"Think not mournfully upon the Past, it cannot return. Wisely improve the Present, it is thine. Go forth to meet the shadowy Future with strong heart and free will."

THERE are few persons who have reached mature life who can look back over the past without mingled emotions. Childhood knows no past; its happy life is rounded out and completed by its present joys. But as we learn the harder lessons in life's school under that stern teacher, experience, our present joys are heightened and our present sorrows deepened by the alternate lights and shadows thrown over them by the past. The happy memories of a mother's tender love are often darkened by the recollection of her losses; we recall our moments of success, only to have our exultation turned into regret by the memory of our failure. Happy would be that man who, in looking back over the years that are his no longer, could raise his eyes toward Heaven and say, in all sincerity, "I have made no mistakes; my conscience tells me that I have been guilty of no wrong either toward God or my fellow-man."

But the human intellect is weak; the human heart is prone to err; and there probably lives no man nor woman who does not wish that at some period of his or her past life, the "still, small voice" of conscience had been heeded, or the dictates of prudence followed.

There is one mode in which such reflections may be made salutary. A careful self-examination, impartially conducted, with a view to discovering past errors and an avoidance of them in the future, will be of great service. But in such an examination into our past lives, there must be no secret desire to cover up or to excuse that which has been blame-worthy. Freely must the heart confess; sternly must the intellect and conscience judge. The resolves for the future, too, must be sincere and earnest.

But after this introspection and the formation of a new determination, let there be no vain and empty regrets over what cannot now be changed. It is worse than foolish to waste time in such fruitless vaporings. The man of firm will should "let the dead past bury its dead;" laying hold upon the present without looking back. You are not called upon to seek to obliterate the recollection of past griefs. Such memories, rightly used, have an ennobling—even a holy—influence. The little empty shoe, the golden curl, the tress of silver hair—these should not be suffered to lie unnoticed and uncared for. They are links in that golden chain which holds you to your true home; they will mutually appeal to you in moments when avarice and passion are struggling to control you, and a voice long silent will make itself heard in your heart. But do not let this grief make you unmindful of present duties, or selfishly indifferent to the claims of others upon you.

In one word, remember the past only to avoid its errors, and cherish its memories only that they may beautify and sanctify your life.

THE PRESENT.

THE Present is the only one of the three divisions of time which any man can safely call his own. The Past has gone from his grasp; the Future he may never reach. To-day belongs to him; and accordingly as he improves or abuses it, will his future be bright with promise or gloomy with recollections of a misspent past. The Present is the seed time, the Future will yield the harvest; and what a man sows to-day he will surely reap, be it sooner or later. "Men do not gather grapes of thorns, nor figs of thistles," is as true in our age as when spoken nineteen hundred years ago. Neglect of duty, self-indulgence, extravagance and improvidence in the present will yield their full harvest of poverty, of suffering and of impotent regrets in the future. To-day's duties must be performed to-day; to-morrow—if it come at all—will have its own calls upon your time and strength. Each moment of life some duty demands to be performed, but for each duty there is a moment of which you can avail yourself:

"One by one the sands are flowing,
One by one the moments fall;
Some are coming, some are going,
Do not strive to grasp them all.

"One by one thy duties wait thee;
Let thy whole strength go to each.
Let no future dreams elate thee;
Learn thou first what these can teach.

"Hours are golden links—God's token,
Reaching Heaven, but one by one;
Take them, lest the chain be broken
'Ere thy pilgrimage be done."

In each period of life, the Present is a time of preparation for the Future; in childhood, we prepare for manhood, and while in the prime of manly strength we seek to provide for the time when the infirmities of age may overtake us. The best preparation always is a careful attention to and conscientious performance of every present duty, however apparently trivial. Present opportunities of self-improvement must not be neglected. A well-stored mind is the best preventive against loneliness and *ennui*. And the recollection of acts of charity and self-denial are the best guards against the reproaches of conscience. A temptation resisted, a tear wiped away from the eye of sorrow, a kind word spoken in the ear of misfortune, a suffering alleviated—these are seeds which will, in the future, bear rich fruit.

THE FUTURE.

IN youth, thoughts of the Future fill the mind. The brain of the boy teems with anticipations and plans for his manhood, and the cheek of the maiden glows with an added flush of loveliness as she looks forward to the proud day when she shall be the queen in her own household. At the threshold of life, as youth emerges from the restraints and fostering care of home, the eye eagerly seeks the most distant horizon, which hope paints for the heart with gorgeous tints. These anticipations are as pleasing as they are natural, and should not be rudely discouraged. Hope for the future gives strength for the present, and a belief in coming happiness lightens the burden of to-day's cares. But as disappointent follows disappointment, our confidence in the absolute certainty of future success becomes lessened, and prudence and foresight succeed to rashness and impetuosity. "Boast not thyself of to-morrow," say the Scriptures, and human experience has demonstrated the wisdom of the advice.

Yet at the same time, there is no call to be constantly foreboding some unknown evil which it is feared that the future may bring. It is true that in summer the wise farmer gathers and stores the fruits of the earth for winter use; yet he would be rightly ridiculed who refused to enjoy the sunshine and flowers of June through his dread of the coming frost and icy blasts of January. Do not "borrow trouble" from some imaginary store which you apprehend may be somewhere in reserve for you. The Future is kindly hidden from our knowledge, and the wise man will not seek to lift the veil which shrouds it. Its joys as well as its griefs, its consolations as well as its trials, will come in their appointed time. Seek, by a wise use of the Present, to prepare yourself to accept its pleasures with thankfulness and moderation, to encounter its misfortunes with resignation and fortitude.

COMPLETE LETTER WRITER.

BY general correspondence is meant all the usual forms in which paper and penmanship are substituted for personal conversation and oral exchange of words. The correspondent should bear in mind that a word is none the less a word, even though quickly and easily spoken; and that it is still only a word—nothing more—even though it be laboriously written, ticked through miles of telegraph wire, spoken by telephone, or signaled by an admiral's flags. The means of expressing and conveying the word have no bearing on its meaning. Therefore, the correspondent should write as if he were speaking to the person whom he is addressing. If it be a business letter, he should be concise, formal, brief, accurate, and yet complete, in expressing his meaning. If it be an invitation, or other form of social acknowledgment, he should be pleasant, polite, not too formal, nor too familiar. If it be a letter to an intimate friend, its contents may be suited in all respects to the degree of attachment between the writer and the recipient of the letter. Epistolary correspondence may be humorous, witty, descriptive, argumentative, or otherwise intended to interest and please. Commercial correspondence should aim to convey information only, plainly yet politely expressed.

Introduction.—If you were about to negotiate a trade with a merchant you would not abruptly begin speaking, but would first address him by name. So with a commercial letter. It must contain at its head the name of the town or city where the letter is written (the county also, if the postoffice where the letter is to be mailed be not well known), the state, the year, month and day. These, taken together, are called in general terms the "date" of the letter, and no letter of any kind should be without it. Next follow the name of the person, or names of the firm addressed, with a brief greeting, such as "Dear Sir," or "Messrs.," or "Gentlemen." The letter should then begin at once, first by acknowledging the receipt of a communication to which the letter is intended as a reply, or otherwise stating the chief subject concerning which the letter is to be written.

The introduction to a social letter from one friend to another should, in the main, be similar to that of a business letter. It is usual in writing to a friend to begin merely with "Dear John," or "Friend William." This will suffice if the communication is a mere note, the transmission of which is sure, and which does not contain anything of importance. All letters, however, are subject to accidents in the mails, and otherwise liable to a possibility of falling into strange hands. Each should, therefore, contain the complete address of the person for whom it is intended, and also that of the writer. Then, should the letter find its way to the dead-letter office, or to the wrong person, it may still be sent to its intended destination or returned to the writer.

Postscripts.— Postscripts [*after-writings*] are nearly always in bad taste, and if possible should be avoided, except in letters between close friends. If it be a letter of importance, and the writer has left out something which he intended to appear before the signature, and he is anxious to convey no bad impression, he will do well to re-write the last page of his letter, so as to include the idea in the body of the letter rather than in a postscript.

Underscoring.—Emphasis, whether in speaking or writing, borders closely upon passion, and therefore should be to a large extent avoided. *Italics* are used in printing to designate *foreign words*, but as a general thing, both in printing and writing, their liberal use pre-supposes a degree of ignorance, or at least a want of cultivation, in the reader. If the reader is educated, as we may suppose he ought to be, he will be fully able to discern the strong passages or fine points of a letter, from the meaning of the words rather than from under-scoring or italics.

Character of Letters.—The first requisite in the conversation of a man of cosmopolitan training is the complete elimination of idioms, slang, provincial phrases, and words of local use, so that you cannot, by hearing him talk or by reading what he has written, guess from what part of the country he came. So it should be with a business letter. It should be so straightforward, concise, and yet easy and direct, as to leave no room for individualities of any kind; and, except for the inevitable personality of the handwriting, it should contain nothing by which the reader can designate the writer.

Epistolary correspondence, on the other hand, needs no such restrictions, and indeed may bristle with the peculiarities of the writer, provided they do not exceed the bounds of good taste, and are not so strongly marked as to prove offensive by strained eccentricity.

Character, however, in spite of the writer, will unerringly mark his letter, just as it will his hand-writing, the crease of his coat, the expression of his eye, and the "set" of his hat. Character is something that none of us can create, but which each of us can preserve. It is a part of us. It remains for him who is wise to so effectually preserve the beauty and truth of his character, and so vigorously to subdue the faults and weaknesses, that in his letters, as in everything else, he will exhibit, at the worst, a strong and manly hold upon the good and the beautiful. In a letter of extended length it would be very difficult for any of us to prevent it from containing something which would cause a friend of long acquaintance to exclaim, "That's just like him!" The important thing is to make our individualities only such as are compatible with culture and refinement.

Use of Capitals.—In writing the date and address, both in the letter and on the envelope, all words except prepositions and rticles should begin with capitals. Otherwise, the use of capitals is, in the great majority of letters, quite excessive. Proper nouns, proper pronouns, the first word in each sentence, and the first word in any parenthesis constituting a sentence, should all and always begin with capitals. With but few other exceptions the use of capitals is unnecessary.

Repetition.—Tautology, both in speech and print, is very awkward. Repetition, therefore, all the more, is intolerable. Say a thing, in your letter, as you want it said. Then don't say it again. Why should you?

Omitting Words.—Always read every letter after you have written it. Then if you find that you have omitted a word, or a few words, you may insert them by interlining and the use of the carat. If this is frequently done, however, it shows that the writer is loose in his habits of thought, and lacking in mental discipline.

HINTS CONCERNING ADDRESSES.

IN the address of a letter, the punctuation mark following the name of the city to which the letter is to be sent should be a dash. After the greeting, should be a colon, as "DEAR SIR:" The word "and" should be spelled out the same as any other word, except in the name of a firm, as "Blue & Gray;" and in the name of a railroad, as "Chicago, Burlington & Quincy," or a canal, as "Wabash & Erie."

Abbreviations rarely look well, and appear as if the writer were as anxious to save himself trouble and time. "Jan." never looks so well as "January," nor "Msrs." so well as "Messrs.," nor "Co." so well as "County." Such abbreviations as "Co." in the title of a firm, "Mr." and "Mrs.," and other established forms in use every day, are to be preferred to the full words spelled out. After every abbreviation there must be a period.

The signature of a firm, followed by another name with the prefix "per" (meaning *by*), indicates that the letter has been written and signed by a clerk, with the authority of the firm. As, "Jones & Robinson, per Jenkins."

Do not be indiscriminate in the use of quotations. Many people fill their letters with quotations, which is both useless and senseless.

Remember that there is no context to indicate the probably correct letters of a name, so that every separate letter in every name must stand for itself, and be written as plainly as possible. An "i" blurred or blotted will change "Miss." to "Mass." An illegible "o" will change "Col." to "Cal.," or "Colo." to "Cala." Here is another illustration of the danger of abbreviations: Never imagine that the postmaster knows where the letter should go by the color of the envelope. He may have a new clerk. Never forget the anathema so frequently uttered in and out of printing offices and postoffices, upon lazy writers—"The man that wrote this ought to die!"

The card of a business man, together with his address, always looks well printed at the head of his commercial correspondence. Unless the printing or lithographing, however, be well and tastefully executed, it is better to do without it than to send out letters bearing a slovenly blotch of bad printing. In writing the date it is not necessary to put the "th" or "d" after the day of the month, if the day is placed after the name of the month. Plain "June 15" is sufficient. In England it is still customary to place the day first, the word "of" being understood; as, "30th September."

The use of titles should be very limited, in America, where democratic institutions prevail. It is questionable taste, to say the least, which betrays an undue fondness for display of this nature. Military and naval titles, also "Hon.," "Rev." and "Dr.," are allowable.

Figures can never be too carefully written. It is better to cross over a wrong figure and write a new one beside it, than to partially erase it, mark it, and leave it in such condition that nobody can tell what it is intended to be. An 8, a 5 and a 3 may thus all be made to look alike, or a 1 may look like a 7.

SAMPLE BUSINESS LETTERS.

COMMERCIAL correspondence is usually expected to be devoid of argument and of glowing comments as to the desirable qualities of goods and products. The goods or samples speak for themselves, and if much talking must be done the "drummer" will do all that is necessary. The business letter should be like the legal document—an epitome of plain facts, except that while the latter is necessarily elaborate and made to include all the words necessary for full description, the former must be limited to a concise brevity, devoid of verbiage and loquacious comment. When numbers of articles and sums of money are to be considered it is best to spell out the words, or to give both words and figures, thus: "Nine hundred dollars ($900)." Technicalities and trade phrases are admissible in case there is no possible doubt that they will be understood. A letter to a firm should not pre-suppose that it will be read and answered by the same person who replied to a previous letter. Most firms have a large number of clerks, and they cannot be expected each to deal invariably with the same customers. Therefore do not make vague or indefinite allusions to something contained in a previous letter. Even if the same person has read both your letters, he may have forgotten the previous one.

The use of frequent paragraphs, in the division of different topics in the same letter, is better than not to have enough.

In all letters of complaint keep your temper as perfectly as you would be expected to do if you were conversing in person.

Politeness pays, in correspondence, society, on the street, in the home, the counting room, and everywhere.

The following are examples of brief business letters:

OFFICE OF DOBSON & SON, Real Estate,
CHICAGO, ILL., January 8, 1885.

MR. WARFIELD, Evanston:
Dear Sir,—Please do not take it as an offense if we remind you that your rent for the month of April is still due, and that our collector has twice called upon you in vain. The owner of the property has repeatedly insisted that we must make our collections invariably in advance, and that failing to do so we must use stringent measures. The collector will call again at your place of business next Wednesday morning.
Respectfully, DOBSON & SON.

JOHNSONVILLE, NEW IBERIA PARISH, LA.,
30th January, 1885.

S. K. & J. N. BOGGS:
Gentlemen,—I have received your circular announcing an advance in upland cotton, and will ship to-morrow per steamer "Vicksburg" nine hundred bales, via New Orleans, consigned to you. Please notify me at once on receipt of the cotton. Deduct your usual commission and send New York draft. Yours truly, JOHN R. STOKES,
Manager Shaw's Plantation.

To S. K. & J. N. BOGGS, Cotton Brokers, 31 Stone Court, Cincinnati, O.

SPRING STATION, KY., January 15, 1885.

MESSRS. ROWE BROTHERS, Chicago:
Gentlemen,—Having heretofore done business with you satisfactorily, and being unable to obtain in Spring Station an article of which I am desirous, I inclose money order of twenty ($20) dollars, for which please send me a lady's gold band ring with large cameo set, the cameo to be white on a black or blue ground. I leave its selection with you, the price not to exceed the amount enclosed. Respectfully, C. H. MCVAY, Lock Box 620.

ROCK ISLAND, ILL., January 6, 1885.

JERSEY & CO., Chicago:
Gentlemen,—The five car-loads of lumber shipped by you have arrived in good condition. Quality satisfactory. Inclosed find New York draft for half the amount ($1,[illegible]), and also my note of hand due in thirty days, as per our agreement. Send me at once three more car-loads of medium oak, 4x6 sills, same grade as that sent last month. Also one car laths and pine shingles, half and half. Yours truly, SAM P. DEXTER.

To L. S. JERSEY & CO., 61 South Canal St., Chicago, Ill.

TERRE HAUTE, IND., January 4, 1885.

MESSRS. H. DEARBORN & CO., New York:
Gentlemen,—I have become impressed with the idea that the New York wholesale men do not sufficiently protect their patrons in the smaller cities from the jobbers in Indianapolis and other large towns, who sell goods in our legitimate territory, under-bidding us on our own ground. This is an important matter, and I must insist on something being done.
Respectfully yours, JAMES T. MARTIN.

OFFICE OF H. DEARBORN & CO., 161 Wall Street, New York,
December 10, 1884.

JAMES T. MARTIN:
Dear Sir,—Concerning your communication of the 4th inst., allow us to assure you that everything possible in this direction is already being done by an energetic committee of the chamber of commerce, which is actively engaged in negotiations with the commissioners of the railroad pools. We will shortly inform you of the result accomplished.
Truly yours, DEARBORN & CO.

To J. T. MARTIN, Terre Haute, Ind.

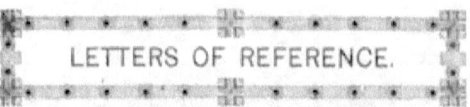

LETTERS OF REFERENCE.

THESE should be concise and not too flowery; for that would indicate that the writer of the letter had some concealed or individual interest in writing so emphatic a recommendation. No one should write a letter of reference except after thorough trial. If a departing employe or acquaintance ask for a letter of reference, and you have had but a limited knowledge of him, it is but justice to yourself to state this in the letter. Following are some examples:

CHICAGO, February 1, 1885.

To Whom it may Concern,—The bearer, John Knox, has been my coachman for two years, during which time he has given me excellent satisfaction in every way. I recommend him to any one in need of a reliable man.

T. R. KIMBLE.

SANDY HOOK, CONN., January 25, 1885.

To Dealers in Dry Goods,—The bearer, Mr. Charles L. Roberts, has been in our employ as a clerk for thirteen months, and we are pleased on his departure to furnish him with this letter of recommendation, bearing testimony to his excellence as a dry goods salesman and his character as a gentleman. He is well posted in the requirements and details of the trade, and we have always found him to be sober, reliable, honest and faithful to our interests.

PAUL WILSON & CO.

THE HERMITAGE BREWERY,
SUNBEAM, MD., January 8, 1885.

This is to say that Mr. Herbert Madison has been a resident of the town of Sunbeam for several years, and is known to us as an industrious and energetic workman. He may refer to us for honesty and sobriety, and we recommend him to all in need of his services.

JAMES SEATH, Treasurer.

NASHVILLE, TENN., February 4, 1885.

The bearer, Miss Jennie King, has been employed by me as a typewriter and cashier in my millinery store. I have found her to be honest and accurate as an accountant, and she has a thorough knowledge of the millinery business.

MRS. MARY HEMINGWAY.

LETTERS OF AFFECTION.

FOR these there is no rule that will govern all cases, and if the affection is of genuine quality it will obey no rule. However, love strives to appear at its best, and is, therefore, usually open to argument. The chief injunction necessary in regard to letters of affection, is toward a degree of reserve and moderation in expressions of endearing terms or declarations of attachment. Be not too lavish of adjectives, nor too liberal in the use of superlative qualifications, descriptive either of your own capacity for affection or of the recipient of the letter. It is well, also, to remember that paper, with the words written upon it, may be preserved long after the sentiments thereon expressed have changed or been proven false. In writing a letter of affection strive to be sensible, straightforward, truthful, manly, and lean rather toward reserve than toward a silly and boyish display of empty words. The following examples are much more brief than will, in general, be satisfactory:

POINT REEF, DAKOTA, February 8, 1885.

Dear Friend,—I arrived here yesterday on my overland journey, safe thus far. I take this opportunity to send another letter assuring you of my unceasing regard, regretting that I am absent from you so long. I look forward hopefully to the receipt of a letter from you at Custer City. It will be indeed a welcome reminder of the existence of one for whom my esteem is too earnest to be expressed except in your presence, to which may good fortune bring me soon. Your best friend, MICHAEL BURK.

LITTLE ROCK, ARK., January 15, 1885.

Dear Mother,—I have been in the city now about two weeks, and intended sooner to let you know of my safe arrival. I hope that you will not be anxious on my account, for I will come home again soon. In my absence I hourly think of you and wonder whether you are well and happy. I will write again shortly and let you know when I may be expected at home again. Your affectionate son, JAMES GREENING.

BUFFALO, N. Y., January 30, 1885.

MRS. JAMES MCCARTHY:

My Dear Wife,—Your note of yesterday is received, informing me of the theft of your new sealskin sacque, and notifying me of the arrival of your sister from Dayton. Please give my best compliments to her, and let the police know of the theft. Take good care of yourself for my sake. Please write again soon. You know that I am always anxious concerning yourself and the children when I am absent from home.

Your true and loyal husband, JAMES MCCARTHY.

BURLINGTON, IOWA, January 1, 1885.

MISS VICTORIA SEYMOUR:

Esteemed Friend,—Allow me to thank you gratefully for the permission accorded me of addressing you, and to take the first opportunity of doing so, hoping that you will condescend to favor me also with a few lines. I must thank you, too, for the courtesy you accorded me during my too brief visit at the house of our mutual friend, where I had the good fortune to meet you, and, I trust, the still better fortune of gaining your friendship. Pardon me if I presume upon a short acquaintance and extend an humble and respectful invitation to a seat at the opera house to-morrow evening. A favorable answer returned by the bearer of this would give much pleasure to your sincere friend, MAURICE MALLORY.

ADVISORY LETTERS.

AN advisory letter from a young to an older person is not in good form, except rarely, when he has had experience on some special subject, on which he has been asked for advice. Letters of counsel from older to younger persons should be kind and gentle in tone; not made odious by an assumption of authority; not patronizing nor dictatorial; and not so austere as to convey the impression that none but a saint could follow it. It is better to make the letter appear as if it were merely conveying information for the benefit of the recipient. No advice, either by letter or speech, will be heeded unless it is welcomed and valued.

INDIANAPOLIS, IND., February 6, 1885.

GEORGE HARRIS, Leadville, Colo.:

My Dear Son,—I write to inform you of my continued good health, and to ask that you will be very careful of yours, for my sake. Let me know frequently concerning your experience there, and notify me instantly of any ill fortune that may occur. I have recently met Mr. Martin, who has just returned from Leadville, and after conversing with him I am more certain that you will get on well, for the sober and well behaved men seem to be the ones who do best there, as indeed they do everywhere. He tells me also that those succeed best in a new country who begin by studying thoroughly its resources, considering well its possibilities, informing themselves widely on the scientific principles governing its minerals and geology, and in all things being ruled by reason rather than by luck, to which no wise man will trust. But if there be such thing, then may good luck attend you.

Your affectionate mother, MARY A. HARRIS.

SAVANNAH, GA., January 20, 1885.

TO JOHNNY AND JIMMY BROWN:

My Little Nephews,—You may be surprised to receive this from me, yet you know that I like you too well not to wish that I could see you. But since I cannot see you at present, I must be content with sending you a letter. I wish you could be here with me as I write, to look out of my window and see the pretty sight which I see. But there are plenty of pretty sights, no doubt, where you are. Heaven and earth are full of beauty, if we will only look for it. The most beautiful of all things, however, is an upright and spotless character, which only the young mind can lay the foundations of with solid hope of the future. Be wise to-day, my dear boys, then will your wisdom count for much profit to you when you are old, besides keeping you happy while you are young. Be studious, virtuous, diligent, shun evil companions, and above all learn to control and command self. Write often to your loving uncle,

H. R. STEEL.

VILLA GROVE, COLO., January 25, 1885.

Miss Ethel Stein,—I am sure that even unsolicited advice from so old and proven a friend as I am will not be taken as an offense. Therefore I feel free to tell you, solely and wholly for your own good, and in strict confidence, that you seem to be extending more than justifiable favor to the person with whom I saw you riding last evening. Not that he is known to me as an actual criminal, but I have heard such allusions made to him and such incidents related as convince me that his character is not above reproach, and his conduct, especially toward young ladies, is questionable, to say the least. It is possible that I am mistaken, but I think not, and deemed best to warn you.

Very respectfully, your friend, ADDIE WATERBURY.

WAUKEGAN, ILL., January 18, 1885.

Dear Brother John,—I consider it proper to let you know that the party with whom you are sharing a room at the Swinton boarding house, in Milwaukee, is not a fit person to be associated intimately with a man who, like you, desires to remain a consistent Christian and an honest man. He is said to be a confirmed gambler, and I know personally that he drinks.

Your brother, THOMAS JONES.

LETTERS OF REQUEST.

LETTERS soliciting favors are so frequently received by persons who have any favors to grant, that the appeals of the deserving often meet a fate which is intended only for the unworthy. Letters of request should, therefore, be very carefully written, lest they include such terms as may be offensive to the reader. Better forego the desired favor than forfeit a valued friendship. But having decided to write a letter of request, so frame it that, even if it be not granted, the matter shall not serve to destroy that friendship. A letter of request should by all means avoid familiarity or presumption. Neither, on the other hand, should it be fawning nor flattering, nor full of self-humiliation.

BLOOMINGTON, ILL., December 28, 1884.

MR. POTTER, C. B. & Q. Railway:

Dear Sir,—I inclose my annual pass for the year 1884, and in view of the large amount of business which I am enabled to divert from other routes to your company, I would be pleased if you could renew the pass for the year 1885. Thanking you for past favors, I remain,

Yours truly, CHARLES GOODWIN.

PRINCETON, MO., January 14, 1885.

HON. THOMAS G. POTTER, Member of Congress, 18th District, Washington, D. C.:

Dear Sir,—I am induced to present herewith a brief petition, bearing the names of thirty-eight residents of Princeton and vicinity, asking your influence in securing my appointment as postmaster. You are aware that I never before troubled you with a petition or request, although you have honored me with your friendship so long. Being feeble from rheumatism I am much in need of such a position as that of postmaster, for which my friends assure me I have every necessary qualification.

Yours respectfully, SOLOMON SEARS.

ROCKVILLE, ILL., January 13, 1885.

My Dear Friend,—I leave next Monday morning for Chicago, where I will arrive at the Rock Island depot at 11:45. If you would meet me there at that time I would esteem it a great favor,

J. S. THOMPSON.

SMITHVILLE, N. Y., January 30, 1885.

MESSRS. JONES & GRAY:

Gentlemen,—I am urgently in need of a copy of Third New York, Vol. III. I have a case pending in Circuit Court in which it would assist me greatly. If you will send me yours by the evening stage, I would esteem it a favor, and return the book soon.

ROBERT ROUNDS.

NEW YORK CITY, N. Y., January 3, 1885.

Dear Sir,—Please mail us at once a copy of your latest quotations in wheat. Also be kind enough to telegraph us Friday your rates on No. 2 red winter. It would be an accommodation for which we would thank you.

MILLER & FINN.

LETTERS OF COMMISERATION.

WHEN a friend is in affliction we can show our sympathy for him in no better way than by means of a letter, judiciously written, sent at the right time; not too cold and business-like in tone, yet not exceeding the limits of simple and unobtrusive sincerity. Your presence at a funeral, or even in a grief-stricken household, may not be noticed by a mind overwhelmed with sorrow, but a letter will reach him when he is prepared to read it, and will be appreciated. It must be free from any kind of ostentation, sparing of needless comment, not lengthy—and would better not be sent at all if it is not a product of genuine kindness and real sympathy.

SHAWNEETOWN, February 8, 1885.

Mr. Oaks,—Accept this small token of my sympathy in your present deep affliction. It was not until yesterday that I learned of the death of your son, whose merits and worth so adorned your family circle. Having myself at one time undergone a similar bitter experience, I can fully feel the extent of your great loss.

Sincerely, your friend, ARTHUR POWERS.

BOSTON, MASS., March 2, 1885.

MISS ETTIE BURKE:

Dear Friend,—I am sure that I am not intruding upon your sorrow when I express my sympathy in the loss of your dear sister. None knew better than I her virtues and womanly traits, her goodness and gentle kindness to all. Aware that her health was not what it could be wished, I still thought and hoped until very recently that she would recover from her illness and live a long and useful life. Our hopes are not fulfilled, but we have a solace in knowing that God is as loving to His children as he is just, and that He has merely removed our loved one to a happier home, where sickness never comes, but where we may one day see her.

Your friend, MRS. LIZZIE CLENDENING.

EVANSVILLE, IND., Februry 18, 1885.

JAMES T. HOBSON:

My Dear Friend,—In the telegraphic columns of the newspapers this morning I learn that by the heavy fire in your city all your hard-earned property, including your home, has been destroyed. Be assured of the heartfelt sympathy of your many friends, of whom I more than ever wish to be counted as one. If there is anything I can do to help you in your difficulty, let me know promptly.

ADDISON BENNETT.

SYRACUSE, N. Y., February 9, 1885.

Dear Cousin,—To my deep regret I learn of the shocking accident of which your father was the victim, last Tuesday. In this trouble you have my entire sympathy. Convey to your mother my deep sense of her loss and grief.

Your cousin, HENRY BUCHANAN.

DETROIT, MICH., January 25, 1885.

My Dear Mrs. Robinson,—It is with pain I find that your little daughter still lingers on a bed of suffering. I had been sanguine that by this time her long illness would give place to renewed health. Be patient and resigned, my friend, in this time of affliction, knowing you have done everything possible. If there is any ground for hope please inform your friend,

JENNIE STILLWELL.

FAMILY LETTERS.

LETTERS between members of a family have too frequently a tendency to enter into details of gossip concerning other families, fault-finding and complaint, morose reflections, and, in short, they partake too much of the nature of that selfish disposition which allows itself to vex the family circle when it would strive to appear at its best among strangers. If you love your relatives do not wait till they are dead and then rear marble shafts over them, but let them know it now. It is not a mark of weakness to express your affection for a worthy object, and surely you can find no more worthy object than the members of the family who have shared your joys and sorrows around the same fireside.

UNIONTOWN, KY., February 9, 1885.

My Dear Son,—I write to say that I am quite well satisfied with your progress thus far in Cincinnati, and am glad that you seem to be pleasing your employers. But remember, my son, that the city is full of temptations which will be new and attractive to you, and which you should guard against carefully. Improve your mind rather than debase it, wherever you go. Be diligent and faithful in business, and know that I have every confidence in you, believing your training has been such that you never can bring dishonor upon the home which is so proud of you. Write regularly. The members of the family all send their love, and wish you the utmost success. Your affectionate father, JOHN MONROE.

CINCINNATI, O., FEBRUARY 15, 1885.

My Dear Father,—Your kind letter was duly received, for which I thank you. I appreciate fully your parental admonition and wise advice. It is such as I have always needed and often received, to my profit. My city experience thus far is, as you seem to think, even more favorable than I had expected. I am doing the best I am able for my employers, and learning many things about the details of business which will be of benefit to me in every way. You may rely upon me fully to pursue an honorable career, limited in success only by my ability. Your son, CHARLES G. MONROE.

DANVILLE, ILL., January 2, 1885.

My Beloved Daughter,—I cannot tell you how much you are missed at home. Your absence, even for so short a time, causes me to feel the more keenly how much I love you. Therefore see to it that your visit is made a pleasant one, and enjoy it fully; otherwise it will not compensate for the regret I feel at seeing each day your empty chair. Yet I want you to be very happy, my dear daughter, so remain as long as you think best. I am sure it will not be necessary to urge or even to remind you to conduct yourself in every way as becomes a daughter of mine, and be always a true lady. Write often to your loving and anxious mother.

SARAH MADDEN.

LAFAYETTE, IND., January 12, 1885.

MRS. SARAH MADDEN, Danville:

Dear Mother,—I thank you for your letter, which was most welcome indeed. I am glad to know how much you love me and think of me. Be assured, dear mother, that I love you quite as much, and wish you could be here with me, enjoying the pleasures which my kind friends are providing for my entertainment. I will probably remain not longer than two weeks, and meanwhile will do my best to please the friends who have received me with such hospitality. I shall let you know the day I will return. Your affectionate daughter,

NELLIE MADDEN.

INTRODUCTORY LETTERS.

IT is customary in introducing one person to another to have very little to say beyond the formal announcement of the names, unless the person who is being introduced is a well known and intimate friend, in which case a very brief recommendation is admissible, as, "Mr. Jones, this is my friend, Mr. Brown." In a letter of introduction the same policy should rule—that of being non-committal concerning the character of the person you are introducing, unless you are so well and favorably acquainted as to be ready to assume the partial responsibility involved in any introduction, which is supposed in almost all cases to carry with it a certain degree of recommendation.

OFFICE OF OSBISTON & CROWELL, 87 College Street, Toledo, O.,
March 3, 1885.

BARBOUR & BROTHERS, New York:

Gentlemen,—This will introduce to you the bearer, Mr. Robert Richardson, who is one of our salesmen. He will spend a short vacation in the metropolis. Please extend to him any courtesies necessary during his stay in the city. Yours very truly,

STEPHENS & SMITH, Per Smith.

VINCENNES, IND., January 8, 1885.

Mr. Johnson,—Permit me to introduce to you my friend, Mrs. Addie Griffith, who will arrive there to-morrow, and is desirous of making some purchases in your line. Any courtesies extended to her will be appreciated by MRS. MARY ROSE.

HYDE PARK, ILL., February 16, 1885.

Miss Eva F. Sanderson,—Allow me to present to you my acquaintance, Mr. Shaw. I am very sure that you will find him an excellent and agreeable gentleman.

Respectfully, SAMUEL CHRISTY.

WHEELING, W. Va., January 16, 1885.

MR. WILLIAM SCANLON, Louisville:

Dear Sir,—The bearer, Mr. Harry Severn, will meet you on your arrival at Frankfort, and conduct you to my residence, where he will entertain you during my absence. I think you will be pleased to form his acquaintance. DAVID STANTON.

MINNEAPOLIS, MINN., February 8, 1885.

Mrs. T. C. Scott,—This letter will introduce to you a lady whose acquaintance you have expressed a wish to form. Miss Harriet Russell. You will find her all that I have described to you, and I am sure you will value her friendship.

Your friend, SALLIE MURDOCK.

DECLINATORY LETTERS.

IT is often necessary to decline a gift, or other offering, and it will usually be found difficult to frame the letter of declination in such manner as will be certain not to give offense. Most people feel their self-esteem wounded when they find their gifts or their sympathy refused. In this they are, perhaps, justifiable, unless very good reasons are shown to exist for making the declination. If a gift is declined, an explicit showing of the cause for it should be made. To decline the acceptance of advice, however, is usually done tacitly, for many people are over-profuse in giving it. When a lady declines the attentions of a gentleman it is optional with her whether or not she states her reasons, but all declinations should be as gently made as possible. If a reason must be given, the truth is always better than a false excuse, the detection of which might cause embarrassment.

WASHINGTON, D. C., February 6, 1885.

MR. R. H. BLAKE, Superintendent X. & Z. Railway:

Dear Sir,—Inclosed I return the annual pass over your road, so kindly sent me last week. Toward you, personally, you cannot doubt that I entertain only the profoundest regard. In view, however, of the fact that a land grant bill involving the interests of your company is to come before congress at this session, and of the further fact that I am expected to give an unbiased vote thereon, you will understand my motives in returning the pass, and will still believe me your friend,

SAMUEL BANCROFT, M. C.

EVANSTON, IND., January 20, 1885.

Mr. Howard Harvey,—With much regret I am obliged to decline your kind invitation, as circumstances over which I have no control make it impossible to accept it.

Very respectfully, ANNIE J. LEMON.

OFFICE OF DE REMER & CLEMENT, 93 Spring St.,
NEW ORLEANS, LA., January 18, 1885.

MESSRS. BROOKS & FISH:

Gentlemen,—Your very complimentary note, offering a desirable position in your service, is at hand. Allow me, while declining your proposal, which is made necessary by my present contract, to express my gratitude for this unsolicited mark of your esteem. On some future occasion I might be at liberty to accept your very favorable offer. I am, gentlemen,

Your obedient servant, JOHN T. O'CONNOR.

CAIRO, ILL., February 7, 1885.

ALDERMEN RICE, FILLMORE, and others:

Gentlemen,—Your favor of this date is at hand, informing me of your intention to propose my name for the office of mayor at the forthcoming municipal convention, and stating your belief that you can accomplish my nomination and election. I must decline your generous offer, gentlemen, for the reason that I seek no office in the gift of the people, though, indeed, I seek the good will of all. In doing so, however, I must confess my surprise at the high place I seem to have attained in your regard, and express my deep thanks for this most unmistakable testimony of your approbation.

Most respectfully yours, HIRAM GOODMAN.

LETTERS WITH PRESENTS.

A LETTER accompanying or explaining a present should be short and concise. It is not necessary to dwell at length on the high opinion held of the person to whom the present is made. The gift speaks for itself, and the letter need not go further than merely to explain the circumstances of the presentation and give the names of the donors. Its object should be a genuine desire to confer pleasure, and never a motive which can possibly be construed as a desire to bias or bribe. The person receiving the gift should use his own judgment in making his reply or acknowledgment. The reply should be returned within a reasonable time, but neither in itself nor in the circumstances under which it is made, should it imply a pecuniary debt.

L. P. & W. T. RAILROAD SHOPS,
COLUMBUS JUNCTION, ILL.,
February 8, 1885.

HENRY B. OSBORN, Master Mechanic:

Dear Sir,—Unwilling to intrude upon your privacy in the sick room to which you are confined, and from which we trust you may soon be liberated, we, your employes in the L. P. & W. T. machine shops, herewith send you by bearer a watch and chain, as a small token of our esteem for you as a man, a citizen and an employer.

THOMAS L. SEYBOLD,
Chief Clerk,
Representing L. P. & W. T. employes.

SEDALIA, MO., February 5, 1885.

REV. JOHN M. TAYLOR:

Dear Friend,—Considering the unusually good fortune which has attended my business efforts of late, I beg leave to remind you, my old friend and pastor, of my continued regard, and request that for the sake of old times you accept the check accompanying this letter.

Yours very truly, J. P. ELDER.

PHILADELPHIA, PA., March 1, 1885.

CHARLES S. ADAMS:

Dear Friend,—For the sake of old times when we were boys together, and for the sake of your estimable wife, I entreat you, in view of your recent deplorable misfortunes, to forget your pride and accept as freely as it is loaned (for we will regard it merely as a loan), the inclosed small draft. By doing so you will greatly please your anxious friend.

THEODORE KRAMER.

DESMOINES, IOWA, February 10, 1885,

MRS. S. E. MOORE:

Dear Teacher,—The beautiful clock accompanying this is a present from your pupils, who desire that you accept it as a testimonial of their esteem.

NETTIE TRELAWNEY,
HARRY G. THOMPSON, } Committee.

KALAMAZOO, MICH., January 14, 1885.

Miss Jessie Graham, Garden Street,—Thinking you might be pleased to attend the roller skating rink this evening, as there are to be unusual attractions, I will, if agreeable, call for you at 7:30 p. m. Very truly, JACOB PALMER.

BEAVER FARM, February 20, 1885.

MASTER JOHNNY SIMS:

Dear Nephew,—I am told that on your recent visit at my farm you much admired the black Shetland pony. Please come again when your school is out, and ride the pony home with you as a gift from your uncle,

LOUIS HAYWORTH.

USING PROFANE LANGUAGE.

THE deplorable prevalence of the habit of using profane language in American society is unhappily such as almost to make it a national characteristic, and is a source of pain, regret and mortification to every one whose patriotism would seek to invest American citizenship, which is the highest citizenship of the world, with the highest dignities and the most elevated moral attributes of manhood, in its most exalted sense. It is often a matter of speculation, how a practice which, when considered by itself, even by those who resort to it, is universally acknowledged to be idle, vicious and degrading, should come to have such a general sway, and that too in spite of the fact that the statutes of every state of the Union make profane language an offense against the laws—to say nothing of the shocking recklessness of divine injunction which is involved. This is probably accounted for by the peculiarities of life on this continent, which so early take the youth away from the wholesome influences of home, and the gentle but effectual restraint imposed by association with mother and sisters, and with general female society. The youth who is thrown upon his own resources, in a strange city, if his mental fibre be not vigorous enough to enable him to hold fast those moral precepts in which the pious training of the mother-love has grounded him—if he have not the wisdom to seize the golden hours of youth and leisure and turn them to his own higher pleasure, advancement and profit; if he have not the prudence to take advantage of his idle time, for his own improvement, by studying the chart of the royal road to health, happiness, wealth, pleasure and prosperity, which the labor of other men and their experience map out before him, in such a book as this: if he have none of these defenses against vicious habits, he will surely fall into company where oaths flow as naturally from the mouths of the hardened and indifferent, as the pestilent and mephitic vapors exhale from the poisonous fermentations of decomposition; and where the habit is acquired, which, against the better judgment and the sense of decency and morality, will cling to him through life, not only lessening his self-respect, but the esteem of others. Even those who use it will acknowledge that it is a vile, abominable, immoral, disgusting, senseless and depraved habit, neither ornamental to the conversation nor essential to the understanding. Every youth should early comprehend these features of profanity, and in life's springtime, cultivate the habit of so guarding his tongue that nothing shall ever escape his mouth, which would shock the prattling innocence of his little sister or give pain to the mother by whose knees he lisped his infantile petitions to the Throne of Grace. Keep ever before the eye of the mind, those words: "Take not the name of the Lord thy God in vain; for the Lord will not hold him guiltless who taketh His name in vain." And bear in mind, too, when tempted to perpetrate or to exercise this impious offense—an offense equally against the laws of God, morality and humanity—those terribly suggestive words of Longfellow:

"The mills of God grind slowly,
But they grind exceedingly small.
With patience, stands He waiting,
With exactness grinds He all."

Let the young man bear in mind, also, that if the heart and the mind and the morals be clean and pure, no such foul utterances can flow from those well-springs of life. Reflect, then, when you find yourself giving way to profanity, that there is a taint of poison in that fountain of existence, upon which the health of your morals, the measure of your self-respect and the happiness of your life depend. Cleanse your thoughts and your conversation at once from this foul impurity, and by exercise of the habit of self-control, and a stern determination to avoid profanity, in deference to decency and what you owe to yourself, if not to your sense of morality, banish from your lips those expressions which are unworthy the dignity of manhood, degrading to intellectual pride and offensive to religion and morals.

LUCKY WEDDING DAYS.

Many people fear to violate marriage superstitions. Certain periods and dates for marriage ceremonies are believed to be more fortunate than others, which is no doubt occasioned by some ancient idea of astrology. But few people are willing to admit they are superstitious, not only in the matter of marriage, but in every other, and when speaking on the subject, not only treat it lightly, but laugh at the very idea, generally terming it an old woman's whim. However, there are undoubtedly but few of any race or religion who can truthfully say they are entirely free from it.

Following is a list of the days which are considered the most fortunate: February 6, 7, 18; March 1, 6, 8; April 6, 11; May 5, 6, 7; June 7, 15; July 7, 15; August 15, 19; September 6, 7; October 6; November 16, 17, and December 15, 16, 17.

STATE NOMENCLATURE.

Nicknames of States, Cities and People.

Arkansas—Bear state.

Atlanta—Gate city.

Baltimore—Monumental city, from the grand monuments.

Boston—Athens of America. The Hub.

Brooklyn—City of Churches.

Buffalo—Queen city of the lakes.

California—Golden state.

Canada—Canuck; a Canadian is so called. Also written Cannuck, and K'nuck, a French Canadian.

Chicago—Garden city.

Cincinnati—Queen city of the west. Porkopolis.

Cleveland—Forest city.

Colorado—Centennial state.

Columbia—Palmetto city; the capital of South Carolina is so called from the arms of the state, which contain a palmetto.

Connecticut—Blue Law state. Nutmeg or Free stone. Land of steady habits.

Delaware—Diamond state. Blue Hen.

Detroit—City of the straits.

Florida—Peninsula state.

Georgia—Empire of the south. Crackers.

Gulf states—Florida, Alabama, Mississippi, Louisiana and Texas.

Illinois—Prairie or Sucker state. Natives called suckers from the habit, in early days, of sucking water from crawfish holes with hollow weeds. Southeastern portion called Egypt, from fertility of the soil, and alleged mental darkness.

Indiana—Hoosier, a corruption of the term husher, applied to rough men from Indiana who exhibited a disposition to hush up their opponents. Applied by the Kentuckians to neighbors in Indiana, who respond to a knock on the door, "Who's yere?"

Indianapolis—Railroad city.

Iowa—Hawkeye state, from old Hawkeye, an Indian chief.

Jayhawker—A cant name for a lawless or other soldier not enlisted.

Kansas—Jayhawker, or Garden of the west.

Kentucky—Blue grass, or Dark and bloody ground. Corn-crackers.

Keokuk (Iowa)—Gate city, from its position on the Mississippi river, a natural center of navigation.

Louisiana—Pelican state. Creole.

Louisville—Falls city.

Lowell (Mass.)—City of spindles.

Maine—Pine Tree state.

Massachusetts—Original name, Massachusetts Bay. Hence, Bay state.

Michigan—Wolverine.

Minnesota—Gopher, or North Star state.

Mississippi—Bayou state.

Missouri—Bullion state, from Senator Benton, who was partial to coin money. He was called Old Bullion. Natives are nicknamed Pukes.

Montreal—City of the Mountain and the Rapids.

Nashville—City of Rocks.

Nevada—Silver.

New Brunswick—Blue Noses.

New Hampshire—Granite state.

New Haven (Conn.)—City of Elms.

New Jersey—Jersey Blues.

New Orleans—Crescent city, because of its shape.

New York—Gotham, so called from the alleged odd erudition displayed by its inhabitants. A descendant of one of the old Dutch families was called a Knickerbocker. (New York was first settled by the Low Dutch, in 1614.)

New York (state)—Empire, or Excelsior. Knickerbocker.

North Carolina—Old North state. Turpentine. Tar Heels.

Nutmeg state—Connecticut, on account of the story that wooden nutmegs are manufactured there for exportation.

Ohio—Buckeye state, from the buckeye tree which grows there.

Oregon—Web-foot state.

Pennsylvania—Keystone state, from its central position as regards the other original states.

Philadelphia—Quaker city. City of Brotherly Love.

Pittsburgh—Iron city.

Portland (Maine)—Forest city.

Quebec—Gibraltar of America.

Rhode Island—Little Rhody.

San Francisco—City of the Golden Gate.

Springfield (Ill.)—Flower city.

South Carolina—Palmetto state.

St. Louis—Mound city, from the mounds found there before the city was built.

Tennessee—Mudheads, the natives of that state are so called. Big Bend state.

Texas—Lone Star, from the single star in the center of the flag of that state. Beetheads.

Toronto—City of Colleges.

Up-country—In New Hampshire, used on the coast.

Utah—Mormon.

Vermont—Green Mountain state.

Virginia—Old Dominion. When a colony, the king called it "The Colony and Dominion of Virginia." Mother of States.

Washington—City of Magnificent Distances.

West Virginia—Panhandle state.

Wisconsin—Badger state.

Origin of the Names of States.

Alabama comes from a Greek work, signifying "The land of rest."

Arkansas is derived from the Indian word Kansas, "Smoky Waters," with the French prefix of ark, "a bow."

California, from a Spanish romance, in which is described "the great island of California where an abundance of gold and precious stones are found."

Colorado, ruddy or blood-red, from the color of the water of Colorado river.

Connecticut was Monegan, spelled originally Qoun-eh-ta-cut, signifying "a long river."

Delaware derives its name from Thomas West, Lord De la Ware, governor of Virginia.

Florida gets its name from Kasquas de Flores, or "Feast of the Flowers."

Illinois' name is derived from the Indian word "Illini," men, and the French affix "ois," making "Tribe of men."

Indiana's name came from that of the Indians.

Iowa signifies, in the Indian language, "The drowsy ones."

Kansas is an Indian word for smoky water.

Kentucky also is an Indian name, "Kain-tuk-ae," signifying, at the head of the river.

Louisiana was so named in honor of Louis XIV.

Maine takes its name from the province of Main, in France, and was so called in compliment to the queen of Charles I., Henrietta, its owner.

Maryland receives its name from the queen of Charles I., Henrietta Maria.

Massachusetts, from the Indian language, signifying the country about the great hills.

Michigan's name was derived from the lake, the Indian name for fish-weir, or trap, which the shape of the lake suggested.

Minnesota, an Indian word for "Cloudy water."

Mississippi derived its name from that of the great river, which is, in the Natchez tongue, "The Father of Waters."

Missouri is an Indian name for muddy, having reference to the muddiness of the Missouri river.

New Hampshire—first called Laconia—from Hampshire, England.

New Jersey was named by one of its original proprietors, Sir George Carter, after the island of Jersey, in the British channel, of which he was governor.

New York was so named as a compliment to the Duke of York, whose brother, Charles II., granted him that territory.

The Carolinas were named in honor of Charles I., and Georgia in honor of Charles II.

Ohio is the Shawnee name for "The beautiful river."

Oregon, from its river, in Indian meaning "River of the West."

Pennsylvania, as is generally known, takes its name from William Penn, and the word "silvania," meaning woods.

Rhode Island gets its name from the fancied resemblance of the island to that of Rhodes in the ancient Levant.

Tennessee is an Indian name, meaning "The river with the big bend."

Vermont, from the Green mountains. (French, *verd mont.*)

Virginia gets its name from Queen Elizabeth, the unmarried, or Virgin Queen.

West Virginia is simply a geographical designation. From its shape, the northern part is called "Panhandle state."

Wisconsin's name is said to be the Indian name for a wild rushing channel.

HOUSEHOLD FAVORITES.

AMONG the brightest attractions of the household are the singing birds which pour forth their cheerful songs, often seeming as if trying to drive away care and banish ill-feeling from the family circle. Waking at the first ray of sunlight, and apparently never conscious that they are in prison, these little pets cheer us by their joy and fill the air with melody. We, therefore, owe them a debt, which is easily paid in good treatment and regular care. But little trouble or work is required each day in attending to their wants, and no creature seems to derive so much happiness from such simple care.

CANARIES.

The canary bird is the most popular and common, the most easily provided for and the most lively of our feathered pets, and has improved in captivity much beyond the wild bird of the Canary Islands. In their native home the birds mate late in March, building the nest at a considerable height above the ground.

The German Hartz canary looks much like the wild bird. The Parisian or Dutch Belgian is longer in the body and legs, its back arched and breast ruffled. Of the former variety there are the bright yellow, the straw colored, the yellowish white, the green or gray, and the cream colored. There are also spotted or mottled canaries, and those called swallows. The cream colored is also known as the filbert.

Of the Belgian canary the Parisian is quite large, the Holland is smaller and with imperfect ruffles, and the Brussels has a rather flat head. The German birds are the best singers, and the best colors are those which are uniform over the whole body. A bird approaching an orange color, with the color the same from head to tail, is rare and costly.

The canary should be given a comfortably large cage, and the fact that he keeps his health in a very small one is no argument against promoting his comfort. If the cage is painted, no mineral should be in the paint, and a green arsenic paint is dangerous. A neat wooden cage, simply oiled with linseed oil, is preferable, and a metal cage is better than an unoiled wooden one, as it gives no harbor for insects. The perches may be of different sizes, but should not be too small. In cleaning the cage use clear cold water, and rub dry. Scrape the perches without washing, and renew the sand. Give the bird clean water to drink and for bathing at least once a day. Canaries thrive best on a mixture of what is called canary seed and rape seed. See that you are not swindled by buying a poor quality of seed. Give hemp seed sparingly. Young birds should have hard-boiled egg from time to time until they are six months old: also flax seed which has been broken for them. The old birds will crack the flax seeds themselves. Do not give sugar and cake regularly nor frequently.

In warm weather vary the diet of the birds with lettuce, sweet apple and chickweed. Cuttle-fish should always be kept in the cage, being fastened with a thin wire. Be careful to avoid bread containing salt or soda, and other such things. The bathing dish should be placed on the floor of the cage. Everything must be kept very clean. The bath may be given by removing the floor of the cage and placing the cage over the bath alone on a table. The sand should be mixed with fine gravel.

The breeding time is from February to April, according to the warmth of your room. Fasten a suitable box in the cage, and place on the floor such stuff as short-cut hemp, manilla, threads, hair, etc., allowing the birds to build the nest themselves. When the birds are breeding give them no baths. Place egg shells in the cage. When the young birds have been hatched supply finely-chopped yolk of eggs, and in a few days mix it with crumbs of crackers and the usual seeds, with a little poppy-seed.

During the moulting time, which occurs once a year, about September, the birds will require especial care. Keep the cage in a sheltered place, obviating all chance of cold. Let the supply of sand and water be frequently renewed. Change the diet frequently, and put a rusty nail and a clove in the drinking water. If the bird's song become husky it has caught cold. Dissolve a small quantity of licorice in the water, and mix some flax seed with the canary and rape seed.

THE MOCKING BIRD.

This is one of the finest songsters in the world; but he is a southern bird, breeding but little farther north than the Ohio river, and not then except on sandy strips of open land, and taking flight at the first sign of cold weather. It is therefore more difficult to keep mocking birds than others, in cold latitudes. The mocking bird lays four eggs, and the young birds are exceedingly voracious, keeping both their parents hard at work to supply them. The mocking bird wants no dainties, but will eat almost anything, including all kinds of insects and fruits. The young birds must be given plenty of spiders. If the young ones can be kept alive till after their first moulting time they are all right, and may live many years; but not more than one out of half a dozen can be so reared, except with the best of attention. Give them plenty of water, and mix oat meal with their wetted corn meal, besides mashed potatoes and hard-boiled eggs. When the birds are older give them the usual "mocking-bird food" obtained of dealers. Mix it with crushed carrots. Give a little pepper now and then.

THE RED BIRD.

The treatment of the red bird should be nearly the same with the mocking bird, which is another very fine singer when he chooses to sing at all. The southern red bird is dark and dingy in color, and is a good singer. The bright red northern bird, though so handsome in appearance, is but a poor songster. Give the red bird plenty of variety in diet, and a large cage. He can be charmed and killed with especial ease by cats. The red bird often lives to a remarkable age.

PIGEONS.

With a good pigeon-house, well sheltered, and clean water near by, with small grains and other such food, pigeons will take care of themselves with very little trouble. Vermin are the chief pests which trouble them; and they will do better if the nests and boxes are lined with slate, or planed smooth and oiled. Cats and hawks are their perpetual enemies. By obtaining a few fancy pigeons, such as pouters, carriers and fan-tails, valuable broods can soon be reared.

PARROTS.

The gray parrots are most hardy, but are sensitive to cold draughts and dampness. Parrots should be kept out of doors in warm weather, and in winter given the benefit of sunshine as much as possible. The perches should never be of metal, but of wood, and sticks of wood should be placed loose in the cage for the parrot to gnaw upon. Give the bird plenty of fruit, also partly boiled corn which has afterward cooled. Vary the diet with all the usual seeds, melons, berries, crackers, nuts, but no meat. Begin the parrot's education as early as possible. If he pulls his own feathers out it shows a lack of cleanliness in his treatment. Give plenty of water.

OTHER PETS.

White Mice.—These little albinos are very easily reared. They will keep themselves wonderfully clean, if they are assisted in this by their cage being cleaned for them. Feed them bread soaked in milk and then squeezed dry; also peas and beans, grain of various kinds, but no meat or cheese. The mice may easily be taught many tricks.

Raccoons.—Do not let dogs or boys annoy the raccoon, as he becomes irritable and will try to bite at every opportunity. Give him a long enough chain, and plenty of water. He is one of the cleanest animals in the world if he has a chance to be.

Squirrels.—Squirrels are usually so neglected in their quarters that they suffer much from want of cleanliness, and lose their neat appearance. They should not be over fed, and should have plenty of exercise and varied diet.

The Aquarium.—The water in an aquarium must be carefully changed every day, by means of a siphon. Once a month carefully place the fish in other vessels and scour out the aquarium thoroughly. Always keep in it a few blades of freshly plucked grass, leaves, or other live plant. Renew the sand and rocks occasionally. If growing plants are in the water it will need changing less frequently. The best food for the fish is raw beef or mutton chopped fine, with no fat; also biscuit crumbs and earth-worms. Feed them every four days.

NAMES AND THEIR SIGNIFICANCE.

Common English Christian Names, with their Signification and Derivation.

Names of Males.

Albert. (Ger.) Illustrious.
Alexander. (Gk.) Defender of men.
Alfred. (Ger.) Good counsellor.
Algernon. (Fr.) With whiskers.
Alphonso. (Ger.) Willing.
Ambrose. (Gk.) Divine.
Andrew. (Gk.) Strong, Manly.
Anthony. (Lat.) Priceless.
Archibald. (Ger.) Holy prince.
Arthur. (Celtic) High, noble.
Aubrey. (Ger.) Ruler of spirits.
Augustus. (Lat.) Exalted, imperial.
Bardolph. (Ger.) Helper.
Bartholomew. (Heb.) Warlike son.
Basil. (Gk.) Kingly, royal.
Benedict. (Lat.) Blessed.
Benjamin. (Heb.) Son of the right hand.
Bernard. (Ger.) Bold as a bear.
Berham. (Ger.) Bright raven.
Brian. (Celtic) Strong.
Caleb. (Heb.) A dog.
Calvin. (Lat.) Bold.
Cecil. (Lat.) Dim-sighted.
Charles. (Ger.) Strong, manly.
Christopher. (Gk.) Bearing Christ.
Clarence. (Lat.) Illustrious.
Claude. (Lat.) Lame.
Clement. (Lat.) Mild.
Conrad. (Ger.) Bold in council.
Cuthbert. (Saxon) Noted for splendor.
Cyril. (Ger.) Lordly.
Cyrus. (Persian) The sun.
Daniel. (Heb.) A divine judge.
David. (Heb.) Beloved.
Donald. (Celt.) Proud chief.
Duncan. (Celt.) Brown chief.
Edgar. (Saxon) Protector of property.
Edmund. (Saxon) Defender of property.
Edward. (Saxon) Guarder of property.
Edwin. (Saxon) Gainer of property.
Egbert. (Ger.) Sword's brightness.
Elijah. (Heb.) Jehovah my God.
Emory. (Saxon) Powerful; rich.
Ephraim. (Heb.) Very fruitful.
Erastus. (Gk.) Lovely; amiable.
Ethan (Heb.) Firmness.
Eugene. (Gk.) Well-born.
Eustace. (Gk.) Healthy.
Ezra. (Heb.) Help.
Felix. (Lat.) Happy.
Ferdinand. (Ger.) Brave; valiant.
Francis. (Fr.) Free.
Frederic. (Ger.) Peaceful ruler.
Gabriel. (Heb.) Man of God.
George. (Gk.) Land-holder.
Gerald. (Ger.) Strong with the spear.
Gideon. (Heb.) A destroyer.
Gilbert. (Ger.) Yellow-bright.
Godfrey. (Ger.) At peace with God.
Gregory. (Ger.) Watchful.
Gustavus. (Swedish) A warrior.
Guy. (Fr.) A leader.
Harold. (Saxon.) A champion.
Henry. (Ger.) Head of a house.
Herbert. Saxon.) Glory of the army.
Herman. (Ger.) A warrior.
Hilary. (Lat.) Merry; cheerful.
Homer. (Gk.) A pledge; surety.
Hobart. (Ger.) Bright in spirit.
Hugh. (Dan.) Mind; spirit.
Humphrey. (Sax.) Home-protector.
Ignatius. (Gk.) Ardent; fiery.
Ira. (Heb.) Watchful.
Isaac. (Heb.) Laughter.
Isaiah. (Heb.) Salvation of the Lord.
Jacob. (Heb.) A supplanter.
James. (Heb.) Same as Jacob.
Jeremiah. (Heb.) Exalted of the Lord.
Jerome. (Gk.) Holy name.
John. (Heb.) Gracious gift of God.
Joseph. (Heb.) He shall aid.
Julius. (Gk.) Soft-haired.
Kenelm. (Saxon.) Defender of kindred.
Kenneth. (Gaelic.) A leader.
Launcelot. (It.) A little angel.
Lawrence. (Lat.) Crowned with laurel.
Leander. (Gk.) Lion-man.
Leonard. (Ger.) Lion-hearted.
Leopold. (Ger.) Bold for the people.
Lewis. (Ger.) Bold warrior.
Lionel. (Lat.) Young lion.
Llewellyn. (Celt.) Lightning.
Louis. (Fr.) Same as Lewis.
Lucian. (Lat.) Born at daybreak.
Ludovico. (Ger.) Same as Lewis.
Luther. (Ger.) Illustrious warrior.
Mark. (Lat.) A hammer.
Martin. (Lat.) Warlike.
Matthew. (Heb.) Gift of Jehovah.
Maurice. (Lat.) Dark-colored.
Meredith. (Celt.) Sea-protector.

Michael. (Heb.) Who is like God.
Miles. (Lat.) A soldier.
Moses. (Heb.) Drawn from the water.
Napoleon. (Gk.) Lion of the forest dell.
Nathan. (Heb.) A gift.
Neal. (Lat.) Dark; swarthy.
Neil. (Celt.) A chief.
Nicholas. (Gk.) Victory of the people.
Obadiah. (Heb.) Servant of the Lord.
Oliver. (Lat.) An olive tree.
Orestes. (Gk.) A mountaineer.
Orlando. (Ger.) Fame of the land.
Oscar. (Celt.) Bounding warrior.
Osmond. (Ger.) Protection of God.
Oswald. (Ger.) Power of God.
Owen. (Celt.) Young warrior.
Patrick. (Lat.) Noble.
Paul. (Lat.) Little.
Peregrine. (Lat.) A stranger.
Peter. (Gk.) A rock.
Philander. (Gk.) A lover of men.
Philemon. (Gk.) Loving; amiable.
Philip. (Gk.) A lover of horses.
Phineas. (Heb.) A mouth of brass.
Quintian. (Lat.) The fifth.
Ralph. (Ger.) Famous hero.
Randal. (Saxon) House-wolf.
Raphael. (Heb.) The healing of God.
Raymond. (Ger.) Wise protection.
Reginald. (Ger.) Strong Ruler.
Richard. (Ger.) Rich-hearted.
Robert. (Ger.) Bright in fame.
Roderic. (Ger.) Rich in fame.
Roger. (Ger.) Famous with the spear.
Roland. (Ger.) Same as Rudolph.
Rudolph. (Ger.) Famous hero.
Rufus. (Lat.) Red; red-haired.
Samson. (Heb.) Splendid sun.
Samuel. (Heb.) Honored of God.
Sebastian. (Gk.) Venerable; reverend.
Seth. (Heb.) Appointed.
Sigismund. (Ger.) Conquering protection.
Silas. (Lat.) Same as Silvanus.
Silvanus. (Lat.) Living in a wood.
Simon. (Heb.) Hearing with acceptance.
Solomon. (Heb.) Peaceable.
Stephen. (Gk.) A crown.
Sylvester. (Lat.) Rustic.
Thaddeus. (Syr.) The wise.
Theobald. (Ger.) Bold for the people.
Theodore. (Gk.) Gift of God.
Theodoric. (Saxon) Powerful among the People.
Timothy. (Gk.) Fearing God
Tristram. (Lat.) Grave, sad.
Tybalt. (Ger.) Same as Theobald.
Ulysses. (Gk.) A hater.
Urban. (Lat.) Of the town; polished.
Uriah. (Heb.) Light of the Lord.
Uriel. (Heb.) Same as Uriah.
Valentine. (Lat.) Strong, healthy.
Victor. (Lat.) A conqueror.
Vincent. (Lat.) Conquering.
Vivian. (Lat.) Lively.
Walter. (Ger.) Ruler of the host.
William. (Ger.) Resolute helmet.
Winfred. (Saxon) Win-peace.
Zabdiel. (Heb.) Gift of God.
Zaccheus. (Heb.) Innocent; pure.
Zedekiah. (Heb.) Justice of the Lord.
Zelobes. (Gk.) A helmet.
Zenas. (Gk.) Gift of Jupiter.
Zephaniah. (Heb.) Hidden of the Lord.

Names of Females.

Abigial. (Heb.) My father's joy.
Achsah. (Heb.) Anklet.
Ada. (Ger.) Happiness.
Adelaide. (Ger.) Same as Adeline.
Adeline. (Ger.) Of noble birth; a princess.
Agatha. (Gk.) Good; kind.
Agnes. (Gk.) Chaste; pure.
Alberta. (Ger.) Feminine of Albert.
Alethea. (Gk.) Truth.
Alexandra. (Gk.) Feminine of Alexander.
Alice. (Ger.) Same as Adeline.
Amabel. (Lat.) Lovable.
Amelia. (Ger.) Busy; energetic.
Amy. (Lat.) Beloved.
Angelica. (Gk.) Lovely; angelic.
Angelina. (Gk.) Same as Angelica.
Ann. / Anna. / Anne. } (Heb.) Grace.
Annette. (Heb.) A variation of Anne.
Antoinette. (Lat.) Inestimable.
Arabella. (Lat.) A fair altar.
Augusta. (Lat.) Feminine of Augustus.
Barbara. (Gk.) Foreign; strange.
Beatrice. (Lat.) Making happy.
Benedicta. (Lat.) Feminine of Benedict.
Bertha. (Ger.) Beautiful; bright.
Betsey. (Heb.) A corruption of Elizabeth.
Blanche. (Fr.) White.
Bridget. (Celt.) Strength.
Camilla. (Lat.) Attendant at a sacrifice.
Caroline. (Lat.) Feminine of Charles.
Catharine. (Gk.) Pure.
Cecilia. (Lat.) Dim-sighted.
Celestine. (Lat.) Heavenly.
Charlotte. (Ger.) Feminine of Charles.
Chloe. (Gk.) A green herb; blooming.
Christina. (Gk.) Christian.
Clara. (Lat.) Bright; illustrious.
Clarice. (Lat.) A variation of Clara.
Clementine. (Lat.) Mild; gentle.
Constance. (Lat.) Firm; constant.
Cora. (Gk.) Maiden.
Cordelia. (Lat.) Warm-hearted.
Cornelia. (Lat.) Feminine of Cornelius.
Deborah. (Heb.) A bee.
Delia. (Gk.) Of Delos.
Diana. (Lat.) Gladness.
Dinah (Heb.) Judged.
Dora. (Gk.) A gift.
Dorcas. (Gk.) A gazelle.
Dorinda. (Gk.) The same as Dorothea.
Dorothea. (Gk.) Gift of God.

Edith. (Ger.) Happiness; rich gift.
Edna. (Heb.) Pleasure.
Eleanor. (Gk.) Light.
Elizabeth. (Heb.) Worshiper of God.
Ella. (Gk.) Diminutive of Eleanor.
Elvira. (Lat.) White.
Emily. (Ger.) Industrious; energetic.
Emma. (Ger.) The same as Emily.
Esther. (Per.) A star.
Ethelinda. (Teut.) Noble snake.
Eugenie. (Gk.) Well-born.
Eunice. (Gk.) Happy victory.
Euphemia. (Gk.) A good report.
Eva. (Heb.) Life.
Evangeline. (Gk.) Bringing gladness.
Eveline. (Heb.) Diminutive of Eva.
Fanny. (Ger.) A diminutive of Frances.
Felicia. (Lat.) Happiness.
Fidelia. (Lat.) Faithful.
Flora. (Lat.) Flowers.
Florence. (Lat.) Blooming; flourishing.
Frances. (Ger.) Feminine of Francis.
Frederica. (Ger.) Feminine of Frederic.
Georgiana. (Gk.) Feminine of George.
Geraldine. (Ger.) Feminine of Gerald.
Gertrude. (Ger.) Spear-maiden.
Grace. (Lat.) Grace; favor.
Hannah. (Heb.) The same as Ann.
Harriet. (Ger.) Feminine diminutive of Henry.
Helen. (Gk.) Light.
Henrietta. (Ger.) Feminine diminutive of Henry.
Hephzibah. (Heb.) My delight is in her
Hester. (Per.) A star.
Honora. (Lat.) Honorable.
Ida. (Ger.) God like.
Inez. (Gk.) The same as Agnes.
Irene. (Gk.) Peaceful.
Isabella. (Heb.) The same as Elizabeth.
Jane. (Heb.) Feminine of John.
Jaqueline. (Fr.) Feminine of James.
Jeanette. (Heb.) The same as Jane.
Joanna. (Heb.) Feminine of John.
Josephine. (Heb.) Feminine of Joseph.
Julia. (Lat.) Feminine of Julius.
Katharine. (Gk.) The same as Catharine.
Keziah. (Heb.) Cassia.
Laura. (Lat.) A laurel.
Leonora. (Gk.) Lightness.
Letitia. (Lat.) Happiness.
Lilian. (Lat.) A lily.
Louisa. (Ger.) Feminine of Louis.
Lucy. (Lat.) Light.
Mabel. (Lat.) A contraction of Amabel.
Madeleine. (Heb.) Same as Magdalen.
Magdalen. (Heb.) Belonging to Magdala.
Margaret. (Gk.) A pearl.
Martha. (Heb.) Ruler of the house.
Mary. (Heb.) Star of the sea.
Millicent. (Lat.) Sweet singer.
Mildred. (Gk.) Mild threatener.
Nancy. A familiar form of Anne.
Nora. A contraction of Honora or Leonora.
Olive. (Lat.) An olive.
Ophelia. (Gk.) A serpent.
Pauline. (Lat.) Feminine diminutive of Paul.
Phœbe. (Gk.) Pure; radiant.
Penelope. (Gk.) A weaver.
Phyllis. (Gk.) A green bough.
Rachael. (Heb.) An ewe.
Rebecca. (Heb.) Of enchanting beauty.
Rhoda. (Gk.) A rose.
Rosa. (Lat.) A rose.
Rosalind. (Lat.) Beautiful as a rose.
Rosamond. (Ger.) House protection.
Roxana. (Per.) Dawn of day.
Ruth. (Heb.) Beauty.
Salome. (Heb.) Peaceful.
Sarah. (Heb.) A princess.
Selina. (Gk.) Moon.
Stella. (Lat.) A star.
Susan. (Heb.) A lily.
Theodora. (Gk.) Feminine of Theodore.
Theodosia. (Gk.) Gift of God.
Tryphena (Gk.) Delicate; dainty.
Tryphosa. (Gk.) Dainty; luxurious.
Ulrica. (Ger.) Rich.
Urania. (Gk.) Heavenly.
Ursula. (Lat.) She-bear.
Victoria. (Lat.) Victory.
Viola. (Lat.) A violet.
Virginia. (Lat.) Virgin; pure.
Vivian. (Lat.) Lively.
Wilhelmina. (Ger.) Feminine of William.
Winifred. (Saxon) Lover of peace.

GEMS

OF

POETRY.

CHOICE SELECTIONS

FROM

Standard Authors.

ELEGY.

WRITTEN IN A COUNTRY CHURCHYARD.

The curfew tolls the knell of parting day,
  The lowing herd winds slowly o'er the lea,
The plowman homeward plods his weary way,
  And leaves the world to darkness and to me.

Now fades the glimmering landscape on the sight,
  And all the air a solemn stillness holds,
Save where the beetle wheels his droning flight,
  And drowsy tinklings lull the distant folds:

Save that from yonder ivy-mantled tower
  The moping owl does to the moon complain
Of such as, wandering near her secret bower,
  Molest her ancient, solitary reign.

Beneath those rugged elms, that yew tree's shade,
  Where heaves the turf in many a mouldering heap,
Each in his narrow cell forever laid,
  The rude forefathers of the hamlet sleep.

The breezy call of incense-breathing morn,
  The swallow twittering from the straw-built shed,
The cock's shrill clarion, or the echoing horn,
  No more shall rouse them from their lowly bed.

For them no more the blazing hearth shall burn,
  Or busy housewife ply her evening care;
No children run to lisp their sire's return,
  Or climb his knees the envied kiss to share.

Oft did the harvest to their sickle yield,
  Their furrow oft the stubborn glebe has broke;
How jocund did they drive their team afield!
  How bowed the woods beneath their sturdy stroke!

Let not Ambition mock their useful toil,
  Their homely joys, and destiny obscure;
Nor Grandeur hear with a disdainful smile
  The short and simple annals of the poor.

The boast of heraldry, the pomp of power,
  And all that beauty, all that wealth e'er gave,
Await alike th' inevitable hour:—
  The paths of glory lead but to the grave.

Nor you, ye proud, impute to these the fault
  If Memory o'er their tomb no trophies raise,
Where through the long-drawn aisle and fretted vault
  The pealing anthem swells the note of praise.

Can storied urn or animated bust
  Back to its mansion call the fleeting breath?
Can Honor's voice provoke the silent dust,
  Or Flattery soothe the dull, cold ear of Death?

Perhaps in this neglected spot is laid
  Some heart once pregnant with celestial fire;
Hands that the rod of empire might have sway'd,
  Or waked to ecstacy the living lyre.

But Knowledge to their eyes her ample page,
  Rich with the spoils of time, did ne'er unroll;
Chill penury repress'd their noble rage,
  And froze the genial current of the soul.

Full many a gem of purest ray serene
  The dark unfathom'd caves of ocean bear:
Full many a flower is born to blush unseen,
  And waste its sweetness on the desert air.

Some village Hampden, that with dauntless breast
  The little tyrant of his fields withstood,
Some mute inglorious Milton here may rest,
  Some Cromwell, guiltless of his country's blood.

Th' applause of list'ning senates to command,
  The threats of pain and ruin to despise,
To scatter plenty o'er a smiling land,
  And read their history in a nation's eyes,

Their lot forbade; nor circumscribed alone
  Their growing virtues, but their crimes confined;
Forbade to wade through slaughter to a throne,
  And shut the gates of mercy on mankind;

The struggling pangs of conscious truth to hide,
  To quench the blushes of ingenuous shame,
Or heap the shrine of luxury and pride
  With incense kindled at the muse's flame.

Far from the madding crowd's ignoble strife
  Their sober wishes never learn'd to stray;
Along the cool sequester'd vale of life
  They kept the noiseless tenor of their way.

Yet e'en these bones from insult to protect
  Some frail memorial still erected nigh,
With uncouth rhymes and shapeless sculpture deck'd,
  Implores the passing tribute of a sigh.

Their name, their years, spelt by th' unletter'd muse,
  The place of fame and elegy supply;
And many a holy text around she strews
  That teach the rustic moralist to die.

For who, to dumb forgetfulness a prey,
  This pleasing anxious being e'er resign'd,
Left the warm precincts of the cheerful day,
  Nor cast one longing lingering look behind?

On some fond breast the parting soul relies;
  Some pious drops the closing eye requires;
E'en from the tomb the voice of nature cries;
  E'en in our ashes live their wonted fires.

For thee, who, mindful of th' unhonored dead,
  Dost in these lines their artless tales relate,
If chance, by lonely contemplation led,
  Some kindred spirit shall inquire thy fate—

Haply some hoary-headed swain may say,
  "Oft have we seen him at the peep of dawn
Brushing with hasty steps the dews away,
  To meet the sun upon the upland lawn;

"There at the foot of yonder nodding beech
  That wreathes its old fantastic roots so high,
His listless length at noontide would he stretch,
  And pore upon the brook that babbles by.

"Hard by yon wood, now smiling as in scorn,
  Muttering his wayward fancies, he would rove;
Now drooping, woeful—wan, like one forlorn,
  Or crazed with care, or cross'd in hopeless love.

"One morn I miss'd him on the 'customed hill,
  Along the heath and near his favorite tree;
Another came, nor yet beside the rill,
  Nor up the lawn, nor at the wood was he;

"The next with dirges due in sad array
  Slow through the churchway path we saw him borne;
Approach and read (for thou canst read) the lay
  Graved on the stone beneath yon aged thorn."

THE EPITAPH.

Here rests, his head upon the lap of earth,
  A youth to fortune and to fame unknown;
Fair Science frowned not on his humble birth,
  And Melancholy marked him for her own.

Large was his bounty, and his soul sincere;
  Heaven did a recompense as largely send:
He gave to Misery all he had,—a tear,
  He gained from heaven—'twas all he wished—a friend.

No farther seek his merits to disclose,
  Or draw his frailties from their dread abode
(There they alike in trembling hope repose),
  The bosom of his Father and his God.

THOMAS GRAY.

A HAPPY LIFE.

How happy is he born and taught
  That serveth not another's will;
Whose armor is his honest thought,
  And simple truth his utmost skill!

Whose passions not his master's are;
  Whose soul is still prepared for death,
Not tied unto the world with care
  Of public fame or private breath;

Who envies none that chance doth raise,
  Or vice; who never understood
How deepest wounds are given by praise,
  Nor rules of state, but rules of good;

Who hath his life from rumors freed;
  Whose conscience is his strong retreat:
Whose state can neither flatterers feed,
  Nor ruin make accusers great:

Who God doth late and early pray
  More of His grace than gifts to lend,
And entertains the harmless day
  With a well-chosen book or friend.

This man is freed from servile bands,
  Of hope to rise, or fear to fall;
Lord of himself, though not of lands;
  And, having nothing, yet hath all.

SIR HARRY WOTTON.

LIFE'S FLEETING JOYS.

"Oh! ever thus, from childhood's hour,
I've seen my fondest hopes decay;
I never lov'd a tree or flow'r,
But 'twas the first to fade away.

"I never nurs'd a dear gazelle,
To glad me with its soft black eye,
But when it came to know me well,
And love me, it was sure to die!

"Now too—the joy most like divine
Of all I ever dreamt or knew,
To see thee, hear thee, call thee mine—
Oh misery! must I lose *that* too?

"Yet go—on peril's brink we meet;
Those frightful rocks—that treach'rous sea—
No, never come again—though sweet,
Though heav'n, it may be death to thee.

"Farewell—and blessings on thy way,
Where'er thou goest, beloved stranger!
Better to sit and watch that ray,
And think thee safe, though far away,
Than have thee near me, and in danger!"

TOM MOORE.

THE LOVE-KNOT.

Tying her bonnet under her chin,
She tied her raven ringlets in;
But not alone in its silken snare
Did she catch her lovely floating hair,
For, tying her bonnet under her chin,
She tied a young man's heart within.

They were strolling together up the hill,
Where the wind comes blowing merry and chill;
And it blew the curls a frolicsome race
All over the happy peach-color'd face,
Till, scolding and laughing, she tied them in,
Under her beautiful dimpled chin.

And it blew a color, bright as the bloom
Of the pinkest fuchsia's tossing plume,
All over the cheeks of the prettiest girl
That ever imprison'd a romping curl,
Or, in tying her bonnet under her chin,
Tied a young man's heart within.

Steeper and steeper grew the hill—
Madder, merrier, chillier still
The western wind blew down and play'd
The wildest tricks with the little maid,
As, tying her bonnet under her chin,
She tied a young man's heart within.

O western wind, do you think it was fair
To play such tricks with her floating hair?
To gladly, gleefully do your best
To blow her against the young man's breast?
Where he as gladly folded her in;
He kiss'd her mouth and dimpled chin.

Oh, Ellery Vane, you little thought,
An hour ago when you besought
This country lass to walk with you,
After the sun had dried the dew,
What perilous danger you'd be in,
As she tied her bonnet under her chin.

AUTHOR UNKNOWN.

GATHER THE ROSEBUDS WHILE YE MAY.

Gather the rosebuds while ye may,
  Old Time is still a flying;
And this same flower that smiles to-day
  To-morrow will be dying.

The glorious lamp of heaven, the sun,
  The higher he's a getting,
The sooner will his race be run,
  And nearer he's to setting.

The age is best which is the first,
  When youth and blood are warmer;
But being spent, the worse and worst
  Times still succeed the former.

Then be not coy, but use your time,
  And while ye may, go marry;
For having lost but once your prime,
  You may forever tarry.

ROBERT HERRICK.

SHELLS OF OCEAN.

One summer eve, with pensive thought,
  I wander'd on the sea-beat shore,
Where oft, in heedless infant sport,
  I gather'd shells in days before,
  I gather'd shells in days before.
The splashing waves like music fell,
  Responsive to my fancy wild;
A dream came o'er me like a spell,
  I thought I was again a child;
A dream came o'er me like a spell
  I thought I was again, again a child.

I stood upon the pebbly strand,
  To cull the toys that round me lay;
But as I took them in my hand,
  I threw them one by one away,
  I threw them one by one away.
Oh thus, I said, in every stage,
  By toys our fancy is beguiled;
We gather shells from youth to age,
  And then we leave them like a child;
We gather shells from youth to age,
  And then we leave them, leave them like a child.

AUTHOR UNKNOWN.

TRUE GROWTH.

It is not growing like a tree
In bulk, doth make a man better be;
Or standing long an oak, three hundred year,
To fall at last, dry, bald, and sere:
    A lily of a day
    Is fairer in May;
Although it fall and die that night—
It was the plant and flower of Light.
In small proportions we just beauties see;
And in short measures life may perfect be.

BEN JONSON.

OH, WHY SHOULD THE SPIRIT OF MORTAL BE PROUD?

Oh, why should the spirit of mortal be proud?
Like a fast-flitting meteor, a fast-flying cloud,
A flash of the lightning, a break of the wave,
He passeth from life to his rest in the grave.

The leaves of the oak and the willow shall fade,
Be scatter'd around and together be laid;
And the young and the old, and the low and the high,
Shall moulder to dust and together shall lie.

The child that a mother attended and loved,
The mother that infant's affection who proved,
The husband that mother and infant who bless'd,
Each, all, are away to their dwellings of rest.

The maid on whose cheek, on whose brow, in whose eye,
Shone beauty and pleasure—her triumphs are by;
And the memory of those who have loved her and praised,
Are alike from the minds of the living erased.

The hand of the king that the sceptre hath borne,
The brow of the priest that the mitre hath worn,
The eye of the sage, and the heart of the brave,
Are hidden and lost in the depths of the grave.

The peasant whose lot was to sow and to reap,
The herdsman who climbed with his goats to the steep,
The beggar who wander'd in search of his bread,
Have faded away like the grass that we tread.

The saint who enjoy'd the communion of heaven,
The sinner who dared to remain unforgiven,
The wise and the foolish, the guilty and just,
Have quietly mingled their bones in the dust.

So the multitude goes, like the flower and the weed,
That wither away to let others succeed;
So the multitude comes, even those we behold,
To repeat every tale that hath often been told.

For we are the same things our fathers have been;
We see the same sights that our fathers have seen—
We drink the same stream, and we feel the same sun,
And run the same course that our fathers have run.

The thoughts we are thinking our fathers would think;
From the death we are shrinking from, they too would shrink;
To the life we are clinging to, they too would cling;
But it speeds from the earth like a bird on the wing.

They loved, but their story we cannot unfold;
They scorn'd, but the heart of the haughty is cold;
They grieved, but no wail from their slumbers will come;
They joy'd, but the voice of their gladness is dumb.

They died—aye! they died, and we things that are now,
Who walk on the turf that lies over their brow,
Who make in their dwellings a transient abode,
Meet the changes they met on their pilgrimage road.

Yea, hope and despondence, and pleasure and pain,
Are mingled together in sunshine and rain;
And the smile and the tear, the song and the dirge,
Still follow each other like surge upon surge.

'Tis the twink of an eye, 'tis the draught of a breath,
From the blossom of health to the paleness of death,
From the gilded saloon to the bier and the shroud—
Oh, why should the spirit of mortal be proud?

William Knox.

ROCK ME TO SLEEP.

Backward, turn backward, O Time, in your flight,
Make me a child again just for to-night!
Mother, come back from the echoless shore,
Take me again to your heart as of yore.
Kiss from my forehead the furrows of care,
Smooth the few silver threads out of my hair;
Over my slumbers your loving watch keep;
Rock me to sleep, mother,—rock me to sleep!

Backward, flow backward, O tide of the years!
I am so weary of toil and of tears,—
Toil without recompense, tears all in vain,—
Take them, and give me my childhood again!
I have grown weary of dust and decay,—
Weary of flinging my soul-wealth away;
Weary of sowing for others to reap;—
Rock me to sleep, mother,—rock me to sleep!

Tired of the hollow, the base, the untrue,
Mother! O mother! my heart calls for you!
Many a summer the grass has grown green,
Blossomed, and faded our faces between,
Yet with strong yearning and passionate pain
Long I to-night for your presence again.
Come from the silence so long and so deep;—
Rock me to sleep, mother,—rock me to sleep!

Over my heart in the days that are flown,
No love like mother-love ever has shone;
No other worship abides and endures,—
Faithful, unselfish, and patient like yours:
None like a mother can charm away pain
From the sick soul and the world-weary brain.
Slumber's soft calms o'er my heavy lids creep;—
Rock me to sleep, mother,—rock me to sleep!

Come, let your brown hair, just lighted with gold,
Fall on your shoulders again as of old;
Let it drop over my forehead to-night,
Shading my faint eyes away from the light;
For with its sunny edged shadows once more
Haply will throng the sweet visions of yore;
Lovingly, softly, its bright billows sweep;—
Rock me to sleep, mother,—rock me to sleep!

Mother, dear mother, the years have been long
Since I last listen'd your lullaby song:
Sing, then, and unto my soul it shall seem
Womanhood's years have been only a dream.
Clasped to your heart in a loving embrace,
With your light lashes just sweeping my face,
Never hereafter to wake or to weep;
Rock me to sleep, mother,—rock me to sleep.

E. A. Allen.

THE LADY'S DREAM.

The lady lay in her bed,
  Her couch so warm and soft,
But her sleep was restless and broken still;
  For turning often and oft
From side to side, she mutter'd and moan'd,
  And toss'd her arms aloft.
At last she started up,
  And gazed on the vacant air
With a look of awe, as if she saw,
  Some dreadful phantom there—
And then in the pillow she buried her face
  From visions ill to bear.
The very curtain shook,
  Her terror was so extreme,
And the light that fell on the broider'd quilt
  Kept a tremulous gleam;
And her voice was hollow, and shook as she cried:

"Oh, me! that awful dream!
That weary, weary walk
  In the churchyard's dismal ground!
And those horrible things, with shady wings,
  That came and flitted round—
Death, death, and nothing but death,
  In every sigh and sound!
And oh! those maidens young
  Who wrought in that dreary room,
With figures drooping and spectres thin,
  And cheeks without a bloom—
And the voice that cried, 'For the pomp of pride
  We haste to an early tomb!
For the pomp and pleasures of pride
  We toil like the African slaves,
And only to earn a home at last
  Where yonder cypress waves;'
And then it pointed—I never saw
  A ground so full of graves!

And still the coffins came,
  With their sorrowful trains and slow;
Coffin after coffin still,
  A sad and sickening show;
From grief exempt, I never had dreamt
  Of such a world of woe!
Of the hearts that daily break,
  Of the tears that hourly fall,
Of the many, many troubles of life,
  That grieves this earthly ball—
Disease and hunger, pain and want,
  But now I dream of them all!
For the blind and the cripple were there,
  And the babe that pined for bread,
And the houseless man and the widow poor,
  Who begg'd to bury the dead!
The naked, alas! that I might have clad,
  The famished I might have fed!
The sorrow I might have soothed,
  And the unregarded tears;
For many a thronging shape was there,
  From long forgotten years,
Ay, even the poor rejected Moor,
  Who raised my childish fears!
Each pleading look, that long ago
  I scann'd with a heedless eye,
Each face was gazing as plainly there,
  As when I pass'd it by;
Woe, woe for me if the past should be
  Thus present when I die,
No need of sulphurous lake,
  No need of fiery coals,
But only that crowd of human kind
  Who wanted pity and dole—
In everlasting retrospect—
  Will wring my sinful soul!
Alas! I have walk'd through life
  Too heedless where I trod;
Nay, helping to trample my fellow-worm,
  And fill the burial sod—
Forgetting that even the sparrow falls
  Not unmark'd of God!
I drank the richest draughts,
  And ate whatever is good—
Fish, and flesh, and fowl, and fruit,
  Supplied my hungry mood;
But I never remember'd the wretched ones
  That starve for want of food·
I dress'd as the noble dress,
  In cloth of silver and gold,
With silk, and satin, and costly furs,
  In many an ample fold;
But I never remember'd the naked limbs,
  That froze with winter's cold.
The wounds I might have heal'd!
  The human sorrow and smart!
And yet it never was in my soul
  To play so ill a part:
But evil is wrought by want of thought,
  As well as want of heart!"

She clasp'd her fervent hands,
  And the tears began to stream;
Large, and bitter, and fast they fell,
  Remorse was so extreme;
And yet, oh yet, that many a dame
  Would dream the Lady's Dream!

THOMAS HOOD.

OFT, IN THE STILLY NIGHT.

Oft in the stilly night,
Ere slumber's chain has bound me,
Fond memory brings the light
Of other days around me;
The smiles, the tears,
Of boyhood's years,
The words of love then spoken;
The eyes that shone,
Now dimm'd and gone,
The cheerful hearts now broken!
Thus, in the stilly night,
Ere slumber's chain has bound me,
Sad memory brings the light
Of other days around me.

When I remember all
The friends so linked together,
I've seen around me fall,
Like leaves in wintry weather;
I feel like one,
Who treads alone
Some banquet-hall deserted,
Whose lights are fled,
Whose garlands dead,
And all but he departed!
Thus, in the stilly night,
Ere slumber's chain has bound me,
Sad memory brings the light
Of other days around me.

THOMAS MOORE.

THERE ARE GAINS FOR ALL OUR LOSSES.

There are gains for all our losses—
There are balms for all our pain
But when youth, the dream, departs,
It takes something from our hearts,
And it never comes again.

We are stronger and are better,
Under manhood's sterner reign;
Still we feel that something sweet
Followed youth, with flying feet,
And will never come again.

Something beautiful has vanished,
And we sigh for it in vain;
We behold it everywhere,
On the earth and in the air,
But it never comes again.

RICHARD HENRY STODDARD.

THE RAVEN.

Once upon a midnight dreary, while I pondered, weak and weary,
Over many a quaint and curious volume of forgotten lore;
While I nodded, nearly napping, suddenly there come a tapping,
As of some one gently rapping, rapping at my chamber-door.
"'Tis some visitor," I muttered, "tapping at my chamber-door—
Only this, and nothing more."

Ah, distinctly I remember it was in the bleak December,
And each separate dying ember wrought its ghost upon the floor.
Eagerly I wished the morrow—vainly I had tried to borrow
From my books surcease of sorrow—sorrow for the lost Lenore—
For the rare and radiant maiden whom the angels name Lenore,
Nameless here forevermore.

And the silken, sad, uncertain rustling of each purple curtain
Thrilled me—filled me with fantastic terrors never felt before;
So that now, to still the beating of my heart, I stood repeating,
"'Tis some visitor entreating entrance at my chamber-door,
Some late visitor entreating entrance at my chamber-door;
This it is and nothing more."

Presently my soul grew stronger; hesitating then no longer,
"Sir," said I, "or Madame, truly your forgiveness I implore;
But the fact is I was napping, and so gently you came rapping,
And so faintly you came tapping, tapping at my chamber-door,
That I scarce was sure I heard you:" here I opened wide the door.
Darkness there and nothing more.

Deep into that darkness peering, long I stood there wondering, fearing,
Doubting, dreaming dreams no mortal ever dared to dream before;
But the silence was unbroken, and the stillness gave no token,
And the only word there spoken was the whispered word, "Lenore!"
Merely this and nothing more.

Back into the chamber turning, all my soul within me burning,
Soon again I heard a tapping, somewhat louder than before.
"Surely," said I, "surely that is something at my window-lattice;
Let me see, then, what thereat is, and this mystery explore.
Let my heart be still a moment, and this mystery explore;
'Tis the wind and nothing more!"

Open here I flung the shutter, when, with many a flirt and flutter,
In there stepped a stately raven of the saintly days of yore.
Not the least obeisance made he; not an instant stopped or stayed he;
But with mien of lord or lady, perched above my chamber-door—
Perched upon a bust of Pallas, just above my chamber-door—
Perched, and sat, and nothing more.

Then this ebony bird beguiling my sad fancy into smiling,
By the grave and stern decorum of the countenance it wore,
"Though thy crest be shorn and shaven, thou," I said, "art sure no craven,
Ghastly, grim, and ancient raven, wandering from the Nightly shore,
Tell me what thy lordly name is on the Night's Plutonian shore."
Quoth the raven, "Nevermore."

Much I marveled this ungainly fowl to hear discourse so plainly,
Though its answer little meaning—little relevancy bore;
For we cannot help agreeing that no living human being
Ever yet was blessed with seeing bird above his chamber-door—
Bird or beast upon the sculptured bust above his chamber-door,
With such name as "Nevermore."

But the raven, sitting lonely on the placid bust, spoke only
That one word, as if his soul in that one word he did outpour.
Nothing further then he muttered; not a feather then he fluttered—
Till I scarcely more than muttered, "Other friends have flown before;
On the morrow he will leave me, as my hopes have flown before."
Then the bird said, "Nevermore."

Startled at the stillness broken by reply so aptly spoken,
"Doubtless," said I, "what it utters is its only stock and store,
Caught from some unhappy master whom unmerciful disaster
Followed fast and followed faster till his song one burden bore—
Till the dirges of his hope that melancholy burden bore—
Of "Never—Nevermore."

But the raven, still beguiling all my sad soul into smiling,
Straight I wheeled a cushioned seat in front of bird, and bust, and door;
Then, upon the velvet sinking, I betook myself to linking
Fancy into fancy, thinking what this ominous bird of yore
Meant in croaking "Nevermore."

This I sat engaged in guessing, but no syllable expressing
To the fowl whose fiery eyes now burned into my bosom's core;
This and more I sat divining, with my head at ease reclining
On the cushion's velvet lining that the lamplight gloated o'er—
She shall press, ah, nevermore!

Then, methought the air grew denser, perfumed from an unseen censer,
Swung by seraphim whose footfalls tinkled on the tufted floor.
"Wretch," I cried, "thy God hath lent thee—by these angels he hath sent thee
Respite—respite and nepenthe from thy memories of Leonore!
Quaff, oh quaff this kind nepenthe, and forget this lost Leonore!"
Quoth the raven, "Nevermore."

"Prophet!" said I, "thing of evil, prophet still, if bird or devil!
Whether Tempter sent, or whether tempest tossed thee here ashore,
Desolate, yet all undaunted, on this desert land enchanted—
On this home by Horror haunted—tell me truly, I implore—
Is there—is there balm in Gilead? Tell me, tell me, I implore!"
Quoth the raven, "Nevermore."

"Prophet!" said I, "thing of evil, prophet still, if bird or devil!
By that heaven that bends above us—by that God we both adore—
Tell this soul with sorrow laden if, within the distant Aiden,
It shall clasp a sainted maiden whom the angels name Leonore—
Clasp a rare and radiant maiden whom the angels name Leonore?"
Quoth the raven, "Nevermore."

"Be that word our sign of parting, bird or fiend!" I shrieked, upstarting—
"Get thee back into the tempest and the Night's Plutonian shore!
Leave no black plume as a token of that lie thy soul hath spoken!
Leave my loneliness unbroken! Quit the bust above my door!
Take thy beak from out my heart, and take thy form from off my door!"
Quoth the raven, "Nevermore."

And the raven, never flitting, still is sitting, still is sitting
On the pallid bust of Pallas just above my chamber-door;
And his eyes have all the seeming of a demon's that is dreaming,
And the lamplight o'er him streaming throws his shadow on the floor,
And my soul from out that shadow that lies floating on the floor,
Shall be lifted, nevermore!

EDGAR ALLAN POE.

MAID OF ATHENS.

Maid of Athens, ere we part,
Give, oh, give me back my heart!
Or, since that has left my breast,
Keep it now, and take the rest!
Hear my vow before I go,
My life, I love you.

By those tresses unconfined,
Wooed by each Egean wind;
By those lids whose jetty fringe
Kiss thy soft cheeks' blooming tinge;
By those wild eyes like the roe,
My life, I love you.

By that lip I long to taste,
By that zone-encircled waist;
By all the token-flowers that tell
What words can never speak so well;
By love's alternate joy and woe,
My life, I love you.

Maid of Athens; I am gone:
Think of me, sweet! when alone.—
Though I fly to Istambol,
Athens holds my heart and soul:
Can I cease to love thee? No!
My life, I love you.

LORD BYRON.

THE RAINY DAY.

The day is cold, and dark and dreary;
It rains, and the wind is never weary;
The vine still clings to the mouldering wall,
But at every gust the dead leaves fall,
And the day is dark and dreary.

My life is cold, and dark, and dreary,
It rains, and the wind is never weary;
My thoughts still cling to the mouldering past,
But the hopes of youth fall thick in the blast,
And the days are dark and dreary.

Be still, sad heart! and cease repining;
Behind the clouds is the sun still shining;
Thy fate is the common fate of all,
Into each life some rain must fall,
Some days must be dark and dreary.

HENRY WADSWORTH LONGFELLOW.

KISSES.

My love and I for kisses play'd:
She would keep stakes—I was content;
But when I won, she would be paid;
This made me ask her what she meant:
"Pray, since I see," quoth she, "your wrangling vein,
Take your own kisses; give me mine again."

WILLIAM STRODE.

THE NEGLECTED CALL.

When the fields were white with harvest, and the laborers were few,
Heard I thus a voice within me, "Here is work for thee to do;
Come thou up and help the reapers, I will show thee now the way,
Come and help them bear the burden, and the toiling of the day."
"For a more convenient season," thus I answered, "will I wait;"
And the voice reproving murmured, "Hasten, ere it be too late."

Yet I heeded not the utterance, listening to lo! here—lo! there—
I lost sight of all the reapers in whose work I would not share;
Followed after strange devices—bowed my heart to gods of stone,
Till, like Ephraim, joined to idols, God well nigh left me alone;
But the angel of His patience followed on my erring track,
Setting here and there a landmark, wherewithal to guide me back.

Onward yet I went, and onward, till there met me on the way
A poor prodigal returning, who, like me, had gone astray,
And his faith was strong and earnest that a father's house would be
Safest shelter from temptation for such sinful ones as he.
"Read the lesson," said the angel, "take the warning and repent;"
But the wily tempter queried, "Ere thy substance be unspent,

"Hast thou need of toil and labor? art thou fitted for the work?
Many a hidden stone to bruise thee in the harvest-field doth lurk;
There are others called beside thee, and perchance the voice may be
But thy own delusive fancy, which thou hearest calling thee—
There is time enough before thee, all thy footsteps to retrace."
Then I yielded to the tempter, and the angel veiled her face.

Pleasure beckoned in the distance, and her siren song was sweet,
"Through a thornless path of flowers gently I will guide thy feet.
Youth is as a rapid river, gliding noiselessly away,
Earth is but a pleasant garden; cull its roses whilst thou may;
Press the juice from purple clusters, fill life's chalice with the wine;
Taste the fairest fruits which tempt thee, all its richest fruits are thine."

Ah! the path was smooth and easy, but a snare was set therein,
And the feet were oft entangled in the fearful mesh of sin;
And the canker-worm was hidden in the rose-leaf folded up,
And the sparkling wine of pleasure was a fatal Circean cup;
All its fruits were Dead Sea apples, tempting only to the sight,
Fair, yet filled with dust and ashes—beautiful, but touched with blight.

"O my Father," cried I, inly, "Thou hast striven—I have willed.
Now the mission of the angel of thy patience is fulfilled,
I have tasted earthly pleasures, yet my soul is craving food;
Let the summons which Thou hast given to Thy servant be renewed;
I am ready now to labor—wilt Thou call me once again?
I will join thy willing reapers as they garner up the grain."

But the still small voice within me, earnest in its truth, and deep,
Answered my awakened conscience, "As thou sowest thou shalt reap;
God is just, and retribution follows each neglected call.
Thou hadst thy appointed duty taught thee by the Lord of all;
Thou wert chosen, but another filled the place assignèd thee;
Henceforth in my field of labor thou mayst but a gleaner be.

"But a work is still before thee—see thou linger not again;
Separate the chaff thou gleanest, beat it from among the grain;
Follow after these my reapers, let thine eyes be on the field,
Gather up the precious handfuls their abundant wheat-sheaves yield;
Go not hence to glean, but tarry from the morning until night;
Be thou faithful, thou mayst yet find favor in thy Master's sight."

HANNAH LLOYD NEALE.

MEETING OF THE WATERS.

There is not in the wide world a valley so sweet
As that vale in whose bosom the bright waters meet;
Oh, the last rays of feeling and life must depart
Ere the bloom of that valley shall fade from my heart!

Yet 'twas not that Nature had shed o'er the scene
Her purest of crystal and brightest of green;
'Twas not the soft magic of streamlet or hill —
Oh, no! it was something more exquisite still.

'Twas that friends, the beloved of my bosom, were near,
Who made every dear scene of enchantment more dear,
And who felt how the best charms of Nature improve
When we see them reflected from looks that we love.

Sweet vale of Avoca! how calm could I rest
In thy bosom of shade, with the friends I love best;
Where the storms that we feel in this cold world should cease,
And our hearts like thy waters be mingled in peace.

THOMAS MOORE.

THE VAGABONDS.

We are two travelers, Roger and I.
  Roger's my dog.—Come here, you scamp!
Jump for the gentleman—mind your eye!
  Over the table,—look out for the lamp!—
The rogue is growing a little old;
  Five years we've tramped through wind and weather,
And slept out-doors when nights were cold,
  And ate—and drank—and starved—together.

We've learned what comfort is, I tell you!
  A bed on the floor, a bit of rosin,
A bit of fire to thaw our thumbs (poor fellow!
  The paw he holds up there's been frozen),
Plenty of catgut for my fiddle
  (This out-door business is bad for strings),
Then a few nice buckwheats, hot from the griddle,
  And Roger and I set up for kings!

No, thank ye, sir,—I never drink;
  Roger and I are exceedingly moral—
Aren't we, Roger?—See him wink!
  Well, something hot, then; we won't quarrel,
He's thirsty, too, see him nod his head!
  What a pity, sir, that dogs can't talk!
He understands every word that's said,—
  And he knows good milk from water-and-chalk.

The truth is, sir, now I reflect,
  I've been so sadly given to grog,
I wonder I've not lost the respect
  (Here's to you, sir!) even of my dog;
But he sticks by, through thick and thin;
  And this old coat with its empty pockets
And rags that smell of tobacco and gin,
  He'll follow while he has eyes in his sockets.

There isn't another creature living
  Would do it, and prove through every disaster,
So fond, so faithful, and so forgiving,
  To such a miserable, thankless master!
No sir!—see him wag his tail and grin!
  By George! it makes my old eyes water—
That is, there's something in this gin
  That chokes a fellow. But no matter!

We'll have some music, if you're willing,
  And Roger (hem! what a plague a cough is, sir!)
Shall march a little.—Start, you villain!
  Stand straight! 'Bout face! Salute your officer!
Put up that paw! Dress! Take that rifle!
  (Some dogs have arms, you see!) Now hold your
Cap while the gentleman gives a trifle,
  To aid a poor old patriot soldier!

March! Halt! Now show how the rebel shakes
  When he stands up to hear his sentence.
Now tell us how many drams it takes
  To honor a jolly new acquaintance.
Five yelps,—that's five; he's mighty knowing!
  The night's before us, fill the glasses!
Quick, sir! I'm ill,—my brain is going!—
  Some brandy,—thank you,—there, it passes.

Why not reform? That's easily said;
  But I've gone through such wretched treatment,
Sometimes forgetting the taste of bread,
  And scarce remembering what meat meant,
That my poor stomach's past reform;
  And there are times when, mad with thinking,
I'd sell out heaven for something warm,
  To prop a horrible inward sinking.

Is there a way to forget to think?
  At your age, sir, home, fortune, friends,
A dear girl's love,—but I took to drink.
  The same old story; you know how it ends.
If you could have seen these classic features,
  You needn't laugh, sir; they were not then
Such a burning libel on God's creatures;
  I was one of your handsome men:

If you had seen HER, so fair and young,
  Whose head was happy on this breast;
If you could have heard the song I sung
  When the wine went round, you would'nt have guessed
That even I, sir, should be straying
  From door to door, with fiddle and dog,
Ragged and penniless, and playing
  To you to-night for a glass of grog!

She's married since;—a parson's wife:
  'Twas better for her that we should part,
Better the soberest, prosiest life
  Than a blasted home and a broken heart.
Have I seen her? Once: I was weak and spent
  On a dusty road: a carriage stopped:
But little she dreamed as on she went,
  Who kissed the coin that her fingers dropped!

You've set me talking, sir; I'm sorry;
  It makes me wild to think of the change!
What do you care for a beggar's story?
  Is it amusing? You find it strange?
I had a mother so proud of me!
  'Twas well she died before. Do you know,
If the happy spirits in heaven can see
  The ruin and wretchedness here below?

Another glass, and strong, to deaden
  This pain; then Roger and I will start.
I wonder, has he such a lumpish, leaden,
  Aching thing, in place of a heart?
He is sad sometimes, and would weep if he could,
  No doubt remembering things that were,—
A virtuous kennel, with plenty of food,
  And himself a respectable cur.

I'm better now; that glass was warming.
  You rascal! limber your lazy feet!
We must be fiddling and performing
  For supper and bed, or starve in the street.
Not a very gay life to lead, you think?
  But soon we shall go where lodgings are free,
And the sleepers need neither victuals nor drink;
  The sooner the better for Roger and me!

J. T. TROWBRIDGE.

BREAK, BREAK, BREAK.

Break, break, break,
  On thy cold, gray stones, O sea!
And I would that my tongue could utter
  The thoughts that arise in me.

Oh, well for the fisherman's boy
  That he shouts with his sister at play!
Oh, well for the sailor lad
  That he sings in his boat on the bay!

And the stately ships go on
  To the haven under the hill;
But oh; for the touch of a vanished hand,
  And the sound of a voice that is still!

Break, break, break,
  At the foot of thy crags, O sea;
But the tender grace of a day that is dead
  Will never come back to me.

ALFRED TENNYSON.

WOODMAN, SPARE THAT TREE.

Woodman, spare that tree!
  Touch not a single bough!
In youth it shelter'd me,
  And I'll protect it now.
'Twas my forefather's hand
  That placed it near its cot;
There, woodman, let it stand,
  Thy axe shall harm it not!

That old familiar tree,
  Whose glory and renown
Are spread o'er land and sea—
  And wouldst thou hew it down?
Woodman, forbear thy stroke,
  Cut not its earth-bound ties;
Oh, spare that aged oak,
  Now towering to the skies!

When but an idle boy,
  I sought its grateful shade;
In all their gushing joy
  Here, too, my sisters play'd.
My mother kiss'd me here;
  My father press'd my hand
Forgive this foolish tear,
  But let that old oak stand!

My heart-strings round thee cling,
  Close as thy bark, old friend!
Here shall the wild bird sing,
  And still thy branches bend.
Old tree! the storm still brave!
  And, woodman, leave the spot;
While I've a hand to save,
  Thy axe shall harm it not!

GEORGE P. MORRIS.

CRABBED AGE AND YOUTH.

Crabbed age and youth
  Cannot live together;
Youth is full of pleasance,
  Age is full of care;
Youth like summer morn,
  Age like winter weather;
Youth like summer brave,
  Age like winter bare.
Youth is full of sport,
Age's breath is short;
  Youth is nimble, age is lame;
Youth is hot and bold,
Age is weak and cold;
  Youth is wild, and age is tame.
Age, I do abhor thee;
Youth, I do adore thee;
  Oh, my love, my love is young!
Age, I do defy thee;
O sweet shepherd! hie thee,
  For methinks thou stay'st too long.

WILLIAM SHAKSPEARE.

LEGEND OF THE HORSESHOE.

A farmer, traveling with his load,
Picked up a horseshoe in the road,
And nailed it fast to his barndoor,
That luck might down upon him pour;
That every blessing known in life
Might come to his homestead and wife,
And never any kind of harm
Descend upon his growing farm.

But dire ill-fortune soon began
To visit the astounded man.
His hens declined to lay their eggs;
His bacon tumbled from the pegs,
And rats devoured the fallen legs;
His corn, that never failed before,
Mildewed and rotted on the floor;
His grass refused to end in hay;
His cattle died or went astray;
In short, all moved the crooked way.

Next spring a great drought baked the sod,
And roasted every pea in pod;
The beans declared they could not grow
So long as nature acted so;
Redundant insects reared their brood
To starve for lack of juicy food;
The staves from barrel sides went off
As if they had the hooping-cough,
And nothing of the useful kind
To hold together felt inclined;
In short, it was no use to try
While all the land was in a fry.

One morn, demoralized with grief,
The farmer clamored for relief;
And prayed right hard to understand
What witchcraft now possessed his land;
Why house and farm in misery grew
Since he nailed up that "lucky shoe."

While thus dismayed o'er matters wrong
An old man chanced to trudge along,
To whom he told, with wormwood tears,
How his affairs were in arrears,
And what a desperate state of things
A picked-up horseshoe sometimes brings.

The stranger asked to see the shoe,
The farmer brought it into view;
But when the old man raised his head,
He laughed outright, and quickly said:
"No wonder skies upon you frown—
You've nailed the horseshoe upside down!
Just turn it round, and soon you'll see
How you and fortune will agree."

The farmer turned the horseshoe round,
And showers began to swell the ground;
The sunshine laughed among his grain,
And heaps on heaps piled up the wain;
The loft his hay could barely hold,
His cattle did as they were told;

Folks say never such ears of corn
  As in his smiling hills were born;
His barn was full of busting bins—
  His wife presented him with twins!

His fruit trees needed sturdy props
  To hold the gathering apple crops;
His turnip and potato fields
  Astounded all men by their yields.

His neighbors marveled more and more
  To see the increase in his store.
And now the merry farmer sings:
"There are two ways of doing things;
And when for good luck you would pray,
  Nail up your horseshoe the right way."

LOVE NOT.

Love not, love not! ye hapless sons of clay!
  Hope's gayest wreaths are made of earthly flowers—
Things are not made to fade and fall away
  Ere they have blossomed for a few short hours.
    Love not!

Love not; the thing ye love may change!
  The rosy lip may cease to smile on you;
The kindly-beaming eye grow cold and strange,
  The heart still warmly beat, yet not be true.
    Love not!

Love not; the thing you love may die—
  May perish from the gay and gladsome earth;
The silent stars, the blue and smiling sky,
  Beam o'er its grave, as once upon its birth.
    Love not!

Love not! oh, warning vainly said,
  In present hours as in the years gone by;
Love flings a hallow round the dear one's head,
  Faultless, immortal, till they change or die.
    Love not!

CAROLINE NORTON.

WHERE ARE YOU GOING, MY PRETTY MAID?

"Where are you going, my pretty maid?"
"I am going a-milking, sir," she said.
"May I go with you, my pretty maid?"
"You're kindly welcome, sir," she said.
"What is your fortune, my pretty maid?"
"My face is my fortune, sir," she said.
"Then I won't marry you, my pretty maid?"
"Nobody asked you, sir," she said.

AUTHOR UNKNOWN.

LAST ROSE OF SUMMER.

'TIS THE LAST ROSE OF SUMMER.

'Tis the last rose of summer,
  Left blooming alone;
All her lovely companions
  Are faded and gone;
No flower of her kindred,
  No rosebud, is nigh
To reflect back her blushes,
  Or give sigh for sigh.

I'll not leave thee, thou lone one!
  To pine on the stem;
Since the lovely are sleeping,
  Go sleep thou with them.
Thus kindly I scatter
  Thy leaves o'er the bed
Where thy mates of the garden
  Lie scentless and dead.

So soon may I follow,
  When friendships decay,
And from love's shining circle
  The gems drop away.
When true hearts lie wither'd,
  And fond ones are flown,
Oh, who would inhabit
  This bleak world alone?

THOMAS MOORE.

A WITHERED ROSE.

A yellow page! a faded line!
  A withered rose, long laid away;
A withered rose, its fragrance gone,
  Reminder of a brighter day.

Once on my breast I wore it, red;
  Strong at my side the giver stood;
Ah! life was young, and hope was sweet,
  And ev'ry sound but murmured good.

The rose is faded, so am I;
  The bloom of youth is long since fled;
The yellow leaf, the dim old words,
  Are ghosts of happiness now dead.

There is a mouldy smell that clings
  Around old papers that have lain;
And love, me thinks, becomes the same,
  When trust in love is ruthless slain.

Sometimes I deem that looking o'er
  The happy days is far more sad
Than bearing heavy burdens now,
  Without one song to make us glad.

Then why should I the past recall?
  Thou'rt ashes now, poor withered rose;
I'll let thee fly like dust, away,
  Thou'lt fall perchance where new love grows.

AUTHOR UNKNOWN.

OLD GRIMES'S HEN.

At last that speckle hen has gone,
  That hen of hens the best.
She died, without a sight or groan,
  While in her downy nest.

Through summer's heat and winter's snow,
  For ten long years she lay,
At morn and eve, old Grimes an egg,
  But none the Sabbath day.

She had a nest behind the door,
  All neatly lined with hay;
Her back was brown and speckled o'er
  With spots inclined to gray.

When e'er the rain came pelting down,
  Or thunder's dreadful roar,
She hid herself in Grimes's hat
  Until the storm was o'er.

Tho' fourteen years of age almost,
  She still looked young and hale,
And like Job's turkey, she could boast
  One feather in her tail.

She never deigned the barnyard beau
  His face to look upon—
But loved that one whose long, shrill crow
  Was heard at early dawn;—

An aged cock, who oft had told
  His descent with a sigh,
From one that crowed when Peter bold
  His Master did deny.

When poor old speckle closed her eye,
  He jumped the fence and cried,
And bade the poultry all good-bye,
  And then lay down and died.

J. M. Barrow.

DAWN.

Juliet.—Wilt thou be gone? It is not yet near day,
It was the nightingale, and not the lark,
That pierced the fearful hollow of thine ear:
Nightly she sings on yon pomegranate tree:
  Believe me, love, it was the nightingale.

Romeo.—It was the lark, the herald of the morn;
No nightingale. Look, love, what envious streaks
Do lace the severing clouds in yonder east:
Night's candles are burnt out, and jocund day
Stands tiptoe on the misty mountain-tops;
  I must be gone and live, or stay and die.

William Shakspeare.

FLOW GENTLY, SWEET AFTON.

Flow gently, sweet Afton, among thy green braes,
Flow gently, I'll sing thee a song in thy praise;
My Mary's asleep by thy murmuring stream,
Flow gently, sweet Afton, disturb not her dream.

Thou stock-dove whose echo resounds through the glen,
Ye wild whistling blackbirds in your thorny den,
Thou green-crested lapwing, thy screaming forbear,
I charge you disturb not my slumbering fair.

How lofty, sweet Afton, thy neighboring hills,
Far mark'd with the courses of clear winding rills;
There daily I wander as noon rises high,
My flocks and my Mary's sweet cot in my eye.

How pleasant thy banks and green valleys below,
Where wild in the woodlands the primroses blow;
There, oft as mild evening weeps over the lea,
The sweet-scented birk shades my Mary and me.

Thy crystal stream, Afton, how lovely it glides,
And winds by the cot where my Mary resides;
How wanton thy waters her snowy feet lave,
As, gathering sweet flow'rets, she stems thy clear wave!

Flow gently, sweet Afton, among thy green braes,
Flow gently, sweet river, the theme of my lays;
My Mary's asleep by thy murmuring stream,
Flow gently, sweet Afton, disturb not her dream.

ROBERT BURNS.

HOPE.

The wretch condemned with life to part,
Still, still on hope relies;
And every pang that rends the heart
Bids expectation rise.

Hope, like the gleaming taper's light,
Adorns and cheers the way;
And still, as darker grows the light,
Emits a brighter ray.

OLIVER GOLDSMITH.

FARE THEE WELL.

Fare thee well! and if forever,
Still forever, fare thee well!
Even though unforgiving, never
'Gainst thee shall my heart rebel.

Would that breast were bared before thee
Where thy head so oft hath lain,
While that placid sleep came o'er thee
Which thou ne'er canst know again:

Would that breast, by thee glanced over
Every inmost thought could show!
Then thou wouldst at last discover
'Twas not well to spurn it so.

Though the world for this commend thee—
Though it smile upon the blow,
E'en its praises must offend thee,
Founded on another's woe—

Though my many faults defend me,
Could no other arm be found
Than the one which embraced me,
To inflict a cureless wound?

Yet, oh yet, thyself deceive not,
Love may sink by slow decay,
But by sudden wrench, believe not
Hearts can thus be torn away;

Still thine own its life retaineth—
Still must mine, though bleeding, beat;
And the undying thought which paineth
Is—that we no more may meet.

These are words of deeper sorrow
Than the wail above the dead;
Both shall live, but every morrow
Wakest from a widow'd bed.

And when thou wouldst solace gather,
When our child's first accents flow,
Wilt thou teach her to say "Father!"
Though his care she must forego?

When her little hands shall press thee,
When her lip to thine is pressed,
Think of him whose prayers shall bless thee,
Think of him thy love had bless'd.

Should her lineaments resemble
Those thou never more may'st see,
Then thy heart will softly tremble
With a pulse yet true to me.

All my faults perchance thou knowest,
All my madness none can know;
All my hopes where'er thou goest,
Whither—yet with thee they go.

Every feeling hath been shaken;
Pride, which not a world could bow,
Bows to thee—by thee forsaken,
Even my soul forsakes me now.

DREAMLAND.

FROM placid lake
As smooth as glass,
Without a sound
The waters pass
Beneath a bridge
Moss grown and brown,
And 'neath huge palms
They wander down
So drowsily,
It almost seems
That this must be
The land of dreams.

But 'tis done—all words are idle—
  Words from me are vainer still;
But the thoughts we cannot bridle,
  Force their way without the will.

Fare thee well—thus disunited,
  Torn from every meaner tie,
Sear'd in heart, and love, and blighted—
  More than this, I scarce can die.

BYRON.

A LITTLE DOUBTFUL.

When a pair of red lips are upturned to your own,
  With no one to gossip about it,
Do you pray for endurance to let them alone?
  Well, may be you do—but I doubt it.

When a sly little hand you're permitted to seize,
  With a velvety softness about it,
Do you think you can drop it with never a squeeze?
  Well, may be you can—but I doubt it.

When a tapering waist is in reach of your arm,
  With a wonderful plumpness about it,
Do you argue the point 'twixt the good and the harm?
  Well, may be you do—but I doubt it.

And if by these tricks you should capture a heart,
  With a womanly sweetness about it,
Will you guard it and keep it, and act the good part?
  Well, may be you will—but I doubt it.

AUTHOR UNKNOWN.

THE COSMIC EGG.

Upon a rock yet uncreate,
Amid a chaos inchoate,
An uncreated being sate;
Beneath him, rock,
  Above him, cloud,
And the cloud was rock,
  And the rock was cloud.
The rock then growing soft and warm
The cloud began to take a form,
A form chaotic, vast and vague,
Which issued in the cosmic egg.
Then the being uncreate
On the egg did incubate,
  And thus became the incubator;
And of the egg did allegate,
  And thus became the alligator;
And the incubator was potentate,
  But the alligator was potentater.

ANONYMOUS.

THE MAY QUEEN.

You must wake and call me early, call me early, mother dear;
To-morrow 'ill be the happiest time of all the glad new year;
Of all the glad new year, mother, the maddest, merriest, day;
For I'm to be Queen o' the May, mother,
I'm to be Queen o' the May.

There's many a black, black eye, they say, but none so bright as mine;
There's Margaret and Mary, there's Kate and Caroline;
But none so fair as little Alice in all the land, they say,
So I'm to be Queen o' the May, mother,
I'm to be Queen o' the May.

I sleep so sound all night, mother, that I shall never wake,
If you do not call me loud when the day begins to break;
But I must gather knots of flowers, and buds and garlands gay,
For I'm to be Queen o' the May, mother,
I'm to be Queen o' the May.

As I came up the valley, whom think ye I should see,
But Robin leaning on the bridge beneath the hazel tree?
He thought of that sharp look, mother, I gave him yesterday—
But I'm to be Queen o' the May, mother,
I'm to be Queen o' the May.

He thought I was a ghost, mother, for I was all in white;
And I ran by him without speaking, like a flash of light.
They call me cruel-hearted, but I care not what they say,
For I'm to be Queen o' the May, mother,
I'm to be Queen o' the May.

They say he's dying all for love, but that can never be:
They say his heart is breaking, mother — what is that to me?
There's many a bolder lad 'll woo me any summer day,
And I'm to be Queen o' the May, mother,
I'm to be Queen o' the May.

Little Effie shall go with me to-morrow to the green,
And you 'll be there too, mother, to see me made the queen;
For the shepherd lads on every side 'll come from far away,
And I'm to be Queen o' the May, mother,
I'm to be Queen o' the May.

The honeysuckle round the porch has wov'n its wavy bowers,
And by the meadow-trenches blow the faint sweet cuckoo-flowers;
And the wild marsh-marigold shines like fire in swamps and hollows gray,
And I'm to be Queen o' the May, mother,
I'm to be Queen o' the May.

The night winds come and go, mother, upon the meadow grass,
And the happy stars above them seem to brighten as they pass;
There will not be a drop of rain the whole of the livelong day,
And I'm to be Queen o' the May, mother,
I'm to be Queen o' the May.

All the valley, mother, will be fresh and green and still,
And the cowslip and the crowfoot are over all the hill,
And the rivulet in the flowery dale 'ill merrily glance and play,
For I'm to be Queen o' the May, mother,
I'm to be Queen o' the May.

So you must wake and call me early, call me early, mother dear,
To-morrow 'ill be the happiest time of all the glad new year:
To-morrow 'ill be of all the year the maddest, merriest day,
For I'm to be Queen o' the May, mother,
I'm to be Queen o' the May.

TENNYSON.

THE LAKE OF THE DISMAL SWAMP.

"They made her a grave too cold and damp
For a soul so warm and true;
And she's gone to the Lake of the Dismal Swamp,
Where all night long, by a firefly lamp,
She paddles her white canoe

"And her firefly lamp I soon shall see,
And her paddle I soon shall hear;
Long and loving our life shall be,
And I'll hide the maid in a cypress tree,
When the footstep of death is near."

Away to the Dismal Swamp he speeds—
His path was rugged and sore,
Through tangled juniper, beds of reeds,
Through many a fen where the serpent feeds,
And man never trod before.

And when on the earth he sank to sleep,
If slumber his eyelids knew,
He lay where the deadly vine doth weep
Its venomous tears, and nightly steep
The flesh with blistering dew!

And near him the she-wolf stirr'd the brake,
And the copper-snake breathed in his ear,
Till he starting cried, from his dream awake,
"Oh when shall I see the dusky lake,
And the white canoe of my dear?"

He saw the lake, and a meteor bright
Quick over its surface play'd—
"Welcome," he said, "my dear one's light!"
And the dim shore echo'd for many a night
The name of the death-cold maid.

Till he hollow'd a boat of the birchen bark,
Which carried him off from shore;
Far, far he follow'd the meteor spark,
The wind was high and the clouds were dark,
And the boat returned no more.

But oft, from the Indian hunter's camp,
This lover and maid so true
Are seen at the hour of midnight damp
To cross the lake by a firefly lamp,
And paddle their white canoe!

THOMAS MOORE.

FROM "LADY OF LYONS."

PAULINE.—I cannot forego pride when I look on thee, and think that thou lovest me. Sweet Prince, tell me again of thy palace by the lake of Como; it is so pleasant to hear of thy splendors since thou didst swear to me that they would be desolate without Pauline; and when thou describest them, it is with a mocking lip and a noble scorn, as if custom had made thee disdain greatness.

CLAUDE MELNOTTE.—Nay, dearest, nay, if thou wouldst have me paint
The home to which, could love fulfill its prayers,
This hand would lead thee, listen! A deep vale
Shut out by Aldine hills from the rude world;
Near a clear lake, margined by fruits of gold
And whispering myrtles; glassing softest skies,
As cloudless, save with rare and roseate shadows,
As I would have thy fate!

PAULINE.—My own dear love!

CLAUDE MELNOTTE.—A palace lifting to eternal summer
Its marble walls from out a glossy bower
Of coolest foliage, musical with birds,
Whose songs should syllable thy name! At noon
We'd sit beneath the arching vines, and wonder
Why Earth could be unhappy, while the heavens
Still left us youth and love! We'd have no friends
That were not lovers; no ambition, save
To excel them all in love; we'd read no books
That were not tales of love—that we might smile
To think how poorly eloquence of words
Translates the poetry of hearts like ours!
And when night came, amidst the breathless heavens,
We'd guess what star should be our home when love
Becomes immortal; while the perfumed light
Stole through the mist of alabaster lands,
And every air was heavy with the sighs
Of orange groves and music from sweet lutes,
And murmurs of low fountains that gush forth
I' the midst of roses! Dost thou like the picture?

PAULINE.—Oh, as the bee upon the flower, I hang
Upon the honey of thy eloquent tongue!
Am I not blest? And if I love too wildly,
Who would not love thee like Pauline?

LADY OF LYONS.

CLAUDE MELNOTTE.—A palace lifting to eternal summer
Its marble walls from out a glossy bower
Of coolest foliage, musical with birds,
Whose songs should syllable thy name!

THE CHANGED CROSS.

It was a time of sadness, and my heart,
Although it knew and loved the better part,
Felt weary with the conflict and the strife,
And all the needful discipline of life.

And while I thought on these as given to me,
My trial-tests of faith and love to be,
It seemed as if I never could be sure
That faithful to the end I should endure.

And thus, no longer trusting to His might,
Who says, "We walk by faith and not by sight,"
Doubting and almost yielding to despair,
The thought arose, "My cross I cannot bear.

"Far heavier its weight must surely be
Than those of others which I daily see;
Oh! if I might another burden choose,
Methinks I should not fear my crown to lose."

A solemn silence reigned on all around;
E'en Nature's voices uttered not a sound;
The evening shadows seemed of peace to tell,
And sleep upon my weary spirit fell.

A moment's pause,—and then a heavenly light
Beamed full upon my wondering, raptured sight;
Angels on silvery wings seemed everywhere,
And angels' music thrilled the balmy air.

Then One, more fair than all the rest to see,
One to whom all others bowed the knee,
Came gently to me, as I trembling lay,
And, "Follow me," He said; "I am the way."

Then, speaking thus, He led me far above,
And there beneath a canopy of love,
Crosses of divers shape and size were seen,
Larger and smaller than my own had been.

And one there was most beauteous to behold,—
A little one, with jewels set in gold,
Ah! this, methought, I can with comfort wear,
For it will be an easy one to bear.

And so the little cross I quickly took,
But all at once my frame beneath it shook;
The sparkling jewels, fair were they to see,
But far too heavy was their weight to me.

"This may not be," I cried, and looked again,
To see if there were any here could ease my pain;
But one by one I passed them slowly by,
Till on a lovely one I cast my eye.

Fair flowers around its sculptured form entwined,
And grace and beauty seemed in it combined.
Wondering I gazed,—and still I wondered more,
To think so many should have passed it o'er.

But, oh! that form so beautiful to see,
Soon made its hidden sorrows known to me;
Thorns lay beneath those flowers and colors fair;
Sorrowing I said, "This cross I may not bear."

And so it was with each and all around,
Not one to suit my need could there be found;
Weeping I laid each heavy burden down,
As my guide gently said, "No cross,—no crown."

At length to Him I raised my saddened heart;
He knew its sorrows, bade its doubts depart;
"Be not afraid," He said, "but trust in Me;
My perfect love shall now be shown to thee."

And then, with lightened eyes and willing feet,
Again I turned, my earthly cross to meet;
With forward footsteps, turning not aside,
For fear some hidden evil might betide;

And there,—in the prepared, appointed way,
Listening to hear, and ready to obey,—
A cross I quickly found of plainest form,
With only words of love inscribed thereon.

With thankfulness I raised it from the rest,
And joyfully acknowledged it the best,—
The only one, of all the many there,
That I could feel was good for me to bear.

And while I thus my chosen one confess
I saw a heavenly brightness on it rest;
And as I bent, my burden to sustain,
I recognized my own old cross again.

But, oh! how different did it seem to be,
Now I had learned its preciousness to see,
No longer could I unbelieving say,
"Perhaps another is a better way."

Ah, no! henceforth my one desire shall be,
That He, who knows me best should choose for me;
And so, whate'er His love sees good to send,
I'll trust it's best,—because he knows the end.

AUTHOR UNKNOWN.

NAUGHTY, BUT SWEET.

Somebody's lips were close to mine,
Thus tempted, I couldn't resist,
Roguish and rosy, a sweet little mouth
Was suddenly softly kissed.

Somebody's eyes looked up and frowned
With such a reproving glance,
"If kisses were wicked?" I asked my pet,
Then the eyes began to dance.

And smiling the little maid answered,
As I knelt there at her feet,
"They must be a little bit naughty,
Or they never would be so sweet."

AUTHOR UNKNOWN.

THE IVY GREEN.

Oh! a dainty plant is the ivy green,
That creepeth o'er ruins old!
Of right choice food are his meals I ween,
In his cell so lone and cold.
The walls must be crumpled, the stones decayed,
To pleasure his dainty whim;
And the mouldering dust that years have made
Is a merry meal for him.
Creeping where no life is seen,
A rare old plant is the ivy green.

Fast he stealeth on, though he wears no wings,
And a staunch old heart has he;
How closely he twineth, how tight he clings
To his friend, the huge oak tree!
And slyly he traileth along the ground,
And his leaves he gently waves,
And he joyously twines and hugs around
The rich mould of dead men's graves.
Creeping where no life is seen,
A rare old plant is the ivy green.

Whole ages have fled, and their works decayed,
And nations scattered been;
But the stout old ivy shall never fade
From its hale and hearty green.
The brave old plant in its lonely days
Shall fatten upon the past;
For the stateliest building man can raise
Is the ivy's food at last.
Creeping where no life is seen,
A rare old plant is the ivy green.

CHARLES DICKENS.

VIRTUE.

The triumphs that on vice attend
Shall ever in confusion end;
The good man suffers but to gain,
And every virtue springs from pain.

As aromatic plants bestow
No spicy fragrance while they grow,
But crushed or trodden to the ground,
Diffuse their balmy sweets around.

OLIVER GOLDSMITH.

JENNY KISSED ME.

Jenny kiss'd me when we met,
Jumping from the chair she sat in;
Time, you thief! who love to get
Sweets into your list, put that in.
Say I'm weary, say I'm sad;
Say that health and wealth have miss'd me;
Say I'm growing old, but add—
Jenny kiss'd me!

LEIGH HUNT.

WHISPERS

In the gloaming when the shadows
 Lengthen o'er the verdant lea,
Oft I wander thro' the meadows,
 And my thoughts are all of thee;
Sweet words then, so long since spoken,
 Breezes seem once more to frame,
And the twilight calm is broken
 By the echo of thy name.
  O, 'tis sweet alone to wander
   'Neath the peeping ev'ning star;
  For, whilst on the past I ponder,
   Whispers reach me from afar.

Is it one afar is speaking
 Of the lonely heart at home,
And his tender words are seeking
 Ears that list across the foam?
Yes; and ere the flowers are dying,
 He will haste again to me:
When I hear the breezes sighing,
 Love, I know they come from thee.
  O, 'tis sweet alone to wander
   'Neath the peeping ev'ning star,
  For, whilst on the past I ponder,
   Whispers reach me from afar.

DETECTING COUNTERFEIT MONEY

THE desire to accumulate property is one of the noblest that nature has implanted in man, and it is through the successful results of this desire we are enabled to point with unerring certainty to the disembarking line, which so surely distinguishes the advanced, educated, refined and civilized man from the wild savage, whose highest desire is to slay and rob his fellow men, and proudly exhibit their scalps, or the plunder he has acquired, as evidence of his cunning or courage.

It is through this inborn desire to accumulate that man is willing to labor, toil, suffer and forego present gratifications for the hope of future greater satisfactions; that has resulted in the building and equipping the mighty ships of commerce, whose white, spreading canvas dots every sea where commerce may be known, or where the interests of God's creatures may best be served. It is through this desire, coupled with unremitting toil, that we owe everything of permanent enjoyment, of enlightenment and of prosperity.

The millions of dollars of paper money which is handled every day as the natural fruit of toil and saving through the many and diversified transactions in the vast, illimitable and ever rapidly developing field of commerce, is but the representative of ownership of property.

If this representative is what it purports on its face to be, each and every one who receives it in exchange for services or commodities owns not merely a piece of paper, with designs, words and promises printed or engraved thereon, but an interest or an undivided whole in a farm, a block of buildings or a store well stocked with merchandise, which, in his estimation, at least, is more desirable to him than the labor or commodity for which he has voluntarily made the exchange; but if, on the contrary, it is other than what it purports on its face to be, he finds that he is the owner of a piece of paper whose value is *nil.*

There is, at the present writing [1885], nearly eight hundred million dollars of paper currency in the United States, consisting of greenbacks and national currency, a great portion of which is in actual circulation, and it has been estimated by eminent authorities who occupy positions of trust in the various departments through which the financial machinery of this vast sea of paper money is daily circulated, that there is in circulation nearly one-fifth of this amount in counterfeit money, or about one hundred and sixty million dollars; and not one dollar of this counterfeit money owes its circulation to any excellence of the work in its manufacture, but wholly to the general ignorance of those who handle it, as to what is required to constitute a genuine bill. The time will come when the United States will redeem all of its issue of paper money, when those who are holding any of this counterfeit money will have to stand the loss to the extent of the sum in their possession.

To all of those who are willing to take a small portion of their time each day for a few weeks in learning just what it takes to constitute a genuine bill, there need be no necessity of ever losing anything by counterfeiters, as it is impossible for them to make bills which will in any way approach the beauty and exactness of the genuine ones. There is not at the present time, nor has there ever been in the past, nor will there ever be in the future, a counterfeit bill made that cannot be detected at sight; and the positive knowledge of how to know at all times when a bill is genuine and when not is within the reach of all those who may have the privilege of reading the following information or infallible rules with a genuine desire to be benefited thereby:

Devices and Frauds.—Various devices are resorted to by a numerous gang or body of persons, to get on in the world without turning their attention to legitimate and useful employments.

This class includes many that are not engaged in the practice of counterfeiting and putting forth bad money, but who make themselves felt in various ways through vain tricks and schemes, which are, to all intents and purposes, frauds.

Business men are generally apt at detecting and turning off petty schemes, but they find it best to have the means with which they may deal successfully as against regular swindlers, forgers and counterfeiters.

Counterfeit and Genuine Work.—As indicated above, counterfeit notes are issued and put into the channels of circulation in abundance every year, by those engaged in the practice of counterfeiting. These notes are often such good imitations of the genuine that it is quite difficult to discern the difference.

That he may protect himself, each business man should have some definite knowledge of a genuine bank note.

The engraving of a genuine note, in most all of its parts, is done by machinery, and it is more exact and perfect. On the contrary, most all parts of counterfeit notes are done by hand.

Counterfeiters cannot afford to purchase machinery, such as is used for the production of genuine notes. The cost of such machinery is between $100,000 and $150,000, and if it were in wrong hands it would be always liable to seizure and confiscation.

DETECTING COUNTERFEIT MONEY.

In order to prevent the forgery of bank notes, a great deal of ingenuity and art has been expended on their production. The principal features of the manufacture are described as a peculiar kind of paper and water mark; an elaborate design, printed with a peculiar kind of ink, and certain private marks, known only by the bank officials.

The work of counterfeiters can never equal that of the makers of genuine notes, whose skill and facilities for producing the highest grade of work known to the art, are the best that the world affords.

Unless one is somewhat learned as to the quality of engraving, that he may be able to distinguish a fine specimen of the art when he sees it, he is likely to become a victim of the counterfeiter's operations.

Lathe Work.—When the genuineness of a bank note is doubted, the Lathe Work on the note should first be closely scrutinized.

The several letters of denomination, circles, ovals and shadings between and around the letters in the words, etc., are composed of numberless extremely fine lines—inclusive of lines straight, curved and net-work. These are all regular and unbroken, never running into each other, and may be traced throughout with a magnifying glass.

Without the skill or machinery by which the genuine is produced, the same quality of work cannot be done. Therefore, in a counterfeit, the lines are imperfect, giving the paper a dull or hazy aspect, that may be all the better appreciated by comparing it with the genuine. The lines in the counterfeit will be found now and then irregular in size, and broken; not uniform in course, sometimes heavy, sometimes light; no two stamps or dies on the same note being exactly alike.

The fine, uniform shade lines, with which the letters on the genuine are embellished, are wrought by a machine that cannot be reproduced by counterfeiters, nor used for other than legitimate purposes, by authority.

Ruling Engine Work.—In Ruling Engine Work, as it is called, the fine line is present, also. The engraving is produced and transferred in the same way as the geometrical lathe work. In this they are parallel and not in circles. Those which constitute the shading of letters are so fine that they form a perfectly even gray shade. They may be printed so that the shading will appear darker, but the aspect will be uniform. The spaces between lines are exact, whether the lines be horizontal or diagonal. The lines are also made crooked or wave-like, not absolutely parallel. Ruling engine work is generally used for shading names of banks, and also for the names of town, state, etc.

Geometrical Lathe.—The fine line is the characteristic of the various and beautiful figures seen on a genuine note. This line is produced by what is called the Geometrical Lathe. The patterns made by the geometrical lathe are of every variety of form. They are not engraven directly upon the bank-note plate, but on pieces of soft steel plate, which are afterward hardened. The impressions are then transferred to a soft steel roller, which, in its turn, is also hardened, and the impressions remain there in relief. This roller is then capable of transferring the same designs to the bank-note plate, by means of the transfer press.

In counterfeit engraving, the design is made directly upon the plate, and not by transfer, as in the production of plates for genuine notes. The essential difference between the two methods of production is, the counterfeit is made by hand, and is inexact and imperfect, while the genuine is made on geometrical principles, and is therefore exact, artistic and beautiful.

In all the government issues the geometric lathe work is liberally used. This should be studied carefully, as it constitutes the chief test of genuineness.

Fine lines, of unerring exactness, never broken, are seen on the genuine medallion heads or shields, upon which the designation

of the note is sometimes stamped. This nicety cannot be given by hand, or with the use of imperfect machinery. By close scrutiny the lines will be found to break off in the pattern, or appear forked, irregular in size, and not well defined throughout.

On most counterfeits the vignettes are not well engraved, and the portraits have a dull appearance; the letters are usually wanting in clearness; the printing is sometimes faulty, by which some features of the note are obscured.

Vignettes.—While lathe work and that of the ruling engine are invariably machine work, and therefore cannot be successfully reproduced by counterfeiters, the Vignettes are chiefly the work of the hands. In all genuine work they are made by first-class artists, who are well paid for their services, and who therefore have no incentive to exercise their skill for illegitimate purposes.

Sometimes water and sky are done with the ruling engine, and when they are, no counterfeiter can successfully imitate them. Fine vignettes are seldom seen on counterfeit notes. If only the lathe and ruling engine work be genuine, an ordinary vignette cannot make a note counterfeit, and if that be counterfeit, no vignette can make the note genuine.

The vignettes on genuine notes are executed by men at the head of their vocation, and are very life-like and beautiful. Counterfeit vignettes usually have a sunken and lifeless appearance. Genuine vignettes, as seen upon government issues, consist of out-door scenes, portraits, historical pictures, and allegorical figures. They are all exceedingly beautiful, and it is not likely that such work will ever be successfully imitated.

Solid Print.—The lettering, or solid print, in genuine work is done by a first-class artist, who makes that kind of work his exclusive concern. The name of the engraving company is always engraved with great pains and is very accurate. It will be seen on the upper and lower margin of the note. This, in counterfeits, is not quite uniform or even. The words "one dollar," as on the one dollar greenbacks, are to be considered as a sample of solid print.

Bank-Note Paper.—Bank notes are printed upon paper composed of linen, the quality of which is not always the same, and it varies in thickness. Therefore the paper is not always a sure test, but it is important. The manufacture of this paper is a profound secret, as carefully kept as the combinations to the great vaults where the government's millions lie awaiting further river and harbor bills. It is made only at the Dalton mill, which dates back almost to colonial days. What its combinations are nobody knows except those intimately connected with its manufacture. The secret of the paper making is jealously guarded, as is also the paper itself. From the moment it is made until it gets into the treasury vaults it is carefully guarded. It goes there in small iron safes, the sheets carefully counted, and all precautions against its loss being taken both by the government officials and by the express companies which carry it.

Counterfeit Signatures.—Sometimes genuine notes are stolen before they are signed; then the only thing about them made counterfeit is the signatures. Those who are familiar with the signatures of officers of the bank where notes are purloined, may not be led into error, as such signatures usually appear more or less cramped or unsteady; but there is no sure protection against a counterfeit of this kind for those who do not have special knowledge of the signatures.

Altered Bank Notes.—Bank notes are altered in two ways, namely: raising the denomination, and changing the name of a broken to that of a responsible bank.

First, in altering a note, it is scraped until it is thin; then figures of larger denomination are pasted over. A pasted note may be detected by holding it up to the light, when the pasted parts will appear darker, as they are thicker.

Second, the denomination of a note is raised by taking out a low one with an acid, and printing in a higher one with a counterfeit stamp. The ink used in genuine bank-note printing is a peculiar kind, and not easily to be obtained by counterfeiters; therefore, their printing will not appear as clear and bright as that of the government, which is done with ink of the finest quality. If the ink is black, it gives a clear and glossy impression, without any of that smutty appearance, as is sometimes seen in counterfeit bank notes. It is almost impossible to imitate the green ink that is used by the government, and it is nearly as difficult to imitate the red and other colors. Counterfeit inks look dull and muddy, while genuine inks have a glossy appearance.

In the case of a note altered by the use of acid, it may be noticed that the acid, by spreading more than was intended by the counterfeiter, has injured parts of other letters, and the paper will appear more or less stained by the acid.

Comparing and Examining Notes.—A counterfeit should be compared with one that is genuine, in order to familiarize one's self with the distinguishing features which have already been indicated.

It is best to acquire the habit of giving each note as received a searching glance, turning it over to see the back, and if there be any defect, it will probably catch the eye. If there be the least suspicion, a critical examination of all its parts should be made.

In case of doubt, the lathe work should be carefully examined, and it may be compared with a perfectly good bill; then examine the shading around the letters, and search for any sign of alteration in the title or denomination of the note. If there are any medallion heads or shields, notice the lines; if there is any red letter work, designed to appear on both sides, look at the character of the work on the face, then turn the note and examine the back. If the printing is not exactly alike on both sides, but varies in any part, the note is counterfeit. Then observe the vignettes and portraits, to see whether their style and perfection compare well with the work on genuine notes. Then examine the solid print and engravers' names, as well as the printing, ink and paper. By such thorough examination, one can hardly be at a loss to determine the status of the note.

Good magnifying glasses are necessary, in most instances, to bring out the fine lines on bank notes. Sometimes a microscope of great power is required to discern the genuine line.

Piecing, etc.—Counterfeiters sometimes make ten bills of nine by what is termed piecing. Thus, a counterfeit note is cut into ten pieces by the counterfeiter, and these pieces are used in piecing nine genuine bills from each of which a piece has been cut. The nine genuine pieces, thus obtained, are then pasted together, and with the tenth counterfeit piece added, make a tenth bill, which is the gain.

Piecing bank bills is not a very successful practice. One who possesses such information as here given, can readily detect the difference between the counterfeit and the genuine. This difference is, however, made less apparent by the counterfeiter, who defaces the counterfeit part, so as to give the note a worn appearance.

Counterfeiting is rendered very difficult in consequence of the remarkable excellence of the work on the government and national currency, as also from the difficulty of imitating the green. But this currency, if successfully imitated by counterfeiters, will repay large outlay and care, as the greenbacks pass anywhere in the nation, and a counterfeit may be carried to other states or sections as it becomes known in any particular locality. National bank currency may be counterfeited by preparing a plate, and then with simple change in the name of the bank, the counterfeit can be adapted to the various towns where banks are located. This much is written, not to lessen the value of or confidence in the issues of the government, but to admonish the public against the dangers of a false security.

THE HORSE.

WHAT CONSTITUTES A GOOD HORSE.

THE horse is at once the noblest, the most intelligent and the most useful of all created animals, and stands the nearest in its relation to man of those whose strength and instinct have been subjected to the power of reason and the force of will which place the human animal on the throne of the animal kingdom. Its noble qualities have in all ages won the praise of poets, the pride of warriors, and the affection of men. It combines in its character and attributes, in an extraordinary degree, strength and docility, power and patience, courage and gentleness, the most acute instinct and the readiest obedience, fleetness of motion and unfailing dependence, the greatest capacity of endurance and a fidelity which rarely fails. It is the almost indispensable coadjutor of man in every sphere of labor, and is essential to all his undertakings of peace or war. Whether in the tilling of the soil, the gathering of the harvest, the marketing of produce, in going to and fro either for profit or pastime, the horse is man's most useful and familiar friend, and the appearance of the horse is generally looked upon as an infallible criterion of the character of his owner for prudence and liberality.

Horses are of many families, and have their geographical homes, with their pertaining distinctive peculiarities, much as the various races of men. The Arabian, for instance, is a true native of Arabia, and wherever acclimatized in other parts of the world preserves its distinguishing characteristics. So, too, with the horses of Normandy, which have given the people of America the valuable class of roadsters known as the Norman-Percheron. The English racer, the stock of Andalusia, the heavy Scotch Clydesdales and the full-blooded flyers of Kentucky are all distinct types, and as easily distinguished by the horseman as the Chinese and the negro.

Of late years general attention has been paid in all advanced communities to the improvement of the native stock by cross-breeding, and re-crossing, till the average standard of American horseflesh has reached a very high period of excellence, and every year is thus adding to the improvement, which affects not only the grade of the stock, but its value and its capacity for purposes of practical utility, and every person who is interested in the possession or raising of horses, will find it the best kind of economy in purchasing for use or propagation, and in breeding, to secure the purest blood that can be obtained in the various classes from which choice is made. For general purposes, the horse kingdom may be divided into four classes: (1) Running horses, (2) trotting horses, (3) roadsters, (4) draught horses.

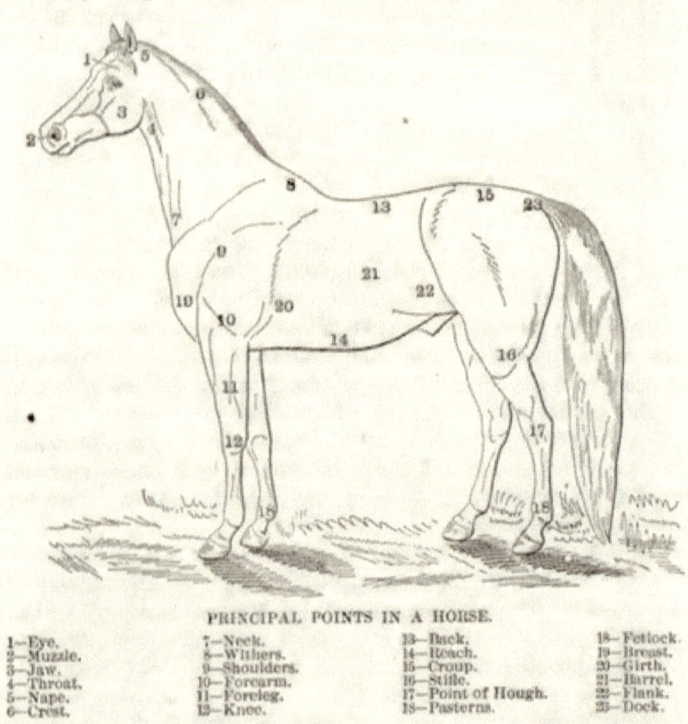

PRINCIPAL POINTS IN A HORSE.

1—Eye.
2—Muzzle.
3—Jaw.
4—Throat.
5—Nape.
6—Crest.
7—Neck.
8—Withers.
9—Shoulders.
10—Forearm.
11—Foreleg.
12—Knee.
13—Back.
14—Reach.
15—Croup.
16—Stifle.
17—Point of Hough.
18—Pasterns.
18—Fetlock.
19—Breast.
20—Girth.
21—Barrel.
22—Flank.
23—Dock.

Points of Excellence.—The points of excellence in a horse, which have general application to all classes, are those of health and symmetry. The former is indicated especially by a bright, clear eye, a clean muzzle, and general ease and freedom in action. The signs of weakness and coarse breeding in a horse are a clumsy muzzle, large ears, thick neck, narrow chest, long and hollow back, sunken flanks, narrow crupper, large joints, and long fetlock, declining backward from the hoof.

Running and Trotting Stock.—Stock which is adapted for fleetness must possess the distinguishing mark of fine blood—fine and mobile muzzle, large and intelligent eye, small ears, slender neck, high withers, clean and shapely shoulders, breadth of chest, with the fore-legs well apart, indicating lung power, short in the back and long in the belly, giving "reach," well rounded and firm, but not too broad in the crupper; legs clean, and fine in the bone, well set up over the hoof; strong and muscular in the fore-legs and stifle, and clean and smooth about the "heels," fetlocks, houghs and pastern.

Roadsters.—Roadsters should possess many of these leading characteristics, but require also indications of strength of a more rugged and enduring character, which, while detracting from their highest speed, give them staying powers suited for their purpose. The roadster should be wider in the muzzle than the racing horse, stronger in the neck, wider in the withers and shoulders, heavier across the crupper, and in the limbs; in height not under fifteen hands, round body, muscular flank, and oblique-set hind quarters.

Draught Horses.—The draught horse is altogether distinguished by the characteristics of strength without regard to speed. Size and weight are of course essential. The neck should be symmetrical, but high in the crest and thick, developing into high broad withers, expansive shoulders, well set out to receive the burden of weight which falls on the collar, back round and broad, body proportionately heavy but round and well shaped, crupper very broad and arching over from the back bone, dock strong and set firm to the crupper, legs thick, large in bone, and well developed in the muscles of the forelegs and stifle, mane, tail and hair of medium fineness, short shanks, broad knees, strong hough and pastern, fetlocks of two inches, strong and thick, well set up upon a round large hoof well open at the heels.

HOW TO ESTIMATE THE HORSE'S AGE.

It is an old saying that politics and horse trading are "mighty onsartin." At all events, it is well to be able to have an approximately correct idea of the age of the horse by the proper marks, as the value of the horse is largely governed by his age. A horse should never be put to hard work or fast driving before the age of four years. Well cared for, he is in his prime from that to ten years of age, when he begins to deteriorate. But with good care, a horse will be serviceable for all ordinary purposes up to fifteen and even to twenty years. Twenty-eight to thirty years is the limit of the horse's age.

The age of the horse is estimated by an examination of the sharp teeth or cutters, but these at ten years old are lost, and another criterion is adopted which is explained further on.

A colt sees daylight with the first and second molar and grinding teeth apparent. When eight days old, the two central cutters come out, and in the next five or six weeks, the two next sharp teeth are supplied. In three months these teeth are all uniform, and a third grinder appears; after his eighth month, the third cutter above and below, on each side, will appear, and the colt then has his full set of front teeth. These teeth have an elevated cutting edge of enamel that is bent inward and over the tooth, so as to form a sort of cavity or depression behind it, that constitutes the mark; it is gradually worn down by nipping the food, and is at length altogether worn away. Ordinarily the animal is young or old in the degree of wear that is observed on this enamel. The teeth that are shed are lost in the order of their coming, the two middle cutters of both the upper and lower jaws being displaced between the second and third years. A three-years-old colt has the permanent middle cutters above the gum, but not even with the transient or adjoining deciduous cutters; these have too a large deep groove containing a black substance crossing the working edge of the corner of the tooth, and the sixth grinder is also coming in view, and at four years it is even with the others; the third transient grinder is last, and the mark is not so plain. At six years the groove on the middle cutters is worn away, but there is left some discoloration; at seven years the mark is worn from the four middle cutters in each jaw, and at eight years the mark is found gone from all the lower cutters. In a stall-fed horse, that eats more of hard substances, as corn and oats, the marks are sooner worn away.

At ten years, the age of a horse is to be known by a wrinkle that comes on the upper corner of the lower eyelid, and for each succeeding year a wrinkle is added, by counting which, and adding the number of them to nine, the age of the animal may be accurately told.

HINTS ON HORSE TRAINING.

A few suggestions, founded on the rules laid down by the celebrated horse trainer Rary, are given in regard to training horses. Always remember the natural laws by which the conduct of the horse is guided. It is the nature of the horse to kick if badly frightened, or to shy if brought suddenly upon something that offends his eyes, his ears or his touch. Accustom the animal to be gently brought into contact with things strange to him. Lead him gradually up to every object at which he becomes frightened, and he will soon learn that there is nothing to fear and will acquire the confidence in his master which will lead him to go anywhere without question. Whipping and spurring are both cruel and useless for any purpose. To gain the good will of a young or strange horse more easily, approach him with the scent of honey, cinnamon or some pleasant smelling oil upon the hands. Never use drugs to tame a horse, as the lesson is only thrown away. Accustom him to uniform kindness and gentleness, which he will repay in kind. Be careful in handling his lips when breaking, as the mouth of the colt is very tender, and rough usage makes him disinclined to accept the bit as a habit. Colts should be broken without the use of blind bridles. Never hitch a colt to anything till it is thoroughly broken. When, by kind usage, the horse has been taught to follow you, put on a backband with the lines through shaft straps, and by gentle means accustom him to the use of the reins for guidance. If the colt is difficult to get under control, throw him, by passing a rope twelve feet long around his body in a running noose, passing it down to the right forefoot through a ring in a spancel. Buckle up the rear forefoot. Take a firm hold of the rope and lead him round till he is tired of three legs then draw up the foot by the rope, giving him a shove with the shoulder, when he will lie down. If he struggle, let him, as he will the sooner find out that he is mastered, and you will have no more trouble. If the young horse develops the kicking habit, fasten a rope round his jaw, passing it through the bellyband and attach to the hind foot. One kick, the weight of which falls on the jaw, will cure him. If the horse prove stubborn, throw him, and let him remain till thoroughly subdued and exhausted.

PACES OF THE HORSE.

In horsemanship, the natural paces of the horse in their proper order are: the walk, the trot. The canter may be added, as it is a pace that belongs to the horse as to other saltatory animals.

The swift pacer will be characterized by great freedom in the angles of the limbs, but particularly so in the elevation of the fore parts, and obliquity of the shoulders; a corresponding length and angularity in the hind legs is also an indication of excellence for the purposes of the pace. The walk, as a pace, should be performed harmoniously, and whether it be quick or slow, each foot is to be dropped flat on the ground. It is a serious defect when, as is too often the case, the toe lights first and then the heel. The training of a horse will have much influence on his method of walking; the angles of his limbs as a natural fact will have much more; while not a little will depend on the hand of the rider. The maximum speed in the true walk of the horse is six miles an hour; as few animals are able to accomplish this, however, five miles is considered a good rate of speed for a fast walker.

After the walk is the trot, a pace that is performed diagonally, the legs being differently employed, in accord with the rate of motion onward, whether fast or slow. There are three varieties of the trot, namely, the moderate, the extended, and the running.

As to the gallop, it may be divided into three varieties which are effected by a propulsive effort of the hind quarters. Gallops are called racing or gallop at full speed, the slow or hand gallop, and the canter, which last, though treated as a separate pace of the horse, is in fact but a slow gallop. Of the varieties, the first or racing gallop is, strictly speaking, a succession of leaps, and after the essential points, described elsewhere, the adaptation of the animal for this pace depends on his power of endurance and freedom and capacity of lungs. This gallop cannot be commenced without the intervention of the slower gallop, in which one of the hinder legs is first advanced to establish a new center, for it would require too great an effort to raise the fore parts at once from a state of rest by means of the loins, and to throw them forward at first to a considerable distance by means of the haunches and thighs; and hence the gallop at full speed is simply a repetition of leaps.

A pace between the amble and racing gallop is the hand gallop, and the latter differs from both in that it is not performed diagonally, and from the legs not being thrown out and contracted equally, one generally taking the lead, as it were, of the other and being projected further forward, while the other is more thrown back making a curve from the shoulder and knee. The canter differs from the gallop in consequence of the movements of the legs, instead of being simultaneous, being directly the reverse. One of the feet is always touching the ground, and the animal is not wholly in the air at any time, from which the peculiar effect of the pace is derived.

USEFUL RECIPES FOR ORDINARY AILMENTS OF HORSES.

The following will be found useful recipes for the cure of the most common ailments of horses. For more serious ailments, to call in the veterinary surgeon is the cheapest and best economy:

VALUABLE RECIPES FOR HORSES.

BEST REMEDY FOR HEAVES.—Balsam of fir and balsam of copaiba, 4 oz. each, and mix with calcined magnesia sufficiently thick to make it into balls, and give a middling-sized ball night and morning, seven to ten days.

CURE FOR COLIC.—Bleed freely at the horse's mouth; then take ½ lb. raw cotton, wrap it around a coal of fire so as to exclude air, and, when it begins to smoke, hold it under his nose till he becomes easy. For obstinate case.—Spirits of turpentine, 3 oz; laudanum, 1 oz.; mix, and administer in one dose.

CURE FOR BOTS.—First give the horse two quarts new milk and one quart molasses. Fifteen minutes later, administer two quarts very strong sage tea; thirty minutes after the tea, enough currier's oil (about three pints) to act as a physic. The first application causes the bots to release their hold; the second puckers them up, and the third carries them away.

COUGH.—See if the hay is not musty, and feed roots and laxative food. Cut cedar boughs fine and mix with his grain; or boil a small quantity of flax-seed and mix it in a mash of scalded bran, sweetening slightly with honey or sugar. HEAVES.—If the cough develop indications of heaves, put a spoonful of ground ginger once a day in his provender, and allow him to drink freely of lime-water.

DISTEMPER.—Take 1¼ gallons of blood from the neck vein; then administer 1½ oz. of sassafras oil. Cure speedy and certain.

FOUNDER.—A horse may be worked the next day after being foundered, and permanently cured in twenty-four hours, by prompt use of the following remedy: Boil or steam stout oat-straw for half an hour; then wrap around the horse's leg quite hot, and keep steam in by binding with woolen cloths. After six hours renew the application and take 1 gallon of blood from the neck vein, and he is cured.

GREASE HEEL.—Boil white-oak bark in wood-ash ley and bark-ooze till quite strong. When cool, is ready for use. Wash leg with castile soap. Apply the ley by a swab on the end of a stick lest the horse kick from the smart. This is a sure cure, but brings off the hair. To restore the hair, make a salve by stewing elder bark with old bacon and mixing with sufficient resin to make it of proper consistency for application.

LOOSENESS OR SCOURING.—For one horse, 1 to 1½ oz. tormentil root powdered and administered in 1 pint of milk; or steep in 1½ pints of milk and administer every four hours till cured.

LOTION.—For cure of the mange, boil 2 oz. tobacco in 1 qt. water; strain; add sulphur and soft soap, 2 oz. each, and apply.

STAGGERS.—Twice a week give the following mess: Bran, 1 gallon; sulphur, 1 tablespoonful; saltpetre, 1 spoonful; boiling sassafras tea, 1 quart; assafœtida, 1½ oz. Keep the horse from cold water for half a day after administering.

SPAVIN.—To cure spavin, make an ointment as follows: Venice turpentine and Spanish flies (cantharides) each 2 oz.; euphorbium and aqua-ammonia each 1 oz.; red precipitate ½ oz.; corrosive sublimate ½ oz.; lard 1½ lbs. Pulverize all the other ingredients and put into the lard; simmer slowly over coals, taking care not to scorch or burn, and pour off free of sediment. Cut off the hair and rub well into the lumps once in 24 hours for three mornings. Previous to each application wash well with castile soap, and with a smooth stick squeeze out the thick yellow matter reduced from the spavin.

SCRATCHES.—Cut the hair off close and wash with strong soap suds or warm vinegar, in which is a strong dissolution of salt. Afterwards dress over with hog lard.

SADDLE AND HARNESS GALLS.—Apply with a brush a mixture made of white lead and linseed oil, which relieves pain, and forming a hard coating enables the wound to heal.

STOPPAGE OF URINE.—Indicated by frequent attempts to urinate, looking around at his side, lying down, rolling and stretching. To cure, take ½ lb. of hops, 3 drachms oil of camphor; gr'nd and mix. Make into three pills and give one every day with a drench made of a small spoonful of saltpetre and 2 oz. water.

TRIUMPHS OF THE TURF.

NOTED TROTTERS AND PHENOMENAL RECORDS.

A GREAT advance has been made in American racing stock within the last twenty years. The fathers of the present generation looked upon Flora Temple as a prodigy of speed, and regarded her 2:19¼ gait as a marvelous achievement. But since the days of that mare (of happy memory) a change has "come o'er the spirit of the dreams" of horse-men, and the racing world is looking forward with strained eyes for the advent of the trotter whose time shall eclipse the 2:09¾ of Maud S. Our English cousins, who used to curl their aristocratic noses in undisguised contempt for everything pertaining to the American turf, or American horsemanship, have learned a lesson which cost them dear, both in pride and in pocket, when Pierre Lorillard's American horse, Iroquois, defeated the best specimens of English blooded stock, again and again, on their own race courses.

As the interest in racing has heightened, a noticeaole change has come over the surroundings of the race-track itself. On the course may now be seen the flower of the very best society, with here and there a sprinkling of the clergy themselves, and on the "grand stand," bright with the gay colors that adorn feminine beauty, gather men eminent in the learned professions, as well as those of the highest station in the world of business. In a word, horse-racing has become a national pastime, equally with the American game of base-ball. This interest inevitably results in a constant effort to improve the racing-stock, and the success which has attended the effort hitherto is best seen by examination of the table on the following page:

Table of the Best Time on Record, at All Distances and All Ways of Going, to December 20, 1884.

TROTTING IN HARNESS.

One mile—Maud S., Lexington, Ky., November 11, 1884, 2:09¾.

Best by gelding—Jay Eye See, Providence, R. I., July 31, 1884, 2:10.

Best by stallion—Maxy Cobb, Providence, R. I., September 30, 1884, 2:13¼.

One mile, by a yearling filly—Hinda Rose, San Francisco, Cal., November 14, 1881, 2:36½.

One mile, by a yearling stallion—Nutbreaker, Lexington, Ky., October 14, 1884, 2:42½.

One mile, by a two-year-old filly—Wildflower, San Francisco, October 22, 1881, 2:21.

One mile, by a two-year-old stallion—Fred Crocker, San Francisco, November 20, 1880, 2:25¼.

One mile, by a three-year-old filly—Hinda Rose, Lexington, Ky., October 10, 1883, 2:19½.

One mile, by a three-year-old stallion—Steinway, Lexington, Ky., August 28, 1879, 2:25¾.

One mile, by a four-year-old filly—Sallie Benton, San Francisco, December 13, 1884, 2:17¾.

One mile, by a four-year-old stallion—Albert W., Oakland, Cal., September 5, 1882, 2:22.

One mile, by a four-year-old gelding—Jay Eye See, Chicago, September 23, 1882, 2:19.

One mile, by a five-year-old filly—Trinket, Dover, Del., September 30, 1880, 2:19¼.

One mile, by a five-year-old stallion—Santa Claus, Sacramento, Cal., September 11, 1879, 2:18.

One mile, by a five-year-old gelding—Jay Eye See, Providence, R. I., September 13, 1883, 2:10¾.

One mile, over a half-mile track—Rarus, Toledo, O., July 20, 1878, 2:16.

Two miles—Monroe Chief, Lexington, Ky., October 21, 1882, 4:46.

Three miles—Huntress, Prospect Park, L. I., September 21, 1872, 7:21¼.

Four miles—Trustee, Union Course, L. I., June 13, 1840, 11:06.

Five miles—Lady Mack, San Francisco, April 2, 1874, 13:00.

Ten miles—Controller, San Francisco, November 23, 1878, 27:23¼.

Twenty miles—Captain McGowan, Boston, Mass., October 31, 1865, 58:25.

Fifty miles—Ariel, Albany, N. Y., May 5, 1846, 3:55:40½.

One hundred miles—Conqueror, Centreville, L. I., November 12, 1853, 8:55:53.

One hundred and one miles—Fanny Jenks, Albany, N. Y., May 5, 1845, 9:42:57.

TROTTING TO WAGON.

One mile—Hopeful, Chicago, October 12, 1878, 2:16¾.

One mile, drawing 2,000 lbs.—Mountain Maid, Long Island, 1865, 3:42¼.

Two miles—General Butler, Fashion Course, L. I., June 18, 1863, 4:56¼, and Dexter, Fashion Course, L. I., October 27, 1865, 4:56¼.

Three miles—Prince, Union Course, L. I., September 15, 1857, 7:53½.

Five miles—Little Mac, Fashion Course, L. I., October 29, 1863, 13:43¼.

Ten miles—John Stewart, Boston, Mass., June 30, 1868, 28:02½.

Twenty miles—Controller, San Francisco, April 20, 1878, 58:57.

Fifty miles—Spangle, Union Course, L. I., October 15, 1855, 3:59:04.

TROTTING UNDER SADDLE.

One mile—Great Eastern, Fleetwood Park, N. Y., September 22, 1877, 2:15¾.

Two miles—George M. Patchen, Fashion Course, L. I., July 1, 1863, 4:56.

Three miles—Dutchman, Beacon Course, N. J., August 1, 1839, 7:32½.
Four miles—Dutchman, Centreville Course, L. I., May, 1836, 10:51.

TROTTING, DOUBLE TEAM.

One mile—Maxy Cobb and Neta Medium, New York, November 13, 1884, 2:15
One hundred miles—Master Burke and Robin, 1834, 10:17:22.

TROTTER WITH RUNNING MATE.

One mile—H. B. Winthrop and Gabe Case, Providence, R. I., August 1, 1884, 2:06
Three miles—Ethan Allen and running mate, 1861, 7:03¼.

THE PACING RECORD.

PACING IN HARNESS.

One mile—Johnston (gelding), Chicago, October 3, 1884, 2:06¼.
One mile—Buffalo Girl, Pittsburgh, Pa., July 27, 1883, 2:12½.
One mile—Cohannet (stallion), Providence, R. I., September 9, 1884, 2:18¾.
Two miles—Defiance and Longfellow, Sacramento, Cal., September 26, 1872, 4:47¾
Three miles—James K. Polk, Centreville, L. I., September 13, 1847, 7:44.
Four miles—Longfellow, San Francisco, December 31, 1869, 10:34½.
Five miles—Onward, San Francisco, December 11, 1874, 12:54¾.

PACING UNDER SADDLE.

One mile—Billy Boice, Buffalo, N. Y., August 1, 1868, 2:14½.
Two miles—James K. Polk, Philadelphia, June 20, 1850, 4:57½.
Three miles—Oneida Chief, Beacon Course, N. J., August 14, 1843, 7:44

PACING TO WAGON.

One mile—Sweetzer, Chico, Cal., November 21, 1878, 2:17¼.
One mile—Pocahontas, Union Course, L. I., June 21, 1855, drawing 265 lbs., 2:17½.
Two miles—Hero, Centreville, L. I., October 17, 1855, 4:59.

THE RUNNING TURF

Fastest Time Recorded to January 1, 1885.

The following is the official record of the fastest time made on the running turf up to January 1 of the present year:

One-half-mile—Olitipa, two years, 97 pounds, Saratoga, N. Y., July 25, 1874, 47¾.

Five-sixths mile—Neyelia two years, 87 pounds, Salem, Oregon, September 18, 1882, 1:00¼, and Jim Renwick, five years, 115 pounds, San Francisco, Cal., November 3, 1883, 1:00½.

Three-fourths mile—Force, five years, 121 pounds, straight track, Louisville, Ky., September 24, 1883, 1:13, and Matinee, two years, 102 pounds straight track, Louisville Ky., September 24, 1883, 1:13¾.

Seven-eighth-mile—Sweetbriar, two years, 107 pounds, San Francisco, Cal., November 3, 1883, 1:28; Joe Murray, five years, 117 pounds, Chicago, Ill., July 17, 1884, 1:28¼, and Miss Woodford, four years, 115 pounds, Sheepshead Bay, L. I., September 6, 1884, 128¾.

One mile—Ten Broeck, five years, 110 pounds, against time, Louisville, Ky., May 24 1877, 1 39¾, and Boardman, four years, 94 pounds, against horses, Sheepshead Bay, L. I. September 21. 1880. 1 40¼

One and one-eighth miles—Roselle, four years, catch-weight, Brighton Beach, Coney Island, August 13. 1881. 1:53¼, and Revoke, 5 years, 145 pounds, Chicago, Ill., August 15, 1884, 1.58½.

One and three-sixteenths-miles—King Earnest-Mimi, colt, three years, 95 pounds, Long Branch, N. J., July 22, 1884, 2.04¼.

One and one half miles—Luke Blackburn, three years, 102 pounds, Monmouth Park, N J, August 17, 1880, 2.34, and Hindoo, three years, 118 pounds, Saratoga, N. Y August 4, 1881, 2 36

Two miles—Ten Broeck five years, 110 pounds, against time, Louisville, Ky., May 29 1877, 3 27½· Wildmoor, six years best in race between horses, Kansas City, Mo September 29, 1882, 3.28 and Malua, five years, 136 pounds, best at the weight, Melbourne, Aus., November 4. 1884, 3.31¾.

Two and one fourth miles—Preakness, aged, 114 pounds, and Springbok, 5 years, 114 pounds dead heat Saratoga, N Y July 29, 1875, 3:56¼.

Two and one-half miles—Aristides four years, 104 pounds, Lexington, Ky., May 13, 1875, 4.27½.

Two and three-fourths miles—Hubbard, four years, 108 pounds, Saratoga, N. Y., August 9 1873, 4.58¾

Three miles—Drake Carter, four years, 115 pounds, Sheepshead Bay, L. I., September 6. 1884, 5.24, and Eole, four years, 120 pounds, Sheepshead Bay, L. I., September 9; 1882, 5 26½.

Four miles—Ten Broeck, four years, 104 pounds, against time, Louisville, Ky., September 27 1876, 7:15¾

Ten miles—Mr Brown six years, 160 pounds ridden by H. C. Peel, match for $1,000 with L L aged 160 pounds, ridden by A. Belmont Purdy, Rancocas, N. J., March 2, 1880, 26 18.

HEAT RACING

One-fourth mile—Suspender, Los Angeles, Cal, April 10, 1883, 23½, 22½.

One half mile—Nora M., four years 113 pounds, Chicago, Ill., August 15, 1884, 49:49; three heats in five, Bluebird aged, 113 pounds, won first and third heats, and Verner, four years 115 pounds, the second, Chicago, Ill., August 9, 1884, 49½, 49½ 49¾

Five-eighths mile—Sudie McNairy, three years, 98 pounds, Chicago, Ill., July 2, 1883, 1:02½. 1 03½

Three-fourths mile—Lizzie S. five years, 118 pounds, Louisville, Ky., September 28, 1883. 1 13½. 1·13¾; Callao aged. 108 pounds. Louisville, Ky., October 10, 1883, 1 13 1 16

One mile—First heat won by Ada Glenn, four years, 106 pounds, others by Dan Sparling, four years, 106 pounds, Sheepshead Bay, L. I., September 21, 1880, 1.41½, 1.42, 1.44¾; Kadi, six years, about 90 pounds, fastest second heat, Hartford, Ct. September 2, 1875. 1:41½: Bounce, four years, 90 pounds, Sheepshead Bay, L. I. September 7, 1881. 1:42, 1:41¼; Gabriel, five years, 115 pounds, best at weight, St. Louis, Mo. June 13, 1881, 1:42½. 1:41¾; Thornhill won first two heats and Thad Stevens, aged, 110 pounds, the others, Sacramento, Cal., July 8, 1873, 1:43. 1:43, 1:43¼, 1:46½, 1:45; John Sullivan, five years, 90 pounds, equaling best third heat, Chicago, Ill., August 12, 1884, 1:43½.

Two miles—Bradamante, three years, 87 pounds, Jackson, Miss., November 17, 1877, 3:32½. 3:29: Miss Woodford, four years, 107½ pounds, Sheepshead Bay, L. I., September 20, 1884, 3:33, 3:31½.

GREAT SEAL OF THE UNITED STATES.

SEALS OF THE STATES OF THE UNION.

STATE OF ARKANSAS.

STATE OF CALIFORNIA.

STATE OF COLORADO

STATE OF CONNECTICUT.

STATE OF DELAWARE.

STATE OF FLORIDA.

STATE OF GEORGIA

STATE OF ILLINOIS

STATE OF IOWA.

STATE OF INDIANA.

STATE OF KANSAS

STATE OF KENTUCKY.

STATE OF LOUISIANA

STATE OF MAINE

STATE OF MARYLAND.

STATE OF MASSACHUSETTS.

STATE OF MICHIGAN.

STATE OF MINNESOTA

STATE OF MISSISSIPPI.

STATE OF MISSOURI.

STATE OF NEBRASKA

STATE OF NEW HAMPSHIRE.

STATE OF NEW JERSEY

STATE OF NEW YORK.

STATE OF NORTH CAROLINA.

STATE OF OHIO.

STATE OF OREGON.

STATE OF PENNSYLVANIA.

STATE OF RHODE ISLAND

STATE OF SOUTH CAROLINA

STATE OF TENNESSEE.

STATE OF TEXAS.

STATE OF VERMONT.

STATE OF VIRGINIA.

STATE OF WEST VIRGINIA.

STATE OF WISCONSIN.

Political History of the United States.

VOCABULARY OF PARTY NAMES, MEASURES, TERMS AND MAXIMS.

ALL TALK AND NO CIDER.—An expression used by disgusted members of the body politic in Bucks county, Pennsylvania, where a company met to test a barrel of cider, presumably during the hard-cider and log-cabin campaign. Political topics were discussed with so much enthusiasm that the barrel of fluid was forgotten until several persons got up to retire from the meeting, saying at the same time that the concern of the speakers was "all talk and no cider."

AMERICAN WHIGS.—First American political party. From 1763 to 1775, the tories favored passive obedience to the crown, but the whigs made manifest their spirit of independence. King George II. declared his American subjects out of their allegiance, when the latter declared their independence of him. The name whig then became synonymous with patriot, and those who supported the crown were called tories.

AMNESTY.—An act of oblivion, by which crimes and offenses against the government up to a certain time are so obliterated that they cannot again be brought against the guilty parties. President Johnson issued a proclamation of amnesty, by which the mass of southern citizens could receive pardon, 29th May, 1865.

ANTI-FEDERALISTS.—See Federalists.

ANTI-MASONRY.—The society of Free Masons was organized in the United States during the last century. William Morgan, of Batavia, New York, having in 1826, written a book against masonry —exposing the secrets of the order—he was seized and taken to Niagara, in September, and nothing further was ever heard of him. The anti-masons, in September, 1831, nominated William Wirt, of

Maryland, and Amos Ellmaker, of Pennsylvania, for president and vice-president respectively. These candidates received the electoral vote of Vermont. See Morgan.

ASSASSINATION OF PRESIDENTS.—Abraham Lincoln was shot through the head by John Wilkes Booth, at Ford's theatre, in Washington, after 10 o'clock on the 14th of April, 1865, and expired at twenty-two minutes past seven o'clock the next morning. An attempt upon the life of Secretary William H. Seward was made at the same time, while he was confined to his bed from the effects of a fall from a carriage; this assassin, Lewis Payne Powell, inflicted severe wounds by striking at the throat of his victim three times, then rushed off to save his own life. James A. Garfield was shot in the upper part of the arm and in the side or back, near the backbone, by Charles Guiteau, at the Baltimore and Potomac depot, in Washington, at 9:20 a.m., on the 2d July, 1881, and after a painful illness of nearly three months, suddenly expired at 10:35 p.m., Monday, September 19, 1881. See Execution of Assassins.

AUTOCRACY.—That form of government in which the sovereign exercises uncontrolled power, uniting in himself the legislative and executive powers of the state. Almost all Eastern nations have this form of government.

BANK OF THE UNITED STATES.—An institution that was incorporated in 1791, but did not go into operation till 1794. It was the first one of the kind in the country, and established at the suggestion of Alexander Hamilton, secretary of the treasury. Its charter was to run twenty years; headquarters in the city of Philadelphia. The capital of the bank was $10,000,000. Its charter expired by limitation in 1811, and the effort to recharter was defeated by one vote in the house, and by the vote of the vice-president in the senate. The second United States bank was chartered in 1816, for the same term, with a capital of $35,000,000. An act of congress in 1832 for extending it was vetoed by President Jackson, who ordered the funds kept in the bank to be withdrawn from it in September, 1833. This act produced much excitement throughout the union. The senate passed a resolution of censure in March, 1834, which was expunged by order of the senate in January, 1837.

BLACK REPUBLICANS.—An epithet used by members of the democratic party in Illinois and elsewhere to distinguish a radical republican. The abolitionists were often called black abolitionists.

BLOODY SHIRT.—Applied to the politician who is disposed to parade acts of violence and murder committed under carpet-bag government.

BLUE LAWS.—An epithet applied to certain supposititious regulations which were imposed upon the inhabitants of the states of Massachusetts and Connecticut in the seventeenth and eighteenth centuries; any law of the puritans, who were so-called from their professing extraordinary purity in worship and conduct.

BORDER RUFFIANS.—Citizens of the border counties of Missouri who invaded the territory of Kansas in the interest of slavery were so called. Frequent raids were made by slave state settlers in 1856, and Lawrence and Ossawottomie were nearly destroyed. John Brown, with thirty men, was successful in opposing five hundred men who attacked Ossawottomie. He was afterward called "Ossawottomie Brown." See Kansas and Nebraska.

BROTHER JONATHAN.—Governor Jonathan Trumbull, the elder, of Connecticut, was the executive of the state named at the time General Washington was in command of the revolutionary army. The general placed much confidence in the wisdom and sympathy of the old governor, who was in a position to aid him in supplying the wants of the army. So the term originated from a remark of Washington, that he must consult "Brother Jonathan." The army was confronting the British before Boston, and Brother Jonathan, on being consulted by the commander, came forward with such aid as rendered the army more effective. When difficulties afterward arose in the army, it became a by-word, "We must consult Brother Jonathan." This term has now become characteristic of the whole country, as John Bull has for England.

BUCKTAILS.—A term applied to the political opponents of De Witt Clinton, a publicly active citizen of New York, who filled the office of mayor in 1815. The bucktails wore in their hats, on certain occasions, a portion of the tail of the deer. Hence the name.

BUGBEAR.—A notion or fancy that is retailed from the stump or through a newspaper by a political sensationalist, to scare the unsophisticated people into the support of a measure or party; a scarecrow; a man of straw; a political sensation.

BULLDOZE.—To intimidate. The term originated in Louisiana, where it was used after the war of 1861–5, in connection with the alleged intimidation of negro voters in that state.

BUNCOMBE.—Speech-making for purposes of political intrigue; mere talk.

CARPET-BAGGER.—One of those unprincipled adventurers who sought to profit by plundering the defenseless people in some parts of the south after the war of 1861–5. The term was used with effect during the period of reconstruction.

"There is another influence equally injurious with theirs (ku-klux), and a great deal more detrimental to the fame and character of the republican party. I allude to what are known as the 'thieving carpet-baggers.'"—Horace Greeley, New York, June 12, 1871.

CAUCUS.—A meeting of the leaders of a political party, to consider and agree upon a plan of action for the campaign.

CHARTER OAK.—A tree in which the colonial charter was secreted, at Hartford, Conn., in 1688. Blown down in 1856.

CIVIL RIGHTS BILL.—A measure, having passed the senate April 2, was adopted by the house contrary to the president's veto by a vote of 122 to 41. This was for the protection of the freedmen, but did not give them the right to vote. For this latter purpose the fifteenth amendment to the national constitution was adopted by congress 26th February, 1869, and having been ratified by three-fourths of the states, was declared effective 30th March, 1870.

CIVIL SERVICE REFORM.—In accordance with an act of congress, passed 3d March, 1871, a board of seven commissioners was appointed by President Grant to inquire into the matter of reforming the civil service. During President Hayes' administration an order was issued to the following effect: "No officer should be required or permitted to take part in the management of political organizations, caucuses, conventions, or election campaigns. Their right to vote and to express their views on public questions, either orally or through the press, is not denied, provided it does not interfere with the discharge of their official duties. No assessment for political purposes on officers or subordinates should be allowed." The credit for starting the movement in favor of this object belongs to President Grant, who recommended it in his second annual message, 5th December, 1870.

COLORED SOLDIERS.—Persons of African descent were received into service of government by authority of congress, 17th July, 1862. In 1864, they were unconditionally accepted as troops, and as many as 186,017 were in the United States' service during the war.

COMMONER.—Henry Clay was so called, as also was Thomas Corwin, by admirers. Clay was also called the great pacificator, from his conciliatory disposition—he, on two occasions, in 1820 and and in 1850, having succeeded in effecting a compromise between the slave states and the abolitionists.

CONFEDERATE STATES.—A separate government formed by the seven southern states which were the first to secede from the national union in 1861. Congress of delegates met February 4, at

Montgomery, Ala., where, by joint action of South Carolina, Georgia, Alabama, Louisiana, Florida and Mississippi (Texas delegates not being appointed till later), a provisional constitution was adopted, and on February 9, Jefferson Davis, of Mississippi, was elected as president, and Alexander H. Stephens, of Georgia, as vice-president. On May 6 the confederate congress passed an act recognizing a state of war with the United States. Virginia, North Carolina, Tennessee and Arkansas, May 6, 1861, passed ordinances of secession. Davis and Stephens were elected to their offices under the permanent constitution, November 6, 1861.

CONFEDERATION, ARTICLES OF.—The articles as adopted, 15th November, 1777, by the second continental congress, and which formed the basis of the federal union in America. This confederation was ratified on the 1st of March, 1781, when the last one of the original states signed the compact.

CONGRESS, COLONIAL.—The first congress held in America. It was composed of delegates from nine of the colonies, who met in New York, October 7, 1765, and published a declaration of their rights and grievances, insisting particularly on the right of exclusively taxing themselves, and complaining loudly of the stamp act, which see. See also Continental Congresses.

CONSTITUTION.—The established form of government in any country, state or community, whether that be a body of written laws, or be founded on prescriptive usage. In regard to political principles, constitutions are (1) democratic, as in the United States, where the sovereign power is vested in the people; (2) aristocratic, when the government is chiefly or entirely in the hands of certain privileged classes; (3) monarchical, when in the hands of one person; (4) of a mixed character, as in Britain, where the sovereign power is distributed over the king, lords and commons.

CONSTITUTIONAL UNION PARTY.—A name adopted in 1860 by the remaining elements of the whig party. May 9, 1860, a convention met and nominated John Bell, of Tennessee, for president, and Edward Everett, for vice-president. The Bell-Everett ticket carried Kentucky, Tennessee and Virginia, but received a very light vote in the north. This was the last vestige of the whig party.

CONTINENTAL.—A term that was used before the American declaration. It had special application to the colonies as a whole. In colonial times a meeting of delegates from the various colonies formed a continental congress. When Ethan Allen was asked by what authority he demanded the surrender of Ticonderoga, he replied: "In the name of the great Jehovah and of the continental congress!"

CONTINENTAL CONGRESSES.—The first continental congress, consisting of fifty-five delegates, from all the colonies except Georgia, met at Philadelphia on the 5th September, 1774. This body, on behalf of the people, as subjects of the British power, framed a declaration of rights and drew up an address to the king, another to the people of Great Britain, and a third to the colonies. The colonists demanded their rights, particularly in relation to a just share in the regulation of their own domestic affairs, and in imposing their own taxes; the right of a speedy trial by jury in the locality in which the offense should be committed, and the right to hold public meetings and petition as against arbitrary rule. The second continental congress met at Philadelphia, 10th May, 1775, and adopted the appellation of the United Colonies. A petition was prepared and sent to England asking for a redress of grievances. The thirteen colonies were, therefore, organized into a federal union, and congress deliberately assumed the general direction of affairs. A declaration was drawn up justifying the course of resistance to British oppression; a loan of money was authorized; the troops were formed into a continental army, and George Washington, a member of the congress from Virginia, was placed in command. The Americans had hitherto been contending, not for independence, but for constitutional liberty. See Declaration of Independence.

CONTRABAND.—In 1861, While General B. F. Butler was in command of Fortress Monroe, a number of slaves having escaped from their master, were brought before him. Each was examined and then set at work for the benefit of the government. When they were applied for by confederate officers on behalf of the owner (Colonel Mallory), the general replied that he should detain the negroes as contraband of war.

CONVENTION OF 1787.—The body of delegates from the original states, which met at Philadelphia, 25th May, 1787, to revise and perfect the fundamental laws of the confederacy. At that time the necessity of a more efficient general government was extensively felt, and after a session of about four months the convention agreed on the federal constitution. That instrument was transmitted by congress to the several states, in nearly its present form, and was, in 1788, ratified by eleven of them (afterward by the other two), and became the constitution of the United States. See Ordinance of 1787.

COON.—The popular emblem of the whigs in the campaign of 1844, when Henry Clay and Theodore Frelinghuysen were candidates for president and vice-president. Mr. Van Buren had been called "the sly fox of Kinderhook." In consequence of his previous candidacies, Mr. Clay had been spoken of as "that same old coon." The whigs were charged with hunting after "that same old coon." Hence the raccoon as an emblem. "A gone coon," said of one whose case is hopeless.

COPPERHEAD.—Northern sympathizers with the confederates were so-called during the civil war of 1861–5.

CORPORAL'S GUARD.—The men in congress who supported President Tyler after he had been renounced by the whigs in 1841.

CRADLE OF LIBERTY.—Faneuil hall, in Boston. The orators of the revolution raised their voices there against British oppression.

CREDIT MOBILIER.—In France, a general society established in 1852, upon the principle of limited liability, under the sanction of the government. The capital was fixed at 60,000,000 francs, divided into shares of 500 francs each. Objects of the society: To aid the progress of public works, and promote the development of national industry, making railways, managing gas companies, and, in fact, becoming a kind of universal trading association, for the buying up of the shares and bonds of existing trading societies and companies, for the purpose of consolidating them into one common stock, and for the transaction of general banking and brokerage operations. The funds for the carrying out of these diverse operations are, (1) the capital of the company, and (2) the deposits received from the society by the public. In the United States, congress passed an act chartering the Union Pacific railway, in 1862. In a speech, delivered in September, 1872, at Indianapolis, Mr. Greeley, as a presidential candidate, made statements substantially as follows: Congress resolved to aid the enterprise generously, and granted the right of way through the public lands, with the right to take materials from any part of the public domain. Then a large grant was made in aid of the road, and bonds of the government calling for $25,000 a mile were loaned to the company, and the first mortgage on the railroad taken therefor; thus the building of the road was provided for with public funds. In a few years, this enterprise having passed into the hands of scheming men, some being members of congress, another step was taken, and congress was prevailed upon to authorize a new loan of $25,000 a mile. A second mortgage of equal amount was taken on the road, and so the security of the first mortgage was destroyed. In a little while a private company was somewhere chartered, entitled the Credit Mobilier of America, and that private company, or ring, was composed of a number of active members of the Union Pacific railroad company, some of them members of congress. No list of this Credit Mobilier was ever published, nor can be obtained. But these gentlemen proceeded to make contracts virtually with themselves, i. e., the same men as officers of the Union Pacific railroad contracted with themselves as officers of the Credit Mobilier of America to construct the road at enormous prices, which absorbed both the bonds loaned by the government and the private loan of the company; this contracting with themselves to pay themselves twice the fair cost of entirely building and equipping the road, and after building the road with the proceeds of the money loaned by the government, they proceeded to divide among themselves the other bonds, equal to the amount which congress had made mortgage on the entire road. By these means twenty or thirty millions of dollars were divided among the parties, and after all that money was so divided and they were called upon to pay, they divided the bonds and built the road with the government bonds, which were a second mortgage on that company. "Now, you see," said Mr. Greeley, continuing, "these gentlemen who engineered through congress this project of making the road cost double what it should cost, and making half the cost a dividend appropriated among themselves, these gentlemen now appear before congress for additional advantages." In February, 1873, the committee appointed by congress to investigate the corrupt Credit Mobilier matter, made a report which amazed the people at large, and a long investigation grew out of this. As a consequence, Oakes Ames and James Brooks of the house were censured, and the reputations of several prominent politicians were somewhat damaged.

COVODE INVESTIGATION.—A committee authorized by the house of representatives to inquire into the chicanery of the Buchanan administration, in attempting to foist the Lecompton constitution upon the people of Kansas. An examination, after the appointment of the committee, 5th March, 1860, resulted in developing the truth of the charges of corruption. See Lecompton Constitution.

DARK HORSE.—No doubt that this phrase originated from the coloring of horses by jockeys in order to bring them into a race under different names and win the prizes. In politics, the successful nominee of a party who is little thought of as the nominee. Hayes and Garfield were "dark horses." (See Surprise Candidate.) "From whence is to come the 'dark horse'? Some say it will be Drummond, some say Hyde, some say Spring, and others Blaine.

The man whom the ring has determined upon to lead the republican party is now engaged in the honest and peaceful occupation of a fisherman, and his name is William P. Frye."—Boston Post, Maine politics, 1882.

DEMOCRATIC PARTY.—The theory of the old democratic-republican party was, popular government, with limitation of the powers of the general or federal government, in order not to restrict the rights of states in the management of local interests. In the last decade of the past century, the party assumed the name of republican, by which it was popularly known until about 1830, when the more radical portion separated from the conservative element, and assumed the name of national republican. The conservatives were called democrats, but that term being regarded as equivalent to republicans, they were known as republicans till about 1830. These parties, until after the election of Jackson, in 1828, claimed the name of republican. The friends of Adams were styled the administration wing, and those of Jackson, the opposition. The Jackson men afterward fixed upon the title of democrat, and there has been no further variation of the name of the party since. The democrats were successful in successive presidential elections until that of 1840, when the whigs, with General Harrison, came into power. President Harrison died in just one month after his inauguration, and the administration under John Tyler became democratic. The administration of James K. Polk was next in order, and then the whigs again succeeded in 1848, when General Taylor was elected. The democrats followed with the election of Franklin Pierce, in 1852, and James Buchanan in 1856. The attempt to force a pro-slavery constitution upon the territory of Kansas, was followed by a split in the democratic party. The popular Illinois senator, Stephen A. Douglas, assumed the leadership of the northern wing, while the pro-slavery men that formed the southern wing were led by the administration. In 1860 the democratic convention, which met at Charleston, April 23, failed to agree upon resolutions and candidates. There were fifty-seven ineffectual ballots, Mr. Douglas, for president, always leading. Many of the delegates withdrew from this convention and met in another hall, adopted resolutions, and adjourned to meet in Richmond, on the second Monday in June. The regular convention adjourned, May 3, to meet at Baltimore, June 18. In the Baltimore convention there arose a disagreement on account of the admission of delegates from the state which had withdrawn from the Charleston convention. The result of it was the withdrawal of a considerable number of delegates, includ-

the chairman of the convention, Caleb Cushing, and Benjamin F. Butler. Stephen A. Douglas was then nominated for president, and Herschel V Johnson, of Georgia, was afterward selected by the executive committee as candidate for vice-president. The delegates who withdrew from the convention at Baltimore, being joined by delegations which had been refused admission, assembled at Maryland institute, June 28, and put in nomination, for president, John C. Breckinridge, of Kentucky, and Joseph Lane, of Oregon, for vice-president. Those who had withdrawn from the Charleston convention met at Richmond, June 11, and adjourned from time to time until the seceders' convention at Baltimore had nominated Breckinridge and Lane, when those nominations were indorsed. The democratic party, thus divided, while the republican party had become a unit against slavery extension and for the union, went before the country with small chances of success. Mr. Douglas took the stump, and in a series of speeches in different sections of the country, expounded his views to great crowds of his countrymen. He was all but idolized by the free-soil democrats, who rallied to his standard with enthusiasm. At the election, the popular vote for Mr. Douglas was very great, but his electoral vote was small. The defeat of Mr. Douglas and the democratic party by the republicans, with Mr. Lincoln as the successful candidate, proved a death-dealing disappointment to Mr. Douglas, whose ambition to rise to the presidency was earnest, and seconded by the ballots of upward of one million three hundred and seventy-five thousand of his friends. In his dying days he made very explicit expressions of loyalty to the federal union and the government of the United States. He died on the 3d of June, 1861, in the forty-ninth year of his age. Since the 3d of March, 1861, to the present time (1885), the republicans have been in possession of the presidential office. As the result of the election of November 4, 1884, the Democrats return to power with Grover Cleveland, of New York, as President, and Thomas A. Hendricks, of Indiana, as Vice-President, on March 4th of this year (1885). See Republican Party.

DON'T GIVE UP THE SHIP.—Said by Captain Lawrence, commander of the United States Chesapeake, after he was mortally wounded, and was being taken below. His vessel was captured by the British ship Shannon, after an action thirty miles from Boston light, 1st June, 1813.

DOUGH-FACE.—An epithet applied to the northern apologist for slavery in the south.

DRED SCOTT DECISION.—A decision given by the United

States supreme court, March 6, 1857, whereby Dred Scott, who had been claimed as a slave in a free state, was remanded to slavery. Of the seven judges, two declared for his freedom. By this decision the Missouri compromise of 1820 was declared unconstitutional, and thereupon arose the popular phrase, "Negroes have no rights that white men are bound to respect."

EXECUTIVE.—The head of the executive department of the government; as, the governor of a state, or president of the United States. Otherwise, the chief magistrate, or the king.

EXECUTION OF ASSASSINS.—David E. Harold, George A. Atzerott, Lewis Payne Powell, and Mrs. E. Surratt, accomplices of Booth in the assassination of President Lincoln, were hung, 7th July, 1865. Others were sent up to Dry Tortugas for life. Henry Wirz, for cruelty to union prisoners at Andersonville, was hung in Washington, 10th November, 1865. Charles Guiteau, for murder of President Garfield, was hung 30th June, 1882. See Assassination of Presidents.

FATHER OF HIS COUNTRY.—George Washington, patriot and first president of the United States, was so called. He was commander-in-chief of the American armies—a man of the happiest union of good qualities. Born on his father's estate, in Westmoreland county, Va., 22d February, 1732, and after a life of unsullied glory, he died, 14th December, 1799.

FEDERALIST.—The name of a political party in the United States, formed in 1788, the members of which claimed to be the peculiar friends of the constitution and federal government. The most distinguished leaders of the federal party were Washington, Adams, Hamilton, and Jay, and the leading federal states were Massachusetts and Connecticut, supported generally by the other New England states. Opposed to this party, were Jefferson, Madison, Monroe, Burr, and Gallatin (republican), who were called anti-federalists, and charged with being indifferent or hostile to the constitution and government. During the contests of the French revolution the federalists leaned to the side of England, the republicans to that of France. The dissolution of the federal party was hastened by reason of its opposition to the second war (1812) for independence. This war came to pass principally from the unjust claims of Great Britain to the right of searching American vessels for deserters and British seamen. As a remedy for the evils which the federalists charged over against the government on account of the war, a convention was held (commencing 15th December, 1814) at Hartford, Conn. This body recommended certain measures to the legislatures of the eastern states, looking to a limitation of the power of the federal government over the militia of the states. It also proposed several amendments to the constitution. But the labors of the convention were brought to a close by the news of the treaty of peace between the United States and Great Britain, signed on the 24th, the ninth day after the assembling of that body. The moral and visible effect of this convention was felt a little later when in 1820, the federal party was completely disbanded.

FIFTY-FOUR FORTY OR FIGHT.—An expression used during the northwestern boundary dispute that arose soon after President Polk's inauguration. The Oregon question, as it is called, was first noticed in a public manner by President Tyler in his message to congress, 5th December, 1842. The territory of the nation known as the Oregon territory, lying on the Pacific ocean, north of the forty-second degree of latitude, was claimed in part by Great Britain. In 1843, a bill was carried through the senate by a majority of one, for taking possession of the whole of the disputed territory, but the house refused to concur in this measure. In his message of 1843, the president (Tyler) asserted the claim on behalf of the United States, in regard to that territory, to the parallel of 54 deg. 40 min. north latitude, and James K. Polk was elected, in 1844, as one disposed to insist upon the 54 deg. 40 min. parallel as the boundary of Oregon. It was understood that the United States were to absorb the whole of the territory—the whole or none, "54–40 or fight." However, the new president felt that it was best to act in the light of previous efforts at compromise, in consequence of which the forty-ninth parallel was to be the northern boundary of the territory of the nation. Finally (18th June, 1846), all previous efforts having failed, an adjustment of the northwestern boundary dispute was reached by means of a convention, proposed by the British minister, which decided upon the forty-ninth degree of north latitude. From the standpoint of those opposed to compromise, this was "the back-down from 54–40."

FILIBUSTER.—A corruption of the English free-booter or buccaneer. "Filibustering," a cant term much used of late years in the legislative assemblies of the United States to designate the employment of parliamentary tactics to defeat a measure, by raising frivolous questions of order, calls to the house, motions to adjourn, etc., in order to weary out the opposite party and to gain time. "Filibusters," the name given to certain adventurers; the most noted filibuster was William Walker, who led an expedition against Nicaragua, in 1855, and succeeded in maintaining himself in that country for nearly two years, but was at length expelled by the union against him of the other Central American states. Walker was subsequently taken and shot at Truxillo, in Central America, in 1860, when engaged on another filibustering expedition.

FINANCIAL PANICS.—The financial history of the country was marked by distress in 1814, when United States treasury notes were seventeen per cent below par. The situation was aggravated by the peace party, whose leaders persuaded the Boston banks to require that the notes on southern banks, then in their possession, be redeemed. In 1819, the financial difficulties were very serious; paper money had run down to fifty-nine per cent, there had been excess of importation, American staples had declined in foreign countries, cotton and breadstuffs were down fifty per cent, and there was general business depression. In 1821, the distress was great west of the Alleghanies, farmers were unable to pay their debts due to government at western land offices. Congress granted relief by permitting portions of land to be surrendered, and the money paid over to be applied on the remainder to secure it. In 1837, a crash came on the heels of a suspension of the New York banks; many other banks went down, corporations shut up their works, business houses failed, the products of the farm declined, and credit gave way for want of confidence. This crisis was due to excessive speculation, large importations, and business depression for want of capital. California felt the strain of depression in February, 1855. August 24, 1857, the Ohio Life Insurance and Trust company failed, many banks soon suspended payments, all owing to land and "railroad" speculation. September 19, 1873, the firm of Jay Cook & Co., of Philadelphia, failed, from which a general financial panic came to pass, destroying confidence, throwing working people out of employment, producing stagnation and misery. The causes assigned in this case were various, including reckless speculation and increasing extravagance of the people, too liberal importations, careless contracts, etc. Many people lost all their earthly possessions, and joined the army of tramps, and the dull tread of that army, little reduced in numbers, is still heard in the land.

FREE SOIL PARTY.—A political party which, as an immediate result of the agitation of the Wilmot proviso, was formed in 1848. The party nominated Martin Van Buren for president and Charles Francis Adams for vice-president. These candidates received the support of nearly 300,000 free-soilers; but the whig party, composed of those who were dissatisfied with the conduct of affairs under the so-called democratic party, carried the election for Taylor and Fillmore. In 1852, the free-soil party named John P. Hale, of New Hampshire, for president, and George W. Julian, of Indiana, for vice-president. These candidates received 155,825 votes. The whigs and free-soilers—the latter having nominated Scott and Graham—were defeated by the straight-out democrats, and General Franklin Pierce, of New Hampshire, and William R. King, of Alabama, were elected to the offices of president and vice-president respectively.

"And then the question of free soil, what shall be the fate of that? I presume there are here some free-soil men [Yes! yes! all free-soil]—I mean those to whom the question of extending or restricting slavery outweighs all other considerations."—Horace Greeley, New York, Sept. 27, 1848.

FUGITIVE SLAVE LAW.—A law enacted in 1850 as a part of the compromise measures of that period. It provided for the return of any slaves who might have escaped. This law was odious in the eyes of every anti-slavery man and woman of the north.

GERRYMANDER.—To fix the political divisions of a state in such manner that one party may obtain an advantage for itself, as against its opponents.

". . . Denounces the action of the legislature in redistricting (gerrymandering) the state solely in the interest of the democratic party as an attempt to disfranchise 190,000 voters, and as a crime against suffrage which should be rebuked at the polls at the next election."—Ext. Report Greenback Convention, Moberly, Mo., May 30, 1882.

GREENBACK.—A form of paper money, issued by the federal government. The act authorizing the issue of greenbacks says that they "shall also be lawful money and legal tender." The honor of the addition of the term greenback to our vocabulary is justly attributable to Salmon P. Chase, secretary of the treasury, 1861-4 It was chiefly his policy that carried the nation through the war of that period. "Greenbacker," an advocate of greenback or paper money.

"HAIL COLUMBIA."—National ode of America; written by Joseph Hopkinson, in the summer of 1798, for a young actor, named Fox, to render on his benefit night.

HALF BREEDS.—An epithet used to distinguish those of the republican party who were friends of Garfield and his administration; followers of Blaine, and other prominent men belonging to the Garfield faction. Opposed to Stalwarts, which see. (See extract under the head of Independents.)

"The election to-day is properly to be regarded as a pitched battle between the stalwart and the half-breed wings of the republican party."—New York Herald, Nov. 7, 1882.

HARD CIDER AND LOG CABIN CAMPAIGN.—The campaign of 1840, which resulted in the election of William Henry Harrison for president, and John Tyler for vice-president, was one of the most exciting, jolly, and interesting of any in the history of the United States. The democrats nominated Mr. Van Buren for re-election, and the abolitionists named James G. Birney as their candidate for president. The orators and journals of the democratic party ridiculed the whig candidate for president (Harrison), and called him an old granny. One of the editorial fraternity unwittingly wrote: "Give him a log cabin and a barrel of hard cider, and he will be content on his farm in Ohio, whose affairs only is he capable of managing." Thereupon the whigs took up the cry of hard cider and log cabin, and the latter became most appropriate and effectual means in joining the issue in favor of the whigs. Log cabins were raised and hard cider was drunk at the various meetings; a paper with the title of Log Cabin was published by Horace Greeley, and the music of Harrison glee-clubs was echoed and re-echoed from hill to dale. At the larger meetings or barbecues, the people were fed during the day without charge, on which occasions animals were roasted bodily, log cabins and barrels of hard cider were mounted on wheels and drawn by oxen or horses in the processions. It was during this campaign that the expression "Tippecanoe and Tyler too" was sounded in song, a stanza of which is here given.

"What has caused this great commotion-motion, motion,
Our country through?
It is the ball a-rolling on
For Tippecanoe and Tyler too;
For Tippecanoe and Tyler too;
And with him we'll beat little Van;
Van, Van, Van is a used-up man,
And with them we'll beat little Van."

To this song was added those other well-known lines, which are commemorative of the whig victory in the state of Maine—

"O, have you heard how Maine went, went, went?
It went h—l bent
For Governor Kent,
For Tippecanoe and Tyler too," etc.

INDEPENDENTS.—Those who take a stand regardless of party, and who are not subject to bias or partisan influence. The term is often applied to those who break away now and then but do not entirely abandon their party.

"As in all civil wars, a good many people who heartily say, 'A plague on both your houses,' are yet forced to take sides, and thus we see some ludicrous spectacles, such as the independents and civil service reformers voting with the half-breed machine, and marching in effect under the banner of Mr. Blaine, who has assumed the leadership of the half-breed army.

"The independents who unwillingly vote with the Blaine machine to defeat the Arthur or Cameron machine still give no signs that they are ready to abandon the republican party."—New York Herald, Nov. 7, 1882.

KNOW-NOTHINGS.—The name of a secret political party which originated in 1853. The party, or rather society, as stated by the New York Times, was first formed by a person of some notoriety, who called himself Ned Buntline—the writer of sea stories. Ned was once a midshipman in the United States navy, but left the service and commenced the business of founding a secret order, of so exclusive a character that none were to be admitted as members whose grandfathers were not natives of the United States. Ned gave instructions to his followers to reply to all questions in respect to the movements of the new party, "I don't know." So they were at first called don't-knows, and then know-nothings, by outsiders. The Crusader, a party organ, printed the principles of the society as follows: Repeal of all naturalization laws; none but native Americans for office; a pure American common school system; war to the hilt on Romanism. In the year 1855-6 the slavery question had assumed paramount importance, and the civil war between the free state men and the pro-slaveryites in the territory of Kansas, so overshadowed the public mind, that foreign citizenship was forgotten, and the know-nothings as a body disappeared. The nearest approach to know-nothingism or Americanism, in 1856 (as indicated by the name), was the American party, whose nominees for president and vice-president were Millard Fillmore, and Andrew J. Donelson of Tennessee. In that year there was a general excitement, and crush of political elements, which resulted in the complete annihilation of the American and whig parties. Thereupon rose the Republican party, which see.

KU-KLUX KLAN.—A secret political organization that arose from the prejudices of unreconciled persons in some portions of the south. It originated in the state of Tennessee, presumably, early in the year 1868, and soon afterward extended its membership and mischievous influence over various sections. The alleged object of the klan was to redeem the south. After its fashion it opposed the enforcement of the reconstruction acts, and endeavored to maintain the dominion of the white race as against the colored race, the male portion of which latter were enfranchised by effect of the fifteenth amendment, 30th March, 1870. Within a few months of its inception the numbers of the various divisions of the klan were increased to a total of 500,000 persons. Later on, the political aspirations of the klan were given up, and members of the order abandoned themselves to schemes of outrage and murder. May 31, 1870, a congressional act was passed, which provided for the protection of the lately enfranchised colored men, as against the "bulldozing" propensities of the ku-klux. In February following a stringent act was passed for a similar purpose, and on the third day of May, 1871, a proclamation against the klan was issued by President Grant. During the next year (1872) efforts were made to expose the klan. A committee was appointed by congress to make an investigation of the ku-klux mystery. Many witnesses were examined by this committee, and the facts were revealed as pertaining to the existence of the ku-klux bands and their horrible doings.

LECOMPTON CONSTITUTION.—An instrument that was framed in convention at Lecompton for the state of Kansas, in September, 1857. It provided for the introduction of slavery, and at an election in December about 6,500 votes (inclusive of many fraudulent ones) were cast for it. The free state men refrained from voting, until the election, 4th January, 1858, when the Lecompton constitution was voted down by 10,000 majority. In July a free constitution was adopted at Wyandot.

LITTLE GIANT.—Stephen A. Douglas, who was of small stature, but a great orator. See Kansas and Nebraska, and Democratic party.

LOBBY.—The individuals who frequent the space in a hall of legislation not used by regular members. (See Logrolling.)

"Indeed, the lobbyists and logrollers around and in congress are accustomed to reckon upon the thermometer in the middle of June every other summer, much as they reckon on twelve o'clock, March 4, in the alternate years."—New York Sun, 1882.

LOCOFOCO.—A term applied to the ultra democracy or tory party in the United States. Lucifer matches were termed locofocos, and the application of the word to this particular political party arose thus: In 1834, a certain number of the extreme democracy met at Tammany hall, New York, and there happening a great diversity of opinion, the chairman left his seat, and the lights were extinguished, with a view to dissolve the meeting; but those in favor of extreme measures produced locofoco matches, rekindled the lights, continued the meeting, and accomplished their object.

"I ask these (free-soilers) what hope they have of keeping slavery out of California and New Mexico with General Cass president and a locofoco congress?"—Horace Greeley, New York, Sept. 27, 1848.

LOGROLLING.—A custom peculiar to lumber regions. In the logging camps of Maine, the several parties help each other at logrolling. In politics, the term denotes an exchange of votes between parties, in order to carry through extravagant measures in which they are interested.

"With all his extravagant notions, General Grant smothered a bill of this kind (river and harbor), when only one-third of the present amount was appropriated; and the respectable press, without distinction of party, has been more decided in condemnation of this logrolling jobbery, by means of which millions are annually squandered and stolen, than of any other measure before congress."—New York Sun, May 20, 1882.

MAINE LAW.—A law enacted in 1846 and amended in 1851 in the state of Maine, being the first to prohibit the sale of intoxicating liquors, and becoming celebrated for her legislation on this subject through the active efforts of General Neal Dow. The Maine law was adopted by other states, notably Kansas. Out of 842 cities and towns in Illinois, 645 were no-license places in 1880.

MASON AND DIXON'S LINE.—A line 39 degrees, 43 minutes and 26.3 seconds north latitude, established in 1764–7, by Charles Mason and Jeremiah Dixon, two English mathematicians and astronomers, in order to decide the disputed question of boundary between Pennsylvania and Maryland.

MISSOURI COMPROMISE.—So called from an act of congress passed in 1820, and approved by President Monroe, 6th March of that year, by which Missouri was permitted to enter the union as a slave-holding state, with the agreement that slavery should be forever prohibited in the territories of the nation lying north of latitude 36 degrees, 30 minutes.

MONROE DOCTRINE.—In 1822, during the presidency of James Monroe, the Spanish-American colonies having fought their way to independence as against Spain, they were recognized as an independent power by the United States. In his annual message to congress in 1823, the president proclaimed the celebrated doctrine of non-interference as follows: "That as a principle, the American continents, by the free and independent position which they have assumed and maintained, are henceforth not to be considered as subjects of future colonization by any European power." This doctrine is attributed to Adams, who was secretary of state under Monroe.

MUGWUMPS.—The word Mugwumps is of Indian origin, and means "chief." It was used by the New England tribes as a term of derision, and by them applied to a man who stood higher in his own esteem than in that of his tribe, a sort of "Big-Injun." In a sense somewhat similar to this, the word has been more or less in use in New England for many years. It was first employed as a political sobriquet in the presidential campaign of 1884, when it was applied by the Republican leaders and press to those "independents" who affiliated and voted with the Democracy. Like many other political nicknames, it was at once accepted and adopted by those on whom it was bestowed.

NATURALIZATION.—The act of conferring upon an alien the rights and privileges of a native inhabitant or citizen. Aliens may become citizens of the United States after residing in the nation for five years. First naturalization act in the colonies was that passed by the assembly of Maryland. A law of this kind was passed by congress, 24th March, 1790.

NULLIFICATION.—Diverse interests which involved the northern and southern sections of the United States in frequent and exciting disputations and contentions, were clearly indicated in the single instance of the "nullification movement." During the first term of President Andrew Jackson, the tariff question assumed quite formidable proportions. The south had no manufactures to foster, and possessed a staple article which it desired to sell, therefore it was opposed to a protective tariff. On the 21st to 25th January, 1830, Robert Y. Hayne, coadjutor of John C. Calhoun, and senator from South Carolina, delivered his great speech in favor of nullification, and the celebrated reply of Daniel Webster was made on the 26th. President Jackson, at a banquet, 13th April, offered the famous toast: "Our federal union: It must be preserved." In 1832, having reached the point of extreme opposition to the tariff, or the increased rate of duties, which congress had laid, the state of South Carolina, in convention, November 19, resolved that the tariff acts were unconstitutional and void. That state at once prepared to resist the national authority by force of arms. President Jackson having been re-elected in 1832, was in office, and determined to execute the laws, which he did by proclamation, issued December 10, and an order for General Scott to proceed to Charleston with all the national troops under his command. He also sent a vessel of war to that port, and had the leaders of the movement informed of his intention to seize and hang them as soon as they should fire the first gun against the national authority. The danger of disunion was, for the time, averted. Henry Clay proposed a compromise measure in the form of a tariff bill, which provided for a gradual reduction of duties during the following decade. The measure became a law, March 2, 1833. See State Rights.

OLD ABE.—Abraham Lincoln was so called. During the war of 1861–5 colored people of the south called him Massa Linkum.

OLD HICKORY.—General Jackson, president of the United States. So called from his tough nature, and his intelligent firmness. Parson Brownlow was called the hickory unionist.

POPULAR SOVEREIGNTY.—The right of the whole people to participate in forming the constitution, and enacting the laws under which they are to live and by which they are to be governed. "Squatter sovereignty," the right of squatters in a territory of the United States to form and regulate their own domestic relations in their own way; the squatter sovereigns of California voted against slavery, and entered the union as a free state. See Kansas and Nebraska.

PRE-EMPTION RIGHT.—The right given to settlers of public lands to purchase them in preference to others. In order to maintain this right, the pre-emptor must have erected a house or entered upon the work of improving the land of which he has taken possession.

RAG BABY.—The idea of making greenbacks the legal, if not the only, money of the nation. Opposed to national-bank money. The greenbackers regard the precious metals as cumbrous and expensive articles for currency. See National Greenbackers.

REPUBLICAN PARTY.—The anti-slavery party that rose into vigorous life during the political upheaval of 1856. The name has been used several times in the history of American politics. (See Democratic Party.) The democrats were the political friends of the south, or of slavery. The republicans were their political opponents. Previous to its organization in 1856, the elements of the republican party opposed the extension of slavery, and generally, were in favor of abolition. The first national convention met at Philadelphia, June 17, of the year named, and nominated Colonel John C. Fremont, of California, for president. William L. Dayton, of New Jersey, was chosen for vice-president. The nominations were made unanimous. The democrats had previously designated their candidates, James Buchanan, of Pennsylvania, for president, and John C. Breckinridge, of Kentucky, for vice-president. The campaign following these and other nominations, was one of great excitement, which the war in Kansas tended to inflame. At the election the republicans polled a very large popular vote, and firmly established themselves as the most formidable party in opposition to the national democracy. The democratic administration that followed was marked by the Dred Scott decision—odious to the republicans—the approval of the Lecompton constitution by President Buchanan, which was as odious, and the execution of John Brown, which aroused the feelings of the abolitionists. Mr. Lincoln, at Springfield, 17th June, 1858, announced that the government could not permanently endure half slave and half free; and later, October 25, in a speech at Rochester, Mr. Seward declared, as between slavery and freedom, there existed an irrepressible conflict. These phrases were often repeated by the republicans, and the southern democrats took notice of them as declarations utterly hostile to the institution of slavery. In the early part of the year, Senator Douglas, of Illinois, the great northern ally of the southern democracy, took issue with the administration on account of the attempt of the ultra democrats to force a pro-slavery constitution upon the people of Kansas. Mr. Buchanan had indorsed the Lecompton scheme, as indicated, and the opposition of Mr. Douglas had the effect to weaken the democratic party in the north. In the elections immediately following this remarkable contest, when most members of the thirty-sixth congress were chosen, the republicans showed increased strength, and the democratic majority of the house was again overthrown. During the year 1859, the breach widened between the north and south, and in 1860, the republican party, all solidified and strong, entered the presidential campaign with renewed vigor. The republican national convention met in Chicago, May 16, and on the 18th the nomination of Abraham Lincoln, of Illinois, for president, and Hannibal Hamlin, of Maine, for vice-president, was made unanimous. Opposed to Lincoln and Hamlin, were Douglas and Johnson (Douglas democracy), Breckinridge and Lane (Breckinridge democracy), and Bell and Everett (Constitutional union). In the election following all these nominations, the free states were carried by the republicans, and Mr. Lincoln received a larger popular vote than that cast for James Buchanan, four years before. When the result was determined, several federal officers in South Carolina resigned their positions, and the people of that state prepared to secede from the union. President Buchanan, by his message, December 4, virtually recognized the right of secession, and one after another various southern states seceded from the union, beginning with South Carolina, December 20, 1860, and ending with the secession of Tennessee, which was effected June 8, 1861. Mr. Lincoln was inaugurated as president 4th March, 1861, when the war for the union was commenced and pushed to a successful termination. From the year 1861 to the time of this writing (1885) the national republican party has been in constant possession of the presidential office. They were, however, defeated in the general elections of November 4, 1884, and retire from office on March 4th of this year (1885), the republican candidates James G. Blaine, of Maine, and Gen. John A. Logan, of Illinois, having been defeated by the democrats whose candidates were Gov. Grover Cleveland, of New York, and ex-Gov. Thomas A. Hendricks, of Indiana. See Democratic Party, and Wide-awakes.

ROOSTER, DEMOCRATIC.—Bird B. Chapman, a politician of repute in Indiana, about 1844, published a democratic paper, and on the occasion of a victory at some local election, was felicitated by an active democrat, who wrote, "Crow, Chapman, crow." These words were used as a headline in his next day's edition, and so the democratic rooster was first introduced as the harbinger of victory.

SALT RIVER.—An imaginary river, up which defeated political candidates are supposed to be sent. The phrase "to row up salt river" had its origin from Salt river, or Salt creek, a small, winding stream in the state of Kentucky. Owing to the many bars and shallows by which it is characterized, it is difficult to row up the stream. The defeated individual is rowed up Salt river.

SLAVERY WAR, OR REBELLION.—The war on account of slavery in the United States, was begun by the confederates, under Beauregard, who opened with thirty heavy guns and mortars on Fort Sumter, in the harbor of Charleston, S. C., 12th April, 1861. During four years, the losses were: killed in battle, 61,362; died of wounds, 34,727; died of disease, 183,287; total died, 279,376; total deserted, 199,105. Confederate soldiers who died of wounds or disease, 133,821; deserted, 104,428—partial figures. Total confederate and union dead, 413,197. Estimated cost of the war, $3,000,000,000. Expenditures arising from the war were, on June 10, 1880, as reported by Secretary Sherman, $6,189,929,908.58. Confederate forces under General Lee surrendered to General Grant, April 9, 1865. President Lincoln was assassinated at Washington, April 14. General Johnston's confederate army surrendered to General Sherman on the 26th, and early in May, 1865, the war ended.

PRESIDENTS AND THEIR CABINETS.

From Washington to Cleveland.

THE following is a complete list of the Presidential Cabinets of the United States, from the first organization of the government of the country under Washington to the election of President-elect Cleveland, and will be found a useful book of reference for the student of history. The list gives the names of the occupants of each cabinet office in the administration, the state from which appointed, and the date upon which he took the oath of office. It includes nearly all the great figures of American political history, many of the cabinet officers having been party leaders and unsuccessful candidates for the Presidency.

First and Second Terms.

President.—George Washington, 1789 to 1797.

Secretary of State.—Thomas Jefferson, Virginia, September 26, 1789; Edmund Randolph, Virginia, January 2, 1794; Timothy Pickering, Pennsylvania, December 10, 1795.

Secretary of the Treasury.—Alexander Hamilton, New York, September 11, 1789; Oliver Wolcott, Connecticut, February 2, 1795.

Secretary of War.—Henry Knox, Massachussetts, September 12, 1789; Timothy Pickering, Pennsylvania, January 2, 1795; James McHenry, Maryland, January 27, 1796.

Attorney-General.—Edmund Randolph, Virginia, September 26, 1789 Wm. Bradford, Pennsylvania, January 27, 1794; Charles Lee, Virginia, December 10, 1795.

Postmaster-General. — Samuel Osgood, Massachussetts, September 26, 1789; Timothy Pickering, Pennsylvania, August 12, 1791; Joseph Habersham, Georgia, February 25, 1795.

[Note.—The position of postmaster-general was a subordinate office under the Treasury department until 1829, when the postmaster-general was made a cabinet officer.]

Third Term.

President. — John Adams, 1797 to 1801.

Secretary of State.—Timothy Pickering, Pennsylvania, continued; John Marshall, Virginia, May 13, 1800.

Secretary of the Treasury.—Oliver Wolcott, continued; Samuel Dexter, Massachusetts, January 1, 1801.

Secretary of War.—James McHenry, continued; Samuel Dexter, Massachusetts, May 13, 1800; Roger Griswold, Connecticut, February 3, 1801.

Secretary of the Navy.—George Cabot, Massachusetts, May 3, 1798; Benjamin Stoddert, Maryland, May 21, 1798.

Attorney-General. — Charles Lee, continued; Theophilus Parsons, Massachusetts, February 20, 1801.

Postmaster-General. — Joseph Habersham, continued.

[Note.—The navy department was created by congress, April 30, 1798. The navy was previously under the department of war.]

Fourth and Fifth Terms.

President.—Thomas Jefferson, 1801 to 1809.

Secretary of State.—James Madison, Virginia, March 5, 1801.

Secretary of the Treasury.—Samuel Dexter, continued; Albert Gallatin, Pennsylvania, May 14, 1801.

Secretary of War.—Henry Dearborn, Massachusetts, March 5, 1801.

Secretary of the Navy.—Benjamin Stoddert, continued; Robert Smith, Maryland, July 15, 1801; Jacob Crowninshield, Massachusetts, May 3, 1805.

Attorney-General.—Levi Lincoln, Massachusetts, March 5, 1801: Robert Smith, Maryland, March 3, 1805; John Breckinridge, Kentucky, August 7, 1805; Cæsar A. Rodney, Pennsylvania, January 20, 1807.

Postmaster-General. — Joseph Habersham, continued; Gideon Granger, Connecticut, November 28, 1801.

SIXTH AND SEVENTH TERMS.

President.—James Madison, 1809 to 1817.

Secretary of State.—Robert Smith, Maryland, March 6, 1809; James Monroe, Virginia, April 2, 1811.

Secretary of the Treasury.—Albert Gallatin, continued; George W. Campbell, Tennessee, February 9, 1814; A. J. Dallas, Pennsylvania, October 6, 1814; Wm. H. Crawford, Georgia, October 22, 1816.

Secretary of War.—William Eustis, Massachusetts, March 7, 1809; John Armstrong, New York, January 13, 1813; James Monroe, Virginia, September 27, 1814; William H. Crawford, Georgia, August 1, 1815.

Secretary of the Navy.—Paul Hamilton, South Carolina, March 7, 1809; William Jones, Pennsylvania, January 12, 1813; B. W. Crowninshield, Massachusetts, December 19, 1814.

Attorney-General. — C. A. Rodney, Pennsylvania, continued; William Pinckney, Maryland, December 11, 1811; Richard Rush, Pennsylvania, February 10, 1814.

Postmaster-General.—Gideon Granger, continued; Return J. Meigs, Ohio, March 17, 1814.

EIGHTH AND NINTH TERMS.

President.—James Monroe, 1817 to 1825.

Secretary of State. — John Quincy Adams, Massachusetts, March 5, 1817.

Secretary of the Treasury.—William H. Crawford, Georgia, continued.

Secretary of War.—George Graham, Virginia, April 7, 1817; John C. Calhoun, South Carolina, October 8, 1817.

Secretary of the Navy.—B. W. Crowninshield, Massachusetts, continued; Smith Thompson, New York, November 9, 1818; John Rogers, Massachusetts, September 1, 1823; Samuel L. Southard, New Jersey, September 16, 1823.

Attorney-General.—Richard Rush, Pennsylvania, continued; William Wirt, Virginia, November 13, 1817.

Postmaster-General.—R. J. Meigs, Ohio, continued; John McLean, Ohio, June 26, 1823.

TENTH TERM.

President.—John Quincy Adams, 1825 to 1829.

Secretary of State.—Henry Clay, Kentucky, March 7, 1825.

Secretary of the Treasury.—Richard Rush, Pennsylvania, March 7, 1825.

Secretary of War.—James Barbour, Virginia, March 7, 1825; Peter B. Porter, New York, May 26, 1828.

Secretary of the Navy.—S. L. Southard, New Jersey, continued.

Attorney-General.—William Wirt, Virginia, continued.

Postmaster-General. — John McLean, Ohio, continued.

ELEVENTH AND TWELFTH TERMS.

President.—Andrew Jackson, 1829 to 1837.

Secretary of State.—Martin Van Buren, New York, March 6, 1829; Edward Livingston, Louisiana, May 24, 1831; Louis McLane, Delaware, May 29, 1833, John Forsyth, Georgia, June 27, 1834.

Secretary of the Treasury.—Samuel D. Ingham, Pennsylvania, March 6, 1829; Louis McLane, Delaware, August 8, 1831; William J. Duane, Pennsylvania, May 29, 1833; Roger B. Taney, Maryland, September 23, 1833; Levi Woodbury, New Hampshire, June 27, 1834.

Secretary of War.—John H. Eaton, Tennessee, March 9, 1829; Lewis Cass, Michigan, August 1, 1831; Benjamin F. Butler, New York, March 3, 1837.

Secretary of the Navy.—John Branch, North Carolina, March 9, 1829; Levi Woodbury, New Hampshire, May 23, 1831; Mahlon Dickerson, New Jersey, June 30, 1834.

Attorney-General.—John M. Berrien, Georgia, March 9, 1829; Roger B. Taney, Maryland, July 20, 1831; Benjamin F. Butler, New York, November 15, 1833.

Postmaster-General.—William T. Barry, Kentucky, March 9, 1829; Amos Kendall, Kentucky, May 1, 1835.

THIRTEENTH TERM.

President.—Martin VanBuren, 1837 to 1841.

Secretary of State. —John Forsyth, Georgia, continued.

Secretary of the Treasury.—Levi Woodbury, New Hampshire, continued.

Secretary of War.—Joel R. Poinsett, South Carolina, March 7, 1837.

Secretary of the Navy.—Mahlon Dickerson, New Jersey, continued; James K. Paulding, New York, June 25, 1838.

Attorney-General —Benjamin F. Butler, New York, continued; Felix Grundy, Tennessee, July 5, 1838; Henry D. Gilpin, Pennsylvania, January 11, 1840.

Postmaster-General. — Amos Kendall, Kentucky, continued; John M. Niles, Connecticut, May 19, 1840.

FOURTEENTH TERM.

President.—William Henry Harrison, March 4, to April 4, 1841; John Tyler, 1841 to 1845.

Secretary of State.—Daniel Webster, Massachusetts, March 5, 1841; Hugh L. Legare, South Carolina, May 9, 1843; A. P. Upshur, Virginia, July 24, 1843; John C. Calhoun, South Carolina, March 6, 1844.

Secretary of the Treasury.—Thomas Ewing, Ohio, March 5, 1841; Walter Forward, Pennsylvania, September 13, 1841; John C. Spencer, New York, March 3, 1843; George M. Bibb, Kentucky, June 15, 1844.

Secretary of War.—John Bell, Tennessee, March 5, 1841; John McLean, Ohio, September 13, 1841, John C. Spencer, New York, October 12, 1841; James M. Porter, Pennsylvania, March 8, 1843; William Wilkins, Pennsylvania, February 15, 1844.

Secretary of the Navy.—G. E. Badger, North Carolina, March 5, 1841; A. P. Upshur, Virginia, September 13, 1841; David Henshaw, Massachusetts, July 24, 1843; T. W. Gilmer, Virginia, February 15, 1844; John Y. Mason, Virginia, March 14, 1844.

Attorney-General.—John J. Crittenden, Kentucky, March 5, 1841; Hugh S. Legare, South Carolina, September 13, 1841; John Nelson, Maryland, July 1, 1843.

Postmaster-General.—Francis Granger, New York, March 6, 1841; Charles A. Wickliffe, Kentucky, September 13, 1841.

FIFTEENTH TERM.

President. — James K. Polk, 1845 to 1849.

Secretary of State. — James Buchanan, Pennsylvania, March 6, 1845.

Secretary of the Treasury.—Robert J. Walker, Mississippi, March 6, 1845.

Secretary of War.—William L. Marcy, New York, March 6, 1845.

Secretary of the Navy.—George Bancroft, Massachusetts, March 10, 1845; John Y. Mason, Virginia, September 9, 1846.

Attorney-General. — John Y. Mason, Virginia, March 5, 1845; Nathan Clifford, Maine, October 17, 1846.

Postmaster-General. — Cave Johnson, Tennessee, March 6, 1845.

SIXTEENTH TERM.

President. — Zachary Taylor, 1849 to 1850; Millard Fillmore, 1850 to 1853.

Secretary of State.—John M. Clayton, Delaware, March 7, 1849; Daniel Webster, Massachusetts, July 22, 1850; Edward Everett, Massachusetts, December 6, 1852.

Secretary of the Treasury. — W. M Meredith, Pennsylvania, March 8, 1849 Thomas Corwin, Ohio, July 23, 1850.

Secretary of War.—George W. Crawford, Georgia, March 8, 1849; Winfield Scott (*ad interim*), July 23, 1850; Charles M. Conrad, Louisiana, August 15, 1850.

Secretary of the Navy.—William B. Preston, Virginia, March 8, 1849; William A. Graham, North Carolina, July 22, 1850; J. P. Kennedy, Maryland, July 22, 1852.

Secretary of the Interior.—Thomas H. Ewing, Ohio, March 8, 1849; A. H. H. Stuart, Virginia, September 12, 1850.

Attorney-General. — Reverdy Johnson, Maryland, March 8, 1849; John J. Crittenden, Kentucky, July 22, 1850.

Postmaster-General. — Jacob Collamer, Vermont, March 8, 1849; Nathan K. Hall, New York, July 23, 1850; S. D. Hubbard, Connecticut, August 31, 1852.

SEVENTEENTH TERM.

President. — Franklin Pierce, 1853 to 1857.

Secretary of State.—William L. Marcy, New York, March 7, 1853.

Secretary of the Treasury.—James Guthrie, Kentucky, March 7, 1853.

Secretary of War. — Jefferson Davis, Mississippi, March 7, 1853.

Secretary of the Navy.—James C. Dobbin, North Carolina, March 7, 1853.

Secretary of the Interior.—Robert McClelland, Michigan, March 7, 1853; Jacob Thompson, Mississippi, March 6, 1856.

Attorney General.-Caleb Cushing, Massachusetts, March 7, 1853.

Postmaster-General. — James Campbell, Pennsylvania, March 7, 1853.

EIGHTEENTH TERM.

President.—James Buchanan, 1857 to 1861.

Secretary of State.—Lewis Cass, Michigan, March 6, 1857; J. S. Black, Pennsylvania, December 17, 1860.

Secretary of the Treasury. — Howell Cobb, Georgia, March 6, 1857; Philip F. Thomas, Maryland, December 12, 1860; John A. Dix, New York, January 11, 1861.

Secretary of War. — John B. Floyd, Virginia, March 6, 1857; Joseph Holt, Kentucky, January 18, 1861.

Secretary of the Navy.—Isaac Toucey, Connecticut, March 6, 1857.

Secretary of the Interior.—Jacob Thompson, Mississippi, continued.

Attorney-General.—J. S. Black, Pennsylvania, March 6, 1857; Edwin M. Stanton, Pennsylvania, December 20, 1860.

Postmaster General.—Aaron V. Brown, Tennessee, March 6, 1857; Joseph Holt, Kentucky, March 14, 1859; Horatio King, Maine, February 12, 1861.

NINETEENTH AND TWENTIETH TERMS.

President.—Abraham Lincoln, 1861 to 1865; Andrew Johnson, 1865 to 1869.

Secretary of State.—William H. Seward, New York, March 5, 1861.

Secretary of the Treasury. — Solon P. Chase, Ohio, March 5, 1861; W. P. Fessenden, Maine, July 1, 1864; Hugh McCulloch, Indiana, March 7, 1865.

Secretary of War.—Simon Cameron, Pennsylvania, March 5, 1861; Edwin M. Stanton, Pennsylvania, January 15, 1862; U. S. Grant (*ad interim*), August 12, 1867; Edwin M. Stanton (reinstated), January 14, 1868; J. M. Schofield, Illinois, May 28, 1868.

Secretary of the Navy.—Gideon Welles, Connecticut, March 5, 1861.

Secretary of the Interior. — Caleb P. Smith, March 5, 1861; John P. Usher, Indiana, January 8, 1863; James Harlan, Iowa, May 15, 1865; O. H. Browning, Illinois, July 27, 1866.

Attorney-General.—Edward Bates, Missouri, March 5, 1831; Titian J. Coffee, June 22, 1863; James Speed, Kentucky, December 2, 1864; Henry Stanbery, Ohio, July 23, 1866; William M. Evarts, New York, July 15, 1868.

Postmaster-General.-Montgomery Blair, Maryland, March 5, 1861; William Dennison, Ohio, September 24, 1864; Alexander W. Randall, Wisconsin, July, 25, 1866.

TWENTY-FIRST AND TWENTY-SECOND.

President—Ulysses S. Grant, 1869 to 1877.

Secretary of State—E. B. Washburne, Illinois, March 5, 1869; Hamilton Fish, New York, March 11, 1869.

Secretary of the Treasury—George S. Boutwell, Massachusetts, March 11, 1869; William A. Richardson, Massachusetts, March 17, 1873; Benjamin H. Bristow, Kentucky, June 2, 1874; Lot M. Morrill, Maine, June 21, 1876.

Secretary of War—John A. Rawlins, Illinois, March 11, 1869; William T. Sherman, Ohio, September 9, 1869; William W. Belknap, Iowa, October 25, 1869; Alphonso Taft, Ohio, March 8, 1876; J. D. Cameron, Pennsylvania, May 22, 1876.

Secretary of the Navy—Adolph E. Borie, Pennsylvania, March 5, 1869; George M. Robeson, New Jersey, June 25, 1869.

Secretary of the Interior—Jacob D. Cox, Ohio, March 5, 1869; Columbus Delano, Ohio, November 1, 1870; Zachariah Chandler, Michigan, October 19, 1875.

Attorney-General—E. R. Hoar, Massachusetts, March 5, 1869; Amos T. Akerman, Georgia, June 23, 1870; George H. Williams, Oregon, December 14, 1871; Edwards Pierrepont, New York, April 26, 1875; Alphonso Taft, Ohio, May 22, 1876.

Postmaster-General—J. A. J. Creswell, Maryland, March 5, 1869; Marshall Jewell, Connecticut, August 24, 1874; James M. Tyner, Indiana, July 12, 1876.

TWENTY-THIRD TERM.

President—Rutherford B. Hayes, 1877 to 1881.

Secretary of State—William M. Evarts, New York, March 12, 1877.

Secretary of the Treasury—John Sherman, Ohio, March 8, 1877.

Secretary of War—George W. McCrary, Iowa, March 12, 1877; Alexander Ramsey, Minnesota, December 12, 1879.

Secretary of the Navy—Richard W. Thompson, Indiana, March 12, 1877; Nathan Goff, Jr., West Virginia, January 6, 1881.

Secretary of the Interior—Carl Schurz, Missouri, March 12, 1877.

Attorney-General — Charles Devens, Massachusetts, March 12, 1877.

Postmaster General — David M. Key, Tennessee, March 12, 1877; Horace Maynard, Tennessee, August 25, 1880.

TWENTY-FOURTH TERM.

President—James A. Garfield, part of 1881; Chester A. Arthur, 1881 to 1885.

Secretary of State—James G. Blaine, Maine, March 5, 1881; Frederick T. Frelinghuysen, New Jersey, December 12, 1881.

Secretary of the Treasury—William H. Windom, Minnesota, March 5, 1881; Charles J. Folger, New York, October 27, 1881; Walter Q. Gresham, Indiana, September 24, 1884; Hugh McCulloch, Indiana, October 31, 1884.

Secretary of War—Robert T. Lincoln, Illinois, March 5, 1881.

Secretary of the Navy—W. H. Hunt, Louisiana, March 5, 1881; William E. Chandler, New Hampshire, April 1, 1882.

Secretary of the Interior—S. J. Kirkwood, Iowa, March 5, 1881; Henry M. Teller, Colorado, April 6, 1882.

Attorney-General—Wayne MacVeagh, Pennsylvania, March 5, 1881; Benjamin H. Brewster, Pennsylvania, December 16, 1881.

Postmaster-General—Thomas L. James, New York, March 5, 1881; Timothy O. Howe, Wisconsin, December 20, 1881; Walter Q. Gresham, Indiana, April 3, 1883; Frank Hatton, Iowa, October 14, 1884.

TWENTY-FIFTH TERM.

President—Stephen Grover Cleveland, elected November, 1884; to be inaugurated March 4. Cabinet not yet announced.

COMPENSATION OF OFFICIALS.

The following shows the present rate of salaries paid by the United States government to its principal officials:

EXECUTIVE.

President	$50,000	Steward	1,800
Vice President	8,000	Usher	1,400
Private Secretary	3,250	Messengers, five	1,200
Assistant Secretary	2,250	Doorkeepers, four	1,200
Executive clerks, two, each	2,000	Watchman	900
Stenographer	1,800	Furnace-keeper	864
Clerks, three, $1,800, $1,400, and	1,200		

HEADS OF DEPARTMENTS.

Secretary of state, secretary of the treasury, secretary of war, secretary of the navy, secretary of the interior, postmaster-general, and attorney-general, each, $8,000.

JUDICIARY.

U. S. SUPREME COURT.

Chief justice	$10,500	Marshal	3,000
Associate justices, nine, each	10,000	Reporter	2,500
Clerk of the court, and deputy, each	2,000		

U. S. CIRCUIT COURTS.

Salaries of nine judges, each	$6,000

U. S. COURT OF CLAIMS.

Chief justice	$4,500	Assistant clerk	2,000
Three associates, each	4,500	Bailiff	1,200
Chief clerk	3,000	Messenger	1,200

DISTRICT JUDGES.

Fifty-three judges, salaries from $3,500 to $5,000.

LEGISLATIVE.

Speaker of the house of representatives, $8,000 per annum and mileage (20 cents per mile).

Senators, 76 in number, each $5,000 and mileage. Representatives and territorial delegates in congress, 300 in number, each $5,000 and mileage.

MINISTERS AND DIPLOMATIC AGENTS

Ministers to Great Britain, Russia, France and Germany, each $17,500.

Ministers to Spain, Austria, Italy, China, Mexico, Brazil and Japan, each $12,000.

Ministers to Chili, Peru and Central America, each $10,000.

Minister Residents in Belgium, Portugal, Netherlands, Denmark, Sweden and Norway, Switzerland, Turkey, Venezuela, Ecuador, Argentine Confederation, Hawaiian Islands, Greece, Colombia and Bolivia, each $7,500.

Consuls and commercial agents, $1,000 to $5,000.

LIBRARIAN.

Librarian of Congress	$4,000
Assistants, two in number, each	2,500
Fifteen clerks, salaries from $1,200 to	1,400

THE WAR DEPARTMENT

Secretary of war, $8,000 per annum.

Lieutenant-general of the army, $916.67 per month.

Adjutant-general, $5,500 per annum; assistant, $3,500; second, third and fourth assistants, each $3,000; chief clerk, $2,000.

Major-general, $625 per month.

Brigadier-general, $458.33 per month.

Inspector-general, $3,500 per annum.

Judge-advocate general, $5,500; assistant, $3,500.

Quartermaster-general, $5,500; deputy, $3,000; assistant, $3,500; chief clerk, $2,000.

Chief of engineer's bureau, $5,500; chief clerk, $2,000.

Surgeon-general, $5,500; assistant, $3,500; chief clerk, $2,000.

Chief of ordnance, $5,500; chief clerk, $2,000.

Paymaster-general, $3,500; deputy, $3,000; assistant, $3,500; chief clerk, $2,000.

Chief signal officer, $5,500.

Commissary-general of subsistance, $5,500; assistant, $3,500; chief clerk, $2,000.

Chief of ordnance, $485.33 per month.

Colonel, $291.67 per month; lieutenant colonel, $250; major, $208.33; captain, $150; first lieutenant, $125, second lieutenant, $116.67; first sergeant, $22; sergeant, $17; private, engineers and ordnance, $20; private, artillery, cavalry and infantry, $13.

THE NAVY DEPARTMENT.

Admiral of the navy, $13,000 per year on sea.

Vice admiral, $9,000 on sea, $8,000 on shore, $6,000 on orders.

Rear admirals, $6,000 on sea, $5,000 on shore, $4,000 on orders.

Commodores, $5,000 on sea, $4,000 on shore, $3,000 on orders.

Captains, $4,500, $3,500, and $2,800.

Commanders, $3,500, $3,000, and $2,300.

Lieutenant commanders, $2,800, $2,400, and $2,000; after first four years, $3,000, $2,600, $2,300.

Lieutenants, after five years, $2,600, $2,200, $1,800.

Masters, after five years, $1,800, $1,500, $1,200.

Ensigns, after five years, $1,400, $1,200, $1,000.

Midshipmen, $1,000, $800, $600.

Seamen, per month, $21.50; ordinary, $17.50; landsmen, $15.50.

DEPARTMENTAL OFFICERS.

Three assistant secretaries of state, $3,500; chief clerk, $2,500; examiner of claims, $3,500; chief of consular bureau, $2,100; chief of indexes and archives, $2,200; chief of bureau of accounts, $2,100; librarian, $1,800.

Two assistant secretaries of the treasury, $4,500; chief clerk, $2,700; first and second comptrollers, $5,000; commissioner of customs, $4,000; six auditors, $3,600; treasurer, $6,000; assistant treasurer, $3,600; register of the treasury, $4,000; commissioner of internal revenue, $6,000; solicitor of internal revenue, $6,000; solicitor of the treasury, $4,500; director of the mint, $4,500; chief of bureau of engraving and printing, $4,500; chief of bureau of statistics, $2,400; supervising architect, $4,500; superintendent of coast survey, $6,000; his assistant, $4,200; supervising surgeon-general, $4,000; superintendent of life-saving service, $4,000; supervising inspector-general of steamboats, $3,500; chief of appointment division, $2,500; chief of warrant division, $2,750; chief of public moneys division, $2,500; chief of customs division, $2,750; chief of internal revenue and navigation, $2,500; chief of loan and currency division, $2,500; chief of revenue marine, $2,500; chief of stationery and printing, $2,500.

Assistant secretary of the interior, $3,500; chief clerk and superintendent, $2,700; assistant attorney-general, $5,000; commissioner land office, $4,000; his chief clerk, $2,000; commissioner pension office, $3,000; his deputy, $2,400; his chief clerk, $2,000, commissioner of patent office, $4,500; his assistant, $3,000; his chief clerk, $2,250; examiners and superintendents of departments in patent office, 27 in number, $2,250 to $3,000; commissioner of Indian office, $3,000; his chief clerk, $2,000; commissioner of education, $3,000; chief clerk, $1,800; superintendent of census bureau, $5,000; auditor of railroad accounts, $5,000; director of geological survey, $6,000; superintendent of government hospital for the insane, $2,500; president Columbia institution for the deaf and dumb, $4,000; architect of U. S. capitol extension, $4,500.

Three assistant postmasters-general, $3,500; chief clerk, $2,200; superintendent of foreign mails, $3,000; assistant attorney-general for postoffice department, $4,000; superintendent of money order system, $3,000.

Subordinates in navy department, 24 in number, $2,400 to $5,000.

Subordinates in department of justice, 5 in number, $2,200 to $7,000.

Commissioner of agriculture, $3,000; chief clerk, $1,900.

Collectors of internal revenue, 125 in number, graduated by collections, $2,125 to $4,500; collectors, 95 in number, paid by fees and commissions, $250 to $12,000.

Surveyors of customs, 26 in number, $395 to $5,000.

United States naval officers, 6 in number, $5,000 to $8,000.

Subordinates at the mints, 9 in number, $2,500 to $4,500.

Ten assistant treasurers of the United States, $4,500 to $8,000.

COUNTIES IN THE UNITED STATES.

The following table shows the number of counties in each state of the Union, as given in the census of 1880. Since the taking of that census, however, a number of new counties have been organized, particularly in those states and territories where the settlement of the country is proceeding most rapidly, as in Dakota, Kansas, Nebraska and Texas. At the present time there are about 2,730 counties in the United States.

STATES.	NO. OF COUNTIES.	STATES.	NO. OF COUNTIES.
Alabama	66	North Carolina	94
Arkansas	75	Ohio	88
California	53	Oregon	26
Colorado	32	Pennsylvania	67
Connecticut	8	Rhode Island	5
Delaware	3	South Carolina	33
Florida	45	Tennessee	94
Georgia	137	Texas	232
Illinois	102	Vermont	14
Indiana	92	Virginia	99
Iowa	99	West Virginia	54
Kansas	113	Wisconsin	63
Kentucky	117		
Louisiana	59	Total	2,472
Maine	16	TERRITORIES.	
Maryland	24	Arizona	7
Massachusetts	14	Dakota	94
Michigan	82	Idaho	13
Minnesota	86	Montana	11
Mississippi	75	New Mexico	14
Missouri	117	Utah	27
Nebraska	80	Washington	25
Nevada	17	Wyoming	7
New Hampshire	10	District of Columbia	1
New Jersey	21		
New York	60	Total	199

OUR NATIONAL ELECTIONS.

In the following Table is given a Summary of the Popular and Electoral Votes in Presidential Elections in the United States.

Year	No. of States.	Total Electoral Vote.	Party.	Candidates.	States.	Popular Vote.	Electoral Vote.
1789	10	73		George Washington			69
				John Adams			34
				John Jay			9
				R. R. Harrison			6
				John Rutledge			6
				John Hancock			4
				George Clinton			3
				Samuel Huntington			2
				John Milton			2
				Benjamin Lincoln			1
				James Armstrong			1
				Edward Telfair			1
				Vacancies			2
1792	15	135	Federalist	George Washington			132
			Federalist	John Adams			77
			Republican	George Clinton			50
			Dem-Repub	Thomas Jefferson			4
			Republican	Aaron Burr			1
				Vacancies			3
1796	16	138	Federalist	John Adams			71
			Dem-Repub	Thomas Jefferson			68
			Federalist	Thomas Pinckney			59
			Republican	Aaron Burr			30
				Samuel Adams			15
				Oliver Ellsworth			11
				George Clinton			7
				John Jay			5
				James Iredell			3
				George Washington			2
				John Henry			2
				S. Johnson			2
				Charles C. Pinckney			1
1800	16	138	Dem-Repub	Thomas Jefferson			73
			Republican	Aaron Burr			73
			Federalist	John Adams			65
			Federalist	Charles C. Pinckney			64
			Federalist	John Jay			1

Year.	No. of States.	Total Electoral Vote.	Party.	For President.	States.	Popular Vote.	Electoral Vote.	For Vice President.	Electoral Vote.
1804	21	176	Dem-Repub	Thomas Jefferson	15		162	George Clinton	162
			Federalist	Chas. C. Pinckney	2		14	Rufus King	14
1808	17	176	Republican	James Madison	12		122	George Clinton	113
			Republican	George Clinton			6	James Madison	3
			Federalist	Chas. C. Pinckney	5		47	Rufus King	47
								John Langdon	9
								James Monroe	3
				Vacancy			1		1
1812	18	218	Republican	James Madison	11		128	Elbridge Gerry	131
			Federalist	De Witt Clinton	7		89	Jared Ingersoll	86
				Vacancy			1		1
1816	19	221	Republican	James Monroe	16		183	D. D. Tompkins	183
			Federalist	Rufus King	3		34	John E. Howard	22
								James Ross	5
								John Marshall	4
								Robt. G. Harper	3
				Vacancies			4		4
1820	24	235	Republican	**James Monroe**	24		231	D. D. Tompkins	218
				John Q. Adams			1	Richard Stockton	8
								Daniel Rodney	4
								Robt. G. Harper	1
								Richard Rush	1
				Vacancies			3		3
1824	24	261	Dem-Repub	**Andrew Jackson**	10	155,872	99	John C. Calhoun	182

Our National Elections—Continued.

Year.	No. of States.	Total Electoral Vote.	Party.	For President.	States.	Popular Vote.	Electoral Vote.	For Vice President.	Electoral Vote.
....	....	....	Republican..	John Q. Adams	8	105,321	84	Nathan Sanford....	30
....	....	....	Republican..	Wm. H. Crawford...	3	44,282	41	Nathaniel Macon....	24
....	....	....	Republican..	Henry Clay..........	3	46,587	37	Andrew Jackson....	13
....	....	....	....	....	....	....		Martin Van Buren..	9
....	....	....	....	....	....	....	....	Henry Clay.........	2
....	....	....	....	Vacancy....	....	....	....	....	1
1828	24	261	Democratic..	Andrew Jackson....	15	647,231	178	John C. Calhoun	171
....	....	....	Nat. Repub..	John Q. Adams......	9	509,097	83	Richard Rush.	83
....	....	....	....	....	....	....	....	William Smith	7
1832	24	288	Democratic..	Andrew Jackson....	15	687,502	219	Martin Van Buren..	189
....	....	....	Nat. Repub..	Henry Clay..........	7	530,189	49	John Sergeant.......	49
....	....	....	Anti-Mason..	William Wirt	1	33,108	7	Amos Ellmaker	7
....	....	....	....	John Floyd..........	1	....	11	Henry Lee.	11
....	....	....	....	....	....	....	....	William Wilkins ...	30
....	....	....	....	Vacancies	....	....	2	....	2
1836	26	294	Democratic..	Martin Van Buren..	15	761,549	170	R. M. Johnson.......	147
....	....	....	Whig	Wm. H. Harrison....	7	736,656	73	Francis Granger	77
....	....	....	....	Hugh L. White......	2		26	John Tyler	47
....	....	....	....	Daniel Webster	1		14	William Smith......	23
....	....	....	....	W. P. Mangum......	1		11	....	
1840	26	294	Whig	Wm. H. Harrison...	19	1,275,017	234	John Tyler	234
....	....	....	Democratic..	Martin Van Buren..	7	1,128,702	60	R. M. Johnson.	48
....	....	....	Liberty	James G. Birney....	....	7,059	....	....	...
....	....	....	....	....	....	....	....	F. W. Tazewell.....	11
....	....	....	....	....	....	....	....	James K. Polk	1
1844	26	275	Democratic..	James K. Polk	15	1,337,243	170	George M. Dallas....	170
..	....	....	Whig	Henry Clay	11	1,299,068	105	T. Frelinghuysen ...	105
....	....	....	Liberty	James G. Birney	....	62,300	...	....	....
1848	30	290	Whig	Zachary Taylor......	15	1,360,101	163	Millard Fillmore	163
...	....	...	Democratic..	Lewis Cass..........	15	1,220,544	127	William O. Butler....	127
....	....	...	Free Soil ...	Martin Van Buren..	...	291,263	...	Charles F. Adams...	....
1852	31	296	Democratic.	Franklin Pierce	27	1,601,474	254	William R. King ..	254
....	....	....	Whig	Winfield Scott.......	4	1,386,578	42	William A. Graham.	42
....	....	....	Free Dem....	John P. Hale........	..	156,149	....	George W. Julian..	...
1856	31	296	Democratic..	James Buchanan....	19	1,838,169	174	J. C. Breckinridge ..	174
...	....	....	Republican..	John C. Fremont....	11	1,341,264	114	William L. Dayton..	114
....	....	....	American....	Millard Fillmore ...	1	874,534	8	A. J. Donelson......	8
1860	33	303	Republican ..	Abraham Lincoln...	17	1,866,352	180	Hannibal Hamlin ...	180
....	....	....	Democratic..	J. C. Breckinridge ...	11	845,763	72	Joseph Lane........	72
....	....	...	Democratic.	S. A. Douglas.......	2	1,375,157	12	H. V. Johnson......	12
....	....	....	Const. Union.	John Bell	3	589,581	39	Edward Everett.....	39
1864	36	314	Republican..	Abraham Lincoln...	...	2,216,067	212	Andrew Johnson...	212
....	...	....	Democratic..	Geo. B. McClellan...	....	1,808,725	21	Geo. H. Pendleton..	21
....	....	....	....	Vacancies	11	....	81	....	81
1868	37	317	Republican..	Ulysses S. Grant ...	26	3,015,071	214	Schuyler Colfax....	214
....	....	....	Democratic..	Horatio Seymour ...	8	2,709,613	80	F. P. Blair, Jr.... ..	80
....	....	....	....	Vacancies	3	..	23	....	23
1872	37	366	Republican..	Ulysses S. Grant	31	3,597,070	286	Henry Wilson.......	286
....	....	....	Dem., Lib. R.	Horace Greeley.....	6	2,834,079	...	B. Gratz Brown.....	47
....	....	....	Democratic..	Charles O'Connor..	....	29,408	....	John Q. Adams	....
...	....	....	Temperance.	James Black.	...	5,608	...	A. H. Colquitt..	5
....	....	....	....	T. A. Hendricks.....	....	....	42	John M. Palmer	3
....	....	....	... .	B. Gratz Brown.....	....	....	18	George W. Julian...	5
....	....	....	....	Chas. J. Jenkins.....	....	....	2	T. F. Bramlette......	3
....	....	....	....	David Davis.........	....	....	1	W. S. Groesbeck	1
....	....	....	....	....	....	....	....	Willis P. Machen....	1
....	....	....	....	....	....	....	....	N. P. Banks.........	1
....	....	....	....	Not counted........	....	....	17	....	14
1876	38	369	Republican..	R. B. Hayes..........	21	4,033,950	185	William A. Wheeler.	185
....	...	....	Democratic..	S. J. Tilden..........	17	4,284,885	184	T. A. Hendricks.....	184
....	....	...	Greenback ..	Peter Cooper........	....	81,740	....	S. F. Cary	...
....	....	....	Prohibition..	G. C. Smith	...	9,522	....	R. T. Stewart.... ...	....
1880	38	369	Republican..	James A. Garfield...	19	4,442,950	214	Chester A. Arthur ..	214
....	....	....	Democratic..	W. S. Hancock	19	4,442,035	155	William H. English..	155
...	....	....	Greenback ..	James B. Weaver...	....	306,867	....	B. J. Chambers......	....
....	....	...	....	Scattering	....	12,576	...	....	....
1884	....	402	Democratic..	Grover Cleveland...	....	4,914,978	219	T. A. Hendricks.	219
....	.. ..	....	Republican..	James G. Blaine.....	....	4,844,252	183	John A. Logan......	183
....	....	....	Prohibition..	John P. St. John ...	.. ..	150,134	....	—Daniel	...
...	....	....	Independent.	Benj. F. Butler......	....	134,028	....	—West...............	....
..	....	....	Woman Suf..	Belva A. Lockwood	....	5	....	....	....

MILITARY RECORD.

GENERALS OF THE ARMY.

THE following list shows the generals who have commanded the army since the year 1775, with the dates of their command, so far as can be found from the official records:

Major-General George Washington, June 15, 1775, to December 23, 1783.

Major-General Henry Knox, December 23, 1783, to June 20, 1784.

Lieutenant-Colonel Josiah Harmer, general-in-chief by brevet, September, 1788, to March, 1791.

Major-General Arthur St. Clair, March 4, 1791, to March, 1792.

Major-General Anthony Wayne, April 11, 1792, to December 15, 1796.

Major-General James Wilkinson, December 15, 1796, to July, 1798.

Lieutenant-General George Washington, July 3, 1798, to his death, December 14, 1799.

Major-General James Wilkinson, June, 1800, to January, 1812.

Major-General Henry Dearborn, January 27, 1812, to June, 1815.

Major-General Jacob Brown, June, 1815, to February 21, 1828.

Major-General Alexander Macomb, May 24, 1828, to June, 1841.

Major-General Winfield H. Scott (brevet lieutenant-general), June, 1841, to November 1, 1861.

Major-General George B. McClellan, November 1, 1861, to March 11, 1862.

Major-General Henry W. Halleck, July 11, 1862, to March 12, 1864.

Lieutenant-General Ulysses S. Grant, March 12, 1864, to July 25, 1866, and as General to March 4, 1869.

General William T. Sherman, March 4, 1869.

Lieutenant-General Philip Sheridan, 1884.

NOTE.—There was a period immediately after the Revolution when the entire army, as organized, consisted of a small corps of artillery, commanded by a captain.

THE GREAT CIVIL WAR.

THE ENROLLMENT IN THE UNITED STATES ARMY.

The following table shows the total number of men furnished by each of the several states for the United States army during the civil war of 1861-1865. The first column of figures shows the number furnished under the call of President Lincoln for 75,000 troops, issued April 15, 1861. The second column shows the aggregate number of white men furnished under all the calls:

STATES.	First Call.	All Calls.	STATES.	First Call.	All Calls.
Maine	771	71,745	Minnesota	930	25,034
New Hampshire	779	34,605	Iowa	968	75,860
Vermont	782	35,246	Missouri	10,501	108,773
Massachusetts	3,736	151,785	Kentucky	....	78,540
Rhode Island	3,147	23,711	Kansas	650	20,097
Connecticut	2,402	57,270	Tennessee	....	12,077
New York	13,906	464,156	Arkansas	....	......
New Jersey	3,123	79,511	North Carolina	....	......
Pennsylvania	20,175	366,326	California	....	7,451
Delaware	775	13,651	Nevada	....	216
Maryland	....	49,731	Oregon	....	617
West Virginia	900	32,003	Washington	....	895
District Columbia	4,720	16,872	Nebraska	....	1,279
Ohio	12,357	317,133	Colorado	....	1,762
Indiana	4,686	195,147	Dakota	...	181
Illinois	4,820	258,217	New Mexico	1,510	2,395
Michigan	781	90,119			
Wisconsin	817	96,118	Total	93,326	2,688,523

The following exhibit gives the number of colored and drafted troops furnished to the Union army by the different states, including the states which were in rebellion; besides which 92,576 colored troops were included (with the white soldiers) in the quotas of the several states. Many who enlisted from the South were credited to Northern States:

STATES AND TERRITORIES.	Colored Troops, 1861-5.	Number Drafted.	Bounties Paid by States.
NEW ENGLAND STATES.			
Connecticut	1,764	12,031	$ 6,887,554
Maine	104	27,324	7,837,644
Massachusetts	3,966	41,582	22,965,550
New Hampshire	125	10,806	9,636,313
Rhode Island	1,837	4,321	820,769
Vermont	120	7,743	4,528,775
TOTAL	7,916	103,807	52,676,605
MIDDLE STATES.			
New Jersey	1,185	32,325	23,868,967
New York	4,125	151,488	86,629,228
Pennsylvania	8,612	178,873	43,154,987
TOTAL	13,922	362,686	153,653,183
WESTERN STATES AND TERRITORIES.			
Colorado Territory	95	......	....
Illinois	1,811	32,085	17,296,205
Indiana	1,537	41,158	9,182,354
Iowa	440	7,548	1,615,171
Kansas	2,080	1,420	57,407
Michigan	1,387	22,022	9,664,855
Minnesota	104	10,796	2,000,464
Ohio	5,092	50,400	23,557,373
Wisconsin	165	38,395	5,855,356
TOTAL	12,711	203,924	60,229,185

Colored and Drafted Troops—*Continued.*

STATES AND TERRITORIES.	Colored Troops, 1861-5.	Number Drafted.	Bounties Paid by States.
BORDER STATES.			
Delaware	954	8,635	1,136,599
District of Columbia	3,269	14,338	134,010
Kentucky	23,703	29,421	692,577
Maryland	8,718	29,319	6,271,992
Missouri	8,344	21,519	1,282,149
West Virginia	196	3,180	864,737
TOTAL	45,184	106,412	10,382,064
SOUTHERN STATES.			
Alabama	4,969	......	....
Arkansas	5,526	......	....
Florida	1,044	......	....
Georgia	......	......	....
Louisiana	8,486	......	....
Mississippi	17,869	......	....
North Carolina	5,035	......	....
South Carolina	5,462	......	....
Tennessee	20,133	......	....
Texas	47	......	....
Virginia	......	......	....
TOTAL	68,571	......	....
GRAND TOTAL	173,079	776,829	285,941,036
At large	733	......	....
Not accounted for	5,083	......	....
Officers	7,122	......	....
TOTAL	186,017	......	....

The various calls for men by the President were as follows, not including the militia brought into service during the different invasions of Lee's armies into Maryland and Pennsylvania:

1861	Call for three-months' men	75,000
1861	Call for three years	500,000
1862	Call for three years	300,000
1862	Call for nine months	300,000
1864	Call for three years, February	500,000
1864	Call for three years, March	200,000
1864	Call for three years, July	500,000
1864	Call for three years, December	300,000
	Total	2,675,000

The Provost-Marshal General in 1866 reported the following as the number of casualties in the volunteer and regular armies of the United States during the war:

Killed in battle, 61,362; died of wounds, 34,727; died of disease, 183,287; total died, 279,376; total deserted, 199,105.

Number of soldiers in the Confederate service who died of wounds or disease (partial statement), 133,821; deserted (partial statement), 104,428.

Number of United States troops captured during the war, 212,608; Confederate troops captured, 476,169.

Number of United States troops paroled on the field, 16,431; Confederate troops paroled on the field, 248,599.

Number of United States troops who died while prisoners, 29,725; Confederate troops who died while prisoners, 26,774.

LAWS OF PUBLIC DISCUSSION.

IN every community occasions arise from time to time in which the citizens find it necessary or desirable to hold a general consultation or meeting, to consider some subject which it is beyond the province of private individuals to decide. Such assemblies include indignation meetings, political meetings and caucuses, meetings to draft petitions or remonstrances, meetings to pass resolutions of all sorts, and, indeed, for a thousand purposes in which united action is needed. In most cases such gatherings are practically spontaneous, and no programme has been made or thought of, so far, at least, as concerns the method of carrying on the business to be transacted. Yet there is a method, and without it the management of a large assembly of men would be difficult, cumbrous and tedious. It is called "parliamentary" practice or rules, being substantially modeled after the manner of proceedings in the English parliament, now in use all over the civilized world. This plan is the one which has been universally adopted after centuries of experiment and practice. Its fundamental principle is the *will of the majority*, and it is with a view to the most perfect authority of that will that every parliamentary rule has been adopted. Very minutely detailed directions have been laid down for the conduct of public bodies, and a ready familiarity with these rules is absolutely necessary in the training of any public man. A full explanation of these rules, with the decisions proper to be made in each of the many complicated cases requiring nice adjustment, would be too prolix for the scope of this work. It is expected, however, that every man who takes an interest in the affairs of the world should be sufficiently posted on the laws of parliamentary usage to understand the leading requisites in the management of a public meeting. Then he need not be made ridiculous by an unexpected election as chairman of some simple meeting, in which position he might otherwise find himself quite helpless.

CALLING THE MEETING.

When a question arises requiring public action, the duty of calling a meeting devolves upon the older and leading citizens, a few of whom, after satisfying themselves of the general wish, give public notice of a meeting, stating a time, place, and the object. Such notice may be given by advertisement, either on posters, dodgers, or in the local newspapers. It should be concise, definite, and wholly non-partisan as regards any subject likely to cause difference of opinion in the meeting. The following may be taken as examples:

PUBLIC MEETING.

To the Editor of the Gazette: Please announce that there will be a public meeting at Jones' Hall, on Water street, Thursday evening, May 10, at 7:45 p. m., for the purpose of taking action concerning the proper observance of the Fourth of July in this city.

JAMES RICE,
ROBERT CONNOR.

NOTICE.

The public is invited to attend a meeting at the east gate of Forest Park, Monday afternoon, April 25, at 3 o'clock, to consider the recent action of the city council in allowing the construction of a railroad through said park.

By request of many citizens.

CHARLES MONROE,
E. H. MARTIN.

It is the duty of the persons calling the meeting to take upon themselves the responsibility of lighting and warming the hall, if necessary, trusting to the meeting to repay them; but if they order a brass band or other luxuries they must be prepared to assume the responsibility themselves.

TEMPORARY ORGANIZATION.

At the appointed hour, if a sufficient number are present, the persons who called the meeting agree upon one of their number to "call the meeting to order." This he does by rising in a prominent place, attracting attention by rapping, if necessary, and announcing: "The meeting will please come to order. Who will you choose as temporary chairman?"

The person who called the meeting to order should be nominated as temporary chairman, and no one else; in which case he will remain silent, and let the person who nominated him "put" the question to the house.

Nominations are made simply in these words: "I nominate Mr. Richard Burk as temporary chairman." If but one name is proposed, the one who called the meeting to order will say: "Mr. Richard Burk has been nominated as temporary chairman of this meeting. All in favor of Mr. Burk as temporary chairman will please say 'Aye.' [A pause.] Contrary, 'No.'" This is called a *viva voce* vote, or vote by the *living voice.*

If more than one nomination have been made, the person presiding will say: "Messrs. Richard Burk and John Locke have been nominated to preside as temporary chairman. Those in favor of Mr. Burk, please rise. [A pause.] They will be seated. [A pause.] Those in favor of Mr. Locke, please rise." This is called a *standing* vote.

If any one move that the election be made by ballot, the person presiding will propose the motion, and if it be carried he will appoint two tellers, who will collect the ballots, count them, and announce the decision. The person elected as temporary chairman will come forward and take the stand. He may make a few remarks, if he deem it appropriate, and will then declare the election of a temporary secretary to be in order.

"CUT AND DRIED" ELECTIONS.

If it be a meeting to consider some important question involving personal interests, or if it be a political meeting, it is likely that a preliminary agreement has been made among a number of those present, by which they are to unite for the election of such persons as will be in favor of their interest. The existence of a clique of this character is sure to show itself to any person of experience in such matters. A novice should be careful as to the part he takes in the organization of the meeting, as he may find, too late, that he has been assisting partisans opposed to him, or hindering those with whom he is in sympathy. A plot of this kind will be best known by the fact that a large number of ballots are in favor of a few chosen men, which could not be the case in a fair informal ballot.

PRELIMINARY BUSINESS.

The temporary chairman will now state the object of the meeting, if it have not already been done. In his remarks and rulings he should take no stand for or against any proposition likely to come before the meeting, and in everything he should be impartial. He will declare out of order any motions or remarks relating to the object of the meeting, until the permanent organization is completed, and will consider only such motions as have regard to the preliminary organization, the arrangement of the hall, etc. He will accept and put to vote any motions for the appointment of the following committees: On *Credentials*, *Order of Business*, and *Permanent Organization*. These motions should be proposed by members of the audience, and if they be agreed to, the temporary chairman will appoint the committees accordingly. The committees will retire, if necessary, for consultation. During their absence the temporary chairman will continue to refuse any business having reference to the main object of the meeting, and if nothing else be proposed a recess may be taken to await the reports of the committees.

THE COMMITTEES.

The person first named for membership on any committee will be the chairman of that committee, will preside over its session in the committee-room, and on its return will report its action to the chairman of the meeting.

The report of the committee on *Permanent Organization* may be in this form:

"Mr. Chairman—Your committee on permanent organization would respectfully recommend that the present organization be made permanent."

Or this

"Mr. Chairman—Your committee on permanent organization recommend the election, by ballot, of a chairman, secretary, assistant secretary, and sergeant-at-arms."

Or, the committee may recommend the appointment of a committee on nominations for effecting the permanent organization.

The committee on *credentials* will report the name of each person entitled to a vote in the meeting. Or, if this is necessary, may report thus:

"Mr. Chairman—Your committee on credentials would recommend that all residents of the Fifth and Ninth Wards be entitled to seats in this convention."

The committee on *order of business* will report in this manner:

"Mr. Chairman—Your committee on order of business recommend the following as the order of business for this meeting: Permanent organization, report of committee on credentials, appointment of committees on resolutions and finance, reception of visitors, reading of papers, addresses, organization of a permanent society."

In small assemblies there is usually no need of committees; but in large bodies they are of very great importance, and their action often decides that of the meeting.

The meeting having been re-called to order by the temporary chairman, the reports of the three committees will be received, and either adopted, amended or rejected. If adopted, the meeting will be conducted in accordance with the reports of the committees. The first thing to be considered is that of the committee on "order of business." Its report having been disposed of and adopted, with or without amendment, the meeting at once has a programme to be followed. The first thing on this programme should be the effecting of a

PERMANENT ORGANIZATION.

by the election of permanent officers. This will be done in one of the three ways above indicated. The quickest way is to "make the temporary organization permanent," which means to retain the temporary officers. The election of officers by means of a "committee on nominations" is often done, but the use of that plan nearly always indicates some hidden motive, as, for instance, the election of officers without allowing the interference of some unfavorable element present in the meeting. Unless objection be made, the permanent officers may be elected by a *viva voce* vote; but the temporary chairman may, in his discretion, order a standing vote, and if it be the wish of the majority (ascertained by *viva voce* vote) the election shall be made by ballot.

The election of the permanent chairman having been effected, the temporary chairman will introduce him to the meeting as such, and will retire.

The permanent chairman will now make any address he deems advisable, and may be allowed some latitude in the expression of opinion, since this will probably be the only chance he will have to do so, unless in a case of a tie vote. The temporary chairman, on the other hand, upon whom we have imposed strict impartiality while in the chair, becomes merely a member of the assembly, like the others, as soon as he retires from the chair, and thenceforth has the same liberty of expression that other members have. The permanent president may at any time appoint any other person to the chair, while he himself makes an address on the subject under discussion; but this privilege is not usually so often resorted to as to give the chairman the same facility of argument and reply as the others.

OTHER OFFICERS.

Even the smallest meeting must have a chairman. It is always advisable also to elect a secretary, for he may be of use. Beyond these two officers, small meetings do not usually need any others. The necessity of many or few officers depends upon the duration of the organization. That is, if it is but a temporary meeting, whose labors will be concluded while it is in one session, few officers need be chosen. But if it be expected to be a permanent body, such as a society, lodge, board of trade, commercial association, fire company, or advisory board, other officers are necessary. In a meeting of a single session, the chairman of the finance committee may be intrusted to act as treasurer; but in a permanent society a treasurer should be chosen. If there be much writing to be done, both a recording and a corresponding secretary may be elected; but in most cases it is better to choose simply a secretary, and let him appoint an assistant. Other officers that may or may not be needed are a financial secretary, marshal or sergeant-at-arms, door-keeper, chaplain, etc. There should be at least one vice-president if more than one session is to be held. If the convention be an important one, consisting of delegates or representatives from different cities, counties or districts, it is the custom to appoint one vice-president for each of these, as a matter of compliment and a recognition of the constituents which the meeting represents. If any officer need an assistant it is a favor to him to let him make the choice, and this should always be done when such appointment is immaterial to other interests.

RECORDS AND DOCUMENTS.

If the association is to be a permanent body, a constitution is needed, setting forth the objects of the union and its limitations, purposes and designs. By-laws must also be prepared, giving detailed rules for the conduct of affairs. Both these tasks are assigned to a committee on *organization and by-laws*, which should be appointed as soon as practicable. Rules of order and standing rules may be added. All these must be left open to amendment.

The secretary has charge of all records and documents, except those of the treasurer. The secretary of every body must keep a record of its proceedings in public sessions. This record is called the *minutes*. The minutes should include a description of everything *actually done*, but should *not* describe debates or arguments, motions not put to vote, resolutions ruled out of order, or other matters on which no *action* is taken. The minutes should include all motions put to vote, all resolutions received, whether they be or be not adopted.

THE TREASURER.

This officer should make reports at frequent intervals, and his records should always be kept in the regular book-keeping style. His transactions should be business-like, and his reports clear and satisfactory.

REPORTS.

All officers of permanent bodies should be required to make annual reports. Semi-annual, quarterly or monthly reports may be provided for in the by-laws.

RULINGS OF THE CHAIR.

The president, or chairman, sits as an impartial judge, deciding between man and man, not according to his own bias of opinion, but so as to conform to the principle already laid down—the *will of the majority*. This can be done only by an adherence to parliamentary rules, as established by universal usage. The president has great power, in the appointment of committees, and in various other ways, and for him to supplement this power by arbitrary rulings is intolerable. Originality is not wanted here, and *precedent* must govern in every possible decision.

MOTIONS AND RESOLUTIONS.

The difference between a *motion* and a *resolution* can be better learned in practice than by description. The chief difference is in their degree of importance. A motion is orally expressed, unless it be of such length or of such peculiar verbiage as to make necessary its reduction to writing. A resolution should *always* be presented in writing. The peculiarity of a resolution lies in its being a declaration of the "sense of the meeting," or the opinion of the body, on some general topic. To illustrate, an order limiting speeches to five minutes, or an order adjourning the meeting, would be passed by a *motion;* while an order censuring or commending an officer, expressing thanks, or making a request, would be done by *resolution.*

AMENDMENTS AND SUBSTITUTES.

Both motions and resolutions, while under consideration and before adoption, are open to amendment. This may consist of a mere insertion or alteration of a word, or a more extended change. It must be remembered that even a small amendment may go a long way in changing the sense of the original motion. Thus, supposing the resolution before the house should be the following:

"*Resolved*, That Mr. Henry Dawson be authorized to represent this society in the meeting of the National Association, and present the claim of the members in this state to a more extended charter."

Then suppose an amendment be offered as follows:

"Mr. Chairman, I move that the resolution be so amended as to substitute the words 'Hiram Robinson' in place of the words 'Henry Dawson.'"

The word "amendment" properly includes both additions and substitutions.

An amendment is also open to amendment, but the chairman must not consider an "amendment to the amendment to the amendment." It is too complicated and confusing. The present amendment must be first disposed of, and any other alterations to the original resolution may then come in as amendments treated separately.

In all cases the amendment to an amendment has precedence of consideration, and must first be put to vote; next, the original amendment, and lastly, the resolution itself.

COMMITTEE OF THE WHOLE.

In committee of the whole the only motions in order are to amend or adopt, and that the committee "rise and report," since it can not adjourn. Neither can it order the ayes and noes. Debate, in committee of the whole, can be limited only by previous agreement.

DEFINITE ANALYSIS.

The important requisite of simplicity, in a deliberative body, is to adopt the motto, "One thing at a time," and to remember that *nothing but the creative power can annihilate.*

Thus, suppose a petition be offered. On a motion it is received. It is then "before the house," and nothing else must be allowed to overcrowd it until it is either laid over, laid upon the table, granted, refused, postponed to a fixed time, indefinitely postponed, or otherwise disposed of, which must be done by motion. Until such motion is adopted nothing else can be heard, with the exception of a motion to adjourn, which is not debatable.

To interrupt the consideration of one thing, in order to take up something else, sets a precedent for the introduction of still other subjects. Thus the questions at issue become so mixed that only the most able chairman, and certainly not a partisan working in the interest of a single proposition, can separate them. An assembly of men, like a horse, can "think of only one thing at a time."

MODES OF OPPOSITION.

Negative action, or opposition to any action proposed, may be conducted by one of the following motions:

To suppress the question—by (1) objection to its consideration; (2) a motion to lay it upon the table.

To suppress debate—by (1) moving the previous question; (2) a motion limiting or closing debate.

To defer action—by (1) postponing to a fixed time; (2) postponing indefinitely; (3) laying it upon the table.

To modify—by (1) a motion to amend; (2) a motion to commit or refer.

The tactics of opposition recently known as "filibustering" consists in a resort to legitimate methods, to accomplish illegitimate results. By illegitimate results, we mean the success of a minority. Thus, a minority on any question at issue in congress, finding they cannot out-vote the majority, will offer amendments or other minor issues, upon which debate may be prolonged for months, and legislation be so obstructed as to amount to a failure in accomplishing the will of the majority.

THE PREVIOUS QUESTION.

The object of a motion for the "*previous question*" is to precipitate a vote upon the question before the house, without further debate. There have been many changes in the form of using this motion, which have given rise to misconceptions. Originally its form was, "Shall the main question be put?" It's form now is, "Shall the main question be *now* put?" Its use in this country is different from that in England. There, the one who moves the previous question votes against it; while here, he votes in favor of it. In America* the motion for the previous question is not debatable, and the discussion is to be resumed if the motion be negatived, the same as if it had not been made. The previous question takes precedence of every debatable one, and can not be amended, committed or postponed. It requires a two-thirds vote for its adoption. It yields to a motion to lay upon the table, and to questions of privilege. When a member moves the previous question the chairman must immediately put it to vote, if it have been seconded.

LAYING UPON THE TABLE.

The passage of a motion to lay any question upon the table does not necessarily mean its defeat, for the majority may at any time subsequently take it from the table. Debate on a motion to postpone to a certain time must be limited to the propriety of postponing it to that time. A motion to take it from the table is not debatable. In some societies a question is prohibited from being taken from the table except by a two-thirds vote.

ORDER OF PRECEDENCE.

1. A motion *to fix the time* to which the assembly shall adjourn takes precedence of every other.
2. A *motion to adjourn* takes precedence of all except No. 1, if it be not qualified. If any qualification is attached, it becomes simply a principal motion.
3. A *question of privilege* takes precedence over any other matter, and if allowed in order by the chair, is disposed of forthwith, the other business being then proceeded with as if it had not been interrupted.
4. A call for the *order of the day* takes precedence of every other question except Nos. 1, 2 and 3, and also excepting a motion to reconsider.
5. *An appeal* from the decision of the chair takes precedence of the question out of which it grows, and yields only to Nos. 1, 2, 3 and 4.
6. An *objection* to the consideration of a question is in order only when it is first introduced.
7. A motion to *suspend the rules* must yield only to Nos. 1, 2, 3 and 4.
8. A request for *leave to withdraw a motion* must yield only to Nos. 1, 2, 3 and 4.
9. A motion *to lay upon the table* any question takes precedence of 10, 11, 12, 13 and 14, but must yield to 1, 2, 3, 4, 5, 6, 7 and 8.
10. A motion for the *previous question* takes precedence of all debatable questions, but must yield to 1, 2, 3, 4, 5, 6, 7, 8 and 9.
11. A motion *to postpone to a certain time* takes precedence only of 12, 13 and 14.
12. A motion to *commit* takes precedence only of 13 and 14.
13. A motion to *amend* takes precedence of nothing except the question which it is proposed to amend.
14. A motion to *postpone indefinitely* takes precedence of nothing except the question which it is proposed to indefinitely postpone.
15. A motion to *reconsider* a vote on 9, 10, 11, 12, 13 or 14 takes precedence of the main question. It must yield to 1, 2, 3, 5, 6, 7 and 8.

MISCELLANEOUS RULES AND HINTS.

In ordinary societies no motion limiting or cutting off debate should be adopted by less than a two-thirds vote.

*In the United States senate it is not allowed. This is sometimes known as the "gag law." In the house of representatives it can be adopted by a majority.

No one may move to reconsider a motion which has been negatived, except a member who voted against it.

No member has a right to have any paper read, without the permission of the assembly. The question of granting such permission cannot be debated or amended.

No member can address the house until he has been recognized by the chair.

A question of privilege is a privileged question, but a privileged question may be either Nos. 1, 2, 3, or 4, in the above list.

A motion to defer action may be debated only with reference to the postponement, and not on the merits of the question which it is proposed to defer.

A motion to reconsider may be made when any other question is before the meeting, but action upon it must be deferred until the present question is disposed of.

In this country, disputes concerning parliamentary rules are decided by a reference to the rules of the house of representatives of the United States.

In the election of an officer from rival candidates, it is not necessary to put the question in such a manner as to compel any member to vote directly *against* any candidate. In a standing vote, or a vote by ballot, each may express his preference *for* one of the nominees, without expressly voting against others, as would be the case in a *viva voce* vote.

When a committee is ready to disperse, it *rises*. When the meeting is ready to disperse, it *adjourns*.

All remarks must be addressed to the chairman, must be confined to the question before the house, and must avoid reflections upon the motives of other members.

In putting a motion to the house to be voted upon, the chairman should state it fully. If he cannot do so he may require the person who made the motion to write it.

If there be no objection, a person who has made a motion may offer an amendment to it, with the consent of the person who seconded it; and it stands in place of the original motion, without the necessity of a vote upon it. No motion can be withdrawn without the consent of the person who seconded it.

PUNCTUATION, CAPITALS AND COMMON ERRORS.

RULES FOR PUNCTUATION.

THERE are two views of the function performed by punctuation, the rhetorical and the grammatical. The former holds that it is the business of punctuation to divide written language into such portions as a correct speaker would divide it; the latter holds that punctuation should attend only to the grammatical structure of a sentence, and not separate the subject from the predicate or the object from the verb that governs it. The latter view is the modern one, and much confusion would be avoided if this would be regarded as the sole function of punctuation. A correct and impressive reader will always make many pauses not indicated by stops, will at times omit a stop where grammatically it would be required, and will vary the length of the pauses according to his idea of the requirements of the passage. The reader's pauses are solely rhetorical, and the punctuation marks are primarily intended as a guide to the eye in taking in the grammatical sense of the passage.

No fixed rule can be given as to the length of time indicated by the marks, only that generally the time decreases in the following order: period, colon, semi-colon and comma.

The tendency in modern English is to use punctuation marks more sparingly than formerly, and to assume that readers possess the ability to find their way through a sentence without signboards at every corner. Compare a writer of even fifty years ago with one of to-day, and it will be found that the latter has not half the number of commas peppered throughout his pages that the former has.

Then, in compound words the tendency is to drop the hyphen, especially in those in which the first word is of one syllable.

Generally it may be said that the period divides a paragraph into *sentences*; the colon and semi-colon divide *compound* sentences into smaller ones; and the comma connects into clauses the scattered statements of time, manner, place and relation belonging to verbs and nouns. Where the sense is clear without commas, it is better to omit them, and then they take the place of the semi-colon in complex and co-ordinate sentences. In few cases are the pauses in good reading indicated by the stopping.

THE COMMA.

(1) Where a short pause is required the comma is used; but it can be dispensed with in short, simple sentences.

(2) When a word is separated from its grammatical adjunct by some intervening phrase, the phrase should be preceded and followed by a comma: as, "The king, wearied by her importunity, granted her request."

(3) Never insert a comma between the subject and predicate. Except when the subject is accompanied by several adjuncts a comma should be introduced immediately before the verb: as, "The injustice and barbarity of this censure on all former editors of the New Testament, will appear," etc.

(4) Two or more words in the same construction are separated by a comma: as, "Reason, virtue, answer one aim," but if the words are closely connected with a conjunction, the comma is omitted: as, "Reason and virtue are one aim."

(5) When words in the same construction are joined in *pairs* by a conjunction, they are separated in *pairs* by a comma: as, "Hope and fear, pleasure and pain, diversify our lives."

(6) Expressions in a direct address, the nominative absolute, and words like hence, beside, first, are separated by commas from the body of the sentence: as, "Come hither, John;" "The sun having risen, we pursued our journey"; "Properly speaking, she was a good natured, reasonable woman"; "Beside, the issue is doubtful."

(7) Nouns in apposition, when accompanied with adjuncts, or nouns attended with participles or adjectives with dependent words, are separated with commas: as, "Paul, the Apostle of the Gentiles, was eminent for his zeal"; "The king, approving the plan, put it in execution."

But if the nouns are single they are not divided: as, "Paul the Apostle suffered martyrdom."

(8) Words placed in contrast to one another are separated by commas: as, "Though deep, yet clear; tho' gentle, yet profound."

(9) Quotations, or expressions resembling quotations, should be marked by commas: as, "It hurts a man's pride to say, I don't know;" we are strictly enjoined, "not to follow a multitude to do evil."

(10) Relative pronouns, except when closely connected with their antecedents, generally admit a comma before them: as, "He preaches sublimely, who leads a good life."

(11) When the infinitive mood or a sentence is the subject of a verb, it generally admits a comma, especially when it follows the verb: as, "It ill becomes wise men, to oppose each other."

(12) When a verb is understood, a comma may often properly be introduced: as, "From law arises security; from security, curiosity; from curiosity, knowledge."

(13) In compound sentences the clauses are separated by commas unless the connection is close: as, "Crafty men contemn studies, simple men despise them, and wise men admire them;" but in the following, where the connection is close and sentence short, no comma is necessary: "Revelation tells us *how* we may attain happiness."

(14) Words repeated require a comma: as, "No, no, no, it cannot be."

(15) Inverted sentences, by throwing words out of their natural order, often require a comma: as, "To God, all things are possible;" but no comma is required in "All things are possible to God."

THE SEMICOLON.

The semicolon is inserted between those members of a sentence less closely connected than those separated by commas, and the parts separated by the semicolon should contain in themselves a complete and independent proposition, while still having a connection with the other parts.

(1) When one clause is explanatory of another it is separated by a semicolon: as, "Study to acquire a habit of thinking; nothing is more important."

(2) When a sentence consists of several complex members separated in turn by commas, the larger divisions are separated by semicolons: for instance, "As the desire of approbation, when it works according to reason, improves the amiable part of our species; so nothing is more destructive, when it is governed by vanity and folly."

(3) When several short sentences, complete in themselves, but having a slight connection in idea, follow in succession, they should be separated by semicolons: as, "Tragedy represents a disastrous event; comedy ridicules the follies of mankind; and elegy displays the tender emotions of the heart."

THE COLON.

The colon is used to divide a sentence into parts less connected than those separated by a semicolon; but not so independent as separate distinct sentences. The general principle, therefore, which regulates the choice of either, is the *closeness of the connection*.

(1) When a member of a sentence is complete in itself, but followed by some supplemental remark or further illustration of the subject, the colon is used: as, "Time is the seed field of eternity: what a man soweth, that shall he also reap."

(2) When one or more semicolons have preceded, and a still greater pause is necessary in order to mark the connecting or concluding clause, a colon is indicated: thus, "As we perceive the shadow to have moved along the dial, but did not perceive it moving; and it appears the grass has grown, although no one has seen it grow: so our advances in knowledge are only perceivable by the distance."

(3) The colon is also used when a direct quotation or speech in introduced: as, "I admire this sublime passage: 'God said, let there be light, and there was light.'"

In case the quotation comes in as a dependent element of the sentence, a comma precedes it: as, "Their fond mother shall cry, ''Tis morn, awake! awake!'"

(4) The presence of a connective word will frequently determine whether a semicolon or colon is indicated: as, "Apply yourself to learning, *for* it will redound to your honor;" but "Apply yourself to learning: it will redound to your honor."

(5) When a general term has several particulars in apposition under it, the general term is separated from the particulars by a colon, the particulars from each other by commas: as, "Nouns have three genders: masculine, feminine and neuter."

(6) After the address in a letter, or the contracted word, "viz," a colon is used: as, "Sir: I have the honor," etc., and "This is used in the following cases, viz.: When," etc.

THE PERIOD.

The period is admissible when the sentences are complete in sense and not connected with each other, in either meaning or grammatical construction; when a very long sentence, which is separated by colons or semicolons, and in case of abbreviations.

In regard to quotation marks, American practice reverses the English order of single and double quotations: thus, in America, we would say: "Never despair," said he "for, as Horace says, '*Nil desperandum.*'" Here, it will be observed, that at first the double quotation marks are used, and a quotation within a quotation is singly marked. The words "said he," are outside the quotation marks, as they should be.

In quoting poetry, it was formerly customary to quote each line; now it is sufficient to quote at commencement of first line, and end of last line.

In quoting an extract, with paragraphs, the first word of each paragraph should be preceded with quotation marks, and in case of the last paragraph, it should close with the marks.

The quotation marks are used whenever a word or phrase is used in an unusual sense, or in a colloquial or slangy manner. It is well, as far as possible, to avoid such a practice.

CAPITALS—WHEN AND WHERE TO USE THEM.

IN the use of capitals there is some diversity in the practice of writers and printers.

The following classes of words usually begin with capital letters:

(1) The first word of every book, chapter, letter or other piece of writing; also, the first word after a period, or after an interrogation or exclamation point, if they close an independent sentence; also, the first word of every line of poetry; also, the first word of a formal quotation: as, "Remember the maxim: 'Know thyself,'" but for an informal quotation, a capital is unnecessary: as, Solomon remarks that "pride goes before destruction."

(2) Proper names; adjectives derived from proper names; titles of honor and distinction, and common nouns personified: as, "There Honor comes, a pilgrim gray."

(3) Words used as titles of the Deity.

(4) Every substantive and principal word in titles of books: as, "The Lady of the Lake."

(5) The pronoun I, and the interjection O.

(6) Other words besides these, when emphatic or the principal subject of discourse.

(7) Generic common nouns, when accompanied by proper nouns included in the genus: as, The Mississippi River, the Supreme Court; the English Government, but not when the words "river," "court, "government," etc., occur by themselves.

(8) Some capitalize "state" and "territory," but it is preferable to follow the rule just given above.

(9) A capital is not required after a period used for contracted words merely: as, "The meeting was adjourned *nem. con.* yesterday."

(10) The tendency to the too frequent use of capitals, a habit often fostered by their very profuse use in book-keeping, is to be avoided.

COMMON ERRORS IN SPEAKING AND WRITING.

IN this article we have aimed to give in a terse form a collection of the most common errors in speaking and writing, and in an equally terse yet clear manner to give the correction—in most cases with reasons therefor, unless the correction be too obvious to require this procedure. A careful perusal of the article will, we hope, "from many a blunder free us."

"I do not know *but what* it is right," should be *but that.*

"The rose smells sweet*ly*," "it sounds grand*ly*," "he looks sharp*ly*."

Here the *ly* is inadmissible, except perhaps in the last sentence, if the reference is to the quality of the act. "He looks sharp," refers to the quality of the agent.

"The mob *were* riotous," should be *was;* but,

"The nobility *were* alarmed," is right. The rule is that collective nouns require a verb in the plural, nouns of multitude require a verb in the singular. Observe that *mob* has a plural, while *nobility* has not.

"I will speak to all, *him* alone excepted," should be *he*. In English the case absolute is the nominative.

"You could do it better than *him* or *me*," should be *he* or *I*.

"He loved him better than *me*," is right, if it signifies that he loved him better than he loved me; but it should be *I* if it signifies that he loved him better than I (loved him).

"Between you and *I*," should be *me*, as it signifies between *you* and between *me*.

"After you and *I*," is right when *after* is an adverb; as in "After you and I go," but it should be *me* when *after* is a preposition; as, "He spoke after you and me."

"*Who* do you vote for?" should be "*For whom* do you vote?"

Solomon, son of David, *who* slew Goliath. (Right.)

Solomon, son of David, *who* built the temple. (Wrong.)

Latter violates the rule that the relative agrees with the nearest word capable of being antecedent.

"Errors are committed by the most distinguished writers with respect to 'shall' and 'will,'" violates the rule that the word or phrase which belongs to the governed word should always be so placed that the *connection* should be clear. The above sentence should read, "Errors in respect to 'shall' and 'will' are committed," etc. This principle of the proper collocation of words is constantly violated, and innumerable instances could be given in illustration of this fault; such as:

"Wanted, a young man to attend horses of a pious turn of mind." "The man was digging a well with a roman nose." "The following verses were written by a young man who has long lain in the grave for his own amusement"; "I saw that the kettle had been scoured with half an eye"; "A public dinnner was given to the inhabitants of roast beef and plum pudding"; "He rode to town, and drove ten cows on horseback."

"Charm he *never* so wisely," should be *ever*.

"He was more beloved (add *than*), but not so much admired, as Brutus"; in this *than* is added on the principle that clauses connected by conjunctions should be grammatically complete.

"To not come," should be "not to come." Rule: Never insert any word between the infinitive sign *to* and its verb.

"If he say *aught*," is preferable to *ought*, on the principle that when usage is divided we should prefer the word which admits of one signification.

"I saw my *contemporary*;" preferable to *cotemporary* on the ground of analogy.

"I cannot accept of this;" *of* should be omitted on the ground of simplicity.

"He displayed great *wrongheadedness*." The last word should be rejected as harsh and unnecessary; "obstinacy in error" is preferable.

"He effected his purpose by *dint of* argument; the italicized words can with advantage be dispensed with.

"I had rather go," is better expressed by "I would rather go." The former includes a solecism and should be avoided.

"The *then* ministry;" better, "the ministry of that time."

"They could *easier* get them by heart;" say *more easily*.

"Thine *often* infirmities;" say *frequent*.

"Jacob loved Joseph more than all his children;" *other* should be inserted after *his*.

"He gave me the *two first* pieces," is correct if it means the two at the beginning; *first two* would signify that the pieces were numbered in pairs.

"The unicorn is a kind of *a* rhinoceros;" *a* should be omitted. Rule: Since a or an denotes one thing of a kind, it cannot be used before the whole kind.

"Everyone must judge of *their* own feelings;" say *his*.

"Let you and *I* endeavor to do better;" say *me*.

"If there is one man worse than another, it is *him* who," etc.; say *he*.

"It is not for such as *us* to try this;" say *we* (are).

"Is she as tall as *me?*" say *I*.

"*Whom* do men say that I am?" say *who*.

"*Who* should we meet the other day but John?" say *whom*.

"He spoke to I don't know *who;*" say *whom*.

"The time shall come *that* he will regret this;" say *when*.

"I have *got* a cold;" avoid the use of *get* or *got* as much as possible: it is generally redundant.

"I cannot *get into* the box;" say *open*.

"I do not say as others *do*," is correct, but be careful about the substitution of *do* for other verbs in cases where the ellipsis of the preceding verb cannot be supplied; as, "I did not say as some have *done;*" should be *said*.

"I have lost this game, though I thought I should *have won* it." Here substitute *win* for *have won*. However far back the *expectation* may be referred, the *seeing* must be considered as *contemporary*, or as *soon to follow*, but cannot, without absurdity, be considered as past.

"The son said to his father that he had sinned against heaven." Where there is obscurity as to the last "he," which grammatically belong to "father," as the nearest antecedent, but in reality is intended to refer to "son." This obscurity should be avoided by a different arrangement, or by inserting the words, "the son," in brackets.

The next sentence is another instance of the same error. "The farmer went to the lawyer, and told him that his bull had gored his ox."

Inelegancy, such as the following, should be avoided:

"They halted with the river at their backs." "Behind them," or, "at the rear," would be better.

"This property has or will be sold." Insert "been" after "has."

"I have bought a house and orchard." Insert "an" before "orchard."

Prepositions are often wrongly used, as in the following:

"Many have profited *from* the misfortunes of others;" say *by*.

"Many customs have been brought *in* use of late." *Into* is required when motion is implied.

"This remark is founded *with* truth;" *on*.

"I find great difficulty *of* writing;" *in*.

"Favors are not always bestowed *to* the most deserving;" *on*.

"This is different *to* that;" *from*.

"He insists *on* it that he is right;" *upon*.

"He should have divided it *between* the three, and not *among* the two." The italicized words should be reversed, as *between* is from by-twain, or by two, and *among* signifies with many.

Completely refers to *degree*, *entirely* to *quantity*. Thus, we should say, "I am *completely* (not *entirely*) tired." "All *are* here," "the whole *is* taken." "All" is plural and collective; "while" refers to the component parts of a body, and is singular.

"*All* men are animals," or "*Every* man is an animal." *All* is collective, *every* distributive.

"An authentic book relates facts as they happened; a *genuine* book is written by the author whose name it bears."

"The vice of covetousness is what enters *deepest* into the soul of any other;" say *deeper*.

"There is one that will think himself obliged to double his kindness and caresses of me." *Kindness* should not be followed by *of* but *to*.

"He attended the *nuptial* of the prince;" say *nuptials*.

"He became *seary* of his money." *Seary* is improperly used for *frightened.*

"His *hauteur* was intolerable." Here a French word is improperly used for *haughtiness.* It is always better, if possible, to stick to plain Anglo-Saxon.

"To make such acquirements as fit them for useful *avocations.*" The impropriety here consists in using avocations for vocations. By the latter is meant "trade," "profession" or "calling;" by the former whatever withdraws or diverts us from business.

"No man had ever *less* friends and more enemies." It should be "*fewer* friends," as *less* refers to quantity, *fewer* to number.

"He sings *a good song,*" is better expressed by "He sings *well;*" as the former strictly implies that the song he sings is a good one, whereas the speaker really means to say, "He sings well."

"Apples will be *plenty* this coming fall;" say *plentiful.*

"I do not suppose that we Americans *want* genius more than other nations." Here *want* is improperly used for *lack.* This word *want* is often improperly used as in the following: "You *want* to be careful," where it is used for *need* or *require.*

"The first proposal was entirely different and inferior to the other." This requires the addition of *from* after *different.*

"To the happiness of possessing such a partner, he soon *had* the satisfaction of obtaining the highest honor the country could bestow." Better to say here, *united* the satisfaction, etc.

"This may be useful to *them* whose chief ambition is to please." Better to say *those,* which stands for a noun not previously introduced.

"My purpose was to *have withdrawn* from commerce;" say *withdraw.*

"He was put to sleep *with* the sound of music;" say *by.*

"The greatest minds often differ among one another." Better, *from each other,* or *one from the other.*

"I have read the Emperor's Charles the Fifth's life." Better, "the life of the Emperor Charles the Fifth."

"It is not for such as *us,*" etc.; better, *we.*

"He was walking *back and forth;*" better, *backward and forward.*

"Whether he will go or *no,*" etc.; should be *not.*

"His argument was *based* upon the fact;" *founded.*

"The money was *ordered paid;*" supply *to be* before *paid.*

"I *calculate* to leave soon;" *intend.*

"He is *considerable* of a scholar;" a *pretty good* scholar.

"He is a *decent* scholar;" better, a *fair* scholar.

"His farm was *convenient* to mine;" *contiguous* or *close.*

"Her situation was distressing *to a degree;*" *extremely* distressing.

"A total *destitution* of capacity;" *want.*

"*Either* of the United States;" should be *any,* as *either* refers to one of *two.*

"Equally *as* well;" omit *as.*

"I *presume* he will go;" say *think* or *suppose.*

"He is in a bad *fix;*" *state* or *condition.*

"Will you *fix* this?" *put in order.*

"What do *folks* think of this?" *people.*

"Talents of the highest *grade;*" better, *order.*

"I *guess* I will do this;" *think.*

"We hope the assistance of God;" hope *for.*

"A *horse* colt; a *mare* colt;" should be, a *colt;* a *filly.*

"This would *illy* accord;" *ill.*

"When did you come *in* town?" *into.*

"A *lengthy* discourse;" *long.*

"Why don't you do *like* I do;" *as.*

TERSENESS IN SPEECH AND WRITING.

THE predominance of the Latin element in the foundation of the English language, invests its vocabulary, beyond any other, written or spoken, with an adaptability for vigor of expression, combined with grace and symmetry of form and simplicity and ease of understanding, which is too often marred by the tendency to redundancy in the use of words and the mistaken idea that floridness is a proper ambition of elegance. He who wishes to write and speak the English language in its purest, best and most classical form, will clothe his words with the greatest power, and conform to the rules for the highest literary excellence, by observing that terseness and simplicity of expression which the student of philology recognizes as the most important and most admirable feature of the language. "Brevity is the soul of wit," is a proverb which, applied to the use of language, has a wider significance, and a more important meaning for him who studies the correct use of it, than its ordinary adaptation implies. In giving the thoughts written or vocal expression, he will achieve the highest excellence who keeps steadily in view that the main object of oral or written utterance is to convey the thought or idea with the greatest force and clearness, in the fewest possible words consistent with a complete expression of the meaning designed to be conveyed, harmony of grammatical arrangement and rhetoric elegance. It is, in fact, simply to study and develop, in its use, the advantages which are inherent in the language. That style of writing and expression which was formerly in fashion in oratory and literature, which lost sight of the object of expression in the desire to embellish speech with ornate and unnecessary flourish, and to exhibit rather the writer's resources of vocabulary than the impression which he designed to reach in the reader's mind, is among the things of the past. Classic elegance and conciseness is now the highest test of excellence, and the best and truest criterion of literary merit. Terseness, conciseness and brevity in writing, are, however, not to be best attained by a series of spasmodic and jerky sentences. They are to be attained without any sacrifice of elegant and euphonious periods, by the choice of the most expressive words, governed by their most appropriate relation to the meaning which the sentence is designed to convey. The redundancy of adjectives is to be avoided, as well as the repetition, in the same sentence, or in succeeding sentences, of the same meaning, conveyed in different words; though it is one of the highest excellences of the use of language to convey in a sentence properly arranged the same effect which is produced by the crude or ill informed writer in several distinct propositions. Lengthy or involved sentences are, as a rule, to be avoided by the ordinary writer. They take him onto a higher ground, which is only safely traversed by the master of the language. It is not given to the ordinary mind to attempt the grasp of language which is the realm of the master mind of a Gladstone, a Beecher or an Ingersoll; and he who attempts, in this way, to soar beyond his capacity, will find himself afloat on Icarius' wings, and will certainly land in discomfiture and disgrace. Cultivate, therefore, brevity—not that brevity which denotes paucity of ideas and language—but the brevity which seeks the greatest power of expression in the fewest words and the greatest simplicity of arrangement. Here is an example in which the same meaning, precisely, is conveyed in two paragraphs, each being grammatically correct and in good form:

"The climate of Illinois is one of the finest in the world. Notwithstanding the extreme cold of the winter months, the people do not suffer the same discomfort in that season as those at the East. This is due to the remarkable dryness of the atmosphere, and the absence of sudden and unforeseen changes. The summer heat, while nearly as great as in the same latitudes at the East, does not entail the same inconvenience and suffering. The cool breezes from the great lake temper the air and prevent that oppressive sultriness which is so much experienced in the Eastern summer. The salubrity of the climate is also remarkable. This is attributable to the large quantity of ozone with which the air is charged."

"The climate of Illinois is one of the finest and most salubrious in the world. The discomforts which attend the changeableness of the weather in the winter, and the extreme sultriness of the summer months, in the East, are avoided—in the former season, by the remarkable dryness of the atmosphere and evenness of the temperature, and in the latter, by the cool breezes from the great lake, which temper the extreme heat. The large percentage of ozone in the atmosphere also renders the climate unusually salubrious."

Observe, that in the former paragraph, there are used one hundred and twenty-two words and seven sentences. The latter, which fully covers the same meaning, in more expressive and elegant shape, contains but eighty-six words and three sentences.

"Such were the considerations, such, I say, were the inducements, which prompted the Democracy in its efforts to send to this chamber a Republican beyond question, since these many long years. If that is the Democracy which gentlemen on that side love, I proclaim my inability to act with them."

Read in this way:

"Such were the considerations, the inducements, which prompted the effort of the Democracy to send to this chamber, one whose Republicanism was, for many years, beyond question. If that be the Democracy which gentlemen opposite love, I proclaim my inability to co-operate with them."

Observe that here is a saving of six words in less than as many lines, an improvement in grammatical and literary construction, with a gain in force and vigor. Let these two principles be borne in mind in cultivating proper brevity: Never sacrifice the force and lucidity of expression to false economy of words. Never sacrifice the true dignity, simplicity and force of expression, to a misplaced idea of what constitutes literary or rhetoric elegance, nor lose your meaning in a sea of words.

OLD SPANISH PROVERBS.

"Taking the wrong sow by the ear."

"Do not leap over the hedge before you arrive at the stile."

"Out of the frying pan into the fire."

"Out of God's blessing into the sun."

"Fair and softly goes far."

"There is nothing sure in this world."

"A man must eat a peck of salt with his friend before he knows him."

"One swallow never makes a summer."

"The itch lives long enough."

"The devil lurks behind the cross."

"You cannot catch old birds with chaff."

"One knows where one's own shoe pinches."

"King's chaff is better than other men's corn."

"The treason pleases, but the traitors are odious."

"Diligence is the mother of success."

"There are always more tricks in town than are talked of."

"There is no striving against the stream."

"Fortune turns round like a mill wheel, and he that was yesterday at the top to-day lies at the bottom."

FLOWERS IN SEASON.

EVERY flower may be supplied with its favorite soil with a little patience and observation. A light soil suits most descriptions very well; and earth, thoroughly well dug, and dressed yearly from a mound of accumulated leaves, rotted with soap-suds, will be found useful generally. A portion of sand should be mixed with it. All bulbs, carnations, pinks, auriculas, ranunculuses, etc., like a mixture of sand. Mix sand well into borders and plats of gardens, and you will have handsome flowers. The addition of powdered charcoal will deepen the colors of most flowers. The following list of common flowers appertaining to each month may assist in filling the borders of gardens :

JANUARY.

Single anemones.
Winter cyclamens.
Michaelmas daisy.
Hepaticas.
Primroses.
Winter hyacinth.
Narcissus of the East.
Christmas rose.

FEBRUARY.

Single anemones.
Forward anemones.
Persian iris.
Spring crocus.
Single yellow gilliflower.
Single liverwort.
Winter aconite.
Hepaticus.

MARCH.

Bulbous iris.
Anemones of all sorts.
Spring cyclamens.
Liverwort of all sorts.
Daffodils.
Crowfoots.
Spring crocus.
Hyacinths of all sorts.
Jonquils.
Yellow gilliflower.
Narcissus of several kinds.
Forward bears'-ears.
Forward tulips.
Single primroses of various colors.

APRIL.

Daisies.
Yellow gilliflowers.
Narcissus of all sorts.
Forward bear's-ear.
Spring cyclamens.
Saffron flowers.
Anemones of all sorts.
Iris.
Pansies.
Daffodils.
Double liverworts.
Primroses.
Honeysuckles.
Tulips.
Hyacinths.
Single jonquils.
Crown-imperial.
Yellow gilliflowers, double and single.
Pasque-flowers.
March violets.

MAY.

Anemones.
Gilliflowers of all sorts.
Yellow gilliflowers.
Columbines.
Asphodels.
Orange or flame-colored lilies.
Double jacea, a sort of cychnis.
Pansies.
Peonies of all sorts.
Ranunculus of all sorts.
Some irises, as those we call the bulbous iris, and the chamoe iris.
Cyanuses of all sorts.
Hyacinths.
Day lilies.
Bastard dittany.
Daisies.
Lily of the valley.
Mountain pinks.
Italian spiderwort, a sort of asphodel.
Poet's pinks.
Backward tulips.
Julians, otherwise called English gilliflowers.

JUNE.

Snap-dragons of all sorts.
Wild tansies.
Pinks.
Irises.
Roses.
Tuberoses.
Pansies.
Larkspur.
Great daisies.
Climbers.
Cyanuses of all sorts.
Fox-gloves of all sorts.
Mountain lilies.
Gilliflowers of all sorts.
Monks'-hoods.
Candy-tufts.
Poppies.

JULY.

Jessamine.
Spanish broom.
Basils.
Bell-flowers.
Indian jacea.
Great daisies.
Monks'-hoods.
Pinks.
Scabiuses.
Nigellas.
Cyclamens.
Lobel's catch-flies.
Lilies of all sorts.
Apples of love.
Comfrey.
Poppies.
Snap-dragons.
Double marigolds.
Amaranthuses.
Pinks of the poets.
Bee-flowers.
Sea-hollies.
Foxgloves.
Wild poppies.
Everlastings.
Roses.
Dittanies.
Bindweeds.
Lilies of St. Bruno.
Tri-colors.
Squills.
Motherworts.
Climbers.
Oculus christi.
Camomile.
Sunflowers.
Belvidere.
Gilliflowers.
Hellebore.
Ox-eyes.
Thorn-apple.
Valerian.

AUGUST.

Oculus christi, or starwort.
Belvideres.
Climbers of all sorts.
Apples of love.
Marvels of Peru.
Pansies.
Ranunculuses.
Double marigolds.
Candy-tufts
Autumn cyclamens.
Jessamines.
Sunflowers.
Indian narcissus.
Fox-gloves.
Cyclamens.
Passion-flowers.
Everlastings.
Tuberoses.
Monks'-hoods.
Indian pinks.
Bindweed.
Pass-velours.
Great daisies.
White bell-flower.
Autumnal meadow-saffron.
Gilliflowers.

SEPTEMBER.

Tri-colors.
Love-apples.
Marvel of Peru.
Monks'-hoods.
Narcissus of Portugal.
Snap-dragons.
Oculus christi.
Basils.
Belvideres.
Great daisies.
Double marigolds,
Monthly roses.
Tube roses.
Amaryilis.
Autumnal narcissus.
White-bell flowers.
Indian pinks.
Indian roses.
Amaranthus.
Pansies.
Passion-flower.
Autumnal crocus.
Thorn-apple.
Carnations.
Ranunculus, planted in May,
Colchicums.

OCTOBER.

Tri-colors.
Oculus christi.
Snap-dragons.
Pansies, sown in August.
Passion-flower.
Colchicums.
Autumn crocus.
Autumnal cyclamens.
Monks'-hood.
Indian pinks.
Pass-velours.
Double marigolds.
Some pinks.
Amaryilis.
Autumnal narcissus.

NOVEMBER.

Snap-dragons.
Double and single gilliflowers.
Great daisies.
Pansies, sown in August.
Monthly roses.
Double violets.
Single anemones of all sorts.
Winter cyclamens.
Forward hellebore.
Golden-rod.

HOW TO TRAVEL.

IN these days of rapid transit the traveler must have information suited to the celerity of his progress and the conventionalities of modern transportation. If he has it not, he is made liable both to ridicule and personal inconvenience. The old easy-going days, when a stage full of impatient people was halted ten minutes to allow for the delay of an old lady whose various band-boxes and parcels were not ready, and when a steamer would make a landing at almost any point to put off a solitary passenger, with his carpet-bag and butter box, are all passed. The public carriers are less accommodating to their patrons than formerly in these respects, but make up for it in others, by requiring those patrons to accommodate each other, in the matter of promptness and undelayed progress. Most of modern travel is by rail. It is usually expeditious and pleasant; yet gives opportunity for the abundant display of selfishness, especially in America, where fifty or more passengers are crowded into the same car. It is in traveling that the genuineness or baselessness of the claim "gentleman" or "lady" is made most apparent.

The Route.—In every railroad station, hotel, or other place where travelers gather, there are sure to be hanging several kinds of maps, showing the course of every railroad in that part of the country. By a glance at these the traveler can be sure of the route he is to take, and avoid uncertainty. The first thing necessary in starting anywhere is to know where you are going.

The Time.—The most uncertain thing of all is the accuracy and comparison of time pieces. The adoption of "standard time" throughout the country has much improved this matter, but still clocks and watches differ enough to cause frequent annoyance. The clock in a ticket agent's office may be relied upon, as the railroad clocks are kept together by telegraph.

Getting Ready.—Trunks, valises, and other baggage, should be packed and transported to the depot in ample time to avoid the confusion which haste is sure to create. If you do not personally know the man who hauls your baggage, make a note of the number of his wagon, so you can find him again if anything goes wrong. Do not let him leave the baggage at some outlying point away from the depot, where thieves may get it.

Avoid Waste.—Waste of temper; waste of money, in letting yourself be swindled when making change; waste of anxiety, by taking more baggage than you need; waste of time, by going to the station an hour before the time for the train, and then waiting impatiently.

DISEMBARKING.

Forethought.—This is worth more than a thousand questions. Have the forethought to ascertain, in advance, just where you will make a change of trains; just which road you are to travel on. Do not suppose, if you are going to Smithville, that *every* train on the Smithville railroad will take you there. Some other train on the same road may be bound for the Jonesville branch, and not going to Smithville at all.

Tickets.—Purchase your tickets before entering the cars. This is the rule of the company, and if you do not obey it you may have to pay the conductor more than the ticket agent. Inform the agent exactly where you want to go, and when. If it is to a point in another state, give the name of the state; for there is probably a town of the same name in some other state or on some other road. Ask the agent the price of the ticket, see that you are not robbed by any one in the crowd at your elbows, and on receiving the ticket, carefully place both it and your money in your safest pocket.

Checking Baggage.—You should see that your trunks are delivered at the door of the baggage room. Having bought your ticket, show it to the baggage master. He will give you a numbered check, placing a duplicate upon each piece of your baggage, and from that moment the responsibility for it devolves upon the railroad company. Bear in mind that a depot check is not a railroad check. That is, your check from your hotel or residence to the depot is given merely by the transfer company, and you must afterward see personally to the checking at the depot. Most railroads limit the weight of baggage carried free to 150 pounds, making a charge for an excess over this weight. After it has arrived at its destination, most railroads give the traveler only twenty-four hours to remove it from the depot. After that time they make a charge for storage, especially in the larger cities. It seems in many cases unjust, especially as the traveler may have received no notification of any such rule. The charge for storage is often increased by an additional one for cartage.

Getting Aboard.—The train comes roaring up to the depot, the crowd is in motion, there are other trains about to leave, and you are likely to become excited. That is precisely what you should not do. If you become excited you are more than ever likely to leave one of your parcels in the depot, get upon the wrong train, meet with an accident, or cause a headache. Be prompt, but cool and business-like. Don't run; there is no need of it. Don't ask strangers for information, but ascertain from the ticket agent, conductor or other railroad employe, which train you should take.

Observation.—It is by observation, rather than by directions, that one can learn to travel comfortably. When a lady, starting on a journey, selects a seat in the smoking car, it shows she has not observed the difference between smoking cars and coaches in the invariable make-up of passenger trains. When a gentleman offers his ticket to the brakeman, it shows he has not observed that the conductor always wears the name "Conductor," on his cap, and may be known at a glance. Observation will show the traveler a thousand little things, if he will notice them, instead of asking innumerable questions. Still, it is better to ask than to be ignorant of what you want to know.

Companions.—If you are traveling with others, do not separate yourself from them in the rush of people, and do not consult your own comfort at the expense or disregard of theirs. If a gentleman is traveling with a lady, he must take upon himself the various little tasks incidental to the trip, such as the purchase of her ticket, the transportation and checking of her baggage, assisting her on board, and procuring a seat for her. You should use your own judgment as to purchases of confectionery or literature, and as to keeping her interested during the journey. Do not imagine that because you are taking a journey you are embarking in some great enterprise which entitles you to distinction. Excited or loud talk at the depot and on the train will subject you to stares and criticisms, which would be fully deserved.

Sleeping Cars.—Berths in sleeping cars should be procured a day or two in advance, if possible, so as to make sure of getting them, and of choosing preferable locations, the same as seats at the theatre. The center of the car is to be chosen rather than the berths near the doors.

General Hints.—If the journey is monotonous, try to find some way of amusing yourself besides that of continually eating, on the cars, or drinking, on a steamer. It is offensive to others for you to be all the time cracking nuts and scattering the hulls upon the floor. Be careful as to the transient acquaintances you form, and make no stranger your confidant. By good judgment, however, you may take part in a conversation, which will make the journey more pleasant. Be careful in stepping on or off the train, or passing from one car to another. The proper way to do so is to have, at each step you take, a firm grip upon the rods with at least one hand. Be especially careful in going to or from a train on a road which has a double track. Make a distinction between authorized railroad employes and outside persons. The man who checks your baggage on the train, however, for removal to a hotel or railroad depot, is an agent for an omnibus or express company, which, though a local concern, is, no doubt, responsible. A hack may belong to a responsible company or to some unknown individual.

European Travel.—Passengers starting for Europe will find it advisable to telegraph in advance to the sea-port city from which they expect to sail, so as to secure a berth in the steamer, having ascertained on which day it is advertised to sail. They can thus plan their journey in its proper order, leaving home at a time suited to the departure of the steamer from New York, or in time to give them a few days of leisure in the city before the day advertised for the steamer's departure.

LANGUAGE OF FLOWERS.

"Nor did I wonder at the lily's white,
Nor praise the deep vermilion of the rose:
They were but sweet, but figures of delight,
Drawn after you, you pattern of all those.
Yet seem'd it winter still, and you away,
As with your shadow, I with these did play."—*Shakspeare.*

Acacia—Concealed love.
Adonis vernalis—Sorrowful remembrances.
Almond—Hope.
Aloe—Religious superstition.

Alyssum, Sweet—Worth beyond beauty.
Ambrosia—Love returned.
Apple blossom—Preference.
Arbor vitæ—Unchanging friendship.

Bachelor's button—Hope in love.
Balsam—Impatience.
Begonia—Deformity.
Bellflower—Gratitude.
Belvidere, Wild (Licorice)—I declare against you.

Blue Bell—I will be constant.
Box—Stoical indifference.
Briers—Envy.
Burdock—Touch me not.

"On woman nature didst bestow two eyes,
Like Heaven's bright lamps, in matchless beauty shining,
Whose beams do soonest captivate the wise,
And wary heads made rare by art's refining."—*Robert Greene.*

Cactus—Thou leavest not.
Camellia—Pity.
Candytuft—Indifference.
Canterbury Bell—Gratitude.
Cape Jessamine—Ecstasy; transport.

Calla lily—Feminine beauty.
Carnation (Yellow)—Disdain.
Cedar—I live for thee.
China Aster—I will see about it.
Chrysanthemum Rose—I love.

"Let not my love be called idolatry,
Nor my beloved as an idol show,
Since all alike my songs and praises be
To one, of one, still such and ever so."—*Shakspeare.*

Cowslip—Pensiveness.
Cypress—Mourning.

Crocus—Cheerfulness.
Cypress and Marigold—Despair.

Daffodil—Chivalry.
Dahlia—Forever thine.
Daisy (Garden)—I partake your sentiment.
Daisy (Wild)—I will think of it.

Dandelion—Coquetry.
Dead leaves—Sadness.
Dock—Patience.
Dodder—Meanness.

Dogwood—Am I indifferent to you?

Ebony—Hypocrisy.
Eglantine—I wound to heal.

Elder—Compassion.
Endive—Frugality.

Evening Primrose—Inconstancy.

"Fair is my love, but not so fair as fickle;
Mild as a dove, but neither true nor trusty;
Brighter than glass, and yet, as glass is brittle;
Softer than wax, and yet as iron, rusty;
A lily pale, with damask dye to grace her,
None fairer, and none paler to deface her."—*Shakspeare.*

Evergreen—Poverty.

Everlasting—Perpetual remembrance.

Fennel—Strength.
Filbert—Reconciliation.
Fir-tree—Elevation.
Flax—I feel your kindness.

Forget-me-not—True love; remembrance.
Fox-glove—Insincerity.
Furze—Anger.
Fuchsia—Taste.

Gentian—Intrinsic worth.
Geranium, Ivy—Your hand for the next dance.
Geranium, Nutmeg—I expect a meeting.
Geranium, Oak—Lady, deign to smile.
Geranium, Rose—Preference.

Geranium, Silver leaf—Recall.
Gilliflower—Lasting beauty.
Gladiolus—Ready; armed.
Golden Rod—Encouragement.
Gorse—Endearing affection.
Gass—Utility.

Harebell—Grief.
Hawthorn—Hope.
Hazel—Recollection.
Heartsease—Think of me.
Heliotrope—Devotion.
Henbane—Blemish.
Holly—Foresight.

Hollyhock—Fruitfulness.
Hollyhock, White—Femal[illegible]on.
Honeysuckle—Bond of Lo[illegible]
Honeysuckle, Coral—The c[illegible] my fate.
Hyacinth—Jealousy.
Hyacinth, Blue—Constancy.
Hyacinth, Purple—Sorrow.

Hydrangea—Heartlessness.

Ice plant—Your looks freeze me.

Iris—Message.

Ivy—Friendship; matrimony.

Jessamine, Cape—Transient joy; ectasy.
Jessamine, White—Amiability.
Jessamine, Yellow—Grace; elegance.

Jonquil—I desire a return of affection.
Juniper—Asylum; shelter.
Justitia—Perfection of loveliness.

Kalmia (Mountain laurel)—Treachery.

Kannedia—Mental beauty.

"Her lips to mine how often has she joined,
Between each kiss her oaths of true love swearing.
How many tales to please me has she coined,
Dreading my love, the loss thereof still fearing!
Yet in the midst of all her pure protestings,
Her faiths, her oaths, her tears, and all were jestings."—*Shakspeare.*

Laburnum—Pensive beauty.
Lady's slipper—Capricious beauty.
Larch—Boldness.
Larkspur—Fickleness.
Laurel—Glory.
Lavender—Distrust.
Lettuce—Cold-hearted.
Lilac—First emotion of love.
Lily—Purity; modesty.
Lily of the Valley—Return of happiness.
Lily, Day—Coquetry.
Lily, Water—Eloquence.
Lily, Yellow—Falsehood.
Locust—Affection beyond the grave.
Love in a Mist—You puzzle me.
Love Lies Bleeding—Hopeless, not heartless.
Lupine—Imagination.

"Alas! how long must true love wait?"
Unto the cruel maid the lover cries.
"Your love for me I rather 'twould turn to hate;"
Which hearing, turns he round and dies.—*Manton*.

Mallow—Sweetness; mildness.
Maple—Reserve.
Marigold—Cruelty.
Marjoram—Blushes.
Marvel of Peru (Four o'clocks)—Timidity.
Mint—Virtue.
Mignonette—Your qualities surpass your charms.
Mistletoe—I surmount all difficulties.
Mock-Orange (Syringa)—Counterfeit.
Morning Glory—Coquetry.

"A merry maid who from her bed arises,
Now greets the sun with open, smiling face,
But later, when cruel night the earth disguises,
She hides her head, leaving to nature but empty space."
—*Manton*.

Maiden's Hair—Discretion.
Magnolia, Grandiflora—Peerless and Proud.
Magnolia, Swamp—Perseverance.
Moss—Maternal love.
Motherwort—Secret love.
Mourning bride—Unfortunate attachment.
Mulberry, Black—I will not survive you.
Mulberry, White—Wisdom.
Mushroom—Suspicion.
Musk-plant—Weakness.
Myrtle—Love faithful in absence.

Narcissus—Egotism.
Nasturtium—Patriotism.
Nettle—Cruelty; slander.
Night Blooming Cereus—Transient beauty.
Nightshade—Bitter truth.

Oak—Hospitality.
Oats—Music.
Oleander—Beware.
Olive-branch—Peace.
Orange-flower—Chastity.
Orchis—Beauty.
Osier—Frankness.
Osmunda—Dreams.

"Sleeping, before me your image I saw,
Pale, haggard, pursued by the Furies it seemed,
And seconds, like years from eternity's store,
Till waking I found that I only had dreamed."—*Manton*.

Pansy—Think of me.
Parsley—Entertainment; feasting.
Passion-flower—Religious fervor; susceptibility.
Pea, Sweet—Departure.
Peach Blossom—This heart is thine.
Peony—Anger.
Pennyroyal—Flee away.
Periwinkle—Sweet remembrances.
Petunia—Less proud than they deem thee.
Phlox—Our souls are united.
Pimpernel—Change.
Pink—Pure affection.
Pink, Double Red—Pure, ardent love.
Pink, Indian—Aversion.
Pink, Variegated—Refusal.
Pink, White—You are fair.
Pomegranate—Folly.
Poppy—Consolation.
Primrose—Inconstancy.

Rhododendron—Agitation.
Rose, Austrian—Thou art all that's lovely.
Rose, Bridal—Happy love.
Rose, Cabbage—Ambassador of love.
Rose, China—Grace.
Rose, Damask—Freshness.
Rose, Jacqueminot—Mellow love.
Rose, Maiden's Blush—If you do love me, you will find me out.
Rose, Moss—Superior merit.
Rose, Moss Rosebud—Confession of love.
Rose, Sweet-briar—Sympathy.
Rose, Tea—Always lovely.
Rose, White—I am worthy of you.
Rose, York and Lancaster—War.
Rose, Wild—Simplicity.
Rue—Disdain.

Saffron—Excess is dangerous.
Sardonia—Irony.
Sensitive Plant—Timidity.
Snap-Dragon—Presumption.
Snowball—Thoughts of Heaven.
Snowdrop—Consolation.
Sorrel—Wit ill-timed.
Spearmint—Warm feelings.
Star of Bethlehem—Reconciliation.
Strawberry—Perfect excellence.
Sumac—Splendor.
Sunflower, Dwarf—Your devout admirer.
Sunflower, Tall—Pride.
Sweet William—Finesse.
Syringa—Memory.

Tansy—I declare against you.
Teazel—Misanthropy.
Thistle—Austerity.
Thorn-Apple—Deceitful charms.
Touch-me-not—Impatience.
Trumpet-flower—Separation.
Tuberose—Dangerous pleasures.
Tulip—Declaration of love.
Tulip, Variegated—Beautiful eyes.
Tulip, Yellow—Hopeless love.

Venus' Flytrap—Have I caught you at last?
Venus' Looking-glass—Flattery.
Verbena—Sensibility.
Violet, Blue—Love.
Violet, White—Modesty.

Wallflower—Fidelity.
Weeping Willow—Forsaken.
Woodbine—Fraternal love.

Yew—Sorrow.

Zennæ—Absent friends.

PALMISTRY, OR HAND-READING.

SCIENCE OF PALMISTRY.

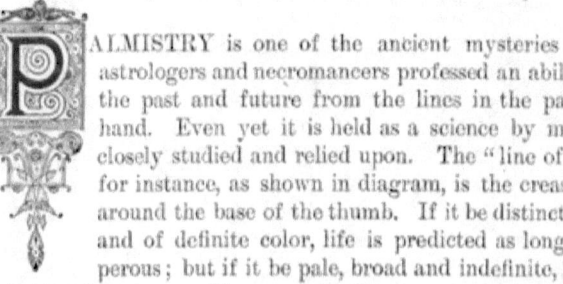

PALMISTRY is one of the ancient mysteries by which astrologers and necromancers professed an ability to read the past and future from the lines in the palm of the hand. Even yet it is held as a science by many, to be closely studied and relied upon. The "line of life," *a c*, for instance, as shown in diagram, is the crease running around the base of the thumb. If it be distinctly marked and of definite color, life is predicted as long and prosperous; but if it be pale, broad and indefinite, life will be full of unhappiness. The years begin at *a* as marked in the diagram, and extend to *c*, in divisions from four to a hundred years. The divisions stand in their consecutive order as follows: 4, 8, 10, 15, 20, 25, 30, 35, 40, 45, 50, 55, 60, 65, 70, 80, 90, 100.

The direction and appearance of *b b*, the line of the head, bears a relation to the mental attributes. If the line be strongly marked, long and definite, there is much strength of character; but if the line is wanting, or incomplete, there is weakness of character and vacillation, and the mind has but little control over the passions and appetites. The line *c o*, is that of the heart. If it be distinct and fully traced, the one on whose hand it is found has a warm heart, full of affection, and will be true to friends. The line *d d*, called saturn or fate, when clear and distinct, and with few if any breaks is considered a sure index of the person being fortunate in most undertakings. The line *e e* is that of the liver, and by its degree of completeness the state of the health is judged. *f f*—in eastern Asia this line's development is watched with much solicitude as the youth advances in years, and if well defined at maturity, there is great rejoicing over the good fortune which it is supposed to indicate. The belt of Venus, shown by *g g*, is an evil line.

The appearance of the lines *m m* are indications by which the length and success of life are foretold. The triple bracelet, *m m m*, having three distinct marks, means a long and happy life.

The varieties in the shape and appearance of the fingers have their subtle meanings, as follows: Smooth fingers, to which belong inspiration, passion, instinct, intuition, grace; the finger with the square tip (L), accompanying theories, methods, intellectual taste, science, combination, literature; the spatulated finger (M), implying a love of things useful and physically perceptible, practical, commercial, agricultural, gymnastic; the conical finger (N), to which belong the plastic arts—painting, sculpture, architecture; the pointed

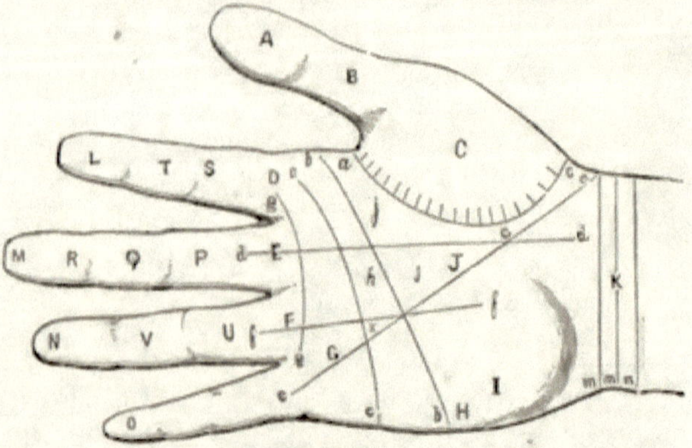

EXPLANATION OF DIAGRAM OF PALM.

A—The Will.
B—Logic
C—The Mount of Venus.
D—The Mount of Jupiter.
E—The Mount of Saturn.
F—The Mount of the Sun.
G—The Mount of Mercury.
H—The Mount of Mars.
I—The Mount of the Moon.
J—The Plain of Mars.
K—The Rascette.

L—Square finger.
M—Spatulate finger
N—Conic finger.
O—Pointed finger.
P—The first phalange.
Q—The second phalange.
R—The third phalange.
S—The first joint (order.)
T—The second joint (philosophy.)
ac—The line of life.

bb—Line of the head.
cc—Line of the heart.
dd—Line of Saturn, or fate.
ee—Line of the liver.
ff—Line of the Sun, or fortune.
gg—Belt of Venus.
h—The quadrangle.
i—The triangle.
j—The upper angle.
k—The inner angle.
m m m—The bracelets of life.

finger (O), which belongs to contemplation, ideality, carelessness of material interests, poetry of the soul and of the heart, a desire for beauty in form and essence.

Similar interpretations are given to the variations in the shape of the hand. There are declared to be seven forms of the human hand, as follows: (1) The hand elementary, or hand with a large palm, the owner of which is content with simple fields of labor, and is not likely to soar above those avocations in which muscle, rather than skill, is required; (2) the hand necessary, or spatulated, which goes a little beyond the first, and aspires to be head gardener, or foreman over the laborer; (3) the hand artistic, or conical, devoted to the fine arts, taste in form and colors, and the beautiful in nature; (4) the useful, or square hand, which is practical, ready for anything, fond of order and system, willing to work either at one thing or another; (5) the knotted hand, which is philosophical, accompanying a delight in the field of research and thought, experiment and application; (6) the psychological, or pointed hand, which loves perfection in mind, and seeks beauty of soul, refinement and culture; (7) the mixed hand, blending the qualities of others of these different types.

The tendencies and traits as shown by the hand should agree with those indicated by the fingers, and also those of the phalanges, or finger joints; just as phrenology and physiognomy agree. The entire hand is read by the palmist, and not simply the lines upon it.

Hands of middle size show a spirit of synopsis, the conception and grouping of details. To large hands often belongs a spirit of minutiæ and trifling detail. The hard stiff hand, which is opened wide and straight with difficulty, indicates intractability, a mind without pliancy, fond of going in grooves.

The person whose fingers tend to bend backward, through suppleness and elasticity, is endowed with sagacity, curiosity and address. Fingers short and thick indicate cruelty. Fingers long and straggling are those of the intriguing and impostors, cheats and sharpers. Persons with very smooth, transparent fingers are curious and indiscreet. If the fingers are smooth and conical it is a sign of talkativeness and levity of mind. The musical mind is accompanied by long, well formed fingers. If the fingers lie perfectly parallel, so that when held together no light can be seen between them, it is a sign of avarice. Strong and knotted fingers mean prudence and capacity.

The swelled muscles or "mounts" in the hand indicate, according to which of them predominate [see explanation] the ruling planets. The sons of Jupiter are strong, easy, jovial, frank; but his step-children are dissipated, vindictive and quarrelsome. The Saturnians are long, thin, pale, gloomy, morose, grumbling. Another class of them are greedy, idle, hungry, sharpers. The children of the Sun are endowed with beauty and grandeur of soul, cheerful but wise. His less favored offspring are small, vain, boasting. The men born under the influence of Mercury are slim, wiry, active, boyish, animated, clever and skillful. The sons of Mars are large, strong-built, red faced, bold, reckless, great eaters and drinkers, fighters, politicians. They may also be burglars, garroters, thieves, brawlers and demagogues. The descendants of the Moon are changeable, capricious, restless, cold, indolent, untruthful, mystical rather than religious, and full of curiosity. The children of Venus are fond of gay clothing, love pleasure, and are amiable, affectionate, compassionate.

NOMS-DES-PLUME.

THE following are the *noms-des-plume* or fictitious names by which the authorship of their works is generally known, of the more noted public writers in the various branches of literature:

A Minute Philosopher—Rev. Charles Kingsley.
An American—J. Fenimore Cooper.
An Irishman—Thomas Moore.
An Old Stager—Mansell B. Field.
Ariel—Stephen R. Fiske.
Artemus Ward—Charles F. Brown.
Arthur Penn (Puck)—H. O. Bonner.
Aunt Fanny—Mrs. Fanny Barrow.
A Yankee—Richard Grant White.

Bab—W. S. Gilbert.
Bailey—Fred Douglass.
Barber Poet—Jacques Jasmin.
Bard of Avon—William Shakspeare.
Bard of Ayreshire—Robert Burns.
Bard of Hope—Thomas Campbell.
Bard of Memory—Samuel Rogers.
Bard of Olney—William Cowper.
Bard of Royal Mount—William Wordsworth.
Bard of Twickenham—Alexander Pope.
Baron Stack—Madame Rattazzi.
Barrabas Whitefeather—Douglas Jerrold.
Benedict Cruiser—George Augustus Sala.
Berwick—James Redpath.
Beulah—Fannie D. Bates.
Boz—Charles Dickens.
Bret Harte—Francis B. Harte.
Brick-top—George C. Small.
Brudder Bones—John F. Scott.

Carl Benson—Charles Astor Bristed.
Carrie Carleton—Mary Booth.
Cecil Davenant—Rev. Davenant Coleridge.
Charlotte Elizabeth—Charlotte Elizabeth Brown.
Chinese Philosopher—Oliver Goldsmith.
Christian Reid—Francis C. Fisher.
Christopher Crawfield—Harriet Beecher Stowe.
Cid Hamet—T. B. Macaulay.
Countess Dash—Viscountess de St. Mars.
Corry O'Lanus—John Stanton.
Cousin Alice—Mrs. Haven.
Currer Bell—Charlotte Bronté.

Dalmocand—George Macdonald.
Dean of St. Patrick—Jonathan Swift.
Dicky Lingard—Harriet Sarah Dunning.
Diedrich Knickerbocker—Washington Irving.
Don John—Jean Ingelow.
Drift-Wood—H. W. Longfellow.

Edward Sexby—Josiah Quincy.
E. H. T.—Earl of Derby.
Elia—Charles Lamb.
Elizabeth Berger—Elizabeth Sheppard.
Elizabeth Wetherell—Susan Warner.
Ellen Louise—Ellen Louise Chandler.
Emile Dalamothe—Emil de Girardin.
English Opium Eater—Thomas de Quincey.
English Palladio—Inigo Jones.
Erodore—Jacob Abbott.
Ethan Spike—Matthew G. Whittier.
Exile of Erin—Rev. M. W. Newman.

Fanny Fern—Sarah Payson Willis (afterwards Mrs. Farrington).
Fanny Forrester—Emily C. Chubbuck (afterwards Mrs. Adoniram Jackson).
Fat Contributor—William Makepeace Thackeray.
Felix Murry—E. A. Duyckinck.
Fitz Noodle (Puck)—B. B. Valentine.
Flaneur—Edmund Yates.
Florence Marryatt—Mrs. Ross Church.
Florence Percy—Elizabeth A. Aken (afterwards Mrs. B. P. Akers).
Francis Herbert—William Cullen Bryant.
Frank Churchill—George Henry Lewes.
Frank Forrester—Henry William Herbert.
Frank Leslie—Frank Collier.

Gail Hamilton—Mary Abigail Dodge.
Galaxy Club—Don Piatt and Mark Twain.
G. A. S.—George Augustus Sala.
Gath—George Alfred Townsend.
Geoffrey Crayon, Esq.—Washington Irving.
George Eliott—Mrs. George H. Lewes.
George Fitz-Boodle—William Makepeace Thackeray.
George Sand—Madame Dudevant.
Gerald Griffin—Dion Boucicault.
Godfrey Sparks—Charles Dickens.
Grace Greenwood—Mrs. L. K. Lippincott.

Hans Breitman—Charles G. Leland.
Hans Yorkel—A. Oakey Hall.
Harry Lorrequer—Charles Lever.
H. E. M.—Cardinal Manning.
Henry Browning—Douglas Jerrold.
Honestus—Benjamin Austin.
Horace Hornem—Lord Byron.

Hosea Bigelow—James Russell Lowell.
Howard Glyndon—Laura C. Belden (afterwards Mrs. Edward C. Searing).
Howard Markham—Mary Cecil Hay.
H. Trusta—Elizabeth Stewart Phelps.
Hugh Littlejohn—John Hugh Lockhart.

Iconoclast—Charles Bradlaugh.
Ikey Solomon, Jr.—William Makepeace Thackeray.
Ik Marvel—Donald G. Mitchell.
Irish Man—Thomas Moore.
Isaac Bickerstaff—Dean Swift.
Isaac Tompkins, Gent—Lord Brougham.
Ivan Ort—Ossian E. Dodge.

Jack Bunsby—Theodore H. Vanderburgh.
Jack Downing, of Downingsville—Seba Smith.
Jack Ketch—Thomas Kibbe Hervey.
James Yellowplush—William Makepeace Thackeray.
Jean Paul—Johann Paul Friedrich Richter.
Jedediah Cheisbotham—Sir Walter Scott.
Jeems Pipes, of Pipesville—Stephen C. Massett.
Jennie June—Mrs. Jennie C. Croly.
J. H. N.—Cardinal Newman.
Joaquin Miller—Cincinnatus Heine Miller.
Josh Billings—Henry W. Shaw.

Kampa Thorpe—Mrs. F. W. Bellamy.
Kate Phusin—John Ruskin.
Kirk White—H. K. White.
Kirwan—Rev. Nicholas Murray.
Kit Carson—Christopher Karson.

Laicus—Rev. Lyman Abbott.
Launcelot Longstaff—Washington Irving.
Launcelot Templeton—Sir Walter Scott.
Learned Blacksmith—Elihu Burritt.
Lemuel Gulliver—Jonathan Swift.
Littlejohn—R. Shelton Mackenzie.
Lord Dundreary—Rev. Charles Kingsley.
Lycidas—John Milton.

Major Jack Downing—Seba Smith.
Malachi Malgrowther—Sir Walter Scott.
Manchester Manufacturer—Richard Cobden.
Margaret Sidney—Mrs. H. B. Stowe.
Marginalia—Edgar Allen Poe.
Marion Harland—Mrs. E. P. Terhune.
Markham Howard—Mary Cecil Hay.
Mark Twain—Samuel L. Clemens.
Max Miller—I. Harley Brock.
Max Mannering—J. G. Holland.
M. de Viellerge—Honoré de Balzac.
Meister Karl—Charles G. Leland.
Michael Angelo Titmarsh—William M. Thackeray.
Miles O'Reilly—Charles G. Halpine.
M. Quad—Charles B. Lewis.
Mrs. Horace Manners—Algernon C. Swinburne.
Mrs. Mary Clavers—Mrs. Caroline M. Kirkland.
Mrs. Partington—B. P. Shillaber.

Ned Buntline—Edward Z. C. Johnson.
Nellie Grahame—Mrs. A. K. Dunning.
Nestor—Sir Richard Steele.
Norma—Elizabeth Aiken.
Nym Crinkle—Andrew C. Wheeler.
Old Bacheldor—George William Curtis.
Old Boy—Thomas Hughes.
Old Public Functionary—James Buchanan.
Old South—Benjamin Austin.
Old Stager—Mansell B. Field.
Oliver Oldschool—Nathan Sargent.
Oliver Optic—William T. Adams.
Oliver Yorke, Esq.—Francis S. Maloney.
Oofty Gooft—Gus Phillips.
Orpheus C. Kerr—Robert H. Newell.
Ossian—James Macpherson.
Ossoli—Margaret Fuller.
Ouida—Louise de la Ramé.
Oxford Graduate—John Ruskin.

Pacificus—Alexander Hamilton.
Parson Brownlow—William G. Brownlow.
Parson Lot—Rev. Charles Kingsley.
Pastor's Wife—Mrs. Austin Phelps.
Paul Prendergast—Douglas Jerrold.
Paul Pry—John Poole.
Peleg Wales—William A. Croffut.
Penholder—Edward Eggleston.
Peter Parley—Samuel G. Goodrich.
Peter Pattieson—Sir Walter Scott.
Peter Pindar—C. F. Lawler.
Peter Plymley—Sidney Smith.
Petroleum V. Nasby—David R. Locke.
Philip Slingsby—Nathaniel P. Willis.
Policeman X.—William M. Thackeray.
Poor Richard—Benjamin Franklin.
Porte Crayon—David H. Strother.

Quaker Poet—John G. Whittier.
Q. K. Philander Doesticks—Mortimer N. Thompson.

Raconteur—Benjamin Perley Poore.
Raoul de Navry—Lady Georgiana Fullerton.
Rev. Dr. Dryasdust—Sir Walter Scott.
Richard Hayward—Fred S. Cozzens.

Sam Slick—Judge T. C. Haliburton.
Saxe Holme—Mrs. Alma C. Johnson.
Seth Spicer—Benjamin F. Gould.
Sir Marmaduke—Theodore Tilton.
Slingsby Lawrence—George Henry Lewes.
Solon Shingle—Caleb Dunn.
Sophie May—Rebecca S. Clarke.
Sparrowgrass—Fred S. Cozzens.
Stedman—Elizabeth C. Dodge (afterwards Mrs. Kinney).
Strauss, Jr.—Kate Field.
Susan Coolidge—Susan C. Woolsey.

Tag, Rag and Bobtail—I. Disraeli.
The Disbanded Volunteer—Joseph Barker.
The Landgrave—Mrs. T. K. Harvey.
The Misses Wetherell—Susan and Anna Warner.
The Vagabond—Adam Badeau.
Thomas Maitland—Robert Buchanan.
Thomas Rowley—Thomas Chatterton.
Tiger Lily—Lillie Devereux Blake.
Timon—Donald G. Mitchell.
Timothy Tickler—John K. Paulding.
Timothy Titcomb—J. G. Holland.
Triangle—Frank Bellew.
T. T.—Theodore Tilton.

U. Donough Outis—Richard Grant White.
Una Savin—Mrs. George H. Hepworth.
Uncle Herbert—T. S. Arthur.
Uncle Jerry—Mrs. Charles E. Porter.
Uncle Paul—Samuel Barham, Jr.
Uncle Toby—Rev. T. H. Miller.
Uncle Willis—Stephen W. Tilton.

Vandianus—Thomas Hughes.
Vanderwerken—William Cooper.
Vandyke Brown—William Penn Brannon.
Veteran Observer—Edward D. Mansfield.
V. Hugo Dusenbury (Puck)—H. C. Benner.
Viator—Benjamin O. Taylor.
Vicar of Bray—S. Alleyn.
Victor Granella—R. Tardieu.
Violet Fane—Mrs. Cecil Singleton.

Walking Gentleman—T. C. Grattan.
Waters—William H. Russell.
Waverley—Sir Walter Scott.
Weaver Poet—William Thorne.
Wetherell—Susan Warner.
What'shisname—E. C. Massey.
Widow Bedott—Frances M. Whatcher.
Wild Edgerton—Brock McVickar.
William Edward Sidney—Beverly Tucker.
Wonderful Quiz—James Russell Lowell.

Yankee—Richard Grant White.
Yawcob Strauss—Charles F. Adams.
Young American—Alexander S. Mackenzie.
Young Rapid—Col. T. Allston Browne.

Z.—Hannah Moore.
Zekel Allspice—John Cooper Vail.
Zeta—James Anthony Froude.

TABLE Showing the Yield Per Acre (in Pounds) of Sundry Fruits, Vegetables and Cereals.

	Yield.		Yield.
Apples	8,000	Oats	1,840
Barley	1,600	Onions	2,800
Beans	2,000	Parsnips	11,300
Cabbages	10,000	Pears	5,000
Carrots	6,800	Peas	1,920
Cherries	2,000	Plums	2,000
Chinque foil grass	9,600	Potatoes	7,500
Grass	7,000	Turnips	8,420
Hay	4,000	Vetches, green	9,800
Hops	46[illegible]	Wheat	1,200
Mangel Wurzel	22,000		

Ages Attained by Various Animals.

Rabbits	5 to 7 years	Deer	18 to 20 years	Ravens average	100 years
Squirrels	6 to 9 years	Bears	18 to 20 years	Eagles average	100 years
Sheep	7 to 10 years	Cows	18 to 20 years	Tortoises average	100 years
Dogs	14 to 20 years	Horses	25 to 30 years	Swans average	300 years
Foxes	12 to 16 years	Porpoises	28 to 30 years	Elephants average	400 years
Cats	12 to 16 years	Lions	60 to 70 years	Whales sometimes attain	1,000 years
Pigs	15 to 20 years	Camels average	100 years		

AUTHOR'S REFERENCES

QUOTATIONS IN PROSE AND POETRY.

JOSEPH ADDISON.

My voice is still for war.
Gods! Can a Roman senate long debate
Which of the two to choose, slavery or death?

A day, an hour, of virtuous liberty
Is worth a whole eternity in bondage.

When vice prevails, and impious men bear sway,
The post of honor is a private station.

And, pleased the Almighty's orders to perform,
Rides in the whirlwind and directs the storm.

FRANCIS BACON.

No pleasure is comparable to the standing upon the vantage ground of truth.

A little philosophy inclineth a man's mind to atheism, but depth in philosophy bringeth men's minds about to religion.

Some books are to be tasted, others to be swallowed, and some few are to be chewed and digested.

Reading maketh a full man, conference a ready man, and writing an exact man.

Knowledge is power.

God made the country, and man made the town.

My Lord St. Albans said that nature did never put her precious jewels into a garret four stories high, and therefore that exceeding tall men had ever very empty heads.

EDMUND BURKE.

There is, however, a limit at which forbearance ceases to be a virtue.

The march of the human mind is slow.

All government, indeed every human benefit and enjoyment, every virtue and every prudent act, is founded on compromise and barter.

He that wrestles with us strengthens our nerves and sharpens our skill.

Our antagonist is our helper.

He was not merely a chip off the old block, but the old block itself.

SAMUEL BUTLER.

Some have been beaten till they know
What wood a cudgel's of by th' blow;
Some kicked until they cou' feel whether
A shoe be Spanish or neat's leather.

Quoth she, I've heard old cunning stagers
Say, fools for arguments use wagers.

To swallow gudgeons ere they're catched,
And count their chickens ere they're hatched.

For those that fly may fight again,
Which he can never do that's slain.

He that complies against his will
Is of his own opinion still.

LORD BYRON.

Maid of Athens, ere we part,
Give, O, give me back my heart.

My native land, good night!

On with the dance! let joy be unconfined.

And there was mounting in hot haste,

Or whispering, with white lips, "The foe!
They come! they come!"

The thorns which I have reaped are of the tree
I planted; they have torn me, and I bleed;
I should have known what fruit would spring from such a seed.

Fare thee well! and if forever,
Still forever fare *thee well*.

My boat is on the shore,
And my bark is on the sea.

He was the mildest-mannered man
That ever scuttled ship or cut a throat.

'Tis strange, but true; for truth is always strange;
Stranger than fiction.

THOMAS CAMPBELL.

'Tis distance lends enchantment to the view,
And robes the mountain in its azure hue.

Another's sword has laid him low,
Another's and another's;
And every hand that dealt the blow,
Ah me! it was his brother's!

'Tis the sunset of life gives me mystical lore,
And coming events cast their shadows before.

Oh, leave this barren spot to me!
Spare, woodman, spare the beechen tree.

COLLEY CIBBER.

Now, by St. Paul, the work goes bravely on.

Off with his head! So much for Buckingham.

Perish that thought! No, never be it said
That Fate itself could awe the soul of Richard.
Hence, babbling dreams! you threaten here in vain;
Conscience, avaunt! Richard's himself again!
Hark! the shrill trumpet sounds to horse; away!
My soul's in arms and eager for the fray.

As good be out of the world as out of the fashion.

We shall find no fiend in hell can match the fury of a disappointed woman—scorned! slighted! dismissed without a parting pang!

This business will never hold water.

Stolen sweets are best.

Possession is eleven points in the law.

Words are but empty thanks.

WILLIAM CONGREVE.

Music hath charms to soothe the savage beast,
To soften rocks, or bend a knotted oak.

Heaven has no rage like love to hatred turned;
Nor hell a fury like a woman scorned.

Thus grief still treads upon the heels of pleasure;
Married in haste, we may repent at leisure.

Defer not till to-morrow to be wise;
To-morrow's sun to thee may never rise.

JOHN DRYDEN.

Whate'er he did was done with so much ease,
In him alone 'twas natural to please.

And all to leave what with his toil he won
To that unfeathered two-legged thing—a son.

Resolved to ruin or to rule the state.

Beware the fury of a patient man.

Better to hunt in fields for health unbought,
Than fee the doctor for a nauseous draught.
The wise for cure on exercise depend;
God never made his work for man to mend.

None but the brave deserves the fair.

Fallen, fallen, fallen, fallen,
Fallen from his high estate,
And weltering in his blood;
Deserted, at his utmost need,
By those his former bounty fed;
On the bare earth exposed he lies,
With not a friend to close his eyes.

Ill habits gather by unseen degrees;
As brooks make rivers, rivers run to seas.

Errors like straws upon the surface flow;
He who would search for pearls must dive below.

Forgiveness to the injured does belong;
But they ne'er pardon who have done the wrong.

When I consider life, 'tis all a cheat;
Yet, fooled with hope, men favor the deceit;
Trust on, and think to-morrow will repay:
To-morrow's falser than the former day;
'Tis worse, and, while it says we shall be blest
With some new joys, cuts off what we possest.
Strange cozenage! none would live past years again,
Yet all hope pleasure in what yet remain,
And from the dregs of life think to receive
What the first sprightly running could not give.

Bless the hand that gave the blow.

As sure as a gun.

BENJAMIN FRANKLIN.

God helps them that help themselves.

Plough deep while sluggards sleep.

Never leave that till to-morrow which you can do to-day.

Three removes are as bad as a fire.

Vessels large may venture more,
But little boats should keep near shore.

He has paid dear, very dear, for his whistle.

ROBERT HERRICK.

Some asked me where the rubies grew,
And nothing I did say,
But with my finger pointed to
The lips of Julia.

Gather ye rose-buds while ye may,
Old Time is still a-flying,
And this same flower that smiles to-day,
To-morrow will be dying.

You say to me-wards, your affection's strong;
Pray love me little, so you love me long.

But ne'er the rose without the thorn.

Attempt the end, and never stand to doubt;
Nothing's so hard but search will find it out.

THOMAS GRAY.

And happiness so swiftly flies,
Thought would destroy their paradise.
No more;—where ignorance is bliss
'Tis folly to be wise.

The curfew tolls the knell of parting day,
The lowing herd winds slowly o'er the lea,
The plowman homeward plods his weary way,
And leaves the world to darkness and to me.

The boast of heraldry, the pomp of power,
And all that beauty, all that wealth e'er gave,
Await alike the inevitable hour,
The paths of glory lead but to the grave.

Full many a gem of purest ray serene
The dark unfathomed caves of ocean bear;
Full many a flower is born to blush unseen
And waste its sweetness on the desert air.

Far from the madding crowd's ignoble strife,
Their sober wishes never learned to stray;
Along the cool sequestered vale of life
They kept the noiseless tenor of their way.

Here rests his head upon the lap of earth,
A youth to fortune and to fame unknown;
Fair Science frowned not on his humble birth,
And Melancholy marked him for her own.

OLIVER GOLDSMITH.

Such is the patriot's boast, where'er we roam,
His first, best country, ever is at home.

Where wealth and freedom reign, contentment fails,
And honour sinks where commerce long prevails.

For just experience tells, in every soil,
That those that think must govern those that toil.

His best companions, innocence and health,
And his best riches, ignorance of wealth.

And in that town a dog was found,
As many dogs there be,
Both mongrel, puppy, whelp and hound,
And curs of low degree.

Good people all, with one accord,
Lament for Madam Blaize,
Who never wanted a good word
From those who spoke her praise.

Measures, not men, have always been my mark.

I'll be with you in the squeezing of a lemon.

I love everything that's old: old friends, old times, old manners, old books, old wine.

Ask me no questions and I'll tell you no fibs.

SAMUEL JOHNSON.

If he does really think that there is no distinction between virtue and vice, why, sir, when he leaves our houses, let us count our spoons.

Sir, a woman preaching is like a dog's walking on his hind legs. It is not done well; but you are surprised to find it done at all.

Much may be made of a Scotchman if he be caught young.

HENRY W. LONGFELLOW.

Tell me not in mournful numbers,
"Life is but an empty dream!"
For the soul is dead that slumbers,
And things are not what they seem.

Art is long, and time is fleeting,
And our hearts, though stout and brave,
Still, like muffled drums, are beating
Funeral marches to the grave.

There is a Reaper whose name is Death,
And, with his sickle keen,
He reaps the bearded grain at a breath,
And the flowers that grow between.

And the night shall be filled with music,
And the cares that infest the day
Shall fold their tents, like the Arabs,
And as silently steal away.

The heights by great men reached and kept
Were not attained by sudden flight,
But they, while their companions slept,
Were toiling upward in the night.

There is no flock, however watched and tended,
But one dead lamb is there;
There is no fireside, howsoe'er defended,
But has one vacant chair.

There is no Death! What seems so is transition;
This life of mortal breath
Is but a suburb of the life elysian,
Whose portal we call Death.

JOHN MILTON.

Where peace
And rest can never dwell, hope never comes
That comes at all.

Awake, arise, or be forever fallen.

Who overcomes
By force, hath overcome but half his foe.

Accuse not Nature, she hath done her part;
Do thou but thine.

How gladly would I meet
Mortality my sentence, and be earth
Insensible! how glad would lay me down
As in my mother's lap!

So may'st thou live, till like ripe fruit thou drop
Into thy mother's lap.

Nor love thy life, nor hate; but what thou liv'st
Live well; how long or short permit to heaven.

Rocks whereon greatest men have oftest wrecked.

The childhood shows the man,
As morning shows the day.

What boots it at one gate to make defense
And at another to let in the foe?

For evil news rides post, while good news baits.

It were a journey like the path to heaven,
To help you find them.

Swinish gluttony
Ne'er looks to Heaven amidst his gorgeous feast,
But, with besotted base ingratitude,
Crams, and blasphemes his feeder.

Fame is no plant that grows on mortal soil.

Sport, that wrinkled Care derides,
And Laughter holding both his sides;
Come, and trip it as you go
On the light fantastic toe.

License they mean when they cry liberty.

THOMAS MOORE.

This narrow isthmus 'twixt two boundless seas,
The past, the future—two eternities.

O, ever thus from childhood's hour
I've seen my fondest hopes decay:
I never loved a tree or flower
But 'twas the first to fade away.
I never nursed a dear gazelle
To glad me with its soft black eye,
But when it came to know me well,
And love me, it was sure to die.

Rich and rare were the gems she wore,
And a bright gold ring on her wand she bore.

Shall I ask the brave soldier who fights by my side
In the cause of mankind, if our creeds agree?

'Tis the last rose of summer,
Left blooming alone.

You may break, you may shatter, the vase if you will,
But the scent of the roses will hang round it still.

My only books
Were woman's looks,
And folly's all they've taught me.

Oft in the stilly night,
Ere Slumber's chain has bound me,
Fond memory brings the light
Of other days around me;
The smiles, the tears,
Of boyhood's years,
The words of love then spoken;
The eyes that shone,
Now dimmed and gone,
The cheerful hearts now broken.

ALEXANDER POPE.

Pleased to the last, he crops the flowery food,
And licks the hand just raised to shed his blood.

Hope springs eternal in the human breast:
Man never is, but always to be blest.
The soul, uneasy and confined from home,
Rests and expatiates in a life to come.

Lo, the poor Indian! whose untutored mind
Sees God in clouds, or hears Him in the wind;
His soul proud Science never taught to stray
Far as the solar walk or milky way.

A little learning is a dangerous thing;
Drink deep, or taste not the Pierian spring:
There shallow draughts intoxicate the brain,
And drinking largely sobers us again.

To err is human, to forgive divine.

He's armed without that's innocent within.

Praise undeserved is scandal in disguise.

Who dares think one thing, and another tell,
My heart detests him as the gates of hell.

He serves me most who serves his country best.

Whatever day
Makes man a slave takes half his worth away.

Know then thyself; presume not God to scan;
The proper study of mankind is man.

Honor and shame from no condition rise;
Act well your part, there all the honor lies.

A wit's a feather, and a chief a rod;
An honest man's the noblest work of God.

'Tis education forms the common mind;
Just as the twig is bent the tree's inclined.

Who shall decide, when doctors disagree,
And soundest casuists doubt, like you and me?

SHAKSPEARE.

There's nothing ill can dwell in such a temple:
If the ill spirit have so fair a house,
Good things will strive to dwell with 't.
—*The Tempest.*

That man that hath a tongue, I say, is no man,
If with his tongue he cannot win a woman.
—*Ibid.*

Why, then the world's mine oyster,
Which I with sword will open.
—*Merry Wives of Windsor.*

The rankest compound of villainous smell that ever offended nostril. —*Ibid.*

Some rise by sin, and some by virtue fall.
—*Measure for Measure.*

Condemn the fault, and not the actor of it.
—*Ibid.*

O, it is excellent
To have a giant's strength; but it is tyrannous
To use it like a giant. —*Ibid.*

The weariest and most loathed worldly life
That age, penury, and imprisonment
Can lay on nature is a paradise
To what we fear of death. —*Ibid.*

What's mine is yours, and what is yours is mine. —*Ibid.*

Benedick, the married man. —*Ibid.*

I thank God I am as honest as any man living that is an old man and no honester than I.—*Much Ado About Nothing.*

O that he were here to write me down an ass!—*Ibid.*

Affliction may one day smile again; and till then, sit thee down, sorrow!—*Love's Labor Lost.*

A lion among ladies is a most dreadful thing.
—*Midsummer Night's Dream.*

They are as sick, that surfeit with too much, as they that starve with nothing.—*Merchant of Venice.*

You take my house when you do take the prop
That doth sustain my house; you take my life
When you do take the means whereby I live.
—*Ibid.*

And so, from hour to hour, we ripe and ripe,
And then, from hour to hour, we rot and rot;
And thereby hangs a tale.
—*As You Like It.*

Blow, blow, thou winter wind,
Thou art not so unkind
As man's ingratitude. —*Ibid.*

He that wants money, means, and content is without these good friends.—*Ibid.*

I had rather have a fool to make me merry than experience to make me sad.—*Ibid.*

Men are April when they woo, December when they wed.—*Ibid.*

Chewing the food of sweet and bitter fancy. —*Ibid.*

No sooner met but they looked, no sooner looked but they loved, no sooner loved but they sighed, no sooner sighed but they asked one another the reason, no sooner knew the reason but they sought the remedy.—*Ibid.*

There's small choice in rotten apples.
—*Taming the Shrew.*

Who wooed in haste and means to wed at leisure. —*Ibid.*

And thereby hangs a tale. —*Ibid.*

My cake is dough.—*Ibid.*

Some are born great, some achieve greatness, and some have greatness thrust upon 'em.—*Twelfth Night.*

MATTHEW PRIOR.

From ignorance one comfort flows;
The only wretched are the wise.

Be to her virtues very kind;
Be to her faults a little blind.

They never taste who always drink;
They always talk who never think.

Who breathes must suffer, and who thinks must mourn;
And he alone is blessed who ne'er was born.

SIR WALTER SCOTT.

O, what a tangled web we weave,
When first we practice to deceive!

O woman! in our hours of ease
Uncertain, coy, and hard to please,
And variable as the shade
By the light quivering aspen made;
When pain and anguish wring the brow,
A ministering angel thou!

"Charge, Chester, charge! on, Stanley, on!"
Were the last words of Marmion.

Sleep the sleep that knows not breaking,
Morn of toil, nor night of breaking.

Sea of upturned faces.

And better had they ne'er been born,
Who read to doubt, or read to scorn.

SIDNEY SMITH.

Daniel Webster struck me like a steam-engine in trousers.

Macaulay is like a book in breeches. . . . He has occasional flashes of silence, that makes his conversation perfectly delightful.

The schoolboy whips his taxed top; the beardless youth manages his taxed horse, with a taxed bridle, on a taxed road; and the dying Englishman, pouring his medicine, which has paid seven per cent. into a spoon that has paid fifteen per cent. flings himself back upon his chintz bed, which has paid twenty-two per cent. and expires in the arms of an apothecary who has paid a license of a hundred pounds for the privilege of putting him to death.

JONATHAN SWIFT.

So, naturalists observe, a flea
Has smaller fleas that on him prey;
And these have smaller still to bite 'em,
And so proceed *ad infinitum.*

And he gave it for his opinion, that whoever could make two ears of corn, or two blades of grass, to grow upon a spot of ground where only one grew before, would deserve better of mankind, and do more essential service to his country than the whole race of politicians put together.

Bread is the staff of life.

Censure is the tax a man pays to the public for being eminent.

I shall be like that tree: I shall die at the top.

ALFRED TENNYSON.

Howe'er it be, it seems to me,
'Tis only noble to be good.
Kind hearts are more than coronets,
And simple faith than Norman blood.

Blow, bugle, blow, set the wild echoes flying;
Blow, bugle; answer echoes, dying, dying, dying.
O love, they die in yon rich sky,
They faint on hill or field or river:
Our echoes roll from soul to soul,
And grow forever and forever.
Blow, bugle, blow, set the wild echoes flying,
And answer, echoes, answer, dying, dying, dying.

'Tis better to have loved and lost
Than never to have loved at all.

There lives more faith in honest doubt,
Believe me, than in half the creeds.

One God, one law, one element,
And one far-off divine event,
To which the whole creation moves.

Ah Christ, that it were possible
For one short hour to see
The souls we loved, that they might tell us
What and where they be.

Theirs not to make reply,
Theirs not to reason why,
Theirs but to do and die.

DANIEL WEBSTER.

Whatever makes men good Christians makes them good citizens.

Sink or swim, live or die, survive or perish, I give my hand and my heart to this vote.

The people's government, made for the people, made by the people, and answerable to the people.

One country, one constitution, one destiny.

I was born in America; I live an American; I shall die an American.

EDWARD YOUNG.

Be wise to-day; 'tis madness to defer.

Procrastination is the thief of time.

Ah! how unjust to nature and himself
Is thoughtless, thankless, inconsistent man.

Man wants but little, nor that little long.

That life is long which answers life's great end.

Death loves a shining mark, a signal blow.

Too low they build who build beneath the stars.

Think naught a trifle, though it small appear;
Small sands the mountain, moments make the year,
And trifles life.

MISCELLANEOUS PROSE QUOTATIONS.

Man proposes, but God disposes.

The real Simon pure.—*Susannah Centlive.*

The balance of power.—*Sir Robert Walpole.*

Facts are stubborn things.—*Tobias Smollett.*

What will Mrs. Grundy say?—*Thomas Morton.*

For a man's house is his castle.—*Sir Edward Coke.*

It is the lot of man but once to die.—*George Herbert.*

Love me little, love me long.—*Christopher Marlowe.*

A delusion, a mockery, and a snare.—*Lord Denman.*

Necessity, the mother of invention.—*George Farquhar.*

Of two evils, the less is always to be chosen. —*Thomas à Kempis.*

Silence is deep as eternity, speech is shallow as time.—*Thomas Carlyle.*

Hanging was the worst use man could be put to.—*Sir Henry Wotton.*

A liberty to that only which is good, just and honest.—*John Winthrop.*

Actions of the last age are like almanacs of the last year.—*Sir John Denham.*

Necessity is the argument of tyrants, it is the creed of slaves.—*William Pitt.*

Put your trust in God, my boys, and keep your powder dry.—*Colonel Blacker.*

An indestructible union composed of indestructible states.—*Salmon P. Chase.*

I could not love thee, dear, so much, loved I not honor more.—*Richard Lovelace.*

That to live by one man's will became the cause of all men's misery.—*Richard Hooker.*

They are never alone that are accompanied with noble thoughts.—*Sir Philip Sidney.*

The world is a comedy to those that think, a tragedy to those who feel.—*Horace Walpole.*

Nothing except a battle lost can be half so melancholy as a battle won.—*Duke of Wellington.*

Certainly, this is a duty, not a sin. "Cleanliness is, indeed, next to Godliness."—*John Wesley.*

To be prepared for war is one of the most effectual means of preserving peace.—*George Washington.*

Let us embrace, and from this very moment vow an eternal misery together.—*Thomas Otway.*

To the memory of the man, first in war, first in peace, and first in the hearts of his countrymen.—*Henry Lee.*

God sifted a whole nation that he might send choice grain over into this wilderness.—*William Stoughton.*

It is a maxim with me that no man was ever written out of reputation but by himself.—*Richard Bentley.*

The noblest mind the best contentment has. —*Edmund Spencer.*
A bold bad man.—*Ibid.*

We join ourselves to no party that does not carry the flag and keep step to the music of the Union.—*Rufus Choate.*

We are ne'er like angels till our passion dies.—*Thomas Dekken.*
Honest labor bears a lovely face.—*Ibid.*

Go poor devil, get thee gone; why should I hurt thee? This world surely is wide enough to hold both thee and me.—*Lawrence Sterne.*

He [Sir John Hampden] had a head to contrive, a tongue to persuade and a hand to execute any mischief.—*Edward Hyde Clarendon.*

Then he will talk—good gods! how he will talk.—*Nathaniel Lee.*
When Greeks joined Greeks, then was the tug of war.—*Ibid.*

There is many a rich stone laid up in the bowels of the earth, many a fair pearl laid up in the bosom of the sea, that never was seen, nor never shall be.—*Bishop Hall.*

It beareth the name of Vanity Fair, because the town where it is kept is lighter than vanity.—*John Bunyan.*
He that is down needs fear no fall.—*Ibid.*

I remember that a wise friend of mine did usually say, That which is everybody's business is nobody's business.—*Izaak Walton.*
No man can lose what he never had.—*Ibid.*

I never could believe that Providence had sent a few men into the world, ready booted and spurred to ride, and millions ready saddled and bridled to be ridden.—*Richard Rumbold.*

Corrupt freemen are the worst of slaves.—*David Garrick.*

Over the hills and far away.—*John Gay.*
While there is life there's hope, he cried.—*Ibid.*

Call things by their right names. * * * Glass of brandy and water! That is the current but not the appropriate name; ask for a glass of liquid fire and distilled damnation.—*Robert Hall.*

Health is the second blessing that we mortals are capable of; a blessing that money cannot buy.—*Francis Quarles.*
The next way home's the farthest way about.—*Ibid.*

When I see a merchant over-polite to his customers, begging them to taste a little brandy, and throwing half his goods on the counter, thinks I, that man has an axe to grind.—*Charles Miner.*

Take a straw and throw it up into the air; you may see by that which way the wind is. —*John Selden.*
Thou little thinkest what a little foolery governs the world.—*Ibid.*

If I were an American, as I am an Englishman, while a foreign troop was landed in my country, I never would lay down my arms—never—never—never.—*Earl of Chatham.*
Where law ends, tyranny begins.—*Ibid.*

He rolls it under his tongue as a sweet morsel.—*Matthew Henry.*
None so deaf as those that will not hear.—*Ibid.*
None so blind as those that will not see.—*Ibid.*

The multitude is always in the wrong.—*Lord Roscommon.*

We grieved, we sighed, we wept; we never blushed before.—*Abraham Cowley.*
Words that weep and tears that speak.—*Ibid.*

Calamity, a man's true touchstone.—*Beaumont and Fletcher's Plays.*
Thou wilt scarce be a man before thy mother.—*Ibid.*
What's one man's poison, signor, is another's meat and drink.—*Ibid.*

The God who gave us life gave us liberty at the same time.—*Thomas Jefferson.*
We mutually pledge to each other our lives, our fortunes and our sacred honor.—*Ibid.*
Error of opinion may be tolerated where reason is left free to combat it.—*Ibid.*

The secret of success is constancy to purpose.—*Benjamin Disraeli.*
Youth is a blunder; Manhood a struggle; Old age a regret.—*Ibid.*
You know who critics are? the men who have failed in literature and art.—*Ibid.*

She [the Roman Catholic church] may still exist in undiminished vigor when some traveler from New Zealand shall, in the midst of a vast solitude, take his stand on a broken arch of London Bridge to sketch the ruins of St. Paul's.—*Thomas B. Macauley.*

The stone that is rolling can gather no moss.—*Thomas Tusser.*
Better late than never.—*Ibid.*
Naught venture, naught have.—*Ibid.*
Look ere thou leap, see ere thou go.—*Ibid.*
For buying or selling of a pig in a poke.—*Ibid.*

He left a paper sealed up, wherein were found three articles as his last will: "I owe much, I have nothing, I give the rest to the poor."—*Francis Rabelais.*
By robbing Peter he paid Paul, * * * and hoped to catch larks if ever the heavens should fall.—*Ibid.*

I do not know what I may appear to the world, but to myself I seem to be only like a boy playing on the seashore, and diverting myself in now and then finding a smooth pebble, or a prettier shell than ordinary, whilst the great ocean of truth lay undiscovered before me.—*Isaac Newton.*

Whatever is worth doing at all is worth doing well.—*Chesterfield.*
I knew one, a very covetous, sordid fellow, who used to say "Take care of the pence, for the pounds will take care of themselves."—*Ibid.*
Despatch is the soul of business.—*Ibid.*

These are the times which try men's souls. —*Thomas Paine.*
The sublime and the ridiculous are often so nearly related that it is difficult to class them separately. One step above the sublime makes the ridiculous, and one step above the ridiculous makes the sublime again.—*Ibid.*

Nothing is more simple than greatness; indeed to be simple is to be great.—*Ralph Waldo Emerson.*
Is not marriage an open question, when it is alleged from the beginning of the world that such as are in the institution wish to get out, and such as are out wish to get in.—*Ibid.*

Their heads sometimes so little that there is no room for wit; sometimes so long that there is no wit for so much room.—*Thomas Fuller.*

They that marry ancient people, merely in expectation to bury them, hang themselves, in hope that one will come and cut the halter. —*Ibid.*

That this nation under God shall have a new birth of freedom, and that government of the people, by the people, for the people, shall not perish from the earth.—*Abraham Lincoln.*

With malice towards none, with charity for all, with firmness in the right, as God gives us to see the right.—*Ibid.*

The newspapers! Sir, they are the most villainous—licentious—abominable—infernal —not that I ever read them. No, I make it a rule never to look into a newspaper.—*Richard Brinsley Sheridan.*

Such protection as vultures give to lambs. —*Ibid.*

Conscience has no more to do with gallantry than it has with politics.—*Ibid.*

Do well and right, and let the world sink.—*Sir John Suckling.*

His bark is worse than his bite.—*Ibid.*

God's mill grinds slow, but sure.—*Ibid.*

Help thyself, and God will help thee. —*Ibid.*

The mouse that has but one hole is quickly taken.—*Ibid.*

A dwarf on a giant's shoulders sees further of the two.—*Ibdi.*

Cæsar had his Brutus, Charles the First, his Cromwell; and George the Third—("Treason!" cried the Speaker)—*may profit by their example.* If *this* be treason, make the most of it.—*Patrick Henry.*

Is life so dear, or peace so sweet, as to be purchased at the price of chains and slavery? Forbid it, Almighty God! I know not what course others may take; but as for me, give me liberty or give me death!—*Ibid.*

The second day of July, 1776, will be the most memorable epoch in the history of America. I am apt to believe that it will be celebrated by the succeeding generations as the great anniversary festival. It ought to be commemorated as the day of deliverance, by solemn acts of devotion to God Almighty. It ought to be solemnized with pomp and parade, with shows, games, sports, guns, bells, bonfires, and illuminations from one end of this continent to the other, from this time forward for evermore.—*John Adams.*

I would do what I pleased, and doing what I pleased, I should have my will, and having my will I should be contented; and when one is contented, there is no more to be desired, and when there is no more to be desired there is an end of it.—*Miguel de Cervantes.*

Blessings on him who invented sleep, the mantle that covers all human thoughts, the food that appeases hunger, the drink that quenches thirst, the fire that warms cold, the cold that moderates heat, and lastly, the general coin that purchases all things, the balance and weight that equals the shepherd with the king, and the simple with the wise. —*Ibid.*

MISCELLANEOUS POETIC QUOTATIONS.

'Tis not the whole of life to live
Nor all of death to die.
—*James Montgomery.*

Did you ever hear of Captain Wattle?
He was all for love and little for the battle.
—*Charles Dibden.*

Except wind stands as never it stood;
It is an ill wind turn none to good.
—*Thomas Tusser.*

Who goeth a borrowing
Goeth a sorrowing. —*Ibid.*

We bear it calmly though a ponderous woe,
And still adore the hand that gives the blow.
—*John Pomfret.*

Heaven is not always angry when he strikes.
But most chastises those whom he most likes.
Ibid.

Delightful task! to rear the tender thought,
To teach the young idea how to shoot.
—*James Thomson.*

Could we forbear dispute and practice love,
We should agree as angels do above.
—*Edmund Waller.*

My God, my Father and my Friend,
Do not forsake me at my end.
—*Earl of Roscommon.*

The world's a theatre, the earth a stage,
Which God and nature do with actors fill.
—*Thomas Heywood.*

'Tis expectation makes a blessing dear,
Heaven were not heaven if we knew what it were. —*Sir John Suckling.*

If she seem not chaste to me,
What care I how chaste she be?
—*Sir Walter Raleigh.*

Young men think old men are fools;
But old men know young men are fools.
—*George Chapman.*

How dear to my heart are the scenes of my childhood;
When fond recollection presents them to view. —*Samuel Wordsworth.*

The old oaken bucket, the iron-bound bucket,
The moss covered bucket which hung in the well. —*Ibid.*

Perhaps it was right to dissemble your love,
But—why did you kick me down stairs.
—*J. P. Kemble.*

True patriots all; for be it understood
We left our country for our country's good.
—*George Barrington.*

You'd scarce expect one of my age
To speak in public on the stage.
—*David Everett.*

Then join in hand, brave Americans all;
By uniting we stand, by dividing we fall.
—*John Dickinson.*

Be England what she will,
With all her faults she is my country still.
—*Charles Churchill.*

The melancholy days have come; the saddest of the year,
Of wailing winds, and naked woods, and meadows brown and sear.
—*William Cullen Bryant.*

When the sun's last rays are fading
Into twilight bright and dim.
—*Theodore L. Barker.*

Come in the evening, or come in the morning;
Come when you are looked for, or come with-without warning.
—*Thomas O. Davis.*

But, spite of all criticising elves,
Those who would make us feel must feel themselves. —*Charles Churchill.*

Care to our coffin adds a nail, no doubt,
And every grin so merry, draws one out.
—*John Wolcot.*

How sleep the brave who sink to rest,
By all their country's wishes blessed!
—*William Collins.*

Immodest words admit of no defense,
For want of decency is want of sense.
—*Earl of Roscommon.*

How much a dunce that has been sent to roam
Excels a dunce that has been kept at home.

A moral, sensible and well-bred man
Will not affront me, and no other can.

I am monarch of all I survey,
My right there is none to dispute.
—*William Cowper.*

'Mid pleasures and palaces though we may roam,
Be it ever so humble there is no place like home. —*J. Howard Payne.*

And I oft have heard defended,
Little said is soonest mended.
—*George Wither.*

Though this may be play to you,
'Tis death to us.
—*Roger L'Estrange.*

He was a man
Who stole the livery of the court of heaven
To serve the devil in. —*Robert Pollok.*

Breathes there the man with soul so dead,
Who never to himself hath said,
This is my own, my native land.
—*Sir Walter Scott.*

And dar'st thou then
To beard the lion in his den,
The Douglas in his hall? —*Ibid.*

Strike—for your altars and your fires,
Strike—for the green graves of your sires;
God and your native land.
—*Fitz-Green Halleck.*

Of right and wrong, wrong he taught.
Truths as refined as ever Athens heard;
And (strange to tell) he practiced what he preached. —*John Armstrong.*

They sin who tell us love can die,
With life all other passions fly,
All others are but vanity.
—*Robert Smither.*

That best portion of a good man's life,
His little nameless, unremembered acts
Of kindness and of love.
—*William Wordsworth.*

The feather, whence the pen
Was shaped that traced the lives of these good men,
Dropped from an angel's wing. —*Ibid.*

Let the world slide, let the world go;
A fig for care, and a fig for woe!
If I can't pay, why I can owe,
And death makes equal the high and low.
—*John Heywood.*

He prayeth best, who loveth best
All things, both great and small.
—*Samuel Taylor Coleridge.*

No man e'er felt the halter draw,
With good opinion of the law.
—*Robert Burns.*

Man's inhumanity to man
Makes countless thousands mourn.
—*Ibid.*

Should auld acquaintance be forgot,
And never brought to min'?
Should auld acquaintance be forgot,
And days o' auld lang syne?
—*Ibid.*

I'm very lonely now, Mary,
For the poor make no new friends;
But oh! they love the better still
The few our Father sends.
—*Lady Dufferin.*

'Tis said that absence conquers love;
But oh! believe it not.
I've tried, alas! its power to prove,
But thou art not forgot.
—*Frederick W. Thomas.*

Backward, turn backward, O Time in your flight,
Make me a child again, just for to-night!

Backward, flow backward, O tide of the years!
I am so weary of toil and of tears,
Toil without recompense—tears all in vain—
Take them, and give me my childhood again!
—*Elizabeth Akers Allen.*

I ne'er could any lustre see
In eyes that would not look on me;
I ne'er saw nectar on a lip
But where my own did hope to sip.
—*R. B. Sheridan.*

A glass is good, and a lass is good,
And a pipe to smoke in cold weather;
The world is good, and the people are good,
And we're all good fellows together.
—*John O'Keefe.*

Drink to me only with thine eyes,
And I will pledge with mine;
Or leave a kiss but in the cup,
And I'll not look for wine.
—*Ben Jonson.*

Underneath this stone doth lie
As much beauty as could die;
Which in life did harbor give
To more virtue than doth live.
—*Ibid.*

Pity the sorrows of a poor old man
Whose trembling limbs have borne him to your door,
Whose days are dwindled to the shortest span;
Oh! give relief and heaven will bless your store. —*Thomas Moss.*

We have lived and loved together
Through many changing years,
We have shared each other's gladness,
And wept each other's tears.
—*Charles Jeffreys.*

Don't you remember sweet Alice, Ben Bolt?
Sweet Alice, whose hair was so brown,
Who wept with delight when you gave her a smile,
And trembled with fear at your frown.
—*Thomas Dunn English.*

Thought is deeper than all speech,
Feeling deeper than all thought;
Souls to souls can never teach
What unto themselves was taught.
—*Christopher P. Cranch.*

But whether on the scaffold high
Or in the battle's van,
The fittest place where man can die
Is where he dies for man.
Michael J. Barry.

'Twas the night before Christmas, when all through the house,
Not a creature was stirring, not even a mouse;
The stockings were hung by the chimney with care
In hopes that St. Nicholas soon would be there. —*Clement C. Moore.*

Ay, tear her tattered ensign down!
  Long has it waved on high,
And many an eye has danced to see
  That banner in the sky.

Nail to the mast her holy flag,
  Set every threadbare sail,
And give her to the god of storms,
  The lightning and the gale.
Oliver Wendel Holmes.

O, would I were a boy again,
  When life seemed formed of sunny years,
And all the heart then knew of pain
  Was wept in transient tears?
—Mark Lemon.

Old Grimes is dead, that good old man,
  We ne'er shall see him more;
He used to wear a long black coat
  All buttoned down before.
—Albert G. Green.

Here lies our sovereign lord the king,
  Whose word no man relies on;
He never says a foolish thing,
  Nor ever does a wise one.

It is a very good word to live in,
To lend, or to spend, or to give in;
But to beg or to borrow, or to get a man's own,
It is the very worst world that ever was known. *—Earl of Rochester.*

And there's a lust in man no charm can tame,
Of loudly publishing our neighbour's shame;
On eagles' wings immortal scandals fly,
While virtuous actions are but born to die.
—Stephen Harvey.

My life is like the summer rose,
  That opens to the morning sky,
But ere the shades of evening close,
  Is scattered on the ground to die.
—Richard Henry Wilde.

Abide with me from morn till eve,
For without Thee I cannot live;
Abide with me when night is nigh,
For without Thee I dare not die.
—John Keble.

Westward the course of empire takes its way;
  The four first acts already past,
A fifth shall close the drama with the day;
  Time's noblest offspring is the last.
—Bishop Berkley.

The good he scorned,
Stalked off reluctant, like an ill-used ghost,
Not to return, or, if it did, in visits
Like those of angels, short and far between.
—Robert Blair.

A mighty pain to love it is,
And 'tis a pain that pain to miss;
But of all pains, the greatest pain
It is to love, but love in vain.
—Abraham Cowley.

Wedlock, indeed, hath of compared been
  To public feasts, where meet a public rout,
Where they are without would fain go in,
  And they that are within would fain go out.
—Sir John Davies.

In bed we laugh, in bed we cry,
And, born in bed, in bed we die;
The near approach a bed may show,
Of human bliss to human woe.
—Isaac De Benserade.

The man that lays his hands upon a woman,
Save in the way of kindness, is a wretch,
Whom 'twere gross flattery to name a coward.
—John Tobin.

Their cause I plead—plead it in heart and mind;
A fellow-feeling makes one wondrous kind.
—David Garrick.

The modest front of this small floor,
Believe me, reader, can say more
Than many a braver marble can,—
"Here lies a truly honest man!"
—Richard Crashaw.

That man may last, but never lives,
Who much receives but nothing gives;
Whom none can love, whom none can thank
Creation's blot, creation's blank.
—Thomas Gibbons.

When stars are in the quiet skies,
  Then most I pine for thee;
Bend on me then thy tender eyes,
  As stars look on the sea.
—Edward Bulwer Lytton.

Give lettered pomp to teeth of time,
  So Bonny Doon but tarry;
Blot out the epic's stately rhyme,
  But spare his Highland Mary.
—John G. Whittier.

O, swiftly glides the bonny boat,
  Just parted from the shore,
And to the fisher's chorus-note
  Soft moves the dipping oar.
—Joanna Baillie.

Come to the sunset tree!
  The day is past and gone;
The woodman's axe lies free,
  And the reaper's work is done.
—Felicia D. Hemans.

On fame's eternal camping ground
  Their silent tents are spread,
And glory guards with solemn sound
  The bivouac of the dead.
—Theodore O'Hara.

In the days when we went gypsying
  A long time ago,
The lads and lassies in their best
  Were dressed from top to toe.
—Edwin Ransford.

But as some muskets so contrive it
As oft to miss the mark they drive it,
And, though well aimed at duck or plover,
Bear wide and kick their owners over.
—John Trumbull.

The last link is broken
  That bound me to thee,
And the words thou hast spoken
  Have rendered me free.
—Miss Fanny Steers.

And the star-spangled banner,
  O long may it wave
O'er the land of the free and the home of the brave. *—F. S. Key.*

Let this great maxim be my virtue's pride—
In part she is to blame that has been tried:
He comes too near that comes to be denied.

But the fruit that can fall without shaking
  Indeed is too mellow for me.
—Lady Mary Wortley Montague.

Let us weep in our darkness, but weep not for him!
Not for him who, departing, leaves millions in tears!
Not for him, who has died full of honor and years!
Not for him, who ascended Fame's ladder so high
From the round at the top he has stepped to the sky.
—Nathaniel P. Willis.

To every man upon this earth
  Death cometh soon or late.
And how can man die better
  Than facing fearful odds,
For the ashes of his fathers
  And the temples of his gods.
—Thomas B. Macaulay.

Which I wish to remark—
And my language is plain—
That for ways that are dark
And for tricks that are vain,
The heathen Chinee is peculiar,
With the smile that was childlike and bland.

A sacred burden is this life ye bear:
Look on it, lift it, bear it solemnly,
Stand up and walk beneath it steadfastly,
Fail not for sorrow, falter not for sin,
But onward, upward, till the goal ye win.
—*Frances Anne Kemble.*

Better trust all, and be deceived,
And weep that trust and that deceiving,
Than doubt one heart, that, if believed,
Had blessed one's life with true believing.
—*Ibid.*

Once to every man and nation comes the moment to decide,
In the strife of Truth with Falsehood, for the good or evil side;
Some great cause, God's new Messiah offering each the bloom or blight,
Parts the goats upon the left hand, and the sheep upon the right;
And the choice goes on forever 'twixt that darkness and that light.
—*James Russell Lowell.*

Go, forget me—why should sorrow
O'er that brow a shadow fling?
Go, forget me—and to-morrow
Brightly smile and sweetly sing.
Smile, though I shall not be near thee;
Sing, though I shall never hear thee.
—*Charles Wolfe.*

Stone walls do not a prison make,
Nor iron bars a cage;
Minds innocent and quiet take
Take that for a hermitage;
If I have freedom in my love,
And in my soul am free,
Angels alone that soar above
Enjoy such liberty.
—*Richard Lovelace.*

When I am dead no pageant train
Shall waste their sorrows at my bier,
Nor worthless pomp of homage vain
Stain it with hypocritic tear.

You shall not pile, with servile toil,
Your monuments upon my breast,
Nor yet within the common soil
Lay down the wreck of power to rest,
Where man can boast that he has trod
On him that was "the scourge of God."
—*Edward Everett.*

AREA, POPULATION AND EDUCATION.

The following is a comparative statement of the area, population and education of the world, by continents and by the principal nations:

BY CONTINENTS

	Area square miles.	Population.
Asia	15,700,000	764,000,000
Africa	11,700,000	172,200,000
Europe	3,900,000	320,500,000
North America	8,860,000	71,500,000
Oceanica	3,700,000	30,900,000
South America	7,000,000	27,500,000
	50,860,000	1,386,600,000

BY NATIONS.

	Area square miles.	Population.	Per cent unable to read or write.
Great Britain and Ireland	121,600	32,250,000	.46
China	4,100,000	410,000,000	.23
Japan	169,000	36,300,000	.16
Russia	8,500,000	98,700,000	.91
Germany	210,000	45,194,000	.12
United States	3,500,000	50,200,000	.20

The comparative density of population of Great Britain and the United States is as follows: Great Britain, inhabitants to the square mile, 289; United States, 14.

ONE DOLLAR

loaned for one hundred years at the following rates of compound interest would realize the sums set opposite each:

1 per cent	$ 2.75	12 per cent	$ 84,675.00
3 "	19.25	15 "	1,174,405.00
6 "	340.00	18 "	15,145,207.00
10 "	13,809.00	24 "	2,551,799,404.00

SIGNALS USED ON RAILROADS.

With the Hands.—Raising the hands to a level with the eyes and parting them with a sweeping motion signifies "go ahead."

Extending the arms and making a downward motion with the hands signifies "stop."

A beckoning with one hand signifies "back up."

With Flags.—Waving red flag or sticking it up by the roadside is a signal of "danger."

The hoisting of a red flag at a station means "stop."

When carried on a locomotive, a red flag conveys a notice that a train (or engine) is following.

With Lanterns.—Swinging a lantern to right angles across the track is a signal to "stop;" swinging it around in a circle, signifies "back;" raising and lowering it means "go ahead."

With the Whistle.—One whistle, "down brakes;" two whistles, "off brakes;" three whistles, a warning that the train is about to "back;" a succession of long whistles means "danger;" a succession of short, quick whistles is a "cattle alarm."

INSTANTANEOUS MEASUREMENT OF LUMBER.

[The figures given in the following Table, represent square feet and inches, and apply to board measurement. They are given for boards up to 30 feet in length, and 25 inches in width. If it be desired to measure a board longer than 30 feet, take from the contents of a board thirty feet long, and add the contents of one of the necessary length, to complete the entire length of the board to be measured. Thus, to find the contents of a board 54 feet long, and of any given width, add the contents of one 30 feet long, and one 24 feet long. Double the figures for 2 inch plank.]

Width.	8 feet long.		9 feet long.		10 feet long.		11 feet long.		12 feet long.		13 feet long.	
	Ft.	In.	Ft.	In.	Ft.	In.	Ft.	In.	Ft.	In.	Ft.	In.
6 inches	4	0	4	6	5	0	5	6	6	0	6	6
7 "	4	8	5	3	5	10	6	5	7	0	7	7
8 "	5	4	6	0	6	8	7	4	8	0	8	8
9 "	6	0	6	9	7	6	8	3	9	0	9	9
10 "	6	8	7	6	8	4	9	2	10	0	10	10
11 "	7	4	8	3	9	2	10	1	11	0	11	11
12 "	8	0	9	0	10	0	11	0	12	0	13	0
13 "	8	8	9	9	10	10	11	11	13	0	14	1
14 "	9	4	10	6	11	8	12	10	14	0	15	2
15 "	10	0	11	3	12	6	13	9	15	0	16	3
16 "	10	8	12	0	13	4	14	8	16	0	17	4
17 "	11	4	12	9	14	2	15	7	17	0	18	5
18 "	12	0	13	6	15	0	16	6	18	0	19	6
19 "	12	8	14	3	15	10	17	5	19	0	20	7
20 "	13	4	15	0	16	8	18	4	20	0	21	8
21 "	14	0	15	9	17	6	19	3	21	0	22	9
22 "	14	8	16	6	18	4	20	2	22	0	23	10
23 "	15	4	17	3	19	2	21	1	23	0	24	11
24 "	16	0	18	0	20	0	22	0	24	0	26	0
25 "	16	8	18	9	20	10	22	11	25	0	27	1

Width.	14 feet long.		15 feet long.		16 feet long.		17 feet long.		18 feet long.		19 feet long.	
	Ft.	In.	Ft.	In.	Ft.	In.	Ft.	In.	Ft.	In.	Ft.	In.
6 inches	7	0	7	6	8	0	8	6	9	0	9	6
7 "	8	2	8	9	9	4	9	11	10	6	11	1
8 "	9	4	10	0	10	8	11	4	12	0	12	8
9 "	10	6	11	3	12	0	12	9	13	6	14	3
10 "	11	8	12	6	13	4	14	2	15	0	15	10
11 "	12	10	13	9	14	8	15	7	16	6	17	5
12 "	14	0	15	0	16	0	17	0	18	0	19	0
13 "	15	2	16	3	17	4	18	5	19	6	20	7
14 "	16	4	17	6	18	8	19	10	21	0	22	2
15 "	17	6	18	9	20	0	21	3	22	6	23	9
16 "	18	8	20	0	21	4	22	8	24	0	25	4
17 "	19	10	21	3	22	8	24	1	25	6	26	11
18 "	21	0	22	6	24	0	25	6	27	0	28	6
19 "	22	2	23	9	25	4	26	11	28	6	30	1
20 "	23	4	25	0	26	8	28	4	30	0	31	8
21 "	24	6	26	3	28	0	29	9	31	6	33	3
22 "	25	8	27	6	29	4	31	2	33	0	34	10
23 "	26	10	28	9	30	8	32	7	34	6	36	5
24 "	28	0	30	0	32	0	34	0	36	0	38	0
25 "	29	2	31	3	33	4	35	5	37	6	39	7

Width.	20 feet long.		21 feet long.		22 feet long.		23 feet long.		24 feet long.		25 feet long.	
	Ft.	In.	Ft.	In.	Ft.	In.	Ft.	In.	Ft.	In.	Ft.	In.
6 inches	10	0	10	6	11	0	11	6	12	0	12	6
7 "	11	8	12	3	12	10	13	5	14	0	14	7
8 "	13	4	14	0	14	8	15	4	16	0	16	8
9 "	15	0	15	9	16	6	17	3	18	0	18	9
10 "	16	8	17	6	18	4	19	2	20	0	20	10
11 "	18	4	19	3	20	2	21	1	22	0	22	11
12 "	20	0	21	0	22	0	23	0	24	0	25	0
13 "	21	8	22	9	23	10	24	11	26	0	27	1
14 "	23	4	24	6	25	8	26	10	28	0	29	2
15 "	25	0	26	3	27	6	28	9	30	0	31	3
16 "	26	8	28	0	29	4	30	8	32	0	33	4
17 "	28	4	29	9	31	2	32	7	34	0	35	5
18 "	30	0	31	6	33	0	34	6	36	0	37	6
19 "	31	8	33	3	34	10	36	5	38	0	39	7
20 "	33	4	35	0	36	8	38	4	40	0	41	8
21 "	35	0	36	9	38	6	40	3	42	0	43	9
22 "	36	8	38	6	40	4	42	2	44	0	45	10
23 "	38	4	40	3	42	2	44	1	46	0	47	11
24 "	40	0	42	0	44	0	46	0	48	0	50	0
25 "	40	8	43	9	45	10	47	11	50	0	52	1

Width.	26 feet long.		27 feet long.		28 feet long.		29 feet long.		30 feet long.	
	Ft.	In.	Ft.	In.	Ft.	In.	Ft.	In.	Ft.	In.
6 inches	13	0	13	6	14	0	14	6	15	0
7 "	15	2	15	9	16	4	16	11	17	6
8 "	17	4	18	0	18	8	19	4	20	0
9 "	19	6	20	3	21	0	21	9	22	6
10 "	21	8	22	6	23	4	24	2	25	0
11 "	23	10	24	9	25	8	26	7	27	6
12 "	26	0	27	0	28	0	29	0	30	0
13 "	28	2	29	3	30	4	31	5	32	6
14 "	30	4	31	6	32	8	33	10	35	0
15 "	32	6	33	9	35	0	36	3	37	6
16 "	34	8	36	0	37	4	38	8	40	0
17 "	36	10	38	3	39	8	41	1	42	6
18 "	39	0	40	6	42	0	43	6	45	0
19 "	41	2	42	9	44	4	45	11	47	6
20 "	43	4	45	0	46	8	48	4	50	0
21 "	45	6	47	3	49	0	50	9	52	6
22 "	47	8	49	6	51	4	53	2	55	0
23 "	49	10	51	9	53	8	55	7	57	6
24 "	52	0	54	0	56	0	58	0	60	0
25 "	54	2	56	3	58	4	60	5	62	6

FAITH.

"Better trust and all be deceived,
And weep that trust and that deceiving
Than doubt that heart that, if believed,
Had blessed one's life with true believing."

—*Frances Anne Kemble.*

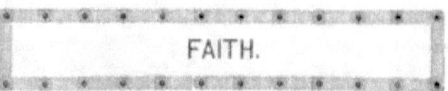

FAITH is one of the brightest and most beautiful attributes cf the human character. Under the most adverse circumstances it rises to the sublimest heights, and commands admiration, love, respect and reverence, even where the feet of the idol in which it worships godlike attributes—the brow of marble and the locks of bronze—are, to every other eye, of the commonest clay. It is the talisman that leads a man, with trust and confidence in the future, steeling his nerves and inspiring his heart, to surmount difficulties and triumph over obstacles which have apparently overwhelmed his fortunes, and keep up a strong heart with which to welcome the turn of the tide of fortune, and a strong arm with which to spread the undaunted canvas on which Faith is inscribed, to catch the rising trade-wind of prosperity. The man who has thorough faith in his future career—who honestly knows himself, by conscious integrity and honesty, by the self-consciousness of doing his duty in the battle of life—will never falter under difficulties, nor will he ever succumb to any disaster. Like the strong swimmer making for the shore, though oft and again buffeted back by the waves of disaster, he will still ultimately reach the solid earth, from which for all the future he can look back from a safe refuge, and thank God for that serene Faith under which he was borne up in difficulties, and by whose aid his fortunes were crowned by the golden garlands of victory, the laurels of social distinction, or the bay-leaves of domestic bliss. How beautiful the faith of the child in the parent, and how much more so the far-seeing faith of the true-hearted and loving wife, who knows her husband better than all the world, and who, in the small days of his early trials in the world, saw before all else the far-off glimmer of the golden dawn awaiting him over the distant hills, when the steeps of adversity were overcome.

Cultivate faith in yourself first of all, if your conscience approve and your self-knowledge justify it, and in all with whom you are brought into contact. Believe in yourself, and seek to justify your belief. Believe in your neighbor, until he himself has shattered the faith with which he was regarded, and even then the exercise of that virtue will be found to have sweetened the memory of the severed friendship, and to soften the disappointment of a broken idol. Tom Moore surely had this divine attribute in his mind's eye when he wrote:

"You may break, you may shatter
The vase, if you will;
But the pefume of roses
Will cling to it still."

He who cultivates Faith will give a generous measure of trust to those around him, which will brighten many paths beside his own. Though he "may not increase his stature by one cubit," he may strengthen himself mentally and morally with this high quality, and, in doing so, will invigorate and lift up others who, weaker in themselves, find in the faith and confidence extended to them in their weakness, the refreshing, revivifying, and grateful influence which the gentle rain sheds upon the drooping plant.

BRIDGE OF FAITH.

I have a bridge within my heart
Known as the bridge of Faith;
It spans by a mysterious art,
The streams of Life and Death.

And when upon this bridge I stand
To watch the tide below,
Sweet thoughts come from a sunny land
And brighten all below.

Then as it winds its way along
Toward a distant sea,
Oh, pleasant is the spirit song
That upward floats to me.

A song of blessings never sere,
Of love beyond compare,
Of pleasures flowed from troublings here
To use serenely there.

And hearing this, a peace divine
Soon shuts each sorrow out;
And all is hopeful and benign.
Where all was fear and doubt.

Oh, often then will brighter flow
The light which round me lies:
I see, from life's beclouded flow
A crystal stream arise.

—*Author Unknown.*

HOPE.

"Who in Life's battle firm doth stand
Shall bear Hope's tender blossoms
Into the Silent Land."

—*Von Salis.*

HOPE springs eternal in the human breast, writes Pope, and truly, if this were not the case, this world would be but a dull and dreary abode for the most of its inhabitants. Hope it is, with its elastic measures, that, painting bright pictures of the future and ever pointing onward and upward, makes men forget the miseries of daily life in the bright anticipations conjured up by the wand of Hope for the future. There is no cavern nor dungeon so deep or so dark that the rays of light from the torch of Hope will not penetrate there and shed its beautiful effulgence through the darksome gloom to lighten the misery of some poor wretch from whom, perchance, all other comfort had fled. Into every condition of men, and into every vicissitude of life, Hope, the comforter, will find its smiling way, cheering men in adversity, encouraging them in success, and, when worldly thrift shall have filled up the measure of prosperity, and there shall seem nothing more to be hoped for, returning at the last to smooth the pillow of the dying, relinquishing all here below, with assurance of eternal gain to be won in the world beyond. From the cradle to the grave, then, Hope stands the nearest to a man of his three guardian angels. It should be appreciated and cultivated accordingly. The hopeful man is like a lamp shining upon the faces of his neighbors. There is an infection in the lightness in his eye, the laughter which springs from his heart to his lips, and the elasticity of his step, which communicates to all around him. It is the spirit which may be regarded as the radiator or diffusor of happiness; and it is also that which finds most readily a home in the hearts of men, and makes the strongest and most direct appeal to their understanding. It is a quality which, taking no denial from Fortune, never recognizes defeat. Elastic as air, it takes new life from every temporary depression; and, finally, by its persistent and unfaltering courage, enables a man to crown his ambition with success. When misfortune strikes you down, friends desert you, children turn their backs upon you, or parents cast you off; when desolation invades your household, ruin points its ghastly skeleton-finger at you, and poverty fastens its cruel and icy fangs upon you; when sickness overtakes your bedside, and the dark and grisly phantoms of the Unknown hover about as if to claim you for their own; when the soul by doubt is tortured, and when all earthly friends have fled, yet still does gentle Hope, with angelic wing, fan the dying embers of life into renewed existence, and from the very gates of destruction raise you up again to health and prosperity, chastened, purged, cleansed—higher, better, and purer than ever. What heat is to the material world so is hope to the social, moral, and mental world. It is estimated that if the sun should withdraw his light and heat for twenty-four hours all animate life would perish miserably in the terrible gloom. So it is in the affairs of life. Without Hope men would succumb at the first adverse breath, and give up the struggle of life miserably. Despair, with its grim and cruel visage, would usurp the place of radiant-faced and bright-winged Hope as man's familiar angel, and its twin-sister, Suicide, would reap to satiety of the dread harvest that she loves. But Hope is still on earth to lighten the burdens of men, and shed light on their path, and will stay with them to the end. But one door is forbidden to Hope, and that is, the entrance to that fearful place of torment of the future world depicted by Danté:

"All Hope abandon, ye who enter here."

Regard Hope always in the spirit of the author of these beautiful lines:

" True Hope is swift;
It flies on eagle's wings;
Kings it makes gods,
And meaner creatures kings."

CHARITY.

CHARITY is the chiefest of the Christian virtues. It is the very crown of a perfect character, and he who possesses it, in its truest and best sense, will possess the chief element of happiness, not only in his own life and surroundings, but for all with whom, in personal, business, or social relations, he may be brought into contact. In its exercise it blesses alike the giver and the receiver, and sheds a mild and beneficent lustre before which the garish lights of wealth and splendor pale, and which illuminates with a divine effulgence the darkest shadows that fall athwart human existence. In its perfection, Charity may be likened to the diamond of the purest water—a complete, harmonious whole, a perfect crystal, without flaw or blemish, and yet, in every aspect, from whatever side it be viewed, reflecting from its perfect depths new lights of radiant beauty. There is no more beautiful, expressive, nor comprehensive description of Charity in literature, than is presented, clothed in the dignity of simplicity, in the following words of St. Paul:

"And though I bestow all my goods to feed the poor, and though I give my body to be burned, and have not charity, it profiteth nothing.

"Charity suffereth long and is kind; charity vaunteth not itself; is not puffed up.

"Doth not behave itself unseemly; seeketh not her own; is not easily provoked; thinketh no evil;

"Rejoiceth not in iniquity, but rejoiceth in the truth;

"Beareth all things, believeth all things, endureth all things.

"Charity never faileth."

It is Charity which moves that spirit of divine compassion which, more or less obscure, slumbers in every human heart, to extend aid to the needy, sympathy to the sorrowing, comfort to the sorely tried, consolation to the afflicted, protection to the persecuted; which lifts up them that fall, encourages them that falter, and lends zeal to them that press forward in the way of life; which is a shield to the weak and tempted, and a sword to the strong and confident; which is a balm for the wounded spirit, a sweet fragrance amid the impurities of sin and suffering, a halo of light which glows with undimmed luster even among the dark and sordid cares of life; which is as deep as ocean, as broad as earth, and as high as heaven. Charity gives alms, but it does not consist of alms-giving.

It clothes the naked and feeds the hungry; seeks out sorrow and succors the distressed; is the protection of husband for the widow, and the care of father for the orphan; and yet suffers not its right hand to know what the left doeth. It avoids ostentation, shuns publicity, shrinks from parade, blushes in the presence of acknowledgment, and does not seek out gratitude. Its true reward is in the inmost chambers of the soul, where it confers an indescribable happiness, that exalts existence and elevates the whole being. It lays hold upon the rewards of religion, and gives to man the nearest appoach to that godlike manhood set forth in the great example of Him who is our highest model of perfection:

"Inasmuch as ye have done it unto the least of these ye have done it also unto me."

It softens the asperities of human nature, and brings out, strengthens, and develops all the higher and better qualities of manhood—intellectual and moral. It imbues the domestic affections with tenderness and consideration, and the social relations with warmth and cordiality. It dignifies and beautifies character, ennobles the whole nature, cements the fidelity of friendships, gives the strength of steel to the silken bonds of love, intensifies the devotion of conjugal worship, and sanctifies filial veneration. Its motto is the Golden Rule, "Do unto others as ye would they should do unto you." Its ways are the footsteps of the Master, and its rewards are both here and hereafter.

THE LADY'S DREAM.

"Each pleading look that long ago
  I scanned with a heedless eye,
Each face was gazing as plainly there
  As when I passed it by;
Woe, woe is me, if the past should be
  Thus present when I die!

"No need of the sulphurous lake,
  No need of the fiery coal,
But only that crowd of humankind
  Who wanted pity and dole—
In everlasting retrospect—
  Will wring my sinful soul!

"Alas I have walked through life
  Too heedless where I trod,
Nay, helping to bury my fellow worm
  And fill the burial rod—
Forgetting that even the sparrow falls
  Not unmark'd of God!"

—*Hood.*

BIOGRAPHICAL CYCLOPEDIA.

BIOGRAPHY is filled with the stories of those who have either sought to become well-known for the sake of notoriety, have acquired fame on account of lofty purpose and earnest spirit, or had greatness thrust upon them by circumstances over which they had no control. In these pages may be found the most interesting tests of the several aspects of force, as above indicated, that are displayed by human nature. Some have been blindly ambitious, as Cæsar, and Napoleon. Others, like Titus, and Washington, are made famous for acts of goodness to mankind; while such as Cincinnatus, and Lady Jane Grey, have had honors thrust upon them, and the pages of history which bear the record of their lives, are not the less attractive for the showing that their honors were well borne.

The names of thousands of the world's most active and eminent men and women are given in this convenient form.

BIOGRAPHICAL COMPENDIUM.

A

Abbott, Jacob, an American author and clergyman. Born Hollowell, Me., 1803.

Abdul Hamid, sultan of Turkey, began his reign August 31, 1876. B. September 22, 1842.

Abelard, *ah-ba-lar*, a learned French priest, lover of Heloise. Born near Nantes, 1079. Died 1142.

Abercrombie, James, a British officer in America. Defeated at Ft. Ticonderoga. B. in Scotland, 1706. D. 1781.

Abernethy, John, an English surgeon. B. in London, 1764. D. 1831.

About, *a-boo*, Edmond Francois Valentin, a French statesman and political writer. B. 1828. D. in Paris, January 18, 1885.

Adams, John, second president of United States. B. in Braintree, Mass., 1735. D. in Quincy, 1826.

Adams, John Quincy, son of John A., sixth president of United States. B. in Braintree, Mass., 1767. D. in Washington, 1848.

Adams, Samuel, an American revolutionist and governor of Massachusetts. B. Boston, 1722. D. 1803.

Addison, Joseph, an English writer. B. Milston, 1672. D. 1719.

Adrian. Six popes of Rome of this name.

Æsculapius, the Greek god of medicine.

Æsop, the fable writer. B. Phrygia about 620 B. C. Date of death uncertain.

Agassiz, *ag-as-se*, Louis John Rudolph, a French naturalist. B. Motiers, Switzerland, 1807. D. Cambridge, Massachusetts, 1873.

Agricola, *a-grik-o-la*, Cnæius Julius, a Roman conquerer. B. Forum Julii, now Frejus, in Provence, A. D. 37. D. Rome, 93.

Agrippa, Marcus Vipsanius, a Roman consul. Naval victory of Actium; dedicated to Jupiter the Pantheon. B. 63. D. 12 B. C.

Agrippina, *ag-rip-e-na*, the elder, wife of Germanicus Cæsar. Died A. D. 34. A., the younger, was mother of Nero, who had her assassinated A. D. 60.

Akbar, the greatest of Moguls in Hindostan. B. 1542. D. 1605.

Alaric I. and II., kings of the Visigoths; the first a great conqueror, the second more pacific. A. I., B. 376.

Albemarle, George Monk, duke, a military and naval officer. B. Potheridge, Devonshire, 1608. D. 1670.

Albert, Prince Consort, married Queen Victoria in 1840. B. Cobourg, Germany, 1819, D. Windsor Castle, 1861.

Albert Edward, prince of Wales, and heir-apparent to British throne. B. in Buckingham Palace, London, 1841.

Albuquerque, *Al'bu-kerke*, Alphonso de, a Portuguese commander. Captured Malacca. B. 1452. D. 1515.

Alcibiades, *al-se-bi-a-dees*, an Athenian general. Defeated Spartans, and was murdered by them, 404 B. C. B. Athens, 450 B. C.

Alcott, *awl'kot*, Amos Bronson, an American educator. B. Wolcott, Conn., 1798. D. Auburndale, Mass., 1859.

Alcott, Louisa May, daughter of Amos, a story writer. B. Germantown, Penn., 1833.

Alden, John, came over in the Mayflower in 1620. D. 1687.

Aldrich, Thomas Bailey, an American poet. B. Portsmouth, N. H., 1836.

Alembert, *da-lam'bair*, John le Rond, a French mathematician; discovered the precession of equinoxes. B. Paris, 1717. D. 1783.

Alexander. Many kings of this name, and eight popes.

Alexander I., emperor of Russia. Beaten by Napoleon at Austerlitz. United armies of Prussia and Russia, were also beaten at Friedland. On the disastrous retreat of Napoleon from Moscow, the allied army entered Paris. Peace—Holy Alliance. B. St. Petersburg, 1777. D. Taganrog, 1825.

Alexander II., emperor of Russia; Abolished serfdom; Victorious in war against Turkey, 1877-8; B. 1818. III. began his reign March 14, 1881; B. March 10, 1845.

Alexander the Great, the most renowned hero in ancient history. Defeated the Persians. B. Pella 356 B. C. D. in his 33d year.

Alexander Severus, a Roman emperor that defeated the Persians. B. in Phœnicia 208. Killed by his troops 235.

Alexander, St., of Alexandria. Condemned Arianism. D. 326.

Alexander, William, an American major-general in revolutionary war. B. New York 1726. D. Albany 1783.

Alexis, Czar of Russia. Reign disturbed by foreign and civil wars. B. Moscow 1630. D. 1676.

Alexis I., Comnenus, emperor of Constantinople. Fought the Turks and Scythians; B. Constantinople, 1048; D. 1118. A. II., succeeded to throne and was murdered by Andronicus. Three others of this name met similar fate.

Alfonso. Many rulers of this name. A. II., the Chaste, of Leon, Castile and Asturias; D. Oviedo, 842, aged 85. III., the Great, fought the Moors; D. Zamora, 910. VI., the Valiant, of Leon and Castile, emperor of Spain. Cid achieved poetical celebrity. A. died at Toledo, 1109. VIII., the Emperor, victor as against the Moors; D. near Toledo, 1157. X., the Learned, king of Leon and Castile; Alfonsine tables drawn under his direction; B. 1203. D. 1284.

Alfonso, of Aragon and Navarre, the Fighter; took immense spoil from the Moors; successful in 29 battles; D. 1134. A. III. established first constitution; D. 1291. V., the Magnanimous, conquered Naples in 1442; B. 1384; D. Naples, 1458.

Alfonso, of Portugal. Freed that state from dependence in which it had been held by Leon and Castile; D. Coimbra, 1185. V., invaded Africa several times; D. Cintra, 1481. Six kings of Portugal.

Alfonso XII., the present (1885) king of Spain; began his reign December 30, 1874. B. November 28, 1857.

Alfred the Great, king of the West Saxons; was engaged in fifty-six battles by sea and land. B. Wantage, in Berkshire, 849. D. 900.

Alger, William Rounsaville, an American Unitarian clergyman. B. Freetown, Massachusetts, 1823.

Ali, *a-le*, the cousin and son-in-law of Mahomet; declared caliph, but was assassinated in 660.

Alison, Sir Archibald, a Scottish historical writer. B. Kenley, Shropshire, 1792. D. near Glasgow, 1867.

Allen, Ethan, an American brigadier-general of the Revolution. B. Litchfield, Connecticut, 1738. D. near Colchester, Vermont, 1789.

Allston, Washington, an American painter. "Jacob's Vision." B. in South Carolina, 1779. D. Cambridgeport, Massachusetts, 1843.

Alvarado, Pedro de, governor of Guatemala; in every battle with Hernando Cortez in conquest of Mexico. B. Badajoz. D. 1541.

Amadeus V., the Great; an umpire in Europe. D. 1323. Nine sovereigns in Savoy of this name.

Ambrose, St., archbishop of Milan. B. Treves, in Gaul, 340. D. Milan, 397.

Ames, Fisher, an American politician and writer. B. Dedham, Massachusetts, 1758. D. there, 1808.

Amherst, Jeffery, an English general; commanded British armies in America, after Abercrombie. B. Kent, 1717. D. 1797.

Amurath I., *a-mu-rath*, a sultan of the Turks; instituted the corps of Janissaries; defeated the Christians. B. 1329; stabbed by wounded Servian, in 1389. Amurath II. defeated Christians and quelled a revolt of the Janissaries. B. 1399; D. 1451. Amurath IV. was the worst ruler over the Ottomans.

Anacreon, *a-nak-re-on*, a Greek lyric writer. B. Teos, in Ionia, 561 B.C.

Anastatius, *an-a-sta-she-us*. Several emperors of the East and several popes of this name.

Anaxagoras, *an-ax-ag-o-ras*, illustrious ancient philosopher. Held that the moon was inhabited. B. near Smyrna, in Ionia, about 500 B. C. D. Lampsacus, Asia Minor, 428 B. C.

Anaximander, *an-ax-e-man-der*, a Greek philosopher. Observed obliquity of the ecliptic. B. Miletus, Asia Minor, 610 B. C. D. 547 B. C.

Anaximenes, *an-ax-im-e-nees*, a Greek philosopher. Held that all things came from the air. D. 504 B. C. Another of this name was philosopher and historian, and native of Lampsacus, Asia Minor. Lived about 320 B. C.

Andersen, Hans Christian, a Danish writer of tales for children. B. Odense, 1805. D. Copenhagen, 1875.

Anderson, Robert, an American major-general. Fort Sumter, S. C. B. Nice, France, 1806. D. 1871.

Andre, *an-dra*, John, a British spy in American revolutionary war. B. London, 1751. Hanged 1780.

Andrew, John Albion, an abolitionist, and governor of Massachusetts five times. B. Windham, Me., 1818. D. 1867.

Andrew, Saint, a disciple of Christ, and apostle. Supposed martyr at Patræ, in Achaia, A. D. 70.

Andronicus, an Athenian architect. Tower of the Winds and weather-cock.

Andronicus, of Rhodes, a philosopher of Aristotleism. Lived 63 B. C.

Angelo, Michael Buonarotti, the great Italian architect and painter. "Last Judgment." B. 1475. D. 1564.

Anne, the British queen. B. Twickenham, near London, 1664. D. 1714.

Anne of Austria, a queen of France. B. 1601. D. 1666.

Anne Boleyn, *bool-en*, the unfortunate wife of Henry VIII. B. 1507. Beheaded 1536.

Anselm, Saint, a book-writer, and arch bishop of Canterbury. B. Piedmont, 1033. D. 1109.

Anthony, Susan B., a celebrated advocate of woman suffrage. B. South Adams, Mass. 1820.

Antigonus, a chief captain of Alexander, defeated and killed in 301, aged 80.

Antiochus *an-ti-o-kus.* Thirteen Syrian kings of this name between 230 B. C. and the empire of the Cæsars.

Antipater, *an-tip-a-ter,* was father of Herod the Great. B. about 398. D. 319.

Antoinette, Marie, queen of Louis XVI. She was archduchess of Austria, and her marriage was brought about to put her country and France on terms of friendly alliance. Was a victim of mobs in 1792, and executed at Paris in 1793, period of the revolution. B. Vienna, 1755.

Antonia. Prominent Roman women of this name. One became the mother of Germanicus Claudius, the emperor, and the bad Livia.

Antoninus, *an-to-ni-nus,* Marcus Aurelius, the best of the Roman emperors. B. Rome, 121. D. Vindobona (Vienna), 180.

Antoninus, Marcus, a great Roman orator. Killed at Rome in 667.

Antony, Mark (Antonius Marcus). Served Cæsar, lover of Cleopatra, defeated at Actium. B. Rome, 83 B. C. Stabbed himself, 30 B. C.

Appleton Daniel, an American book publisher. B. Haverhill, Mass., 1785. D. 1840.

Aquinas, Saint Thomas, a theologian, and called the Angelic Doctor. B. castle of Aquino, It., 1224. D. near Terracina, 1274.

Arago, Francois Jean Dominique, a French scientist. B. near Perpignan, 1786. D. Paris, 1853.

Arbuthnot, Alexander, a Scottish clergyman. B. Arbuthnot, 1538. D. 1735.

Archimedes *ar-ki-me-dees,* the inventor, of Syracuse. Screw, burning-glass, other inventions. B. about 287 B. C. Killed during an assault by the Romans, 212 B. C.

Argand, Aime. Invented the lamp of that name. B. Geneva, Switz., 1782. D. 1803.

Aristophanes, *ar-is-tof-a-nees,* an Athenian comic dramatist. Lived 400 B. C.

Aristotle, the Grecian philosopher, and head of the Peripatetics. B. Stagira, Macedonia, 384 B. C. D. Chalcis, island of Eubœa, 322 B. C.

Arius, *a-re-us,* the founder of the Arian sect. Lived about 300.

Arkwright, Sir Richard, an English inventor. Made first machine for carding and spinning cotton. B Preston, Lancashire, 1732. D 1792.

Arminius, or Herman, the deliverer of Germany. Assassinated A. D. 20, aged 39.

Armstrong, John, an American brigadier-general, and member of President Madison's cabinet. D. Red Hook, N. Y., 1843, in his 85th year.

Armstrong, Sir William George, the inventor of the gun of that name. B. 1810.

Arnold, Benedict, an American major-general and traitor. B. in Connecticut. D. London, 1801. A great Swiss patriot of this name gained the liberty of Switzerland, 1386.

Arthur, Chester Allan, the twenty-first President of United States. B. Fairfield, Vt., October 5, 1830.

Audubon, John James, an American naturalist. B. in Louisiana, 1780. D. New York, 1851.

Augustine Saint, a father of the Christian church. B. Tagaste, in Africa, 354. D. 430.

Augustulus, Romulus, the last emperor of the West, being conquered in 476.

Austin, Saint, the first bishop of Canterbury. D. 608.

B

Bach, John Sebastian, a German musician. Had eleven sons, all musicians. B. Eisenach, 1685. D. Leipsic, 1754.

Bache, *batch,* Alexander Dallas, Superintendent United States coast survey. B. Philadelphia, 1806. D. Newport, R. I., 1867.

Bacon, Sir Francis, a profound thinker for his age. Pope said he was "the wisest, brightest, meanest of mankind." B. London, 1561. D. 1626.

Bacon, Nathaniel, an American patriot of Virginia. B. in England. D. 1677.

Bacon, Roger, an experimental philosopher. Made some discoveries, and invented air-pump and gun-powder. B. Ilchester, 1214. D. 1292.

Bailey, Gamaliel, an American journalist. National Era. B. Mt. Holly, N. J., 1807. D. 1859. Jacob Whitman B., an American naturalist; B. Ware, Mass., 1811; D. West Point, N. Y., 1857. Theodorus, an American naval officer war 1861-5; B. Plattsburgh, N. Y., 1805; D. Washington, 1877.

Bailly, *bail-ye,* Jean Sylvain, a French astronomer. B. Paris, 1736. Guillotined by Jacobins, 1793.

Baily, Francis, an English astronomer. B. 1774. D. 1844.

Bainbridge, Captain William, an American naval officer that first hoisted the American flag in the harbor of Constantinople. B. Princeton, N. J., 1774. D. Philadelphia, 1833.

Baird, Spencer Fullerton, an American professor of natural history. B. Reading, Penn., 1823.

Baker, Osmon Cleander, an American clergyman; B. Marlow, N. H., 1812; D. 1871. Edward Dickinson B. was an American politician and soldier; B. London, 1811; Killed at Ball's Bluff, Va., 1861. An African traveler of this name discovered Lake Albert Nyanza in 1864.

Baldwin. Several kings of Jerusalem of this name, and emperors of Constantinople.

Bales, Peter, a great master of penmanship; taught at Oxford and London. B. 1547. D. about 1610.

Ball, Sir Alexander John, a British officer in first American war; D. 1809. Thomas R., an American carver in marble; B. Charlestown, Mass., 1819.

Ballou, Hosea, an American Universalist clergyman, and founder of Universalism in the United States. B. Richmond, N. H., 1771. D. 1852.

Bancroft, Hubert H., an American historian. B. Granville, O., 1832. George, an American historian and poetical writer. B. Worcester, Mass., 1800. Richard, was Archbishop of Canterbury, and abused the Puritans. B. Farnsworth, Lancashire, 1544. D. 1610.

Bangs, Nathan, an American clergyman and book-editor. B. Stratford, Ct., 1778. D. 1862.

Banks, Nathaniel Prentiss, an American major-general, defeated Confederates in Louisiana. Was defeated at Sabine Cross Roads B. 1816.

Barbarossa was a famous pirate. Seized Algiers, but was beaten and killed in 1535.

Barker, Jacob, an American senator, and founder Exchange Bank in Wall st. B. Kennebec Co., Me., 1779. D. Philadelphia, 1871.

Barlow, Joel, an American poet. B. Redding, Ct., 1754. D. near Cracow, Poland, 1812.

Barnabas, St., a companion of St. Paul, was stoned to death in Cyprus, his birth place.

Barnes, Albert, an American writer of theology. B. 1798. D. 1870.

Barnum, Phineas Taylor, an American showman. B. Bethel, Ct., 1810.

Barre, Isaac, a British officer. Friendly to American colonists. B. Dublin, 1726. D. 1802.

Barrett, Benjamin Fisk, an American clergyman. B. Dresden, Me., 1808. George Horton, an American tragedian. B. Exeter, Eng., 1794. D. New York, 1860. Lawrence, the American actor. B. Ireland.

Barron, James, an American naval officer that fought a duel with Decatur, killing him. B. Virginia, 1768. D. 1851.

Barry, John, an American naval officer and commander of the Alliance. B. Wexford, Ireland, 1745. D. Philadelphia, 1803.

Bartholomew, St., one of the twelve; was probably flayed alive in Armenia.

Bartlett, John Russell, author of the Dictionary of Americanisms. B. Providence, Rhode Island, 1805. Josiah was a member of the Continental Congress. B. Amesbury, Massachusetts, 1729. D. 1795.

Barton, Benjamin Smith, was founder of natural history in America. B. Pennsylvania, 1766. D. 1815. Clara, an American humanitarian. B. Oxford, Massachusetts, 1830. William, captured the British general Prescott in 1777. B. Providence, 1750. D. 1831.

Bates, Edward, an American statesman; was in Lincoln's cabinet. B. 1793. D. 1869.

Bayard *bi'ard*, Thomas Francis, the Delaware statesman. B. Wilmington, 1828. Several other members of the family were senators before him.

Bayer, Johann, a German Scientist. B. Bavaria, about 1572. D. Augsburg, 1660.

Bazaine, *ba-zan'*, Francois Achille, a French general in Crimean and other wars; surrendered to Germans at Metz. B. Versailles, 1811.

Beauregard, Peter Gustavus Toutant, a confederate general; defeated United States troops under McDowell at Bull Run, war of 1861-5. B. near New Orleans, 1818.

Becket, Thomas a, an English prelate and archbishop of Canterbury. B. London, 1119. Murdered in the cathedral, 1170.

Bedford John, duke of, an English officer that aided in bringing Joan of Arc to the torch. B. 1390. D. Rouen, 1435.

Beecher. Lyman, the father of Harriet Elizabeth (Stowe), who wrote Uncle Tom's Cabin. The former born at New Haven, Connecticut, 1775. D. 1863. The latter was born in Litchfield, Connecticut, 1812. Henry Ward, the son and brother, an American theologian. B. Litchfield, 1813.

Beer, Wilhelm, a German scientist. Brother of the great Meyerbeer. B. Berlin, 1797. D. 1850.

Beethoven, *bait-ho-ven*, Ludwig von, a German musical composer. B. Bonn, 1770. D. Vienna, 1827.

Bell, John, an American senator. Leader constitutional union party, 1860. B. near Nashville, Tenn., 1797. D. in that state, 1869.

Bellows, Henry Whitman, an American clergyman. Started a Unitarian paper in New York. B. Boston, 1814.

Benedict, Saint, founder of the Benedictines. B. Nursia, 480. Died about 543.

Bennett, James Gordon, an American current writer. Founder of New York *Herald*. B. Scotland, 1795. D. 1872.

Benton, Thomas Hart, an American statesman. He loved coin, and was called Old Bullion. B. near Hillsborough, N. H., 1782. D. Washington, 1858.

Bergh, Henry, an American humanitarian. B. New York, 1823.

Berkeley, Sir William, the royal governor of Virginia. B. near London. D. Twickenham, 1677.

Beust, *boost*, Frederick Ferdinand, Baron von, the German friend of liberty. D. Dresden, 1809.

Bias, was one of the most active of the seven wise men. B Priene, about 570 B. C.

Biela, *bee-a-la*, William, Baron von, discovered comet bearing his name. B. Stolberg, 1782. D. 1856.

Bierstadt, *beer-stat*, Albert, an American painter. Yosemite Valley scenes. B. Dusseldorf, Ger., 1829.

Bigelow, *big-e-low*, Erastus Brigham, an American inventor. B. 1814. D. 1879.

Birney, *bur-ne*, James G., one of the liberal party in United States. Twice a presidential nominee. B. Danville, Ky., 1792. D. Perth Amboy, N. Y., 1857.

Bismarck-Schonhausen, *bees-mark shern-hou-sen*, Otto Edward Leopold, the German imperial chancellor. Made Prussia the strongest power in Germany. B. Schonhausen, near Madgeborg, 1815.

Black, Jeremiah S., an American politician. Secretary of state under Buchanan. B. Glades, Penn., 1810. D. York, Penn., 1883.

Black Hawk, a Pottawatomie chief. Friend of British, war 1812. B. 1767. D. in Iowa, 1838.

Blackstone, Sir William, an English lawyer, and author of Commentaries. B. London, 1723. D. 1780.

Blaine, James Gillespie, an American statesman. Republican nominee for president in 1884. B. Washington county, Penn., 1830.

Blair, Francis Preston, an American politician and editor at Washington. B. Abingdon, Va., 1791. D. 1876. Montgomery, his son, was postmaster-general in Lincoln's cabinet.

Blake, Robert, a celebrated British admiral. B. Bridgewater, 1598. D. 1657.

Blanc, *blong*, Louis, a French politician. History of French Revolution. B. Madrid, 1812.

Bland, Richard, an American patriot in colonial legislature of Virginia. B. early in last century.

Blucher, *fon bloo'ker*, Gebhard Leberecht, a Prussian general that aided in defeat of Napoleon. B. Rostock, 1742. D. Kribiowitz, Silesia, 1819.

Bode, Johann Elert, a German astronomer. Bode's Law of Planetary Distances. B. 1747. D. 1826.

Boleyn. See Anne Boleyn.

Bolingbroke, Henry St. John, an English writer, and possessed of great eloquence. B. Battersea, 1672. D. there, 1751.

Bolivar, Simon, a South American soldier and liberator. B. Caracas, 1783. D. San Pedro, 1830.

Bonaparte. Name of the French imperial family. Napoleon, the man of singular fortunes, was emperor. Defeated the armies of Austria, overran Italy, Egypt and part of Syria, and crossed the Alps. In 1803 he gained a series of victories at Ulm, Wagram, Jena, Friedland, Austerlitz, etc., and became in effect dictator of Europe. In 1812 he advanced to Moscow and lost his army. In 1815 he defeated the Prussians and English separately, but at Waterloo was crushed by allied armies under Wellington, Blucher and Bulow. B. Ajaccio, Corsica, 1769. D. St. Helena, 1821. Napoleon III. had extreme experiences as president and emperor in France. B. Paris, 1808. D. Chiselhurst, Eng., 1873.

Bond, William Cranch, an American astronomer. B. Portland, Me., 1789. D. Cambridge, Mass., 1859.

Bonheur, *bon-hur*, Rosa, a French painter. "Horse Fair." B. Bordeaux, 1822.

Boniface, Saint, was sent by Gregory II. to convert the barbarians of the north to Christianity. B. Devonshire, 680. Killed in Friesland, 754. There were nine popes of this name.

Boone, Daniel, an American pioneer. Fought the savages in Kentucky. B. Bucks County, Pa., 1735. D. Missouri, 1820.

Booth, Edwin, an American tragedian: B. 1833. Junius Brutus, tragedian, was father of Edwin; B. London, 1796; D. 1852.

Borgia, *bor-je-a*, Lucrezia, sister of the profligate Cæsar Borgia. Said to have been very wicked. D. Ferrara, 1523.

Bossuet, *boo-swa*, Jacques Benigne, Bishop of Meaux, an eloquent French preacher. B. Dijon, 1627. D. Paris, 1704.

Boudinot, *boo-de-not*, Elias, first President American Bible Society. B. Philadelphia, 1740. D. Burlington, N. J., 1821.

Boutwell, George Sewell, an American financier. B. Brookline, Mass., 1818.

Bouvier, *boo-veer*, John, publisher of a dictionary of law in United States. B. Codognan, France, 1718. D. Philadelphia, 1851.

Bowditch, Nathaniel, an American navigator. Published a translation of Laplace's Mecanique Celeste. B. Salem, Mass., 1773. D. 1838.

Boylston, Zabdiel, an American physician that introduced the practice of inoculation for the small-pox in Boston, about 1721, the year in which Lady Mary Wortley Montague practiced it in England. B. Brookline, Mass., 1680. D. 1676.

Braddock, Edward, a British general in America. Defeated and mortally wounded at Fort Duquesne, near the site of Pittsburg, Penn. B. Perthshire, in Scotland, 1715. D. 1755.

Bradford, William, an American artist. Sea views. B. New Bedford, Mass, 1827.

Bragg, Braxton, an American general in Mexican war and war 1861-5. Defeated Rosecrans at Chickamauga, Tenn. B. Warren county, N. C, 1817. D. Galveston, Texas, 1876.

Brahe, *bra*, a Danish speculator on astronomy. B. Knudstorp, Sweden. 1546. D. Prague, 1601.

Breckinridge, John Cabell, an American statesman. Confederate secretary of war. B. near Lexington, Ky., 1821. D. 1875.

Brewster, Sir David, a Scotchman that invented the kaleidoscope. B. Jedburgh, 1781. D. 1868. William, known as Elder Brewster, came to America as a Pilgrim.

Bright, John, an English statesman, friendly to America. B. Rochdale, Lancashire, 1811.

Brooks, Noah, an American newspaper man and story writer. B. Castine, Me., 1830.

Brown, Benjamin Gratz, an American editor and senator from Missouri. B. Lexington, Ky., 1826.

Browne, Charles Farrar, an American writer known as Artemus Ward. B. Waterford, Me., 1834. D. Southampton, Eng., 1867.

Browning, Elizabeth Barrett, an English poet. Wrote Aurora Leigh. B. London, 1809. D. Florence, 1861.

Bruce, Robert, the hero and king of Scotland. Beat the English at Bannockburn. Reigned 23 years. B. 1274. D. Bardross, 1329.

Brunswick. Name of one of the oldest German families, of which the royal family now living in England is a branch.

Brutus, Lucius Junius, a Roman patriot, was made consul 500 B. C. Killed by the Tarquins. Marcus Junius B. joined in killing Cæsar.

Bryant, William Cullen, an American poet. "Thanatopsis." B. Cummington, Mass, 1794. D. New York, 1878.

Buchanan, James, fifteenth president (Democrat) of the United States. Minister to St. Petersburgh. United States senator. B. Stony Batter, Penn., 1791. D. Lancaster, 1868.

Buckingham, George Villiers, duke of, an English politician that was favored by James I. B. Brookesley, Leicestershire, 1592. D. Portsmouth, 1628. His son, of the same name, a duke, was a favorite of Charles II.

Buell, Don Carlos, an American Major-General that operated against the Confederate forces in Kentucky and Tennessee, war 1861-5. B. near Marietta, O., 1818.

Buffon, Georges Louis Leclerc, a great naturalist—the Pliny of France; wrote 36 volumes natural history. B. Montbard, Burgundy, 1707. D. Paris, 1788.

Bull, Ole Borneman, a famous Norwegian violinist. B. Bergen, 1810. D. Norway, 1880.

Bulwer-Lytton, Edward George, Earl Lytton, Baron, an English novel and play-writer. B. Norfolk, 1805. D. London, 1873. Edward Robert, son, an English politician and poet. B. 1831. "Lucile."

Bunyan, John, wrote "Pilgrim's Progress." B. Elstow, near Bedford, Eng., 1628. D. London, 1688.

Burgoyne, John, a British general that surrendered his army at Saratoga, N. Y., 17th October, 1777, to General Gates. B. about 1730. D. London, 1792.

Burke, Edmund, a native of Dublin, made a great figure in English politics; in 1785, he impeached Hastings. B. 1730. D. Beaconsfield, 1797.

Burlingame, Anson, an American diplomat; minister to China. B. New Berlin, N. Y., 1822. D. St. Petersburg, 1870.

Burns, Robert, the inimitable Scottish poet. B. near Ayr, 1759. D. 1796.

Burnside, Ambrose Everett, an American major-general that captured Roanoke Island and Beaufort, N. C., in the war, 1861-5. B. Liberty, Ind. 1824. D. Bristol, R. I., 1881.

Burr, Aaron, an American politician; an enemy of the Federalists; murderer of Hamilton. B. Newark, N. J., 1756. D. "unwept, unhonored and unsung," on Staten Island, N. Y. 1836.

Butler, Benjamin Franklin, an American major-general, war 1861-5. A people's nominee for president in 1884. B. Deerfield, N. H., 1818.

Byron, George Gordon, Lord, a British poet. "Don Juan." B. London, 1788. D. Missolonghi, 1824.

C

Cabot, John, a British navigator that discovered North America. Flourished in 1497. Sebastian, son of the above, was with his father, and afterward sailed along the North American coast. B. Bristol, about 1477. D. 1557.

Cadwalader, John, an American brigadier-general, trusted by Washington. B. Philadelphia, 1743. D. 1786.

Cæsar, *se-zar*, Caius Julius, the first Roman emperor. In his eight years' war against the Gauls, Germans, Helvetians, and Britons, three million men were slain. Defeated Pompey at Pharsalus. He was assassinated in the senate house, which event involved the city of Rome in confusion, and paved the way to the revolution by which the people lost their liberty as a republic, and became subject to absolute monarchy. B. 100 B. C. Slain 43, B. C. See BRUTUS and CASSIUS.

Calhoun, John Caldwell, an American statesman and senator, vice-president with Adams and Jackson. He became a leader of the nullification party, that afterward bore its fruit of secession. B. district of Abbeville, S. C., 1782. D. Washington, 1850.

Caligula, Caius Cæsar Augustus Germanicus, the third emperor of Rome. a bad man. B. A. D. 12. Assassinated in the year 41.

Cameron, Simon, an American statesman. Secretary of war in Lincoln's cabinet. B. Lancaster county, Penn., 1799.

Camillus, Marcus Furius, a Roman dictator—a second Romulus. D. 365 B. C.

Camoens, Luiz de, the most celebrated poet of Portugal. B. Lisbon, 1524. D. 1580.

Campbell, Alexander, son of Rev. Thomas B. Founder of the Campbellite sect. B. County Antrim, Ire., 1786. D. Bethany, W. Va., 1866. William C., an American brigadier-general that opposed Cornwallis. B. Augusta, Va., 1745. D. Yorktown, 1781.

Campbell, Thomas, a pure British poet. B. Glasgow, 1777. D. Boulogne, 1844.

Canby, Edward Richard Sprigg, an American major general and in three wars; killed by the Modoc Captain Jack, in Siskiyou county, California. B. in Kentucky, 1819.

Canonicus, a Narragansett Indian chief, whose tribe was ever at peace with the whites. B. about 1565.

Canute, or Knut, the Great, king of Denmark; proclaimed king of England, 1017, on the death of Edmund. B. in Denmark, about 995; D. Shaftesbury, 1035. Canute IV., the Pious, king of Denmark, was slain by his subjects for making extraordinary grants of land to the church, 1087.

Caracalla, *kar-a-kal-la,* Marcus Aurelius, Antonius, a bad Roman emperor that caused wholesale butchery for base purposes; murdered by his successor, Macrinus, in 217, at Edessa. B. Lyons, A.D. 188.

Carey, Henry Charles, an American writer on political economy. B. Philadelphia, 1793; D. 1879.

Carlos, Don, son of Charles IV. of Spain; tried to get the crown. B. 1788; D. 1855.

Carlotta, wife of Maximilian, which see.

Carlyle, Thomas, a British author and lecturer. "Heroes, Hero-Worship, and the Heroic in History." B. in Ecclefechan, Scotland, 1795; D. 1881.

Carnot, *kar-no,* Lazaris Nicholas, a prominent actor in the French revolution; opposed the imperial power of Napoleon. B. in Burgundy, 1753; D. Magdeburgh, 1823.

Caroline, Amelia Elizabeth, wife of George IV. of England; was separated from him and traduced. B. 1768; D. 1821.

Carroll, Charles, of Carrollton, an American senator; last to die of the signers of the American Declaration. B. Annapolis, Maryland, 1737; D. 1832.

Carson, Christopher (Kit), an American ranger, and brigadier general, war 1861-5. B. in Kentucky, 1809; D. 1868.

Cartwright, Peter, an American clergyman that was indefatigable in the Methodist cause. B. in Virginia, 1785; D. Pleasant Plains, Illinois, 1872.

Carver, John, the first governor of Plymouth Colony, arriving there in the Mayflower Nov. 11, 1620. D. 1621.

Carey, Alice, and Phœbe, her sister, American poets. Alice born near Cincinnati, 1820; D. New York, 1871. Phœbe born 1824; D. Newport, 1871.

Cary, Lott, a negro preacher that aided in starting the colony of Liberia. He was a slave in the Old Dominion. B. 1780. D. 1828.

Casabianca, Louis, a captain in the French navy. He was commander of the Orient in Napoleon's expedition to Egypt, and perished with his son of ten years at the battle of the Nile. "The boy stood on the burning deck." B. Bastia about 1755.

Casimir, *kas-i-meer.* Name of several kings of Poland

Cass, Lewis, an American senator, and presidential nominee that opposed Gen. Taylor. B. Exeter, N. H., 1782. D. Detroit, 1867.

Cassius, *kash-e-us,* Longinus Caius, one of the slayers of Cæsar. He was brother-in-law of Brutus. Distinguished himself in the Parthian war. Believing the battle at Philippi to be lost he had himself killed by a servant, 42 B. C.

Castillo, Bernal Diaz del, an adventurer that accompanied Cortes in Mexico. B. near close sixteeth century. D. 1560.

Castro, Ines de, was the mistress, and in succession the wife, and lastly, in death, the crowned Queen of Pedro of Portugal, the Cruel, her corpse being taken from the tomb to be saluted and crowned as queen. Murdered four years before by the nobles. Camoens tells her story in "Lusiads." Lived fourteenth century.

Catherine I., empress of Russia, wife of Peter the Great; B. Livonia, 1686; D. 1727. II., Catherine Alexievna, married grandson of Peter the Great, had him deposed and was proclaimed empress; B. 1729; D. 1796.

Catherine de Medici, *kat-er-ine de med-e-che,* a French queen that instigated the butchery of the Huguenots in 1572. B. Florence, 1519. D. Blois, 1589.

Catiline, Lucius Sergius, a Roman that conspired against Rome, and was unmasked by Cicero. Killed, 62 B. C.

Cato, Marcus Porcius, a Roman statesman and patriot; became consul; B. Tusculum about 234 B. C. Cato, the Younger, a patriot, though rich, was frugal in his habits; B. Rome, 95 B. C.; killed himself 46 B. C. to escape from Cæsar.

Cavour, *ka-voor,* Camillo Benso, Count, an Italian statesman. B. Turin, 1810. D. 1861.

Caxton, William, a London mercer that introduced the printers' art in England. B. Kent about 1412. D. London, 1492.

Cervantes, *ser-van-tez,* a Spanish novelist. "Don Quixote." B. Alcala de Henares, 1547. D. 1616.

Chandler, Zachariah, an American senator. B. Bedford, N. H., 1813. D. Chicago, 1879.

Channing, William Ellery, an American clergyman, Unitarian. B. Newport, R. I., 1780. D. Burlington, Vt., 1842.

Chapin, Edwin Hubbell, an American clergyman, Universalist; B. Union Village, Washington county, N. Y., 1814. D. New York, 1880. Stephen C. was a Congregationalist and then Baptist; B. Milford, Mass., 1778; D. Washington, 1845.

Charlemagne, *sharl-e-main,* or Charles the Great, emperor of the West. His Dominion reached from the Baltic to the Mediterranean. B. Bavaria, 742. D. Aix-la-Chapelle, 814.

Charles Martel, a sovereign of France for twenty-five years during the nominal reigns of the last of the Merovingians. Overthrew the Saracens at the battle of Poitiers, by which he probably saved Europe from the infidel yoke. B. about 694. D. Quercy sur Oise, 741.

Charles. There were many other sovereigns of this name in France, Germany, Naples, Sardinia, Spain, Sweden and other countries. Charles V., of France, was wise, and VII. was victorious against the English. VIII. conquered Italy, and was king of Naples and Emperor of Constantinople. IX. reigned during massacre of St. Bartholomew. I., of England, on throne 1625, much involved in wars; defeated and executed.

Chase, Salmon Portland, an American financier. The greenback currency is attributed to him. Secretary treasury under Lincoln. B. Cornish, N. H., 1808. D. New York, 1873.

Chaucer, Geoffrey, the earliest of British poets, and a man of extraordinary genius. B. London, 1328. D. 1400.

Cheatham, B. F., an American commander of confederate troops in Georgia, war 1861-5.

Chesterfield, Philip Dormer Stanhope, Earl of, a British statesman and polished writer. B. London, 1694. D. 1773.

Child, Lydia Maria, an American writer. B. Medford, Massachusetts, 1802. D. Wayland, 1880.

Chilo, *ki-lo*, one of the seven wise men. D. 597 B.C.

Choate, Rufus, an American pleader and senator. B. Ipswick, Massachusetts, 1799. D. Halifax, 1859.

Christiern, *kris-te-ern*, name of nine Danish sovereigns. IX., king of Denmark, began his reign November 15, 1863. B. April 8, 1818.

Church, Frederick Edwin, an American artist; landscapes. B. Hartford, Connecticut, 1826.

Cibber, Colley, a British dramitist of great merit. B. 1703. D. on the water, near Ireland, 1758.

Cicero, Marcus Tullius, a Roman orator and consul: joined Pompey against Cæsar; proscribed by Mark Antony, pursued, and murdered, 43 B.C. B. Arpinum, 106 B.C.

Cincinnatus, Lucius Quintius, a Roman farmer patriot; twice made dictator of Rome. B. about 519 B.C.

Clarke, James Freeman, an American clergyman. B. Hanover, New Hampshire, 1810.

Claudius. Name of many Roman sovereigns and generals. Appius, a magistrate, was struck at sight of Virginia, the beautiful daughter of Virginius, and tried to possess her; he was foiled by the father, who killed Virginia that she might be saved from the clutches of Appius, who afterward died in prison, 449 B.C.

Clay, Cassius Marcellus, an American major general and abolitionist. B. Madison county, Kentucky, 1810. D. 1872.

Clay, Henry, an American senator, and presidential nominee for president four times; a whig. B. near Richmond, Virginia, 1777. D. Washington, 1852.

Cleburne, Patrick R., an American major-general, confederate service, 1861-5.

Clement, *klem-ent*, name of fourteen popes.

Cleobulus, *kle-ob-u-lus*, one of the seven wise men of Greece. D. 560 B. C.

Cleopatra, Queen of Egypt, was successively the mistress of Julius Cæsar and of Anthony. With her ended the kingdom of Egypt. She put an end to her existence by the bite of an asp 30 B. C. B. 69 B. C.

Cleveland, Stephen Grover (Democrat), twenty-second President of the United States. James G. Blaine, of Maine, being the unsuccessful (Republican) candidate for that office. C. was governor of New York. Elected President 1884. B. Essex, N. J., March 18, 1837. Richard, father of the above, was educated for the Presbyterian ministry.

Clingman, Thomas L., an American statesman in confederate service 1861-5. B. Huntsville, N. C., about 1812.

Clinton, Sir Henry, a British general that served in America; took Charleston in 1780; B. 1738; D. 1795. James C. was member of the convention for the adoption of the present constitution of the United States; B. New York, 1736; D. 1812. George was vice-president United States, a brigadier-general, governor New York; B. New York, 1739; D. Washington, 1812. DeWitt, nephew of George, was an American senator, mayor of New York, governor of that state; B. Little Britain, Orange county, N. Y., 1769; D. 1828.

Clovis I., *klo-ve*, the founder of a new monarchy whose capital was Lutetia, or Paris. Clotilda, a Christian princess, was his queen. B. Tournai about 465. D. Paris, 511.

Cole, Thomas, an American artist; landscape. "Voyage of Life." B. Lancashire, Eng., 1801. D. Catskill, N. Y., 1848.

Coleridge, Samuel Taylor, a British poet. B. Ottery, St. Mary, Devonshire, 1772. D. London, 1834.

Colt, Samuel, the inventor of revolver of same name. B. Hartford, Connecticut, 1814. D. 1862.

Colfax, Schuyler, vice-president United States, and speaker in the national house. Distinguished as a public lecturer. Delivered his last lecture on "Landmarks of Life" before the students of the Metropolitan Business College at Chicago and died of heart disease a few days afterward at Mankato, Minn., January 13, 1885. B. New York, 1823.

Columbus, Christopher; discovered the American continent in 1492. B. Genoa, 1441. D. Valladolid, 1506.

Commodus, Lucius Aurelius Antonius, a Roman emperor and a bad man. B. A.D. 161; put to death 192.

Conde, Louis II., of Bourbon, Prince of, called the Great; defeated the Spaniards at Rocroi; active and full of resources. B. Paris, 1621. D. Fontainebleau, 1686.

Confucius, the Chinese philosopher; was born about 550 B.C. D. 479 B.C.

Conkling, Roscoe, an American statesman; an independent Republican or Stalwart; United States senator from New York. B. Albany, October 30, 1828.

Conrad. Name of several kings of Germany.

Constantine, the Great, emperor of Rome, a Christian; called the council at Nice. B. Nissa, 272. D. near Nicomedia, 337. There were other emperors of Rome and the East of this name.

Cook, Captain James, a British navigator; explored various regions. B. Marton, Yorkshire, 1728; killed and eaten by savages on Sandwich islands, 1779.

Cooper, James Fenimore, an American author. B. Burlington, New Jersey, 1789. D. Cooperstown, 1851.

Cooper, Peter, an American inventor; National nominee for president in 1876, receiving over 81,000 votes; founder of the Institute named for him. B. New York, 1791. D. 1883.

Copernicus, Nikolaus, a celebrated Prussian astronomer, and restorer of the true system of the world. B. Thorn, 1472. D. Frauenburg, 1543.

Corday, Charlotte. See MARAT.

Cornwallis, Charles, Lord, a British general that served in America, and surrendered at Yorktown, Virginia, 1781. B. 1738. D. Ghazepore, 1805.

Cortes, *kor-tecz*, Hernando, the Spanish conqueror of Mexico. B. Medellin, 1485. D. near Seville, 1547.

Corwin Thomas, an American statesman, United States senator, secretary treasury with Fillmore. B. in Kentucky. D. Washington, 1865, in his 71st year.

Cox, Samuel Sullivan (Sunset), an American statesman. B. Zanesville, O., 1824.

Cowper, *koo-per*, William, a pleasing British poet. B. Hertfordshire, 1731. D. East Dereham, Norfolk, 1800.

Cranmer, Thomas, a celebrated reformer, and archbishop of Canterbury. B. Aslacton, in Nottinghamshire, 1489. Brought to the stake March 21, 1556.

Crittenden, John Jordon, an American statesman, and long a United States senator. B. Woodford county, Ky., 1787. D. near Frankfort, 1863.

Cromwell, Oliver, the protector of the commonwealth of England. Succeeded nominally to the sovereign authority. B. Huntingdon, 1599. D. Hampton Court, 1658.

Crook, George, an American general of cavalry in war 1861-5. B. near Dayton, O., 1828.

Curtis, George William, an American journalist. Leader of independent Republicans in opposition to Blaine, the nominee for president in 1884. B. Providence, R. I., 1824.

Cushing, Caleb, an American statesman and diplomat; B. Salisbury, Mass., 1800; D. Newburyport, 1879. William B., an American naval officer that destroyed the confederate ram Albemarle. B. Wisconsin, 1843.

Cushman, Charlotte Saunders, a famous American tragedian. B. Boston, 1816. D. 1876.

Cuvier, *koo-ve-a*, Georges Chretien Leopold Frederic Dagobert, Baron, a French naturalist. "Animal Kingdom." B. Montbeliard, 1769. D. Paris, 1832.

Cyrus, the Great, dethroned his grandson and overcome Crœsus of Lydia, took Babylon, and founded the great Persian Empire. Rivers of blood were shed in his conquests. B. about 600 B. C.

D

Daggett, David, an American judge and senator. B. Attleboro, Massachusetts, 1764. D. New Haven, Connecticut, 1851.

Daguerre, *da-gare*, the French discoverer of the process of taking pictures. B. in France, 1789. D. 1851.

Dahlgren, John Adolph, an American naval officer; made a rear admiral in 1863. B. Philadelphia, 1809. D. Washington, 1870.

Dallas, Alexander James, an American statesman; in Madison's cabinet as secretary of treasury. B. Jamaica Island, 1759; D. Trenton, N. J., 1817. George Mifflin, son, an American statesman, senator, vice-president. B. 1792. D. 1864.

Dana, James Dwight, an American naturalist. B. Utica, New York, 1813. Richard Henry, an American writer of poetry. B. Cambridge, Massachusetts, 1787. D. Boston, 1879.

Dante, the most powerful of the Italian poets. B. Florence, 1265. D. in exile at Ravenna, 1321.

Danton Georges Jacques, one of the most active demagogues of the French revolution; vanquished by Robespierre. B. Arcis sur Aube, 1759; guillotined 1794.

Dare, Virginia, was born at Roanoke, August 18, 1587; named for the Virginia districts; first English child born on the American continent.

Darius I., king of Persia; destroyed Babylon; defeated at Marathon; D. 485 B.C. Codomanus, the last king of the ancient Persian empire, was conquered by Alexander.

Darwin, Charles Robert, an English naturalist; he believed in the ascent of man from lower forms of life; evolution. B. Shrewsbury, 1809. D. 1882.

Davis, Henry Winter, an American statesman; a friend of national union during late war 1861-5. B. Annapolis, Maryland, 1817; D. Baltimore, 1865. Jefferson Davis, an American statesman; president of southern confederacy, 1861-5. B. Todd county, Kentucky, 1808. Jefferson C., an American general, war 1861-5. B. Clark county, Indiana, 1828.

Davy, Sir Humphrey, the most original and able chemist of his time. B. Penzance, Cornwall, 1778. D. Geneva, Switzerland, 1829.

Dayton, William Lewis, an American senator and diplomat. B. Basking Ridge, N. J., 1807. D. Paris, 1864.

Decatur, Stephen, Jr., an American commodore that was killed in a duel with Commodore James Barron. B. Sinnepuxent, Md., 1779. Killed at North Bladensburg, Md., 1820.

Defoe, Daniel, the British author, famous for writing "Robinson Crusoe." B. London, 1661. D. 1731.

Delaware, Thomas West, the first governor of Virginia. The state of Delaware was named for him in 1610. D. 1618.

Demosthenes, *De-mos-the-neez*, the most admired of Greek orators, and an Athenian patriot. B. Pæania, in Attica, about 385. To save himself from Antipater he took poison, 322 B. C.

De Quincey, Thomas, a British author and opium eater. B. near Manchester, 1786. D. Edinburgh, 1859.

Descartes, Renatus, a celebrated French metaphysician, mathematician and natural philosopher. B. La Haye, Touraine, 1596. D. Stockholm, 1650.

De Soto, Fernando, an adventurer that discovered the Mississippi river. B. Xerxes du Caballeros, in Estremadura, 1496. D. 1542, and was buried in Mississippi river.

Dickens, Charles, the famous British novelist. "David Copperfield," "Little Dorritt." B. Landport, 1812. D. near Rochester, 1870.

Dickinson, Anna Elizabeth, an American reader and actress; has appeared in "Hamlet;" B. Philadelphia, 1842. Daniel Stevens D., an American statesman; B. Goshen, Ct., 1800; D. Binghamton, N. Y., 1866.

Diderot, *de-da-ro*, Denis, a powerful French philosophical writer. B. Langres, 1713. D. Paris, 1784.

Diogenes, *di-odj-e-neez*, one of the celebrated Greek philosophers. B. in Asia Minor about 412 B. C. D. 323 B. C.

Disraeli, *diz-ra-el-e*, Benjamin, Earl of Beaconsfield, a British prime minister, and leader of the conservatives in England. B. London, 1804. D. 1881.

Dix, John Adams, an American statesman; governor of New York, senator, and major general war 1861-5. B. Boscawen, New York, 1789. D. New York, 1879.

Domitian, Titus Flavius Domitianus Augustus. See TITUS.

Donati, *do-na-tee*, Giovanni Battista, a modern Italian astronomer; discovered comet of his name, June 2, 1858. B. Pisa, 1826. D. Florence, 1873.

Dore, *do-ra*, Paul Gustave, a French painter; has illustrated "Paradise Lost." B. Strasburg, 1833.

Douglas, Stephen Arnold, an American statesman and political orator; senator from Illinois; affectionately called "the Little Giant." B. Brandon, Vermont, 1813. D. Chicago, 1861.

Dow, Neal, an American general, war 1861-5; a temperance reformer. B. Portland, Maine, 1803.

Drake, Sir Francis; sailed round the world in 1577-80, and afterward served as admiral. B. Tavistock, Devonshire, 1545; D. at sea, West Indies, 1595. John Rodman, an American poet. B. New York, 1795. D. 1820.

Draper, John William, an American chemist and writer; made research in spectrum analysis. B. St. Helens, near Liverpool, 1811.

Dryden, John, an illustrious British poet; translated Virgil. B. Aldwinkle, Northamptonshire, 1631. D. 1700.

Dumas, *du-ma*, Alexander Davy, a French writer of stories and plays. B. Villers-Cotterets, 1803. D. Puyneur, Dieppe, 1870. Alexander, his son, a French writer of stories. B. Paris, 1824.

Dyer, John, a British poet that wrote "Grongar Hill" and "The Fleece." B. Carmarthenshire, 1700; D. 1758. George D., a poet and antiquary, was born 1755; D. 1841.

E

Eads, *eeds*, James Buchanan, an American civil engineer. Designer St. Louis bridge. B. Lawrenceburg, Ind., 1820.

Early, Jubal A., an American general in confederate service, war 1861-5. B. Virginia about 1815.

Edison, Thomas Alva, an American electrician and inventor. His phonograph, telephone and electric light have made him famous. B. Milan, O., 1847.

Edmunds, George Franklin, an American statesman and senator. B. Richmond, Va., 1828.

Edward. Name of seven kings of England.

Eliot, George (Marian Evans), a well-known British novelist; "Romola." B. about 1820; D. 1880. Samuel, an American writer; "History of Liberty;" B. Boston, 1821.

Elizabeth, queen of England, was the daughter of Anne Boleyn; she was rather heartless, and a true child of Henry VIII; she was last of the Tudor line that reached from A.D. 1485 to 1603. B. Greenwich, 1533. D. Richmond, 1603.

Emerson, Ralph Waldo, an eminent writer of prose and poetry. B. Boston, 1803.

Emmet, Robert, an Irish patriot; tried to make Ireland free. B. Dublin, 1780; executed, 1803.

Ericsson, *er-ik-son*, John, the great Swedish inventor and engineer. Iron-clad Monitor was constructed by him. B. Wermeland, 1803. D. Stockholm, 1889.

Euclid, *u-klid*, a Grecian whose name is immortalized for his work on "The Elements of Geometry," fifteen volumes. B. Alexandria, about 300 B.C.

Evarts, *ev-arts*, William Maxwell, an American statesman; counsel for Andrew Johnson in the impeachment trial. B. Boston, 1818.

Everett, Edward, an American orator and senator. B. Dorchester, Massachusetts, 1794. D. Boston, 1865.

Ewell, Richard Stoddard, an American general in confederate service, Bull Run, Gettysburg. B. Washington, 1823. D. in Tennessee, 1872.

Ewing. Thomas, an American statesman and senator; organized the Interior department under Harrison and Tyler. B. Ohio county, Virginia, 1789. D. Lancaster, Ohio, 1871.

F

Fagnani, *fag-na-nee*, Joseph, an American portrait painter. B. Naples, 1819. D. New York, 1873.

Fahrenheit, *fa-ren-hite*, Gabriel Daniel, a German philosopher that improved the thermometer. B. in Dantzic, about 1690. D. Amsterdam, 1736.

Faneuil, *fun-il*, Peter, an American merchant that erected the famous hall of that name in Boston. B. New Rochelle, New York, 1700. D. Boston, 1743.

Farragut, *far-a-gut*, David Glascoe, an American admiral, in the public service in 1812, and at New Orleans and Mobile Bay, war 1861-5. B. near Knoxville, Tennessee, 1801. D. Portsmouth, New Hampshire, 1870.

Fenton, Reuben E., an American statesman, governor of New York, and United States senator. B. Carroll, N. Y., 1819.

Fessenden, William Pitt, an American statesman, member congress, senator, secretary treasury in President Lincoln's administration. B. Boscawen, N. H., 1806. D. Portland, Me., 1869.

Field, Cyrus West, the founder of the ocean telegraph; B. Stockbridge, Mass., 1819. David Dudley, brother, an American jurist; B. Haddam, Conn., 1805.

Fillmore, Millard, thirteenth president of the United States. Elevated from the vice-presidency on the death of Taylor. B. Cayuga county, N. Y., 1800. D. Buffalo, 1874.

Floyd, James Buchanan, an American statesman. Secretary of war under President Buchanan. Confederate general war 1861-5. B. Montgomery, Va., 1805. D. Abington, Va., 1863.

Foote, Andrew Hull, an American admiral. Captured Ft. Henry on Tennessee river war 1861-5. B. New Haven, Conn., 1806. D. New York, 1863.

Foster, Stephen Collins, an American writer of songs. Author of "Old Kentucky Home," "Oh, Susanna," etc. B. Pittsburg, 1826. D. New York, 1864.

Fowler, Orson Squire, an American phrenologist. B. Cohocton, N. Y., 1809.

Francis Joseph I., the emperor of Austria and Hungary, began his reign December 2, 1848. B. August 18, 1830.

Franklin, Benjamin, Dr., an American politician; an active minister of state. B. Boston, 1706. D. Philadelphia, 1790.

Franklin, Sir John, a British arctic explorer; lost his life in the North, as a record indicates, in 1847. B. Spilsby, Lincolnshire, 1786.

Frederick William, the emperor of Germany, began his reign January 2, 1861. B. March 22, 1797.

Fremont, John Charles, an American major-general, explorer, senator, nominee for president. B. Savannah, Ga., 1813.

Fulton, Robert, the famous American inventor; applied steam to the propelling of boats. B. Little Britain, Penn., 1765. D. New York, 1815.

G

Gadsden, Christopher, an American patriot leader; a delegate to first continental congress, in 1774. B. Charleston, S. C., 1724. D. 1805.

Gage, Thomas, the British commander of the royal troops in North America, and last governor of Massachusetts for the English crown. D. England, 1787.

Gaines, *ganz*, Edmund Pendleton, an American officer of the revolution. B. Culpepper county, Va., 1777. D. New Orleans, 1849. Myra Clark, born New Orleans, 1805. Gained property there worth six million dollars.

Galilei, Galileo, the founder of mechanical philosophy, was born at Pisa in 1564. Discovered the pendulum as a measure of time, Jupiter's moons, Venus' phases and the ring of Saturn, and followed these astonishing discoveries by constructing the microscope. In 1611 he discovered at Rome the spots on the sun, and in 1615 he was arraigned before the inquisition. Again arraigned and tortured in 1632. Became blind in 1636. His last discoveries were the moon's librations and the cause. D. Arcetri, 1642.

Gambetta, Leon, a French republican leader. B. Cahors, 1838. D. 1882.

Garfield, James Abram, twentieth president of the United States, senator from Ohio, major-general war 1861-5. B. Orange, Cuyahoga county, O., 1831. Shot by Charles Guiteau, July 2, 1881, and died at Elberon, Long Branch, September 19.

Garibaldi, *gar-e-bal-de*, Giuseppe, a modern Italian patriot and general. Was conspicuous in the Italian war of 1859 against the Austrians. Engaged in an ill-advised and unsuccessful attempt, in 1867, to free Rome from the Papal government. B. Nice, 1807. D. 1882.

Garland, Augustus H., an American senator from Arkansas. Was a member of the confederate congress. B. Tipton county, Tenn., 1832.

Garrison, William Lloyd, an American abolitionist and advocate of woman suffrage. The Liberator, started in Boston in 1831 was his paper. B. Newburyport, Mass., 1804. D. 1879.

Gates, Horatio, an American general of the revolution; defeated General Burgoyne at Saratoga, and forced him to surrender with his whole army; was defeated at Camden, South Carolina, by Cornwallis; he emancipated his slaves. B. in England, 1728. D. New York, 1806.

Gatling, Richard, an American inventor; gun. B. Hertford county, North Carolina, 1818.

Geary, John White, an American general. B. 1819. D. 1873.

George I., king of Greece, began his reign June 6, 1863. B. December 24, 1845.

Germanicus, Cæsar, a nominal Roman emperor; at the head of the Roman army in Germany when Augustus died; defeated Arminius; he was father of CALIGULA, which see; probably poisoned by order of Tiberius, at Antioch, A.D. 19, in his 34th year.

Giddings, Joshua Reed, an American politician; representative from Ohio in congress; elected to congress about eleven times. B. Tioga Point, now Athens, Pennsylvania, 1795; D. Montreal, Canada, 1864.

Girard, Stephen, an American merchant. At his death he left $9,000,000 for public purposes. A college is named for him. B. near Bordeaux, 1750. D. Philadelphia, 1831.

Gladstone, William Ewart, the British premier and chancellor of the exchequer. The Earl of Beaconsfield resigned April 28, 1880, when Gladstone became his successor. B. Liverpool, 1809.

Goldsmith, Oliver, a British poet and dramatist. "The Genius of Love," "She Stoops to Conquer." B. Pallas, Ire., 1728. D. London, 1774.

Goodrich, Chauncey Allen, an American educator, author of a grammar; B. 1790; D. 1860. Samuel Griswold, a writer for young folks, was the well-known "Peter Parley;" B. Ridgefield, Conn., 1793; D. New York, 1860.

Goodyear, Charles, an American inventor that discovered the process of vulcanizing India rubber. B. New Haven, Conn., 1800. D. New York, 1860.

Gough, John B., an American temperance lecturer. B. Sandgate, Kent, Eng., 1817.

Gould, Jay, an American speculator. A great railroad magnate. B. Roxbury, N. Y., 1837.

Grant, Ulysses Simpson, eighteenth president of the United States. Held office for two terms, from 1869 to 1877. Famous for his successes in the war 1861-5. General Grant traversed the globe in 1879. B. Point Pleasant, O., 1822.

Gray, Thomas, a British poet. Author of the beautiful Elegy. B. Cornhill, London, 1716. D. London, 1771.

Greeley, Horace, an American journalist. Founder of New York Tribune. A presidential nominee in 1872, and defeated by General Grant. B. Amherst, N. H., 1811. D. Pleasantville, N. Y., 1872.

Greene, Nathaniel, an American general of the Revolution; was in the battles of Trenton, Princeton, Germantown and Brandywine; much esteemed by Washington. B. Potowhommet, R. I., 1742. D. near Savannah, Ga., 1786.

Greenough, Horatio, an American sculptor that made a colossal statute of Washington. B. Boston, 1805. D. 1852. Ogden, an American scholar, and soldier in war 1861-5; an able lawyer, writer and orator. B. Marshall, Ill., 1840. Killed before Kenesaw, Ga., 1864.

Gregory. There were sixteen popes of this name.

Grey, Lady Jane, a talented woman that learned many languages; had the honors of the English crown thrust upon her, and was proclaimed queen, July 10, 1553; reigned nine days; her husband and herself were, in February, 1554, beheaded by the relentless Mary, who began to reign July 6, 1553, and died in 1558. Lady Jane was born at Bradgate hall, in Leicestershire, 1537.

Gustavus, Adolphus, the greatest king of Sweden; he protected the Lutherans in Germany, and humbled the house of Austria by his victories. Fell in the battle of Lutzen, in 1632. B. Stockholm, 1594.

Gutenberg, *goo'ten-ba-erg*, Johann, the partner of Faust (which see), inventor of printing. B. Metz, 1400. D. 1468.

H

Hahnemann, Samuel Christian Frederick, the founder of the Homœopathic system of medicine. B. Saxony, 1755. Died Paris, 1843.

Hale, Nathan, an American patriot, war of the Revolution. B. Coventry, Ct., 1755. Captured as a spy, and executed by order of Sir William Howe, in New York, 1776.

Hall, Charles Francis, an American explorer in the North; the principal figure of several expeditions. B. Rochester, N. H., 1821. D. Greenland, 1871.

Halleck, Fitz Greene, an American poet. "Marco Bozzaris." B. Guilford, Connecticut, 1795; D. 1867. Henry Wager, an American major general; Grant's chief of staff. B. Waterville, New York, 1815. D. Louisville, Kentucky, 1872.

Hamilton, Alexander, an American statesman; secretary of the treasury on the organization of the federal government in 1789. B. Nevis, in the West Indies, 1757; D. New York, 1804.

Hampton, Wade, an American senator; lieutenant general in confederate service, war 1861-5. B. Columbia, South Carolina, 1818.

Hancock, John, an American statesman; was president of the continental congress in 1775; first to sign the American Declaration. B. Quincy, Massachusetts, 1737. D. 1793.

Hancock, Winfield Scott, an American general that served in the Indian territory, Mexico, and war 1861-5; a presidential nominee of the Democratic party in 1880 against Garfield. B. Montgomery county, Pennsylvania, 1824.

Hannibal, a famous Carthaginian general that took Saguntum in 219 B.C., and gained the battle of Cannæ, in Apulia, in 216; defeated near Zama by Scipio, in 202, and so ended the second Punic war. B. 247 B.C.; poisoned himself to escape the Roman victors, 182 B.C.

Hardee, William J., an American general in confederate service, war 1861-5; compiler of Tactics that is named for him. B. Savannah, Georgia, 1818. D. Wytheville, Virginia, 1873.

Harrison, William Henry, ninth president of the United States; defeated the Indians at battle of Tippecanoe. Mass-meetings and processions first came in vogue. B. Berkeley, Virginia, 1773. D. Washington, 1841, one month after his inauguration, and was succeeded by Vice President John Tyler, who was the tenth president of the United States. The latter was born in Charles City county, Virginia, 1790. D. Richmond, 1862.

Harte, Francis Bret, an American author; writer of poetry. B. Albany, New York, 1839.

Hawthorne, Nathaniel, an American author. "The Scarlet Letter." B. Salem, Mass., 1804. D. Plymouth, N. H., 1864.

Hayes, Rutherford Birchard, nineteenth president of the United States; major-general; governor of Ohio; B. Delaware, O., 1822. Isaac Israel H. was an American explorer of the Arctic regions; B. Chester county, Pa., 1832; D. 1881.

Hendricks, Thomas Andrews, an American statesman. Vice-president of the United States with Cleveland. United States senator from Indiana. Defeated by Morton for governor in 1859, and again in 1868. Elected governor in 1872, and re-elected, serving till 1877.

Holmes, Oliver Wendell, an American writer of prose and poetry. B. Cambridge, Mass., 1809.

Homer, the father of poetry, and supposed author of the Iliad and Odyssey. Was a native of Chios or Smyrna, and probably died there. Lived about 907 B. C.

Hood, John B., an American general in the confederate service, war 1861-5. Defeated at Nashville. B. Bath county, Ky., 1830. D. New Orleans, 1879.

Henry. Name of eight English kings, and various sovereigns of France and Germany. I. and II. of England were good and amiable. III. was pusillanimous. IV. a usurper. V. formed the design of conquering France; won the battle of Agincourt. VI., son of preceding, an imbecile. VII., usurper and tyrant. VIII., cruel; disgraced England by his robberies and horrible executions to gratify his lust. See ANNE BOLEYN. IV., the Great, of France, defeated the Duke of Mayenne at Ivry, but lost the results of the victory; satisfied the Catholic party by abjuring the Protestant faith in 1593; five years from that year were spent in securing his throne, when, in 1598, he issued the edict of Nantes, granting toleration to Protestants; B. Pau, capital of Bearn, 1553; assassinated in Paris in 1610, after a glorious reign of twenty-one years. See MARIE DE MEDICI.

Henry, Patrick; an American statesman and orator that exclaimed, "Give me liberty or give me death" B. Studley, Hanover county, Virginia, 1736. D. Red Hill, Charlotte county, 1799.

Herodotus, the first Greek historian, and father of history. Lived about 450 B. C.

Herschel, Sir William, one of the greatest of modern astronomers. Discovered Uranus in 1781, its satellites in 1787. B. Hanover, 1738. D. Windsor, Eng., 1822.

Hewitt. Abram Stevens, an American statesman. Representative from New York in the forty-fourth and forty-fifth congresses. B. Haverstraw, N. Y., 1822.

Hooker, Joseph, an American general in the war 1861-5. Commander of Army of the Potomac, 1863. B. Hadley, Mass., 1815. D. Garden City, N. Y., 1879.

Hosmer. Harriet Goodhue, an American sculptor. "Zenobia." B. Watertown, Mass., 1831.

Houston. Sam, an American general and governor of Texas. B. Lexington, Va., 1793. D. Huntersville, Texas, 1863.

Howard, Oliver Otis, an American general war 1861-5. Distinguished himself at Gettysburg B. Leeds, Kennebec county, Me., 1830.

Howe, Elias, an American inventor. Sewing machine. B. Spencer, Mass., 1819. D. Brooklyn, N. Y., 1867.

Hull, Isaac, an American commander on the waters; captured the British frigate Guerriere. B. Derby, Connecticut, 1775. D. Philadelphia, 1843.

Humbert, king of Italy, began his reign January 9, 1878. B. March 14, 1844.

Humboldt, Friedrich Heinrich Alexander, Baron von, an eminent German philosopher and traveler; creator of the science of comparative geography, and reviewer of the study of the natural sciences. B. Berlin, 1769. D. 1859.

Hume. David, a Scotch writer that treated of history and metaphysics. B. Edinburgh, 1711. D. 1776.

Huxley, Thomas Henry, a British scientist that has written of man's place in nature. B. Middlesex, 1825.

I

Ingersoll, an American orator of the iconoclastic persuasion. B. Dresden, New York, 1833.

Innocent. A title assumed by thirteen popes.

Irving, John Henry Brodrib, a British tragedian. B. near Glastonbury, 1838. Washington, an American writer of sketches and history. B. New York, 1783. D. Sunnyside, 1859.

Isabella of Castile, a queen of Spain. The discovery of America by Columbus was made during the reign of Isabella and Ferdinand V., king of Aragon, who married and reigned together. B. 1450. D. 1504.

Ismail, *is-ma-eel*, Mohammed Tewfik, the present khedive of Egypt. B. 1852.

J

Jackson, Andrew (new Democratic party), the seventh president of the United States, served two terms, 1829-36, inclusive. He defeated the British at New Orleans, in 1815; United States senator twice; executed the law against the nullification scheme in Charleston, S. C. B. Waxhaw, N. C., 1767. D. Hermitage farm, near Nashville, Tenn., 1845.

Jackson, Thomas Jonathan, better known as Stonewall, was an American general that served against the Seminoles and in Mexican war, and the war of 1861-5, in which latter he was a confederate lieutenant-general. B. Clarksburg, Va., 1824. D. near Fredericksburg, 1863.

Jay, John, chief justice of supreme court of the United States, the first. Served 1789-95; member of congress of the United Colonies. B. New York, 1745. D. 1829.

Jefferson, Thomas (Democratic-Republican), third president of the United States. Served two terms, 1801-8, inclusive. Author of Notes on Virginia; drew up the American Declaration. B. Shadwell, Va., 1743. D. Monticello, 1826.

Joan of Arc, *zhan-dark*, the illustrious Maid of Orleans; raised the siege of Orleans, and assisted at the coronation of King Charles VII., at Rheims. She afterward fell into the hands of the execrable Duke of Bedford, Regent of England, and was by him burnt as a sorceress at Rouen, in 1431. B. Domremy, Lorraine, about 1411.

Johnson, Andrew (Democrat), the seventeenth president of the United States. Served from April 15, 1865, till the inauguration of President Grant, in 1869; elevated second term of Lincoln. B. Raleigh, N. C., 1808. D. near Elizabethtown, Tenn., 1875.

Johnston, Joseph Eccleston, an American general that opposed the national troops in the war of 1861-5; served against the Indians in Florida, and in the Mexican war in 1847, being wounded twice; surrendered his confederate army to Sherman, April 26, 1865. B. in Prince Edward county, Virginia, 1807.

K

Kane, Elisha Kent, an American explorer of the ice region; made a search for Sir John Franklin, 1853. B. Philadelphia, 1820. D. Havana, 1857.

Kellogg, Clara Louisa, an American musician that is eminent in opera. B. Sumter, South Carolina, 1842.

Kepler, Johann, an eminent German astronomer, whose fame rests upon his discovery that the planets' orbits are elliptical. B. Weil, Wirtemberg, 1571. D. Ratisbon, 1630.

Kilpatrick, Judson, an active cavalry officer in the United States service in 1861-5. B. 1832.

Knox, Henry, an American general of artillery, war of the Revolution; secretary of war with Washington. B. Boston, 1750. D. Thomaston, Me., 1806. John K. was the great champion of the Scottish reformation. B. Gifford, East Lothian, 1505. D. Edinburgh, 1572.

L

Lafayette, *laf-a-et*, Maris Jean Paul Roch Yves Gilbert Motier, Marquis de, a celebrated soldier and patriot, whose talents and energy were thrown into the American service as against the British domination; distinguished himself in Virginia and at the siege of Yorktown. B. Chavagnac, dept. Haute-Loire, 1757. D. Paris, 1834.

Lamar, Lucius Quintus Cincinnatus, an American statesman; United States senator. B. Jasper county, Ga., 1826.

Lamb, Charles, a distinguished English essayist and humorist. B. London, 1775. D. Edmonton, 1834.

La Salle, *la-sal*, Robert Cavelier Sieur de, a French explorer that discovered the mouth of the Mississippi river in 1691. B. Rouen, 1643. Killed in 1687 by his men while on the way to Canada.

Law, John, a schemer that started the Mississippi company and involved much ruin in France. Saved himself by flight. B. Edinburgh, 1681. D. Venice, 1729.

Lawrence, James, an officer of the American navy. With the Hornet he took the British brig Peacock. Received a mortal wound on the Chesapeake while in action with the frigate Shannon. B. Burlington, N. J., 1781. D. 1813.

Lee, Ann, the founder of Shaker associations in America, was born in Manchester, Eng., 1736; D. Watervliet, N. Y., 1784. Richard Henry was an eloquent speaker, and United States senator; B. Stafford, Va., 1732; D. Westmoreland county, Va., 1794. Robert Edward, one of the best of American generals; "Light Horse Harry" Lee, also an American general, was his father; Robert E. became chief commander of the confederate army in northern Virginia; surrendered to Grant at Appomattox, April 9, 1865; B. Stafford, Va., 1807; D. Lexington, Va., 1870.

Leibnitz, Gottfried Wilhelm, Baron, a German metaphysician and scientist. A profound and masterly controversial theologian. B. Leipsic, 1646. D. Hanover, 1716.

Leo. Name of six emperors of Constantinople, between the years 457 and 886. The name of thirteen popes; the last was proclaimed in 1878, and was born in Carpineto, Italy, in 1810.

Lesseps, *dah-la-sep*, Ferdinand, Viscount de, a French diplomat that cut the Ishthmus of Suez and opened communication by water between the Red sea and the Mediterranean. B. Versailles, 1805.

Lever, Charles James, an Irish writer of stories. "Charles O'Malley." B. Dublin, 1809. D. 1872.

Leverrier, *leh-va-re-a*, Urbain Jean Joseph, a modern French astronomer, celebrated for his discovery of the planet Neptune. B. St. Lo., France, 1811. D. 1877.

Lewes, *lu-is*, George Henry, a British author; married Marian Evans. See ELIOT, George.

Lewis, Dio, an American writer on the laws of health. B. Auburn, New York, 1823. Edmonia, an American carver; made bust of Longfellow. B. near Albany, New York, 1845. Ida, saved four men from a watery grave near Newport, Rhode Island, where she was born in 1841.

Liebig, *fon le-big*, Justus, Baron von, a distinguished German chemist. "Familiar Letters on Chemistry." B. Darmstadt, 1803. D. Munich, 1873.

Linnæus, *lin-ne-us*, or Linn, Charles von, the most celebrated of modern naturalists; explored Lapland. B. Rashutt, 1707. D. 1778.

Livingstone, David, a distinguished African traveler; verified the existence of Lake Ngama. B. Scotland, 1813. D. Itala, Central Africa, 1873.

Lincoln, Abraham, the sixteenth president of the United States; elected twice, 1860 and 1864; hero of the war of 1861-5; signed the emancipation proclamation that made free all the slaves in the United States. Assassinated in Washington, by J. Wilkes Booth, April 14, 1865. B. Hardin county, Kentucky, 1809. Robert, son, an American politician; secretary of war in the cabinet of President Arthur. B. Springfield, Illinois, 1843.

Lind, Jenny, a celebrated Swedish musician; began to sing at ten; visited the United States in 1850. B. Stockholm, 1821.

Lippincott, Sarah Jane, better known as Grace Greenwood, an American writer for young people. B. New York, 1823.

Liszt, Franz, an eminent Hungarian composer. B. Raiding, 1811.

Livy, or Livius, Titus, a celebrated Roman historian, "History of Rome." B. Territory of Patavium, now Padua, 59 B. C. D. A. D., 17.

Locke, John, an English political and philosophical writer; wrote essay on human understanding. B. near Bristol, 1632. D. Otes, 1704.

Lockyer, Joseph Norman, a British astronomer; viewed the eclipse in Sicily, in 1870, for the government. B. Rugby, 1836.

Logan, John Alexander, an American statesman; United States senator from Illinois; nominee for vice-president on the Blaine ticket, in 1884. B. Jackson Co., Ill., 1826.

Longfellow, Henry Wadsworth, an eminent American poet. "Excelsior." B. Portland Me., 1807. D. 1882.

Longstreet, James, an American lieutenant-general in the Confederate army, war 1861-5; was in the Mexican war. B. South Carolina, 1820.

Longworth, Nicholas, an American lawyer that became a maker of wines, and was a millionaire. B. Newark, N. J., 1782. D. Cincinnati, 1863.

Lopez, *lo-pes*, Don Francisco Solano, succeeded his father, Don Carlos, as president of Paraguay, in 1862; was beaten by allies and made to flee in 1869; a bad man. B. near Asuncion, 1827. Killed in 1870.

Lossing, Benson John, an American writer of history. "Pictorial History United States." B. Beekman, N. Y., 1813.

Louis. Name of German and French sovereigns. XVI. of France was unfortunate, and met his death on the scaffold in 1792; the queen was executed in 1793, and his sister in 1794. XVII., brother of the preceding in the reign of terror, and that of Bonaparte, was obliged to leave his country. Twice replaced on the throne by the allied Powers. D. in 1825. Philippe of France, *fe-leep*, first of the Orleans line, was forced to flee, and finally sailed for America in 1796. After a checkered career, he was placed on the throne in 1830, which he held for 17 years. Harrassed by illiberal restrictions, his people broke out in revolution in 1848, and he fled from Paris in disguise. B. Paris, 1773. D. Claremont, Eng., 1850.

Lover, *luv-er*, Samuel, an Irish writer. "Handy Andy." B. Dublin, 1797. D. 1868.

Lowell, James Russell, an American poet; "Biglow Papers;" B. Cambridge, Mass., 1819. Maria, his wife, was a poet; B. Watertown, Mass., 1821; D. Cambridge, 1853.

Loyola, Ignatius de, celebrated as the founder of the order of Jesuits. B. Guipuzcoa, Spain, 1491. D. Rome, 1556.

Luther, Martin, a celebrated reformer of Germany. Declared the pope the "man of sin" set forth in Scripture. B. Eisleben, Lower Saxony, 1483. D. 1546.

Lycurgus, a celebrated Spartan legislator that is supposed to have been born 926 B. C. An Athenian orator of this name lived about 408 B. C.

Lucretia, a Roman matron, was the wife of Collatinus, and the cause of the revolution of Rome from a monarchy to a republic. Sextus Tarquinius, who tried to prevail over her virtue, had recourse to a scheme by which he succeeded in violating her person. The next day she acquainted her husband and kindred of the transaction, and, in spite of their soothing remonstrances, drew a dagger and stabbed herself. The bloody poinard, with her dead body exposed to the senate, was the signal of Roman liberty. The expulsion of the Tarquins, and the abolition of the regal dignity was instantly resolved upon and carried into execution. Died 509 B.C.

Lysander, a famous Spartan general that defeated the Athenian fleet when the 27 years' war came to an end. Killed in action 396 B. C.

Lytton, Edward George, Earl. See BULWER-LYTTON.

M

Macaber, an early German poet. "Dance of Death," consisting of dialogues between Death and a number of personages belonging to various ranks of society.

Macadam, John Loudon, a Scotch surveyor that invented the system of road-making called after his name. B. Ayr, 1756. D. Moffat, Dumfriesshire, 1836.

Macaulay, Thomas Babington, Lord, a celebrated British historian and poet. Wrote ballads. B. Rothley Temple, Leicestershire, 1800. D. Holly Lodge, Campden Hill, 1859.

Macbeth, a Scottish king that was beaten at Dunsinane by the English in 1054. Defeated and killed at Lumphanan.

MacDonald, James Wilson Alexander, American sculptor and artist. B. Steubenville, Ohio, 1830.

Macmahon, Marie Edme Patrice Maurice, duke of Magenta; president French republic, 1873-9. B. near Autun, 1808.

Macready, William Charles, a British tragedian. B. London, 1793. D. Somersetshire, 1873.

McDonald, Joseph E., an American senator, from Indiana. B. Butler county, Ohio, 1819.

McDowell, Irwin, an American general under Beauregard. B. Franklin county, Ohio, 1818.

McClellan, George Brinton, an American general; captured Yorktown; Antietam, 1862; nominee for president in 1864. B. Philadelphia, 1826.

McPherson, an American general. B. Clyde, Sandusky Co., Ohio, 1828; killed in action, 1863.

Madison, James, the fourth president of the United States. B. King George, Virginia, 1751. D. Montpelier, Virginia, 1836.

Magalhaens, *ma-gal-ya-ens*, or Magellan, Fernando, a Portuguese navigator; discovered the straits named for him. B. Opporto, 1470; killed by natives of Philippine islands, which he discovered, 1521.

Mahomet, or Mohammed, the founder of the Mahometan faith; proclaimed the koran in his fortieth year. B. Mecca, in 569 or 571. D. 632, and was buried at Medina. I., sultan or emperor of the Turks; restored the power of the Ottomans to its ancient glory; B. 1374. II., the Great, born in 1430; took Constantinople in 1453. D. 1481.

Maintenon, *mant-non*, Frances d'Aubigne, Marchioness of, a woman of great personal beauty; mistress King Louis XVI. D. St. Cyr, 1719.

Manlius Capitolinus, Marcus, a famous Roman consul. The geese awoke him in time to save the Roman capitol from sudden attack at night. For trying to obtain the sovereignty of Rome, he was thrown from the Tarpeian rock, 381 B.C. Torquatus slew a Gaul, and took his chain (torques) from his neck; hence he assumed the name of Torquatus; lived 340 B.C.

Mann, Horace, an American senator that was interested in the cause of education; school system was reformed by him; president of Antioch college. B. Franklin, Massachusetts, 1796. D. Yellow Springs, Ohio, 1859.

Mansfield, William Murray, Earl of, a British chief justice. B. Perth, 1704. D. London, 1793, having filled his office for thirty-two years.

Manutius, Aldus, invented the type known as *italic*. B. Bassiano, 1449. D. Venice, 1515.

Marat, Jean Paul, a French revolutionist of 1793. Assassinated by Charlotte Corday. Marat born at Baudry, Switz., 1744. Assassinated, 1793.

Marcellus, Marcus Claudius, Roman general. Successfully encountered Hannibal in second Punic war. Captured Syracuse, in Sicily. B. about 268 B. C. Killed in ambuscade, 208 B. C.

Marcy, William Larned, an American statesman. Secretary of war under Polk. B. Southbridge, Mass., 1786. D. Ballston Spa, N. Y., 1857.

Maria Louisa, ex-empress of France. Napoleon Bonaparte's second wife. B. 1791. D. 1847.

Maria Theresa, empress of Germany and queen of Hungary; had a stormy reign. She was secured in her rights by the peace made at Aix-la-Chapelle. Called mother of her country. B. Vienna, 1717. D. 1780.

Marie de Medici, *me-de-che*, wife of Henry IV. of France. After the king's murder, became regent. Reign disgraced by the countenance she afforded to unworthy favorites; forced to leave France by Richelieu. B. Florence, 1573. D. Cologne, 1642.

Marius, a Roman general; was six times consul; butcher. D. 86 B. C.

Marlborough, John Churchill, Duke of, celebrated British general. Principal victories: Blenheim, in 1704; Ramillies, 1706; Oudenarde, 1708, and Malplaquet, 1709. B. Ashe, Devonshire, 1650. D. London, 1722.

Marquette, Jacques, a French missionary that explored the Mississippi. B. Laon, 1637. D. on the shore east of Lake Michigan, 1675.

Marshall, John, the fourth chief justice of United States Supreme Court; served, 1801-35. B. Fauquier county, Va., 1755. D. Philadelphia, 1835.

Martineau, *mar-te-no*, Harriet, a British writer on various subjects. B. Norwich, 1802. D. Ambleside, 1876.

Mary, the mother of the Savior, daughter of Joachim and Anna, of the tribe of Judah, was married to Joseph of the same tribe. Of the royal house of David.

Mary (Bloody), Queen of England; her reign was stained with the blood of many martyrs; in four years, 227 persons were burned. B. Greenwich, 1516. D. St. James palace, 1558. Mary Stuart, Queen of Scots. After nineteen years captivity in England, she was executed in Fotheringay castle, 1587. B. Linlithgow palace, 1542.

Maury, Matthew Fontaine, American officer; published a physical geography of the sea, in 1856. B. Spottsylvania county, Virginia, 1806. D. Lexington, Virginia, 1873.

Maximilian, Ferdinand Maximilian Joseph, archduke of Austria and emperor of Mexico; married Carlotta Marie Amelie, who was born 1840, and shot, in Mexico, 1866. B. Vienna, 1832; shot, Queretaro, 1867.

Mazarin, Jules, a political churchman; succeeded Cardinal Richelieu, prime minister of France, which he governed till his death at Paris, in 1661. B. Piscina, Naples, 1602.

Mazzini, *mat-see-nee*, Guiseppe, a modern Italian politician and patriot. B. Genoa, 1808. D. 1872.

Meade, George Gordon, American general; commanded army of the Potomac at Gettysburg; Cold Harbor, Spottsylvania, Wilderness. B. Cadiz, Spain, 1815. D. Philadelphia, 1872.

Medici, *med-e-che*, Cosmo de, the Elder, and Father of his Country, a merchant and founder of an illustrious family at Florence; governed Florence from 1428 to 1464; B. 1389; D. 1464. Lorenzo de, the Magnificent, son of Peter, grandson of Cosmo, and brother of Julian de Medici; these brothers enjoyed an almost absolute power in Florence. Julian was assassinated at the instigation of Ferdinand I. and Pope Sextus IV., 1478. Lorenzo was wounded, but escaped with his life; accounted the Mæcenas of his age. B. 1448. D. 1492.

Mehemet Ali, pacha of Egypt; conquered Syria, and was kept out of Constantinople by European intervention. B. Cavalla Roumelia, 1769. D. Cairo, 1849.

Meissonier, *ma-so-ne-a*, Jean Louis Ernest, a celebrated French artist. B. Lyons, 1812.

Melancthon, Philip, Reformer; associate of Luther. B. Brettin, Baden, 1497. D. Wittenberg, 1560.

Mendelssohn-Bartholdy, Felix, German composer. B. Hamburg, 1809. D. Leipsic, 1847.

Mesmer, Frederich Anton, German physician, after whom animal magnetism is named. B. Merseburg, Swabia, 1734. D. 1815.

Metternich, Clement Wenceslas, Prince, an Austrian diplomat. B. Coblentz, 1773. D. Vienna, 1859.

Meyerbeer, *mi-er-ba-er*, Giacomo, great German composer. B. Berlin, 1794. D. 1864.

Michelet, *me-sheh-la*, French historian. B. Paris, 1798. D. Hyeres, 1874.

Mill, John Stuart, an eminent writer on political economy. B. London, 1806. D. Avignon, France, 1873.

Miltiades, a celebrated Athenian general; gained the battle of Marathon, in 490, against the Persians. Lived about 500 B.C.

Milton, John, author of "Paradise Lost," and "Paradise Regained." B. London, 1608. D. 1674.

Mirabeau, *me-ra-bo*, Count de, eloquent French orator. B. near Nemones, 1749. D. Paris, 1791.

Modjeska, *mo-jes-ka*, Countess, Polish actress. B. Cracow, 1844.

Mohammed. See MAHOMET.

Moliere, *mo-le-air*, Jean Baptiste, a very eminent French dramatist; wrote comic plays. B. Paris, 1622 D. 1673.

Mollhausen, Baldiun, a German writer of stories; visited United States. B. Bonn, 1825.

Moltke, *molt-keh*, Helmuth Karl Bernhard von, a German general. Received the title of count after the success at Metz, Franco-German war. B. Mecklenburg, 1800.

Monroe, James (Democratic-Republican), the fifth president of the United States. United States senator in 1790. Minister to France, London and Spain. Governor of Virginia. Secretary of state. Served two terms as president, 1817-25. B. Westmoreland county, Va., 1758. D. New York, 1831.

Montagu, Lady Mary Wortley, an English authoress. B. Thoresby, Nottinghamshire, about 1690. D. London, 1762.

Montezuma, the last king of Mexico. Conquered by Cortez. Stoned to death in 1520 for having proposed to surrender to the Spanish. B. about 1480.

Montgomery, Richard, an American major-general. Took Montreal. Fell at Quebec, 1775. B. near Raphoe, Ire., 1736.

Moore, Sir John, a British general, killed 1809 at the battle of Corunna. B. Glasgow, 1761.

Moore, Thomas, eminent Irish poet. Wrote history of Ireland. B. Dublin, 1779. D. 1852.

More, Hannah, an eminent English author; B. near Bristol, 1745; D. Clifton, Gloucestershire, 1833. Sir Thomas, English statesman and writer; B. London, 1480; beheaded, 1535.

Moreau, *mo-ro*, Jean Victor, French revolutionary general. Joined the allied sovereigns against France in 1813, and was killed before Dresden. B. Morlaix, 1763.

Morgan, Daniel, American general, defeated the British at the Cowpens. B. New Jersey, 1736. D. Winchester, Va., 1802.

Morrison, William R., an American statesman, and colonel in war 1861-5. Wounded at Ft. Donelson. Elected to congress three times. B. Monroe county, Ill., 1825.

Morse, Samuel Finley Breese, an American inventor. Invented electric telegraph in 1832. Made a line between Baltimore and Washington in 1844. Made first submarine cable. B. Charlestown, Mass., 1791. D. New York, 1872.

Morton, Oliver Perry, an American senator. War governor of Indiana. B. Wayne county, 1823. D. Indianapolis, 1877.

Motley, John Lothrop, an American historian. B. Dorchester, Mass., 1814. D. England, 1877.

Mozart, *mote-sart*, Wolfgang Amadeus, a famous German composer. B. Salzburg, 1756. D. Vienna 1791.

Murray, Lindley, American author of grammar of the English language. B. Swatara, Penn., 1745. D. near York, England, 1826.

N

Napier, *na-pe-er*, John, Baron, a celebrated Scotch mathematician. Invented logarithmic tables. B. Merchiston Castle, near Edinburgh, 1550. D. there 1617.

Nast, Thomas, an American caricaturist. B. Landau, Bavaria, 1840.

Nelson, Horatio, Lord, an illustrious English admiral; was killed at Trafalgar, Spain, where he gained a great victory, 1805. B. Norfolk, 1758.

Nero, wicked emperor of Rome; persecuted the Christians. B. Antium, A. D., 37. Killed himself in 68.

Newton, Sir Isaac, English philosopher and mathematician. B. Woolsthorpe, Lincolnshire, on Christmas day, 1642. Discovered the law of gravitation; analyzed light. D. near London, 1727.

Ney, Michel, bravest of Napoleon's marshals. Executed in 1815. B. Sarre Louis, 1769.

Nicholas I., became emperor of Russia in 1825; defeated the shah of Persia soon afterwards; aided Greeks to gain their independence; defeated Turks in war of 1828. B. St. Petersburg, 1796. D. 1855, during Crimean war.

Nightingale, Florence, the English humanitarian in the Crimea, from 1854 to 1856. B. Florence, 1820.

North, Lord, a British prime minister for twelve years, in the reign of George III. Introduced a bill in 1778, in which assumption of right of Great Britain to tax the colonists, led to the American war of Independence. B. 1732. D. 1792.

O

O'Connell, Daniel, known in his time as the Liberator of Ireland. Was born in County Kerry, 1775. D. Genoa, 1847.

Oglesby, Richard J., an American general; elected governor of Illinois in 1864, re-elected, 1872, and in 1884; United States Senator, 1873. B. Oldham county, Ky., 1824.

Oldcastle, Sir John, the first author and martyr of the reformation. B. in reign of Edward III. Burned 1418.

Optic, Oliver, an American writer for the young people; published a magazine. B. Medway, Mass., 1822.

Orange, William of Nassau, Prince of, founder of the Dutch Republic. B. 1533. Assassinated, Delft, 1584.

Orsini, Felice, Italian patriot; in 1858, tried to kill the French emperor, and was executed. B. Meldola, 1819.

Osman, or Othman I., called the Victorious; founder of the race that reigns at Constantinople. B. Sakut, Bithynia, 1259. D. 1326. See ABDUL HAMID.

Otho I., called the Great, emperor of Germany; was elected in 936. B. 912. D. Memleben, Thuringia, 973.

Ovid, Publius Ovidius Naso, Latin poet; banished by Augustus. B. Sulmo, 43 B.C. D. Tomi, A.D. 18.

Owen, Robert, British philanthropist and founder of socialism. B. Newton, Montgomeryshire, 1771. D. 1858.

P

Paine, Thomas, American philosopher. D. New York, 1809.

Pakenham, Sir Edward, a British general that was killed in battle at New Orleans in 1815.

Palmer, *pah-mer*, Erastus Dow, an American sculptor; made a statue of Robert Livingstone. B. Pompey, N. Y., 1817.

Palmerston, *pah-mer-stun*, Henry John Temple, Viscount, a British statesman and well-known foreign minister; prime minister twice. B. London, 1784. D. Brockett Hall, Herts, 1865.

Parnell, Charles Stewart, Irish leader in parliament. B. County Wicklow, 1846.

Parton, James, an American writer and biographer. B. Canterbury, Eng., 1822.

Pascal, Blaise, French philosopher. B. Clermont, 1623. D. Paris, 1662.

Payne, John Howard, an American dramatist; author of "Home, Sweet Home." B. New York, 1792. D. Tunis, 1852.

Peabody, George, an American millionaire that endowed many institutions. Peabody institute. B. Danvers, Mass., 1795. D. London, 1869.

Peel, Sir Robert, son of the cotton-spinner of that name; was a celebrated British statesman; several times at the head of affairs; settled the Oregon question with the United States. B. Bury, Lancashire, 1788. D. London, 1850.

Pemberton, John C., a confederate general, 1861-5; surrendered to Grant at Vicksburg. B. Philadelphia, 1817.

Pendleton, George H., an American senator from Ohio. B. Cincinnati, 1825.

Penn, William, the founder and legislator of Pennsylvania. B. London, 1644. D. Ruscombe, Berkshire, 1718.

Pericles, an Athenian orator. B. 495 B.C. D. Athens, 429 B.C.

Perry, Oliver Hazard, American naval officer; gained a victory on Lake Erie. B. Rhode Island, 1785. D. West Indies, 1820.

Peter I., Alexievitsch, the Great, emperor of Russia. B. Moscow, 1672; D. St. Petersburg, 1725. II., reigned after the two years of Catherine, who succeeded Peter the Great. III., strangled, 1762.

Phillips, Wendell, a celebrated American orator and humanitarian. B. Boston, 1811. D. 1884.

Pierce, Franklin (Democrat), the fourteenth president of the United States, 1853-7; brigadier general in Mexican war. B. Hillsborough, N. H., 1804. D. Concord, 1869.

Pitt, William, Earl of Chatham, made a speech, in 1778, against the American war, and died from exhaustion. His second son was the equally-famous William Pitt that became prime minister twice, last time in 1804. B. at Hayes, 1759. D. Putney, 1806.

Pius. Name of nine popes. IX. died in 1878.

Pizarro, Francisco, Spanish freebooter; conquered Peru and founded Lima in 1535. B. Truxjillo, 1471; killed by enemies, at Lima, 1541.

Plato, Greek philosopher. B. Athens, about 429 B.C. D. 348.

Pliny, Caius Plinius, the Elder; classic author. B. 23 A.D. D. 79.

Plutarch, *plu-tark*, Greek biographer and historian. B. Chæronea. D. about A.D. 140.

Pocahontas, an Indian princess; is celebrated in the history of Virginia for her heroic attachment to the colonists. B. about 1595. D. Gravesend, Eng., 1617.

Poe, Edgar Allan, American poet. B. Boston, 1809. D. Baltimore, 1849.

Polk, James Knox (Democrat), eleventh president of the United States. B. Mecklenburgh county, N. C., 1795; D. Nashville, 1849. Leonidas, confederate general. B. Raleigh, N. C., 1806; killed by a cannon ball, near Marietta, Ga., 1864

Pope, Alexander, British poet. B. London, 1688. D. 1744.

Pompey, Cneius Pompeius Magnus, rival of Cæsar.

Powers, Hiram, an American sculptor. B. Woodstock, Vt., 1805. D. Florence, Italy, 1873.

Priestley, Dr. Joseph, British philosopher. B. in Yorkshire, 1733. D. Northumberland, Penn., 1804.

Ptolemy, *tol-e-me*, Sagus, one of the generals of Alexander the Great; obtained Egypt as his share of the spoils. D. 285 B.C.

Putnam, Israel, an American major general, war of the revolution; active in French and Indian wars at an earlier period. B. Salem, Mass., 1718. D. Brooklyn, Ct., 1790.

Pythagoras, *pi-thag-o-ras*, the earliest Greek philosopher, geometrician and astronomer. B. Samos, about 580 B.C.; aged about eighty.

Quitman, John Anthony, American general conspicuous in taking Pueblo and Mexico. B. Dutchess county, N. Y., 1799. D. Natchez, 1858.

R

Racine, Jean, French dramatist. B. Ferte-Milon, Aisne, 1639. D. Paris, 1699.

Raleigh Sir Walter, an illustrious English navigator; discoverer of Virginia; defeater of the Spanish Armada. B. Hayes, Devonshire, 1552. Beheaded in 1618.

Raphael, a celebrated Italian artist. B. Urbino, 1483. D. Rome, 1520.

Reade, Charles, a British story writer of force and originality. B. Ipsden, 1814. D. 1884.

Red Jacket or Sagoyewatha, celebrated Indian chief, of the Senecas. B. Old Castle, N. Y., 1752. D. Seneca village, near Buffalo, 1830.

Rembrandt van Ryn, Paul Harmens, Dutch painter. B. Leyden, 1607. D. Amsterdam, 1669.

Renan, *reh-non*, Joseph Ernest, author of "Life of Christ." B. Treguier, 1823.

Richelieu, *reesh-le-uh*, Armand Jean Duplessis, Duke of, a celebrated French cardinal and statesman; managed affairs for Louis XIII. B. Paris, 1585. D. 1642.

Robespierre, *ro-bes-pe-air*, Maximilian Joseph François Isidore, head of the Jacobins. B. Arras, 1759. Beheaded, 1794.

Roebling, John Augustus, designer of the Brooklyn Bridge, New York. B. Prussia, 1806. D. Brooklyn, 1869.

Rogers, John, English biblical scholar; burned for his Protestantism in 1515, at Smithfield.

Rosecrans, William Starke, an American major-general, war 1861-5. B. Kingston, O., 1819.

Rosse, Earl of, British astronomer. B. York, 1800. D. Ireland, 1867.

Rousseau, *roos-so*, Jean Jacques, French philosopher. B. Geneva, 1712. D. Paris, 1778.

Rubens, Peter Paul, illustrious Flemish painter. B. Siegen, Germany, 1577. D. Antwerp, 1640.

Russell, William, Lord, an English politician, was beheaded for his Protestanism, in London, 1683. B. 1639.

S

Scott, Sir Walter, voluminous writer of tales and romantic histories, in verse and prose. B. Edinburgh, 1771. D. Abbotsford, 1832.

Scott, General Winfield, a commander-in-chief of the United States army; he gained the battles of Chippewa and Lundy's Lane; 1816, gained several victories in the Mexican war, besides his capture of the City of Mexico in 1847. B. Petersburg, Va., 1786. D. West Point, 1866.

Semmes, *sems*, Raphael, Confederate commander of the "Alabama." B. Charles county, Md., 1809. D. 1877.

Seward, William Henry, an American statesman; governor of New York; United States senator; secretary of state in Lincoln's cabinet. B. Florida, N. Y., 1801. D. Auburn, 1872.

Shakspeare, William, the immortal English dramatist. B. Stratford-upon-Avon, Warwickshire, 1564. D. 1616.

Shelley, Percy Bysshe, a British poet. B. near Horsham, Sussex, 1792. Met his death by drowning in Spezia bay, in 1822.

Sheridan, Philip Henry, an American general of cavalry and infantry, war 1861-5; became lieutenant-general in 1869, commander-in-chief, 1884. B. Somerset, O., 1831.

Sherman, William Tecumseh, an American commander-in-chief; his greatest exploits were the campaign of 1864, that ended in the capture of Atlanta, and the march to the sea and through the Carolinas. B. Lancaster, O., 1820.

Silliman, Benjamin, an American scientist; published a book on chemistry. B. Trumbull, Ct., 1779. D. New Haven, 1864.

Sixtus. Name of five popes, the last of whom was the founder of the Vatican library.

Saint Anthony was founder of monastic institutions. B. near Heraclea, 251; lived one hundred and five years.

Santa Anna, Antonio Lopez de, a Mexican general and statesman, was president of the republic of Mexico several times, before 1848; defeated by Generals Scott and Taylor; from 1852 to 1855 he again held power, but was driven into exile by General Carrera, who turned against him. B. in Jalapa, 1798. D. 1876.

Schenck, Dr. Noah Hunt, an American clergyman. D. in Brooklyn, January 5, 1885.

Smith, Gerrit, an American humanitarian and writer. B. Utica, N. Y., 1797, D. New York, 1874. John, founder of Virginia. B. Willoughby, Lincolnshire, 1579. D. London, 1631.

Socrates, *sok-ra-teez*, Greek philosopher; the priesthood had him poisoned, at Athens, in 399 B.C. B. near that place, about 470 B.C.

Solon, Athenian law-giver; one of the seven wise men of Greece. B. Isle of Salamis, 638 B.C. D. Athens, 559 B.C.

Sophocles, *sof-o-kleez*, a celebrated Greek tragedian. B. Athens, about 496 B.C. D. 406.

Spencer, Herbert, a British scientist. Evolution. B. Derby, 1820.

Spenser, Edmund, a British poet. "Fairie Queen." B. London, 1553. D. 1599.

Spinoza, Benedict, a learned Jewish philosopher. B. Amsterdam, 1632. D. at the Hague, 1677.

Stafford, William Howard, Viscount, a British statesman; perished on the scaffold, no doubt as an innocent man. B. 1612.

Stephen. Name of ten popes.

Stephens, Alexander Hamilton, vice president of the southern confederacy, in 1861. B. in Georgia, 1812. D. Atlanta, 1883.

Stephenson, George, a British inventor; the locomotive for the rail was contrived by him. B. Wylam, Northumberland, 1781. D. near Chesterfield, Derbyshire, 1848.

Stewart, Charles, an American rear admiral; commanded the "Constitution," in the war of 1812, and captured the British war vessels "Picton," "Cyane," and "Levant." B. Philadelphia, 1778. D. Bordentown, N. J., 1869.

Stoddard, Richard Henry, a poet. B. Hingham, Mass., 1825.

Story, Joseph, an American jurist that was associate justice of the United States supreme court. B. Marblehead, Mass., 1779. D. Cambridge, 1845.

Stowe, Harriet Elizabeth. See Beecher.

Stuart, Gilbert Charles. B. Rhode Island, 1756. D. Boston, 1828. Name of English and Scotch sovereigns.

Sumner, Charles, an American statesman and senator. B. Boston, 1811. D. Washington, 1874.

Swedenborg, Emanuel, a Swedish philosopher. B. Stockholm, 1688. D. London, 1772.

T

Tacitus, Caius Cornelius, Roman historian. B. about 55 A.D. D. 117.

Tamerlane, or Timur, a celebrated Tartar that gained many victories, and claimed that his power was over three-fourths of the world. B. near Samarcand, 1336. D. 1405.

Tasso, Torquato, eminent Italian poet; became a lunatic. B. Sorrento, 1544. D. 1595.

Taylor, Zachary (Whig), the twelfth president of the United States; major in the war of 1812; colonel in Black Hawk war; commander of United States army in Florida war. B. Orange county, Va., 1784. D. Washington, 1850, after serving as president four months. See Fillmore.

Tecumseh, an Indian chief; fought on the side of the British in the war of 1812-15. B. Ohio, about 1770. Killed in battle of Thames, 1813.

Tell, William, Swiss patriot; chief of the revolution that delivered the Swiss Cantons from the German yoke, in 1307. D. 1354.

Tennyson, Alfred, British poet laureate. Became a peer in 1884. B. Somersby, Lincolnshire, 1810.

Thackeray, William Makepeace, a Britsh novelist. B. Calcutta, 1811. D. London, 1863.

Theodosius, the Great; last Roman emperor; a convert to Christianity. B. in Spain, about 346 A.D. D. Milan, 395.

Thiers, *tee-air*, Louis Adolphe, president of the French republic, 1871-3, and was succeeded by McMahon. B. Marseilles, 1797. D. 1877.

Thomas, George Henry, an American commander, 1860-65. B. Southampton county, Va., 1816. D. San Francisco, 1870.

Titus. Flavius Sabinus Vespasianus, a Roman emperor that reigned two years, from A.D. 79. B. A.D. 40. D. 81.

Tyler, John. See Harrison, W. H.

Tyndall, John, a British scientist that witnessed the solar eclipse in Algeria in 1870 by order of the government. B. County Carlow, Ireland, 1820.

Tyng, Stephen Higginson, an American clergyman, and writer on theology. B. Newburyport, Mass., 1800.

V

Van Buren, Martin (Democrat), the eighth president of the United States; served, 1837-41; senator in 1821, and governor of New York in 1828; secretary of state with Jackson; minister to England. B. Kinderhook, N. Y., 1782. D. Kinderhook, 1862.

Van Dyke, Sir Anthony, the prince of portrait painters, was born at Antwerp in 1599. D. 1641.

Verne, Jules, an eminent French romancer. "Twenty Thousand Leagues Under the Sea." B. Nantes, 1828.

Victor Emanuel, king of Italy. B. Turin, 1820. D. 1878.

Victoria Alexandrina, queen of England, began her reign, June 20, 1837. B. Kensington palace, 1819.

Virginia. See CLAUDIUS.

Voltaire, François Marie Arouet de, the great French writer; was for fifty years the most popular in Europe. Œdipus. B. Paris, 1694. D. 1778.

W

Wade, Benjamin Franklin, an American senator from Ohio; vice-president of the United States, after the elevation of Andrew Johnson to the presidency. B. Springfield, Mass., 1800. D. Jefferson, O., 1878.

Wagner, Richard, an eminent German musician. "Flying Dutchman." B. Leipsic, 1813. D. 1883.

Watt, James, a British inventor; made improvement in the steam engine. B. Greenock, Scotland, 1736. D. near Birmingham, 1819.

Washington, George (Federalist), commander-in-chief of American army; father of his country, and first president of the United States. Served two terms, from 1789 to 1797. B. Westmoreland county, Va., 1732. D. Mt. Vernon, 1799.

Wayne, Anthony, an American major general in the revolution; captured Stony Point. B. Waynesborough, Penn, 1745. D. Erie, Penn. (then Presque Isle), 1796.

Webster, Daniel, a renowned American statesman; United States senator, 1824; secretary of state with Harrison, again senator, and secretary of state under Fillmore in 1850. B. Salisbury, N. H., 1782. D. Marshfield, Mass., 1852.

Wellington, Arthur Wellesley, Duke of, an illustrious British general. B. near Dublin, 1769. D. near Deal, Eng., 1852.

Whittier, John Greenleaf, an American poet. "Snow Bound." B. Haverhill, Mass. 1807.

William I., the Conqueror. B. Falaise, Normandy, 1027. D. 1087.

Wolfe, James, a British general. D. 1759, in his 34th year. B. Westerham, Kent.

X

Xenophon, *zen-o-fon*, a Greek general. Supposed birth, 444 B. C.

Xerxes, *zerks-eez*, a Persian king, called the great. Reigned in fifth century, B. C. Slain 465.

Y

Youmans, Edward Livingstone, an American writer on natural history and science. B. Coeymans, N. Y., 1821.

Young, Brigham, the late head of the Mormons in Utah. B. Whitingham, Vt., 1801. D. Salt Lake City, 1877.

TABLE Showing the Railway Distances, Railway Fares, and Mail Time from New York to the Chief Cities of the United States.

Place.	R'y Distance.	R'y Fares.	Mail Time.	Place.	R'y Distance.	R'y Fares.	Mail Time.
	Miles.	$ cts.	H. M.		Miles.	$ cts.	H. M.
Albany, N. Y.	145	3 10	4 15	Fort Wayne, Ind.	765	16 50	20 0
Atlanta, Ga.	881	25 50	32 15	Galveston, Texas	1783	40 50	97 15
Auburn, N. Y.	319	6 58	9 30	Harrisburg, Penn.	182	5 50	5 0
Baltimore, Md.	188	6 20	6 0	Hartford, Conn.	112	2 65	2 30
Bangor, Me.	478	12 00	19 40	Indianapolis, Ind.	824	18 25	29 45
Boston, Mass.	225	6 00	8 0	Kansas City, Mo.	1349	32 50	60 0
Bridgeport, Conn.	58	1 50	2 0	Keokuk, Iowa	1128	26 10	48 15
Brooklyn, N. Y.	2	02	0 35	Leavenworth, Kan.	1352	32 75	62 0
Buffalo, N. Y.	424	9 25	14 0	Little Rock, Ark.	1417	42 50	54 10
Burlington, Iowa	1139	27 25	47 0	Louisville, Ky.	867	21 90	34 30
Burlington, Vt.	301	8 00	11 0	Lowell, Mass.	241	7 00	9 0
Charleston, S. C.	806	24 00	33 0	Memphis, Tenn.	1251	32 00	50 0
Chicago, Ills.	917	20 00	35 0	Milwaukee, Wis.	997	22 50	41 0
Cincinnati, O.	732	18 00	28 0	Mobile, Ala.	1286	40 55	51 00
Cleveland, O.	589	13 00	20 0	Montgomery, Ala.	1065	32 80	45 15
Columbus, O.	631	16 25	22 0	Nashville, Tenn.	1060	29 60	43 0
Concord, N. H.	278	7 12	10 30	Newark, N. J.	10	0 25	0 30
Council Bluffs, Iowa	1389	35 25	55 0	Newburgh, N. Y.	62	1 80	2 35
Davenport, Iowa	1095	26 10	41 20	Newburyport, Mass.	274	7 00	9 0
Dayton, O.	706	17 50	24 45	New Haven, Conn.	77	1 75	2 45
Denver, Col.	1985	60 00	92 10	New Orleans, La.	1368	42 75	58 0
Des Moines, Iowa	1271	31 15	51 0	Newport, R. I.	187	2 00	10 0
Detroit, Michigan	774	15 00	24 0	Norfolk, Va.	370	8 25	18 30
Dubuque, Iowa	1103	26 50	42 30	Northampton, Mass.	152	3 60	6 10
Easton, Penn.	85	2 40	2 30	Norwich, Conn.	130	2 00	5 30
Elmira, N. Y.	277	7 25	8 45	Ogdensburgh, N. Y.	274	9 60	14 0
Evansville, Ind.	991	24 90	26 0	Omaha, Neb.	1412	36 00	56 10
Philadelphia, Pa.	80	2 50	2 0	Savannah, Ga.	946	25 00	39 0
Pittsburgh, Pa.	447	12 50	14 30	Springfield, Ills.	1041	24 00	42 15
Pittsfield, Mass.	160	3 25	6 0	Springfield, Mass.	141	3 00	4 30
Portland, Me.	340	9 10	13 50	Syracuse, N. Y.	298	6 26	8 15
Poughkeepsie, N. Y.	75	1 52	3 0	Terre Haute, Ind.	869	21 20	22 0
Providence, R. I.	189	5 00	6 15	Toledo, O.	716	16 25	24 0
Richmond, Va.	341	12 80	13 0	Trenton, N. J.	56	1 75	1 45
Rochester, N. Y.	375	9 50	9 30	Troy, N. Y.	151	3 75	4 15
Sacramento, Cal.	3121	136 00	146 15	Utica, N. Y.	239	4 65	7 35
St. Louis, Mo.	1066	24 25	37 0	Vicksburg, Miss.	1236	30 25	63 15
St. Paul, Minn.	1349	31 25	54 0	Washington, D. C.	229	7 50	8 0
Salt Lake City, Utah	2458	116 25	129 0	Wheeling, W. Va.	515	14 00	21 0
San Antonio, Texas	1950	67 50	123 30	Wilmington, Del.	117	3 10	3 0
San Francisco, Cal.	3260	136 00	132 0	Worcester, Mass.	192	4 55	7 30

NOTE—The foregoing "railway fares" and "mail time," are to be considered approximations only; the rates of fare are frequently altered, and the mail time varies by different routes as well as by different trains.

LENGTH OF THE PRINCIPAL RIVERS OF THE WORLD.

Rivers.	Miles.	Rivers.	Miles.	Rivers.	Miles.
Amazon	3,600	Rhine	950	Columbia	1,200
Nile	3,000	Kansas	900	Nebraska	1,200
Missouri	2,900	Tennessee	800	Red River	1,200
Mississippi	2,800	Red River of the North	700	Susquehanna	500
Lena	2,600	Cumberland	600	Potomac	500
Niger	2,600	Alabama	600	James	500
Obi	2,500	Arkansas	2,000	Connecticut	450
St. Lawrence	2,200	Volga	2,000	Delaware	400
Madeira	2,000	Rio Grande	1,800	Hudson	350
Colorado (Cal.)	1,100	Danube	1,600	Kennebec	300
Yellow Stone	1,000	San Francisco	1,300	Thames	233
Ohio	950				

MERCANTILE VOCABULARY.

A

Abandonment, the surrendering of a ship or goods insured to the insurer.

Abatement, discount allowed on damaged goods, or for the payment of money before due.

Acceptance, the formal agreement to pay a draft or bill according to its terms.

Accommodation, the loan of money or of one's name upon which money may be raised.

Account, a systematic arrangement of debits and credits, under the name of a person, species of property, or cause. Bookkeeping is the *science* of accounts.

Account-Current, a running or unsettled account; a statement in detail of the transaction between one person and another, in the form of debtor and creditor. Sometimes it is used to show only the Dr. side of the account, each party rendering to the other an account of his debits only. In this case the debit of the one is the credit of the other.

Account-Sales, a statement in detail of goods sold on commission, together with the charges thereon.

Accountant, one skilled in accounts, or engaged in keeping books.

Actuary, the active officer in a life insurance company; one skilled in the science of annuities.

Adjustment, the settlement of a loss incurred by the insured; a general settlement.

Administrator, one who administers upon an estate by order of the Probate Court.

Adulteration, the act of debasing by mixing any spurious commodity with a genuine article.

Ad valorem, according to the value; a term used in fixing the rates of duties on imports.

Adventure, a speculation; usually applied to the shipment of goods on account of the shipper.

Advance, increase in price; money paid on goods before they are delivered.

Advice, information given with reference to a shipment or other important matter.

Agent, one who acts; usually applied to a person who does business for and in the name of another.

Agio, a term used to denote the difference between the real and nominal value of money.

Allowance, deduction made from weights, etc. *See* FARE.

Amalgamation, the operation of forming amalgam; mixing mercury with any metal.

Antedate, to date before hand.

Appraisal, a value set upon goods or property of any kind.

Appraiser, one who appraises.

Aqueduct, a channel or conduit for the conveyance of water.

Arbitration, the hearing of a cause between parties in controversy; estimating the value of exchange negotiated through direct channels.

Assay, the trial or proof of the purity of metals.

Assets, resources of any kind; available means.

Assessment, a valuation of property or profits for the purpose of taxation.

Assessor, one who assesses or values property.

Assignee, a person properly appointed to transact business or receive property for or on account of any person or estate.

Assignor, one who makes an assignment or transfers property or interest.

Assignment, the act of making over property or trust to an assignee.

Association, the union of persons in company for the transaction of business.

Assortment, a variety of sorts or kinds adapted to various wants.

Assurance, a guarantee or indemnity. *See* INSURANCE.

Attachment, a legal warrant for seizing a man's person or goods.

Auction, a method of selling goods to the highest bidder.

Auctioneer, one who sells goods at auction.

Auditor, a person appointed and authorized to examine accounts, compare vouchers, etc.

Average, a term used to denote damages or expenses resulting from accidents at sea; the mean time for the payment of several items due at different times.

Avoirdupoise, the common standard of weight for all commodities except precious metals and drugs.

B

Balance, a term used to denote the difference between the sides of an account, or the sum necessary to make the account balance; an account in the ledger showing resources and liabilities.

Balance of Trade, the difference between the value of imports and exports.

Ballast, a heavy substance placed in the hold of a ship to keep her steady in the water.

Banking, the business of a bank.

Bankrupt, one who is unable to pay his debts.

Bill, a general name given to a statement in writing.

The following are some of the technical names of bills:

Bill of Exchange, an order drawn on a person in a distant place, requesting the payment of a sum of money.

Bill of Entry, a written account of goods entered at the custom house.

Bill of Right, a form of entry at the custom house by which the importer may examine his goods.

Bill of Lading, a formal receipt from the master of a vessel, signed by himself or his clerk, for goods received by him for transportation, with an agreement to deliver the same, under certain exceptions, in like good order and condition as when received by him.

Bill of Parcels, an account, given by the seller to the buyer, of articles and prices.

Bill of Sale, a writing given by the seller of personal property to the buyer, equivalent to the deed.

Bill of Health, a certificate from the proper authorities as to the state of health of a ship's company on leaving port.

Bill of Mortality, a certified account of the deaths at a certain place during a certain period.

Bill of Credit, a document for raising money on the credit of a state.

Blank Credit, the permission which one house gives to another to draw on it at any time to a certain extent.

Board of Trade, an association of business men for the general advancement of commercial interests.

Bona fide, in good faith.

Bond, a deed by which the party binds himself, his heirs, executors and assigns, to the performance of certain conditions.

Bonded Goods, those which remain in the custom warehouse until the duties are paid.

Bottomry Bond, a mortgage on the bottom of a vessel—that is, on the vessel itself, for the repayment of money loaned.

Broker, a middleman employed to transact business or negotiate bargains between different merchants or individuals; a trader in stocks, moneys or other commodities.

Brokerage, the commission or percentage charged by a broker for services.

C

Capital, investment in business.

Carat, the weight which expresses the degree of fineness of gold.

Cargo, the lading or freight of a vessel.

Cashier, one who keeps the cash account; the financial officer of a bank, railroad, or mercantile house.

Carrier, a person, company or corporation engaged in the transportation of goods from one place to another, and who are bound, for a stipulated or reasonable hire, to receive and carry the goods of all persons, and to be responsible for their care while in their possession, as well as for their safe delivery.

Charter, an instrument bestowed with form and solemnity, bestowing certain privileges and rights.

Charter-party, a contract in writing between the owner or master of a ship and the freighter, by which the former lets the ship or a part of it to the other for the conveyance of goods.

Clearance, a certificate from the custom house that a ship has permission to sail.

Clearing, the obtaining of permission for a ship to leave port; the exchanging of drafts and settlement of balances between different houses

Clearing-House, the place where the operation of clearing is performed.

Coasting, the trade carried on between different ports of the same country.

Coin, pieces of metal, usually gold or silver, impressed with a public stamp, and used as money.

Commerce, the exchange of commodities.

Commission, a percentage for the sale of goods or other service.

Company, an association of persons for a common enterprise.

Compound, to settle with a creditor by paying a part of the debt.

Compromise, an agreement embracing mutual concessions.

Consignee, one to whom goods are consigned.

Consignment, goods consigned to be sold on account.

Consignor, one who consigns goods.

Consols, an abbreviation of the term "consolidated funds," applied to the chief public stocks of England.

Consul, an agent for a government in a foreign land.

Contraband, an article prohibited from being imported, exported, bought or sold.

Contract, an agreement between two or more parties, upon sufficient consideration, to do or not to do a certain thing.

Contra, on the opposite side.

Copartnership, the legal relations existing between two or more persons consequent upon their sharing the profits or losses of some adventure or business engagement between them; partnership.

Copyright, the exclusive right allowed by law to an author or his representative, of printing, publishing and selling any literary composition during a certain period of time.

Counterfeit, a spurious article resembling the genuine.

Coupon, a French word signifying *cut-off*. It is applied to interest warrants attached to public stocks, bonds, etc. When paid they are cut off from the bond.

Course of Exchange, the current price paid in one place for bills of exchange on another place.

Credential, the official warrant of a delegating power authorizing the holder to act in a specified capacity.

Credit, trust given to one who owes.

Currency, a term used to express the collective amount of money used in the business of buying and selling.

Current, a term used to denote the present time, or time in its successive stages of transition.

Customs, the tariff charged by law on imports and exports.

Custom House, the office where the business connected with customs is transacted.

D

Damaged goods, in the language of customs, are goods subject to duties that have received injury, either in the voyage home or the bonded warehouse.

Days of Grace, the time allowed by law and usage between the written date of maturity of a note or draft and the date upon which it must be paid.

Debenture, a certificate of drawback entitling the importer to return duties on goods shipped again.

Debt, an amount owing from one party to another.

Decimal, from the Latin *decem*, signifying ten; any system of counting by tens.

Decimal Fractions, fractions having any power of ten for their denominator.

Deed, a written contract, signed, sealed and delivered.

Defalcation, diminution, deducted from.

Defaulter, one who fails to account for money or valuables entrusted to his care.

Delivery, the passing of goods or money from one to another.

Demand and Supply, terms used to denote the relations existing between consumption and production.

Demurrage, allowance made to the owner or master of a vessel by the freighter for the detention of a vessel in port beyond the time agreed upon.

Denier, a small French copper coin.

Deviation, the departure of a vessel from the course specified in her insurance policy.

Diplomacy, the art of conducting negotiations.

Discount, consideration allowed for the payment of a debt before it is due.

Dishonor, to refuse or neglect to accept, or to pay a bill on its maturity.

Dividend, division of profits among stockholders.
Drawback, an amount remitted which has been previously paid as duties.
Draft, an order for the payment of money.
Drawee, the person on whom a draft is drawn.
Drawer, the person who draws a draft.
Duplicate, a copy or transcript of anything.
Duty, a government tax.

E

Effects, property of any kind.
Embargo, a prohibition laid by the government on ships to prevent their leaving port.
Embezzlement, the illegal appropriation of the funds of a principal by an agent or employee.
Emporium, a commercial center; a mart.
Encumbrance, liabilities resting on an estate.
Endorse, to subscribe to anything; to write one's name on the back of a note.
Endorsee, the person to whom a bill is endorsed; the legal holder of a bill after its endorsement.
Endorser, the person who endorses.
Engross, to monopolize; to buy up produce with a view of affecting the market; to copy in manuscript.
Entry, the record of a transaction in a book of accounts; the act of reporting a vessel or cargo at the Custom-House, upon its arrival in port, by delivery of proper documents.
Exchange, the fundamental principle of trade; the species of paper by which debts are paid without the transmission of money; premium and discount arising from the purchase and sale of funds.
Executor, a person appointed to execute or carry into effect the will of a testator.
Exports, goods or produce carried abroad.
Express, a messenger or vehicle sent on a special errand; a regular conveyance for packages.

F

Fabric, manufactured cloth.
Face, the amount expressed on a note or draft.
Factor, an agent employed to transact business for another.
Factory, a house or place where factors reside; a building for the manufacture of goods.
Fac-simile, an exact resemblance.
Failure becoming insolvent.
Fancy Stocks, usually applied to the stocks of joint companies subject to fluctuation in price.
Favor, the polite term of a letter received; a note or draft is in *favor* of the person to whom it is to be paid.
Fee simple, an estate held by a person in his own right.
Finance, pertaining to money; the public revenue.
Financier, an officer of revenue; one skilled in money matters.
Firm, the general title of a copartnership.
Firkin, a measure equal to nine ale gallons.
Flotsam, the cargo of a wrecked vessel which has not yet been washed to shore, but continues floating on the surface of the waves, to distinguish it from *jetsam*, which denotes that the goods are sunk beneath the surface of the water, and *logan*, when they are sunk, but tied to a cork or buoy to be found again.
Foreclose, to cut the mortgagor off from the equity of redemption.
Forestalling, buying up produce before it gets to market to enhance the price.
Form, a particular arrangement; a systematic method of expressing facts.
Forecastle, the part of the upper deck of a ship forward of the mast.
Folio, page of a book; usually applied to the two pages opposite each other.
Franc, a French coin, equal to about eighteen cents American money.
Free Trade, the policy of conducting international commerce without duties.
Freight, goods being transported; the price of transportation.
Fund, a stock or capital, a sum of money appropriated to some special enterprise used in the plural to denote wealth generally.

G

Gauging, the art of measuring the contents of a cask or other receptacle.
Gain, profit; increase in wealth.
Gratuity, a free gift; a donation.
Guarantee or Guaranty, an undertaking or engagement by a third person, that the agreement between two parties shall be observed; a surety.

H

Harbor, a place where ships may lie at anchorage and in safety; a port for loading and unloading.
Hawker, an itinerant peddler of merchandise.
Highway, a public road or thoroughfare.
High Seas, the waters of the ocean without the boundaries of any country.
Honor, to accept or pay when due.
Hypothecate, to pledge as security.

I

Import, to bring from a foreign country.
Importation, the act of importing; the thing imported.
Indemnity, a guarantee against loss.
Indenture, a written instrument.
Infant, a person under twenty-one years of age.
Insolvency, the condition of bankruptcy.
Insurance, indemnity from loss; the rate paid for indemnity.
Installment, part of a sum of money paid or to be paid at a certain time.
Interest, the use of money; commonly defined as a percentage allowed by the borrower to the lender.
International, relating to intercourse between different nations.
Intestate, without a will; a person dying without having disposed of his estate by will.
Inventory, a list of goods enumerated in detail.
Investment, the laying out of money in the purchase of property.
Invoice, a bill of goods bought or sold.

J

Jettison, goods thrown overboard to lighten a ship in a storm.
Jointure, an estate in lands settled on a woman in consideration of marriage.
Joint-stock, property held in common by a company.
Journal, the chief book of the current entries in business.
Judgment, the decree of a competent court.
Jurisdiction, the power or right of exercising authority.

L

Land Waiter, a custom-house officer, whose business it is to attend to the landing of imported goods, to weigh, measure or otherwise examine and take an account of them.

Law, Commercial, customs acknowledged and recognized by all commercial nations, and constituting part of the general laws of a country.
Lease, a contract demising the use of property for a certain time.
Leasehold, property held under a lease.
Ledger, the merchant's book of accounts.
Legacy, a bequest; money or property given by will.
Letter of Credit, an open letter of request authorizing the holder to receive money on account of the writer.
Letter of Advice, a letter giving notice or information of any business transaction.
Liability, a debt or claim against a person.
License, a legal permission to do a certain act, such as selling goods, etc.
Lien, security on land or other property.
Lighter, a large, open, flat-bottomed boat used to carry goods to or from a vessel when loading or unloading.
Lighterage, a charge or commission for carrying goods in a lighter.
Liquidate, to pay or satisfy demands.
Loan, that which is lent for a temporary purpose.
Lucre, gain in money or goods.

M

Manifest, a list of the articles comprising a vessel's cargo.
Manufacture, the process of converting raw materials into articles of use and sale.
Manufactory, the place were goods are manufactured.
Marine, a general name for the navy of a kingdom or a state.
Maritime Law, law relating to harbors, ships and seamen.
Mark or Marc, a weight in European countries for estimating gold and silver.
Maturity, the date when a note or draft falls due.
Maximum, the highest price or rate.
Mercantile Law, law pertaining to business transactions.
Merchandise, goods; the common articles of barter.
Merchant, one who speculates in merchandise.
Minimum, the lowest price or rate.
Mint, the place where money is coined.
Monopoly, the sole right to make or use a certain article.
Monetary, relating to financial matters.
Mortgage, the transfer of property to secure the payment of a debt.
Mortgagee, the person to whom the transfer is made.
Mortgagor, the one who makes the transfer.

N

Navigation, the science of conducting ships or other vessels from one port to another.
Negotiate, to put into circulation. To negotiate a bill means to pass or dispose of the same; to convert into money.
Net or **Nett,** that which remains of a weight or quantity after certain deductions.
Net Proceeds, the amount due a consignor after deducting charges attending sales.
Nickel, a scarce metal resembling silver; used in the composition of the five cent coin of the United States.
Notary Public, an officer whose chief business it is to protest paper for non-payment.
Note, an incidental remark made for the purpose of explanation; a written obligation to pay money or goods.

O

Obligation, a bond with a penalty attached; a contract; an act which binds one to some performance.
Obligee, the person to whom another is bound.
Obligor, the person who is bound or who binds himself to the obligee.

P

Par, equal value.
Partnership, an agreement between two or more persons to share in the profit and loss of any enterprise.
Pawn, a deposit; a pledge; something given as security for money borrowed, or for the fulfillment of a promise.
Pawnbroker, a person who advances money on goods, having power to dispose of the same if the money is not refunded as per contract.
Payee, the party to whom or to whose order a note or bill is made payable.
Policy of Insurance, contract between the insurer and the insured.
Portage, the amount paid by a captain in running his vessel; the price of carrying.
Post, to transfer from the journal, or some other book of entry, to the ledger; a messenger, particularly a letter-carrier.
Premium, the sum paid for insurance; the excess of value above par.
Price Current, a list of merchandise, with market value.
Principal, an employer; the head of a commercial house; the sum loaned upon which interest accrues.
Promissory Note, a written promise to pay, absolutely and unconditionally, to a certain person or to his order, a definite sum of money, at or before a specified time.
Protest, a formal notice to the securities of a note or draft, stating that the same was not paid at maturity; or to the drawer of a draft, stating that the same was not accepted upon presentation.

Q

Quarantine, restraint of intercourse to which a ship is subjected, upon the supposition that she may be infected with disease.

R

Rate, price; amount above or below par.
Rebate, reduction for prompt payment.
Receipt, a written acknowledgment of having received money or other value.
Remittance, bills or money sent from one house to another; the act of remitting or transmitting funds from one place to another.
Reprisal, the act of seizing ships or property as indemnity for unlawful seizure or detention.
Resources, effects; property of any kind.
Retail, to buy and sell in small quantities.
Revenue, the annual produce of rents, excise, customs duties, etc., collected by a state or nation.

S

Salvage, an allowance made by law for the saving of a ship's cargo from wreck or fire.
Sample, a specimen.
Schedule, an inventory; a catalogue; a list.
Seaworthy, in a proper condition to venture to sea.
Seize, to take possession of by legal process.
Set of Exchange, three bills of the same tenor and date, forwarded by different conveyances, to prevent failure of transmission, any one of which being accepted or paid, the others are void.

Shipment, goods shipped; the act of loading a vessel for voyage.
Sight, the time of presenting a bill to the drawee.
Signature, the name of a person written by himself.
Sine Die, without fixing the day.
Smuggling, the offense of secretly importing or exporting goods without the payment of the government duties.
Solvent, sound; able to pay all liabilities.
Sounding, trying the depth of the sea and the nature of the bottom.
Stock, capital in trade; the title of the proprietor of a business.
Stocks, shares in joint stock companies, and negotiable debts of governments and corporations, drawing interest.
Stock-jobber, one who deals in stocks.
Supercargo, an officer in a merchant vessel, appointed to superintend the commercial transactions of the voyage.
Surety, indemnity against loss; a person bound for the performance of a contract by another.

T

Tare, an allowance or discount for the weight of boxes and other receptacles of merchandise.
Tariff, a list of prices; duties on imports and exports.
Tender, an offer for acceptance; a legal tender is an offer of such money as the law prescribes.
Teller, an officer in a bank who receives or pays money.
Tonnage, the weight of a ship's lading; the capacity of a vessel.
Transfer, to convey from one to another.
Trustee, a person trusted; one to whom some special business or interest is committed.

U

Underwriter, an insurer; one who insures property against loss; so called from his *underwriting* or subscribing the policy of insurance.
Usance, business custom or habit which is generally conceded and acted upon.
Usury, illegal interest; formerly any consideration for the use of money.

V

Vend, to sell or transfer for a consideration.
Voucher, a written evidence of an act performed, such as the payment of money.

W

Wages, compensation for services.
Warehouse, a building in which goods are stored.
Wares, merchandise of any kind.
Wharfage, money paid for the use of a wharf.
Wreck, the ruins of a ship stranded.
Wreckers, persons employed in saving property from a wreck.

ABBREVIATIONS.

Adv .... Adventuro
Acct .... Account.
Agt .... Agent.
Am't .... Amount.
Ans .... Answer.
Apr .... April.
Ass't'd .... Assorted.
Aug .... August.

Bal .... Balance.
B. B .... Bill Book.
Bbl .... Barrel.
B. Pay .... Bills Payable.
B. Rec .... Bills Receivable
Bl'k .... Black.
Bo't .... Bought.
Bro't .... Brought.
Bu. or *Bush* .... Bushel.

Cap .... Capital.
C.-B .... Cash-Book.
Co. .... Company.
Col'd .... Colored.
Com .... Commission.
Cons't .... Consignment.
C. S. B .... Commission Sales-Book
Cr .... Creditor.
Cts .... Cents.

D. B .... Day-Book.
Dec .... December.
Dep .... Deposit.
D'ft .... Draft.
Dis. or *Disc* .... Discount.
Do .... The same.
Doz .... Dozen.
Dr .... Deistor.
D's .... Days.

Ea .... Each.
E. E .... Errors excepted.
E. & O. E .... Errors and omissions excepted.
Emb'd .... Embroidered.

Jan .... January.
Jour .... Journal.
J. F .... Journal Folio.

Lab .... Labor.
Lbs .... Pounds.
Leg. .... Ledger.
L. F .... Ledger Folio.

Mar .... March.
Mdse .... Merchandise.
m. or *mo.* .... Month.
mos .... Months.

No. .... Number.
Nov .... November.
Eng .... English.
Ent .... Entry.

Ex .... Example.
Exch .... Exchange.
Exp .... Expenses.

Fav .... Favor.
Feb .... February.
Fig'd .... Figured.
Fol .... Folio.
For'd .... Forward.
Fr .... From.
Fr't .... Freight.

Gal .... Gallon.
Gro. or *gro* .... Gross.

Hhd .... Hogshead.
Hk'f .... Handkerchief.

I. B .... Invoice Book.
i. e .... That is,
Ins .... Insurance.
Inst .... Instant,
Int .... Interest.
Inv't .... Inventory.

Oct .... October.
O. I. B .... Outward Invoice Book

p .... Page.
pp .... Pages.
Pay't .... Payment.
P. C. B .... Petty Cash Book
Pd .... Paid.
Pkg .... Package.
Pr .... Pair.
pr or *per* .... By.
Prem. .... Premium.
Prox. or *prox* .. Proximo.
Ps .... Pieces.
P. & L .... Profit & Loss

Qr. or *qr* .... Quarter.

Rec'd .... Received.
Rec'ble .... Receivable.
R. R .... Rail Road.

S. B .... Sales Book.
Sept .... September.
Sh .... Share.
Ship't .... Shipment.
Str .... Steamer.
Stor. .... Storage.
Sunds .... Sundries.
Sup .... Superfine.

ult .... The last.

viz .... To wit—namely.
vs .... Versus—against.

Yds .... Yards.
Yr .... Year.

OLD SPANISH PROVERBS.

THE following quaint old Spanish proverbs are selected from popular quotations then current, used by Don Miguel de Cervantes, the celebrated author of Don Quixote, some three hundred years since :

"He that would not when he may,
When he would, he shall have nay."

"It is ill talking of halters in the house of a man that was hanged."

"A close mouth catches no flies."

"Who can hedge in a cuckoo."

"Little said is soon mended."

"It is a sin to belie the devil."

"Misunderstanding brings lies to town."

"There is no padlocking peoples' mouths."

"Many think to find flitches of bacon and find not so much as the racks to lay them on."

"Let them that say it eat the lie and swallow it with their bread."

"It is no bread and butter of mine."

"Never thrust your nose into other men's porridge."

"He that buys and lies finds it in his purse."

"Let him that owns the cow take her by the tail."

"The wise man keeps himself to-day for to-morrow."

"A wise man will not venture all his eggs in one basket."

"Do not expect pears from an elm tree."

"It cannot be night at ten o'clock in the morning."

"After meal comes mustard."

"A leap from a hedge is better than the prayer of a good man."

"Where one door shuts another opens."

"Evil to him who evil seeks."

"He who seeks danger perishes therein."

"Covetousness breaks the sack."

"To the grave with the dead, and the living to the bread."

"A mouth without cheek teeth is like a mill without a millstone."

"Keep with good men and thou shalt be one of them."

"Never cringe nor creep
For what you by force may reap."

THEMES FOR DEBATE.

FOLLOWING are one hundred and fifty topics for debate. The more usual form in their presentation is that of a direct proposition or statement, rather than that of a question. The opponents then debate the "affirmative" and "negative" of the proposition. It is well to be very careful, in adopting a subject for debate, to so state or explain it that misunderstandings may be mutually avoided, and quibbles on the meaning of words prevented.

THEMES FOR DEBATE.

Which is the better for this nation, high or low import tariffs?

Is assassination ever justifiable?

Was England justifiable in interfering between Egypt and the Soudan rebels?

Is the production of great works of literature favored by the conditions of modern civilized life?

Is it politic to place restrictions upon the immigration of the Chinese to the United States?

Will coal always constitute the main source of artificial heat?

Has the experiment of universal suffrage proven a success?

Was Grant or Lee the greater general?

Is an income tax commendable?

Ought the national banking system to be abolished?

Should the government lease to stock-growers any portion of the public domain?

Is it advisable longer to attempt to maintain both a gold and a silver standard of coinage?

Which is the more important to the student, physical science or mathematics?

Is the study of current politics a duty?

Which was the more influential congressman, Blaine or Garfield?

Which gives rise to more objectionable idioms and localisms of language, New England or the West?

Was the purchase of Alaska by this government wise?

Which is the more important as a continent, Africa or South America?

Should the government interfere to stop the spread of contagious diseases among cattle?

Was Cæsar or Hannibal the more able general?

Is the study of ancient or modern history the more important to the student?

Should aliens be allowed to acquire property in this country?

Should aliens be allowed to own real estate in this country?

Do the benefits of the signal service justify its cost?

Should usury laws be abolished?

Should all laws for the collection of debt be abolished?

Is labor entitled to more remuneration than it receives?

Should the continuance of militia organizations by the several states be encouraged?

Is an untarnished reputation of more importance to a woman than to a man?

Does home life promote the growth of selfishness?

Are mineral veins aqueous or igneous in origin?

Is the theory of evolution tenable?

Was Rome justifiable in annihilating Carthage as a nation?

Which has left the more permanent impress upon mankind, Greece or Rome?

Which was the greater thinker, Emerson or Bacon?

Which is the more important as a branch of education, mineralogy or astronomy?

Is there any improvement in the quality of the literature of to-day over that of last century?

Should the "Spoils System" be continued in American politics?

Should the co-education of the sexes be encouraged?

Which should be the more encouraged, novelists or dramatists?

Will the African and Caucasian races ever be amalgamated in the United States?

Should the military or the interior department have charge over the Indians in the United States?

Which is of more benefit to his race, the inventor or the explorer?

Is history or philosophy the better exercise for the mind?

Can any effectual provision be made by the State against "hard times"?

Which is of the more benefit to society, journalism or the law?

Which was the greater general, Napoleon or Wellington?

Should the volume of greenback money be increased?

Should the volume of national bank circulation be increased?

Should the railroads be under the direct control of the government?

Is the doctrine of "state rights" to be commended?

Is the "Monroe doctrine" to be commended and upheld?

Is the pursuit of politics an honorable avocation?

Which is of the greater importance, the college or the university?

Does the study of physical science militate against religious belief?

Should "landlordism" in Ireland be supplanted by home rule?

Is life more desirable now than in ancient Rome?

Should men and women receive the same amount of wages for the same kind of work?

Is the prohibitory liquor law preferable to a system of high license?

Has any state a right to secede?

Should any limit be placed by the constitution of a state upon its ability to contract indebtedness?

Should the contract labor system in public prisons be forbidden?

Should there be a censor for the public press?

Should Arctic expeditions be encouraged?

Is it the duty of the State to encourage art and literature as much as science?

Is suicide cowardice?

Has our government a right to disfranchise the polygamists of Utah?

Should capital punishment be abolished?

Should the law place a limit upon the hours of daily labor for working men?

Is "socialism" treason?

Should the education of the young be compulsory?

In a hundred years will republics be as numerous as monarchies?

Should book-keeping be taught in the public schools?

Should Latin be taught in the public schools?

Do our methods of government promote centralization?

Is life worth living?

Should Ireland and Scotland be independent nations?

Should internal revenue taxation be abolished?

Which is of greater benefit at the present day, books or newspapers?

Is honesty always the best policy?

Which has been of greater benefit to mankind, geology or chemistry?

Which could mankind dispense with at least inconvenience, wood or coal?

Which is the greater nation, Germany or France?

Which can support the greater population in proportion to area, our Northern or Southern States?

Would mankind be the loser if the earth should cease to produce gold and silver?

Is the occasional destruction of large numbers of people, by war and disaster, a benefit to the world?

Which could man best do without, steam or horse power?

Should women be given the right of suffrage in the United States?

Should cremation be substituted for burial?

Should the government establish a national system of telegraph?

Should the electoral college be continued?

Will the population of Chicago ever exceed that of New York?

Will the population of St. Louis ever exceed that of Chicago?

Should restrictions be placed upon the amount of property inheritable?

Which is more desirable as the chief business of a city—commerce, or manufactures?

Which is more desirable as the chief business of a city—transportation by water or by rail?

Should the rate of taxation be graduated to a ratio with the amount of property taxed?

Will a time ever come when the population of the earth will be limited by the earth's capacity of food production?

Is it probable that any language will ever become universal?

Is it probable that any planet, except the earth, is inhabited?

Should the state prohibit the manufacture and sale of alcoholic liquors?

Should the government prohibit the manufacture and sale of alcoholic liquors?

Should the guillotine be substituted for the gallows?

Was Bryant or Longfellow the greater poet?

Should the jury system be continued?

Should the languages of alien nations be taught in the public schools?

Should a right to vote in any part of the United States depend upon a property qualification?

Can a horse trot faster in harness, or under saddle?

Should the pooling system among American railroads be abolished by law?

Is dancing, as usually conducted, compatible with a high standard of morality?

Should the grand jury system of making indictments be continued?

Which should be the more highly remunerated, skilled labor or the work of professional men?

Which is the more desirable as an occupation, medicine or law?

Should the formation of trade unions be encouraged?

Which has been the greater curse to man, war or drunkenness?

Which can man the more easily do without, electricity or petroleum?

Should the law interfere against the growth of class distinctions in society?

Which was the greater genius, Mohammed or Buddha?

Which was the more able leader, Pizarro or Cortez?

Which can to-day wield the greater influence, the orator or the writer?

Is genius hereditary?

Is Saxon blood deteriorating?

Which will predominate in five hundred years, the Saxon or Latin races?

Should American railroad companies be allowed to sell their bonds in other countries?

Should Sumner's civil rights bill be made constitutional by an amendment?

Does civilization promote the happiness of the world?

Should land subsidies be granted to railroads by the government?

Which is the stronger military power, England or the United States?

Would a rebellion in Russia be justifiable?

Should the theatre be encouraged?

Which has the greater resources, Pennsylvania or Texas?

Is agriculture the noblest occupation?

Is legal punishment for crime as severe as it should be?

Can democratic forms of government be made universal?

Should the formation of monopolies be prevented by the State?

Has Spanish influence been helpful or harmful to Mexico as a people?

Which is of more importance, the primary or the high school?

Will the tide of emigration ever turn eastward instead of westward?

Should the art of war be taught more widely than at present in the United States?

Was slavery the cause of the American civil war?

Is life insurance a benefit?

Should gambling in grain be prohibited by law?

Does "prohibition" prohibit?

Should the general government restrain the destruction of our forests?

Is the accumulation of wealth a curse to society?

Is ærial navigation desirable?

Which is the more potent, the ballot or the bullet, as a civilizer?

Should the tenure of office of the president be extended to six years?

Which develops the more elevating or beautiful scenery, the ocean or the mountains?

Which is the more elevating in influence, the poet or the painter?

BUSINESS FORMS.

FOR the more convenient transaction of business and the greater security of those engaged in it against fraud and error, various forms of written instruments have been adopted, founded on experience and sanctioned by the law of custom. No person engaged in commercial pursuits, or in the transaction of business in any way or upon any scale, can afford to be ignorant of those Business Forms, and no prudent man will affix his signature to any document, or form of agreement, without fully and thoroughly comprehending all that is involved in it, and the nature and extent of the obligation which his signature so made carries. One of the most common and successful methods adopted by the class of unscrupulous swindlers known as confidence men, is that of securing the signatures of the unsophisticated and unsuspecting, to forms which purport to mean one thing, but which are readily altered or construed to a totally different meaning, to the robbery and often ruin of the man whose confidence in the honesty of others is thus taken advantage of. The only safety against the impositions of the designing and dishonest, is for every man to be master of the standard and recognized business forms, and to refuse to sign any undertaking or obligation whatever, except it be in the form with which he is familiar, and which he knows is an honest and reliable form of agreement, note, order, check or other business engagement. These forms, one or other, or all, which enter into every man's business, consist of the following:

Bills.	Due Bills.	Orders.	Drafts.
Receipts.	Notes.	Checks.	Bills of Exchange.

BILLS.

A BILL is an itemized statement of account of goods bought or sold, or labor or services performed, with the price and the date of each article or act of service, the amount of the whole, and the date at which the bill is rendered. The first line on the bill is the name of the city, town or village in which the business of the person or firm rendering the bill is situated. This may be, at choice, accompanied, as in the following form, by the street and number. Then follows the name of the person to whom the bill is rendered, written from the left hand of the page. Then follows the name of the person or firm by whom the service or article has been furnished, which should be preceded by the word To at the left hand of the line, and the word Dr. at the right hand. It is customary to place beneath this the card of business of the party as well. The following is the form :

FORM OF BILL FOR SERVICES.

227 Market St.,
Chicago, June 24, 1885.

Mr. William C. Whitney,

To *George B. Culver,* **Dr.**

1885. *Barrister, Conveyancer, Etc.*

May	*7*	*To examining abstract of title,*	*$10*	*00*		
June	*1*	*" Counsel in case Moore,*	*50*	*00*		
		" Expenses, trip to Springfield, in connection with above,	*9*	*60*	*$69*	*60*
		Received Payment, George B. Culver.				

They are generally used in printed form. If the bill is made out for services rendered, use abbreviation "Dr." and "Cr." Bills for goods sold commonly have "Bought of," in place of "Dr." If service is performed by the day or hour, specify the number of days or hours, with the rate per day or hour in each entry. When there is only one item place in the total column; otherwise, carry the total over as above. In making out a bill care should be taken that every detail is perspicuous. Neatness in form and absolute correctness should also be observed. Nothing is so injurious to the reputation and success of a business man as carelessness, and inaccuracy in rendering bills.

FORM OF MERCHANTS' BILL.

Folio 214.
Salesman, W. H. M.

Chicago, February 10, 1885.

Messrs. Thompson & Smith,
Evanston, Ill.

Bought of *BROWN, JONES & CO.*
Wholesale Grocers,

212 Randolph St., Chicago.

June	*1*	*5 Boxes Toilet Soap,*	*3.80*	*19*			
		10 Boxes Servian Prunes, 1000 lbs.	*07*	*70*			
		1 Case Cal. Smok. Tob., ¼ & ½, 100 lbs.	*35*	*35*			
		1 Bbl. N. O. Molasses, 42 gal.	*86*	*36*	*12*	*160*	*02*
		Int. on ½ bill for 63 days, 8%,				*1*	*12*
		Received Payment,				*161*	*24*
		By Note, 60 days,		*81*	*18*		
		" Cash,		*80*	*06*		
		Brown, Jones & Co.					
		Per Robinson.					

When a bill has been paid by note, or otherwise than by cash, it should be so stated in the bill. Wholesale merchants and jobbers send a bill with each purchase. Retail merchants usually render a bill on the first of each month for the past month's purchases. When bills of goods sold during the month are rendered from time to time, and settlement made monthly, a *Statement* is rendered at the close of the month, which shows the amounts and dates of the several bills, but not the items.

RECEIPTS.

WHEN money is paid for settlement of or application on a debt, or claim, payment of rent, or money advanced on contract, the business man should not wait to be asked for a receipt, but give it as a matter of course. The party paying money should always require a receipt. Parties may die, witnesses move away, and all evidence of payment be removed, where there is no receipt, and thus in settlement of an estate much difficulty is experienced. A receipt written in pencil is legal, but a careful business man will not give a receipt in pencil, nor will a prudent man accept one. The receipt should state clearly and fully what the payment was for; if on contract or note, specify what contract or note; if for rent, state what premises and *from* what date *to* what date the rent is paid. If in part payment, state what is the full amount on which to be applied, and specify the debt—rent, note or contract.

FORM OF RECEIPT.

Chicago, June 12, 1881.

Received of .... *John Wilson,* ....

Eighty-four and .... $\frac{35}{100}$ *Dollars,*

in full of all demands to date.

$84.35. *Edward Langdon.*

A receipt, though apparently so, is not always a certain proof of payment, as it may be inoperative from mistake or fraud, and is open to explanation or contradiction. A release differs from a receipt in this, that it cannot be contradicted by evidence, except for fraud. An entry in the creditor's books does not constitute a receipt. A release is a contract, and, except in case of fraud, must be taken to mean what is written. A receipt that contains any writing, to the effect of an agreement that the money paid is to be applied to a particular purpose, debt or note, even if paid beforehand on the score of future transactions, is legal and not to be modified by parole evidence. A receipt for the consideration of money, in a sale of real property is conclusive against the seller, and equivalent to a bond for a deed. Where payment is made in the shape of note, check or other than current legal tender, the receipt should specify the acceptance of such consideration. Otherwise, if the check or note be dishonored, or the money be found to be of an insolvent bank, the creditor is entitled to return it and demand to be paid again.

BANK CHECKS.

SAFETY, convenience and other considerations, induce most business men to keep an account at a bank, depositing the cash receipts of each day, reserving only a sufficient sum for needs of the evening or morning. Paymentsof most kinds, except for trivial accounts and expenses, are thus almost altogether made through the bank. The person receiving a check may transfer it to another by indorsement, and thus it may pass through several hands before finding its way to the bank on which it is drawn, when it is charged up to the party by whom it was drawn and canceled. In filling out a check the amount should be expressed, both in the margin and in the body of the note, as a precaution against errors. If the words expressing the amount do not fill up the line entirely, draw a heavy stroke or wave line with the pen, so as to prevent any dishonest person into whose hands the check might fall, from raising or altering it.

FORM OF A BANK CHECK.

No. 1730. *Chicago, March 7, 1885.*

TENTH NATIONAL BANK,
Of Chicago,

Pay to the order of .... *Edward Johnstone,* ....

Seventy-eight and .... $\frac{75}{100}$ *Dollars.*

$78.75. *George B. Anderson.*

Canceled checks are usually returned once a month to the drawer, by whom they should be carefully preserved, as they constitute evidences of payment. The object of payment may be specified on the body of the check, thus constituting its payment a receipt for the particular debt or service. If the person accepting a check does not require to use the money he may get it "certified" at the bank, which renders it equivalent to cash, by the guarantee of the bank.

The facility of having checks cashed, opens a door to dishonesty, which has been guarded against by the system of crossed checks. A wishes to send B a check for $1,000 and is doubtful of the honesty of his messenger. He knows B banks with, say the Marine Bank, of Detroit. He makes out his check in the usual form and then writes across it the words "Marine Bank of Detroit." A's bank will then only pay this check when presented by or through the Marine Bank. Checks are to be presented for payment without unreasonable delay. There is no payment unless the check is honored. The bank or party on whom a check is drawn is obliged to pay it if he have funds in his possession to the amount named on the check, belonging to the drawer. It is a fraud to draw a check where the drawer has no funds, and no arrangement by which he is entitled to draw checks on the bank named. A bank is responsible for the loss in case of a forged check if the check be honored by it. A check not drawn within the state where the bank is situated is subject to the law governing bills of exchange. The holder of it must protest in writing, usually through a notary, against all parties liable for any loss or damage by its non-payment.

DUE BILLS.

DUE bills are used for money borrowed, or in effecting settlement of accounts, and should state whether payable in merchandise or cash, and are made in this shape:

> *$15.75. Chicago, March 5, 1885.*
>
> *Due Samuel M. Jennings, on demand, Fifteen Dollars and Seventy-five Cents.*
>
> *James Brown.*

Another form is the I. O. U., which is in this shape:

> *$17. Chicago, March 5, 1885.*
>
> *James W. Smith, Esq.:*
>
> *I. O. U. Seventeen Dollars.*
>
> *James Edwards.*

This form of paper differs from a promissory note, which usually contains a promise to pay, at a time specified therein, a sum of money to a certain person, or to his order, for value received.

PROMISSORY NOTES.

Promissory notes are essential to the system of credit in business and are of four kinds as explained below:

FORM OF NEGOTIABLE NOTE.

> *$1,000.00. Chicago, Ill., March 15, 1885.*
>
> *Thirty days after date I promise to pay to the order of ....*
>
> *Jacob Rindskopf.*
>
> *One Thousand .... 00/100 Dollars,*
>
> *value received, with interest at six per cent per annum until paid.*
>
> *Due April 7, 1885. John W. Durand.*

FORM OF NOTE NOT NEGOTIABLE.

$230 00.	*Chicago, March 5, 1885.*
Sixty days after date I promise to pay to John J. Dunscombe, Two Hundred and Thirty $\frac{00}{100}$ Dollars, payable at my office, 17 Clark street. Value received.	
	Francis Whitcombe.

FORM OF DEMAND NOTE.

$100.	*Chicago, March 5, 1885.*
On demand I promise to pay James Calendar or order, One Hundred Dollars, value received, with interest at 6 per cent.	
	Philip Coleman.

FORM OF JOINT NOTE.

$325.	*Chicago, March 5, 1885.*
Three months after date, we, or either of us, jointly and severally promise to pay Henry Porter, or order, Three Hundred and Twenty-five Dollars, value received, without interest.	*John A. McDonald.*
	Charles C. Tupper.

The first form of note is negotiable, and is payable to the person holding it, when properly indorsed, at the time of its maturity. The second is payable only to the person in whose favor it is drawn. A promise to pay is not invalidated by any informality. Unless a note be made payable to bearer the name of payee must be specified. If a note be not dated, the time is computed from the day the knowledge of it is first gained. If there be any difference between the words and figures in the amount for which the note is made, the words prevail. A note does not bear interest till after it matures, unless so written. One who cannot write should have a witness when he makes his + mark. A note is void if procured from the maker while in a state of intoxication or otherwise irresponsible. If no time be specified a note is payable at once. A note by a minor is not collectable in law. Payment of a note must be made on the last day of grace, by the holder, or his authorized agent, in business hours, at the place of business of the maker, unless otherwise stated. In case of non-payment at 3 o'clock on the last day of grace, it should be handed to a notary for protest, and immediate notice sent to the indorser, if any. A note that has been accidentally destroyed may be recovered upon adequate proof. In case of loss, notice must be given and payment demanded as if the note was still secure in form.

ORDERS.

An order is a written request from one person or firm to another, for the delivery of a sum of money or articles of merchandise. These orders are usually drawn by one merchant on another, or by persons in the same town or neighborhood, and are a kind of informal draft, not intended to be transferred by indorsement, nor circulate as do the several forms of negotiable paper. The person or firm on whom an order is drawn, must in filling it know that it is genuine, and the order itself should then be carefully preserved as a voucher, in case disagreements should ever arise.

Kalamazoo, Mich., January 29, 1885.

Messrs. Paul & Thomas,

Please deliver to bearer with bill, for me,

1 pr. Calf Boots, No. 8.
2 prs. Kid Slippers, No. 7.

John Barden.

Statute of Limitations in Each State and Territory and Canada, for Notes, Judgments, Open Accounts, Sealed Instruments, and Actions for Assault and Slander, with a List of the Penalties for Usury in all the States and Territories.

States and Territories.	Statute of Limitations.					Penalties for Usury.
	Open Accounts.	Notes.	Judgments.	Assault and Slander.	Sealed Instruments.	
	Yrs.	Yrs.	Yrs.	Yrs.	Yrs.	
Alabama	3	6	20	1	10	Forfeiture of entire interest.
Arizona	2	4	5	......	4	
Arkansas	3	5	10	1	10	Forfeiture of principal and interest.
California	2	4	5	1	5	
Colorado	3	3	6	1	6	
Connecticut	3	3	6	3	17	
Dakota	6	6	20	2	20	Forfeiture of interest.
Delaware	3	6	20	1	20	Forfeiture of principal.
Dist. Columbia	3	6	12	1	12	Forfeiture of entire interest.
Florida	4	5	20	2	20	
Georgia	4	6	7	1	20	Forfeiture of excess.
Idaho Ter	4	5	5	2	6	Forfeiture of three times the amount paid; fine, $300 or six months' imprisonment, or both.
Illinois	5	10	20	1	20	Forfeiture excess interest.
Indiana	6	10	20	2	20	Forfeiture excess interest.
Iowa	5	10	20	2	10	Forfeiture of entire interest.
Kansas	3	5	5	1	15	Forfeiture of excess.
Kentucky	2	5	15	1	15	Forfeiture of entire interest.
Louisiana	3	5	10	1	10	Excess above 8 per cent, after maturity, forfeits entire interest.
Maine	6	6	20	2	20	
Maryland	3	3	12	1	12	Forfeiture of excess.
Massachusetts	6	20	12	2	12	
Michigan	6	6	10	2	10	Forfeiture of excess, if over 7 per cent.
Minnesota	6	6	10	2	20	Forfeiture of entire debt.
Mississippi	3	6	7	1	7	Forfeiture of entire interest.
Missouri	5	10	20	2	20	Lender forfeits entire interest; borrower pays 10 per cent to school fund.
Montana	2	6	6	2	6	
Nebraska	4	5	10	1	5	Forfeiture of entire interest.
Nevada	2	4	5	2	5	
New Hampshire	6	6	20	2	20	Forfeiture of three times the excess and costs.
New Jersey	6	6	20	2	6	Forfeiture of entire interest.
New Mexico	......	......	......	1	......	Forfeiture of excess.
New York	6	6	20	2	20	Voids contract, and is a misdemeanor.
North Carolina	3	3	11	1	10	Forfeiture of entire interest; party paying may recover double the amount paid.
Ohio	6	15	15	1	15	Forfeiture of excess.
Oregon	6	6	10	2	10	Forfeiture of original sum and costs.
Pennsylvania	6	6	20	1	20	
Rhode Island	6	6	20	1	20	
South Carolina	6	6	20	2	20	Forfeiture of all interest.
Tennessee	6	6	10	1	10	Forfeiture of excess, fine and imprisonment.
Texas	2	4	10	1	10	Forfeiture of all interest.
Utah	2	4	5	1	5	
Vermont	6	6	8	2	8	Forfeiture of excess.
Virginia	2	5	20	1	20	Forfeiture of all interest.
Washington Ter.	3	6	6	2	6	
West Virginia	3 to 5	6	10	1	20	Forfeiture of excess.
Wisconsin	6	6	20	2	20	Forfeiture of all interest.
Wyoming Ter	4	5	21	1	5	
Canada	1 to 5	6	6	2	20	Misdemeanor.
New Brunswick	6	6	20	......	20	Misdemeanor.
Nova Scotia	6	6	20	......	20	Misdemeanor.

Legal Rates of Interest in the States and Territories, With Exemptions from Judgment, Etc.

States and Territories.	Legal Rate p. c.	Contract Rate p. c.	Exemptions from Judgments, Inter-State Regulations, etc.
Alabama	8	8	Judgments of other states limited to 20 years. Exemptions—Personal property, $1,000; homestead, $2,000.
Arizona	10	Any	Exemptions from $1,000 to $5,000.
Arkansas	6	10	Judgments required to be renewed every three years. Exemptions, $200 to $2,500.
California	7	Any	On judgments for money loaned, 7 per cent only. Exemptions, from $1,000 to $5,000.
Colorado	10	Any	If debts are contracted within the state, the statute of limitations extends six years. Exemptions, $300 to $2,000.
Connecticut	6	Any	Exemptions, $200 to $500.
Dakota	7	12	Exemptions, $1,500.
Delaware	6	6	Exemptions, $75 to $275.
Dist. Columbia	6	10	Exemptions, $300 to $400.
Florida	8	Any	Exemptions, $1,000 to $2,000.
Georgia	7	8	Exemptions, $1,600.
Idaho	10	18	Exemptions, $100 to $5,000.
Illinois	6	8	Exemptions, $400 to $1,000.
Indiana	6	8	Judgments must be renewed, within five years. Exempt, $600.
Iowa	6	10	On notes, if partial payment has been made, date of limitation begins from last payment. Exemptions—County, 40 acres; city, one-half acre with buildings, regardless of value.
Kansas	7	12	On open accounts, limitation extends but two years for non-residents of the state. Exemptions, $300 to $400.
Kentucky	6	8	Exemptions, $500 to $1,500.
Louisiana	5	8	Judgments may be renewed at any time before expiration. Exemptions—None in cities; country, homestead, $2,000.
Maine	6	Any	If notes are witnessed, 20 years. Exemptions, $500.
Maryland	6	6	Exemptions, $100.
Massachusetts	6	Any	Notes witnessed, 20 years. Exemptions, $300 to $800.
Michigan	7	10	Executions on judgments not entered within two years must be renewed. Exemptions, $150 to $1,500.
Minnesota	7	10	Judgment liens expire after five years if not attached. Exemptions, $500 to $1,000, besides homestead of 80 acres in country, and one lot to one-half acre in cities.
Mississippi	6	10	Exempt. $250 to $500. Residence in city, $2,000; country, 80 acres.
Missouri	6	10	Exemptions—$300; homestead in country, 160 acres; in cities, homestead in value from $1,500 to $3,000.
Montana	10	Any	Exemptions, $800 to $2,500.
Nebraska	7	10	Action on foreign judgments must be commenced within five years. Exemptions—Personal property, $500; country, 160 acres; cities, two lots.
Nevada	10	Any	Merchants' or store accounts, one year only after last purchase. Exempt.—$200 to $500; homestead, to head of family, $5,000.
New Hampshire	6	6	Actions on judgments must be brought within two years. Exemptions—$100 to $400; interest in homestead to wife during life, $500.
New Jersey	6	6	Exemptions—Personalty, 200; homestead under statutory notice, $1,000.
New Mexico	6	12	Exemptions, to head of family residing on property, $1,000.
New York	6	6	Corporations barred defense in actions for usury. Exemptions—$250; homestead, if recorded, $4,000.
North Carolina	6	8	Executions must be renewed within one year and one day from date of issue. Exempt.—Personalty, $500; homestead, $1,000.
Ohio	6	8	Exemptions, $500 to $1,000.
Oregon	8	10	Exemptions, $400 to $700.
Pennsylvania	6	6	Exemptions, $300.
Rhode Island	6	Any	No higher rate than 6 per cent interest can be collected by law. Exemptions, $230 to $500.
South Carolina	7	7	Exemptions—Personalty, $500; homestead, $1,000.
Tennessee	6	6	Exemptions—$250; homestead, $1,000.
Texas	8	12	Exemptions—Furniture and farming implements and 200 acres; in cities, real estate, $5,000.
Utah	10	Any	Exemptions—Personalty, $200 to $400; homestead, $1,000, and $250 additional to each member of family.
Vermont	6	6	Exemptions—Personalty, $250; homestead, $500.
Virginia	6	6	Exemptions—Personalty, $200; homestead, real or personal property, $2,000.
Washington Ter.	10	Any	Exemptions—Personalty, $150 to $500; homestead occupied by family, $1,000.
West Virginia	6	6	Exemptions—Personalty, $50 to $200; homestead, if recorded before creation of debt, $1,000.
Wisconsin	7	10	Exemptions—Personalty, $200 to $250; printing materials, $1,500; homestead, country, 40 acres; town or city, ¼ acre.
Wyoming Ter.	12	Any	Exemptions—$500 to $800, and wearing apparel for every person; homestead, occupied, 160 acres; town lots, $1,500.

TABLES OF WEIGHTS AND MEASURES.

AVOIRDUPOIS WEIGHT.

16 drams make 1 ounce.
16 ounces make 1 pound.
25 pounds make 1 quarter.
4 quarters make 1 hundred weight.
20 hundred weight make 1 ton.

DRY MEASURE.

2 pints make 1 quart.
8 quarts make 1 peck.
4 pecks make 1 bushel.
36 bushels make 1 chaldron.

LINEAR (or Long) MEASURE.

12 inches make 1 foot.
3 feet make 1 yard.
5½ yards (16½ feet) make 1 rod.
40 rods make 1 furlong.
8 furlongs make 1 mile.

TIME MEASURE.

60 seconds make 1 minute.
60 minutes make 1 hour
24 hours make 1 day.
7 days make 1 week.
4 weeks make 1 lunar month.
13 lunar months, or 12 calendar months,* or 52 weeks, make 1 year.
365 days, 5 hours, 48 minutes and 49 seconds, make 1 solar year.
366 days make 1 leap year.

*A calendar month is either 28, 29, 30 or 31 days. In computing interest, 30 days is reckoned as a month.

CIRCULAR MEASURE.

60 seconds make 1 minute.
60 minutes make 1 degree.
30 degrees make 1 sign.
90 degrees make 1 quadrant.
4 quadrants (or 360 degrees) make 1 circle.

TROY WEIGHT.

24 grains make 1 pennyweight.
20 pennyweight make 1 ounce.
12 ounces make 1 pound.

APOTHECARIES' WEIGHT.

20 grains make 1 scruple.
3 scruples make 1 dram.
8 drams make 1 ounce.
12 ounces make 1 pound.

LIQUID (or Wine) MEASURE.

4 gills make 1 pint.
2 pints make 1 quart.
4 quarts make 1 gallon.
31½ gallons make 1 barrel.
2 barrels (63 gallons) make 1 hogshead.

SQUARE MEASURE.

144 square inches make 1 square foot.
9 square feet make 1 square yard.
30¼ square yards make 1 square rod.
40 square rods make 1 rood.
4 roods make 1 acre.

CUBIC MEASURE.

1728 cubic inches make 1 cubic foot.
27 cubic feet make 1 cubic yard.
128 cubic feet make 1 cord (of wood.)
40 cubic feet make 1 ton (shipping.)
2150.42 cubic inches make 1 standard bushel.
268.8 cubic inches make 1 standard gallon.
1 cubic foot is equal to four-fifths of a bushel.

SURVEYOR'S MEASURE.

7.92 chains make 1 link.
25 links make 1 rod.
4 rods make 1 chain.
10 square chains (160 square rods) make 1 acre.
640 acres make 1 square mile.

CLOTH MEASURE.

2¼ inches make 1 nail.
4 nails make 1 quarter.
4 quarters make 1 yard.

LIST OF MISCELLANEOUS MEASURES.

3 inches make 1 palm.
4 inches make 1 hand.
6 inches make 1 span.
18 inches make 1 cubit.
21.8 inches make 1 bible cubit.
2½ feet make 1 military pace.
12 articles make 1 dozen.
12 dozen make 1 gross.
12 dozen dozen make 1 great gross.
20 articles make 1 score.
10 years make 1 decade.
100 years make 1 century.
16 pounds make 1 stone.

THE RAPID CALCULATOR.

BY means of the table on the following page, it will be found easy to ascertain the amount of interest on any given sum for any given time. The first column shows the amount on which the interest is to be computed; the second column gives the respective rates at which the computation is to be made, and the remaining columns contain the amount of interest on the sums indicated for the periods named above them.

ILLUSTRATION.—What is the interest on $60 for six months at eight per cent? Look in the left hand column of the table for the *amount*, $60; find the figure 8 in the group opposite $60 in the second column, which shows the *rate per cent;* then run the finger along this line toward the right, until the column headed "6 months" is reached. The figures there found ($1.80) give the required answer. Of course, if the rate named had been 6, 7 or 10 per cent, the line commencing with the proper figure should have been followed.

In the table, computations have been given only at six, seven, eight and ten per cent, these being the rates most common in business transactions. Interest at other rates may, however, be easily computed from the figures given. Thus, interest at four per cent is one-half that at eight; five per cent one-half of ten; twelve per cent double six, etc., etc.

If it be desired to ascertain the interest on an amount not specifically named in the table, it may be easily found by combining the figures given for two or more amounts whose sum will equal the amount sought.

ILLUSTRATION.—To find the interest on $146 for one year, nine months and eighteen days at seven per cent.

Interest on $100 for 1 year at 7 per cent	$7 00
Interest on $100 for 9 months at 7 per cent	5 25
Interest on $100 for 15 days at 7 per cent	25
Interest on $100 for 3 days at 7 per cent	06
Interest on $40 for 1 year at 7 per cent	2 80
Interest on $40 for 9 months at 7 per cent	2 10
Interest on $40 for 15 days at 7 per cent	16
Interest on $40 for 3 days at 7 per cent	02
Interest on $5 for 1 year at 7 per cent	35
Interest on $5 for 9 months at 7 per cent	26
Interest on $5 for 15 days at 7 per cent	01
Interest on $5 for 3 days at 7 per cent	00.02
Interest on $145 for 1 year, 9 months, 18 days at 7 per cent	$18 26.02

To ascertain the interest on $200, $500, $1,200, etc., multiply that given in the table for $100 by the proper number.

As notes are so frequently made at 30 days' time, a separate column has been included in the table, giving the amount of interest for 33 days, allowing for the usual three days of grace. It is believed that this feature will render the table still more convenient for reference.

Instantaneous Computation of Interest on Given Amount for any Number of Days or Months.

Amount.	Rate per cent.	TIME FOR WHICH INTEREST IS COMPUTED.																										
		DAYS.															MONTHS.											
		1	2	3	4	5	6	7	8	9	10	15	20	25	30	33	1	2	3	4	5	6	7	8	9	10	11	12
$1	6	0	0	0	0	0	0	0	0	0	0	0	0	0	0	1	0	1	1	2	2	3	3	3	4	4	5	5
	7	0	0	0	0	0	0	0	0	0	0	0	0	0	1	1	1	1	2	2	3	3	4	4	5	5	6	6
	8	0	0	0	0	0	0	0	0	0	0	0	0	0	1	1	1	1	2	2	3	3	4	5	6	7	7	8
	10	0	0	0	0	0	0	0	0	0	0	0	1	1	1	1	1	2	3	3	4	5	6	7	8	8	9	10
$2	6	0	0	0	0	0	0	0	0	0	0	1	1	1	1	1	1	2	3	4	5	6	7	8	9	10	11	12
	7	0	0	0	0	0	0	0	0	0	0	1	1	1	1	1	1	2	4	5	6	7	8	9	11	12	13	14
	8	0	0	0	0	0	0	0	0	0	0	1	1	1	1	1	1	3	4	5	7	8	9	11	12	13	15	16
	10	0	0	0	0	0	0	0	0	0	1	1	1	1	2	2	2	3	5	7	8	10	12	13	15	17	18	20
$3	6	0	0	0	0	0	0	0	0	0	1	1	1	1	2	2	2	3	5	6	8	9	11	12	14	15	17	18
	7	0	0	0	0	0	0	0	0	1	1	1	1	1	2	2	2	4	5	7	9	11	12	14	16	18	19	21
	8	0	0	0	0	0	0	0	1	1	1	1	1	2	2	2	2	4	6	8	10	12	14	16	18	20	22	24
	10	0	0	0	0	1	1	1	1	1	1	1	2	2	3	3	3	5	8	10	13	15	18	20	23	25	28	30
$4	6	0	0	0	0	0	0	1	1	1	1	1	1	2	2	2	2	4	6	8	10	12	14	16	18	20	22	24
	7	0	0	0	0	0	0	1	1	1	1	1	2	2	2	2	2	5	7	9	12	14	16	19	21	23	26	28
	8	0	0	0	0	1	1	1	1	1	1	1	2	2	3	3	3	5	8	11	13	16	19	21	24	27	29	32
	10	0	0	0	0	1	1	1	1	1	1	2	2	3	3	4	3	7	10	13	17	20	23	27	30	33	37	40
$5	6	0	0	0	0	0	1	1	1	1	1	1	1	2	3	3	3	5	8	10	13	15	18	20	23	25	28	30
	7	0	0	0	0	0	1	1	1	1	1	1	2	2	3	3	3	6	9	12	15	18	20	23	26	29	32	35
	8	0	0	0	0	1	1	1	1	1	1	2	2	3	3	3	3	7	10	13	17	20	23	27	30	33	37	40
	10	0	0	0	1	1	1	1	1	1	1	2	3	3	4	5	4	8	13	17	21	25	29	33	38	42	46	50
$10	6	0	0	1	1	1	1	1	1	2	2	3	3	4	5	6	5	10	15	20	25	30	35	40	45	50	55	60
	7	0	0	1	1	1	1	1	2	2	2	3	4	5	6	7	6	12	18	23	29	35	41	47	53	58	64	70
	8	0	0	1	1	1	1	2	2	2	2	3	4	6	7	7	7	13	20	27	33	40	47	53	60	67	73	80
	10	0	1	1	1	1	2	2	2	3	3	4	6	7	8	9	8	17	25	33	42	50	58	67	75	83	92	1.00
$20	6	0	1	1	1	2	2	2	3	3	3	5	7	8	10	11	10	20	30	40	50	60	70	80	90	1.00	1.10	1.20
	7	0	1	1	2	2	2	3	3	4	4	6	8	10	12	13	12	23	35	47	58	70	82	93	1.05	1.17	1.28	1.40
	8	0	1	1	2	2	3	3	4	4	4	7	9	11	13	14	13	27	40	53	66	80	93	1.07	1.20	1.33	1.47	1.60
	10	1	1	2	2	3	3	4	5	5	6	9	12	14	17	19	17	33	50	67	84	1.00	1.17	1.33	1.50	1.67	1.84	2.00
$30	6	1	1	2	2	3	3	4	4	5	5	8	10	13	15	17	15	30	45	60	75	90	1.05	1.20	1.35	1.50	1.65	1.80
	7	1	1	2	2	3	4	4	5	5	6	9	12	15	18	20	18	35	53	70	88	1.05	1.23	1.40	1.58	1.75	1.93	2.10
	8	1	1	2	3	3	4	5	5	6	7	10	13	17	20	22	20	40	60	80	1.00	1.20	1.40	1.60	1.80	2.00	2.20	2.40
	10	1	2	2	3	4	5	6	7	7	8	12	17	21	25	27	25	50	75	1.00	1.25	1.50	1.75	2.00	2.25	2.50	2.75	3.00
$40	6	1	1	2	3	3	4	5	5	6	7	10	13	17	20	22	20	40	60	80	1.00	1.20	1.40	1.60	1.80	2.00	2.20	2.40
	7	1	2	2	3	4	5	5	6	7	8	12	16	19	23	25	23	47	70	93	1.17	1.41	1.63	1.87	2.10	2.33	2.57	2.80
	8	1	2	3	4	4	5	6	7	8	9	13	18	22	27	30	27	53	80	1.07	1.33	1.60	1.87	2.13	2.40	2.67	2.93	3.20
	10	1	2	3	4	5	7	8	9	10	11	16	22	27	33	36	33	67	1.00	1.34	1.67	2.00	2.33	2.67	3.00	3.33	3.67	4.00
$50	6	1	2	3	3	4	5	6	7	8	8	13	17	21	25	28	25	50	75	1.00	1.25	1.50	1.75	2.00	2.25	2.50	2.75	3.00
	7	1	2	3	4	5	6	7	8	9	10	15	19	24	29	32	29	58	88	1.17	1.46	1.75	2.04	3.33	2.63	2.92	3.31	3.50
	8	1	2	3	4	5	7	8	9	10	11	16	22	27	33	36	33	67	1.00	1.33	1.67	2.00	2.33	2.67	3.00	3.33	3.67	4.00
	10	1	2	4	6	7	8	10	11	13	14	21	28	35	42	46	42	83	1.25	1.67	2.08	2.50	2.92	3.33	3.75	4.17	4.58	5.00
$60	6	1	2	3	4	5	6	7	8	9	10	15	20	25	30	33	30	60	90	1.20	1.50	1.80	2.10	2.40	2.70	3.00	3.30	3.60
	7	1	2	3	4	5	6	7	8	9	11	18	24	30	35	38	35	70	1.05	1.40	1.75	2.10	2.45	2.80	3.15	3.50	3.85	4.20
	8	1	3	4	5	7	8	9	11	12	13	20	27	33	40	44	40	80	1.20	1.60	2.00	2.40	2.80	3.20	3.60	4.00	4.40	4.80
	10	2	3	5	7	8	10	12	13	15	17	25	33	42	50	55	50	1.00	1.50	2.00	2.50	3.00	3.50	4.00	4.50	5.00	5.50	6.00
$70	6	1	2	4	5	6	7	8	9	11	12	18	23	29	35	39	35	70	1.05	1.40	1.75	2.10	2.45	2.80	3.15	3.50	3.85	4.20
	7	1	3	4	5	7	8	10	11	12	14	20	27	34	41	45	41	82	1.23	1.63	2.04	2.45	2.86	3.27	3.68	4.08	4.49	4.90
	8	2	3	5	6	8	9	11	12	14	16	23	31	39	47	52	47	93	1.40	1.87	2.33	2.80	3.27	3.73	4.20	4.67	5.13	5.60
	10	2	4	6	8	10	12	14	16	17	19	29	39	49	58	64	58	1.17	1.75	2.33	2.92	3.50	4.08	4.67	5.25	5.83	6.42	7.00
$80	6	1	3	4	5	7	8	9	11	12	13	20	27	33	40	44	40	80	1.20	1.60	2.00	2.40	2.80	3.20	3.60	4.00	4.40	4.80
	7	2	3	5	6	8	9	11	12	14	16	23	31	39	47	52	47	93	1.40	1.87	2.33	2.80	3.27	3.73	4.20	4.67	5.13	5.60
	8	2	5	8	11	13	16	19	21	24	27	40	53	67	80	88	80	1.60	2.40	3.20	4.00	4.80	5.60	6.40	7.20	8.00	8.80	9.60
	10	2	5	7	9	11	13	16	18	20	22	33	44	56	67	73	67	1.33	2.00	2.67	3.33	4.00	4.67	5.33	6.00	6.67	7.33	8.00
$90	6	2	3	5	6	8	9	11	12	14	15	23	30	38	45	50	45	90	1.35	1.80	2.25	2.70	3.15	3.60	4.05	4.50	4.95	5.40
	7	2	4	5	7	9	11	12	14	16	18	26	35	44	53	58	53	1.05	1.58	2.10	2.63	3.15	3.68	4.20	4.73	5.25	5.78	6.30
	8	2	4	6	8	10	12	14	16	18	20	30	40	50	60	66	60	1.20	1.80	2.40	3.00	3.60	4.20	4.80	5.40	5.80	6.40	7.20
	10	2	5	7	10	12	15	17	20	22	25	37	50	63	75		75	1.50	2.25	3.00	3.75	4.50	5.25	6.00	6.75	7.50	8.25	9.00
100	6	2	3	5	7	8	10	12	13	15	17	25	33	42	50	55	50	1.00	1.50	2.00	2.50	3.00	3.50	4.00	4.50	5.00	5.50	6.00
	7	2	4	6	8	10	12	14	16	18	19	29	39	49	58	64	58	1.17	1.75	2.33	2.92	3.50	4.08	4.67	5.25	5.83	6.42	7.00
	8	2	5	7	9	11	12	16	18	20	22	33	44	56	67	73	67	1.33	2.00	2.67	3.34	4.00	4.67	5.33	6.00	6.67	7.33	8.00
	10	3	6	8	11	14	16	19	22	25	28	42	56	69	83	92	83	1.67	2.50	3.33	4.17	5.00	5.83	6.67	7.50	8.30	9.17	10.00

TABLE showing the Quantity of Various Kinds of Seeds needed for Planting, per Acre, and Mode of Planting.

Kind of Seed.	Mode of Planting	Quantity Needed.	
		Measure.	No.
Asparagus	12 inch drills	Qts*	16
Asparagus plants	4 x 1½ feet apart	Plts	8,000
Barley		Bus.	2¼
Beans, bush	30 inch drills	Bus	1¼
Beans, pole, Lima	4ft. apart each way	Qts	20
Beans, Carolina, prolific, etc	4 x 3 feet apart	Qts	10
Beets and mangold	30 inch drills	Lbs.	9
Broom corn	In drills	Lbs	12
Cabbage	Outside, for transplanting	Oz	12
Cabbage	Sown in frames	Oz	4
Carrots	30 inch drill	Lbs	4
Celery seed		Oz	8
Celery plants	4 x ½ feet apart	Plts.	25,000
Celery, white, Dutch		Lbs	13
Clover, Aliske		Lbs	6
Clover, large red		Lbs	16
Clover, large red, with timothy		Lbs	12
Clover, Lucerne		Lbs	10
Corn, field		Qts	8
Corn, salad	10 inch drills	Lbs	25
Corn, sugar		Qts	10
Cucumbers	In hills	Qts	3
Flax	Broadcast	Qts	20
Grass, timothy		Qts	10
Grass, timothy, with clover		Qts	6
Grass, orchard		Qts	25
Grass, red top or beads		Qts	20
Grass, blue		Qts	28
Grass, rye		Qts	204
Grass, lawn		Lbs.	35
Lettuce	In 30 inch rows	Lbs.	3
Melons, citron	In hills, 4 feet apart each way	Lbs.	2
Melons, water	In hills, 8 feet apart each way	Lbs.	3
Oats		Bus	2
Onions	In beds or sets	Lbs.	50
Onions	In rows for large bulbs	Lbs.	7
Parsnips	30 inch drills	Lbs	5
Parsley	24 inch drills	Lbs	4
Peas	Broadcast	Bus	3
Peas, short varieties	In drills	Bus	2
Peas, tall varieties	In drills	Bus	1to1½
Pepper-plants	1 x 2½ feet apart	Plts	17,500
Potatoes		Bus	8
Pumpkins	In hills, 8 x 8 feet apart	Qts	2
Radishes	24 inch drills	Lbs	10
Rye	Broadcast	Bus	1½
Rye	In drills	Bus	1¼
Squash, bush	In hills, 4 x 4 feet apart	Lbs	3
Turnips	In 24 inch drills	Lbs	3
Turnips	Broadcast	Lbs.	3
Tomatoes	In frames	Oz	3
Tomatoes	Seeds in hills, 3 feet apart each way	Oz	8
Tomato plants		Plts	3,800
Wheat	Broadcast	Bus	2
Wheat	In hills	Bus	1½

* Qts., quarts; Plts., plants; Bus., bushels; Lbs., pounds; Oz., ounces.

TABLE showing the Number, Diplomatic Titles, and Salaries of the various Foreign Ministers of the United States.

Country.	Resid'ce.	Title.	Sal'y.
			$
Argentine Republic	Buenos Ayres	Min. Res	7,500
Austria-Hungary	Vienna	E. E. and Min. Plen.	12,000
Belgium	Brussels	Min. Res	7,500
Bolivia	La Paz	Min. Res	5,000
Brazil	Rio de Janiero	E. E. and Min. Plen	12,000
Central Americ'n States	Guatemala*	E. E. and Min. Plen	10,000
Chili	Santiago	E. E. and Min. Plen	10,000
China	Pekin	E. E. and Min. Plen	12,000
Colombia	Bogota	Min. Res	7,500
Corea	Seoll	E. E. and Min. Plen	5,000
Denmark	Copenhagen	E. E. and Min. Plen	5,000
France	Paris	E. E. and Min. Plen	17,500
Germany	Berlin	E. E. and Min. Plen	17,500
Great Britain	London	E. E. and Min. Plen	17,500
Greece, Rouma'ia & Servia	Athens*	Min. Res	6,500
Hawaiian Islands	Honolulu	Min. Res	7,500
Hayti	Port-au-Prince	Min. Res	7,500
Italy	Rome	E. E. and Min. Plen	12,000
Japan	Tokio (Yeddo)	E. E. and Min. Plen	12,000
Liberia	Monrovia	E. E. and Min. Plen	3,000
Mexico	City of M	E. E. and Min. Plen	12,000
Netherlands	The Hague	Min. Res	7,500
Paraguay and Uruguay	Mont'deo	Min. Res	5,000
Persia	Teheran	Min. Res	5,000
Peru	Lima	E. E. and Min. Plen	10,000
Portugal	Lisbon	Min. Res	5,000
Russia	St Petersburgh	E. E. and Min. Plen	17,500
Siam	Bangkok	Min. Res	5,000
Spain	Madrid	E. E. and Min. Plen	12,000
Sweden & Norway	Stock'o'm	Min. Res	7,500
Switzer'd	Berne	Min. Res	5,000
Turkey	Constantinople	E. E. and Min. Plen	7,500
Venez'ela	Caracas	Min. Res	7,500

*Ministers reside at the capital of the country to which sent; except that the Minister to the Central American States (including Costa Rica, Guatemala, Honduras, Nicaragua and Salvador) resides at the capital of Guatemala, and the Minister to Greece, Roumania and Servia, resides at the capital of Greece.

[Explanation of Abbrevations: E. E. and Min. Plen., Envoy Extraordinary and Minister Plenipotentiary; Min. Res., Minister Resident.]

WRITING MADE EASY.

WRITING is indeed a part of the art preservative, and in this age of accomplishment, the ability to write well, with speed, and so clear that it can be read with ease, should be acquired by each individual, no matter what may be his busines or place in the world.

Communication between man and man must now be more frequent as it becomes universal, and every accountable being will, at once, find that there is the utmost need of knowing how to handle the pen.

First, learn to write a plain, round business hand. Let it be neat and accurate; do not yield to the habit of botch-work or bungling. Pay due respect to your correspondent by sending a letter that is free of a stupid or awkward address, whether inside or outside of the envelope. Be punctilious about spelling the words that you choose to employ. Few are so smart that a dictionary of words is of small or no use. Have a dictionary close by as well as your bible, and do not grow up or continue a victim of bad spelling.

MATERIALS FOR WRITING.

To a suitable table or desk, with light free at the point of the pen, is to be added the prerequisite materials of pens, ink and paper.

Steel pens are in general use, and are best for most persons. Gold pens are to be valued for always producing the same quality of writing, while steel pens, new or old, produce finer or coarser lines, and better lines as the steel point adheres to the paper. One will require a coarse pen, and another a fine one; the pen should be adapted to the hand, whether it be one of the elastic series or less flexible. There are all grades, shapes, and sizes to suit the fancy or style of all. Pens are to be selected by trying one or two of several kinds before buying a full supply. Write a few lines or a page with the different points and then compare the writing. If it be shaded too much, take a less flexible pen, if the hair lines are too delicate, take a coarser pen.

Use black ink, free from sediment, that flows well; an inkstand with broad base and small neck to save it from upsetting and absorbing the dust of the room. A fluid ink that does not appear black at once, but continues to grow black and durable, is preferred by business men and accountants. Fancy colored inks should be avoided.

Paper is abundant and cheap, and it is a mark of bad taste to write on an inferior article. Bad writing on good paper is better than good writing on bad paper. Foolscap is best for the practice of penmanship, as it may be easily sewed into book-form, with cover of some different color, and serve the purpose very well. The paper should have a medium surface. A few extra sheets beside the writing book are needed for use in testing the pens and practicing the movement exercises. There should be many thicknesses of paper under the pen of the writer, and a large sized blotter under the hand.

Study gives form

Have the will to learn, to study, and to practice. Aimless or careless practice never made a good writer. The forms of the models should be well conceived by the mind. These must be clearly formed in the mind if you would execute the pen-work so that the writing will appear neat and plain. Study comes before practice, or with it. But practice does not come before study in learning anything. The form of each letter should be studied and its various parts fairly analyzed, then practiced.

POSITION OF THE BODY.

Sit squarely before the desk with feet firmly on the floor, and both arms on the desk, is the best position for practice in writing, or correspondence. Otherwise, the right side may be placed to the desk, with the right arm only resting thereon, and some persons prefer this position. Do not cross the feet, sit on the edge of the chair, or assume any careless attitude. Sit erect, but slightly inclined forward, that the eye may follow the pen closely. This is the only proper or healthful position. When wearied by sitting and the effort of writing, rise from the desk and take exercise by walking about the room or in the open air; then come back refreshed and ready to take new interest in the practice of writing. Let the light fall from the left side, unless you are left-handed.

SHADING.

Shading has its value, but business men, clerks and telegraph operators find a uniform and regular style of writing, without shade, the best, even though it may not be as artistic.

UNIFORMITY.

This is a necessary element in all good penmanship. There must be no irregularity in the slope of letters and words that form a written page. Uniformity in the size of letters, all letters written

on the line, and of uniform hight, are some of the essentials of good pen work.

SLANT.

Writing may be more or less positive in its angle of slant, and that will not matter so much if all the letters are made to conform exactly to the same slant. Writing that is nearest to the perpendicular is most legible, and therefore best for business purposes. But for ease in execution, the writing should slant, but ought to be made as nearly perpendicular as is consistent with ease of execution. The slant of writing should not be less than sixty degrees from the horizontal.

LEGIBILITY.

In learning to write, the pains that are taken to make it legible should not be offset by the bad habit of making all manner of meaningless flourishes. The business man does not look with favor upon shades and flourishes in writing, but in his estimation writing is injured by them. A plain, regular style that can be written rapidly, and read at a glance, is demanded for business purposes.

POSITION OF BODY WHILE STANDING.

A PRACTICAL bookkeeper finds it advantageous to do his writing while standing. Where entries are to be tranferred from one book to another, as is the case where large books are in use, the work cannot be done in a business-like manner in other than a standing position. While writing in large books, the writer must place his left side to the desk, since cumbrous books must lie squarely on the desk, for convenience, if not to make the most of space.

FINISH.

Good pen-work consists in attention to small details; each letter and word correctly formed, makes the beautiful page. By careless making of one letter, or part of a letter of a word, oftentimes the word is mistaken for another, and the entire meaning changed. Particular attention should be given to the finish of some of the small letters, as the dotting of the i and the crossing of the t. Blending the lines which form a loop, often causes the letter to appear as a stem, as if it were a t or d, or an e becomes like an i. If the small cross be left off the capital F the letter will be a T; the W often becomes an M, or vice versa, and the I a J. Each letter has an identity of its own, that by study and careful practice will be preserved.

POSITION OF HAND AND PEN.

Rest the right arm on the muscles just below the elbow, and the wrist should be elevated so as to move free from paper and desk. Turn the hand so that the wrist will be level, or so that the back of the hand will face the ceiling. The third and fourth fingers turned underneath the hand will form its support and the pen; these fingers and the muscles of the arm near the elbow form the only points of rest, or contact, on desk, or paper. The pen should point over the shoulder, and should be so held that it may pass the root of the nail on the second finger, and about opposite the knuckle of the hand. Teachers concur in the one position above described. Any other or

unnatural position is opposed to good writing. Avoid an awkward or cramped position, or drawing the forefinger up into a crooked shape. Hold the pen firmly but lightly. Have the will to acquire the habit of holding the pen correctly, not grasping it as if it were about to escape, and with practice you will soon be able to write with ease.

RAPIDITY

An essential feature of a practical business style of writing must be rapidity of execution. Merchants require that their clerks do their writing well and rapidly, and the letters to be answered, bills to be made out, or items to be entered on the books of account, make it needful that the clerks move the pen with dexterity and ease. In acquiring speed in writing, one should gradually increase the speed until the desired rate is accomplished.

BEAUTY.

As in other things, the element of beauty in the handwriting is largely a matter of taste and education. To the man of business, the most beautiful handwriting is that that is written with ease, and expresses plainly and neatly the thought of the writer. To the professional or artistic taste no writing would be considered beautiful unless it was made to conform to rule as to proportion, shade and spacing. In the practical art of writing, it may be fair to measure its beauty largely by its utility

MOVEMENT

In the office or counting room, where the clerk or correspondent must write from morning till night, the finger movement cannot be used. Writing by use of the fingers as the motive power, is entirely inadequate to the requirements of business, since the fingers soon become tired and the hand becomes cramped. The whole arm or free arm movement, in which the arm is lifted from the desk and completes the letter with a dash or swoop, is necessary in ornamental penmanship, but has no place in a practical style of business writing. For the practical purposes of business, the muscular movement, in which the arm moves freely on the muscles below the elbow, is best adapted. The third and fourth fingers may remain stationary on the paper, and be moved between words or from time to time, where careful and accurate writing is desired, but in more rapid, free and flowing penmanship, the fingers should slide over the paper.

MOVEMENT EXERCISES.

To obtain control of the pen and train the muscles, a series of movements must be practiced. Circular motion, as in the capital O, reversed as in the capital W, vertical movement as in f, long s and capital J, lateral motion as in small letters. This is to enable one to move the pen in any direction, up, down, or sidewise. Try the simplest exercise in movement; follow around in the same line as as nearly as possible, without shading.

Same exercise with ovals drawn out and slight shade added to each down stroke.

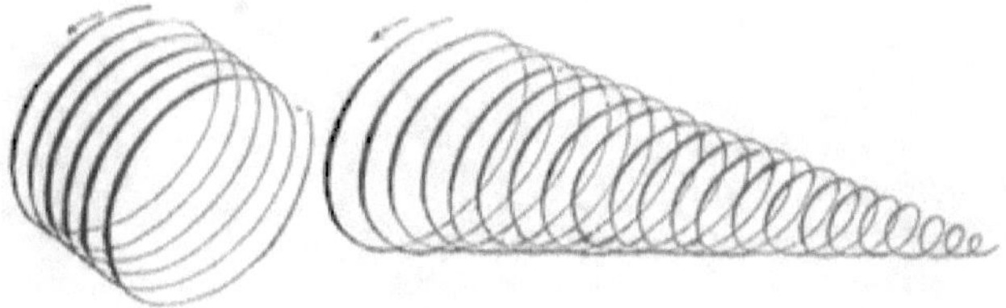

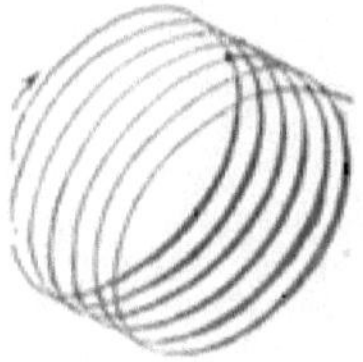

Continuation of exercise for reverse practice.

Side of ovals should be even, making a straight lie. Reverse the movement. Note the arrows.

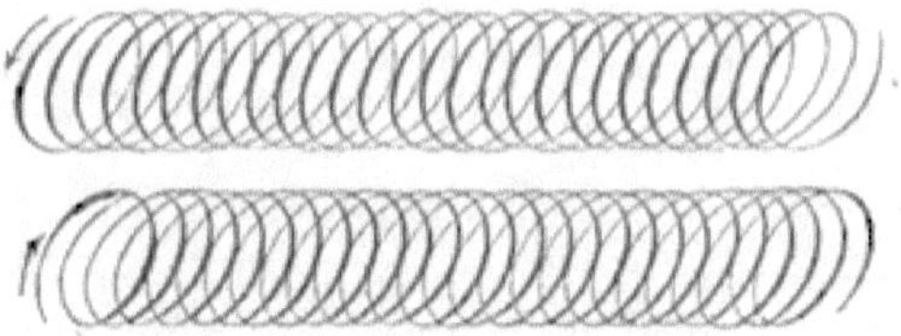

Essential elements of capital letters are as shown in the following three exercises, which should at first be made large for the purposes of movement.

Capital O, down strokes parallel.

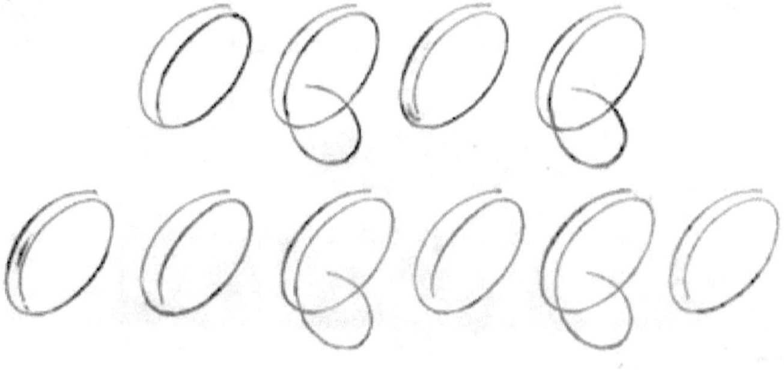

Capital stem. Down stroke curved, shade low, finish with a dash.

Capital loop. Curves parallel. First curve highest.

Lateral movement, by which one writes long words without lifting the pen.

Down strokes straight, even and resting on line.

Third and fourth fingers should slide on the paper. Avoid the finger movement. Combine the movements in various forms.

Lateral and rolling movement combined. Vertical movement and rolling movement combined. Do not shade the circles. Lines should be parallel.

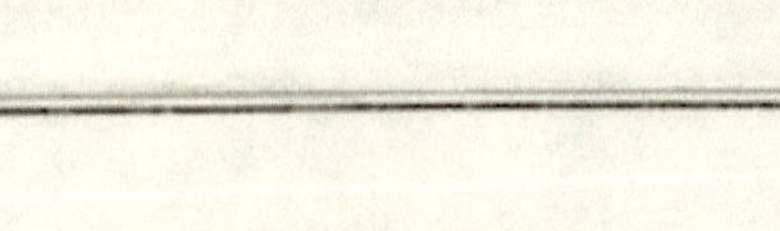

Repeating many of the small letters, as m, u, e, r, s, a, d, h and c; also capitals D, J, P, etc., forms an excellent exercise for the learner.

PRINCIPLES IN WRITING.

Essential parts of all letters of the alphabet are here shown, by which the learner can examine, analyze and criticise his writing.

Study the principles well; the form of each should be fixed in the mind. Then make a scale by dividing the distance between the blue lines on the paper into equal spaces, as shown in the diagram, and write the letters down as they appear there.

Contracted letters, as a, c, e, m, n, o, r, s, u, v, w, x, that occupy one space, and that part of d, g, h, q and y, found in the first space, are all well rounded and developed. These and part of letters found in the first space, form the essential part of all writing, and therefore deserve special care.

Notice that the loop letters, b, f, h, k and l, extend two and one-half spaces above the blue line, while the loop below the line, as g, f, j, q, y and z, extends one and one-half spaces below the blue line. If all loops are made exact or within the space for them, then the loops on one line will just meet the lower loops of the line above, but never conflict, to the destruction of neat body writing.

Telegraph operators, some of whom are among our best business penmen, make all extended letters very short, while accountants and business men, favor the style of short loops, well developed letters, and capitals made small.

Apply the principles. Observe regularity.

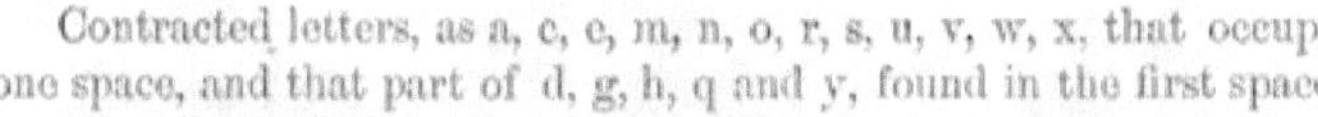

Muscular movement.

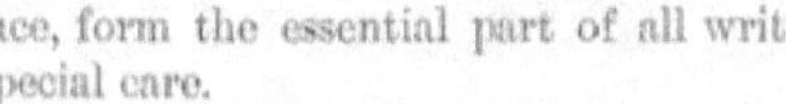

Down strokes straight. Up strokes curved.

Well formed loop. Make letters even.

Practice these exercises with the muscular movement until they can be made with regularity and ease.

Let third and fourth fingers slide. Notice the top of the r.

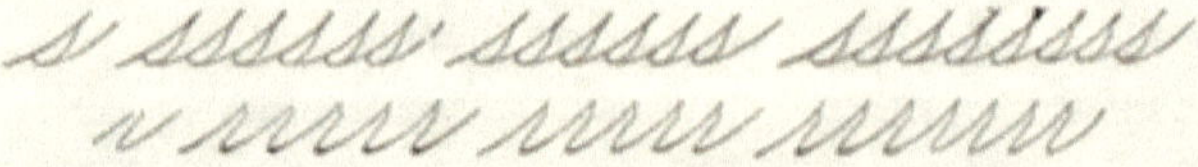

Small o closed at the top. No retracing in a.

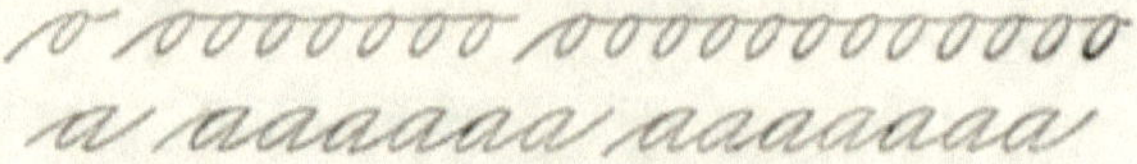

Two spaces high. Down strokes straight.

Mark the principles. Do not retrace.

Notice form. In w, last part narrow. Make without raising the pen.

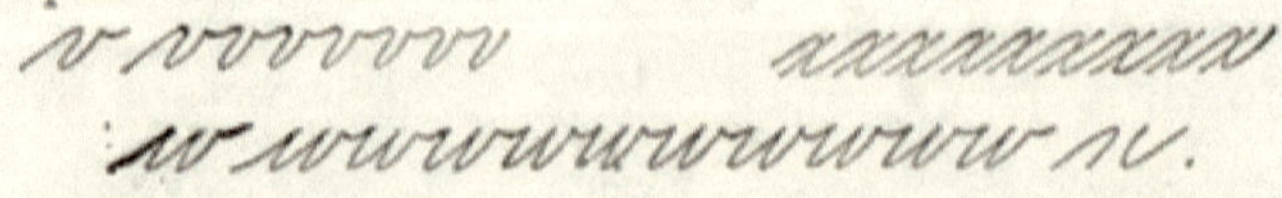

Extend two spaces above the line, and one below.

Retracing is an error. The only exception to this is in d, t, p and x, where it becomes necessary.

b b b blending blooming

k k kick kicking

f find fund fame flame

Upper loops have their crossing at the height of one space, while lower loops cross at the blue line.

y your youth y j journey

fs effs efffs afsure z zone

tune time tanner dru

Place the capital letters on the scale, analyze them according to principles 6, 7 and 8, and notice their relative proportions.

A B C D E F G

H I J K L M

Practice the oval letters.

O. D. C. E. P. B. R.

ORNAMENTAL PENMANSHIP.

Most beautiful forms may be drawn with the pen, as elegant out lines of the bird, landscape, swan or reindeer, but ornate writing or pen-work has no connection whatever with the practical business of life. To do that kind of work, one must have the skill of an expert and the eye of an artist. The appended illustration, a fac-simile of pen-work, will show what a degree of artistic elegance can be attained in the use of the pen by the careful study and constant practice of the rules laid down in this book.

Ovals must be made full and round. No corners or flat sides.

O Olean Orleans Ohio

C Church Currency C

P Prince Prayer P P

Letters in which the capital stem, or seventh principle forms a leading part, are as follows:

H. K. F. T. S. L. G.

In H and K, the capital stem is almost straight on the down stroke, in F, and T, it is a little more of a wave line, and in S and L the line is much of a compound or double curve

hurt hint hand heart
head hundred hhh

Capital I, and also J, which is a modified I, is sometimes closed among the capital stem letters, from the resemblance of the I to this principle in all but the top.

Independence Jamestown

ORNAMENTAL PENMANSHIP.

WEATHER SIGNS.

A rosy sky at sunset presages fine weather; a red sky in the morning, bad weather, probably rain. In the morning, if gray dawn, fine weather; low dawn, fair weather; high dawn, wind. A bright blue sky denotes fine weather; dark blue sky, wind. Soft looking clouds presage fine weather, with light breezes. Clouds with hard looking edges denote strong wind. At sunset, if bright yellow sky, expect hard wind; rain, if pale yellow. Clouds that are small and black indicate rain; scurrying clouds, wind or rain. Following clear weather, if light streaks or mottled patches of white clouds appear, followed by growing cloudiness, wind or rain may be sure to follow.

RELATIVE DURABILITY OF VARIOUS KINDS OF WOOD.

The figures given below were ascertained by experiment. A square piece of each variety, 1½ inches square and two feet in length, was driven into the ground to within one-half inch of its entire length. At the end of five years, these pieces were taken up and examined, and their condition was found to be, respectively, as follows:

Ash, elm, fir, oak, soft mahogany and every variety of soft pine were found to be entirely decayed.

Hard pine, larch and teal-wood, were sound at the core but rotten on the outside.

Cedar of Lebanon and hard mahogany were in fairly good condition, decay being slight.

Virginia cedar and locust were found unaffected, being as sound, in all respects, as when driven into the ground.

Easy Rules for Computing Simple Interest.

RATE.	Multiply Principal by	Divide product by
Four per cent....	Number of days to run, and point off the right-hand figure	Nine.
Five per cent.....	Number of days to run	Seventy-two.
Six per cent......	Number of days, and point off the right-hand figure.....	Six.
Seven and three-tenths per cent*	Twice the number of days	....
Eight per cent...	Number of days	Forty-five.
Nine per cent....	Number of days, and separate the right-hand figure	Four.
Ten per cent.....	Number of days	Thirty-six.
Twelve per cent..	Number of days, and separate the right-hand figure	Three.

* At this rate $100 earns two cents per day.

Showing the Length (in feet) of Iron Wire Per Bundle.*

Gauge, or size.	Length, feet.	Gauge, or size.	Length, feet.	Gauge, or size.	Length, feet.
No. 0..........	213	No. 7..........	717	No. 14	3,426
No. 1..........	273	No. 8	858	No. 15..........	4,404
No. 2..........	315	No. 9..........	1,028	No. 16..........	5,892
No. 3..........	363	No. 10..........	1,290	No. 17..........	7,620
No. 4..........	429	No. 11..........	1,587	No. 18..........	9,450
No. 5..........	510	No. 12..........	2,100	No. 19..........	12,555
No. 6..........	609	No. 13..........	2,409	No. 20..........	14,736

* The weight of iron wire per bundle is uniformly 63 pounds; its length depends upon its fineness, or, in other words, its size.

ABBREVIATIONS AND CONTRACTIONS
USED IN
WRITING AND PRINTING.

A

A., or *Ans.* Answer.
A. A. G. Assistant Adjutant General.
A. B. Bachelor of Arts (See B. A.)
Abp. Archbishop.
Abr. Abridged.
A. C. *Before Christ.*
A. D. In the year of our Lord.
Adjt. Adjutant.
Admr. Administrator.
Admx. Administratrix.
Æ., or *Æt.* Of age; aged.
Af., or *Afr.* Africa, African.
Agr. Agriculture.
Agt. Agent; Against.
Ala. Alabama.
Ald. Alderman.
A. M. Master of Arts; Before noon; In the year of the world.
Am., or *Amt.* Amount.
Anal. Analysis.
Anat. Anatomy.
Ang.-Sax. Anglo-Saxon.
Anon. Anonymous.
Anat. Anatomy.
Apl. April.
Apoc. Apocalypse.
App. Appendix.
Aq. Water.
Ark. Arkansas.
Art. Arctic.
Asst. Assistant.
Astrol. Astrology.
Astron. Astronomy.
Att., *Atty.* Attorney.
Atty. Gen. Attorney General.
Aug. August.
Aust. Austria, Austrian.
Av. Average.
Ave. Avenue.
Avoir. Avoirdupois.

B

B. Base, or bass (*in music*); Book; Baron; Born; Buy.
B. A. Bachelor of Arts; British America (See A. B.).
Bal. Balance.
Bar. Barrel.
Bart., or *Bt.* Baronet.
Bbl. Barrel, barrels.
B. C. Before Christ.
B. C. L. Bachelor of Civil Law.
B. D. Bachelor of Divinity.
Bd. Bond; Bound.
Belg. Belgian.
Benj. Benjamin
Bib. Bible; Biblical.
Biog. Biography; Biographical.
Bk. Book.
B. L. Bachelor of Laws.
B. LL. Bachelor of Laws (See LL. B.).
B. M. Bachelor of Medicine
Bor. Born; Borough.
Bot. Botany, botanical, botanist.
Bp. Bishop.
Braz. Brazilian.
Brig. Brigade, Brigadier.
Brig. Gen. Brigadier General.
Bro. Brother.
Burl. Burlesque.
B. V. Blessed Virgin.
B. V. M. Blessed Virgin Mary.

C

C. Carbon; Church; Congress; Consul; One hundred; Cent; Chapter.
Cal. Calendar; California.
Cam., or *Camb.* Cambridge.
Can. Canada.
Cap. Chapter; Capital.
Caps. Capitals.
Capt. Captain.
Card. Cardinal.
Cash. Cashier.
Cat. Catalogue.
Cath. Catholic; Catharine; Cathedral.
C. B. Companion of the Bath.
C. E. Civil Engineer.
Cent. A hundred.
C. G. Captain of the Guard; Commissary General; Counsel General.
C. H. Court House; Custom House.
Ch. Church.
Chal. Chaldron.
Chanc. Chancellor.
Chap. Chapter.
Chas. Charles.
Chr. Christopher; Christian.
Chron. Chronicles; Chronology.

Cic. Cicero.
Civ. Civil.
C. J. Chief Justice.
Clk. Clerk.
C. M. Common Meter.
Co. Company; County.
C. O. D. Cash (or collect) on delivery.
Col. Colonel; Colonial; Colossians; Column.
Coll. College; Collector; Collection; Colleague.
Colloq. Colloquial.
Com. Commissioner; Committee; Commentary; Common; Commodore.
Conj. Conjunction.
Conn. Connecticut.
Const. Constable; Constitution.
Cor. Mem. Corresponding Member.
Cor. Sec. Corresponding Secretary.
C. S. A. Confederate States of America; Confederate Army.
Ct. Connecticut; Court; Count.
Cts. Cents.
Cwt. Hundred-weight.
Cyc. Cyclopedia.

D

D. David; Duke; Duchess; Dowager; Dutch; A penny or pence.
Dan. Danish; Daniel.
D. C. District of Columbia; (in music) From the beginning.
D. C. L. Doctor of Civil (or Canon) Law.
D. D. Doctor of Divinity.
Dea. Deacon.
Dec. December.
Def. Definition.
Deft. Defendant.
Del. Delaware.
Dem. Democrat; Democratic.
Den. Denmark.
Dep. Deputy.
Dept. Department; Deponent.
Deut. Deuteronomy.
Dft. Defendant.
D. G. By the grace of God.
D. H. Dead-head.
Dict. Dictionary; Dictator.
Dis. Distant; Distance.
Disct. Discount.
Dist. District.
Dist. Atty. District Attorney.
Div. Divided; Division; Divisor; Dividend.
D. M. Doctor of Music (see Mus. Doc.).
Do. The same.
Dols. Dollars.
Doz. Dozen.
D. P. Doctor of Philosophy (see P. D., also Ph. D.).
Dpt. Deponent.
Dr. Debtor; Doctor; Dram; Drachms.
D. S. (In music) From the sign.
D. T. Dakota Territory.
Dub. Dublin.
D. V. God being willing.
Dwt. Pennyweight, or Pennyweights.

E

E. East; Eastern; Earl.
Ea. Each.
Eccl. or *Eccles.* Ecclesiastes.
Eccl. Hist. Ecclesiastical History.
Ed. Editor; Edition.
Edin. Edinburgh.
Edw. Edward.
Eg. Errors excepted.
E. Eg. Ells English.
E. Fl. Ells Flemish.
E. Fr. Ells French.
E. G. For example.
E. I. East Indies.
Elec. Electricity.
Eliz. Elizabeth.
E. Lon. East Longitude.
Emp. Emperor; Empress.
Ency. or *Encyc.* Encyclopedia.
Encyc. Amer. Encyclopedia Americana.
Encyc. Brit. Encyclopedia Britannica.
E. N. E. East Northeast.
Eng. England; English.
Env. Ext. Envoy Extraordinary.
Ep. Epistle.
Eph. Ephesians.
Epiph. Epiphany.
Eq. Equal; Equivalent.
E. S. Ells Scotch.
E. S. E. East Southeast.
Esq. Esquire.
Et al. And the others; and elsewhere.
Et seq. And the following.
Ex. Example; Exception; Exodus.
Exec. Executor.
Execx. Executrix.
Exod. Exodus.
Ezek. Ezekiel.
E. & O. E. Errors and ommissions excepted.

F

F. France; Follow; Folio; Friday; Florin; Foot.
Fa. Florida.
Fahr. Fahrenheit.
F. A. M. Free and Accepted Masons.
Far. Farthing; Farriery.
Fcp. Foolscap.
Fer. Iron.
Feb. February.
Fec. He did it.
Feud. Feudal.
Fig. Figure; Figurative; Figuratively.
Fir. Firkin.
Fl. Flemish; Florida.
Fl. Florin; Florins; Flourished.
Fr. France; French; Franc; Francis; From.
F. R. C. S. Fellow of the Royal College of Surgeons.

Fri. Friday.
Fath. Fathom.
Fur. Furlong.
Fut. Future.

G

G. Genitive; Guinea; Gulf.
Ga. Georgia.
Gal. Galatians; Galen.
Gal. Gallon; Gallons.
Galv. Galveston.
G. B. Great Britain.
G. B. and *I.* Great Britain and Ireland.
G. C. Grand Chapter.
Gen. General; Genesis; Geneva.
Gent. Gentleman.
Geo. George.
Geog. Geography; Geographer.
Geol. Geology; Geological; Geologist.
Geom. Geometry.
Ger. or *Germ.* German.
Gi. Gill or Gills.
G. L. Grand Lodge.
G. M. Grand Master.
G. O. Grand Order.
Gr. Great; Greek; Gross; Grain.
Gram. Grammar.
G. S. Grand Secretary; Grand Scribe; Grand Sentinel.
G. T. Good Templar; Grand Tyler.

H

H. High; Height; Harbor; Hour.
Hab. Habakuk.
Hag. Haggai.
H. B. M. Her (or His) Britannic Majesty.
H. C. House of Commons.
Hdkf. Handkerchief.
Heb. Hebrew; Hebrews.
H. G. Horse Guards.
H. H. His (or Her) Highness; His Holiness (the Pope).
Hhd. Hogshead.
H. I. H. His (or Her) Imperial Highness.
Hind. Hindoo; Hindostan.
Hist. History; Historical.
H. L. House of Lords.
H. M. His (or Her) Majesty.
H. M. S. His (or Her) Majesty's Steamer, Ship or Service.
Ho. House.
Hon. Honorable.
Hon'd. Honored.
Hort. Horticulture.
Hos. Hosea.
H. P. Horse-power; Half-pay; High-Priest.
H. R. House of Representatives.
H. R. E. Holy Roman Empire.
H. R. H. His (or Her) Royal Highness.
H. R. I. P. Here rests in peace.
Hum. Humble.
Hun. Hungary.
Hund. Hundred.
Hyd. Hydrostatics.
Hydraul. Hydraulics.
Hypoth. Hypothesis; Hypothetical.

I

I. India; Iceland.
Ib. or *Ibid.* The same.
Ice. or *Icel* Iceland; Icelandic.
Id. The same.
I. T. Idaho Territory.
I. E. That is.
I. H. S. Jesus, the Savior of Men.
Ill. or *Ills.* Illinois.
Imp. Imperial.
Imp. or *Imper.* Imperative.
Imp. or *Imperf.* Imperfect.
In. Inch; Inches.
Incog. Unknown.
Ind. India; Indian; Indiana.
Ind. or *Indic.* Indicative.
Ind. T. or *Ind. Ter.* Indian Territory.
Inf. Infinitive.
I. N. R. I. Jesus, of Nazareth, King of the Jews.
Ins. Inspector; Insurance; Instant.
Ins. Gen. Inspector General.
Inst. Instant (the present month).
Int. Interest.
Introd. Introduction.
Ia. Iowa.
I. O. O. F. Independent Order of Odd Fellows.
I. O. S. M. Independent Order of the Sons of Malta,
I. O. U. I owe you—an acknowledgment for money.
Irreg. Irregular.
I. S. Inside Sentinel.
Is. or *Isa.* Isaiah.
Is. or *Isl.* Island.
I. T. Indian Territory.
It. or *Ital.* Italy; Italian; Italic.

J

J. Judge.
Jam. Jamaica.
Jan. January.
Jas. James.
J. C. Jesus Christ; Julius Cæsar.
J. D. Junior Deacon.
Jer. Jeremiah.
J. G. W. Junior Grand Warden.
J. H. S. Jesus, the Savior of Men (See I. H. S.).
Jno. John.
Jona. Jonathan.
Jos. Joseph.
Josh. Joshua.
Jour. Journal; Journeyman.
J. P. Justice of the Peace.
J. Prob. Judge of Probate.
Jr. Junior.
Jul. July.
Jun. June; Junior.
Just. Justice.
J. W. Junior Warden.

K

K. King; Knight.
Kan. Kansas.
K. B. Knight of the Bath.
K. C. King's Counsel.
K. C. B. Knight Commander of the Bath.
K. L. H. Knight of the Legion of Honor.
K. M. Knight of Malta.
Kin. Kingdom.
Knick. Knickerbocker.
K. P. Knights of Pythias.
Kt. Knight.
K. T. Knight Templar.
Ky. Kentucky.

L

L. Lady; Latin; Lord; Law; Book; Lake.
L. or *lb.* A pound (in weight).
L. or £. A pound sterling.
La. Louisiana.
Lat. Latin.
Ld. Lord.
Lev. Leviticus.
Lib. Book.
Lieut., or *Lt.* Lieutenant
Lieut.-Col. Lieutenant-Colonel.
Lieut.-Gen. Lieutenant-General.
Lieut.-Gov. Lieutenant-Governor.
Liq. Liquid; Liquor.
Lit. Literature; Literary; Literally.
LL.B. Bachelor of Laws. See B. L. and B.LL.
LL.D. Doctor of Laws. See D.LL.
Lon., or *Lond.* London.
Lon., or *Long.* Longitude.
L. S. D. Pounds, Shillings, Pence.
Lt. Inf. Light Infantry.
Lv. Livres.

M

M. Marquis; Middle; Monday; Monsieur; Morning; Thousand; Meridian, or Noon; Masculine; Month; Minute; Mile.
Mac., or *Macc.* Maccabees.
Macad. Macadam.
Mach. Machinery.
Maj. Major.
Maj.-Gen. Major-General.
Manuf. Manufacturing.
Mar. March.
Marq. Marquis.
Masc. Masculine.
Mass. Massachusetts.
Math. Mathematics; Mathematician.
Matt. Matthew.
M. C. Member of Congress; Master of Ceremonies.
M. D. Doctor of Medicine.
Md. Maryland.
Mdlle. Mademoiselle.
M. E. Methodist Episcopal; Mechanical Engineer.
Me. Maine.
Mech. Mechanics.
Med. Medicine.
M. E. G. H. P. Most Excellent Grand High Priest.
Mem., or *Memo.* Memorandum.
Meth. Methodist.
Mex. Mexico; Mexican.
Mich. Michigan.
Min. Minute; Minutes.
Min. Plen. Minister Plenipotentiary.
Minn. Minnesota.
Miss. Mississippi.
M. M. Their Majesties.
Mme. Madame.
Mo. Missouri.
Mod. Modern.
Mon., or *Mond.* Monday.
Mons. Monsieur, or Sir.
M. P. Member of Parliament; Member of Police; Municipal Police.
MS. Manuscript.
MSS. Manuscripts.
Mts. Mountains.
Mus. Doc. Musical Doctor.
M. W. Most Worthy.
M. W. P. Most Worthy Patriarch.
M. W. G. M. Most Worthy (or Most Worshipful) Grand Master.
M. W. S. Member of the Worshipful Society.
Myth. Mythology; Mythological.

N

N. Noon; North; Note; Name; Number; New.
N. A. North America.
Nah. Nahum.
Nap. Napoleon.
Nat. Natural; National; Natal.
Nat. Hist. Natural History.
Naut. Nautical.
N. B. Note well, or take notice; New Brunswick.
N. C. North Carolina.
N. E. North-east; New England.
Neb. Nebraska.
Neg. Negative.
Neh. Nehemiah.
Nem. Con. No one contradictory; unanimously.
Neth. Netherlands.
New Mex. New Mexico.
N. F. Newfoundland.
N. H. New Hampshire.
N. J. New Jersey.
N. Lat. North Latitude.
N. O. New Orleans.
N. P. Notary Public.
N. S. Nova Scotia.
N. T. Nevada Territory.
N. W. North-west.
N. Y. New York.
N. Z. New Zealand.

O

O. Ohio.
Obit. Died.
Obad. Obadiah.
Obs. Observatory.
Obt., or *Obdt.* Obedient.
Oct. October.
O. F. Odd Fellows.
Old Test. Old Testament.
Op. Opposite.
Or. Oregon.
Ord. Ordinance; Ordinary.
Orig. Original.
O. S. Old Style; Outside Sentinel.
Oxf., or *Oxon.* Oxford.

P

P. Pole; Pope; Pint; Page.
Pa. Pennsylvania.
Parl. Parliament.
Part. Participle.
P. B. Bachelor in Philosophy.
P. C. Privy Council.
P. D. Doctor of Philosophy.
P. E. Protestant Episcopal.
P. E. I. Prince Edward's Island.
Penn., or *Penna.* Pennsylvania.
Per cent. By the hundred.
P. G. Past Grand.
Pg. Portuguese.
Phar. Pharmacy.
Ph. B. Bachelor of Philosophy.
Ph. Doc. Doctor of Philosophy.
Phila. Philadelphia.
Pk. Peck; Pecks.
P. M. Postmaster; Post Meridian (or afternoon).
P. M. G. Postmaster-General.
P. O. Postoffice.
P. O. D. Postoffice Department.
Port. Portugal; Portuguese.
P. R. Prize Ping; Porto Rico.
Pres. President.
Prof. Professor.
Prot. Protestant.
Pro tem. For the time being.
P. S. Postscript; Privy Seal.
Pt. Pint; Pints.
Pub. Public.
Pub. Doc. Public Documents.

Q

Q. Question.
Qu. Query; Question; Queen.
Q. B. Queen's Bench.
Q. C. Queen's Counsel; Queen's College.
Q. E. D. Which was to be demonstrated.
Q. M. Quartermaster.
Q. M. G. Quartermaster-General.
Qr. Quarter (28 lbs.).
Qt. Quart. *Qts.* Quarts.
Qu. Queen; Question.
Q. V. Which see.
Qy. Query.

R

R. Railway; River; Rood; Rod; King; Queen.
R. A. Royal Academy; Rear Admiral; Royal Arch.
Rad. Radical; Root.
Rec'd. Received.
R. C. Roman Catholic.
Recpt. Receipt.
Rec. Sec. Recording Secretary.
Rect. Rector; Receipt.
Ref. Reformer; Reformed; Reformation; Reference.
Ref. Ch. Reformed Church.
Reg. Register; Regular.
Regt. Regiment.
Rep. Representative; Republican; Reporter.
Repub. Republic.
Retd. Returned.
Rev. Revelations; Revolution; Revenue; Review.
Rev., or *Revd.* Reverend.
Rhet. Rhetoric.
R. I. Rhode Island.
Richd. Richard.
Riv. River.
R. N. Royal Navy.
Robt. Robert.
Rom. Roman; Romans.
Rom. Cath. Roman Catholic.
Rt. Right.
Rt. Hon. Right Honorable.
Rt. Rev. Right Reverend.
Rt. Wpful. Right Worshipful.
Russ. Russia.
R. W. Right Worthy; Right Worshipful.

S

S. Sign; South; Saint; Sunday; Second; Shilling.
S. A. South America; South Africa; South Australia.
Sans., or *Sansc.* Sanscrit.
Sat. Saturday.
Sax. Saxon.
S. C. South Carolina.
Sc. Namely, To-wit.
Sci. Science; Scientific.
Scr. Scruple.
S. D. Senior Deacon.
S. E. South-east.
Sec. Secretary; Second; Section.
Sen. Senior.
Sep., or *Sept.* September.
Serg., or *Serj.* Sergeant.
Serv., or *Servt.* Servant.
Sh. Shilling.
Shak. Shakspeare.
Sing. Singular.
S. J. Society of Jesus.
S. Lat. South Latitude.
S. M. J. His (or Her) Imperial Majesty.
S. of Sol. Song of Solomon.
Soc. Society.

Sol. Gen. Solicitor General.
Sq. Square.
Sq. ft. Square feet.
Sq. in. Square inch.
Sq. m. Square miles.
Sq. rd. Square rods.
Sq. yds. Square yards.
Sr. Senior.
S. S. Sunday School.
S. S. E. South South-east.
S. S. W. South South-west.
St. Saint; Stone; Street.
S. T. D. Doctor of Sacred Theology.
Sun. Sunday.
Sup. Superior; Supplement; Superfine; Superlative.
Supr. Superior.
Supt. Superintendent.
Surg. Surgeon.
Surg. Gen. Surgeon General.
Surv. Surveyor.
Surv. Gen. Surveyor-General.
S. W. South-west.
Sw. Sweden; Swedish.
Switz. Switzerland.
Syn. Synonym; Synonymous.
Synop. Synopsis.
Syr. Syria.

T

T. Tuesday; Town; Territory.
Tan., or *Tang.* Tangent.
T. E. Topographical Engineers.
Tex. Texas.
Th. Thursday.
Theo. Theodore; Theodosia.
Theol. Theology.
Tim. Timothy.
Topog. Topography; Topographical.
Tr. Translation; Translator; Transpose; Trustee.
Treas. Treasurer.
Tri. Trinity.
Tu. Tuesday.
Turk. Turkey; Turkish.
Typ., or *Typo.* Typographer.
Typog. Typography.

U

U. Unitarian.
U. K. United Kingdom.
Ult. Last, or of the last of the month.
Unit. Unitarian.
Univ. University.
U. S. United States.
U. S. A. United States of America; United States Army.
U. S. L. United States Legation.
U. S. M. United States Mail; United States Marine.
U. S. M. A. United States Military Academy.
U. S. N. United States Navy.
U. S. S. United States Senator; United States Ship, or Service.
U. S. V. United States Volunteers.
U. T. Utah Territory.

V

V. Viscount; Victoria; Verb; Verse; Village; Volume.
V., or *vs.* Against.
V. A. Vice Admiral; Vicar Apostle.
Va. Virginia.
V. C. Vice Chancellor; Vice Chairman.
V. D. L. Van Diemen's Land.
Ven. Venerable.
V. G. Vicar General; Vice Grand.
Vice Prest. Vice President.
Vis., or *Visct.* Viscount.
Vol. Volume.
V. P. Vice President.
V. R. Queen Victoria.
Vt. Vermont.
Vulg. Vulgar; Vulgarly.

W

W. West; Wednesday; Warden; Week.
W. A. West Africa; West Australia.
Wed. Wednesday.
W. G. M. Worthy Grand Master.
W. G. S. Worthy Grand Secretary.
Whf. Wharf.
Wk. Week.
W. I. West Indies.
Wis. Wisconsin.
W. Lon. West Longitude.
W. M. Worshipful Master.
W. N. W. West North-west.
W. P. Worthy Patriarch.
W. S. W. West South-west.
W. T. Washington Territory.
W. Va. West Virginia.

X

X. Christ.
Xmas. Christmas.
Xn. Christian.
Xt. Christ.

Y

Y., or *Yr.* Year.
Yd. Yard.
Yds. Yards.
Y. M. C. A. Young Men's Christian Association.
Yr. Your.
Yrs. Yours.

Z

Zach. Zachary.
Zech. Zechariah.
Z. G. Zoological Gardens.
Zin. Zinc.

FOREIGN WORDS AND PROVERBS.

FEW mistakes are more common than the misuse of words or phrases borrowed from foreign languages. As a rule, it is wiser for those who are familiar with no language but their own to confine themselves, in conversation, to the use of their mother tongue, since even if the foreign word or phrase be appropriately used, the danger of mispronunciation yet remains. There are, however, some words or quotations in such common colloquial use that to be ignorant of their meaning is nearly as mortifying as to missapply them. There is another class of quotations not in such general use, but which are frequently encountered in literature, the correct understanding of which adds much to the pleasure of the reader.

The following list embraces selections from both these classes, and contains those most commonly used in conversation and most frequently seen in English books and periodicals. The language to which they belong is indicated by the following abbreviations: (Fr.) French; (It.) Italian; (Lat.) Latin; (Sp.) Spanish.

A

Ab ovo usque ad mala. (It.) (Used originally of a dinner.) From the egg even to the apple; i. e., from beginning to end.
A cheval. (Fr.) On horseback.
A discretion. (Fr.) At pleasure; without restriction.
Ad astra. (Lat.) To the stars.
Ad interim. (Lat.) In the meanwhile.
Ad libitum. (Lat.) At pleasure.
Ad nauseam. (Lat.) To disgust; or until one becomes disgusted.
A la Francaise. (Fr.) In the French manner.
Al fresco. (It.) To the shade; to the open air; cool.
Alia tentanda via est. (Lat.) Another way must be tried.
Allegro. (It.) Sprightly; cheerful.
Alter ego. (Lat.) Another self.
Alto relievo. (It.) In high relief.
Ante bellum. (Lat.) Before the war.
A pied. (Fr.) On foot.
A pis aller. (Fr.) At the worst.
A priori. (Lat.) From the former; i. e., from cause to effect.
Au régle. (Fr.) According to rule; correctly; properly.
Aut Cæsar, aut nullus. Either Cæsar or no one; i. e., first, or nothing.
A votre sante. (Fr.) To your health.
Beaux esprits. (Fr.) Gay spirits; men of wit.

B

Beaux yeux. (Fr.) Handsome eyes; i. e., attractive looks.
Bel esprit. (Fr.) A brilliant mind; a person of wit or genius.
Bella femina chi ride, vuol dire, borsa che piange. (It.) The smiles of a beautiful woman are the tears of the purse.
Bella, horrida bella! (Lat.) Wars, horrid wars.
Ben vienes si vienes solo. (Sp.) Welcome, if thou comest alone. (Spoken of misfortune.)
Billet de banque. (Fr.) A bank note.
Bis dat qui cito dat. (Lat.) He gives twice who gives quickly.
Bis vincit qui se vincit in victoria. (Lat.) He restrains himself in the moment of triumph.
Blasé. (Fr.) Palled; surfeited; incapable of further enjoyment.
Bon ami. (Fr.) Good friend.

Bona fide. (Lat.) In good faith; honestly.
Bon trovato. (It.) Well found; an ingenious selection; a happy thought.
Bravo. (It.) Well done. (An exclamation.)

C

Carbonari. (It.) Members of a secret political society.
Caret initio et fine. (Lat.) It wants beginning and end.
Ce ne que le premier pas qui coute. (Fr.) It is not the first step which is difficult.
C'est a dire. (Fr.) That is to say.
C'est une autre chose. (Fr.) That is another thing.
Ceteris paribus. (Lat.) Other things being equal.
Chaque a son gout. (Fr.) Each to his taste.
Chateaux en Espagne. (Fr.) Castles in Spain; castles in the air.
Chef de cuisine. (Fr.) Head cook.
Chemin de fer. (Fr.) Railroad.
Cher ami. (Fr.) Dear friend.
Chevalier d'industrie. (Fr.) A knight of industry; one who lives by persevering fraud.
Chi tace confessa. (It.) Silence is confession.
Chi responde presto sa poco. (It.) He who answers suddenly knows little.
Con amore. (It.) With love; earnestly.
Con spirito. (It.) With spirit.
Contra bonos mores. (Lat.) Against good manners.
Couleur de rose. (Fr.) Rose color; hence, an aspect of beauty or loveliness.
Coup de grace. (Fr.) A finishing stroke.
Coup de main. (Fr.) A sudden enterprise or effort.
Coup d'etat. (Fr.) A stroke of policy; a violent measure of state in public affairs.
Crimen falsi. (Lat.) Falsehood; perjury.
Cui bono? (Lat.) For whose benefit? What good is it?

D

De bon augure. (Fr.) Of good omen.
Dei Gratia. (Lat.) By the grace of God.
De jure. (Lat.) By law; rightfully.
De mal en pis. (Fr.) From bad to worse.
De mortuis, nil nisi bonum. (Lat.) Concerning the dead, let only good be spoken.
Deo volente. (Lat.) God being willing.
De profundis. (Lat.) Out of the depths.
Dernier resort. (Fr.) The last resort.
De trop. (Fr.) Too much; in the way; not wanted.
Dies non. (Lat.) A day on which judges do not sit.
Dieu défend le droit. (Fr.) God defend the right.
Dieu vous garde. (Fr.) May God protect you.
Di grado in grado. (It.) Step by step; by degrees.
Diis aliter visum. (Lat.) To the gods it seemed otherwise.
Distingue. (Fr.) Distinguished; eminent.
Dolce far niente. (It.) Sweet doing-nothing; sweet idleness.
Domino. (It.) A mask robe.
Drap d'argent. (Fr.) Silver lace.
Drap d'or. (Fr.) Gold lace.
Droit des gens. (Fr.) The law of nations.
Ducit amor patriæ. (Lat.) The love of country leads.
Due teste vagliano piu che una sola. (It.) Two heads are better than one.
Dum vivimus, vivamus. (Lat.) While we live, let us live.
Dux femina fuit. (Lat.) A woman was the leader of the deed.

E

Ecattivo vento che non e' buono per qualchuno. (It.) It is an ill wind that blows nobody any good.
Ecce homo. (Lat.) Behold the man. (Used of Christ.)
Ecce signum. (Lat.) Behold the sign.
El corazon manda las carnes. (Sp.) The heart bears up the body.
E meglio cader dalle finistre che dal tetto. (It.) It is better to fall from the window than the roof. In other words, of two evils choose the least.
En avant. (Fr.) Forward.
Enfans perdus. (Fr.) Lost children.
Enfin. (Fr.) At last; finally.
En masse. (Fr.) In a body.
Ennui. (Fr.) Tired; bored.
Entre nous. (Fr.) Between ourselves.
Esto perpetua. (Lat.) Let it be perpetual.
Et id genus omne. (Lat.) And everything of that kind.
Ex uno, disce omnes. (Lat.) From one, learn all.

F

Faber suæ fortunæ. (Lat.) The architect of his own fortune; a self-made man.
Facile princeps. (Lat.) Easily first, the admitted chief.
Facilis descensus Averni. (Lat.) The descent of Avernus (Hell) is easy.
Faire sans dire. (Fr.) To do without saying; *i. e.*, unostentatiously.
Fait accompli. (Fr.) A thing accomplished.
Fantoccini. (It.) Dramatic representations with puppets.
Far niente. (It.) Doing nothing.
Fauteuil. (Fr.) An easy chair.
Femme de chambre. (Fr.) A chambermaid.
Feræ naturæ. (Lat.) Of wild nature (said of beasts.)
Fiat justitia ruat coelum. (Lat.) Let justice be done, though the heavens fall.
Fiat lux. (Lat.) Let there be light.
Fidus Achates. (Lat.) Faithful Achates; a true friend.
Fille de joie. (Fr.) A woman of licentious pleasure.
Flagrante delicto. (Lat.) In the commission of the crime; in the very act.
Fra. (It.) Brother; friar (applied chiefly to monks of the lower order).
Franco. (It.) Free from postage; post free.
Functus officio. (Lat.) Having performed the duties of his office; hence, out of office.
Furor scribendi. (Lat.) A rage for writing.

G

Gaieté de coeur. (Fr.) Gaiety of heart.
Gallicé. (Lat.) In French.
Garcon. (Fr.) A boy.
Garde a cheval. (Fr.) A mounted guard.
Gauche. (Fr.) Awkward.
Gaucherie. (Fr.) Awkwardness.
Gaudet tentatione virtus. (Lat.) Virtue rejoices in temptation.
Gens d' armes. (Fr.) Armed police.
Gentilhomme. (Fr.) A gentleman.
Giovine Italia. (It.) A young lady.
Giovine santo, diavolo vecchia. (It.) A young saint, an old devil.
Gloria in excelsis Deo. (Lat.) Glory to God in the highest.
Gloria Patri. (Lat.) Glory be to the Father.
Guerre a l' outrance. (Fr.) War to the uttermost.

H

Hic et ubique. (Lat.) Here and everywhere.
Hic jacet. (Lat.) Here lies. (Used in epitaphs.)
Hoc loco. (Lat.) In this place.
Homme des lettres. (Fr.) A man of letters; a literary man.
Homme d'etat. (Fr.) A statesman.
Homo sui juris. (Lat.) A man who is his own master.
Honi sort qui mal y pense. (Fr.) Evil be to him who evil thinks.

Hora e' sempre. (It.) It is always time.
Hora fugit. (Lat.) The hour flies.
Hors de combat. (Fr.) Out of condition to fight.
Hotel Dieu. (Fr.) The name of a large hospital in Paris.
Humanum est errare. (Lat.) To err is human.
Hurtar para dar por Dios. (Sp.) To steal in order to give alms.

I

Ich dien. (Ger.) I serve.
Id est. (Lat.) That is; abbreviated *i. e.*
Il a le diable en corps. (Fr.) He has the devil in him.
Il sabio muda conseio, il nescio no. (Sp.) A wise man sometimes changes his opinion, a fool never.
Il n'est sauce que d'appetit. (Fr.) Hunger is the best sauce.
Improvisatore. (It.) An impromptu poet.
Incognito. (It.) In disguise; unknown.
In dubito. (Lat.) In doubt.
In esse. (Lat.) In being.
In hoc signo spes mea. (Lat.) In this sign is my hope.
In hoc signo vinces. (Lat.) In this sign you shall conquer.
In pecto. (It.) In the breast; in reserve.
Insouciance. (Fr.) Indifference; carelessness.
Inter alia. (Lat.) Among other things.
Inter nos. (Lat.) Between ourselves.
Ira furor brevis est. (Lat.) Anger is a short madness.
Ita lex scripta est. (Lat.) The law is so written.

J

Jacta est alia. (Lat.) The die is cast.
Jardin des Plantes. (Fr.) The botanical garden in Paris.
Je suis parit. (Fr.) I am ready.
Jeu de mots. (Fr.) A play on words; a pun.
Jeu d' esprit. (Fr.) A witticism.
Joco di mano, joco villano. (It.) A practical joke is a vulgar joke.
Joli. (Fr.) Pretty.
Jus civile. (Lat.) Civil law.
Jus gentium. (Lat.) Law of nations.
Junta. (Sp.) A state council in Spanish countries.
Juxta. (Lat.) Near by.

L

Laissez faire. (Fr.) Let it alone.
Lapis philosophorum. (Lat.) The philosopher's stone.
La poverta è la madra di tutte di arti. (It.) Poverty is the mother of all the arts.
Lapsus linguæ. (Lat.) A slip of the tongue.
L'argent. (Fr.) Money.
La speranza è il pan di miseri. (It.) Hope is the poor man's bread.
Laus Deo. (Lat.) Praise be to God.
Le beau monde. (Fr.) The fashionable world.
Les beaux yeux. (Fr.) Soft glances.
Le tout ensemble. (Fr.) All together; the whole appearance; the general effect.
Lettre de cachet. (Fr.) A sealed letter; a royal warrant.
Lex non scripta. (Lat.) Unwritten law; the common law.
Lex talionis. (Lat.) The law of retaliation.
L' inconnu. (Fr.) The unknown.
Lis litem generat. (Lat.) Strife begets strife.
Locale. (Fr.) A place or station.
Locus in quo. (Lat.) The place in which.
Locus penitentiæ. (Lat.) Place for repentance.

M

Ma chere. (Fr.) My dear. (Used in addressing females only.)
Ma foi. (Fr.) Upon my faith.
Magna civitas, magna solitudo. (Lat.) A great city is a great desert.
Magnus Apollo. (Lat.) Great Apollo; one of high authority.
Maladie de mer. (Fr.) Seasickness.
Mala fide. (Lat.) With bad faith; treacherously.
Mal a propos. (Fr.) Ill-timed.
Mal de tete. (Fr.) Headache.
Mauvaise honte. (Fr.) False modesty.
Mauvais sujet. (Fr.) A bad subject; a worthless fellow.
Me judice. (Lat.) I being judge; in my opinion.
Mens sana in corpore sano. (Lat.) A sound mind in a sound body.
Menu. (Fr.) A bill of fare.
Mon ami. (Fr.) My friend.
Mon cher. (Fr.) My dear (used in addressing males).
Mors omnibus communis. (Lat.) Death is common to all.
Multum in parvo. (Lat.) Much in little.
Mutatis mutandis. (Lat.) The necessary changes being made.

N

Naissance. (Fr.) Birth.
Natale solum. (Lat.) Native soil.
Naiveté. (Fr.) Ingenuousness.
Née. (Fr.) Born. (As Mrs. Brown, *née* Smith, or whose maiden name was Smith.)
Ne exeat. (Lat.) Let him not depart.
Niaserie. (Fr.) Foolishness.
Nil admirari. (Lat.) To wonder at nothing.
Nil desperandum. (Lat.) Never despair.
N'importe. (Fr.) It matters not.
No hay cerradura si es de oro la ganzua. (Sp.) There is no lock but a golden key will open it.
No es todo oro lo que reluze. (Sp.) All is not gold that glitters.
Nom de plume. (Fr.) A literary title.
Non compos mentis. (Lat.) Not of sound mind.
Non mi recordo. (It.) I do not remember.
Non est inventus. (Lat.) He has not been found.
Non omnia possumus omnes. (Lat.) We can not all of us do all things.
Notre Dame. (Fr.) Our Lady.
Nous verrons. (Fr.) We shall see.
Nulla nuoba, buona, nuova. (It.) The best news is no news.
Nulla vestigia retrorsum. (Lat.) No steps backward.
Nullius filius. (Lat.) The son of no one; a bastard.

O

Obiit. (Lat.) He or she died.
Obiter dictum. (Lat.) A thing said by the way.
Œil de boeuf. (Fr.) A bull's eye.
Ogni uno per si medesimo, e Dio per tutti. (It.) Every man for himself and God for us all.
Olla podrida. (Sp.) An incongruous mixture.
Omnia vincit amor. (Lat.) Love conquers all things.
On connait l'ami au besoin. (Fr.) A friend is known in time of need.
On dit. (Fr.) They say; a flying rumor.
Ora et labora. (Lat.) Pray and work.
Ora pro nobis. (Lat.) Pray for us.
Otium cum dignitate. (Lat.) Ease with dignity; dignified leisure.
Oublier je ne puis. (Fr.) I can never forget.

P

Pace tua. (Lat.) By your consent.
Padrone. (It.) Ruler, protector.
Par example. (Fr.) By way of example.
Par excellence. (Fr.) By way of eminence.
Partout. (Fr.) Everywhere.
Parvenu. (Fr.) A newcomer; an upstart.
Passe partout. (Fr.) A master key.

Passim. (Lat.) Everywhere.
Paterfamilias. (Lat.) The father of a family.
Pater noster. (Lat.) Our Father, the Lord's prayer.
Peccavi. (Lat.) I have sinned.
Penchant. (Fr.) Inclination; desire.
Pendente lite. (Lat.) Pending the suit.
Per capita. (Lat.) By the head.
Per centum. (Lat.) By the hundred.
Per contra. (Lat.) Contrariwise; on the other hand.
Per diem. (Lat.) By the day.
Perdu. (Fr.) Lost.
Per gradus. (Lat.) Step by step.
Peu-à-peu. (Fr.) Little by little; by degrees.
Poca robba, poca pensiero. (It.) Little wealth, little care.
Post mortem. (Lat.) After death.
Porte crayon. (Fr.) A pencil case.
Pour passer le temps. (Fr.) To pass away the time.
Presto maduro, presto podredo. (Sp.) Soon ripe, soon rotten.
Prima donna. (It.) The principal female singer or actress.
Pro bono publico. (Lat.) For the public good.
Pro et con. (Lat.) For and against.
Proh pudor. (Lat.) Oh! for shame.
Projet de loi. (Fr.) A scheme of law; a legislative bill.
Pronunciamento. (Sp.) A public declaration; a proclamation.
Protégé. (Fr.) One patronized or protected by another.
Punica fides. (Lat.) Punic faith; treachery.

Q

Quære. (Lat.) Query; inquiry.
Quantum sufficit. (Lat.) As much as is necessary; a sufficient quantity.
Quasi. (Lat.) As if; in a manner.
Quelque chose. (Fr.) Something; a trifle.
Quid pro quo. (Lat.) One thing for another; tit for tat; an equivalent.
Quid times. (Lat.) What do you fear?
Quen pregunta, no yerra. (Sp.) Who asks errs not.
Qui m'aime, aime mon chien. (Fr.) Love me, love my dog.
Qui en sabe. (Fr.) Who knows?
Qui va là? (Fr.) Who goes there?
Quod vide. (Lat.) Which see. Abbreviated *q. v.*

R

Radix. (Lat.) A root.
Raison d'état. (Fr.) A reason of state.
Recoje tu heno mientras que el sol auziere. (Sp.) Make hay while the sun shines.
Régime. (Fr.) Mode of living; government; system.
Rencontre. (Fr.) Encounter.
Rendezvous. (Fr.) Appointment to meet; a place of meeting.
Rerum primordia. (Lat.) The first elements of things.
Res gestae. (Lat.) Exploits; accomplished facts.
Résumé. (Fr.) An abstract or summary.
Revenons à nos moutons. (Fr.) Let us return to our subject.
Rio. (Sp.) A river.
Rôle. (Fr.) Character in a drama.
Roué. (Fr.) A dissipated fellow; a libertine.
Rus in urbe. (Lat.) The country in town.

S

Salon. (Fr.) A saloon; a drawing room.
Sang froid. (Fr.) Indifference; apathy.
Sans ceremonie. (Fr.) Without ceremony.
Sans changer. (Fr.) Without changing.
Sans culottes. (Fr.) Ragged men; the lower classes.
Sans Dieu rien. (Fr.) Nothing without God.
Sans souci. (Fr.) Without care; free and easy.
Savant. (Fr.) A man of learning.
Savoir faire. (Fr.) Ability; contrivance; skill.
Secundum artem. (Lat.) According to rule; scientifically.
Semper felix. (Lat.) Always happy; always fortunate.
Semper fidelis. (Lat.) Always faithful.
Semper idem. (Lat.) Always the same.
Senor. (Sp.) Lord; sir.
Sic semper tyrannis. (Lat.) Ever thus to tyrants.
Sic transit gloria mundi. (Lat.) So passes away earthly glory.
Siesta. (Sp.) Sleep after dinner; rest.
Signora. (It.) Lady.
Similia similibus curantur. (Lat.) Like things are cured by like.
Sine die. (Lat.) Without a day appointed.
Sine qua non. (Lat.) An indispensable condition.
Sobriquet. (Fr.) A nickname.
Soi-disant. (Fr.) Self-styled.
Soirée. (Fr.) An evening party.
Status quo. (Lat.) The state in which.
Sub pœna. (Lat.) Under a penalty.
Sub rosa. (Lat.) Under the rose; privately.
Suggestio falsi. (Lat.) Suggestion of a falsehood.
Sui juris. (Lat.) In one's own right.
Summum bonum. (Lat.) The chief good.
Suppressio veri. (Lat.) The suppression of the truth.

T

Tableau vivant. (Fr.) A living picture. (A representation of a scene by persons properly grouped, who remain silent and motionless.)
Tache sans tache. (Fr.) A work without a stain.
Tant mieux. (Fr.) So much the better.
Tant pis. (Fr.) So much the worse.
Te judice. (Lat.) You being judge; in your opinion.
Tel maître, tel valet. (Fr.) Like master, like man.
Tempora mutantur, et nos mutamur in illis. (Lat.) Times are changed, and we are changed with them.
Tempus edax rerum. (Lat.) Time, the devourer of all things.
Tempus fugit. (Lat.) Time flies.
Tempus omnia revelat. (Lat.) Time reveals all things.
Tenez. (Fr.) Take it; hold, wait.
Terra cotta. (It.) Baked earth.
Terra firma. (Lat.) Solid earth; a safe footing.
Terra incognita. (Lat.) An unknown country.
Toga virilis. (Lat.) The gown of manhood.
Tot homines, quot sententiæ. (Lat.) So many men, so many minds.
Toujours prêt. (Fr.) Always ready.
Tour de force. (Fr.) A feat of strength or skill.
Tout-à-fait. (Fr.) Entirely; wholly.
Tout-à-l'heure. (Fr.) All at once; instantly; suddenly.
Tout à vous. (Fr.) Wholly yours.
Tout bien ou rien. (Fr.) The whole or nothing.
Tout de même. (Fr.) Precisely the same.
Tout de suite. (Fr.) Immediately.
Tout ensemble. (Fr.) The whole taken together.
Tristesse. (Fr.) Sadness; sorrow.
Tuum est. (Lat.) It is your own.

U

Ubi supra. (Lat.) Where above mentioned.
Ultima thule. (Lat.) The utmost boundary or limit.
Ultimatum. (Lat.) The last or only condition.
Unâ voce. (Lat.) With one voice; unanimously.
Un bien fait n'est jamais perdu. (Fr.) An act of kindness is never lost.
Un cabello haze sombra. (Sp.) The least hair makes a shadow.
Une affaire flambée. (Fr.) A gone goose.
Uno animo. (Lat.) With one mind; unanimously.
Ubi infra. (Lat.) As below.
Ut supra. (Lat.) As above stated.

V

Vade mecum. (Lat.) Go with me; a constant companion.
Væ victis (Lat.) Woe to the vanquished.
Vale. (Lat.) Farewell.
Valet anchora virtus. (Lat.) Virtue serves as an anchor.
Valet de chambre. (Fr.) A body servant.
Veni, vidi, vici. (Lat.) I came, I saw, I conquered.
Vera pro gratus. (Lat.) Truth before favor.
Verbatim. (Lat.) Word for word and letter for letter.
Verbum sat sapienti. (Lat.) A word is enough for a wise man.
Verdad es verde. (Sp.) Truth is green.
Veritas prevalebit. (Lat.) Truth will prevail.
Vestigia nulla retrorsum. (Lat.) No steps backward.
Via. (Lat.) By way of.
Vice. (Lat.) In place of.
Videlicit. (Lat.) To-wit; namely. (Abbreviated viz.)
Vide et crede. (Lat.) See and believe.
Vi et armis. (Lat.) By force and arms; by main force.
Vigilate et orate. (Lat.) Watch and pray.
Vin. (Fr.) Wine.
Vincit qui se vincit. (Lat.) He conquers who overcomes himself.
Vinculum matrimonii. (Lat.) The bond of matrimony.
Vis atergo. (Lat.) A pushing force from behind.
Vis-à-vis. (Fr.) Opposite; facing.
Vis inertiae. (Lat.) The power of inertia.
Vivat. (Fr.) A shout of "Long live."
Vive la republique. (Fr.) Long live the republic.
Vive le roi. (Fr.) Long live the king.
Voila. (Fr.) Behold, look there.
Voila tout. (Fr.) Behold all; that's all.
Volenti non fit injuria. (Lat.) No injustice is done to the person who consents (i. e., is willing that it should be done to him).
Vox et praeterea nihil. (Lat.) A voice and nothing more; sound without sense.
Vulgo. (Lat.) Commonly.

Z

Zonam solvere. (Lat.) To loose the virgin zone.

SHALL WE MEET AGAIN?

The following from the pen of the lamented George D. Prentice is well worth reproduction. It was regarded as meritorious when it first appeared, and age seems to have but added to its beauty:

"The flat death is inexorable. No appeal for relief from the great law which dooms us to dust. We flourish and fade as the leaves of the forest, and the flowers that bloom, wither, and fade in a day have no frailer hold upon life than the mightiest monarch that ever shook the earth with his foot-steps. Generations of men will appear and disappear as the grass, and the multitude that throng the world to-day will disappear as footsteps on the shore. Men seldom think of the great event of death until the shadow falls across their own pathway, hiding from their eyes the faces of loved ones whose living smile was the sunlight of their existence. Death is the antagonist of life, and the thought of the tomb is the skeleton of all feasts. We do not want to go through the dark valley, although its dark passage may lead to paradise; we do not want to go down into damp graves, even with princes for bed fellows. In the beautiful drama of Ion, the hope of immortality, so elequently uttered by the death-devoted Greek, finds deep response in every thoughtful soul. When about to yield his life a sacrifice to fate, his Clemanthe asks if they should meet again; to which he responds: I have asked that dreadful question of the hills that look eternal—of the clear streams that flow forever—of stars among those fields of azure my raised spirits have walked in glory. All are dumb. But as I gaze upon thy living face, I feel that there is something in love that mantles through its beauty that can not wholly perish. We shall meet again, Clemanthe."

HORSE POWER.

A most important term in mechanical engineering is that of horse-power, which is used to indicate the strength of steam engines, computed on a standard fixed by the power allowed to be exercised by a horse. Though different engineers differ in opinion as to the power of the horse, as a standard of strength, the celebrated engineer, James Watt, fixed it at one constant point; and from his theory, a horse can elevate a mass weighing 33,000 pounds one foot high in one minute of time. The horse-power exercised by falling water is calculated by multiplying the cubic quantity of the water by the altitude of the fall, and the product thus derived by sixty-two and one half pounds, this being the weight of a cubic foot of water. The strength of a steam-engine is reckoned by multiplying together the area, in inches, of the piston, the average pressure in pounds to the square inch, the length of the stroke in feet, and the number of strokes a minute; then dividing by 33,000.

PRACTICE OF BOOK-KEEPING.

BOOK-KEEPING is the science of accounts and the method of recording the every day transactions that arise therein, in such a manner that one may be able to determine, at any time, his resources and his liabilities, as well as his gains and losses for any given time.

RESOURCES consist of all a person owns, such as merchandise, amounts due from others, either in notes or on account, cash, real estate, etc.

LIABILITIES consist of all debts owing individuals, firms or corporations.

NET CAPITAL is the excess of one's resources over their liabilities.

NET INSOLVENCY is the excess of liabilities over their resources.

PROFITS OR LOSSES.—There cannot be a gain or a loss in one's business without some change in the value or quantity of the resources or liabilities. Gains arise from an increase in the value or the quantity of the resources, or from a decrease of the liabilities. Losses arise from a decrease in the quantity or value of the resources, or from an increase of the liabilities without a corresponding increase of the resources.

Debit and credit serve merely to distinguish the left from the right hand side of an account. Debit items are placed on the left and credit items on the right hand side of an account. Any person, item or thing that costs value must be debited or, which is the same thing, must be placed on the left hand side of the account in question. Any person, item or thing that produces value must be credited, or placed on the right hand side of the account in question.

Every kind of goods usually handled by merchants, with a view to profit, would be placed under the title of merchandise. The notes and written obligations of others than the proprietor of the business whose books are being kept by the parties making the entries, should be placed under the title of bills receivable, and all notes or written obligations of the above designated proprietor should be entered under the title of bills payable.

Houses, lands, farms, and all permanent fixtures thereto, should be entered under the title of real estate. Other items with which dealings may be had, should be entered under titles indicated by the respective items in question.

By carefully tracing the entries found on the following pages, from the day book to the journal, and from the journal to the ledger, and noting the instructions for balancing and closing the ledger as well as examining and studying the accompanying statements, any person may in a short time comprehend the practice of double entry bookkeeping.

RULE.—Debit whatever is received, or costs value. Credit whatever is disposed of, or that produces value.

1885.

Jan.	1	Luther Johnson commenced business this day with a Cash capital of		3500	

As the business has received cash, debit that account. Credit Luther Johnson as he has produced value to the business.

	1	Cash Dr.	3500			
		To Luther Johnson			3500	

Jan.	2	Bought of Field, Leiter & Co.,			
		50 doz. Men's Linen Shirts, $26.00	$1300.00		
		100 doz. Ladies' Linen Handkerchiefs, $5.00	500.00		
		2 Cases Paper Cambric, 4000 yds. 15c	600.00		
		200 yds. Bleached Cotton, 20c	40.00	2440	
		Gave in payment my Note at 10 days for $600.			
		Cash for balance, 1840.			

Debit Merchandise as it has cost value. Credit Bills Payable, as our note has produced the business value in Merchandise. Credit Cash, as it has also produced value in Merchandise.

Jan.	2	Mdse. Dr. to Sundries,	2440			
		To Bills Payable			600	
		" Cash			1840	

Jan.	3	Bought of J. V. Farwell, on account,			
		50 yds. Irish Linen, $1.15	$57.50		
		100 yds. Sheeting, 17c	17.00	74	50

Debit Merchandise as it has cost value. Credit J. V. Farwell as he has produced value.

Jan.	3	Merchandise Dr.	74	50		
		To J. V. Farwell			74	50

1885.

Jan.	4	Sold to W. O. Thomas, on account, 10 doz. Men's Linen Shirts, $28.00 5 yds. Irish Linen, $1.25	$280.00 6.25	286	25

Debit W. O. Thomas as he has cost the business value. Credit Merchandise as it has produced the business the amount Thomas owes.

Jan.	4	W. O. Thomas, Dr. To Merchandise	286	25	286	25

Jan.	5	Sold to Dodd & Brown, St. Louis, on their Note, 1 Case Paper Cambric, 2000 yds. 17c 10 doz. Ladies' Linen Handkerchiefs, $6.00	$340.00 60.00	400	00

Debit Bills Receivable as the note has cost value. Credit Merchandise as it has produced the note.

Jan.	5	Bills Receivable, Dr. To Merchandise	400		400	

Jan.	7	Bought of Hamlin, Hale & Co. on my Note, 30 days, 1000 yds. Gingham, 10c 55 " Black Silk, $2.75 100 " Broadcloth, 6.50	$100.00 151.25 650.00	901	25

Debit Merchandise as it has cost value. Credit Bills Payable as your note has produced value in Merchandise.

Jan.	7	Merchandise, Dr. To Bills Payable	901	25	901	25

Jan.	9	Sold to G. R. Rathbun, Omaha, on account, 30 yds. Black Silk $3.25 15 " Irish Linen $1.25	$97.50 18.75	116	25

Debit G. R. Rathbun as he has cost the business value. Credit Merchandise as it has produced value in Rathbun's personal account.

Jan.	9	G. R. Rathbun, Dr. To Merchandise	116	25	116	25

Jan.	11	Paid Field, Leiter & Co. Cash for my Note of the 2d.	600	

Debit Bills Payable as your note has cost value. Credit Cash as it has produced value.

Jan.	11	Bills Payable, Dr. To Cash	600		600	

1885.

Jan.	12	Sold to H. Russell, Jolliet, Ill.,				
		50 yds. Sheeting, 20c		$10.00		
		200 " Gingham, 12c		24.00		
		10 doz. Men's Linen Shirts, $28.00		280.00	314	
		Received in payment, Cash	$150.00			
		Balance due on account	164.00			

Debit Cash and J. H. Russell as they have cost value. Credit Merchandise as it has produced value.

Jan.	12	Sundries Dr. to Mdse.			314	
		Cash	150			
		H. Russell	164			

Jan.	15	Sold to M. R. Johnson, for Cash,			
		14 yds. Broadcloth, $7.25	$101.50		
		1 Case Paper Cambric, 2000 yds. 17c	340.00	441	50

Debit Cash as it has cost value. Credit Merchandise as it has produced value.

Jan.	15	Cash, Dr.	441	50		
		To Merchandise			441	50

Jan.	16	Received Cash of W. O. Thomas on account,	75	

Debit Cash as it has cost value. Credit W. O. Thomas as he has produced value.

Jan.	16	Cash, Dr.	75			
		To W. O. Thomas			75	

Jan.	18	Sold to G. R. Rathbun, Omaha, on account,			
		100 yds. Bleached Cotton, 22c	$22.00		
		20 doz. Men's Linen Shirts, $27.50	550.00	572	

Debit G. R. Rathbun as he has cost value. Credit Merchandise as it has produced value.

Jan.	18	G. R. Rathbun, Dr.	572			
		To Merchandise			572	

Jan.	19	Received of H. Russell, Joliet, his Note, on his account,	100	

Debit Bills Receivable as the note has cost value. Credit H. Russell as he has produced value.

Jan.	19	Bills Receivable, Dr.	100			
		To H. Russell			100	

1885.

Jan.	20	Sold to F. E. Arnold, Rockford,			
		20 yds. Irish Linen, $1.20	$ 24.00		
		800 " Gingham, 12c	96.00		
		16 " Broadcloth, $7.50	120.00	240	
		Received in payment,			
		J. V. Farwell's order on me for $ 60.00			
		Balance due on account 180.00			

Debit J. V. Farwell and F. E. Arnold as they have cost the business value. Credit Merchandise as it has produced value.

Jan.	20	Sundries Dr. to Mdse.			240	
		J. V. Farwell	60			
		F. E. Arnold	180			

Jan.	22	Received of G. R. Rathbun, Omaha, on account,			
		Cash,	$125.00		
		His Note for	200.00	325	00

Debit Cash and Bills Receivable as they have cost the business value. Credit G. R. Rathbun as he has produced value to the business.

Jan.	22	Sundries Dr. to G. R. Rathbun			325	
		Cash	125			
		Bills Receivable	200			

Jan.	24	Sold to H. Russell, Joliet, on account,			
		50 yds. Sheeting, 18c	$ 9.00		
		50 doz. Ladies' Linen Handkerchiefs, $6.00	300.00		
				309	

Debit H. Russell as he has cost the business value. Credit Merchandise as it has produced value.

Jan.	24	H. Russell,	309			
		To Mdse.			309	

Jan.	25	Received of F. E. Arnold on his account Cash,	75	

Debit Cash as it has cost value. Credit F. E. Arnold as he has produced value to the business.

Jan.	25	Cash, Dr.	75			
		To F. E. Arnold			75	

Jan.	26	Paid Hamlin, Hale & Co. Cash on my Note of 7th inst.	450	

Debit bills payable as your note has cost value. Credit cash as it has produced your note.

Jan.	26	Bills Payable, Dr.	450			
		To Cash			450	

1885.

Jan.	27	Sold to W. O. Thomas, 10 doz. Men's Linen Shirts, $27.75 Received in payment his Note, for J. V. Farwell's order on me Cash for Balance due on account	 $150.00 75.00 25.00 27.50	277	50

Debit Bills Receivable for the amount of the note, J. V. Farwell for the amount of his order, Cash for the amount of cash received, and W. O. Thomas for the amount he still owes you. As these accounts have cost the business value, credit Merchandise, as it has produced value.

Jan.	27	Sundries Dr. to Mdse. Bills Receivable J. V. Farwell Cash W. O. Thomas	 150 75 25 27	 50	277	50

Jan.	29	Received of Dodd & Brown, Cash on their Note,	150	

Debit cash, as it has cash value. Credit Bills Receivable as the note has produced value.

Jan.	29	Cash, Dr. To Bills Receivable	150		 150	

Jan.	30	Paid Cash for following expenses, Clerks' Wages to date Gas Bill for month Advertising in Chicago Bulletin to date Robert Law for 2 tons Coal	 $225.00 10.80 150.00 22.00	407	80

Debit expense, as that account has cost value. Credit cash from the fact of its having produced the various items of value named in Day Book entry.

Jan.	30	Expense, Dr. To Cash	407	80	 407	 80

Jan.	31	Received Cash on accounts, of W. O. Thomas, G. R. Rathbun, F. E. Arnold.	 $105.00 200.00 50.00	355	00

Rule.—Debit Cash as it has cost you the personal accounts. Credit each of the persons named in the Day Book entry as they have produced you cash.

Jan.	31	Cash, Dr. to Sundries To W. O. Thomas " G. R. Rathbun " F. E. Arnold	355		 105 200 50	

Inventory of Merchandise unsold January 31, 1875.

70 yds. Broadcloth @ $6.50	$455.00
25 " Black Silk @ 2.75	68.75
100 " Bleached Cotton @ 20c	20.00
10 " Irish Linen @ $1.15	11.50
40 doz. Ladies' Linen Handkerchiefs @ 5.00	200.00
	755.25

INSTRUCTIONS FOR POSTING.

In posting, an account is opened in the Ledger with every item found in the Journal. Every debit item in the Journal must be placed on the Dr. side of its account in the Ledger, and every credit item in the Journal on the Cr. side of its account in the Ledger. The date of the item in the Journal is carried with it to the Ledger. In posting debit items, write as an explanation in the Ledger account, *To* the name of the credit item; if Sunds. are credited, write *To Sunds.*; and in posting credit items, write as an explanation in the Ledger account, *By* the name of the debit item, or if Sundries are debited, write *By Sunds.* The page of the Journal is entered in the Ledger, and the page of the Ledger is entered in the Journal.

The proprietor's or partners' accounts should, for convenience, always be placed first in the Ledger, and are generally followed by Cash, Merchandise, and other accounts in the order of their importance.

Dr. LUTHER JOHNSON. Cr.

1885.					1885.				
Jan.	31	To Profit & Loss	111	80	Jan.	1	By Cash	3500	00
"	31	" **Balance**	3388	20					
			3500	00				3500	00
					Feb.	1	By balance	3388	20

Dr. MERCHANDISE. Cr.

1885.					1885.				
Jan.	2	To Sundries	2440		Jan.	4	By W. Thomas	286	25
"	3	" J. Farwell	74	50	"	5	" Bills Rec.	400	
"	7	" Bills Payable	901	25	"	9	" G. Rathbun	116	25
"	31	" **Profit & Loss**	**296**		"	12	" Sundries	314	
					"	15	" Cash	441	50
					"	18	" G. Rathbun	572	
					"	20	" Sundries	240	
					"	24	" H. Russell	309	
					"	27	" Sundries	277	50
					"	31	" **Balance**	**755**	**25**
			3711	75				3711	75
		To balance	755	25					

Dr. CASH. Cr.

1885.					1885.				
Jan.	1	To L. Johnson	3500		Jan.	2	By Mdse.	1840	
"	12	" Mdse.	150		"	11	" Bills Payable	600	
"	15	" "	441	50	"	26	" "	450	
"	16	" W. Thomas	75		"	30	" Expense	407	80
"	22	" G. Rathbun	125		"	**31**	" **Balance**	**1598**	**70**
"	25	" F. E. Arnold	75						
"	27	" To Mdse.	25						
"	29	" Bills Rec.	150						
"	31	" To Sundries	355						
			4896	50				4896	50
Feb.	1	To Balalance	1598	70					

BILLS PAYABLE.

Dr. 1885.					Cr. 1885.				
Jan.	11	To Cash	600		Jan.	2	By Mdse.	600	
"	26	" "	450		"	7	" "	901	25
"	31	" **Balance.**	**451**	**25**					
			1501	25				1501	25
					Feb.	1	By Balance	451	25

J. V. FARWELL.

Dr. 1885.					Cr. 1885.				
Jan.	20	To Mdse.	60		Jan.	3	By Mdse.	74	50
"	27	" "	75		"	31	" **Balance**	**60**	**50**
			135	00				135	00
Feb.	1	To Balance	60	50					

W. O. THOMAS.

1885.					1885.				
Jan.	4	To Mdse.	286	25	Jan.	16	By Cash	75	
"	27	" "	27	50	"	31	" "	105	
					"	13	" **Balance**	133	75
			313	75	"			313	75
Feb.	1	To Balance	133	75					

BILLS RECEIVABLE.

1885.					1885.				
Jan.	5	To Mdse.	400		Jan.	29	By Cash	150	
"	19	" H. Russell	100		"	31	" **Balance**	**700**	
"	22	" G. Rathbun	200						
"	27	" Mdse.	150						
			850					850	
Feb.	1	To Balance	700						

G. R. RATHBUN, Omaha.

1885.					1885.				
Jan.	9	To Mdse.	116	25	Jan.	22	By Sunds.	325	
"	18	" "	572		"	31	" Cash.	200	
					"	31	" **Balance**	**163**	**25**
			688	25				688	25
Feb.	1	To Balance	163	25					

H. RUSSELL, Joliet.

1885.					1885.				
Jan.	12	To Mdse.	164		Jan.	19	By Bills Rec.	100	
"	24	" "	309		"	31	" **Balance**	**373**	
			473					473	
Feb.	1	To Balance	373						

F. E. ARNOLD,

1885.					1885.				
Jan.	20	To Mdse.	180		Jan	25	By Cash	75	
					"	31	" "	50	
						31	" **Balance**	**55**	
			180					180	
Feb.	1	To Balance	55						

EXPENSE.

1885.					1885.				
Jan.	30	To Cash	407	80	Jan.	**31**	**By Profit & Loss**	**407**	**80**

PROFIT & LOSS.

1885.					1885.				
Jan.	31	To Expense	407	80	Jan.	31	By Mdse.	296	
					"	**31**	" **L. Johnson**	**111**	**80**
			407	80				407	80

After all the items have been posted, the next step is to take a

TRIAL BALANCE,

or Proof-Sheet, to test the accuracy of the transfers. This is done by writing the name of each account with corresponding aggregate debit and credit amounts that do not balance or cancel each other, then finding the sum of the debits and also of the credits. If the footings agree, the Ledger is probably correct. Not certainly, however, because an entry may be posted to a wrong account, or omitted entirely

Trial Balance, January 31, 1885.

L. F.					
	Luther Johnson			3500	
	Merchandise	3415	75	2936	50
	Cash	4896	50	3297	80
	Bills Payable	1050		1501	25
	J. V. Farwell	135		74	50
	W. O. Thomas	313	75	180	
	Bills Receivable	850		150	
	G. R. Rathbun	688	25	525	
	H. Russell	473		100	
	F. E. Arnold	180		125	
	Expense	407	80		
		12410	05	12410	05

CLOSING THE LEDGER.

Make out an Inventory of property on hand. In business this process is called "taking an account of Stock," and consists in actually enumerating the articles, and affixing values thereto.

Credit the account or accounts representing this property, with the amount on hand, as if it had been sold at the valuation given, making the entry in red ink, *By Balance*. Add this amount to the total credits of the account, find the difference between this sum and the total debits and write the difference on the smaller side, in red ink, *To* or *By Profit and Loss*.

Close all the remaining accounts, except the proprietor's or partners', which is the last closed, by entering the difference between the two sides of each account in red ink on the smaller side. If the difference represents a resource or liability, as Cash, Bills Payable, Bills Receivable, and personal accounts, use the expression either *To* or *By Balance;* if a gain or loss, as Expense, Interest, Discount, Premium, and property accounts, use the expression either *To* or *By Profit and Loss*.

When all the accounts are thus closed (except the proprietor's), open an account with Profit and Loss, if there is not one already open, and transfer all the Profit and Loss red ink entries to the opposite side of the Profit and Loss account, making the entry in black ink, *To* or *By* whatever account transferred from.

Close Profit and Loss account by entering the difference in red ink on the smaller side, *To* or *By* the proprietor's name, and transferring same to the opposite side of the proprietor's account; make the entry in black ink, *To* or *By Profit and Loss*. If it be a partnership business, the partners' names will be entered separately in the Profit and Loss account, instead of the proprietor's, and the net gain or net loss will be divided according to the terms of the copartnership, and the proportion belonging to each transferred to his account.

Close the proprietor's or partners' accounts by entering the difference on the smaller side in red ink, *To* or *By Balance*. All transferable entries should be made in red ink, and in transferring them to another account, change sides with each entry, as each one must be placed on its original side, and make the entry in black ink. Rule the accounts as shown in the foregoing Ledger, foot the two sides of each account, and place the amount in black ink beneath the columns which produced them. Then make out a

BALANCE SHEET.

which is a statement of the condition of the business, and should be preserved for future reference. It contains under the head of RESOURCES all amounts due or belonging to the firm, also the amounts withdrawn by the proprietor for his private use; and under the head of LIABILITIES all amounts owed by the concern, also the amount invested by the proprietor. Making an exception of the proprietor's account, the Resources will be all red ink *Balance* entries found on the Cr. side of the accounts, and the Liabilities will be all red ink *Balance* entries, found on the Dr. side of the account. The difference between the Resources and Liabilities will show the net gain or net loss which must agree with the Profit and Loss account in the Ledger; and the proprietor's investment plus or minus the net gain or net loss will equal the proprietor's net capital at closing, which must agree with the proprietor's account in the Ledger.

Balance Sheet, January 31, 1885.

L. F.		Dr.		Cr.	
	RESOURCES.				
	Merchandise per inventory	755	25		
	Cash on hand	1598	70		
	J. V. Farwell owes on account	60	50		
	W. O. Thomas " " "	133	75		
	Bills Receivable, Notes on hand	700			
	G. R. Rathbun owes on account	163	25		
	H. Russell " " "	373			
	F. E. Arnold " " "	55		3839	45
	LIABILITIES.				
	Bills Payable, Notes unpaid	451	25		
	Luther Johnson's net investment	3500		3951	25
	Net Loss			111	80
	Luther Johnson's investment	3500			
	" " Net Loss	111	80		
	" " Net Capital			3388	20

NOTE.—In the above Balance Sheet have been placed all the personal accounts which occurred in the Ledger; this in business is not done, unless they are but few, but instead of entering them separately a schedule of the personal accounts is made out, and the total amounts of this schedule entered as "Sundry Personal Accounts due us," and "Sundry Personal Accounts owed by us."

If the business is to be continued, bring down the Balances as shown in the Ledger, on the opposite sides of the accounts in black ink.

ANALYSIS OF LEDGER ACCOUNTS.

PROPRIETOR'S OR PARTNER'S ACCOUNTS.—Debit side shows amounts withdrawn from the business, or obligations assumed for the partner by the firm; the amount of loss if any, and net capital. Credit side shows the amount invested on commencing business and all additional investments, the amount of gain, if any, and net insolvency.

CASH ACCOUNT.—Debit side shows the amount of cash received; the credit side the amount paid out or disposed of. Closed BY BALANCE, as the Dr. side must be equal to or greater than the Cr. Difference shows the amount of Cash on hand.

BILLS RECEIVABLE ACCOUNT.—Debit side shows the amount of Notes and Drafts received against others; credit side the amount disposed of. Closed BY BALANCE as the debit side must equal or exceed the credit. Difference shows the amount of notes on hand.

BILLS PAYABLE ACCOUNT.—Credit side shows the amount of your own notes and acceptance issued; debit side the amount taken up or redeemed. Closed TO BALANCE as the Cr. side must equal or exceed the debit. Difference shows the amount of notes outstanding.

PERSONAL ACCOUNTS.—Debit side shows their indebtedness to you; Credit side your indebtedness to them. Closed either To or BY BALANCE.

PROPERTY ACCOUNTS.—Debit side shows the cost and charges of the property; Credit side the sales, or what it has produced. Credit BY BALANCE for amount on hand, and closed To or BY PROFIT AND LOSS.

EXPENSE ACCOUNT.—Credited BY BALANCE for everything remaining on hand at time of closing which has been previously entered in the Expense account, closed into Profit and Loss.

PREMIUM AND DISCOUNT.—Debit side shows what each has cost you; Credit side shows what each has produced you. Closed into Profit and Loss.

INTEREST ACCOUNT.—Debit side shows what Interest has cost you; Credit what it has produced you. Credited BY BALANCE for accrued interest on other notes and obligations due you. Debited TO BALANCE for accrued interest on your own outstanding notes and obligations. Closed into Profit and Loss.

PROFIT AND LOSS ACCOUNT.—Debit side shows amount of your loss, also your net gain; Credit side shows your gains, also your net loss. Closed To or BY the proprietor or To or BY each partner.

THE RELIGIOUS RECORD.

RELIGIONS OF THE WORLD.

Buddhists	482,600,000
Christians	388,250,000
Pagans	227,000,000
Mohammedans	122,400,000
Brahminical Hindoos	120,000,000
Jews	7,700,000
Parsees	1,000,000

CHRISTIAN DENOMINATIONS.

Roman Catholics	202,368,000
Protestants	108,630,000
Greek Church	70,482,000
Eastern Christians	6,770,000

RELIGIONS IN THE UNITED STATES.

Roman Catholics		6,832,954
Methodist	1,680,779	2,736,504
South	828,013	
Protestant	118,170	
Colored	74,195	
Wesleyan	17,847	
Free	12,130	
Primitive	3,370	
Independent	2,100	
Baptist	2,132,044	2,250,431
Free Will	76,706	
Anti-Mission	40,000	
Seventh-Day	8,606	
Six-Principle	2,075	

RELIGIONS IN THE UNITED STATES—CONT'D.

Presbyterian	573,377	891,458
South	119,970	
Cumberland	111,855	
United	80,236	
Reformed	6,020	
Lutheran		684,570
Christian		567,448
Congregational		383,685
Episcopal	323,876	334,335
Reformed	10,459	
Reformed Church, U. S.	154,742	233,659
America	78,917	
Jews		230,457
United Brethren		155,437
United Evangelical		144,000
Mormon		110,379
Evangelical Association		99,007
Dunkards		90,100
Adventists	11,100	89,333
Second	63,500	
Seventh-Day	14,733	
Friends		67,643
Universalist		37,945
Church of God		29,224
Unitarian		17,960
Moravian		16,112
New Jerusalem		4,734
New Mennonites		2,990
American Communities		2,838
Shakers		2,400

DISTRIBUTION OF CHRISTIANS.

COUNTRIES.	Roman Catholics.	Protestants.	Greek Christians.	Eastern.	Total.
Russia	7,546,144	4,400,000	54,000,000		65,946,144
Germany	15,371,227	26,835,558			42,206,785
United States	6,832,954	30,000,000			36,832,954
France	35,500,000	600,000			36,100,000
Austria	27,904,308	3,558,000	3,052,000		34,514,308
South America	26,754,000	2,000,000			28,754,000
Italy	26,658,700	40,000			26,698,700
Spain	16,870,000	45,000			16,870,000
Mexico and Central America	12,196,677				12,196,677
Turkey		40,000	11,625,000		11,665,000
Oriental Nations				6,770,000	6,770,000
Sweden-Norway		5,908,600			5,908,600
Belgium	5,518,146				5,518,146
Portugal	4,745,124				4,745,124
Canada	1,962,600	1,800,000			3,762,600
Holland	1,313,084	2,198,000			3,511,084
West Indies	2,911,000				2,911,000
Switzerland	1,084,400	1,558,000			2,642,400
Denmark		1,865,000			1,865,000
Greece			1,442,000		1,442,000
India and Ceylon	1,600,000	300,000			1,900,000
Africa	1,106,200	719,000			1,825,200
Australia and Polynesia	434,000	1,000,000			1,434,000
China and Japan	800,000	300,000			1,100,000
Arabia and Persia	1,000,000	89,000			1,089,000

THE FARMYARD.

THE SHEEP.

WITHOUT doubt, the sheep is a most useful animal to man as food, and the most necessary to his health and comfort. In the absence of the cow, it furnishes him with milk and a sound but rather inferior quality of cheese, and its fat gives him light, its fleece broadcloth, kerseymere, blankets, gloves and hose. From the primitive stock ELEVEN varieties of domesticated sheep are reared, and by their several advocates are supposed to possess some

Special Qualities.—These eleven species embrace the following: Shetland or Orkney, Dun-Wooled, Black Faced, Moorland of Devonshire, the Cheviot, Horned of Norfolk, The Ryeland, South-Down, Merino, Old Leicester, and The Teeswater. But of late years the number has been reduced to the following four: The South-Down, The Leicester, The Black-Faced, and the Cheviot. The South-Downs derive their name from the breezy range of light chalky hills running through the southwest and south of Sussex and Hampshire, England, and known as the South-Downs. This species, for symmetry of shape, constitution and early maturity, ranks with any stock in the world. They have no horns; head small, and legs and face a grayish color. However, it is considered deficient in depth and breadth of chest. It is covered with a fine wool of from two to three inches in length. A marked feature of this breed is that its hind quarters are higher than the fore, and weigh generally from fifteen to eighteen pounds.

The Leicester.—This breed is regarded as the largest example of the improved breeds, being very productive, and yielding a good fleece. He has small head, covered with short, white hairs, clear muzzle, open countenance, full clear eye, long thin ear, tapering neck, and straight back, its weight being about ninety-five pounds.

The Black-Faced.—This is a strong, hardy race of sheep. The face and legs are dark, horns spiral in shape, a small second tuft of light colored wool is on forehead. The eye is sparkling, bright, and well open; body long, round, and firm; limbs stout; wool thin, coarse and light.

The Cheviot.—A sheep of remarkable vigor and sound constitution, capable of enduring great privation, and producing a valuable fleece. Neither sex have horns; white face, legs long and clean, head erect, neck and throat well covered, ears long and open, with animated face. They are small boned, but are wanting in depth of chest, which seems to be their only defect.

THE COW.

IN the animal kingdom the cow is certainly one of, if not the greatest blessings God in his infinite wisdom and goodness has seen fit to bestow upon the human family; and is justly termed the poor man s friend. Breeders seem to attach more value to what are termed Short Horns, than any others, though coming under this general head there are many varieties. Mr. Dickson thus describes the Short Horns: The external appearance of the Short Horned breed is very attractive. The exquisitely symmetrical form of the body in every position, bedecked with a skin of the richest hues of red, so arranged or commixed as to form a beautiful fleck or delicate roan, and possessed of the mellowest touch; supported on clean, small limbs, showing, like those of the race-horse and the greyhound, the union of strength with firmness; and ornamented with a small, lengthy, tapering head, neatly set on a broad, firm, deep neck, and furnished with a small muzzle, wide nostrils, prominent, mildly beaming eyes, thin, large, binal ears set near the crown of the head, and protected in front with semi-circularly bent, white or brownish colored, short (hence the name), smooth-pointed horns. All these points combine to form a symmetrical harmony which has never been surpassed in beauty and sweetness by any other species.

Mr. Youatt says the colors of the improved pure Short Horns are but two, red or white, or a mixture of both. Coming under this head, and which are considered to rank as first, are the Durhams, the Alderneys, the Suffolk Duns, and also those called Cream Pots, an American breed. The Alderneys, prized mainly for the richness of their milk, but in quantity small; therefore those preferring quality to quantity can find it in the Alderney. Mr. Jaques thus describes the Cream Pots: I purchased a native cow in consequence of her superior quality as a milker, averaging about fifteen quarts a day. Continuing, he says: My Cream Pots are full in the body, deep in the flank, not quite as straight in the belly, nor as full in the twist, nor quite as thick in the thigh as the Durhams; but in other respects like them. They excel in affording a large quantity of rich cream, capable of being converted into butter in a very short time.

A writer in the *Farmer's Magazine* several years ago, thus described the good qualities of the Short Horns. "She's long in her face; she's fine in her horn; she'll quickly get fat, without cake or corn; she's clean in her jaws, and full in her chin; she's heavy in flank, and wide in her loin; she's broad in her ribs, and long in her rump; she's wide in her hip, and calm in her eyes; she's fine in her shoulders, and thin in her thighs; she's light in her neck, and small

in her tail; she's wide in the breast, and good at the pail; she's fine in her bone, and silky of skin; she's a grazier's without, and a butcher's within." Farmers as a rule pay too little attention to the care of their stock, and especially is this true in the care of their cows. Every farmer should understand that in order to get good results, their stock should have good, dry, clean quarters, and it is of the utmost importance that there should be good water accessible at all times. Just so certain as these essentials are neglected, will the effects be seen and felt in the pocket of the master. In order that a good crop of wheat or corn may be had from a certain piece of ground, it is not only necessary to plant the seed, but it also must be tended from time to time, for if neglected the result will be no harvest. And this is not only true in this particular, but in everything pertaining to the successful operation of the farm.

THE HOG.

OF the various kinds of hogs the following list of breeds can be accepted as the best, presenting severally the qualities affecting both the breeder and consumer: Berkshire, Essex, York and Cumberland, also the Chinese. Among the breeders of hogs the black pig is generally regarded as the best. It has much the finest and most delicate skin, and is less affected by the heat of summer. It also is less subject to disease than the other colors, and, being of a more kindly nature, will fatten much easier. The chief points in selecting a good hog are the following: Breadth of chest, depth of carcass, width of ribs, chine and loin, of compact form, docile, cheerful and general fine appearance.

A well-bred hog has medium head in length, the forehead narrow, full cheeks, fine snout, small mouth, eyes bright and small, ears sharp, thin and short and pointing forward; a full, broad neck, and especially so on the top, joining very broad shoulders; the loins, ribs and haunch should be in a line; also a well-set tail, not too high nor too low; a nearly straight back, deep, broad and prominent chest, with thick, short legs, and, when in good flesh, the belly should nearly touch the ground; long, thin, fine hair, with but few bristles, and of uniform color. The above is considered a true type of a perfect hog. Hogs, when confined in a pen, should have plenty of cinders, or something of that nature, not only to exercise their jaws upon, but to aid their digestion.

POULTRY.

THE GAME FOWL.—This species was regarded by the Greeks and Romans with great respect, and even awe. The former people practiced divination by means of this bird. Before going into battle, there being doubt in the camp as to the fittest day to commence operations, the letter would be placed, face downward, of every day in the week, and a grain of corn placed on each—then the sacred cock would be brought out and the time for battle regulated according as he picked the corn. But upon one momentous occasion some person inimical to priestly interest, examined the grain and was a little surprised to find that the corn lying on the letters not wanted were made of wax, and the bird of course, preferring the genuine article, left the false ones untouched. After this discovery the custom fell into disuse. These birds were bred for the sport of fighting many years before the Christian era. And the custom has continued on down to the present time.

The Dorking.—This bird takes its name from a town in Surrey. The Dorking's chief characteristic is that it has five claws on each foot. Pure white is its true color, long in body, short in legs, and a good layer.

The Poland. — This is a native of Holland, and a favorite with fowl keepers who have an eye to profit, their chief value being in the great number of eggs they produce, being quite generally known as "the everlasting layers." But their eggs, although being of good size, lack greatly in nutriment.

The Cochin-China.—For elegance of shape, or quality of flesh, the Cochin cannot compare with our handsome dunghill. However, our poultry breeders are gainers by the introduction of the ungainly celestial, owing to new blood having been infused into the chicken family.

The Speckled Hamburg.—In color a golden or orange-yellow, each feather having a glossy dark brown or black tip. They are beautiful birds and the hens fine layers.

Black Spanish.—This fowl is recognized by its uniform black color, with tints of green, white face and large comb. An authority says the best are those with blue legs and black feathers, large white face, and large high comb, and which should stand erect in the cock, though pendant in the hens. The hens are good layers, and their eggs large though they are small bodied.

The Bantam.—We close our items on fowls with but few words on this diminutive species. The thoroughbred is considered next to the game cock for animation, plumage and courage, and are considered great favorites, as also pets, with many people.

CENSUS OF OUR CITIES.

The following table shows all the cities and towns in the United States, alphabetically arranged, which have, according to the census of 1880 a population of ten thousand or over:

City.	County.	State.	Population. 1870.	Population. 1880.	City.	County.	State.	Population. 1870.	Population. 1880.
Akron	Summit	Ohio	10,006	16,512	Council Bluffs	Pottawattamie	Iowa	10,020	18,063
Albany	Albany	New York	69,422	90,758	Covington	Kenton	Kentucky	24,505	29,720
Alexandria	Alexandria	Virginia	13,570	13,659	Cumberland	Allegany	Maryland	8,056	10,693
Allegheny	Allegheny	Pennsylvania	53,180	78,682	Dallas	Dallas	Texas	.....	10,358
Allentown	Lehigh	Pennsylvania	13,884	18,063	Danbury	Fairfield	Connecticut	8,753	11,666
Altoona	Blair	Pennsylvania	10,610	19,710	Davenport	Scott	Iowa	20,038	21,831
Amsterdam	Montgomery	New York	7,706	11,710	Dayton	Montgomery	Ohio	30,473	38,678
Atchison	Atchison	Kansas	7,054	15,105	Denver	Arapahoe	Colorado	4,759	35,629
Atlanta	Fulton	Georgia	21,789	37,409	Des Moines	Polk	Iowa	12,035	22,408
Auburn	Cayuga	New York	17,225	21,924	Detroit	Wayne	Michigan	79,577	116,340
Augusta	Richmond	Georgia	15,389	21,891	Dover	Strafford	New Hampshire	9,294	11,687
Aurora	Kane	Illinois	11,162	11,873	Dubuque	Dubuque	Iowa	18,434	22,254
Baltimore	Baltimore	Maryland	267,354	332,313	East Cambridge	Middlesex	Massachusetts	.....	16,134
Bangor	Penobscot	Maine	18,289	16,856	Easton	Northampton	Pennsylvania	10,987	11,924
Bay City	Bay	Michigan	7,064	20,693	East Saginaw	Saginaw	Michigan	11,350	19,016
Belleville	St. Clair	Illinois	8,146	10,683	Eau Claire	Eau Claire	Wisconsin	2,293	10,119
Biddeford	York	Maine	10,282	12,651	Elizabeth	Union	New Jersey	20,832	28,229
Binghamton	Broome	New York	12,692	17,317	Elmira	Chemung	New York	15,863	20,541
Bloomington	McLean	Illinois	14,590	17,180	Erie	Erie	Pennsylvania	19,646	27,737
Boston	Suffolk	Massachusetts	250,526	362,839	Evansville	Vanderburg	Indiana	21,830	29,280
Bridgeport	Fairfield	Connecticut	18,969	27,643	Fall River	Bristol	Massachusetts	26,766	48,961
Brooklyn	Kings	New York	396,099	566,663	Fitchburg	Worcester	Massachusetts	11,260	12,429
Buffalo	Erie	New York	117,714	155,134	Fond du Lac	Fond du Lac	Wisconsin	12,764	13,094
Burlington	Des Moines	Iowa	14,930	19,450	Fort Wayne	Allen	Indiana	17,718	26,880
Burlington	Chittenden	Vermont	14,387	11,365	Galesburg	Knox	Illinois	10,158	11,437
Cambridge	Middlesex	Massachusetts	39,634	52,669	Galveston	Galveston	Texas	13,818	22,248
Camden	Camden	New Jersey	20,045	41,659	Georgetown	.....	Dist. Columbia	11,384	12,578
Canton	Stark	Ohio	8,660	12,258	Gloucester	Essex	Massachusetts	15,389	19,329
Cedar Rapids	Linn	Iowa	5,940	10,104	Grand Rapids	Kent	Michigan	16,507	32,016
Charleston	Charleston	South Carolina	48,956	49,984	Hamilton	Butler	Ohio	11,081	12,122
Chattanooga	Hamilton	Tennessee	6,093	12,892	Hannibal	Marion	Missouri	10,125	11,074
Chelsea	Suffolk	Massachusetts	18,547	21,782	Harrisburg	Dauphin	Pennsylvania	23,104	30,762
Chester	Delaware	Pennsylvania	9,485	14,997	Hartford	Hartford	Connecticut	37,180	42,015
Chicago	Cook	Illinois	298,977	503,185	Haverhill	Essex	Massachusetts	13,092	18,472
Chillicothe	Ross	Ohio	8,920	10,938	Hoboken	Hudson	New Jersey	20,297	30,999
Cincinnati	Hamilton	Ohio	216,239	255,139	Holyoke	Hampden	Massachusetts	10,733	21,915
Cleveland	Cuyahoga	Ohio	92,829	160,146	Houston	Harris	Texas	9,382	16,513
Cohoes	Albany	New York	15,357	19,416	Hyde Park	Cook	Illinois	3,644	15,716
Columbia	Richland	South Carolina	9,298	10,036	Indianapolis	Marion	Indiana	48,244	75,056
Columbus	Muscogee	Georgia	7,401	10,123	Jackson	Jackson	Michigan	11,447	16,105
Columbus	Franklin	Ohio	31,274	51,647	Jacksonville	Morgan	Illinois	9,203	10,927
Concord	Merrimac	New Hampshire	12,241	13,843	Jersey City	Hudson	New Jersey	82,546	120,722

Joliet	Will	Illinois	7,263	11,657	Newport	Campbell	Kentucky	15,087	20,433
Kalamazoo	Kalamazoo	Michigan	10,447	13,552	Newport	Newport	Rhode Island	12,521	15,693
Kansas City	Jackson	Missouri	32,260	55,785	Newton	Middlesex	Massachusetts	12,825	16,995
Keokuk	Lee	Iowa	12,766	12,117	New York	New York	New York	942,292	1,206,299
Kingston	Ulster	New York		18,344	Norfolk	Norfolk	Virginia	19,229	21,966
Knoxville	Knox	Tennessee	8,682	10,947	Norristown	Montgomery	Pennsylvania	10,753	13,063
La Crosse	LaCrosse	Wisconsin	7,785	14,505	Norwich	New London	Connecticut		15,112
Lafayette	Tippecanoe	Indiana	13,506	14,860	Oakland	Alameda	California	10,500	34,555
Lake	Cook	Illinois	3,360	18,290	Ogdensburg	St. Lawrence	New York	10,076	10,341
Lancaster	Lancaster	Pennsylvania	20,233	25,769	Omaha	Douglas	Nebraska	16,083	30,518
Lawrence	Essex	Massachusetts	28,921	39,151	Orange	Essex	New Jersey	9,348	13,207
Leadville	Lake	Colorado		14,820	Oshkosh	Winnebago	Wisconsin	12,663	15,748
Leavenworth	Leavenworth	Kansas	17,873	16,546	Oswego	Oswego	New York	20,910	21,116
Lewiston	Androscoggin	Maine	13,600	19,083	Paterson	Passaic	New Jersey	33,579	51,031
Lexington	Fayette	Kentucky	14,801	16,656	Peoria	Peoria	Illinois	22,849	29,259
Lincoln	Lancaster	Nebraska		13,003	Petersburg	Dinwiddie	Virginia	18,950	21,656
Little Rock	Pulaski	Arkansas	12,380	13,138	Philadelphia	Philadelphia	Pennsylvania	674,022	847,170
Lockport	Niagara	New York	12,426	13,522	Pittsburg	Allegheny	Pennsylvania	86,076	156,389
Logansport	Cass	Indiana	8,950	11,198	Pittsfield	Berkshire	Massachusetts	11,112	13,364
Long Island City	Queens	New York		17,129	Portland	Cumberland	Maine	31,413	33,810
Los Angeles	Los Angeles	California	5,728	11,183	Portland	Multnomah	Oregon	8,293	17,577
Louisville	Jefferson	Kentucky	100,753	123,758	Portsmouth	Scioto	Ohio	10,592	11,321
Lowell	Middlesex	Massachusetts	40,928	59,475	Portsmouth	Norfolk	Virginia	10,590	11,390
Lynchburg	Campbell	Virginia	6,825	15,959	Pottsville	Schuylkill	Pennsylvania	12,384	13,253
Lynn	Essex	Massachusetts	28,233	38,274	Poughkeepsie	Dutchess	New York	20,080	20,207
Macon	Bibb	Georgia	10,810	12,749	Providence	Providence	Rhode Island	68,904	104,857
Madison	Jefferson	Indiana	10,709	8,945	Quincy	Adams	Illinois	24,052	27,268
Madison	Dane	Wisconsin	9,176	10,324	Quincy	Norfolk	Massachusetts	7,442	10,570
Manchester	Hillsborough	New Hampshire	23,536	32,630	Racine	Racine	Wisconsin	9,880	16,031
Memphis	Shelby	Tennessee	40,226	33,592	Reading	Berks	Pennsylvania	33,930	43,278
Meriden	New Haven	Connecticut		15,540	Richmond	Wayne	Indiana	9,445	12,742
Milwaukee	Milwaukee	Wisconsin	71,440	115,587	Richmond	Henrico	Virginia	51,038	63,600
Minneapolis	Hennepin	Minnesota	13,066	46,887	Rochester	Monroe	New York	62,386	89,366
Mobile	Mobile	Alabama	32,034	29,132	Rockford	Winnebago	Illinois	11,049	13,129
Montgomery	Montgomery	Alabama	10,588	16,713	Rock Island	Rock Island	Illinois	7,890	11,659
Muskegon	Muskegon	Michigan	6,002	11,262	Rome	Oneida	New York	11,000	12,194
Nashua	Hillsboro	New Hampshire	10,543	13,397	Sacramento	Sacramento	California	16,283	21,420
Nashville	Davidson	Tennessee	25,865	43,350	Saginaw	Saginaw	Michigan	7,460	10,525
New Albany	Floyd	Indiana	15,396	16,423	Saint Joseph	Buchanan	Missouri	19,565	32,431
Newark	Essex	New Jersey	105,059	136,508	Saint Paul	Ramsey	Minnesota	20,030	41,473
New Bedford	Bristol	Massachusetts	21,320	26,845	Salem	Essex	Massachusetts	24,117	27,563
New Brighton	Richmond	New York		12,679	Salt Lake City	Salt Lake	Utah	12,854	20,768
New Britain	Hartford	Connecticut		11,800	San Antonio	Bexar	Texas	12,256	20,550
New Brunswick	Middlesex	New Jersey	15,058	17,166	Sandusky	Erie	Ohio		15,838
Newburg	Orange	New York	17,014	18,049	San Francisco	San Francisco	California	149,473	233,959
Newburyport	Essex	Massachusetts	12,595	13,538	San José	Santa Clara	California	9,089	12,567
New Haven	New Haven	Connecticut	50,840	62,882	Savannah	Chatham	Georgia	28,235	30,709
New London	New London	Connecticut	9,576	10,537	Schenectady	Schenectady	New York	11,026	13,655
New Orleans	Orleans	Louisiana	191,418	216,090	Scranton	Lackawanna	Pennsylvania	35,092	45,850

www.ingramcontent.com/pod-product-compliance
Lightning Source LLC
Chambersburg PA
CBHW022104300426
44117CB00007B/581
* 9 7 8 3 3 3 7 2 1 9 9 6 3 *